CW00673851

ANGUS

MONUMENTAL INSCRIPTIONS

(pre-1855)

Volume 1

STRATHMORE

edited by

Alison Mitchell

for

The Scottish Genealogy Society, 15 Victoria Terrace, Edinburgh, EH1 2JL

1979

Published by the Scottish Genealogy Society

First published 1979
Reprinted 1993 & 1996

Cover design by Craig Ellery, showing Glamis Castle & Edzell Castle

© Scottish Genealogy Society

All rights reserved. No part of this publication may be reproduced, stored in a retrieval system, or transmitted in any form, or by any means, electronic, mechanical, photocopying, recording or otherwise, without prior consent of the copyright holder.

ISBN 0 901061 20 4

ERRATA

AIRLIE	Iohn Rid 1686? (excavated 1989)
FORFAR	Alexr Whytlaw, not Quhytlawe
GLAMIS	Iohn Blear in the Thorntoun, not Blaer in the Thorntown
	Christan Burn, not Christian.
	Kilmundei, not Killmundie
KETTINS	Thos Bruce died Jan. 29 1667, not 22.
	James Fyfe at Miln of Aiedlair, not Ardlar.
	David Dick died 1692, not 1699 as Jervise says.
	No sign of Andrew Semon, 1756.
KINNETTLES	Margarit Garland was aged 35 years.
LINTRATHEN	Jn Dickson's stone does not bear a cordiner's knife, etc. It looks like IT
NEVAY	Alexr Neave's stone has a shield & skull, not two heads.
	Jn Riven died 1645
RUTHVEN	The 2nd inscription on Christian Irland's stone is rude, not "exceedingly well executed". We have some confusion here! Anna Gibb died Apriel the 25 day 1735.
	Jas Lounie died 4 Nov. 1679.
	IB, presumably the wife of -S, brewer, died 1702 her age ...

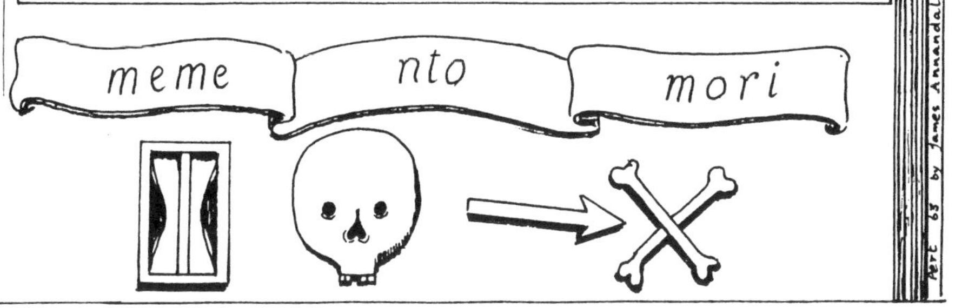

P R E – 1 8 5 5
G R A V E S T O N E
I N S C R I P T I O N S
i n
A N G U S

V O L U M E O N E
S T R A T H M O R E .

listed
by

David C. Cargill
Sydney Cramer
Jean Davidson
Michael Dun
Charles Millar
Alison Mitchell
Andrew Mitchell
Angus Mitchell
Ann Mitchell
John F. Mitchell
Sheila Mitchell
Anne Pinkerton
W. J. Shaw
Marshall Sloan
Lorna Thomson

in the burial grounds of

1a Aberlemno
1b Aldbar
2 Airlie
3a Brechin cathedral
3c Magdalen chapel
3b cemetery
4 Careston
5 Clova
6a Cortachy
6b Glen Prosen
7 Dun
8 Dunnichen
9 Eassie
10 Edzell
11a Farnell
11b Kinnaird
12 Fern
13a Forfar parish church
13c St. John's
13b cemetery
13d Restenneth
14 Glamis
15 Glenisla
16a Guthrie
16b Kirkbuddo
17a Inverarity
17b Meathie-Lour
18 Kettins
19 Kingoldrum
20a Kinnell
20b Friockheim cemetery
21 Kinnettles
22 Kirkden (Idvie)
23a Kirriemuir par:church
23b St. Mary's
23c cemetery
23d Kinloch mausoleum
24 Lethnot
25 Lintrathen
26 Lochlee
27a Logiepert
27b Logie-Montrose
27c Pert
28 Menmuir
29 Navar
30 Nevay (St.Ringan's)
31 Newtyle
32 Oathlaw (Finhaven)
33a Rescobie
33b Balmadies
34 Ruthven
35 Stracathro
36 Tannadice

P R E F A C E

Before 1855, when the registration of births, marriages and deaths became compulsory throughout Britain, genealogical records in Scotland were often scanty. This Index attempts to collect the old gravestone records before they are destroyed or are lost underground in the northern parts of Angus.

It summarises the genealogical information on all the gravestones which record deaths before 1855 and includes some adjacent stones which are obviously related. Symbols of trade are included, the commonest being the plough share and coulter for a farmer, a shuttle or handloom for a weaver, a crown and hammer for all types of smith, a crown and curved knife for a leather worker, a goose (iron) and scissors for a tailor.

Human error, our own, the mason's or the family's, may be discovered. Carving illegible on a dry dull day may become legible on a damp sunny day. Buried stones may be revealed by the bleaching of grass above in a summer drought. Further search at the site may be rewarding!

Willsher & Hunter, "Stones - 18th Century Scottish Gravestones" (Canongate, 1978), supplemented by Dr D Christison's articles in the Proceedings of the Society of Antiquaries, Scotland (PSAS) vol 36 & 39 (1901 & 1904) are the best introduction to the symbolism of the sculpture.

Essential guidebooks for genealogical research are
G Hamilton-Edwards, "In Search of Scottish Ancestry" (Phillimore, 2nd ed. 1977)
Donald Steel, "Sources for Scottish Genealogy" (Phillimore, 1971)
Neil Craven, "A Bibliography of Angus" (Forfar, 1975)

We have also found applicable to this book
J P S Ferguson, "Scottish Family Histories Held in Scottish Public Libraries"
Donald Whyte, "Introducing Scottish Genealogical Research"(Edinburgh, 1978)
F Davidson, "An Inventory of 17th Century Tombstones in Angus" (1977, ten copies only, held at the National Library and the Ancient Monuments Commission both in Edinburgh, at Dundee Central Library, & at the Latter Day Saints genealogical Library in Salt Lake City - it records the older stones in meticulous detail with many illustrations).
Andrew Jervise, "Land of the Lindsays" (1853),
"Memorials of Angus & the Mearns" vol i & ii (1885) ed by J Gammack,
"Epitaphs & Inscriptions from Burial Grounds & Old Buildings in the North East of Scotland" vol i (1875) & vol ii (1879),
Mss Collection 530/53 (Forfarshire) in the Library of the Society of Antiquaries, Scotland in Edinburgh (perhaps intended to be vol iii of the "Epitaphs...")

Old Parochial (i.e.Parish) Registers (OPR) with the Registrar General, Princes Street, Edinburgh, are noted for each parish.

Other church records, deposited in the Scottish Record Office, Charlotte Sq. Edinburgh, are also noted for each parish. CH2 series is for congregations which remained Church of Scotland throughout, CH3 is for seceding congregations which later rejoined the Church of Scotland, HR is for Heritors Records.

Testaments deposited in the Scottish Record Office have been indexed to 1823. In this book, as a sample of one category of ms material available to researchers, we include a selection from the Registers 1514-1800 published by the Scottish Record Society. Until 1823 each Angus parish was in the Commissariot of either Brechin or St.Andrews, but up to about 1610 Angus people often registered testaments with the Commissary of Edinburgh. For 1801-23 there is a ms index and for 1846-67 there is a HMSO index (vol v for Forfarshire), both in the Scottish Record Office.

Fasti, Ewing and Small give brief biographies of Church of Scotland, Free Church and United Presbyterian church ministers respectively.

T H E   A B B R E V I A T E D   S C H E M E

" John Gray, fa Alex, mo Mary Reid, w Agnes Black 12.1840 40, s Jas (w Eliz Brown, s And (s Jas)),s Chas "

would mean that the relationship of names within brackets (that is, Eliz Brown and Andrew Gray) is to the name immediately before the bracket (that is, James Gray, their husband and father respectively) and names outwith brackets are related to the first person mentioned in the group (that is, John Gray whose parents were Alexander Gray and Mary Reid, whose wife Agnes Black died in December 1840 aged 40 years, and whose sons were James and Charles). This is a four- generations group, as James Gray has a grandson James son of Andrew.

Relationship groups are separated by a semi-colon ;

A single date after a name is a date of death, but two dates together are for date of birth and date of death respectively. Age in years (or in months, weeks, days as specified, or stillborn) may follow the date.

Uncertain words, letters or figures are in brackets thus (_ _).

Missing phrases, words, letters or figures are shown as - or - - - - - .

The burial ground sketch maps are <u>not</u> drawn to scale, but may indicate where family graves are clustered together. At Careston, for instance, it appears that different farms were allotted a part of the ground marked by wall plaques.

ABBREVIATIONS

Relationships

bro..brother
ch...child
1ch..eldest child
2ch..second child
chn..children
da...daughter
1da..eldest daughter
er...elder
fa...father
gchn.grandchildren
gda..granddaughter
gfa..grandfather
gs...grandson
h....husband
mo...mother
s....son
sis..sister
w....wife, usually spouse
1w...first wife
2w...second wife
wid..widow
yr...younger
yt...youngest
unm..unmarried

First names

Alex...Alexander
And....Andrew
Archd..Archibald
Cath...Catherine
Chas...Charles
Dond...Donald
Edw...Edward
Elis..Elisabeth
Eliz..Elizabeth
Geo...George
Jas...James
Kath..Katharine
Margt.Margaret
Patk..Patrick
Richd.Richard
Robt..Robert
Thos..Thomas
Wm....William

Other Abbreviations:

b.......born
bart....baronet
by......erected by
cem.....cemetery
col.....colonel
CT......chest tomb
d.......died or day/s
Davidson: Inventory of 17th century tombstones in Angus
DD......Doctor of Divinity
DNB.....Dictionary of National Biography
EICS....East India Company's Service
esq.....esquire
Ewing: Annals of the Free Church 1843-1900, 2 vol.
Fasti Ecclesiae Scoticanae 1915 et seq, 8 vol.
FC......Free Church of Scotland
fr......farmer
FS......flat stone
gen.....general
HR......heritors' records
imo.....in memory of
inf.....infant/infancy
int.....interred
Jervise: Epitaphs & Inscriptions from Burial Grounds in North east Scotland, 1875-9, 2 vol.
KS......kirk session
LLD.....Doctor of Law
lieut...lieutenant
m......month/s
MA.....Master of Arts
maj....major
manuf..manufacturer
md.....married
MD.....Doctor of Medicine
mert...merchant
min....minister of religion
mr.....mister
NSW....New South Wales, Australia
NZ.....New Zealand
ob.....obelisk
OPR....Old Parish Registers with the Registrar General, Edinburgh
par....parish
PSAS...Proceedings of Society of Antiquaries, Scotland
regt...regiment
rev....reverend
RN.....Royal Navy
Small: History of the Congregations of the UP Church 1733-1900, 2 vol.
SRO....Scottish Record Office
tent...tenant
Testaments: Commissariot Record, Registers (Scottish Record Society)
TS.....table stone
UP.....United Presbyterian
w......week/s
W & H..Willsher & Hunter, "Stones"(1978)
WS.....Writer to the Signet (solicitor)
y......year/s

1a ABERLEMNO

The parishes of Aberlemno and Aldbar were united early in the 17th century. The present parish church of Aberlemno was erected in 1722 and restored in 1856. It is well kept and visited frequently because of the notable cross slab with Pictish symbols in the burial ground.

The pre-1855 inscriptions were surveyed in August 1977.

National Grid reference: NO 523 556

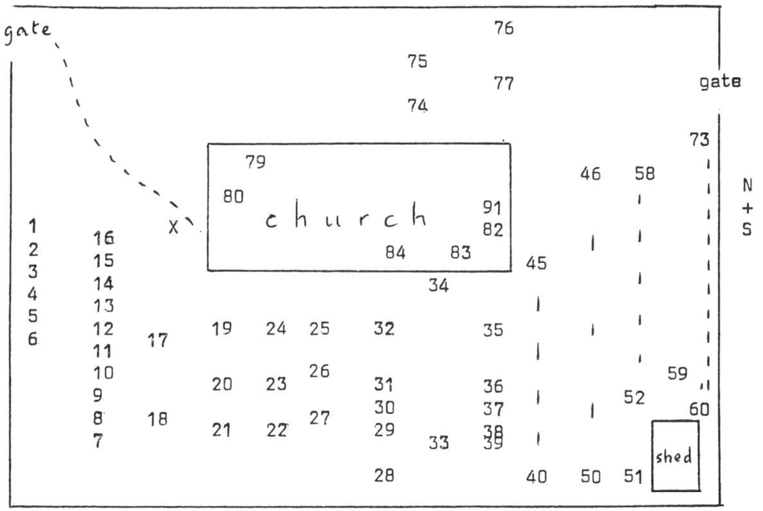

1 1850. John McDougan innkeeper 14.11.1849 36, w Susan Urquhart 7.9.1875 74, da Eliz 5.4.1862 22

2 by Mary Stirling, fa David Stirling weaver Whinniedrum 1.3.1737, mo Kath Eadie 9.11.1759, bro & siss Margt d nonage, Isabel 4.8.1789 50, Geo 1.9.1796 64, Mary 12.1.1798 62; (west side) emblems

3 David How sometime tent Bevellgreen 24.6.1752 45, by Isobel Jolly his - - -; D H I J ; IoH DH WH IH

4 IF IC ; 1768 RF ; IF MB ; IoF EF IanF IF AnF DF WF RF; IoF IeF IF DF MF WF AF ;
by Jas, John & Robt Fotheringhames sometime subtenant to Jas Peter in Balbinie d 3.1734, their mo Agnes Deor (or Deer) also the aforesaid Jas Fotheringhames wives & chn viz. Anne Gurley & Eliz Byres his spouses & John, Eliz, Janet, Jas, And Fotheringhames his chn

5 1827. by Helen Bain residing at Framedrum of Pitkennedy 21.12.1838 72, h Jas Fairweather 10.2.1826 65

6 by John & Jas Fanums imo fa John Fanum sometime subtenant in Nether Melgund 12.1746 46; David Fanum 2.1763 26;
IeF MF IoF EF DF IF

7 1865. by family, fa Chas Davidson sometime tent farm of Murton, par of Forfar d there 12.11.1825 38, mo Margret Donald d Southtown of Melgund 11.6.1864 76, bro Chas d Kirktoun this par 2.1839 26

8 184-. John Davidson 15.6.1839 40, da Margery 21.7.1839 8m, s John 25.12.1839 2, by w Helen Wyllie

9 John Davidson mert Henwellburn 14.3.1876 72, w Isabella Cuthbert 28.6.1887 80, s John 5.8.1909 63, s And 15.7.1913 73

10 by John & Jas Davidson, fa John Davidson sometime resident Henwellburn 16.11.1830 62, mo Jean McGregor 7.6.1816 41

11 1748. crown & hammer, anvil & pincers; -C -S ; IaC IoC IsC MC MC SC ; HC IC MC AC GC ;
their chn Isobel Cowie (24).9.1747 15, Geo Cowie; also aforesaid Geo Cowie d 1762; Jannet Smith 31.6.1771

12 Heir lyes the corps of Hilon Black who departed this lyf the 12 of Febrwari 1705 of hir age 28 year; (west side) GB YM ; GB IB HB IB

13 1834. Jas Bertie 10.1.1833 77, da Helen 4.1801 9m, s Walter d Arbroath 17.11.1829 28, by da

14 1742. by David Finlay & Margret Scott in Collerdrume of Ballgaes, chn Margret 13.8.1730 7, Margret 8.4.1734 3, s Jas 31.1.1738 2; (west side) DF ♡ MF 1742; stretcher & shuttle; MF AF DF MF MF IF ; KF ; emblems

15 1823. by Alex Gibb, w Jean Hutcheon 11.9.1820 28; David Hutcheon 19.9.1850 53

16 Jas & David Bell

17 W A I K ; by Wm Allexander tent Hillside of Balgavis & w Janet Ker, chn Jean 4.12.1765 19m, Hellen 11.3. aged 11m; (west side) share & coulter; WA IK CA IA HA ; emblems; text

18 Chas Henderson sometime tent Pitkennedy 11.3.1815 78, by w Elspeth Davidson, their chn then alive Ann, Elspeth, Margt, Janet, Sarah, Jas, Isabel, Jean & Chas; above Elspeth Davidson 25.3.1820 69; Jas Henderson, w Isabel Reid 24.1.1830 48

19 by David Mill & Janet Moleson, s Thos 28.12.1746 23; Thos Mill 1.12.17-- (30); Janet 8.2.1754 59; David Mill 2.2.1755 58; ThsM AndM DaM GeoM JanM IamM IsM; (west side) two fat children; text

20 Geo Ross sometime tent Blibberhill 15.4.1774 68, w Eliz Fairweather 25.6.1778 63; (west side) G R E F ; 1775; hammer

21 1851. by Chas Ross mechanic Dundee, fa David Ross d Muirside Auldbar 11.1808, mo Isabella Cuthill 3.1830, bros Wm 10.1828 & David 6.1845, w Bathina Petrie d Dundee 7.1849 48, their two ss David 3.1837 inf, Jas 13.9.1842 5y6m

22 1733. D H ; heir lyes the corpse of David Hood - - - sometime in Crosto - of Aberlemno & his maired w Agnes Fitchit lived with him 33y aged 79 & he died 26.1.1733; HH AH HH IH WH AH ; (east side) here also lie the ss of the aforesaid David Hood viz. Alex sometime tent Laws 6.1751 67, John sometime tent Crosstoun 4.1745 56, Wm sometime tent Balgarrok 5.1755 64; emblems

23 1813. by John Smith late tent Nether Turin, w Elis Findlay 24.11.1812 65, two ss John & Thos d nonage; John Smith 18.12.1812 77;
(west side) And Smith fr Nether Turin for 44y d 21.10.1844 72; And Smith da Jean 16.2.1831 19

24 heir lyes Henrie Inverarity sometime tent Framedrum 2.2.1766 88, w Agnes Wood 1723 35, another w Marget Black 28.4.1767 72, his chn John 17(3)6 18, Agnes nonage, Eliz 26.8.1741 3; (west side) emblems

1a ABERLEMNO

25 David Paterson late fr of Tillywhandland 25.1.1841 92, w Jean Barry d Lunanhead 9.5.1853 84, chn Jas d Arbroath 23.9.1880 78 int Abbey burying ground, Jean d Lunanhead 31.1.1888 84, David d there 31.8.1891 91 both int here

26 by John Webster sometime in Carsbank, fa Wm 2.1756 76; (west side) implement  ; IW IB 1781; Io, E, M, Is, Io, W, Io Websters

27 1843. David Mitchell late tent Waterside Newton 30.6.1833 76, by w Mary Hood 8.1.1850 86, da Janet 9.6.1842 48; Elis Hood 2.1854 93, wid of John Findlay supervisor of inland revenue (see SRO "The Scottish Excise Department" microfilm)

28 - - - - - K- - - - of Milg- - - - of their - - - - - died in 8.4. 1815 5y; (west side) 1815

29 by David, Isobel & Wm to bro John Nicol wevere in Lochhead 3.5.1728 35; Jas Nicol weaver Lochhead, w Isobel Dall, chn Jas & Alex; (west side) shuttle, stretchers & loom; text

30 1802. by Jas Nicol sometime tailor Henwelburn, w Marget Esplin 13.1. 1747 43; Agnes Davidson 21.11.1766 32; Jas Nicoll 13.2.1794 93; (west side) MN IsN TN JanN

31 1832. by Jas Irvine, fa Jas 10.7.1830 75, mo Janet Farquhar 29.3.1831 81, also Chas 20.7.1831 19

32 Alex Milne in Turin Hill, da Katherine 6.2.1837 21

33 Jas Hall quarrymaster Turin Hill 5.9.1881 86, w Janet Inverarity 15.9. 1843 43, da Jane 1.2.1915 77 (h Jas Stewart 28.5.1914 72, da Jessie Inverarity 23.7.1881 12, s Jas 4.12.1893 20, da Margt 17.4.1930 55)

34 mural. Wm Jaffray parochial schoolmaster here for 51y d 22.9.1824 74, w Jannet Brown 22.12.1822 72, da Helen 26.11.1808 23, Jannet 14.9.179(3) 10y

35 John Cattanach blacksmith Cottertoun of Balgavies 28.7.1869 43, w Isabella McGregor 23.9.1919 60, da Grace 27.2.1909 52, s Jas A of Birch Cottage Balgavies 18.12.1939 76

36 Chas Mann Cattanach 6.6.1966 74, w Sheila Sinclair 14.12.1973

37 John Catanach blacksmith 13.4.1858 75, w Eliz Paterson 16.4.1859 71, s Chas received injury in a leg on Aberdeen railway d Montrose Infirmary 27.3.1848 27

38 Jas Cattanach in North Mains of Balgavies 9.3.1900 74, w Isabella Mann 26.8.1898 74, s Chas 1878 25, da Jessie 1885 29, da Eliza 1885 37, da Mary-Ann 1914 58, s John 1940 76 (w Matilda Wishart 1899 31)

39 Alex Jas Laing Cattenach 1974 80

40 Margt Scott 16.6.1854 75, by chn

41 1862. Wm Spence fr Fonnab 5.12.1859 54

42 1756. Wm Spence lived sometime in Broomhill of Ballgavies 25.3.1755 63, w Elis Steven 25.2.1755, chn Wm 3y, Kathren 23y, David 15y, by s John in West Milldens (w Grisall Colvill 9.3.1757 34); This old race of Spences came there about the year 1438 where they & their offspring resided from father to son till the year 1820; John Spence lived & died in ground of Balgavies 1809 84 being the last of the name of Spence who lived in the ground of Balgavies, w Janet Ford 1782 41 after giving birth to five ss & five das; revised by s Andrew in Broughty Ferry; (east side) share & coulter; IS GC ; WS ES WS KS IS DS TS ; IsS IoS TS

DS AS ES ; Here lyes an honest old race / Who in Ballgavies land had a place / Of Residence, as may be seen / Full years three hundred and eighteen; Jas Spence tent Fonnab 5.11.1828 65, w Janet Anderson 29.11.1845 82

43 John Neish Jarron 7.7.1907, w Annie Kydd 6.2.1879

44 1845. John Jarron tent Mains of Melgund 7.8.1837 69, w Margt Hunter 16.11.1862 87, chn Robt, Isabel, Jean & Barbara all inf, Jas d of typhoid fever at Greenock on his return from England 23.10.1838 22 int Greenock; Mary Ann Jarron or Cable 28.9.1892 84

45 1797. Jas Peter tent Mains of Melgund 22.10.1796 46, da Betty 29.1.1784 3, by w Agnes Smith & da Mary; In hopes in peace his Lord to meet/ Here lies interrd in dust / One in his temper ever kind / In all his dealings just, / Kind to the poor, the widow's friend / He always did remain,/ Till Heaven's great Lord by his decree / Recalled his life again.

46 1756. David Cramond tent Moorside of Melgond 7.2.1755 38, by w Jean Gib

47 Chas Gordon tent Muirside of Melgond 9.8.1841 81, w Eliz Gibson 25.10.1857 86, s Jas 4.6.1806 9, s David d America 5.10.1819 26, da Margt 11.1.1822 28, by da Jean

48 - - M S ; 1748 ; G A E M ; G A M W G A A A C A IsA IoA B A ; Geo Anderson tent Clattie Mill & w Eliz Morton, s Geo pickieman at Balgarvock 9.3.1747; all buried here ; mill rhind & millstone pick; thistles & roses

49 Wm Burns d Netherton of Melgund 8.3.1930 89, w Beatrix Findlay 17.11.1937 92

50 1815. Wm Burns smith Nethertoun, w Margt Thomson 26.6.1814 31, four surviving chn Elis, David, Margt, Joseph; (east side) Wm Burns smith Nethertown of Melgund for 42y d 4.6.1845 78

51 Joseph Petrie 19.4.1862 74, w Mary Scott 7.1.1837 54, chn Janet, Margt & Jane inf, gs Joseph King 3.9.1854 3

52 1780. by Wm Findlay tent Melgam & w Agnes Black & s Jas, s Wm 12.9.1772 20; square & compasses, axe, saw; WF AB IaF KF MF AF IF

52a by And Langlands & Agnes Hunter sometime in Southtown of Melgund, das Margt 26.8.1824 25, Reynold 8.6.1817 15

53 I L ♡ I B 1732 ; share & coulter; IL IeL IoL GL AllL ML DL AL; (east side) by John Langlands & Janet Ballbirnie she d 5.1744 47 in Haugh of (Thoneve<u>n</u>), s Jas 12.1730 11, s David (<u>4</u>.172<u>8</u>), da Ann 1740

54 1788. by John Langlands then tent Bogarda, w Eliz Scott 6.7.1787 2(<u>8</u>) & her chn Alex b 17.5.1783, David b 20.6.1785, Ann b 20.6.1787; IL ES

55 A C I C 1785; - - - - - - - - - - ary 176(<u>8</u>) - - - - - abb the - - - - - - - Crabb

56 by David - - - - - - - - - - - ; (east side) shuttle, stretchers & heddle; AM IM DM EP ; John Milne; Helen Milne; John Milne; Isbel Milne; David Milne; Jean Milne; Janet Milne; David Milne; John Milne; 1745 (but see no.88 infra)

57 Wm Robertson in Eastsghiel Pitkennedy d Auldbar Cottage 6.12.1881 79, w Janet Matthew d Auldbar Cottage 14.12.1885 84, chn Jas d Australia 18.3.1871 44, Wm d Newtown of Melgund 30.12.1863 34, Mary Ann d Eastsghiel 11.8.1842 15, John Matthew d Largo 28.2.1881 41

58 1826. Jas Kennedy 11.2.1821 55, by w Jean Burnet, da Janet 16.2.1807 10m, s And 18.5.1809 6

59 John Gowans tent Woodend of Auldbar 17.6.1793 75, fa Jas, bro Jas, sis Agnes all int here, by w Jean Saunders & Geo McAllie; (west side) I G I S

60 Peter Bell esq of Balconnel for upwards of 30y tent Crosstown Aberlemno 13.1.1850 67, bro Jas at Balnacake 27.12.1824 44, by s Geo of Balconnel, s Peter 10.1.1845 21

61 by Jas Davidson in Pitkennedy & w Isobel Irvine 1.12.1821 76, da Jean 13.4.1791 16, s Alex 16.2.1796 14, s Robt 20.11.1797 18, da Isabel 15.9.1815 24

62 - - - - - - - (flaked)

63 AC IC DC MC IC AC ; John Craik 1775 76, w Margt Storrock sometime in Corstowne of Aberlemno 1795 92, chn Alex 10.5.1730 2, Margt 10.3.1739 4, Alex 28.8.1740 1, Mary 1803 62, Jas 1808 70, John tent Balglaysie 6.6.1777 47 (w Margt 1.10.1813 68, 6 chn d inf of whom two of name John, Margt 29.9.1813 43)

64 John Stewart sklater lived in Turin 16.7.1717 66, w Isobel Hutchen 26.10.1717 57; I S I H ; DS IS IS MS ; Thos Thornton in Kirkton here 17.7.1732 40; T T ♡ M S; IH IH TH ; slater's tools

65 FS heir rests ane faithful sister qvha livit vith hir mariet hesbent Veliam Alerdys borges in Dundie 29 zeiris calit Ianet Ademson qvha depertit in this paries the 19 day of Iuli anno 1600; W A I A ; a field charged for Allardyce(as in no.66; this inscription is elucidated in Jervise vol i p8)

66 FS V A ; heir rests ane faithful brother V A qvha departit this lyfe the 17 day of Avgvst anno Christi - - - - - - ; I A ; field charged for Allardyce (see Jervise i 9, also Jervise "Memorials of Angus" (1885 2nd edition) for the family of Allardyce.)

67 FS heir rests in the Lord ane faithful brother Alexander Watson sumtym in Crostvovn departit 28 of Febrvarii 1622 aige 51; A W M D V W; I live to die - I die to live. (see Jervise i 9)

68 FS John Dalgetie 13.2.1697 8(0), w Margt Philp ; two shields, ID MH ; Wnder this ston thir Mortals doe remain / Whil Chryst be Pleased to reas them up again / Altho by death they be in Prison cast / The Prince of Lyfe vill reas them up again / And giv them Lyf vhich no more vill Decay / An habitation vhich passeth not away.

69 TS tipped up. I W ♡ I I ; C W A D 1739 IW MW IW ; by Jas & John W - - - er, fa Jas - - - - who lived in Cro - - - Aberlemno & d 27.(5) 1737 (67), w - - - - - - - - - 17(20) 58y also - - - - - - d 1.1721 29, da Margt 27.12.172(0) - -, also bro aged - - - - -

70 TS faithfull sister Agnes All(an) - - - - - - - - - - - - - - (Joh)n Allan who lived sumtim in the - - - - - - - -

71 here rests in God a faithful brother Wm Dorwart 3.6.1623 61

72 I P IC 1758 ; I^{am}; I^{an}; M; I^{s} Peter; John Peter tent South Melgund, by s Jas, da Isobel 19.11.175- 23 (see Jervise i for poem epitaph)

73 1788; share & coulter; poem (quoted in Jervise i); (side against wall) I T I F ; by Jas, John & Joseph Taylor, fa Jas tent Wandershill 2.1785 75, & their bro David 22.11.1774 22; John Taylor 28.6.1790 28; Jas Taylor in Li- - field (2.7.)1862 74

74 Geo Jarron fr Mains of Melgund 13.7.1874 70, by w Agnes Hunter 2.2.1882 76, s Geo d Bonnyton Inverarity 6.2.1900 54

75 Alex McKenzie gardener Turin for 27y d Turin Gardens 6.7.(1901) 72, w Margt Hay d there 12.11.1887 70, chn Geo d Turin 19.10.1867 19, Alex d Bonnington 12.6.1853 15m, Alex d Coulmony 10.4.1863 9, Margt inf

76 And Henderson fr Woodrae for 54y 1.1787 1870, w Barbara Jarron 10.1799 9.1876, s And 2.6.1866 32, Geo 6.7.1866 24, das Joanna 5.1848 3, Anne 18.10.1901 75, Agnes Jarron 26.1.1921 81

77 Jas McLaren fr Balgarrock 6.4.1901 85, w Agnes Jarron 11.9.1898 83, chn Margt 16.1.1842 30.9.1846, Alex 30.4.1843 29.3.1848, Jas 15.6.1845 15.4. 1848, Jessie 9.10.1850 26.9.1870; John McLaren of Balgills 17.1.1848 11.6.1918

78 1852. by Wm Cooper contractor to his foreman Bohn Flaxman of Brighouse near Halifax Yorkshire 19.6.1852 38

79 mural in church. mr Thos Ml ordained 1714; mr And Ml ordained 1750; mr Jas Michl ordained 1794; by mr Thos Mitchel min here d 9.1.1750 59 & w Marie Miller, two chn Thos & Agnes d nonage, s rev And 4.1.1794 64 (w Jean Craw 27.9.1809 86, s rev Jas 13.5.1841 71); said rev Jas Mitchel, 1w Eliz Sedgwick 3.5.1821 53, her chn Eliz Burnett, Alex, Marmaduke, And, Jean Craw, Georgina, Margt, Eliza Tailyour & Frances Nicol all of whom except Alex & And d before her, 2w Janet Webster, her da Eliz

80 mural in church. 1803. Geo Jarron of Balbinnie 5.1.1793 65, by chn Geo, John, Robt, Ann & Jean; Geo Jarron, w Barbara Wallace 15.4.1797 33, da Barbara d nonage; also of chn Robt & Isabel (note - Jervise i 8 has "also of Robt & Isabel Jarron's children" in error)

81 mural in church, in Latin. Wm Chalmers of Auldbar d vii id jul (ie. 9 July) 1765, w Cecilia Elphinston d non mart (ie. 7 March) 1761 58, by s (see Jervise i 8: Wm Chalmers was s of Chalmers of Hazelbank in Aberdeenshire & was a successful merchant in Spain; his wife was daughter of Elphinston of Glack descended from Arthur brother of bishop Elphinston founder of Kings College Aberdeen; Wm Chalmers bought Aldbar in 1753 & was succeeded by s Patk sheriff of Forfar 1774-1819)

82 mural in church. Patk Chalmers esq of Auldbar advocate 15.2.1824 87; virtuous & learned, polished & refined / Of pleasing manners and enlightened mind / Beloved in Life, lamented at his end/ Below / Here sleeps the Sire the Grandsire, and the Friend.

83 mural in church. Isabel Tindal 2.11.1811 67

84 mural in church. 1604. J B E M (Jervise i 10 says this stone was believed to have come from Melgund Castle & to represent Jas Beaton of Melgund (gs of cardinal Beaton) & his w Eliz Menzies; see St Andrews Testaments: Jas Bethune of Melgund, 1613)

The following inscriptions were not seen in 1977 and are taken from And Jervise "Epitaphs & Inscriptions" vol i pp 9-10

85 FS heir rests ane fa - - - - - - - - - - - - - - - - - - riet vyf Janet vobster 6.1605 66

86 FS - - - - - as Daigati qvha leavet v^{t} his m - - - - - ther day - - - - Alexandr Daigati, John Daigati

87 FS And Dalgetie - - - - 89 age 70, w Euphan Bell 24.12.1672 41

88 1734. David Milne; poem

89 the arms & initials of Margt Ogilvy, the mo of cardinal Beaton's chn,

are on the ruins of Melgund Castle

90 a monogram of initials of Geo first earl of Huntly & of his w Henrietta Stewart is built into the farm offices of Mains of Melgund

N o t e s

Jervise: "Epitaphs & Inscriptions...." vol i devotes pp 7-10 to some local history of Aberlemno with tombstone inscriptions 29, 42, 45, 48, 65-8, 72-3 and 79-90 or parts of them

Fasti vol v 276: ministers from 1567 including three generations of Mitchells who were ministers in succession from 1716 to 1841.

Davidson: "An Inventory ...." has descriptions of stones no. 65 & 66

Edinburgh Testaments: a random selection includes
Walter Bellie, his spouse Margt Newton in Tulliquhandlane, 1598;
William Bellie at the Mylne of Drummis par of Aldbar, spouse Isobel Watt, 9.2.1598-9

St.Andrews Testaments: a random selection includes
Geo Allan at Woodside of Aldbarr, 1778;
Thos Anthony cottarman in Claschbenny, 1607;
John Davidson in the Muirsyde of Melgund, 1675;
Elspet Dempster spouse to John Bellie in Nethertowne of Melgum, 1638;
Gelis Esplin spouse to David Symson in Balgaie, 1606;
Henry Esplin in Kirktoun of Guthrie par Aberlemno, 1746;
Wm Ochterlony in Milnehill of Kellie, spouse Isobel Somer, 1613;
Robt Young of Aldbar, 1734.

Ewing: "Annals of the Free Church..." A congregation was formed at Aberlemno in 1843, but no minister was appointed until 1857.

OPR with the Registrar General:
269 Aberlemno - Births 1706-16, 1745-1854
Marriages,1707-10, 1745-1854
Deaths, 1706-14, 1724-29

SRO: CH2/5 minutes & accounts 1731-1893
CH3/6 Aberlemno FC KS minutes 1857-1924
HR 310 Heritors records minutes 1854-1931

I n d e x

Ademson	65
Alerdys	65-6
Alexander	17
Allan	70.Notes
Allardyce	65-6
Anderson	42.48
Anthony	Notes
Bain	5
Ballbirnie	53
Barry	25
Beaton	84.89
Bell	16.60.87
Bellie	Notes
Bertie	13
Black	12.24.52
Brown	34
Burnet	58
Burns	49-50
Byers	4
Cable	44
Cat(t)anach	35-8
Cattenach	39
Chalmers	81-2
Colvill	42
Cooper	78
Cowie	11
Crabb	55
Craik	63
Cramond	46
Craw	79
Cuthbert	9
Cuthill	21

1a ABERLEMNO

Daigati 86
Dalgetie 68.87
Dall 29
Davidson 7-10.18.30.61.Notes
Deer/Deor 4
Dempster Notes
Donald 7
Dorwart 71

Eadie 2
Elphinston 81
Esplin 30.Notes

Fairweather 5.20
Fanum 6
Farquhar 31
Fin(d)lay 14.23.27.49.52
Fitchit 22
Flaxman 78
Ford 42
Fotheringhame 4

Gib(b) 15.46
Gibson 47
Gordon 47
Gowans 59
Gurley 4

Hall 33
Henderson 18.76
Hood 22.27
How 3
Hunter 44.52a.74
Huntly 90
Hutche(o)n 15.64

I. 69
Inverarity 24.33
Irvine 31.61

Jaffray 34
Jarron 43-4.74.76-7.80
Jolly 3

K. 28
Kennedy 58
Ker 17
King 51
Kydd 43

Langlands 52a-54

McAllie 59
McDougan 1
McGregor 10.35
McKenzie 75
McLaren 77

Mann 38
Matthew 57
Menzies 84
Mill 19
Miller 79
Milne 32.56.88
Mitchel(l) 27.79.Notes
Moleson 19
Morton 48

Nicol(l) 29-30

Ochterlony Notes
Ogilvy 89

P. 56
Paterson 25.37
Peter 4.45.72
Petrie 21.51
Philp 68

Reid 18
Robertson 57
Ross 20.21

S. 48.64
Saunders 59
Scott 14.40.51.54
Sedgwick 79
Sinclair 36
Smith 11.23.45.
Somer Notes
Spence 41-2
Steven 42
Stewart 33.64.90
Stirling 2
Storrock 63
Symson Notes

Taylor 73
Thomson 50
Thornton 64
Tindal 83

Urquhart 1

Vobster 85

W. 69
Wallace 80
Watson 67
Watt Notes
Webster 26.79.85
Wishart 38
Wood 24
Wyllie 8
Young Notes

1b A B E R L E M N O , A L D B A R

Aldbar and Aberlemno parishes were united early in the 17th century. The ruin of Aldbar pre-Reformation church was rebuilt in 1853 as a chapel for Chalmers of Aldbar and is again ruinous. The site is in the den, difficult to reach and overgrown with nettles.

All Inscriptions were listed in June 1978.

National Grid reference: NO 573 583

1 cross. John Inglis Chalmers of Aldbar 2.8.1809 15.5.1868

2 Patk Chalmers of Aldbar, da Frances 8.6.1805 10.1.1872

3 Jas Inglis esq of Jamaica, relict Mary Jane d Brechin 11.4.1852 72

4 sarcophagus. Patk Chalmers 31.10.1802 23.6.1854

5 cross. John Inglis, w Margt Chalmers, s Patk 1.1841 1925, & Ellen M Chalmers 17.4.1936

6 Patk & Ellen Chalmers of Aldbar Brechin, s Wolseley b 31.10.1876 d 27.7. 1914 at Santa Cruz Mexico

7 - - - - fallen - - - -

The following were not seen in 1978 but are taken from Jervise and from rev Chas Rogers:"Monuments & Monumental Inscriptions in Scotland"

8 brass in chapel. Patk Chalmers esq of Aldbar many y mert London b here 1777 d here 8.12.1826, w Frances Inglis d here 10.2.1848 69

9 brass in chapel. Patk Chalmers esq of Aldbar,late capt 3rd dragoon guards, sometime MP Montrose Burghs, author "The Sculptored Monuments of Angus", re-edified this chapel 1853, d Rome 23.6.1854 int outside this chapel (see DNB; Jervise notes his bro John Inglis Chalmers d 1868)

10 on old tower of Aldbar Castle. STL DED (for sir Thos Lyon & dame Euphemia Douglas (da of the earl of Morton)

11 on lintel at Blackiemill. 1698 RY AG (for Robt Young & Ann Graham)

N o t e s

see Aberlemno

I n d e x

Chalmers	1-2.4-6.8-9	Inglis	3.5
Douglas	10	Lyon	10
Graham	11	Young	11

2 A I R L I E

The parish church was dedicated to St. Medan in 1242. The pre-Reformation church was overbuilt by a new church about 1603, and this was replaced by the present church in 1783.

The pre-1855 inscriptions were surveyed in June 1976.

National Grid refernce: NO 313 514

2 AIRLIE

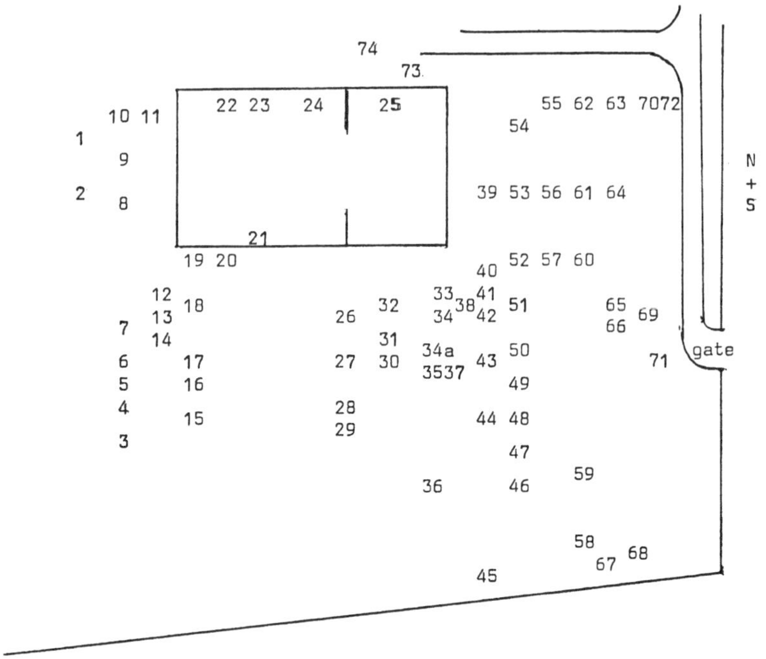

1 Wm Ramsay 6.3.1876 71, w Margt Robertson 8.8.1886 84, da Margt L 7.1853 4½, s Wm 14.7.1879 36, da Cath Robertson 16.2.1897 55

2 David Ramsay in Muirhouses here 8.1.1909 69, w Isabella Newton d Litchfield farm Enstone 7.5.1940 88, s John inf, da Christina 21.9. 1973 86

3 1874. David Davie for many y tent Brae of Airlie 22.9.1865, w Cath D d Airlie 2.3.1904 86, chn Jessie 22.8.1852 5, David McLaren 20.5. 1855 3w, Wm d Pallamacottah India 16.2.1870 26, Annie 17.6.1845 2.6. 1885 (h Wm Ramsay), gchn Mary Salter Ramsay 12.9.1878 9.11.1949 (h Jas Kinnear) & Margt Eliz Ramsay 20.4.1873 10.10.1953 (h Hugh Frazer Rankin OBE)

4 1835. John Davie 12.1.1835 69, w Eliz Maclaren 18.6.1834 74, by chn David & Janet in Wester Brae of Airlie; (west side) plough, three corn sheaves

5 John Davie 1848 1914, w Isabella Gordon 1852 1928, chn David 1877 1877, Isabela Sim 1876 1917, Cath Salter 1878 1948, James Gordon 1883 1958 (w Janet G Lyon), Wm 1881 1966 (w Alexina Coventry), Annie 1885 1974

6 A G Kinnear d Johannesburg 8.3.1953 ashes here, w Margt Gordon Davie of Krugersdorp South Africa d in her native land 16.9.1932

7 1761. by Thos Davie & w Isobel Myle in Wardend of Lentrathen, s Patk 19.7.1760 11; (west side) cherub, emblems, shield with shoe; T D   I M   PD   ID   ID ; poem (see Jervise i 162 for poem)

8 FS (marginal) David Sandyman in Grange of Airly 27.11.1733 65, w Isobel

Myles 2.12.1733 60; two cherubs; WS MS GS MS ; emblems; shield with oxenyoke and D S I M

9 1854. Robt Smith 3.1.1853 55, by w Margt Whitton of Cardean Mill & s Wm

10 FS an honest man Alex Marshall 20.9.1727, w Agnas Layon; emblems

11 John Dawson butler Lendertis for 23y d there 10.2.1846, w Margt Young 27.7.1841

12 FS (marginal) Jas Adam tent Waster Camsie in the Parsie (ie. parish) of Lintrathen 4.1730 39 leaving behind him two ss & three das, by w Jean Wright; emblems ; I A I W ; IA TA IA HA IA

13 TS hire lyes ane honest man callit John Adam who lived in Clintlo 8.12. 1678 53, w Isobel Gibbon; I A I G ; TA AA EA (for da Alspit see Lintrathen inscription no. 30)

14 FS Geo Adam sometime in Di - - ent 4.4.1695 66, w Christan Henderson; G A C H ; IA WA HA WA GA IA ; emblems ; epitaph

15 FS John Broun in Kearlenwale 15.6.1682 80 & Janet Barnet 29.1.1688 62; emblems; I B I B

16 TS two cherubs; yoke, share & coulter; (west) 1750; monogram; (south) RL IL ; (marginal) by Robt Lounan fr Lindertis & w Margt Nicol, s Robt 2.9.1746 13 (see Jervise i 162 for poem)

17 Fs (marginal) Jas Ducher, w Agnas Lunan 1634 26

18 FS by - - - - - - - - - - - Androw Wallace - - - - - - - - - - - -26.8.167(<u>3</u>) 80y; A W A R ; (central) - - - - - age 80y

19 FS originally with 20 in the enclosure beside 38. John Nicoll sometime tent Lenross, w Isobell Watson 16.3.1695 69; John Nicoll tent Nevay 1788 80; emblems

20 FS originally beside 38. 1736. Jas Nicol sometime in Kinalty 10.1733 61, w Isobell Hood 3.1719, by chn Elspeth, John, Jas, Margt & Janet & at desire of s Wm d 5.1735 18, also chn Isobel, Alex, Jean & Frederick d in their minority. 1849. revised by Alex Nicol tent Littelton

21 over door of enclosure. This burial builded by E M Villiam Malcolm 1609; emblems; M W M G M (see 24 infra)

22 - - - - illegible - - -

23 marble mural. John Hill of Cotton of Craigs 1804 over 90y, s John yr 31.7. 1803 41 (w Margt Playfair 24.11.1853 85); other John Hill 24.6.17(<u>9</u>)3 27.12.1847; Kath Hill 25.4.1796 10.3.1816; Ann Hill 23.9.1797 10.11. 1840 (h Jas Thomas writer Perth); Chas Hill 10.4.1795 12.1795; David Hill 27.8.1801 7.6.1860

24 mural. Girsel Mathou 23.2.1609 38, wife of maister Villiam Malcolm min here (see Fasti v 247)

25 ministers int here: rev Frederick Lyon MA 9.1699 47; rev Wm Lyon 4.1. 1743 67; rev Jas Stormonth MA 27.12.1809 56; rev Robt Aikman 8.7.1832 67; rev David White 29.12.1873 66 (see Fasti v 247-8)

26 FS Thos Mustart lived in Cookston 22.8.1675 32, w Margret Watson; emblems ; T M

27 fallen

28 Wm Watson potato mert Lownie 9.10.1911 62, fa John d Blackhill here 27.5. 1870 62, mo Betsy Burnett 24.10.1884 61

29 loom & shuttle; (west side) by Jas Watson, fa John d Blackhill Bre(dill-ven) 1796 81, (w) Isobel Smith 60y, chn Robt, Hellen & Thos inf

30 A L; Patk Smith hamarman Baickie, w Agnes Long 11.1.1674 53, (s) John 11.1.1679 (w Janet Smith); emblems

31 FS by (Robt Smith). w Isobel Adam 16.4.1748 35, s John - - - - - ; two cherubs; crown & hammer; R S I A 174- ; HS $J^{O}S$ -S

32 TS (marginal) lyes John Chaiplaine 9.11.1659 22, s of John in Cingoldrowme & Elane Smale his mo

33 FS sword, horn & shield; cross ; - - - ter Roger & Yofan Rolok who d in Ridie 1640 (see Jervise i 162 & C Rogers "Monuments.." ii 195; also "The Scottish Branch of the Norman House of Roger" (1872) p 20; Edinburgh Testaments - David Roger in Redie, 26.2.1581; 1s Wm his executor, 2s David, gs John got the lease of the farm & his s Jas executed a will in 1610 by which his daughters were to inherit if their husbands took the name of Roger. The Roger family remained at Aitlie till the beginning of the 19th century)

34 And Archer hird in Blakston, w Agnes Fairweather 5.2.1735 46, chn David 24.9.1722 1y, Jas 5.8.1722 4, Johanna - - - ; cherub; (west side) A A A F 1735; cherub

34a FS (marginal) by John Archer & Margt Low of (Drumished) to his fa And 76y & his mo Agnes Far(weather) who d 1764; oxen yoke, share & coulter; (see Jervise i 162 for poem)

35 coped stone. I A I A 1754 ; emblems; (south panel) heir lyis Ihon Allen d in anno 16(3)1 and of his aige - -; (north panel) Iscbel Th(omson) wha d ano (1641) and of hir age 6(2) (see Davidson p 6)

36 TS (marginal) by - - - - (Fairwe)at(her) - - Isabel Adam tents in Fort(h)ink to da Iannet (Fair)weather d (24).12. 1778 2(C or 6); emblems

37 TS (marginal) heir lyes David Wighton shoemaker sometime indweller in Brydstoun 14.2.1692 70, w Janet Broun 7.10.1692 54; D W I B

38 ob Alex Nicoll fr Littleton d there 22.12.1861 68, w Janet Small d there 14.2.1846 43, chn Alex, Eliz, Janet, Jessie d inf, Isabella Hunter 14.1. 1857 24, Jane Johnston or mrs Mundell 16.2.1858 26, Geo d Kildinny par of Forteviot 18.3.1874 34; (south side) Thos Munro Nicoll fr Littleton b 12.8.1842 d 21.2.1912, w Jane Reid 22.3.1844 17.1.1928; Thos Reid Nicoll 12.5.1898 15; (north side) John Nicoll fr Reedie 1837 1901, w Margt Pattullo 1847 1906; Herbert Hunter Nicoll d Reedie 3.10.1885 4m (see also inscriptions 19 & 20)

39 TS 1735; (marginal) by Wm Fenton imo da Janet a young woman of excellent virtue 26.4.1764 20 diservedly regretted by all

40 by Wm & Chas Stewart, fa John 6.9.1815 61

41 And Milne fr Dillavaird 22.5.1861 49, by w Mary Lamond 10.8.1898 84

42 sarcophagus. Alex Irvine 26.3.1868 46, w Ann Ogilvy Lamond 3.10.1917 36

43 Francis Lamond fr East Mains of Airlie 6.11.1864 71, w Isabella Hendry 13.1.1883 81, chn John 1842 17, Mary 14.12.1848 16m, Margt 11.1854 12

44 Wm Nicoll in Lenros, fa John Nicol 25.4.1673 23; I N I W ; emblems

45 leaning against wall. by Thos Low tylor in Gallie Hill imo w Cathron Lounan

11.6.1749 77; DL KL EL IL IL BL ;
tailor's goose and scissors

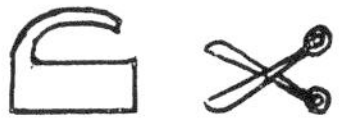

46 by rev Thos Reid in 46th y of ministry here d 11.12.1889 86, w Jessie Fenton 19.3.1848, s Jas 4.6.1868; Hugh Munro Pattullo 16.5.1961 86, 1w Jeannie Nicoll 3.6.1913 38, 2w Eleanor Johnstone Boyd 28.12.1960 83, s Kenneth Davidson 17.10.1929 26; Jean Reid Hodgson nee Pattullo d Port Elizabeth South Africa 4.6.1974 73 (see Fasti v 248)

47 by Robt Stewart in West Mill, two ss Jas 6.12.1829 15 & David 25.12.1832 20; (west side) 1833

48 1837. Wm Grimmond in Grange of Airly 12.1838 54, w Jean Miller 17.2.1837 45, s John 22.8.1833 19, da Margery 18.2.1835 17, s Jas 3.3.1835 6, da Emily 5.3.1866 29, Margt 2.2.1874 58

49 1870. Robt Thomson d Manse Cottage 31.10.1911 98, w Helen Hickson d there 13.12.1881 75, s Peter 17.10.1853 15, da Helen 13.5.1861 10, s Robt 25.2.1869 25, s Jas 24.5.1883 52, da Ann 27.10.1894 58; Thos Thomson fr Hatton Ogilvy 28.6.1910 68 int Glamis cem; their da Jane Reid 2.1.1925 78

50 by Jas Thomson fr in Middle Campsie, imo da Beatrix 18.12.1745 12m; JT; oxenyoke, share & coulter

51 FS E K R F ; 15(96) ; ?skull

52 FS (marginal) heir lyis Androv Vright qha depairted this lyf Agust anno 16(3 or 5)6 & of his age 61 ; A W E C (but Jervise i 162 gives 1506, and Davidson gives 1636)

53 FS heir lyis Ihon Wright who depairtit this lyfe in Dec. anno 16(33) and of his age - - ; heir lyis also his spous Margrat -t-vmbe- wha diet 12. 16(3)3 & of hir aige -6

54 FS by Jannet Whyte, h John Wright tent Castleton 2.2.1657 80; repaired by Robt Wright imo Agnes Graham his mo 3.1.1818 77

55 FS (marginal) heir lyes ane honest woman called Elspet Cardean spouse to Thos Barnit in Cants mil 8.4.1644 and of hir age 24 zeirs; TB EC

56 FS (marginal) David Cardeain 3.5.1662 74; Elspat Stil 4.6.1662 68; DS ; ICHL

57 Thos Cardean tent Easter Dunnoon 1.1771 63, two das Isobel & Helen, by his w Helen Malcolm;
Oxen yoke, share and coulter; TC HM

58 by John Palmer 11.3.1875 67, w Margt Chambers 30.12.1860 49, ss Thos 5.12.1860 17, Joseph 25.8.1869 at Fenagh Lodge in County Carlow Ireland 33y (w Eliz Burton 17.6.1864 32 both int Fenagh churchyard), Wm 8.12.1853 19, David 4.2.1854 5, da Eliz 29.6.1854 11m, da Ann 31.1.1856 18

59 Peter Moncur d Burnside of Airlie 14.6.1849 71, by w Eliz Robertson

60 Wm Mershal sometime in Miln of (cuming) 15.10.1757 73, by w Isoball Nicoll & chn Wm, Patk & Janet

61 TS W M - N ; cherubs ; oxenyoke, share & coulter

62 FS heir lyes Androw Ba+ter in Weltoun of Airly who departed upon the 25th of May 1649 his age 8(2) & Janet Mustert his spouse d (26).6.1656 hir age 61; A B I M ; emblems

63 TS John Hood who lived in Readie 16.1.1669 62, w Janet Irnes; IH II AH

64 TS Jas Hood who lived some time in Reedie 2.3.1673 33, 2s of John; emblems

65 TS W H E R; mantling; cherubs; (marginal) here lye Wm Hood somtyme in Neather Logy who departed this lyfe the 28 day of Febrruary 1758 aged 56 y & his wife Elspeth Ratry who departed this lyfe 31. - - - -

66 TS 1748; John Thomson 16.4.177(6 or 4), w Margret Kinoch 2.2.1806; Wm Thomson d (3 or 5).2.1787; John, James, Wm, Alex, Thomas Thomsons

67 cherub; A G A C ; poem; loom, shuttle, emblems; (on top) 1732; (west side) by And Glendy, imo w Agnes Constable 30.3.1732 58

68 emblems; M N A N C P ; (other side invisible against south wall)

69 by Alison Lowdon 1.11.1892 81 in Kirkton of Airlie, imo mo Ann McCraw 15.11.1832 50, fa Wm Lowdon 2.9.1867 81, her bros Jas 16.11.1834 19, John 8.12.1834 18, aunt Alison Lowdon 7.11.1843 69; Alison McAndrew 10.12.1847 10

70 1835. David Paterson architect & tent Newton of Airlie 2.10.1834 42, 2s David 4.10.1823 4; (west side) 1835

71 1845. Geo Gray at Getside in par of Glamis 18.3.1844 86, w Isabell Young 4.4.1845 81, chn Isabell 1796 4m, Jas 25.2.1813 19

72 by David Rattray fr Bakie, w Eliz Stevenson, chn Jas 16.10.1830 3.3.1835 Eliz 5.5.1832 10.3.1835, Margrey 2.7.1833 13.3.1835, Margt 20.4.1837 16.6.1841

73 1728. by John Arnot fr Pitterro & Janet Arnot fr Ingleston of Bridgtun, imo fa Jas sometime fr Bridgton 20.2.1791 66; (west side) mantling, shield, J A M W

74 Jas Grive & I May Findlater in Chri-stie, s Jas 30.7.1828 2(4); Jas Grave, w May Findlater 19.7.1829 44

The following was not seen in 1976 and is taken from And Jervise "Epitaphs & Inscriptions..." vol i p 162:

75 1748. Robt Cairns, his wife d leaving a husband and children; poem

N o t e s

Jervise: "Epitaphs & Inscriptions...." vol i refers to inscriptions nos. 7, 16 21, 24, 34a, 33, 52, 56, 75.

Rev Wm Wilson: "Airlie, a Parish History" (1917)

Fasti: vol v p246 - ministers from 1587

Ewing ii 154 - Airlie FC ministers from 1843

Edinburgh Testaments: a random selection includes
Alexander Dick in Gallowhill par of Nether Airlie, 1591;
James Hill in Cairneywell, 1603;
Helen Roger sometime spouse to Wm Smyth elder in Cardene, 1583.

St. Andrews Testaments: a random selection includes
Christian Adam in Brydistoune, 1618;
Margaret Adam spouse to Walter Great in Cotton of Kynnaltie, 1618;
Christian Bonar spouse to John Edward, 1598;
John Mustard at Myln of Cookstoun, 1681;
Robert Mustard son of deceased David in Carden, 1618;
Thos Mustart in Easter Cuikston, his spouse Marjorie Piggott, 1614;
William Mustard in Carden, 1614
And Nicol in Auchendorie, 1617

2 A I R L I E

Christian Nicol spouse to Henry Smyth in Bakie, 1617;
Isobel Nicol spouse to John Mitchell in Balkie, 1613
David Ogilvie of Kinaltie, 1675 & 1693
James Ogilvie in Dillavaird, 1649;
Menry Smith in Lundis, 1732;
John Wilkie in Cookston, his spouse Isobel Haldane, 1740;
Andrew Wright in Reidie, 1637;
James Wright at the Mylne of Cuikston, 1624.

OPR with the Registrar General, 270 Airlie:
Births 1682-1713, 1717-21, 1723-1854
Marriages 1682-1854
Deaths 1706-1854
KS minutes 1682-1847 & other matters 1814-24

SRO CH3 nil
HR170 minutes 1861-1927
GD 16/46/95 & GD 16/47/12 concerning church, manse & school from 1781-1887 (Airlie Muniments)

Index

Adam 12-4.31.36.Notes
Aikman 25
Allen 35
Archer 34.34a
Arnot 73

Barnet/it 15.55
Baxter 62
Bonar Notes
Boyd 46
Broun 15.37
Burnett 28
Burton 58

C. 52.56
Cairns 75
Cardean 55-7
Chaiplane 32
Chambers 58
Constable 67
Coventry 5

Davie 3-7
Dawson 11
Dick Notes
Ducher 17

Edward Notes

F. 51
Fairweather 34.34a.36
Fenton 39.46
Findlater 74

Gibbon 13
Glendy 67
Gordon 5
Graham 54
Grave 74
Gray 71
Great Notes
Grimmond 48
Grive 74

Henderson 14
Hendry 43
Hickson 49
Hill 23.Notes
Hodgson 46
Hood 20.63-5

Irnes 63
Irvine 52

K. 51
Kinnear 5-6
Kinoch 66

L. 56
Lamond 41-3
Layon 10
Long 30
Lounan 16.45
Low 34a.45
Lowdon 69
Lunan 17
Lyon (see Layon) 5.25.

M. 61
McAndrew 69
McCraw 69
McLaren, Maclaren 3-4
Malcolm 21.24.57
Marshall 10
Mershal 60
Mathou 24
Miller 48

2 AIRLIE

Index continued

Milne	41	Roger	33.Notes
Mitchell	Notes	Rolok	33
Moncur	59	Salter	5
Mundell	38	Sandyman	8
Mustart	26. Notes	Sim	5
Mustert	62	Smale	32
Myle(s)	7-8	Small	38
N.	61.68	Smith	9.29-31.Notes
Neil	65a	Stevenson	72
Newton	2	Stewart	40.47
Nicol(l)	16.19-20.38.44.46 60.Notes	Stil	56
		Stormonth	25
Ogilvie	Notes	Thomas	23
P.	68	Thomson	35.49-50.65a-66
Palmer	58	W.	44.73
Paterson	70	Wallace	18
Pattullo	38.46	Watson	19.26.28-9
Piggott	Notes	White/Whyte	25.54
Playfair	23	Whitton	9
R.	18	Wighton	37
Ramsay	1-3	Wilkie	Notes
Rankin	3	Wright	12.52-4.Notes
Ratry	65	Young	11.71
Rattray	72		
Reid	38.46.49		
Robertson	1.59		

3a BRECHIN CATHEDRAL KIRK

In the dark ages the Celtic missionaries set up a mission station here for evangelizing south Pictland, and in the 12th century King David I founded the Cathedral, dedicated to the Holy Trinity, on the site of the Culdee monastery. As the Cathedral was also the parish kirk it was adapted for Reformed worship in the 16th century. The surrounding burial ground thus has a long history of congestion, and the Kirk Session from at latest 1619 regulated the burials, and the erection of stones. The Kirk Session records indicate that very many monumental must now be deep underground. After 1870 burial was limited to relatives of those already interred there.

This list of pre-1855 and allied inscriptions is based on the ms list made by Sydney Cramer in May 1959, with a few corrections and additions noted in 1977. Cramer's numbering has been retained.

National Grid refernce: NO 597 601

A This tomb was built in 1787 by Robt Speid of Ardovie upon the burying ground of his family where 8 generations have been buried since 1519 when his predecessor Thos Speid exchanged his lands of Cuikston at Kinnaird, of which he & his predecessors had been proprietors past all memory, with Robt Carnegie of Kinnaird for the lands of Ardovie. Here lyes Jas Speid son to Robt Speid

3a BRECHIN CATHEDRAL KIRK

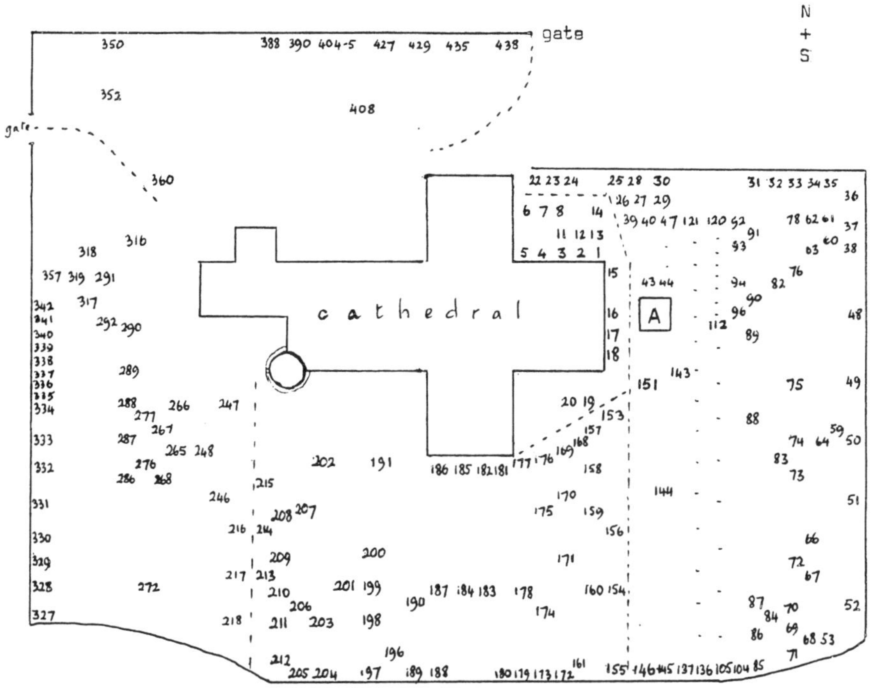

1 mural. 1806. capt David Ferrier commander of a ship in East Indies, sailed round the world in the 'Dolphin', d here 1804 60, by bro Alex Ferrier of Kintrocket (see inscription no.427; D H Edwards, "Guide to Brechin" for stories of the captain's great strength)

2 mural in Latin. Laurence Dundas professor in Edinburgh 29.4.1734 55y7m, w Helen Ogilvie, 4 ss & 3 das of whom only s Laurence & da Isabella reached their majority. Geo Dundas; Thos Dundas of Fingask; Henry Guild writer in Edinburgh; April 1704. (see Edinburgh Testaments: mr Lawrence Dundas professor of Humanity, 16.1.1735)

3 mural. Thos Fraser mert Brechin 12.1826 nearly 78y, by nephew Thos Fraser of London

4 mural. Andrew Will lieut 92nd Highland regt after serving 4y in Peninsular war where he was severely wounded in the head & at battles of Quatre Bras & Waterloo, fell in Jamaica 7.10.1819 a victim to the climate

5 mural. Wm Shiress 52y solicitor here b Falkirk 1.1.1804 d here 21.1.1881, w Mary Will b Jamaica 28.2.1809 d here 9.4.1847 (see Edwards "Guide" 3rd ed. p 199 "his business hours were ... from 7 in the morning till 10 at night"

6 Geo Farquharson plasterer 12.4.1907 83, w Jane Leighton 11.8.1867 47, s Geo 1853 7, da Jessie 1854 3, s Joseph 1858 11, 4da Eliz d Victoria Australia int Hamilton cem there (h John McFadyen)

7 Chas Mann 60y servant in Aldbar home farm including 28y as manager b 14.3.1808 d 27.1.1891, w Mary Hampton, his fa (James) Mann d (5).1829

3a BRECHIN CATHEDRAL KIRK

8 Jas Milne 9.12.1886 83, w Isabella Barnet 28.5.1851 78, da Hannah 5.5.1840 $5\frac{1}{2}$, da Isabella 20.7.1849 $12\frac{1}{2}$, 2ss & a da d inf, da Helen 24.2.1901 67, s David 2.6.1904 58 int Sighthill cem Glasgow, da Ann 8.4.1906 75 - Helen & Ann were int New cem Brechin

9 David Clark crofter Little Brechin b Strathmartine 10.5.1800 27.12.1882, 1w Helen Smith 26.11.1837 38, 2w Helen Ferrier 22.5.1870 66

10 Jas Lindsay at Auldbar 8.4.1854 58, da Jessie 3.9.1835

11 John Whyte 23.12.1879 73, w Jean Dickson 6.8.1886 73, s Alex 6.4.1842 inf s Jas 8.1.1854 $2\frac{1}{2}$, s Wm 17.1.1854 7, s Geo 18.1.1854 $4\frac{1}{2}$

13 1829. by Chas Oswald tobacconist, chn Jas & Jean d inf

14 Alex Henderson 31.12.1868 76, w Betsy Hay 15.1.1842 46, s John 29.10.1875 42, s Chas 20.6.1845 19, da Annie Calder 15.9.1869 40, s Jas 9.6.1877 46, s David Moir 7.3.1881 45, by da Jane 25.1.1899 74

16 by Alex Greig weaver Gallowhill Brechin, w Mary Belford 28.7.1827 (53), chn Mary, Margt, Helen & Geo int here. Jas Greig tailor 5.5.1854 54, w Jean Crabb, da Mary 13.1.1826 4m, s Jas 26.3.1836 8, s Alex 19.(2).18(5)2 20y

17 David Jack 9.2.1843 59, w Isabell Ogilvie 14.4.1853 66, 2 ss & 3 das d inf, by s Jas, 50 Union Street Brechin 17.11.1899 75 int New cem (w Eliz Robertson 16.12.1896 73, s Allan 6.5.1868 $1\frac{3}{4}$, da Isabell 21.1.1871 16y5m, da Helen M 19.9.1872 8y5m, yt s John Traill 1.7.1885 15y10m)

18 John Duncan fr Side Stracathro 3.1.1823 66, w Margt Ferrier d Brechin 26.7.1856 88, chn John & Helen d inf, s John d Brechin 20.7.1851 43, s Jas d Jamaica 5.9.1854 41; David Hunter Duncan fr Friock-Mains 14.10.1882 76, w Isabella Smith d Middleton 8.9.1849 44, s Alex Scott d Barry Mills 23.5.1867 33

19 Wm Bruce mert 8.11.1884 79, w Isabella Bruce 27.1.1876 66, da Margt 8.1841 1y, s Wm 11.1852 9m, s John 3.1854 4y5m, da Ann 4.2.1864 19, da Isobel 10.9.1869 27. Jane Craik or Bruce 1.2.1917 89

20 Wm Turner innkeeper 2.10.1834 64, w Ann Bruce 2.1.1860 80, da Mary 1.6.1828 27, da Jane 3.6.1854 33, by s Wm of Dunlop Queensland NSW

22 by Robt Mitchell late - - - - Dalgety imo Alex Mitchell tent East Mains of Dod 28.3.1800 101y2m, 1w Cathren -nst- - by whom two ss & one da, 2w - - - Nave- - - - das, two ss of whom - - - - is the yt; said Alex Mitchell's fa was fr Kirton of Neivie d 96y & gfa was fr Brydeston par of - -irly d 98y & his ancestors were farmers in which 500y (There is a farm called Braideston in par of Airlie)

23 by - - - - - - & Berthier Morrison imo their sis Eliz Monroy b London 16.3.1772 d here 28.6.1830 having served her latter 17y to the family of Patk Chalmers esq, Auldbar

24 FS (marginal) John - - - wheilwright burges in Brechin 20.3.1709 73, w Margt - - - - - (8)8y & three of their chn; (central) I MK ♥ M M M B
I B ♥ M MK I B ;

axe, square, compasses

25 FS tipped up & broken. - - - - - west - - - - - - - - imo his - - - - - sometyme - - - - in West Mill - - - - Jan 1766; also his mo Eliz Crighton 27.1.1750 50; Nicol Bouack 16.12.1798 77 tent in West Burkle, w Jean Dorward 29.7.1779 56

26 David Smith 6.8.1874 63, w Anne Catenoch 25.1.1866 51, da Mary Ann d inf, da Jessie 13.11.1884 35, da Jean 4.11.1911 68 int New cem, gmo Jane Clark 1.1.1845 75

3a BRECHIN CATHEDRAL KIRK

27 David Tosh 6.1.1868 72, w Mary Whamond 3.6.1848 44

28 Benjamin Mitchell mert Fettercairn b Navar 22.6.1788 d here 3.5.1851, w Agnes Duncan 19.2.1801 27.11.1852, da Margt 5.1848 17, da Jane d London 12.3.1855 27 (h Jas Carr engineer)

29 David Lawson 3.3.1835 72, w Ann Stockwell 8.2.1843 82, by chn D & A Lawson

30 Chas Hill 1.7.1854 42, w Ann McDonald 11.5.1886 74, s David 12.9.1863 24, s Wm 18.4.1879 41, s John 2.2.1897 57 int Camberwell cem London, da Jane 2.5.1904 60

31 mural. rev Alex Leith Ross Foote DD min Brechin 6.9.1878 74, 1w Margt Dingwall Fordyce d Clifton Bristol 29.4.1842 29, 2w Jessie Murray 9.10.1855 36, 1s Robt Jas 26.12.1857 9, 3w Alison Keir Cunningham 4.4.1862 36, s Archibald 14.1.1863 11m (see Edwards "Guide" 3rd ed. p 64 for anecdotes of Dr Foote; his portrait then (1904) by Herdman in the Mechanics Hall Brechin)

32 David Leighton esq of Bearhill 1.5.1846 63, w Agnes Ann Valentine 16.10.1854 62, yr s Geo drowned in crossing the Arroyo de San Francisco near Paysandu 29.10.1865 29 int British cem Buenos Ayres

33 mural. rev Nathaniel Morren min here from 1843 d 28.3.1847 48 in 24th y of ministry, w Mary Shand d Greenock 16.7.1875 74 (see Fasti v 378)

34 mural. Jas Molison tent Hillhead of Burghill d here 4.10.1862 85, sis Mary d Hillhead of Burghill 8.11.1850 65

35 mural. rev Jas Goodwin 1st min the Relief now the UP church High Street Brechin b Kilsyth 1799 ordained 21.12.1831 d Sabbath 4.7.1847 (see Edwards "Guide" 3rd ed. p 64 for particulars of his sudden death). rev Peter Davidson min UP church High Street, da Cath Harvey 1.1862 1¾

36 Alex Laing 14.5.1787 14.10.1857 (Author of "Wayside Flowers" & editor of Burns and Tannahill; DNB)

37 Wm Mustard esq Viewbank 12.9.1850 69, w Susan Simpson 17.1.1862 74

38 rev Geo Alexander rector Grammar School 54y b Monquhitter par 2.2.1786 d here 17.5.1877, w Sarah Durward 1.12.1850 75 (see Edwards "Guide" 3rd ed. p 187; his portrait by Colvin Smith was in the Mechanics Hall Brechin)

39 John Hampston mason 3.5.1866 70, w Jean Fotheringham 13.11.1842 42

40 Alex Brough mason 2.1.1901 70, w Mary Ann Byers 26.4.1826 20.1.1889, s Wm 19.4.1863 29.5.1863, da Mary Ann 20.2.1857 7.1.1871, s John 21.12.1868 2.2.1871, da Margt 5.5.1864 4.2.1871, s Alex Smith lost at sea off Socotra Island by the sinking of SS Curfew 22.6.1896 (s Wm Hammond 29.4.1867 7.1.1920). Wm Byers 8.7.1846 63, w Ann Walker 3.3.1856 67, ss Wm, Thos, Geo & David, 1s Jas 2.1.1878 66, s John 10.6.1901 82 (w Cath E Young 18.4.1890 59, s Wm 10.4.1865 6)

41 1851. by David Troup mason, s Chas Kinnear 25.9.1847 6, s Thos 18.7.1854 3¾

42 Wm McLeod 21.9.1867 49, w Jessie Black 26.4.1903 85, s Wm 16.2.1873 15, s Chas d West Hoboken New Jersey USA 4.7.1899 49

43 David Valentine 1.9.1843 78, w Betsy Spalding 18.2.1844 76, da Jean 10.10.1872 67 (s Alex Smith residenter 28 River Street Brechin 27.4.1905 67)

45 Jas Glen RHA fought at Waterloo 1815, pensioner d 23.10.1876 85, w Eliz Cameron 7.4.1876 76, da Agnes 13.3.1925 90, gs Jas Glen d Prince Albert

Saskatchewan Canada 8.1.1896 26, by family

46 Alex Keeler pensioner, w Janet Law 16.11.1845 45, 2 chn d inf

47 John Grey d by boring shot in Southesk quarry 26.2.1850 56, s John 1839 13

51 Jas Crichton 9.9.1845 77, w Isabella Millar 22.12.1822 48, s John 2.4.1824 30, da Ann 1802 1859, s Jas 9.1.1862 57 (w Ann Grant 8.11.1873 73) da Isabella Crichton or Brodie 10.7.1878 86, gs Jas Crichton d inf, gda Mary Crichton d inf

53 Wm Fleming tent Pitforthie 11.12.1848 59, w Margt Samson 7.12.1860 68

54 Robt Bruce flourmiller Meikle Mill 4.12.1845 54, w Margt Burnett 13.7.1866 71, 1s Jas d Mills of Morphie 1818 1½, 9s Geo 21.11.1842 5, 4s Robt 19.9.1867 44, 3s John 27.5.1870 49, 2s David 24.6.1876 57

56 Jas Peter fr Tillygloom 30.7.1877 82, w Isabel Ker 21.7.1886 84, s David 7.8.1836 4, da Eliz 10.6.1905 60, s Hendry Fairweather d Tillygloom 2.5.1927 89 int New cem, gda Eliz Ker Peter 8.7.1871 4, sis Mary 13.11.1879 81

58 by John Dear, w Isobel Scott 27.5.1822 77, chn David, John, Robt, Eliz, Jas, Margt, Christian, Wm, Agnes & Mary

59 John Dear 18.12.1887 83 (see Edwards "Guide" 3rd ed. p 216 " many years town's mason & a very ready witted man...."), w Jean Fisher 27.6.1850 47, s Joseph 25.9.1889 53, by ss Joseph, John & Jas

61 our parents Robt Cowie 1893 & Margt Jane Birse 1940 & our grandparents all of Little Keithock all int here

62 David Cowie blacksmith, w Helen Howie, da Jane 28.9.1842 7m, da Margt 21.6.1843 3, da Mary 2.7.1843 4¾

63 Alex Spaddie mason 15.9.1853 53, w Clementina Bean 6.7.1795 19.3.1880 84, (her sis Cath Bean 9.11.1883 93), by da Jane

65 Jas Kidd 6.4.1852 52, w Margt Adam 11.3.1862 64, chn Mary & Peter d inf, by s And baker Dundee

66 1826. Wm Addison, w Ann Walls, s Alex 3.10.1810 4, s John 12.4.1813 1y, s Wm 8.10.1813 15, da Margt 4.1.1820 24

67 John B Stewart 4.7.1891, w Betty Ross 19.8.1876 75, fa John Stewart 26.4.1833 67, mo Mary Webster 11.12.1840 74, gda Margt B Stewart 1.3.1878 1y & many relatives & friends int here

68 John Ferrier 19.2.1849 49, by w Ann Watson, s Geo 30.4.1837 ¾, da Mary 10.8.1842 5, s Jas 22.8.1851 24

69 John Aitken mason 2.1.1832 52, w Margt Guthrie 6.6.1841 64, s Alex d Fettercairn 20.6.1856 43, da Helen 13.6.1856 56, s capt John of the Steam Boat Tubal Cain d 30.5.1886 70

70 Jas Hood manuf 9.2.1846 51, w Isabella Jarron 26.5.1860 64, s Jas Webster b 12.9.1827 d same day, da Jane 1.5.1831 10.2.1903 at Clifton int Arno's Vale cem Bristol

71 John Wyllie fr Drumachlie 6.1842 82, sis Susan Wyllie 1.1857 90, w Kath Deas 6.1836 77, s John 1.1854 54, s David 31.12.1869 76, da Kath 22.12.1884 86, da Margt 2.5.1876 84 (h lieut Alex Young 21st regt of Foot 22.10.1832 49, da Isabella Deas 28.9.1866 38 (h Richd Smith), by s Alex Forbes 17.2.1902 78)

72 1886. John Gall, the Latch of Brechin 3.1840 76, w Agnes Low 5.5.1857 93, s Joseph 5.8.1845 42 (w Isabella Greig 2.2.1886 83, s Geo 27.12.1897 68, gs John Mitchell 6.11.1859 4)

73 Wm Carrie 8.6.1879 75, w Janet Carrie 16.12.1860 72, da Mary 6.4.1836 3y3m. Jas Black 14.2.1883 70, w Margt Carrie 1.9.1898 78

74 1875. Jas Fenton 25.12.1857 62, w Betsy Hendry 22.10.1866 72, da Sarah 7.4.1849 19, s John 21.4.1860 27, chn Wm & Jane d inf. Wm Willocks 11.10.1898 74, w Mary Fenton 9.1.1899 76, s Geo 21.8.1858 2, da Jane Ann 28.3.1862 3

75 John Hood carrier 30.9.1843 61, w Margt Scott 27.6.1849 57, chn David, Eliz, Isabella & Mary. John 8.12.1889 67, w Susan Christie 12.12. 1877 49, s David 31.1.1860 $\frac{1}{4}$, da Susannah 30.1.1940 78

76 John Pullar Fyfe 9.5.1865 59, w Ann Duncan 5.10.1877 72, s Robt d in America, s Jas drowned in America at the Pier of Pennsylvania

77 1825. by Chas Christie, w Eliz Deuchars 20.5.1823 64y4m, da Mary 3.5. 1823 27. Chas Christie 21.6.1835 82. Amelia Christie 3.8.1851 & Eliz Christie 21.5.1852

78 by David Smart imo bro Jas d aged 12y, fa John 15.10.18(30) (58), gmo Isobel S - - ess 26.(2).1835

79 by Alex Gordon tailor, da Mary 28.10.1825 14

81 Jonathan Davidson 14.12.1895 81, w Martha Rattray 8.2.1887 80, da Martha 12.7.1842 6, s Wm 30.6.1868 27 lies in Boleskin Inverness, da Jane 22.2.1847 4, by s Joseph

82 John Mitchell 19.8.1871 70, w Betsy Randall 10.6.1862 59, s J R 4.7. 1856 21

84 1844. Barbray Black 19.2.1864 75, s Wm R Forrest 19.5.1866 49, her uncle Wm Robb mert 24.3.1837 70 & Isobell Robb 8.1.1837 83

86 Jas Adamson, w Helen Guthrie, s Robt tent Middledrums 11.7.1848 80,(1w Ann Guthrie 14.2.1824 40, 2w Mary Thomson 24.10.1862 75 (wid of Geo Anderson solicitor, see inscription no.396)

87 Robt Duncan mert 21.3.1844 78, w Isabella Ritchie 18.5.1846 74, 2s Ebenezer John Collet 13.9.1848 50, da Margt 10.5.1862 65 (h Jas Gaul d Philadelphia 42y)

88 1881. Jas Taylor 13.9.1879 71, w Jane Allan 14.9.1880 72, da Jane 27.3. 1849 3, s Geo 10.4.1867 27, s Wm 9.1.1870 28, s Jas 10.1832 19.11.1885

89 Alex Dundas mert 3.1843 70, w Ann Brown 3.1842 43 (her sis Helen Brown 2.11.1872 63) da Ann 1.3.1836 6, s Alex Foote d inf

90 Jas Watson mert 23.2.1787 87, w Margt Deuchar d 6y after him. Jas Watson baker 17.9.1755 21.9.1828, w Margt Gardiner 12.2.1837 81

91 Jas Duncan 11.12.1860 73, w Margt Pyper 25.6.1847 57. - - - - - her husband Jas Jarvis 15.6.1880 70, da Mary 22.11.1867 13, s Wm 20.9. 1884 45, da Margt 18.1.1895 51; Catherine 3.11.1898 79

92 1845. Jas Wood labourer 6.9.1833 60, s John grocer South Port 26.9.1843 41, s Jas 29.1.1848 37, s Robt 23.1.1865 67

93 Wm Ferrier, w Ann Black, s capt Wm at the barque F W Cochrane d at sea on voyage from Jamica to Liverpool 18.5.1871 (by w Louisa Ferrier)

94 Chas Mitchell mert 12.5.1785 15.2.1871, w Isabella Hendery 1795 9.11.1853, da Margt 6.5.1824 10.5.1852, da Mary Ann 8.9.1829 1.8.1830, da Agnes 29.6. 1831 10.2.1835, s Chas 12.7.1841 6.1846

95 FS Alex Low manuf (13).2.1830, da Margt 17.3.1807 12, da Mary 1.6.1808 1$\frac{1}{2}$, s David (1).6.1815 16, s Jas 27.8.1818 13, s And (28.9.)1829 18, s Alex 17.7.1796 17.7.1840, wid Margt Dundas 19.7.1840 63

96 1845. by Alex Ritchie, w Eliz Mitchell 30.8.1844 70

97 Wm Preshaw 1763 1826, w Margt Mathers 1776 1860 84, by s Wm F

98 David Hobb mert 28.4.1861 83, w Mary Low 20.5.1854 69, s David 25.6.1818 2, s Wm 8.2.1826 2, s Joseph 13.8.1851 36, da Isabella 3.11.1871 54, da Janet 6.2.1883 63

99 1838. Geo Scott fr East Pittendriech 14.8.1847 91, w Elis Couttie 9.1. 1837 73, 3 of their chn Wm, Geo & Cath. Robt Scott tent East Pittendriech 13.12.1866 70, w Jean Watson 9.10.1834 26, s Jas also tent East Pittendriech 20.9.1896 62

101 Wm Pennycook, Bridgend Brechin 15.3.1863 83, w Jean Ferrier 24.1.1868 74, da Isabell Binny 28.5.1835 12, da Ann 8.2.1836 5, s Wm Ferrier 18.7.1854 25, da Eliz 21.3.1864 41, by da Cath Ferrier Pennycook or Duncan

102 John Lamb wright 1802 82, s Robt 26.1.1833 76 (w Ann Reid 26.11.1844 87, da Isoble inf, da Ann inf, s Jas 18.7.1809 17, da Jean 12.12.1842 53). David Lamb mert, s Jas Henry 6.1833 7m, da Jane Ann 2.12.1839 5y2m, s Martin Drydon MD Indian Army d Missoorie 21.6.1860 33

103 rev John Lamb UP Church Errol d Brechin 19.10.1875 88, w Jane Will 22.8. 1873 69

104 1880. Geo Greig 14.12.1868 81, w Eliz Webster 26.12.1868 81, s Joseph drowned Alloa 1837 21, s Geo 10.7.1880 53, chn Geo, David & Agnes d inf, da Eliz 8.4.1886 64, da Mary Ann 29.9.1894 76 int Eastern Necropolis Dundee, da Margt 18.3.1899 75 (h Geo Callender 2.4.1899 69)

105 - - - d Donaldson sometime - - - - Brechine 8.3.1724, w Isabell Fletcher 1723 59, (only) s - - - - d 1772 67

106 Alex Fairweather dyer Brechin 25.3.1821 25, s Alex 29.3.1855 34

107 17-8. by Jas Inverarity, mo Margt Mill d 1.17(46) 53.
17--. Jas Mill & - - - - Donaldson, their chn John, Isobel, (Janet), - - - - - & Robt Mills - - - -. John Mill & Ann - - - - their chn Margt, Ann, - - - - , Isobel & Je - - (see Brechin Testaments: Jas Innerarity mert & tanner in Brechin, 19.6.1795)

108 1830. Geo Alexander 20.6.1794 32, w Mary Carnegie 2.1844 76 (her bro David Carnegie slater 4.4.1828 74, his w Mary Davidson 8.11.1824 70), by s David slater 5.4.1841 48 (w Ann Low 10.1.1859 71, s Joseph 27.12.1847 26, s John 18.1.1837 9, s Chas 6.6.1842 9)

109 David Shepherd manuf 6.11.1841 72, w Mary Galdie 24.2.1862 80, 3 of their chn David, Margt & Mary d inf

111 TS David Duncan 2.2.1791 86, s John Duncan esq of Rosemount 7.3.1831 79 (see Edwards "Guide" 3rd ed.pp 127 & 214 - punchbowl was presented to the Council in 1785 by dr Duncan proprietor of Rosemount who realised a fortune in India; Jervise "Brechin" pp 10-11)

112 TS David Reedie late physician in Brechin 1.7.1816 24, by w Mary Lyon

114 1878. Wm Hunter 11.3.1877 71, w Susan Greig 29.12.1884 77, da Isabell d inf, s Wm inf, s David d Boston Mass USA 28.2.1882 36 int Forrest Hills

115 Patk Soutar of Little Keithock 12.12.1831 83, w Jean Baillie 14.12.1830 80, by nephew Jas Soutar mert Dundee

116 TS Patk (Watson) - - - - - - - , w mrs Mary (Murray)

118 Robt Mills 20.10.1861 49, w Agnes Jamieson 9.12.1817 12.1.1885, s Geo 15. 11.1838, da Agnes 6.3.1840, s Adam 12.3.1856, s John 12.9.1863 22, s Robt d Toronto Canada 7.1.1884 40, da stillborn Montrose 6.12.1836, s Robt 18. 9.1837 18.10.1837

121 John Maich 25.8.1846 70, 1w Ann Burnett 30.4.1841 60, 2w Eliza Calder , s Joseph 27.6.1846 ¼, her s Alex Christie 23.2.1848 4m

122 Wm Ayre mert 16.8.1785 16.4.1830, w Agnes Gordon b Goul Tannadyce 26.5. 26.5.1855, s John 1827 10, s Jas 1828 2, da Agnes 1832 10, chn Geo & Mary d inf, s Robt Mackenzie d Benduck-Hay NSW 2.11.1892 65, s Alex d London 4.1880

123 1852. John Scott 17.7.1889 83, w Nicola Thow 18.6.1890 87, s Jas 10.10. 1851 13¾, ss John & Jas d inf, da Mary Robert 11.6.1876 (h John Cromar Shirburn, Oxfordshire)

124 Wm Caution d Oathlaw 19.2.1837 51, w Cath Steven d Brechin 5.8.1870 81, da Isabella 30.6.1889 75, da Mary 3.4.1891 68, da Margt 14.8.1849 23 (by da Isabella Smart in USA)

125 CT David Allardice mert 12.8.1822 79, w Mary Spence 14.6.1780 27, s John 8.1780 1y5m, da Margt 11.1.1792 16, & David. David Allardice d Edinburgh 16.1.1854 76 int Dean cem, w Christian Straton d Edinburgh 30. 6.1859 81, da Christian Jean 4.7.1820 8m, da Margt Graham 4.2.1830 16 int here (see inscription no.388)

126 cross. Ann Allardice 6.7.1900 85, by nephews & nieces

127 FS Robt Allardice mert bailie 15.11.1737 63, w Eliz Lyon (see Brechin Testaments: Eliz Lyon, 24.4.1754), ys David of Memus 27.9.1783 67 (w Isobel Spence (see Brechin Testaments: Isobel Spence relict of David Allardice of Memus mert, 20.6.1797), chn John, Isobel & Benjamin d inf, chn John, Robt, Mary & Helen also lie here, s Wm of Murlingden 8.11.1837 71 (1w Cath Lowe, s David inf, s Chas 9y, 1s Alex surgeon EICS d Cochin East Indies 1.7.1839 36, 2w Ann Molison 22.11.1851 62, 1da Ann 6.7.1900 85)) (see inscription no.165; Edwards "Guide" 3rd ed.p 70; Scottish Antiquary xiv p 15)

128 John Valentine wright 18.3.1868 75, w Jane Singers 14.6.1874 72, s David 1837 ¾, da Eliz 13.9.1871 41, da Margt 28.12.1871 45, s Geo 1.5.1872 47, gs John Kinnear 1.10.1859 5½

129 David Lyon mert 9.6.1809 75, w Isabella Greig 27.5.1790 48, da Margt 25. 3.1835 61, da Isabella 29.1.1851 81

130 David Millar seaman capt of Heather Bell of Aberdeen d at sea 9.3.1852 26, fa Jas Millar senior bailie stoneware mert 27.3.1839 51, gmo Eliz Miller 5.6.1842 79

131 - - ld Millar shoemakers deacon 7.6.1752 71, w Helen Burn, da Agnes 7.7. 1722 5, da Eliz 1757 inf ; D M H B; AM KM DM AM IM EM

132 Chas Black mert 2.2.1800 57, by w Louisa Davidson 9.5.1845 83, only ch Margt 27.4.1800 1, his yt bro Alex mert 18.6.1790 43 (w Isobel Millar)

133 Jas Duncan 20.4.1858 74, w Eliz Fotheringham 27.10.1842 47, ss Wm, Jas, Frank & Alex. David Shepherd 19.7.1890 67, w Ann Duncan 20.2.1909 84, s Jas 17.11.1863 1y, s David 27.12.1874 8, da Eliz Ann 23.8.1895 31

136 Robt Cairncross & w Janet Gowans int Kinkell, s John mert he served in Peninsular campaign, principal clerk Artillery office HQ until the Duke of Wellington's army left France b 15.5.1783 d 14.6.1853 (w Agnes 10.6. 1796 21.10.1876 (da of Thos Strachan & Helen Don int here), da Agnes 29. 6.1829 31.3.1856, s David Milne 10.3.1825 10.4.1848, s John 25.5.1827 d 15.1.1858 at Melbourne Australia, s Robt Grieve 24.4.1834 22.5.1899 at 463 Central Park West New York City USA) by Wm Hovels Cairncross in 1908 d 37 St David Street Brechin 31.1.1915 78

138 Jas Strachan 8.11.1827 29.7.1893, w Eliz Burnett 8.11.1827 28.5.1877, da Mary 5.6.1885 32

139 Alex Strachan 30.6.1817 77, w Ann Dickson 6.6.1826 85, by Isabella Strachan the only surviving branch of the family

140 Samuel Strachan 9.9.1878 74, w Janet M Strachan 16.2.1887 85, da Eliza 16.9.1841 10m, s John 6.4.1859 21, da Annie 4.5.1860 25, da Jessie 20.11.1875 43, yt s Robt 29.12.1883 38, s Chas 24.12.1897 57, s Samuel 22.9.1908 69 both int Newington cem Edinburgh. James M 15.3.1909 69

141 John Joe 20.4.1766 3.2.1840, w Eliz Crocket 19.3.1767 20.9.1848, s Alex wright 30.8.1801 3.1871 (w Isobel Oakenhead, s Alex mason 6.10.1879 47 (w Jane Thomson 21.6.1882 49, s John 17.1.1951 81 lies in New cem)), da Mary 13.6.1889 83 (h Robt Symington mert 11.3.1882 71)

142 FS John Martin of the Swan Inn 13.5.1836 76, w Ann Strachan 21.1.1826, 3 ss & 1 da; Eliz 3.18-- ; John (Str)achan - - - - 65y (see Fasti i 106 for their son rev Jas Martin)

144 John Stevenson tent Mains of Melgund 18.5.1744 59

145 1880. John Dakers manuf 13.10.1794 28.8.1887, w Martha Steel 22.3.1802 8.4.1884, da Mary d inf, s John 28.11.1832 12.6.1858, s Jas 14.2.1838 13.7.1878, s Peter 26.5.1841 15.10.1884 (see Edwards "Guide" 3rd ed.p 215)

146 John Gordon 27.8.1860 61, w Mary Baillie 12.4.1849 49, s Jas 12.5.1862 35, s David inf, s Wm 17.12.1899 67 (s John inf), s John 23.1.1907 81 (da Ann inf, s Jas 24.10.1866 6); by John, Wm & Alex

147 John Oakenhead 4.12.1801 47, s John 9.1.1823 23, s Robt 15.11.1861 65 (w Eliz Stevenson 11.5.1866 72)

148 Jas Valentine, Montrose Street Brechin 4.5.1810 2.12.1884, w Helen Don Strachan 7.10.1807 4.9.1898, s Jas 16.8.1842 3, s Alex 29.6.1846 14

149 Geo Fairweather fr Smithyhill, da Jenny 19.1.1797 28 (h Jas Strachan mert 3 chn Jeany, David & Helen 6.1.1797 1y1m)

150 1825. John Bruce grammar school master, session clerk 10.5.1783 60, w Helen Bisset 9.1784 51, chn Alex, Jean, Wm, Mary, And, John & Helen all int here, by da Ann (h Skene Walker 11.1.1824 66) (see Brechin Testaments: Helen Bisset relict of John Bruce schoolmaster, 1785)

150a - - - - - - - children - - - - - - - - Margaret - - - - - - ; (west side) Ia E, M E, (P)E, - - - - -

151 by surviving family imo their mo Margt Smart 24.3.1853 51; Thos Hogg & Isobella Kinear, da Margt 21.8.1853 1½

153 David Bruce coachman Brechin castle & vintner 11.12.1830 37, by wid Agnes Davidson

154 David Davidson 3.1831, w Mary Thomson 5.1846, by chn

155 Francis Wallace 3.5.1798 61, w Margt Carnegie 5.12.1834 80, s Wm seaman navigator & mathematician 3.3.1843 54, da Helen 22.12.1843 64, by da Betty

156 1757. I C E M ; 4 ; I C D C I C M C

157 Peter Smith 1.8.1810 48, w Janet Middleton d Andover 8.1839 77, by ss John & Peter, Andover, Massachusetts

158 1853. Margt Cairns, Haughmuir 4.5.1851 63

159 Jas Douglas surgeon Brechin 22.4.1767 18.11.1832, w Ann Lyall 29.11.1772 4.2.1848, s Robt MD of St Anns 26.2.1806 3.11.1881 (w Anne Buchanan 28.10.1818 14.7.1892), s Jas 14.12.1795 25.12.1796, da Margt 25.8.1802 7.3.1803, s John 6.6.1808 9.6.1816, da Margt 8.1.1799 3.9.1858, da Isabel 8.1.1799 30.10.1872, da Anne 12.5.1804 29.1.1874, s rev Alex min at Farnell 4.3.

1801 28.6.1839

160 Alex Black 38y tent in Waulk Mill of Arbuthnot d here 24.12.1855 88, w Eliz Garvie d here 13.9.1851 83, by s Alex bookseller

161 CT John Sandieman surgeon Royal Artillery 14.9.1840 55

162 David Lyall, Kintrockat 22.12.1870 64, w Isabella Webster 11.8.1879 73, s Wm 26.10.1854 5, s David 10.2.1867 31

163 Alex Mitchell 14.1.1863 65, w Eliz Blues 26.1.1874 68, s Colin S 10.10. 1850, by surviving s Alex

164 CT 1777. Francis Molison mert 28.7.1769, w Kath Spence 9.9.1764, David who survived his fa a few years only, by s John mert 19.5.1789 (w Fergusia Todd, survived by one s & one da) (see Brechin Testmants: Francis Molison late bailie Brechin, 9.2.1722; John Molison late provost Brechin, 21. 6.1791)

165 John Molison, s Thos col Eastern Forfarshire Militia & provost of Brechin 1760 1815(w Ann Burslem 1800, s John 1791 1809, da Christina 1793 1811 s Thos MD 1796 1835 (see Edwards "Guide" 3rd ed.p 69: he d in Edinburgh unmarried), da Ann 1789 1851(h Wm Allardice esq of Murlingden (see no. 127)), da Mary Curzon 1794 1865 (h rev Robt Smith DD senior min Old Machar Aberdeen)), da Mary 1774 1856 (h rev Geo Watson min here) (see Edwards "Guide" pp 62, 69 & 191)

166 1761. by Wm Laing mert & shoemaker, w Kath Low 27.11.1760 41, only ch Isobel

167 Patk Laing tanner 1813, w Jean Gowans 1838. Wm Wright of the Excise, w Eliz Riddoch 1802 int Abbey Yard a native of Monzievaird, da Jean 121. 1854 (h Jas Laing surgeon Brechin, also 3 of their chn). Jas Laing 16.3.1854 60. Alex Riddoch Laing 6.11.1826 14.1.1886

168 provost John Smith, w Cecilia Chalmers, s Jas (w Margt Irvine, da Margt 1889 89 (h Thos Ogilvy grain mert 1797 1879, s Patk Chalmers 1822 1855, other chn d childhood, da Eliz Martin 1832 1923, s Francis Chalmers 1843 1932, gs Laurance Murray Ogilvy 25.9.1928 70, gda Lizzie Williams Ogilvy d London 25.9.1928 70 (see Edwards "Guide"3rd ed.p 70; see no. 334)

169 Robt Gillies mert in Brechin d Perth 1779 where a tablet was placed by 1s John LLD, w Margt Smith 5.9.1812 82 had a numerous family, 1s John LLD (see DNB), by yt s the hon Adam senator College of Justice (see DNB), 2s Colin esq 1.7.1826 77, da Mary 30.5.1829 71, da Joanna 3.6.1833 75 (see Edwards "Guide" 3rd ed.pp 61-2 & 71: Robt Gillies of Little Keithock was s of rev John Gillies min of Careston & bro of dr John Gillies author of "Historical Collections of the Gospel"; see also DNB for Margt Gillies)

170 1829. David Rickard mert 4.2.1801, by wid Isabella Gillies, s capt Joseph EICS d here 29.6.1829 (da Isabella Gillies 8.2.1829)

171 Isabel 3.5.1886 55. Clement Gay Rickard 19.4.1915. Mary Cath Rickard 17.5.1916

172 Patk Guthrie mert 30.9.1871 64, w Margt Watson 15.1.1888

173 ob David Guthrie mert sometime provost of Brechin 17y 29.10.1786 28.5.1854, w Anne Burns 14.9.1870 86. Helen, Jane & Clementine das of the 1st provost Guthrie lie here (see Edwards "Guide" 3rd ed.pp 62-3, 70)

174 1824. David Guthrie mert provost 12.3.182(4) 63, w Clementina Gay 18.5. 1841 77, 7s rev Thos Guthrie DD 1803 1873 int Grange cem Edinburgh (see DNB: preacher & philanthropist; Memoir by his ss David Kelly & Chas John Guthrie (1874)), 8s maj Chas 46th regt EICS d India from wounds received in action 1804-1843 (see also inscription no. 229)

175 Alex Guthrie surgeon in Brechin 58y, provost 22.8.1869 77, w Mary 5.3. 1869 74 & those of their family int here (see Edwards "Guide" 3rd ed.p 63: Alex Guthrie, provost David 1786 1854 & Patk d 1871 were all ss of David Guthrie merchant who d 1824 & descendants of David Guthrie tent Balbirnie Mill who went to Menmuir before 1731)

178 Geo Ross distiller 19.8.1850, w Ann Fullerton 17.10.1876, s Jas d Catalina Newfoundland 6.9.1864, s Wm d Alexandria 7.12.1858, da Georgina 7.1872 (h Chas Ross, Cork), s Alex last heard of at Bahia & said to have d of yellow fever there, da Patricia Gordon 4.1884, s John Valentine d Christchurch NZ 25.12.1893

179 Jas Gray Arnot 30.11.1858 64, w Christina Hodge 22.9.1851 62, da Mary 15.11.1900 80 (h Geo Wyllie 4.10.1891 82)

180 Geo Arnot 18.5.1842 64, w Isabella Kinnear 16.11.1839 48, 1s John d West Bourne England 11.9.1861 38

182 Geo Macbain, Swan Inn 4.5.1840 39, w Ann Rose 23.11.1883 79.
Robt Macbain 1.11.1842 48

183 John Smart manuf 8.11.1855 67, w Ann Grim 27.10.1855 58, da Jane 13.6. 1848 20, da Margt 23.2.1851 27, da Ann 21.6.1852 30, s John 3.7.1853 23, s Alex 16.3.1863 30, da Helen 16.11.1891 66

184 Jas Reid slater 26.1.1833 83, w Agnes Machir 16.11.1841 82, s Wm inf, da Mary inf, s Jas 1809 18, s Geo tobacconist 28.8.1868 81, s David 2.4. 1876 86; mrs Jean Reid or Arnot 2.5.1852 57

185 Jas Farquhar 1850 30, w Jane Mitchell 43 Mill Street Paisley 9.12.1896 78 int Woodside cem Paisley, s Geo 1855 18 int Sighthill cem Glasgow, s Wm 1859 17, da Agness 1874 35 int Spithill cem Aberdeen, da Annie 1886 37 at Paisley, s Jas 1912 64 int Woodside Paisley

186 Thos Birse surgeon 22.4.1813 54, w Anna Shepherd 23.12.1812 50, s David d Trinidad 20.3.1825 23, da Margt d Arbroath 13.1.1854 56, s Jas Shepherd surgeon 28.3.1845 52 (w Margt Smith 26.12.1826 30)

187 David Duthie 30.11.1797 17.7.1877, w Margt Gordon 25.1.1803 5.1.1879, s John 17.2.1843 2, 1da Mary Mathers 26.2.1832 17.5.1905

188 by Geo Stewart hammerman Nether Tennements imo mo Agnes Ogilvie (4).9. 1753 61 & 3 chn d nonage John, Jas & Katren; "Here Agnes lys claid with a mournful shade / Hath left her friends and loving husband sad;/ And now is gone above the stars to sing / Eternal praise to her Immortal King."

189 TS John Shires slater 1724 87, w Eliz Bruce 3.5.1698 55, chn who survived them: John, Ann, Eliz, Jas slater 1736 57 (w Jean Wishart 1750, chn John, Isobel, Kath, Jean, David slater 25.4.1794 81 (w Isobel Maule 24.3.1802 76, s Wm slater 23.2.1837 81 who revised this stone in 1831, s John 17.5. 1835 72, s David 22.7.1848 (77) (s David Sime Shiress 26.4.1880 55), da Isobel, da Jean, da Kath, da Margt, da Eliz, da Mary)) (see Edwards "Guide" 3rd ed.p 61: Shiress ia variously spelt Seras, Scheres, Ceres in old papers ... The name existed here from 1560 in which year Peter Seres was a bailie)

191 John Edgar of Keithock 4.4.1788 63, yt s Jas d at sea 9.6.1841 64, 1da Cath Margt 11.5.1845 82 (wid of Jonathan Watson bishop of Dunkeld, s John d at sea 24.6.1840 36, da Cath Mary d Edinburgh 7.1.1884 82) (see Jervise "Inscriptions"p 22 for Edgars of Keithock & bishop Watson; also in "Land of the Lindsays"; see Brechin Testaments: David Edgar of Keithock, 13.9.1723 & relict Eliz Guthrie also relict of David Guthrie of Seatoun, 30.10.1723)

3a BRECHIN CATHEDRAL KIRK

192 John Wall burges shoemaker in Brechin, w Eliz Steill 17.3.1730 38, chn Jean, Eliz, John & And d inf (see Edwards "Guide" 3rd ed.p 57 has "Watt" in error, and quotes poem; Jervise "Inscriptions" p 12)

193 Chas Fettes 13.3.1831 74, w Jean Tindall 21.5.1846 83, da Mary 31.8.1876 81, s Jas surgeon Laurencekirk erected this stone

194 1861. John Valentine mert, twin ss b 28.1.1835 John d 1y4m, Chas d 4y

195 1782. Alex Smith, w Isobel Milne, s Robt 22.8.1779 48 (wid Agnes Lighton, 4 chn d inf, Alex, - - - , Margt & P - - -, also Ann - - - - - survives (see perhaps Brechin Testaments: Robt Smith weaver & bleacher in Brechin, 28.2.1781)

196 1886. Geo Wright 26.7.1844 48, w Ann Craig 9.2.1878 80, chn Robt & Eliz erected this stone, four ss & two das d inf, da Mary 4.4.1886 56 (wid of Jas Nicol) Annie Kennedy Nicol 23.1.1935 74. Eliz Smart Nicol 23.11. 1953 90

198 Wm Tindall 11.12.1810 51, w Margt Walker 5.2.1820 52, s Wm 6.8.1817 22, da Jean 10.6.1819 12, s David 4.5.1820 20, s Burns 16.11.1822 19, s Jas 28.10.1836 42

199 Robt Baillie tent Kincraig & w Cath Edgar both d 4.1799 (ed. they had a s Wm writer to the Signet sheriff substitute Dumfriesshire d Edinburgh 13.2.1855 87)

200 in Latin. John Ouchterlony, w - - enar Edgar 10.3.1726 36 (see perhaps Brechin Testaments: John Ouchterlony mert Brechin, 20.8.1747 & Nicholas da of late John Ouchterlony mert in Brechin, 22.10.1782)

201 CT John Spence mert burges of Brechin d some years after his w Jean Henderson 24.5.1634 34, s John town clerk of Brechin 29.10.1689 (1s Geo 11.1717 56 (only s John & da Mary)).
John Spence town clerk of Brechin 10.11.1773 77, only s John town clerk & clerk to Justice of the Peace of the court of Forfar 1.5.1790 67 to whose memory this stone was re-erected & the former inscription renewed, (1s John clerk of Brechin 12.1814 (see Edwards "Guide 3rd ed.p 61 who has "1815" in error, he d childless), chn Alex & Eliz int here) (see Brechin Testaments: John Spens commisar clerk of Brechin & Eliz Lyon his spouse, 23.10.1691; John Spence late commisary of Brechin, 8.7. 1791)

202 Wm Mackay artillery pensioner imo w Mary Bain 2.12.1836 42; "Ye children who this motto read / I pray you to your ways take heed / And do not do as some have done - /Hurry your mother to the tomb. /All feuds by me are now forgiven - /Resting in hope of peace in heaven;/Then ere too late think on your end -/As death you leaves doth judgment find." (see Edwards "Guide" 3rd ed.p59: Old Mackay was a man of considerable ingenuity, & notwithstanding that he had lost one eye & both hands in the service of his country, he not only followed the trade of handloom weaver, but dressed fly-hooks & plaited fishing line with an incredible amount of care & beauty)

203 Jas Nairn 4.8.1867 70, w Betsy Findlay 7.6.1852 53, by da Ann (h David Soppet 2.11.1865 53, 3 chn d inf, s David d Letham 6.1884 38)

204 1799. Francis Finlay, Middleshade near Brechin 31.3.1730 1.6.1798, by wid Janet Brown (see Brechin Testaments: Brancis Findlay at Middleshade, 13.7.1798)

205 Jas Wood mert Brechin 8.-.1782 60

206 Wm Hebenton shoemaker 13.7.1861 64, by wid Agnes Rose

207 1848. David Hebenton flesher 20.8.1879 77, 1w Jane Craig 23.5.1848 45,

s John 11.4.1846 2, s Geo 21.4.1837 4, da Margt 4.2.1843 1y, s Joseph 13.3.1844 5, s Robt 22.9.1844 4, 2w Cath Mathers 21.12.1892 82

208 TS Jas Scott, High Street 12.10.1855 63, w Janet McKinlay 28.11.1854 63

209 Thos Ramsay 25.6.1850 58, w Helen Walker 14.8.1875 84, by da Mary d Stirling 10.3.1909 82 (h Hugh Hunter d Brechin 10.6.1899 73, s David d Australia 20.2.1889, s Thos d America 4.1899)

210 Jas Macher tent Ardovie, s And 1721 7; David 1743 21 ; Wm Machir 31.7.1800 75

211 Alex Wood, w Eliz Anderson 17.12.1746 46, da Helen 11.10.1736 11, chn David, Eliz & Kath d inf; (west side) A W E A ; IW, HW, AW, DW, EW, IW, MW, MW, KW. 1756

212 Daniel McIntosh 5.3.1851 60, w Jean Napier 7.10.1858 66, da Mary 28.4.1879 53 (by s Jas McIntosh (s Jas 3.12.1878 5, s Wm 2.5.1879 1m both int New cem))

213 by Robt Rodger, w Margt Lawrie d Drumbartnot 12.12.1869 45, da Agnes 16.5.1852 4

214 1837. Jas Rodger fr Drumbartnot 31.8.1815 69, w Jean Baillie 31.5.1834 81, by s Robt (s Wm d inf, s David 19.2.1839 4)

215 Robt Rodger fr Drumbartnot 5.5.1848 59, w Jean Rodger 19.8.1846 54, by s Jas (his aunt Jean Rodger, Burnside of Cairnbank 9.2.1860 79)

216 Alex Sievwright 15.7.1870 75½, w Mary Ann Barclay 8.9.1858 62, da Margt 5.1839 5, da Susan Bremner 6.1.1865 26, by family in 1870

217 Wm Doig 1.1.1801 18.3.1860, w Christian Sievwright 11.5.1798 1.10.1884, da Betsy 3.10.1839 16.11.1841, da Christian Murray 30.6.1833 28.2.1889, da Jean Japp 28.6.1841 9.3.1906, da Mary 8.9.1827 8.3.1911, by 1s John P in 1890

218 large granite. Alex Low mert 24.4.1783 73, w Cath 2.3.1763 (da of Francis Molison & Eliz Donaldson), da Cath 1789 48 (h Colvin Smith, Maison Dieu 1811 76, only ch John mert 17.12.1837 73 (w Cecilia Gillies 31.7.1839 75, 1s Colvin RSA d Edinburgh 21.7.1875 79 (see DNB), s rev Robt DD senior min Old Machar d Aberdeen 11.11.1877 80 int here with w Mary Curzon Molison & several of their chn (see no.165))). maj gen John Smith, Bengal Staff Corps (nephew of Colvin Smith RSA), 1da Mary Harriet Gillies 11.1.1919 (see Edwards "Guide" 3rd ed.pp 59, 62, 70)

221 painted boards. GIFTS: 1615 Andrew bishop of Brechin, pulpit chandelier;
1616 John Muirton mert, £66; 1617 Thos Coupare, £66;
1620 Elspate Lows alias Kinnimond, £200;
1623 Robt Rollock & da Mary, £100;
1622 Kath Langwill mortified a yeard; 1630 Jas Webster maltman, £66;
Jas Pieres mert, £133 & for helping to call the great bell, £66, & Agnes Cargill his spouse, £66 (see Brechin Testaments: Jas Perron & relict Agnes Cargill, 1630; Jas Peirrs & spouse Agnes Cargill, 1629);
1633 Alex Collie shoemaker, £10; 1641 Christian Laing, £10;
1643 John Tulloch mert, £66; mr Alex Bisset min gifted silver communion cup (see Fasti v 375); 1644 John Greig maltman, £40;
1648 mr Wm Raitt min gifted silver communion cup (see Fasti v 375);
Normand Fairlie younger, £33; 1649 David Clark mert, £33;
Elspat Gray spouse to David Watt maltman, £40;
1651 Jas Dempster calive, £66; 1655 mr Laurence Skinner min, great Bible (see Fasti v 376); 1660 John Mil church officer, three tinne basins for serving in administration of the Sacraments;
1664 Alex Anderson the Haugh, £20 (see Brechin Testaments);
1665 David Strang bishop of Brechin gifted the Orledge on the steeple;

1660 John Wattson mert £100; 1673 John Bellie mert £66 (see Brechin Testaments) ; 1676 Kath Fenton relict of provost John Skinner £33 (see Brechin Testaments); 1678 dr John Innes, £33;
1680 Walter Jameson bailie & kirkmaster, 2 tinne quart stoops for Communion Tables;
1680 Isobel Nicol relict of John Mill tayleour, £6.13.4;
1682 Anna Barclay reclict of David bishop of Brechin, £33 (see Brechin Testaments; also Jervise: she was da of Barclay of Mathers & sis to 1st Barclay of Urie, she md David Strachan in 1649);
1682 John Gairdner wheelwright £33 (see Brechin Testaments: John Gardner & Cath Mather his spouse, 3.2.1682);
1684 mr Robt Carnegy son of David dean of Brechin, £100 (see Brechin Testaments, 1679; also Jervise "Inscriptions" p 32: David Carnegy dean d 1677 77, his w Helen Lindsay (her Testament, spouse to mr David Carnegy min of Farnell, 27.10.1656));
1688 Cath Mader spouse to Jas Allan bailie, £33 (see Brechin Testaments);
1689 Jas Allan bailie, £33 (see Brechin Testaments, 21.10.1690);
1690 master John Glendei dean of Cashels & prebend of St Michaels Dublin, £40; 1692 John Mill wheelwright, Hospital Master, £33 (see Brechin Testaments: John Mill lint wheelwright burgess late master of the Hospital & Jean Mill his spouse, 1692 & 8.7.1693);
1702 Thos Sivewright mert Edinburgh, £100; Wm Fanes glover,to the poor, £133; John Leonard chapman, Angus, to the poor, £66;
1711 Geo Carnegy glover London, to the poor, £60;
1728 bailie David Doig of Cookston, folio bible;
1732 rev John Johnston for school & other pious uses, £1000 (see Fasti v 380); 1744 rev Wm Shanks for school use, £66 (Fasti v 380; Brechin Testaments);
1751 Helen White relict of provost Robt White, to the poor, £66 (see Brechin Testaments); 1765 Alex Young burges, to the poor, £26;
1772 Wm Shepherd mert, to the poor, £65

225 mural. rev David Blair 20.4.1769 68 (about 1760 he founded the first Sabbath evening school in Scotland), w Christian Doig 9.1753 43 (da of John Doig of Cookstone magistrate here), 7 chn lie here & 4 chn d abroad & 1 ch int in churchyard here, by s David of Cookstone mert Dundee (see Fasti v 376; Brechin Testaments; inscription no.389 infra; Edwards "Guide" 3rd ed. pp 106, 112)

229 rev Jas Burns 1st min here 2.1.1837 61 in 38th y of min, w Christina Chalmers 6.10.1837 62, 1da Ann 1810 1899 (h rev Thos Guthrie DD 1803 1873 (see DNB; inscription no. 174 ante) (see Edwards "Guide" 3rd ed. pp 67-8: rev Jas Burns' fa was surveyor of taxes, Bo'ness & had 8 ss of whom Jas, Wm H, Robt & Geo were ministers)

230 mural. rev Robt Coutts 2nd min here 18.6.1803 31 (see Fasti v 381; Edwards "Guide" 3rd ed. pp 66-7: he md in 1801 a da of dr Macculloch of Dairsie; her memoirs were edited by dr Hetherington)

245 John Knox mert provost 7.6.1754 83, w Margt Donaldson 7.2.1755 83 with 5 ss & 5 das (see Edwards "Guide" 3rd ed. pp 69-70)

246 Thos Oakers private 71st Foot regt 26.2.1856 76, w Christian Ogilvy 8.3. 1846 66, da Mary d inf (see Edwards "Guide" 3rd ed. p 215)

247 1827. Ernest Fiddler vintner Arbroath, w Sarah Black 12.8.1799 35, das Ann & Margt d inf, das Isobel, Eliz & Ann survive; Marjory 20.2.1825

248 Geo Young 5.12.1864 68, w Helen Leighton 6.4.1873 66

249 David Young 15.12.1887 83 (see Edwards "Guide 3rd ed. p 216: "Laird" Young, long Deacon of the Weavers .. resided in St.Mary Street for .. over 60 y & was the last survivor of the heads of old & well-known fam-

ilies connected with the west end of the "Upper Wynd" - St.David Street), w Ann Mathers 19.1.1867 69, s Chas 8.11.1829 2y10m, s David 1.10.1826 1y, da 13.12.1839 inf, da Mary 16.1.1834 2½, s 13.12.1839 inf, da Mary 23.7. 1859 22¾, s David d Montreal 27.7.1872 38, last survivor Ann 5.9.1912 83

250 1864. John Dakers shoemaker 29.8.1864 93, w Isabella Dakers 28.9.1827 55, da Isabella 28.4.1807 1y, da Ann 28.5.1808 4, da Isabella 5.2.1808 26.4. 1871, by s Jas

251 rev Jas Gowans UF Chruch Kilwinning 2.5.1874 82, w Eliz Dakers 29.2.1884 73, da Eliza 20.10.1851 1, s Samuel Black 16.9.1882 26

252 Jas Dakers 17.9.1899 81, w Marjory Mill 15.2.1893 71, s Jas 24.3.1872 24, s David 8.2.1869 8

253 Jean Crammond 10.9.1841 21, her sis Sophia 12.1.1860 (h David Blues seaman). And Williamson joiner 6.3.1892 75

254 Wm Jamie 23.12.1859 72, w Ann Crammond 21.6.1874 87, by s David

255 Wm Dakers wood mert 17.1.1866 92, w Annie Black 20.8.1854 68, da Mary 1.6.1871 70, s Jas mert Fettercairn 29.7.1875 71

256 1755. D W I M ; by David Watson dyer at Mickle Mill of Brechin, chn David & Isobel d nonage

257 Wm Sievwright city missionary Edinburgh, w Margt Mathers d after bearing a stillborn son 17.3.1852, da Jean Mathers 19.9.1850 5.4.1867

258 by David Low imo mo Cathrine Shiress 23.3.1822 69, his s Jas 22.12.1827 ½y, s David 22.12.1833 4½

259 Thos Mathers 2.2.1799 64, w Cathrine Fisher 2.4.1795 60, by s John (w Isobel Hobb 30.5.1810 28, s David 2.4.1819 10y7m)

260 by David Low shoemaker & family in 1823

261 David Lowe leather mert 26.8.1851 60, w Jane Christison 23.9.1852 59, da Kath 29.12.1859 37, s John 2.1.1864 29, s Jas 10.5.1884 56, da Margt 4. 2.1900 75, s Wm Shiress d Battry Park Isle of Wight County, Va USA 7.3. 1903 77, da Jane Anne d Arbroath 13.2.1917 85

262 Alex Grubb, Summer Bank Brechin d Edinburgh 13.7.1865 80 int Warriston cem there, w Jane Lowe 5.5.1862 68, s David Reid solicitor Edinburgh

263 1847. Joseph Low mert 28.9.1846 33, w Eliz Don d Edinburgh 25.12.1893 80 int Warriston cem there, s Geo 16.5.1842 inf

264 Wm Mudie 17.4.1844 48, w Margt Low 10.2.1875 78, 1s Jas d inf, ys Alex 28.9.1842 4

265 Alex Smart 14.2.1853 37, w Jane Hodge 4.2.1890 77, da Agnes 1855 9

266 Wm Hodge 12.2.1884 64, w Mary Burnet 13.6.1894 73, s Wm 13.12.1879 28

268 1857. Alex Walker mason 2.9.1840 29, by w Agnes Smart, s Wm 17.1.1844 7, s David 7.12.1855 16

269 David Smart slater 3.1848 97, w Margt Geekie 12.1853 75, by gs Chas Cowie 23.1.1865

270 Wm Gordon residenter 26.5.1823 67, 4 das d inf, by s Wm; "Like leaves on trees the race of man is found,/ Some withring green, some withring on the ground;/ Another race the following spring supplies-/ They fall successive, and successive rise."

271 Francis Stuart 14.5.1884 73, w Eliz Stuart 10.10.1885 80, 1s Alex Gordon 2.4.1871 33, s Jas 27.10.1880 41

272 1846. John Gordon 1.4.1823 71, w Martha Kinnear 10.6.1823 67, da Helen

14.2.1827 38, by s Robt blacksmith Montrose d Airlie Street Brechin 6.10.1885 95 (w Eliz Webster 20.6.1871 80)

273 John Webster fr Dubton 7.2.1855 88, w Isabel Gordon 27.6.1819 42, chn Alex, Eliz, Jas, John, Robt, Jessie, Robt & Geo; (s?)Wm Webster d Westbank 17.2.1875 77,(w Jane Gordon 6.5.1875 44),da Isabel 21.5.1882 72, da Agnes d Trusta 7.9.1893 94

274 1756. Alex Kaithnes 38y, by w Jean Webster, her das Margt 4.5.1755, Jean 13.2.1752 30

275 John Willox tent Netherpitforthie, by w Agnes Wood 5.4.1772 61, chn Chas, John, Wm, Jean, Margt, Christean, Helen & Agnes

276 John Wisheart burges 30.(11). 1742 63, by Hellen - - - - - ; John Wisheart weaver burges 27.6.175(7) (75)

277 FS Jas Scott tent Newton St Vigeans 11.1778 70, w Kath Livie 3.1782 73, da Margt 1.1784 44, da Magdalen (2).12.1792 57 (h Wm Neish tent Linthank, 3 of their chn viz Isobel, Cath & Alex d inf)

281 convener Alex Mitchell, w Ann Mill, s David convener (w Eliz Ferrier, da Margt Ann, s Wm F d Bloemfontein SA, s professor Alex F DD LLD min Dunnichen for 46y, professor St Mary's College St Andrews, moderator in 1885 d 22.3.1899 76 (w Margt Tweedie Johnstone 12.11.1900 74, s Robt Haldane d S Australia 15.1.1876 22, s Jas Ferrier 16.8.1909 46, da Eliz Margt 29.11.1919 54))

282 Jas Monro 1760 1841, 1w Amn Smith, s Alex 1.1869 80 (w Helen Barclay 3. 1856 60, s Jas, s John Barclay, da Margt, da Helen, by 'myself' (chn Alex, Jas, Hugh Aird, John Macpherson)), 2w Margt Webster

284 1862. David Mitchell 5.1.1861 67, w Mary Junor 1.6.1868 75, da Mary 4. 1.1822 15.8.1825, s Jas 11.10.1823 22.1.1843, s Robt 15.8.1829 12.6.1847 by s John

285 1829. Robt Carnegie 3.4.1828 40, by w Cath Junor, da Isabella 14.2.1828 ½y

286 Samuel Gordon, Woodside Little Brechin 14.12.1884 87, w Mary Ramsay 22. 12.1808 16.1.1894 at Montrose, s John d inf, s Jas 10.12.1854 18, yt da Mary Ann 1.1854 24.5.1903 at Broughty Ferry, s David Stewart Ramsay mert Valparaiso Chile 25.8.1845 12.6.1903 at Edinburgh, da Eliz 20.9.1838 19.8.1909 at Rothesay Bute (h Jas M Hardy), da Jane d Brantford Canada 26.11.1910 76 (h Hudson Cleator of Cleator's Creek), da Agnes d Edinburgh 6.11.1912 79 (h Jas Leishman)

287 Isobell Wobster dearly beloved spouse to Wm Maule gardiner at the Castle of Brechine who running the course of her life by unfeigned piety, unshaken patience, singular prudence, true Christian charity, worshipping God & magnifying her lawful affairs, surrendered her soul to God ye 2 of June 1752 aged 66y. She was the mo of 12 chn, 4 of whom d inf & are here int

288 John Edwards 11.11.1855 82, w Mary Moug 4.1.1858 75, s Wm 2.1825 1m, s Alex 5.1835 22, da Eliz 11.1857 50, da Ann 7.1861 57, s Robt 11.4.1866 64 (w Cath Mitchell 25.9.1885 80)

288a David Ferrier 1828 59, w Christina Roger 1829 62, s Michael 2.7.1863 64, da Margt 28.9.1871 75, da Christian 22.9.1805 17.1.1880 (s David F 1836 inf, da Margt M 12.4.1849 9, h Alex Scott senior 22.5.1877 73)

289 Wm Ferrier 1850, w Margt Joe 15.10.1901 86, da Mary b 24.6.1838, s Michael b 18.8.1839, s Jas b 16.1.1842, da Jean Ann b 16.4.1846 all int here, s Wm sole partner of Chas Mitchell & Son mert 5.11.1849 25.3.1913

290 John Anderson 26.10.1872 73, w Jane Ferrier 5.1.1883 79, by s David Ferrier JP mert 5.4.1897 59 (w Isabella Stott d at Trinity 22.11.1916 82, s

Wm 3.5.1865 24.1.1867, s David 26.1.1867 12.2.1867, 3s Geo d Denver Colorado 10.1.1905 36), da Christina 6.4.1848 14

291 Jas Windrim at Burn of Keithock 2.10.1841 73. John Black, Keithock Burn 24.1.1869, w Mary Rodger 29.12.1868

291a listed by Jervise "Inscriptions" p 20 as being buried next to 291 & Edwards "Guide" 3rd ed.p65 notes it was later fastened inside the old chancel wall: in Latin. John Winram 1.2.1619 36, by w Margt Wat

292 Alex Singer 11.5.1851 52, w Isobel Marr 24.7.1870 74, s Geo d inf, s John 18.2.1843 5, s Alex 11.5.1881 54, s Robt d India 14.11.1880 39 servant to capt Sandeman 78th highlanders, s Jas 6.2.1887 55 (w Anne Baillie 7.2.1892 72)

293 1789. by Jas Howie mert, w Mary Strachan 30.8.1788 57, had 6 chn, 2 of whom both called John d young & int here (see Edwards "Guide"3rd ed. p 58 for poem); square & compasses

294 Jas Black 1.7.1840 72, w Betsy Craig 12.3.1855 84, da Mary 4.4.1881 75, by s Wm wright 13.3.1892 81 (w Isabella Mudie 19.4.1898 89, s David 24.2.1854 3, da Betsy 27.3.1895)

295 David Black wright 9.8.1877 77, w Jessie Wilson 15.11.1888 72, 1s Jas 15.2.1866 26

296 Alex Arnott, Upper Tenements 3.3.1875 79, w Jane Lindsay 9.3.1858 63, had 3 ss & 3 das: Eliz, Anne, Jas & Alex d inf, da Mary Ann 20.3.1907 (h Wm Mitchell 3.2.1895 73, chn Jas, Mary Ann & Lindsay d inf), s Wm d New Jersey City USA 3.10.1894 70

297 Chas Arnot weaver Nether Tenemants of Caldham 10.3.1740 53, w Agnes Fettes 17.1.1748 55, had 10 chn: Chas, Jas & Chas d inf, Margt, John, Robt, Anne, Isabel, Jean & David survived

298 Wm Peterkin mert 2.1847 71, w Eliz Laurence 6.3.1856 73, s Jas confectioner 23.7.1877 65 (da Ann 27.11.1851 4m). Ann Peterkin 9.9.1880 67

299 by Robt Lowrance, da Eliz 6.2.1780 22

300 David Alexander bookseller & printer 8.3.1859 43, w Margt Peterkin 2.2.1892 77

301 by Wm Gordon writer, s John Alexander 14.2.1830 4m

302 John Ferrier - - - - 72y, - - - -t Hill 18(<u>75</u>) 66, s Wm wright (<u>13</u>).6.1867 (<u>68</u>) - - - - - - - - - - - - - chn David & Ann - - - - -- yt s Wm - - - - -6.February - - -

304 Jas Craig kirk officer here 39y d 17.6.1849 70, w Jean Balfour 26.10.1845 64, ss David & Geo d inf (see Edwards "Guide" 3rd ed.p 163-4: he was bellringer .. an upright man --; a s James, Aberdeen, was alive in 1849)

305 Jas Wood, Upperpitforthie 1751, w - - -et Nish 10.7.1765 80

305a Jas Wood & Margt Nish late tents Upperpitforthie, s Alex 8.1.1756, chn John, And, Margt, Isobel, Jannet, Ann & Jean

306 Wm Peter tent East Drums 31.7.1826 68. Wm Sharpe surgeon, da Christina 5.2.1836 2y4m

307 Wm Smith, West Drums 30.8.1859 79, w Jean Barclay 30.11.1843 64, s Wm 1.10.1892 73

308 Jas Speid 26.2.1749 79, w Mary Milne 14.5.1745 70, by s John tent Pitpullox (see Brechin Testaments: Margt Bell spouse to Jas Speid in Pitpullokis, 22.12.1612; John Speid elder in Pitpulokis heritable proprietor of the lands of the back of the Crage of the Hill of Balnabreich, 26.12.1649 etc etc)

309 Jas Baxter 1.4.1867 74, w Helen Adamson 22.11.1883 66, s Robt 5.1.1868 27, da Helen 14.5.1870 32

310 1846. Jas Baxter 16.4.1836 82, w Mary Sime 13.2.1828 75, s Alex 14.12. 1807 24

311 by Jas Dunbar, w Janet Gordon 18.3.1835 42, s Robt 8.3.1837 10, s Wm 17.6.1841 8, s Alex 25.3.1849 20, sis Ann Dunbar 29.11.1848 52

312 Jas Crockett dyker 23.10.1866 62, w Martha Proctor 1.8.1877 66, s Thomson 22.9.1846 2, s David 24.11.1880 46, s Joseph (s Jas 17.10.1888 17, s Wm 15.8.1891 20). A.Crockett, Brechin

313 Alex Crockat 28.2.1748 63, w Barbary Smith 2.2.1748 60, by s John (w Isabel Balfour, s David 13.10.1763 13)

314 1869. Wm Binny of Forfar, da Helen 20.11.1843, da Isobel 26.9.1850, da Janet 11.5.1862, by da mrs Speid

315 John Garden mert 24.2.1746 72, w Marion Sime 12.12.17(48), by heirs (see Brechin Testaments)

316 Jas Strachan baker, w Barbara Mill 1855 53

317 John Reid weaver 29.3.1860 64, w Isabel Stevenson 27.6.1865 71, twins Jas & Jane both d 31.10.1830 1y, da Agnes 2.6.1837 5

318 John Low 26.4.1891 88, w May Sievwright 16.6.1873 70, da Betsy 25.10. 1842 inf, da Isabella 25.7.1853 20, da Cath 28.7.1853 15, s Jas C 11.8. 1853 17

319 Jas Skea tent Mountboy 21.3.1843 77, w Margt Hay 14.12.1862 82, s Alex 6.6.1822 3, da Eliz 22.12.1854 39, s David 21.7.1857 57, s Jas 17.10. 1857 52 (da Margt 19.5.1866 26), s Joseph 19.8.1865 45, s Thos 13.1.1869 65, s Wm 1.11.1873 64, da Ann 16.1.1879 70, da Mary 9.3.1882 80 (h Thos Nicol mert), da Margt 20.5.1883 85 (h Alex Norie woollen spinner). Thos Nicol mert 9.8.1895 90

320 John Henry blacksmith Kintrockat d St Anns 21.1.1865 87, w Margt May 19. 2.1872 92, by son

321 John Kidd 11.3.1868 70, w Eliz Soutar 11.10.1867 67, chn Cecilia, Eliz, Jane, Ann & Jas d inf

322 1866. John Soutter 20.1.1781 15.5.1849 md 4.6.1810 to Mary Mitchell 22. 9.1785 8.1.1865, by chn John, Mary, Joseph, Alex, Eliz & Jas, said Eliz d 15.2.1904 80 (h Wm O'Neil)

323 Jas Soutter 8.2.1833 80, w Margt Hastings 1.4.1826 71, da Margt 12.12. 1878 96 (h Peter Carnegie gardener Ardovie 3.1.1824 39, da Jean 23.4. 1828 13, da Eliz 15.12.1890 (78))

324 1879. David Scott, Springfield 23.1.1850 62, w Cath Cooper 19.5.1867 78

326 rev David Blackadder 4.8.1843 72 in 40th y of ministry, fa mr Thos d here 1.1809 77 native of Blackadderton Edron par in Berwickshire, by 2nd United Secession Congregation Brechin as a tribute (see Edwards "Guide" 3rd ed.p 60-1 for full isncription)

327 FS tipped up. Patk Mitchell mert burgess 31.3.1712 59; P M, I D ; KM, MM, -M

328 Alex Low mert, das Isoble, Agnes, Margrat d - - - - 17(11)

328a FS tipped up. (~~marginal~~)- - - - - - - - - - - - - - ; (central) -- , I M

329 David Crab 12.1766 72, by ss Thos & David; Thos Crab, w Margt Trail, three chn int here viz David, Isabel & Agnes; Helen Crab 25.12.1781 1y8m

330 John Couts vintner 9.6.1807 96, by wid Susan Couts imo da Susan 2.8.1810 3

331 1847. Geo Scott manuf 31.1.1876 88, w Margt Ronald 11.3.1846 60, da Mary 1823 1y, da Margt 1824 8, da Jane 3.4.1853 42, da Margt Scott or Buyers 5.1.1904 73

332 FS tipped up. (marginal) Thos Hutchon, w Isobel Spence 16(6-) (80)y; Jas Nicol in Dubton & Thos Hutchon burges in Brechin(Edwards "Guide": "1668")

334 John Smith mert, w Cecilia Chalmers imo four of their chn, John 27.6.1762 2¼, Geo 26.9.1763 2m, John 4.10.1768 2, Christian 6.9.1771 3w (see no.168)

335 Jas Eaton, Nether Tenemants 5.1.1863 80, w Mary Wood 14.7.1860 72, s Chas 25.3.1856 21, s in law Alex Durie 26.9.1866 50 (s John 11.2.1887 47). Cath Eaton 13.5.1882 73

336 Robt Eaton mason Coldham Tenemants, w Eliz Burnet 23.7.1753 55, da Kath d inf, da Mary 15.10.1753 22. by Alex Wood junior mason ; mason's tools

337 Alex Murray cabinetmaker 16.6.1853 58, w Mary Burnett 30.7.1872 67, 3 chn d inf, s Jas d Edinburgh 10.4.1873 29

338 John Burnett wright 8.2.1814 77, w Margt Findlay 27.7.1780 32, s John wright 27.9.1847 76 (w Christina Leslie d Edinburgh 8.3.1882 int Grange cem, by ss John & Robt)

338a FS tipped up. Heir rests in the Lord a faithful bro John Mathie sometime in Naither Pitforthie d 3.1653 87; skull, crossbones, sandglass etc

339 1795. David Paterson. Ann Arnot

340 1866. David Paterson feuar Nether Tenements Caldhame 12.1803, w Ann Arnott 5.1795 both in advanced age, s David feuar & mert Nether Tenements 14.9.1846 87 (w Isobel Arnot 18.8.1862 88, da Isobel b 1801 d at an early age, da Eliz 17.9.1898 83)

341 FS tipped up & broken. Geo Weath, w Agnis Caldonhead 25.12.1749 45 had 7 chn: John, Wm, Ann, Margt, Jean, Agnes & Isobell; Wm Weath weaver, w Eliz Beal 28.3.1782; above Geo Weath schoolmaster Pitpullocks 15.7.1767 73 (see Brechin Testaments: John Waith in Dubton, 1643; Margt Langlands relict of Jas Weath shoemaker Brechin, 1773)

341a FS tipped up. Alex Li(ttlejohn) citizen of Brechin 20.8.1668 62; poem; C P, I A, M D, - - - - (see Brechin Testaments: Alex Littlejohn burgess in Brechin & Christian Paterson his spouse, 5.3.1669 & 27.3.1671)

342 mural. 1860. Alex Currie, Bearhill 18.5.1793 64, w Rachel Palmer 1.3.1802 74, s Jas, da Jean, da Helen (h Wm Weath, childless), da Rachel, s John, s Alex, da Mary, da Rebecca (h David Gordon, only ch Alex Currie) all int Brechin, 2s David, West-Port 10.3.1800 42 (w Jean Allan 8y his wife & 50y his widow d Edinburgh 20.3.1850 79, chn Rebecca & John d inf, s Jas d childless in London 7.7.1856 59 int Kensal Green cem, by 1s Alex advocate Edinburgh sheriff of Banffshire, Clerk of Session 1856-67, 5.1.1793 7.11.1868 in Edinburgh, da Jean 17.9.1798 12.3.1869 at Careston manse (h Alex Baxter of Alyth, s Alex Currie))

343 Geo Scott banker 9.2.1875 69, sis Jean Scott 9.6.1856 48, w Isabella Duke 27.1.1833 31, da Ann 17.1.1841 10, da Jeannie 1.12.1915 82

344 John Duke bleacher 28.7.1850 55, w Marjory Middleton 21.1.1879 87, 1s David manuf 23.7.1877 55, da Isabella 30.10.1903 79 (see Edwards "Guide" 3rd ed.p 58: David & his bro Robt Duke erected Denburn Linen Works)

345 Jas Simpson, w Isabel Craw, by ss Geo, John & David, s rev Geo, Free Church Kintore (see Ewing i 316: Robert (sic) Simpson DD b Brechin 1791 md in 1833 Harriet Mary Brown, d 1870), s John fr Broomfield Monymusk d 1845, s David, Crossfield 21.8.1856 60 (w Kath Erskine 1.2.1866 76, (da) Isobel Crowe Simpson d London 19.3.1891 65, da Jane Anderson-Simpson 6.3.1892 64

346 Alex Hampton 5.8.1855 66, w Mary Lonmuir 26.11.1882 82, da Mary 19.10. 1837 1y10m, da Mary 27.2.1845 1½, s Jas Langmure 4.4.1847 1y1m, s John d Kimberley South Africa 29.11.1887 57, s Thos d Glasgow 17.8.1896 56, da Helen 27.5.1901 72, da Margt d Forfar 9.9.1902 68 (h And Shepherd), da Rose last of family 20.9.1914 76

347 Jas Craig wright 19.11.1827 50, w Jean Rennie 9.5.1856 91, s John 3.1. 1844, da Susan 1.10.1857 (h Robt Fleming teacher Glasgow). Eliz Sim 10.10.1890 96, h John Craig

348 - - - - - - - Aiseann imo - - - MacDonald d - -ember 1853 33 - -- pipe major - - highlanders --- - - - - - - former commanding officer col Maule (see Edwards "Guide" 3rd ed.p 57: he was Lord Panmure's piper)

350 mural. David Hunter eesq of Blackness d Eskmount 19.10.1809 67, by wid

351 rev Alex Davidson, Scots Episcopal min Brechin & Menmuir 29.6.1782 int church aisle of Menmuir, wid Margt Stewart 11.1.1820, s Alex writer Brechin 14.1.1819 (w Ann Hood 13.4.1864 81)

352 ob.right hon Wm Ramsay Maule baron Panmure of Brechin & Navar 27.10.1771 13.4.1852, by The People (see DNB: he was born Ramsay but adopted the surname Maule in 1787)

353 by Jas Lennox imo bro Wm (nephew of the late Wm Baird) 4.4.1859 25

354 Wm Baird, Swan Inn Brechin 26.6.1853 45, wid Isabella Hunter, his niece Jane Baird Lennox 3.7.1858 20

355 John Davidson saddler 31.10.1884 79, w Ann Murray 29.10.1847 33, s Jas Walker inf, s John Murray inf, da Isabella 18.8.1852 9

357 Jas Lyall 23.5.1858 66, by s Jas B, Andover Mass USA

358 David Reid 5.3.1855 75, w Jean Baillie 18.12.1822 37, s David d Liverpool 7.3.1842 26, s Wm d Trinidad 1843 30, s Joseph 23.3.1897 78, by da Jean

359 Geo Walker 23.1.1858 49, w Cecilia Soutar 21.4.1871 82, s John 6.3.1854 2y10m, da Sarah 1912, bro John 7.9.1884 87

360 Helen Crockatt d Barrelwell 16.1.1826 86, 2h Robt Soutar & his chn Agatha, Cecilia & James & her chn by her 1st h: Wm, Margt, Agnes & Helen Geekie all erected this

361 Jas Greig mert 17.9.1855 49, w Margt Ker 15.11.1879 75

362 1830. David Ker mert 9.7.1839 80, w Eliz Fairweather 22.11.1829 63, da Isabel, da Margt, da Eliz 20.6.1880 73

366 David Macher cooper 31.12.1821 79, w Eliz Peter 12.4.1823 85, da Jean (h John Taylor mert)

367 by Jonathan Mitchell, w Margt Neish 24.11.1843 62

368 1848. Francis Baillie tent Dalgety 15.9.1846 68, w Eliz Fiddes 25.8. 1863 82, s Alex 23.5.1851 37, s John 2.11.1859 44, s Jas 25.1.1875 63, da Eliz 24.11.1900 82

369 Thos Allan, w (Eliza Burns) 12.(12).182(9) (42), s Thos 1.3.1818 7

370 Wm Smyttan surgeon Royal Navy sometime practitioner here 27.7.1819 32, da Louisa 11.12.1817 6m

371 David McKenzie mert 30.11.1836 41, w Rebecca Watson 14.7.1854 57, da Helen 8.1.1830 5, s Robt 1.5.1831 9, da Margt 10.9.1842 10, by ss Jas, Chas, David & Robt

372 Robt McKenzie mert 2.12.1818, by wid Margt Ruxton, chn Jas, Margt, Isobel, Chas & Margt

373 David Moir bishop of Brechin b 2.10.1777 consecrated 1837 d 21.8.1847, also died chn Jean, Wm, Helen, Anne, Peter, Mary & Robt (see Edwards "Guide" 3rd ed.pp 51 & 53: he was the son of a mason & crofter at Culbach in par of Fordoun ....;there is also a memorial tablet in the Episcopal Church- w Janet 1856, ss Chas d St Kitts 1854, David d Ceylon 1857, John d inf)

374 1846. by Wm Fitchett, w Mary Smart 28.4.1840 52, chn John, Margt & Ann d inf, s John fr Hillhead of Burghill d in old age (w Jane Wilkie d in old age)

375 1847. 1838. Jas Michie watchmaker d Kirrymuir 2.4.1839 64, w Jean Gordon 22.8.1838 63, s Jas writer d Kirrymuir 13.11.1837 28, by surviving child Jane in 1839 (h John Loudon manuf Kirrymuir) (see John Smith "Old Scottish Clockmakers")

377 1849. Wm Strachan 13.10.1877 59, w Lizzie McEwan 15.5.1890 68, da Margt 16.10.1859 8, da Mary Ann 24.10.1859 5½, s Wm inf, s Geo d Valley Falls RI USA 17.3.1916 74, s David 1859 1925, Matilda S Wilson 1848 1928, Helen S Collie 1856 1930 the three last named int in Boston Mass USA

378 by Wm Johnston, w Jean Webester 21.5.1840 47

379 David McIntyre 1.11.1801 13.8.1881, w Margt Watson 15.7.1806 17.12.1894, yda Mary Ann 21.9.1841 12.4.1853, 1s David 6.12.1835 27.12.1859

381 Angus Stewart baker 17.12.1831 60, by wid Margt Robertson

382 John Christie 31.10.1836 67, by s John (da Margt 26.2.1834 2)

383 Jas Christie 31.10.1836, wid Cath Farquhar 25.12.1858 57 (her 2h Solomon Caldwell 24.3.1872 63, s John 15.1.1851 11), da Cath Anderson 5.1836 16d, s Jas 3.1839 2y

384 by Wm Nairn, s Wm 8.7.1847 35

385 by Jas Robertson innkeeper, w Eliz McKenzie 23.1.1836 69

386 by Geo Hammond, w Georgina Gordon Trimble 16.3.1849 49, 1s Geo factor Drummuir estate Banffshire 29.8.1852 29 int Botriphnie, 5s Thos 26.2.1853 17, 4s Jas d Leven Fife 28.7.1864 31, 6s Gordon MD staff assistant surgeon d Bathurst coast of Africa 18.8.1866 28, 3s Wm MD d Edinburgh 27.4.1875 43 int Warriston cem, 7s Alex, Transfer dept North British Railway Co Edinburgh 2.5.1875 34 int Dean cem

387 John Henderson nurseryman 6.11.1840 72, w Agnes Thomson 9.12.1846 76, 1s And 27.1.1852 51 (w Mary Fullerton 23.4.1858 60), 2s Geo 24.4.1879 76 (w Eliz Low 7.8.1876 69) (see Edwards "Guide" 3rd ed.p 257: Geo Henderson of the Den Nurseries designed the New Cemeteries at Brechin, Forfar and Arbroath)

388 mural. rev Geo Straton 25y clergyman Episcopal congregation Brechin d 2.1.1820 76 (see "Scottish Antiquary" xiv p 96, Episcopal Births, Deaths & Marriages 1796-1819; he md 15.9.1776 Margt da of capt John Graham of Duchray who d 10.8.1781 leaving das Christy, Mary & Jean)

389 rev David Blair min here, s John esq of Providence Essequibo (1s John Croydon 29.3.1840 55 (wid Isobel 13.12.1866 73 int Kensal Green cem, da Magdalen killed in her 5th year)) (see Fasti v 376; also inscription no.225 ante)

390 mural. mrs Anne Gib 1842 49, da Christina Eliz 9.11.1822 10 (see Edwards "Guide" 3rd ed.p56 for poem),sgen sir Wm Anthony Gib KCB Indian Army 9.1.1827 18.9.1915 (w Sarah Caroline 30.11.1910 (fa gen Howard Dowker Madras Army))

391 lieut Chas Binny Gib 1st regt TLI drowned at Palamcottah 1845 24, sis Anne Benny Gib 21.3.1859 44

392 Wm Mill 25.8.1791 63, w Eliz Crichton 18.2.1818 60, by s John (s John 1.11.1821 6d)

393 Joseph Gillam, Dunstew Oxford 12.4.1849 68, da Helen 16.3.1816 6m, da Ann 20.5.1819 9w, s Wm 8.6.1851 (43)

395 John Anderson blacksmith 1.1.1822 28.11.1883, w Cath Bowick (her mo Lizzie Lindsay 20.1.1780 2.4.1845, bro Chas Bowick 21.5.1810 12.10.1866)

396 Geo Anderson writer 1.12.1822 47, s Jas d London 11.3.1833 17, s Alex d Mansefield Victoria 29.12.1859 47 (see inscription no.86 ante)

397 Wm Anderson writer 2.6.1866 83, da Eliz int New cem Brechin (h David Cargill shipowner Arbroath, da Clementina 19.8.1854 19.6.1855, s David 28.9.1856 15.6.1862, da Eliz 28.10.1851 27.5.1863, s Jas 18.9.1858 14.11.1876, s Wm Anderson 18.11.1852 d Bristol 30.9.1879 int Arnos Vale cem)

399 John Duncan 10.4.1795 19.6.1878, w Agnes Lyall 16.11.1794 13.5.1840. Jane L Duncan 22.3.1830 13.7.1830. Jas L Duncan 1.10.1834 2.6.1889. Helen Speid Duncan 14.11.1831 3.1.1917. Mary Speid Duncan 5.9.1825 15.2.1917

400 Jas Neish tailor 8.5.1814 54, wid Magdalene Stott, by bro Wm

401 Jas Don blacksmith 27.1.1833 59, w Mary Carnegie 21.2.1869 90, da Mary 7.6.1814 1y2m, s Wm 27.1.1820 12½, da Mary 15.12.1902 86

402 Thos Don fr Balzeordie 1.7.1878 75, w Ann Low 30.12.1903 85, da Maria d Station Hotel Carlisle 1.12.1872 24, s Wm Carnegie 1877 24 int Quincey Iowa USA

403 Jas Don mert 28.5.1874 72, w Jean Webster 27.3.1887 81, da Jane 23.7.1846 12, da Isabella 19.1.1884 45, s Wm mert Calcutta 30.7.1899 56, by surviving chn Jas, Mary Don or Young, & David in 1903

404 mural. 1847. John Don JP banker 22.10.1899 94, w Jane Davidson 26.4.1846 38, yt s David 30.12.1848 4y7w, 2s Jas 3.3.1849 10y10m, 3s Chas banker 1.8.1876 34, s rev J D d King Williamstown South Africa 7.5.1903 69 (see Ewing i 139: John Davidson Don b 1834, ordained Calcutta 1862, md 1865 Cath Neville Baylie & 1889 Cath Isabella Brownlie) (3s lieut Alex D B killed in action France 10.1916 24, 1s John Baylie d Edinburgh 11.12.1947 81, 2s Chas Davidson d King Williamstown South Africa 7.3.1959 84), 1da Mary Anne 24.2.1917 84

405 mural. Ann Carnegie 17.7.1822 25

406 Jas Sturrock served the late Lord Panmure many years d 25.4.1853 69, wid Betsy Mitchell 13.12.1869 71

407 Jas Thomson fr Findowrie 17.5.1792 22.3.1871, w Lucy Miln 31.12.1798 28.2.1840, 2da Isabella 31.8.1828 1.11.1866, 3da Jane 18.10.1831 17.3.1899 (see inscription no.51 in Dun churchyard)

408 TS Wm Low mert 2.2.1849 79, w Kath Reid 18.6.1857 86, s Jas 13.9.1819 17, s Wm 29.5.1822 15, da Mary 7.4.1888 79, da Jean 11.10.1879 74 (h Wm Mill cabinetmaker 31.5.1869 61)

409 1814. Jas Will, s John 22.3.1814 inf, s Jas 16.4.1814 2y9m

410 Robt Duncan pensioner 1st regt of Foot, w Eliz Cutthill 11.2.1844 62, s David 22.10.1823 inf

412 Jas Kinnear plumber 17.12.1862 65, w Jane Arbuthnot 12.7.1870 75, s Alex 21.5.1842 15, das Agnes & Eliz d inf, da Mary Cath 28.9.1904 75

413 1841. John Leighton mert 18.4.1841 49, w Eliz Cuthill 5.9.1874 71 (2h

David Craig solicitor provost 16.5.1871 67)

414 Mathew Jamieson surgeon 4.6.1820 59, w Jean Downie 28.1.1833 73, da Mary inf

415 Alex Edwards 18.3.1880 73, w Margt Byars 8.5.1900 87, da Mary Scott 21.1.1849 10, da Isabella 1.12.1852 4

416 by Jas Edward, da Mary 8.6.1842 9y8m, fa in law Robt Grant 18.8.1842 73

417 by Jas Duncan, s Wm 7.5.1836 5, da Mary Ann 10.5.1836 2

418 John Ogilvy mert 8.1.1841 70, 1w Eliz Findlay 19.5.1807 30, 2 chn inf, 2w Margt Dakers 17.1.18- 68, only ch Margt 3.4.1860 48 (h Geo Anderson 27.9.1873 59)

419 rev John Craig, w Cath Pringle 28.9.1829 31 (see Jervise "Inscriptions" p 18 - da Cath Pringle Craig, poetess)

421 1845. Jas & David Fergusons

422 Alex Jenkins messenger at arms 17.9.1856 62, w Marjory Miller 15.2.1893 78, da Eliza 24.6.1844 6, s Wm 28.8.1866 16; Jas Jenkins d Glasgow 2.8.1919 71, w Susan Carver 8.7.1915 66; Ann Jenkins 23.8.1916 81 int New Cem (wid of Daniel Murray)

423 Wm Machar mert Brechin d Bankhead Menmuir 13.8.1859 71, w Mary Byars 29.2.1836 37, s Jas inf, s John d 2 St Mary Street Brechin 11.6.1880 48 fr Bankhead Menmuir & Mill of Tannadyce (s Wm 10.10.1867 4 int Tannadice)

424 And Millikin methodist min 1824 28, s Samuel 1831 8, by wid Cath Forbes

425 David Lyon mert 10.11.1823 65,1w Eliz Downie 26.4.1817 72, by 2w Isabella Glen

426 Alex Guthrie tent Maisondieu 9.7.1882 83, w Isabella Kydd 3.1.1883 86, da Margt 22.2.1831 1y10m, s Thos 18.5.1853 20, s Jas d Edzell 9.3.1879 53, 3s Alex deputy surgeon general RMS d Chatham 3.3.1886 54, s John d Cardiff

427 mural. by Jas imo bro Alex Ferrier esq of Kintrocket formerly surgeon EICS 29.6.1809 59; epitaph (see inscription no.1 ante; also Edwards "Guide" 3rd ed.p 66)

428 Jas Ferrier 22.6.1907 89 int New cem, 1w Isabella Hood 18.2.1849 28, 2w Agnes Smart 11.9.1897 78

429 Walter Ferrier 24.3.1857 65, w Jean McGill 11.4.1858 63, da Jean 19.6.1854 38 (h John Towns), s Alex d Australia 12.11.1868 42, da Eliz Gowans 3.6.1888 52, da Jessie Douglas 3.3.1890 56 both int New cem, da Cath d Lyndoch Valley South Australia 3.5.1902 73 (wid of dr Richter), s Geo d Riverton South Australia 21.6.1906 73, s Jas 22.6.1907 89, da Helen 5.1.1908 85 (wid of Wm Blackhall)

429a mural. Jas Ferrier of Kintrockat afterwards of Broadmire 28.1.1828 85, w Eliz Gowens 5.10.1805 49, 13 chn: David 6.1796 15, Jas 12.1804 24, Grizell 10.6.1808 31 (h Jas Cuthill), Alex d India 1817 32 (see Jervise Ms 530 in Scottish Antiquaries Library p 635: Alex was capt EICS), Ann 2.2.1820 21, Margt 2.1.1837 41 (h Jas Low mert Brechin), Kath 10.3.1839 54, John 17.4.1855 76, Walter 24.3.1857 65, Eliz 2.10.1863 76 (h David Mitchell, Brechin) (see Jervise Ms 530 p 635: they were parents of professor Mitchell, St Andrews), Wm formerly of Huntingdon Park d Runniss Shropshire 7.2.1867 77, Jean 24.1.1868 74 (h Wm Pennycook), Geo 15.5.1885 94, by Wm & Geo in 1864

430 by Robt Welsh plasterer, w Rachel Strachan 19.3.1819 60, da Rachel 15.8.1798 5. Robt Welsh bailie 13.1.1845 76, yts Thos 21.10.1846 56, 1s & only surviving s Jas min New Deer inscribed this

431 John Smith senior d Aberdeen 15.1.1845 69, w Margt Bowman d Rosemount Place Aberdeen 3.8.1846 69, s John brewer Den brewery Brechin d on his birthday 16.3.1837 23, s Wm mert Bahia for 18y d there 2.7.1852 42

432 Jas Bisset 14.9.1868 66, w Magdalen Bisset 22.7.1884, da Eliz 2.5.1853 2

433 Alex Durie mert wright , w Agnes Davidson, da Isobel 6.11.1761 18, da Margt 3.2.1763 21; poem

434 Jas Baxter brewer 19.7.1848 63, w Cathy Durie 8.12.1833 31, nephew David Baxter 17.1.1874 63 (w Lilly Archibald 4.1.1883 67, da Mary 15.8.1874 18, da Eliz 8.5.1891 51)

435 FS tipped up. (marginal) And Dounie weaver burgess 6.1.1696 65; (central) two cherubs; A D, I R; loom & shuttle; E H, K D, A D, I D, A D; poem

435a TS Robt Leitch 1800 75; Cath Hitherwick 1805 84; Eliz Leitch 1851 85; - - - Erskine 8.2.18 - - - - - tona West Indies - - - - - his spouse - - - - - - - - - -2.182 -, da Eliz 13.2.18 - 82y

436 John Mitchell 58y wright feuar Little Brechin 7.5.1865 89, w Isabel Gray 10.12.1850 70

437 Chas Will 4.5.1836 mert, 1w Mary Memes 30.4.1833, his sisters Eliz & Margt Will int here, s Chas 1827 inf, s Chas Davidson 16.8.1842, da Isabella d Blairathole 27.9.1839 (h John Acton), da Clementina 29.6.1861, by s David, 2w Jane Low 20.1.1838

438 in Latin. Wm Linton AM rector of Brechin Grammar School for 55y d 14.11.1832 80, by his grateful pupil Alex Currie sheriff of Banffshire in 1845 (see Jervise "Inscriptions" pp 14-5 & Edwards "Guide" 3rd ed.p 50: he was a native of Montrose & graduated at Aberdeen University)

The following are listed in Jervise "Inscriptions from the Burial Grounds of Brechin & Magdalen Chapel" (1864) and were not seen in 1959 or 1978:

439 (p 5) built into outer side of boundary wall. arms of bishop Shoreswood 1454-62

440 (p 11) Jas Dirrow 1723 66; poem "the stone & gravel did him much torment, till his last sand was run & breath was spent." (note - Dirrow = Durie; see Brechin Testaments: Isobel Wishart relict of James Dirrow mert & late Town Treasurer of Brechin, 12.6.1751)

441 (p 16) Patk Bowie esq of Keithok 9.3.1809 62

442 (p 17) David Donaldson bailie here, w Bessie Watt, das Elspet & Jean; 1647 (note- the three women were said to have died of the plague; Donaldson was commissioner for Brechin to the Scots Parliament in 1644; see Brechin Testaments, 1686)

443 "Luna quater crescens / Seccentos peste peremptos, / Disce mori! vidit. Pulvis et umbra sumus." (note - this commemmorated 600 persons who died of the plague in 1647)

444 John Hutchen, wife d 1668 "In Death no difference is made / Betwein the Sceptre & the Spade."

The following was noted by Jervise ms 530 p 633 in Scottish Antiquaries Library:
445 Chas Willocks in Haughmuir 1738 58, w Isobel Kaithness, 3 chn

The following was listed by Rogers ii 202 and not seen in 1959:
446 unmarked grave in the south aisle. rev Wm Guthrie min Fenwick 1620 10.10.1665 (he was 1s of the laird of Pitforthie; see Brechin Testaments)

3a BRECHIN CATHEDRAL KIRK

The following is noted in Edwrdrds "Guide" 3rd ed.p 65 & was not seen in 1959:
447 Here lies John Smart mason in Brechin who d 30 August aged 50 & of his spouse Agnes Brown d 1712 aged 43

The following is mentioned in Douglas "Description of the East Coast of Scotland" (1782) on the north wall of a ruinous aisle:
448 Jas Thom late dean of guild of Brechin & his wife - - - (note - he was Dean of Guild in 1700)

Index

Acton	437
Adam	65
Adamson	86.309.396
Addison	66
Aitken	69
Alexander	38.108.300
Allan	88.221.342.369
Allardice	125-7.165
Anderson	211.290.395.418
Arbuthnot	412
Archibald	434
Arnot	179-80.184.296-7 340
Ayre	122
B.	24
Baillie	115.146.199.214.292 368
Baird	353-4
Balfour	304.313
Ballie	358
Barclay	216.221.282.307
Barnet	8
Baxter	309-10.434
Baylie	404
Beal	341
Bean	63
Belford	16
Bell	308
Bellie	221
Benny	391
Binny	101.314.391
Birse	61.186
Bisset	150.221.432
Black	42.73.84.93.132.160 247.255.291.294-5
Blackadder	326
Blair	225.389
Blues	163
Bouack, Bowick	25.395
Bowie	441
Bowman	431
Bremner	216
Brodie	51
Brough	40
Brown	89.204.447
Bruce	19-20.54.150.153.189
Buchanan	159
Bumet	336
Burn	131
Burns	173.229.369
Burnett	54.121.266.337-8
Burslem	165
Byars, Byers	40.331.415.423
Cairncross	136
Cairns	158
Caithness, see Kaithness	
Calder	121
Caldonhead	341
Caldwell	383
Callendar	104
Cameron	45
Cargill	221.397
Carnegie	108.155.221.285.323. 401.405
Carr	28
Carrie	73
Catenoch	26
Caution	124
Cay	174
Chalmers	23.168.229.334
Chapman	221
Christie	75.77.121.382-3
Christison	261
Clark	9.26.221
Cleator	286
Collie	377
Coupar	221
Couttie	99
Coutts	230.330
Cowan	136
Cowie	61-2.269
Crab(b)	16.329
Craig	196.207.304.347.413.419
Craik	19
Crammond	253-4.321
Craw	345
Crichton	392
Crighton	25.51
Crockatt, Crocket	141.312-3.360
Croydon	389
Cunningham	31
Currie	342.438
Cut(t)hill	410.413.429a

3a BRECHIN CATHEDRAL KIRK

Index continued

D. 327
Dakers 145.246.250-2.255.418
Davidson 35.81.108.132.153-4 289.351.355.404.433.437
Dear 58-9
Deas 71
Deuchar(s) 77.90
Dickson 11.139
Dirrow 440
Doig 217.221.225
Don 136.263.401-4
Donaldson 105.107.218.245.442
Dorward 25.38
Douglas 159
Dowker 390
Downie 414.425.435
Drydon 102
Duke 343-4
Dunbar 311
Duncan 18.28.76.87.91.101.111 133.399.410.417
Dundas 2.89.95
Durie 335.433-4.440
Duthie 187

E. 150a
Eaton 335-6
Edgar 191.199-200
Edward(s) 288.415-6
Erskine 345.435a

Fairlie 221
Fairweather 56.106.149.362
Fanes 221
Farquhar 185.383
Farquharson 6
Fenton 74.221
Ferguson 421
Ferrier 1.9.18.68.93.101.281 288-90.302.427-9a
Fettes 193.297
Fiddes 368
Fiddler 247
Findlay 203-4.338.418
Fisher 59.259
Fitchett 374
Fleming 53.347
Fletcher 105
Foote 31
Forbes 44.424
Forrest 84
Fotheringham 39.133
Fraser 3
Fullerton 178.387
Fyfe 76

Gairdner 221
Galdie 109
Gall 72
Garden 315
Gardiner 90
Garvie 160
Gaul 87
Geekie 269.360
Gib 390-1
Gillam 393
Gillies 169-70.218
Glen 45.425
Glendel 221
Goodwin 35
Gordon 79.122.146.178.187.270-3 286.301.311.342.375
Gowans 167.251.429a
Graham 125.388
Grant 51.416
Gray 47.221.436
Greig 16.72.104.114.129.221 294.361
Grieve 136
Grim 183
Grubb 262
Guthrie 69.86.172-5.191.229.426 446

H. 435
Hampton 7.39.346
Hardy 285
Harvey 35
Hastings 323
Hay 14.319-20
Hebenton 206-7
Henderson 14.201.387
Hendry 74.94
Henry 320
Hill 30.302
Hitherwick 435a
Hobb 98.259
Hodge 179.265-6
Hogg 151
Hood 70.75.351.428
Howie 62.293
Hunter 114.209.350
Hutchen, Hutchon 332.444

Innerarity 107
Iollie, see Jollie
Irvine 168

Jack 17
Jamie 254
Jamieson 118.414
Japp 217
Jarron 70
Jarvis 91
Jenkins 422
Joe 141.289

Johnston 221.282.378
Jollie 221
Junor 284-5

Kaithness 274.445
Keeler 46
Keir 44
Kerr 56.361-2
Kidd, Kydd 65.321.426
Kin(n)ear 41.128.151.180.272.412
Knox 245

Laing 36.166-7.221
Lamb 102-3
Langlands 341
Langwill 221
Law 46
Lawrie 213
Lawson 29
Laurence 298
Leighton 6.32.248.413
Leishman 285
Leitch 435a
Lennox 353-4
Leslie 338
Lighton 195
Lindsay 10.221.296.395-7
Linton 438
Littlejohn 341a
Livie 276
Lonmuir 346
Loudon 375
Low(e) 72.95.98.108.127.166 218.221.258.260-4.318 328.387.402.408.429a.437
Lowrence 299
Lyall 159.162.357.399
Lyon 112.127.129.201.425

M. 24.328a
MacBain 182
Macculloch 230
McDonald 30.348
McEwan 377
McFadyen 6
McGill 429
Machar 184.210.366.423
McIntosh 212
McIntyre 379
Mackay 202
Mackenzie 122.371-2.385
McKinlay 208
McLeod 42
Mader 221
Maich 121
Mann 7
Marr 292
Martin 142.168
Mathers 97.187.207.221.249.257 259
Mathie 338a
Maule 287.352
Memes 437
Michie 375
Middleton 157.344
Mill(s) 107.118.221.252.281.316 392.408
Millar 51.130-2.422
Miln(e) 8.136.195.308.407
Mitchell 22.28.72.94.96.163.185 281.284.288-9.296.322 327.367.406.429a.436
Moir 373
Molison 34.127.164-5.218
Monro 282
Monroy 23
Morren 33
Morrison 23
Moug 288
Mudie 264.294
Muirton 221
Murray 31.116.217.337.355.422
Mustard 37

Nairn 203.384
Napier 212
N(e)ish 277.305.367.400
Nicol 196.221.319.332
Norie 319

Oakenhead 141.147
Ogilvie/y 2.17.168.188.246.418
O'Neil 322
Oswald 13
Ouchterlony 200

Palmer 342
Panmure 352.406
Paterson 340.341a
Pennycook 101.429a
Perron 221
Peter 56.306.366
Peterkin 298.300
Pieres, Pierss 221
Preshaw 97
Pringle 419
Proctor 312
Pyper 91

R. 435
Raitt 221
Ramsay 209.286.352
Rattray 81
Reedie 112
Reid 102.184.317.358.408
Rennie 347
Richter 429
Bickard 170-1
Riddoch 167
Ritchie 87
Robb 84
Robertson 17.381.385

3a BRECHIN CATHEDRAL KIRK

Index continued

Ro(d)ger 213-5.288a.291
Rollock 221
Ronald 331
Rose 182.206
Ross 178
Ruxton 372

Samson 53
Sandieman 161.292
Scheres 189
Scott 18.58.75.99.123.208 277.288a.324.331.343
Seras 189
Shand 33
Shank 221
Sharp 306
Shepherd 109.133.186.221.346
Shirburn 123
Shires(s) 5.78.189.258.261
Shoreswood 439
Sievwright 216-7.221.257.318
Sime 310.315
Simpson 37.345
Singer(s) 128.292
Skea 319
Skinner 221
Smart 78.124.151.183.265 268-9.374.428.447
Smith 9.18.26.43.71.157 165.168-9.186.195 218.282.307.313.334 431
Smyttan 370
Soppet 203
Soutar 115.321-3.359-60
Spaddie 63
Spalding 43
Speid A.308.314.399
Spence 125.127.164.201.332
Steel,Steill 145.192
Steven 124
Stevenson 144.147.317
Stewart 67.188.351.381
Stockwell 29
Strachan 136.139-40.142.148-9 221.293.316.377.430
Straton 125.388
Stott 290.400

Stuart 271
Sturrock 406
Symington 141

Taylor 88.366
Thom 448
Thomson 86.154.387.407
Thow 123
Tindall 193.198
Todd 164
Tosh 27
Trail 329
Trimble 386
Troup 41
Tulloch 221
Turner 20

Valentine 32.43.128.148.178.194

Waith, see Weath
Walker 40.150.198.209.268.359
Wall(s) 66.192
Wallace 155
Watson 68.90.99.116.172.191.221 256.371.339
Wat(t) 192.291a.221.442
Weath 341-2
Webster 67.70.104.162.221.272-4 282.378.403
Welsh 430
Whamond 27
White 221
Whitson 165
Whyte 11
Will 4-5.409.437
Williamson 253
Willocks/x 74.275.445
Wilson 377
Windrim, Winram 291.291a
Wishart 189.276.440
Wobster 287
Wood 92.205.211.275.305 335-6
Wright 167.196
Wyllie 71.179
Wynram, see Windrim

Young 40.71.221.248-9.403

3b BRECHIN CEMETERY

The New Cemetery, designed by George Henderson on part of the Den Nursery, was opened for burials in October 1857 and has been enlarged since.

National Grid refernce: NO 600 605

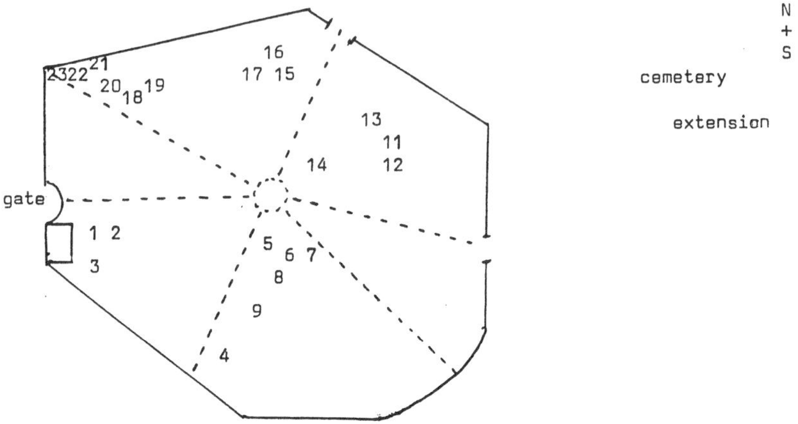

1 Alex Whitton 25.9.1823 30.3.1850, w Mary Adam 15.8.1822 7.9.1879, s Geo d Newton Abbott 13.1.1904 57

2 David Main d Laurencekirk 22.11.1815 51, w Eliz Leighton d Laurencekirk 22.12.1836 65, da Jane 16.10.1861 58 (by da Sarah Belford 11.2.1905 79)

3 Jas Taylor 2.1.1793 8.1.1871, da Margt 20.10.1828 14.9.1879 (h Alex Aberdein 4.10.1828 20.7.1852 int Marykirk); Thos Maxwell, w Margt Hogg Aberdein 21.5.1851 22.8.1884; Thos & Chas Maxwell d inf; Jas Taylor Aberdein 4.12.1914 61

4 Wm Colvin 21.6.1836 57, w Margt Wilson 16.5.1864 75, chn Anne & Helen 27.5.1836 9y & 7y, John 6.2.1840 26, Margt 19.8.1868 53, Jane 29.3.1871 (<u>52</u>), Wm 1.12.1879 62, Wm & Jas d inf, Alex 28.8.1897 64

5 ob by Michael Ferrier 15.9.1828 17.11.1898, w Johanna Lyall Fullerton 9.7.1835 12.1.1881, his mo Ann Laing 1803 19.11.1848, bros David 1831 11.6.1855 & John 1834 29.9.1835, sis Isabella Clark 1844 22.2.1847, s Jas Paterson 6.4.1863 14.8.1863, s Wm Fullerton 7.12.1871 8.3.1878, 2s John Wm 18.3.1861 8.6.1921 (w Jeannie Ferrier Anderson 30.7.1864 10.2.1931, s John Anderson 3.1.1894 15.2.1971)

6 Chas Roberts 6.5.1838 63, w May Duncan 24.5.1860 79, da Ann mrs Burgess (da Ann mrs Thomson 4.4.1874 27, uncle Philip Duncan wright Barrelwell 30.12.1878 78 (his w Janet Cowie 2.9.1875 93))

7 next 6. Jas Burgess 50y wright Barrelwell 14.8.1808 8.8.1885, w Ann Roberts 13.3.1822 d Linlithgow 22.7.1903

8 Jas Skene 25.11.1865, w Mary Henderson 24.5.1891 77, 1da Jean 31.12.1842 10

9 Jas Duthie 7.5.1875 75, w Abigail Martin 21.6.1904, s And 13.6.1853 14 int Lethnot, da Margt 8.5.1861 28

10 ob John Lyall skinner Brechin 8.3.1841 38, w Eliz Edward d R Infirmary of Edinburgh 25.5.1865 57 having on the 10th undergone excision of the

tongue which she bore with great Christian spirit, by s Jas M d Boston US 11.12.1873 37, da Margt 31.12.1855 21, s Adam 31.8.1866 27 (s Jas d inf, w Margt Meldrum 19.1.1905 66 (her 2h John Hosea, s David 7.8.1880 5y9m)); Edw Lyall 20.11.1936 72, w Lucretia M Coutts 5.8.1938 71

11 Thos Kinnear fr Hillside Stracathro 13.9.1862 77, by w Mary Taylor 16.11.1783 2.9.1875, da Cath d Hillside 3.1824 3, 1da Mary 7.9.1875

12 John Ferguson 22.5.1883 62, w Eliza Watson 3.4.1898 75, chn Robt d Melbourne 28.9.1881 31, Jane 1857 5, twins Joan & Martha 1863 13d, Jas d Melbourne 28.5.1912, 1da Eliza 24.2.1929, da Mary 17.2.1943

13 John Black, Meiklestrath d Fettercairn 16.8.1843 66, w Eliz Fraser, Kirktoun of Logie Part d Fettercairn 1826 49, s John 30.3.1819 17.1.1908 (w Betsy Low b Hillfaulds Edzell 2.8.1820 d 3 Trinity Road Brechin 16.2.1902), ss Robt & Jas int Fettercairn

14 Jas Napier crofter Cauldford 15.6.1860 75, w Jean Black 18.2.1881 88, chn Helen 1823 1y, Margt 1837 5, Isobell 1861 32, Helen 14.5.1863 27, Eliz 29.11.1882 62

15 Jas Jolly 9.10.1863 74, w Jean Robie 15.11.1869 73, s Alex drowned while bathing Geelong Australia 29.3.1840 22, da Isabella 17.2.1899 78 (wid of Jas Speid) (see Jervise "Inscriptions from ... Brechin" p 25: Alex Jolly was educated for the medical profession, went to the whale fishing during the college vacation as surgeon on board the "Viewforth" in 1835-6 & was ice-bound in the Davis Strait)

16 Jas Collins d Montrose 8.4.1820 48, w Ann Crane 16.3.1863, da Helen 5.6.1866 50, by da Eliz

17 John Smith 3.1844 47, w Jane Kinnear 11.1877 85, by s Jas

18 Alex Durie fr Arratsmill 20.12.1811 int Stracathro, w Eliz Christie d St James Park Brechin 28.11.1860 83, 1da Eliz 8.9.1876 72, yt da Jessie 28.7.1885 74 (h Chas Durie, Dubton of Stracathro, da Eliza 20.11.1890 57), 3da Isabella 10.7.1891 82

19 next 18. John Durie fr Denstrath, w Rose Lindsay both int Fettercairn, s Jas Gibb d St James Park Brechin 28.10.1877 19

20 Robt Wyllie, Pearse Street Brechin 6.5.1858 76, w Eliz Soutar 24.7.1896 91, ss Robt 18.11.1840 16.7.1876, Alex d Cedar Forest Virginia 10.1.1899 56, da Eliz 20.11.1920 88, Mary Ann 23.1.1941 95

21 David Scott, Newington 9.11.1812 7.1.1890, w Mary Ann Munro 25.3.1817 17.3.1894, chn Alex Munro 22.11.1841 7.9.1852, Jas Munro 28.6.1854 27.10.1854, Hugh Aird 13.7.1857 22.6.1858

22 David Lamb mert Brechin 29.11.1874 77, w Ann Brydon 22.12.1882 79, s Jas Henry 8.6.1833 7m, Jane Ann 2.12.1839 5, Martin Brydon MD HEICS d Missourie India 21.6.1860 33, Annabella 29.11.1932 86, Geo Scott 8.4.1933 89 (see Brechin Cathedral Kirk inscription no 102 ante)

23 Francis Stewart d Bervie 6.10.1851 48, w Margt Guthrie 7.10.1885 80, chn Thos 1.2.1839 2, Jas 16.11.1847 18

I n d e x

Aberdein 3
Adam 1
Aird 21
Anderson 5
Belford 2
Black 13.14
Brydon 22
Burgess 6-7

3b BRECHIN CEMETERY

Index continued

Christie 18
Clark 5
Collins 16
Colvin 4
Coutts 10
Cowie 6
Crane 16

Duncan 6
Durie 18-19
Duthie 9

Edward 10

Ferguson 12
Ferrier 5
Fraser 13
Fullerton 5

Guthrie 23

Henderson 8
Hosea 10

Jolly 15

Kinnear 11.17

Laing 5
Lamb 22
Leighton 2
Lindsay 2
Low 13
Lyall 5.10

Main 2
Martin 9
Maxwell 3
Meldrum 10
Munro 21

Napier 14

Paterson 5

Roberts 6-7
Robie 15

Scott 21
Skene 8
Smith 17
Soutar 20
Speid 15
Stewart 23

Taylor 3.11
Thomson 6

Watson 12
Whitton 1
Wilson 4
Wyllie 20

3c MAGDALENE CHAPEL BRECHIN

No trace of the medieval chapel also known as Maidlin chapel, chapel of Caldhame and chapel of Arrat, now remains and its burial ground is completely neglected. The long grass probably hides many stones as only five headstones were visible in 1978. Burials took place here until at least 1850. It is beside the road A 935 east of Brechin. National Grid reference: NO 646 591

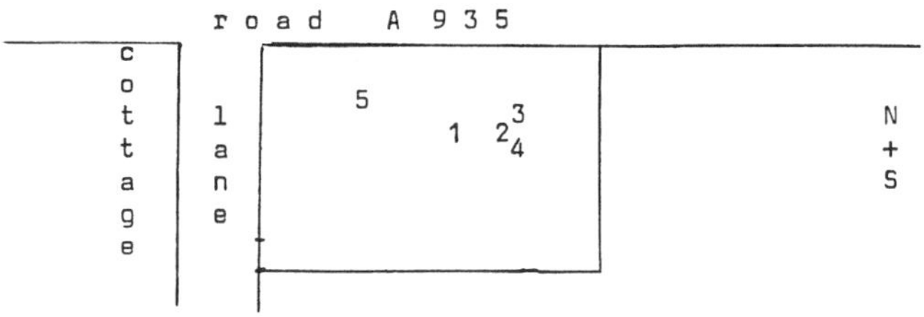

1 John Kirkland tent Isaackston, w Jean Lyel 31.1.1756 4(8); (west side) I K, I L ; plough; IK RK GK IK DK EK IK WK 1756; "Let all who see this monument / Remember evrey day / That death will shortly on them (sere) / And in the dust them lay."

2 "The trumpet doth sound, The Dead shall rise / To meet the Lord unto the Skies." Here lyes John Rob lawfull son to John Rob tennant in Arats Mill who dyed 20.-.173(0) 23y & Ann d 173- 10y, Alex (Rob) d 1737 2y, Jesbel Rob 17-9 7y, (Jam late) in grave - - - - -
(west side) "Of all Imployments that may be found / Husbandrie ought to be crowned." This stone was set up by John Robb tenant in Arrats Mill in the year 1740; I R, E G ; John R, Ann R, Alex R, I R

3 Thos Rob dyster mert in Brechin, w Jean Mitchel 25.2.1761 34 having 4 chn procreate betwixt them viz - - , Eliz, John & Jean d inf; emblems of mortality; (west side) E R, J R, M R, J R

4 1772. Wm Robb tent Kinnairds Mill 19.3.1763 48, by w Jean Skeir, int with 6 of their chn viz Alex, John, Christian, - blank -, Eliz, Alex, - blank -, & Mary d inf; (west side) W R, I S; plough; A R, A R, J R, M R, J R, J R, W R, E R, C R, A R, H R, M R; poem

5 - - - - - - - - (18th century)

The following were noted by Jervise "Inscriptions from Brechin & the Magdalen Chapel" (1864) and were not seen in 1978:

6 John Erskine who died of the affliction ("perhaps the plague of 1647")

7 near NW corner. Wm Crofts late wright Issackston 11.6.1798 42 (Jervise notes that Isaacstown was probably just to the west of Magdalen Chapel as the field bears that name)

8 1808. by Robt Law weaver Brechin, two das

9 next 8. John Fife tent Hill of Hedderwick 12.11.1742

Index.

Crofts	7	Law	8
Erskine	6	Lyel	1
Fife	9	Mitchel	3
G.	2	Rob(b)	2-4
Kirkland	1	Skeir	4

3 BRECHIN

Notes

In 1978 there was nothing to mark the sites of the Kirk of Butherkill (Burghill, Grid refernce: NO 602 593) and of the Kirk of Kilmoir demolished to make way for the Castle offices (National Grid reference: NO 597 600)

Register of Testaments. A few citizens of Brechin are recorded outwith the Commissariot of Brechin. Prior to 1609 especially, Brechiner testaments may be recorded with the Commissariot of Edinburgh, as with the following selection:
Thos Bell in Wester Balnabreich, spouse Margt Baxter, 1607
capt Thos Bowman citizen, 1595
mr David Carnegy of Kinnaird, 1598-9, last spouse Janet Henryson relict of Alex Guthrie common clerk of Edinburgh, 1600
Marjorie Carnegy relict of Thos Smyth citizen of Brechin, 1596
John Chalmer citizen in Brechin, 1590
Agnes Crawmound spouse to Alex Lour citizen of Brechin, 1596
John Daw in Louchland, 1586
John Dempster citizen, 1578
Eliz Donaldson relict of John Low elder citizen in Brechin, 1578
Thos Erskine in Tayok, 1592
Andro Fentoun, 1565
Kath Fentoun spouse to Thos Speid of Auchdowey, 1584-5
John Finlay in Isakstoun, 1578
James Fyfe in Wester Balnabreiche, 1601, his relict Margt Gold, 1602
Wm Galloway, Craigend of Bannabreich, 1594
Jas Grahame in Leuchland, spouse Kath Fullartoun, 1607
Robt Kinnear of Bothers, 1603
etc. etc.

OPR with the Registrar General: 275 Brechin

Births	1612-3, 1620-1854
Marriages	1700-3, 1721-4, 1727-8, 1743-53, 1758-
Deaths	nil

SRO:	CH2/40	Records of the Presbytery of Brechin	
	CH2/41	Brechin East Church (FC from 1843)	Minutes 1838-1909 Managers Minutes 1837-44
	CH3/439	Relief Session (High Street) & Bank Street UP, St.Ninians Church of Scotland	KS minutes 1832-1963 DC minutes 1830-1963 baptisms 1832-1962 marriages 1834-1856 proclamations 1932-63 church records 1847-64
	CH3/440	Brechin Associate Session, City Road, UP, United Free	KS minutes 1764-1952, 1856- Managers Minutes 1764-1914
	CH3/590	Maison Dieu Lane (Burgher), UP	Managers Minutes 1800-45 Congregational Minutes 1844-7
	CH3/623	Brechin West FC, United Free.	minutes 1843-1948 church records 1846-50 etc
	HR 752	Brechin heritors records	minutes 1807-1925 buildings 1748-1905 poor relief etc 1837-1841

"Scottish Antiquary" xiv 96: Scottish Episcopalian Church, Brechin, births marriages and deaths 1796-1819. (ms copy also in the Brechin Diocesan Library deposited at Dundee University library, original not traced.) New Spalding Club Miscellany i 307 mentioned a register of episcopal baptisms from 1812, then (1887-90) "in the hands of the incumbent."

3 BRECHIN

Brechin Kirk Treasurer's Accounts from 1633)
Brechin Kirk Session Register from 1615) with the Session Clerk,
Lair book) Cathedral Kirk
Burial Register 1782-97, 1818-32)
Marriages, baptisms & burials, charges, 1.10.1783-29.5.1791, 1.6.1791-9.1794

Brechin Museum: Hammermen Corporation Book 1600-
Brechin Town Council Minutes 1672-

D.D.Black "History of Brechin to 1864" (1867) includes a list of the Town councillors from 1672-1864

And. Jervise "The Inscriptions from the Burial Grounds of Brechin and Magdalen Chapel" (Brechin 1864)

D.H.Edwards "Historical Guide to Brechin" 3rd ed.(Brechin 1904)

David B Thoms "The Kirk of Brechin in the Seventeenth Century" (Brechin 1972)

Fasti v 374 ministers from 1562
v 382 Brechin East church ministers 1837-43, then FC till 1856; ministers from 1859

Ewing ii 164 Brechin South church ministers from 1852
Brechin West ministers from 1843
Brechin East ministers from 1843

Small i Brechin City Road Antiburgher, 1768
Maisondieu Burgher, 1804
Bank Street Relief, 1831

4 CARESTON

The parish, originally Caraldston, was disjoined from Brechin in 1641. Many gravestones were removed by order of George Skene of Skene about 1770 and the yard is comparatively empty.
National Grid reference: NO 528603

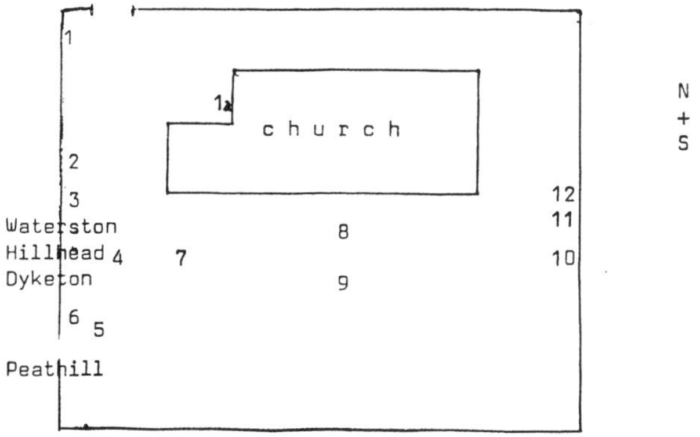

4 CARESTON

1a panel above church door. shield

(Sir Alexander Carnegie of Balnamoon endowed the church in 1640)

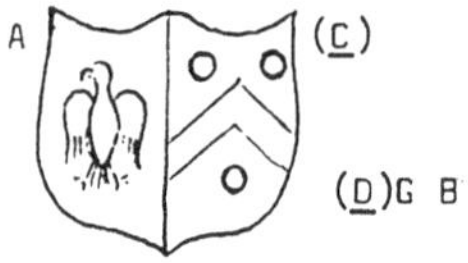

1 Alex Burnett min here d - - - (see Jervise i 259 & Fasti v 384: he d 25.1.1800, was appointed minister by Geo Skene of Skene)

2 mr John Gillies ord min Carraldstone in 9.1716 d 1.3.1753 72, five chn d inf int here, s Thos 1.3.17(3)6 13, w Mary Watson survived him as did chn John min in Glasgow, Robt mert Brechin, Mary, Isobel & Janet (see Fasti v 383; Jervise "Epitaphs" i 259 &"Land of the Lindsays" p 219)

3 rev David Lyell ord min here 1800 d 15.7.1854 85, w hon Cath Arbuthnott 16.12.1853 65, s Stuart Thos surgeon EICS d Ballary India 17.7.1853 45 (see Fasti v 384; Jervise "Epitaphs" i 259 for a brief biography)

4 1853. John Laing tent Whiteside 23.6.1833 49, w Agnes Hewitt 26.11.1846 46 both int here, by chn Jas, John, Alex, Anne & Agnes

5 Alex Peter tent Parkside, elder, 10.8.1861 86, w Isabel McGonachie 30.10.1834 59, s John tent Parkside 2.8.1879 70 (w Mary Cobb 12.4.1881 54, s John 5.4.1881 22 int Aberlemno). 1872

6 John Wood 22.4.1832 64y10m, s Alex 6.12.1805 5y3m, by w Jean McLeish

7 Alex Fyfe late tent Whiteside of Careston 12.7.1871 62, chn Wm 22.3.1852 19, Isabella 24.4.1852 13, Alex 27.7.1867 32, Jas & John d inf, by w Isabella Richard d Arbroath 12.9.1893 84 int here & surviving family

8 David Buchan for 45y tent Whiteside here d 14.2.1890 77, w Isabella Peter 18.3.1878 60, s John 27.3.1882 21, da Mary 20.9.1854 7

9 John Cove d at Marous 13.5.1877 73, da Christina 28.5.1854 6

10 John Mitchell in Haughs of Kinnaird drowned while bathing 6.1820 int here, w Eliz Mitchell d Edinburgh 28.6.1860 78, da Anne d Portobello 17.1.1834 17¾ (h rev John Housby), only s John MD 1st class state surgeon d Crimean War from over-exertions amongst the wounded soldiers at battle of Alma 24.9.1854 45, 1da Christina d Aberdeen 28.5.1872 65, by da Eliz

11 by Alex Mitchell tent Nether Careston, fa Alex formerly tent there d 13.9.1823 86, mo Isabel Guthrie 7.2.1828 79, s David 9.3.1821 11, da Elis 20.3.1822 19; 1828

12FS by Geo Mitchell, fa Geo M -(marginal inscription buried)- -, mo Janet Jervise "Epitaphs" i 260 has Elspet in error) Fairweather 1736 80; GM IF; IM, TM, IM, CM, AM; AM, IM, MM, EM, IM; Agnes Gal 1731 35; poem; flowers

The following were noted by Jervise "Epitaphs & Inscriptions in Northeast Scotland" i 259-60 and wre not seen in 1978:

13 FS set up against front wall of kirk. John Ritchie, chn Mary 9y, David 7m, Margt near 5y, Jean 7y, Eliz 2y7m all chn d between 8 & 25.3.1767

14 fragment of 17th century. John Woode ("Wood is one of the oldest family names in Careston")

15 by Jas Clark & Agnes Bean; poem

The following was noted in 1978 on the adjoining cottage chimney:

16 GS, M F ; 58

4 C A R E S T O N

N o t e s

And. Jervise, Epitaphs & Inscriptions ..." vol i pp 259-60 quotes inscriptions no. 1-3.12-5; also describes the hand-bell inscribed "A F, C F, 1756" given to the parish by Alex Fairweather in Balglassie.

Testaments from Careston are recorded with the Commissariot of Brechin. The following is a selection:

Jas Black son of deceased And Black in Hillhead of Caraldstone, 1704
mrs Eliz Campbell & husband rev Gilbert Skene min Carraldstone, 1679
mr Wm Chaplain at the Mill of Carreldstone & spouse Christian Duncan, 1705
Elspet Deuchar spouse to Thos Lyell in Nether Caraldstone, 1684
John Espline in Hillhead of Caraldstoune, 1710
Elizabeth Espline daughter of deceased John as above, 1718
John Findlay in Mains of Corretstoune 1600
David Findlayson in Tenements of Carestoun & spouse Christian Fraser parish of Brechin, 1632
Isobel Forsyth & husband John Willie in Carestoun, 1626

Wm Gardner in Carraldstoun, spouse Isobel Tyre, 1579
John Hood in Dyktoune, 1670
John Hood smith indweller in Dyktoune of Carraldstone, relict Cath Thomson 1671
Jas Lyell at Milne of Caraldstone & spouse Banet Lowe, 1681
Geo Skene of Skene, 1783 etc. etc. etc.

Testaments recorded with the Commissariot of St.Andrews include:

Isobel Lindsay spouse to Alex Seatoun lawful son to Geo Seatoun of Carestoun, 1682

OPR with the Registrar General: 277 Careston

	Births	1714-1854
	Marriages	1714-96, 1798-1815, 1817, 1821-54
	Deaths	1773-1806, 1813, 1815, 1818-54
SRO:	CH2/55	minutes 1733-53, 1760-1937
		cash book 1716-33
	CH3	nil
	HR	no records
Fasti v 383		Ministers from 1639
Ewing ii		nil

I n d e x

Arbuthnott 3
Bean 15
Black Notes
Buchan 8
Burnett 1
Campbell Notes
Chaplain Notes
Clark 15
Cobb 5
Cove 9
Deuchar Notes
Duncan Notes
Espline Notes
Fairweather 12.Notes
Findlay Notes
Findlayson Notes
Forsyth Notes
Fraser Notes
Fyfe 7
Gardner Notes
Gillies 2
Guthrie 11
Hewitt 4
Hood Notes
Housby 10
Laing 4
Lindsay Notes
Lowe Notes
Lyell 3.Notes
McGonachie 5
McLeish 6
Mitchell 10.2
Peter 5.8
Richard 7
Ritchie 13
Seatoun Notes
Skene 1.Notes
Thomson Notes
Tyre Notes
Watson 2
Willie Notes
Wood(e) 6.14

5 C L O V A

The parish was united with Cortachy in 1618, and disjoined from Cortachy in 1860. The parishes are now re-united.

The parish church of Clova was dedicated to St Mary and was rebuilt in 1855, at Milton of Clova. National grid reference: NO 326 730

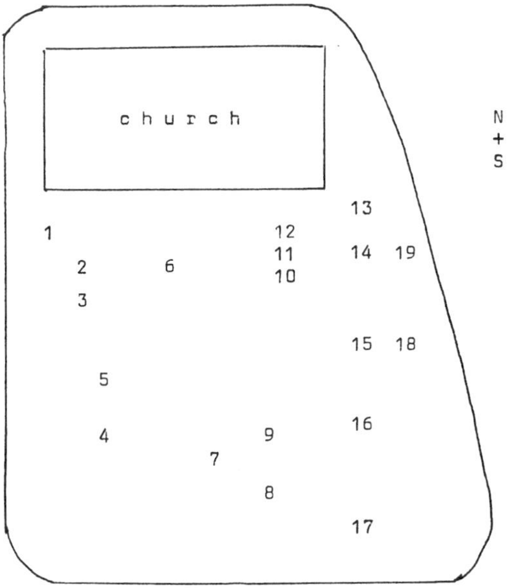

1 John Crichton at Bonhard 11.2.1895 88, fa John 15.9.1856 79, mo Jean Esplin 3.1838 71, sis Margt 27.9.1830 21

2 by Jane Lindsay, h Wm Duncan late fr Adylen 21.11.1860 83, s Jas 6.1.1846 40, Thos 3.1832 25

3 J M

4 rev John Mechie for 10y missionary min here & Glenprosen d 11.8.1854 (Fasti v 279: his name spelt Michie, he d unmarried)

5 T C ; I L

6 1787. here lyes John Ogilvy d jaun 2 1786 72, by w Kathren Ego, his das Jean & Helen; John Ogilvy let tenant in the Arlots

7 Margt Whyte teacher New Pitsligo d Laurencekirk 11.12.1894 75 int here, fa Alex fr Mains 28.2.1846 88, mo Jane Wilson 27.4.1867 80

8 Archd Whyte in Braedownie d Nether Hayston Glamis 29.1.1882 86, w Agnes Ogilvy d Braedownie 18.2.1877 79

9 1835. by Archd Whyte at Braedownie, fa Alex 2.4.1817 64, bros & sis John 22.5.1812 22, Jas 31.7.1812 25, Wm 13.1.1813 21, Alex 1.2.1814 26, Helen 4.9.1817 16; the four bros int inside the church west end below the gallery.

10 1778. by Jas, David & Thos Lindsay, fa late tent Nether Agie 26.2.1778 79, mo Jean Lucas 20.2.1777 49; (west side) share, coulter & ox yoke; emblems

11 Thos Lindsay late fr Rottal 4.3.1835 81,int on 7.3.1835

12 broken. Jas Lindsay late fr Glen C- -g 16.9.1826 37, by w Helen McDonald & s Thos

13 very small. E W

14 rev Wm Ewart min here & Glenprosen 29.1.1844 42 in 16th y of ministry, by mo mrs Isabella Ewart at Inverquech & Wm Ewart mert Alyth & - - - - - - - - 1849. Wm Brown fr Pluckerstone (see Fasti v 279 for rev Wm E. b Mill of Queich Alyth about 1800 s of Wm Ewart fr & miller, d unmarried; see also North Perthshire Monumental inscriptions, Alyth no.52)

15 Jas Lindsay late fr Greenordie 21.7.1848 65, w Jannet Lucas d Letham 20.4.1869 82, da Eliz d Edinburgh 10.10.1862 36, ss Jas, Wm & Alex d inf, da Jane d Charleston 27.2.1867 56

16 by Margt Kennedy in Kirktown of Clova, mo Ann Lindsay d Bouhard 12.10. 1862 76, uncle David Lindsay 13.5.1835 44; John Lindsay 1842; Jas Lindsay late fr Bouhard 27.11.1862 80

17 John Kennedy d Kirktown of Clova11.2.1870 69, w Margt Crichton d Northmuir of Kirriemuir 1.3.1882 77 also int here

18 Jas Robbie late fr Kilburn 17.3.1856 82, w Betty Lindsay 3.10.1854 67, chn Jane 16.2.1856 37, And 4.7.1856 34 int Kirkmichael churchyard Banffshire, John 4.1.1861 40

19 Wm Robbie late fr Kilburn 28.12.1897 66, w Mary Ann Ogilvy 25.1.1904 63, da Jessie 24.3.1869 in 1st y, s And 16.9.1887 3, s Wm 23.7.1901 35, da Maryann Sim 2.1.1923 60, da Eliza 13.5.1942 61 (h J B Walker) d Johannesburg, s Jas d Kilburn 27.1.1944 66, da Isabella d Perth 7.2.1951 76

The following is noted by Jervise "Epitaphs & Inscriptions .." ii 117 as being the oldest stone in the churchyard, but was not seen in 1977:

20 Wm Duncan 1787

The following is noted by And Jervise "Land of the Lindsays" p 281 as a panel on the mansion of Clova:

21 D O I G 1684 ("for sir David Ogilvy, 3s of the 1st earl of Airlie, & his wife Jean Guthrie")

N o t e s

Testaments: the following is a selection from the Record of the Commissariot of Brechin -
David Crichton in Caldhame & spouse Margt Shirrell, 1700
Robt Duncan in Braedounie, 1718
John Howe in Easter Kirktown of Clova & spouse Christian Ogilvy, 1702
John Lucas sometime tent Longholm & spouse Jean Robie, only da in life Jean who was spouse to David Ogilvie tent Tarriebuckle, 1770
David Ogilvie of Clova, 1726
sir David Ogilvie of Clova, relict Isobel Guthrie, 1698
sir David Ogilvie, w dame Margt Hamilton, 1669
Thos Shaw in Arntiber, 1681
John Stormonth deceased in Acharn, da Elizabeth, 1752

5 C L O V A

OPR with the Registrar General: 278 Cortachy & Clova
Births ? to 1709, 1711-32, 1738-40, 1746 1854
Marriages ? to 1708, 1713-6, 1725-32, 1746-74, 1781-1809, 1817-19, 1825-54
Deaths 1751-1854

278 Clova
Births 1820-54
Marriages 1741-51

SRO: see the notes for Cortachy

Fasti v 278 Ministers 1578-1616 and from 1811

I n d e x

Brown 14

C. 5
Crichton 1.17.Notes

Duncan 2.20.Notes

Ego 6
Esplin 1
Ewart 14

Guthrie 21.Notes

Hamilton Notes
Howe Notes

Kennedy 6.17

L. 5
Lindsay 2.10-2.15-6.18
Lucas 10.15.18.Notes

M. 3
McDonald 12
Mechie,Michie 4

Ogilvy 6.8.19.21.Notes

Rob(b)ie 18.19.Notes

Shaw Notes
Shirrell Notes
Stormonth Notes

W. 13
Walker 19
Webster Notes
Whyte 7-9.
Wilson 7

6a C O R T A C H Y

The parish church burial ground is sheletered by trees above the gates of Cortachy castle.
National Grid reference NO 395 597

1 1815. Collen Macdonald 1.8.1811 75, by ss Donald, Jas & Wm

2 Jas Lindsay fr Glenug 16.9.1826 36 int Clova, w Helen Lindsay at present (ie in 1849) tent Newton of Inshewan, only s Thos fr Newton of Inshewan 22.2.1849 23 int here

3 1804. Jas Young late dyer Eastmill of Cortachy 4.3.1796 75, w Eliz Low 12.9.1803 64

4 John Young of Eastmill, 1da Mary 28.6.1833 23; eulogy

5 John Young of Eastmill, 2s John 11.4.1835 37 of Honduras "leaving in a foreign land ... a widow & four chn to lament the premature death of an

6a C O R T A C H Y

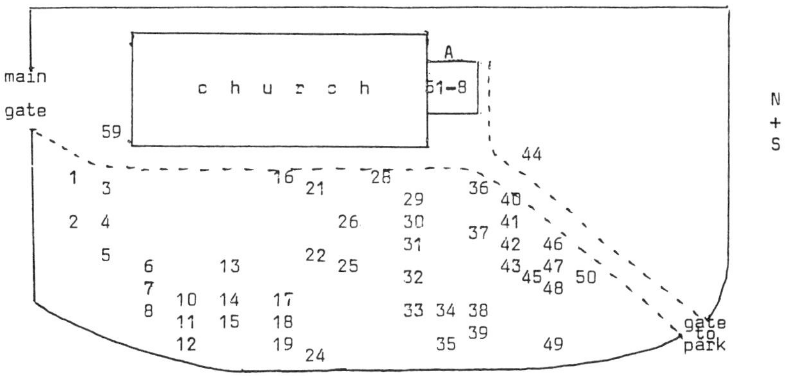

affectionate husband & indulgent parent", by surviving relatives whom he had returned to visit after an absence of 19 years; above named John Young, 1da Louisa Frances Lyell 12.7.1835 6

6 John Duncan fr Runtaleave 1806 55, w Margt Lindsay 7.4.1844 78, s Chas 9.1816 23

7 1798. Jas Stewart 4.7.1797 75 & int 8th inst, by w Christiana Buchan

8 in French. Francois poraz, w Jane Wilson d Cortachy 29.9.1832 35 (see Jervise "Epitaphs" ii: Poraz d 1868 72y int New cem Dundee); poem

9 Thos Dickson late tent of the farm of Cossacks 13.4.1802 72, by w Jean Low & ss Wm, David & John

10 by Alex Cameron miller Eastmill of Cortachy, chn Alex 14.1.1848 4, Charlotte 19.1.1848 7, Jas 21.1.1848 10, John 25.1.1848 2

11 Wm Wheatley officer of excise d Cortachy 10.9.1840 33, by w A G

12 1785. Chas Young 12.11.1775 63, w Yoophan Rob 1.12.1784 70, by s Jas in Dalhip; David Young 25.6.1785 3; Jean Young 8.1785 (5)8; (west side) square & compasses

13 Jas Steele tent Cants Mill 8.1828 81, w Marjory 25.1.1837 82, s David tent Redheugh 5.5.1854 67

14 Janet Whyte

15 by Jas Whyte imo w Margt Lindsay 10.1812, da Jane 10.1812

16 FS Chas Fleming at Brae(side) imo w Isobel Ogilvie (25.1.)18(09 2)4y

17 Robt Thomson writer in Kirriemuir 7.6.1839 38, by mo mrs Jean Tosh or Thomson & sisters Jean & Barbara

18 1779. by Jas Thomson gardiner in Cortachy & w Ann Gourly, s Alex 9.1.1779 10; (west side) tree & plants

19 under turf. Margt Robbie 3.18 - 27y

20 Here lyes James Dunkan 18.12.1707 59, w Margt Jak 8.3.1726 78

21 1833. Chas Hendry d at Gella 12.7.1827 87; Chas Hendry at Tarry Buckle, w Ann Ogilvy 25.9.1831 41, s Alex 23.4.1824 9m; Chas Hendry 22.1.1866 75

22 1848. Jas Bearn tent Eastmill of Downie Park 3.1.1848 75, s Jas 20.6.1814 8

23 Jas Young 23.6.1783 3;   Jean Young 8.1875 38

24 by Jas Nicoll, West Roods of Kirriemuir, w Margt Grewar 17.12.1833 60

25 rev Wm Ogilvy b in par Newtyle 2.2.1794, licensed to preach 1817, settled min United par of Cortachy & Clova 26.7.1826, d 27.7.1848 (see Fasti v)

26 John G(rant), w Margt Christie 7.7.1754 79, s David fr Fichill 12.1773 - - - (rest of inscription buried) - - -

27 Elspet Smith 18.4.1856 59, also her das Ann & Mary d inf

28 Jas Kidd, Cortachy gardens, s Jas 31.3.1861 6m

29 David Robbie fr Nethertown of Inshewan 19.1.1843 74, w Isobel Reid 5.9.1841 73, da Mary 1809 4, by chn Jas, David & Betsy in Nethertown of Inshewan

30 1786: by David Peter Smith, w Margt Smith 31.10.1785 59, s David 21.11.1785 33

31 John Lindsay late tent Lethnot 7.3.1837 74, w Agnes Findlay 11.3.1837 71 s Wm 27.4.1806 9, da Ann 15.5.1806 5, s John 18.1.1817 22, s Jas 21.7.1825 34, gs Jas 10.5.1843 18, s in law Jas Findlay late tent of East Lethnot 17.7.1845 57, da Euphemia 13.7.184(6) 47

32 Agnes Lindsay 22.1.1864 13

33 Mary Duncan or Lindsay 28.2.1855 66, by chn John, Agnes & Stewart Lindsay; David Lindsay tent Craigton 20.12.1858 75

34 1826. rev John Gourlay late min Cortachy & Sarah Ann Hunter his wife do rest in their graves. Mr Gourlay was yt s of mr John Gourlay (Fasti v 281 has: mr Jas Gourlay) a burgess of Brechin, b 1756 d 69y, for more than 30y assistant min Arbuthnott hence he was removed to be min Lintrathen & was translated to the Pastor in charge of this par about 7y before his decease; (west side) Mrs Gourlay was yt da of mr John Hunter, Millplough of Allardice, Arbuthnott, b 1765, surbived her father's family & d 55y, da Mary d childhood int Arbuthnott, surviving chn John & Wm (Fasti v 281: rev John Gourlay d 27.7.1819, w Sarah Ann Hunter d 14.3.1822)

35 FS of two panels with marginal inscriptions. Heir lyis James Wollom wak marchant in Cortachie who departed 21 of 1611 Ianwaria and his aig 58; scales; MB IW ; "Soli Deo". ; skull ; woolsack
Heir lyis Marget Wollom spws to Thomas Philp in Cortachie who departed the 21 of November 1616; pincers, hand/glove, - - ; TP MW; "..Honor et Gloria"; skull (see Jervise "Epitaphs" ii 114 for illustration)

36 John Ogilvy late fr Powmire 1.8.1825 77, w Janet Findlay 1.3.1820 62; David Ogilvy fr Middle Hill, da Janet 3.6.1834 12

37 TS by Alex Winter tent in the Doal imo his fa's bro Jas d in Peathaugh in par Glenisla 3.1.1732 72; I W 1732; buckler & sword; by Jas Winter, Dykehead 1885; "Here lyes Jas Vinter who died at Peathaugh / Who fought most valiantly at ye Water of Saugh /Along wt Ledenhendry who did command ye day They vanquis the enemy and made them Runn away." (see Jervise "Epitaphs" ii 114: Ledenhendry was John M'Intosh farmer there; see Fern inscription no.45)

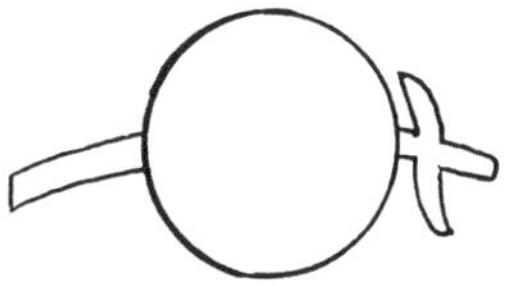

38 Geo Gordon tent in Buckwood, w Eliz Mitchell 3.9.1837 65; Geo Gordon 10.6.1843 82

39 Thos Gossens fr Dykehead 27.9.1864 67

6a CORTACHY

40 John Watt tent in Cullow 15.6.1836 97, w Janet Shaw 24.5.1819 74, s Duncan fr Coilamy & Clova 12.8.1859 89 (w Eliz Mealmaker 1816 44, s John lieut 93rd Foot 1838 35, s Jas min Cortachy & Clova 22.10.1861 61)

41 1743 (born 1671). David Watt sometime indweller in Dykehead 17.11. 1742 71; IW, IW, AW, HW, DW, GW, MW, AW, IW, MW, TW (west side) D W, H F ; share & coulter; poem (see Jervise "Epitaphs" ii 114: notes '41y' in mistake for '71y')

42 by John Watt tent Wellbank, w Ann Smith d Wellbank 9.7.1846 57, s Jas 20.11.1834 17; John Watt 20.1.1866 78

43 Wm Milne fr of Cowhillock 17.4.1816 69, w Susan Kennedy 27.2.1835 78, Wm late mert Kirriemuir 12.3.1836 45

44 1851. David Stewart shoemaker Kirriemuir 22.6.1818 32, w Isobel Harris 12.11.1850 60, by chn Helen, Jas & David

45 W B

46 Wm Duncan fr Adylin 21.11.1860 84 int Clova, w Jane Lindsay 8.3.1866 86, gs Jas Low 14.9.1865 3y9m

47 by John, Joseph & Peter Gordon imo sis Jane Gordon 18.3.1820 13

48 1815. Jas Ogilvie sometime tent Rashie Bogg d - - - - 58y, by s David

49 1817. Alex Walker sometime tent East mill of Kenalty 3.6.1815 54, by w Martha Ferguson

50 1832. G Coutts

A The Airlie mausoleum lintel: This edifice was erected Anno Domini 1828 by David 7th Earl of Airlie on the - - - - the old - - - - - David Paterson architect; Peter Scott builder (see Jervise "Epitaphs" ii 110: IH with arms of Heron; GM with arms of Mercer; IO with arms of Ogilvy, also DO; MV with arms of Wood; possibly for David 3s of Lord Ogilvy)

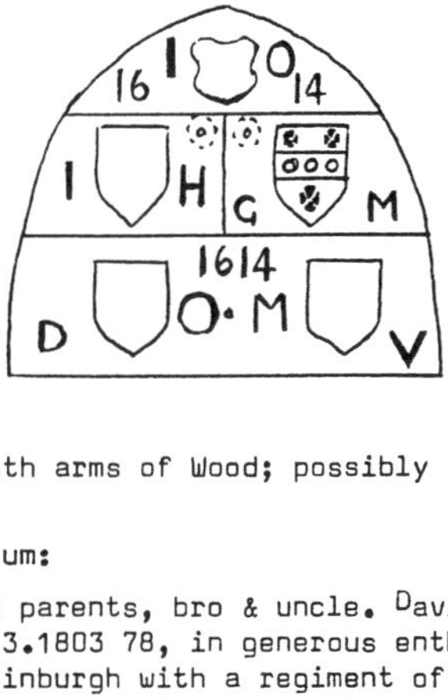

The following nos 51-8 are in the mausoleum:

51 mural. by David 7th earl of Airlie imo parents, bro & uncle. David 5th earl of Airlie d Cortachy castle 3.3.1803 78, in generous enthusiasm of youth joined the Chevalier at Edinburgh with a regiment of 600 men & continued loyal & true to the cause. He afterwards entered the French service in which he obtained rank of lieut general. In 1778 HM George III was pleased to restore him to his country & estates. (see DNB)

52 mural. capt John Ogilvy of 1st regt of Foot d Berice 24.8.1809 25

53 mural. Walter 6th earl of Airlie d Cortachy castle 10.4.1819 85 & Jane his Countess 11.6.1818 56

54 mural. Clementina countess of Airlie d London 1.9.1835 40, by s David earl of Airlie (Jervise "Epitaphs" ii 110 notes: she was only da of Gavin Drummond of Keltie d 1809, her s lord Walter, da lady Arbuthnott-Ogilvy)

55 mural. by David Graham Drummond 8th earl of Airlie imo fa David 7th earl 29.8.1849 64

6a CORTACHY

56 mural. Margt Bruce countess of Airlie d Brighton Sussex 18.6.1845 39, twin ss d 16 June, she left 4 ss to h David earl of Airlie, int 9.7.1845

57 mural. hon Donald Ogilvy of Clova, w Maria d Leamington (9.4.1843 52)

58 mural. David Ogilvy - - - (Jervise "Epitaphs" ii has:b 10.4.1826 d 20.7.1857)

59 a loose marble tablet lying at the foot of the church wall, in Latin. rev Wm Badenoch min here, w Ann Farquharson 10.3.1710 27.10.1736; "Corpus Sudera Mortem"

The following are noted in Jervise "Epitaphs" ii but were not seen in 1977:

60 FS John - - - - in Clachneybrain d 10.-.16505 (for 1655) 65y, w Janet Cant 6.5.1644; emblems; I P (?for Philip?) C C

61 Jas Sime gardener here, w Kath Lewchars 1749 "a prudent mother"

62 W R ; rev Wm Ramsay min here from 1795 till 1818 (see Fasti v 281)

Notes

Testaments from Cortachy are recorded with the Commissariot of Brechin. The following is a selection:

David Allan in Rotwell, 1651
John Allan in Ficheill, 1637 & his spouse Christian Ogilvie, 1629
Robt Anderson in Loanhead of Collow, 1741
Jas Bruce in Rottuall & w Janet Glen, 1613
Alex Donald in Fedderege & spouse Margt Mitchell, 1611
Alex Donald in Glenmoy & spouse Annas Edward, 1628
Alex Donalt in Shank of Glenmoy, spouse Janet Froster, 1657
Jas Donald in Ogie & spouse Janet Fentoun, 1611
Alex Donald in Feythregy, 1578
John Duncan in Rottuall & spouse Janet Robie, 1651
Thos Duncan in Rottwall, spouse Margt Lindsay, 1611
John Gall sometime shoemaker in Dykehead of Cortachy, 1725
Alex Howe grieve at Cortachy, 1792
David Lindsay in Dykheid of Tullo, 1612
David Lindsay in Fetteregie, 1778
Jas Lindsay in Colow, 1670
Jas Lindsay in Collone, 1691
Jas Lindsay in Roymantis in Rottuall par Kincardine, w Bessie Lucas, 1637
John Lindsay in Glaplet, 1712
Robt Lindsay sometime in Romants, 1750
Thos Lindsay in Fedderege, 1610, widow Christian Strachan, 1610
Thos Lindsay in Rochtache, 1637, w Margt Mitchell 1624
Alex Mitchell in Bukood of Cortachie & spouse Isobel Burne, 1688
David Myll sometime in Braelaus, widow Janet Soutar, 1711
Alex Ogilvie in Glenmoy & spouse Isobel Findlay, 1658
Andrew Ogilvie in Fichell par Cortoquhie, spouse Janet Findlay, 1624
Jas Ogilvie in Shank of Glenmoy, 1661
Wm Ogilvie in Eolzeune, spouse Alison Robert, 1610
David Robbie in Eglismagien & spouse Elspet Robbe par Costachy, 1637
David Robbie in Fetteregie & spouse Margt Edward, 1688
Alex Robertson alias Nilson in Doll, 1665
Duncan Shaw in Milntoun of Cortachie, 1779 & 1796
Jas Volome at Kirktown of Cortachy, widow Margt Bowman, 1680
John White in Rottuall & spouse Elspet Robbie, 1637
Thos White in Rottuall, 1629
Alex Winter in Shank, spouse Margt Donald, 1684
David Wolom, 1675

6a C O R T A C H Y

OPR with the Registrar General: 278 Cortachy - Births 1662-75,1677-
Marriages 1662-75, 1677-

278 Cortachy & Clova - Births -1709, 1711-32, 1738-40, 1746-1854
Marriages -1708, 1713-16, 1725-31, 1746-74, 1781-1809, 1817-19, 1825-54
Deaths 1751-1854

SRO CH2/561/1 Cortachy 1659-79, Cortachy & Clova 1679-87, 1697-1702
proclamations & certificates (2 pages) 1709-10
baptisms (1 page) 1709-10
minutes 1702, 1748-1826, 1795-1901
poor's money 1816-25; cash book 1800-6, 1827-34, 1852-98
baptismal register 1741-1855

HR 384 Cortachy & Clova, rental of parish of Cortachy 1826, buildings 1797-1927 etc

CH3/497 Memus FC minutes 1843-65 ; C R 1857-70
(FC parish embraced Cortachy, Kirriemuir, Oathlaw & Fern

Ewing ii 157 Memus ministers from 1844

Fasti v 279 Cortachy ministers from 1571

I n d e x

Airlie 51-6
Allan Notes
Anderson Notes

Badenoch 59
Bearn 22
Bowman Notes
Bruce 56.Notes
Buchan 7
Burne Notes

Cameron 10
Cant 60
Christie 26
Coutts 50

Dickson 9
Donald Notes
Duncan 6.33.46
Dunkan 20

Edward Notes

Farquharson 59
Fentoun Notes
Ferguson 49
Findlay 31.36.Notes
Fleming 16
Froster Notes

G. 11
Gall Notes
Glen Notes
Gordon 38.47
Gossens 39
Gourl(a)y 18.34
Grant 26
Grewar 24

Harris 44
Hendry 21
Howe Notes
Hunter 34

Jak 20

Kennedy 43
Kidd 28

Lewchars 61
Lindsay 2.6.15.31-3.46.Notes
Low 9
Lucas Notes
Lyell 5

Macdonald 1
M'Intosh 37
Mealmaker 40
Mill Notes
Milne 43
Mitchell 38.Notes

Nicoll 24

Ogilvie 16.48
Ogilvy 21.25.36.51-8. Notes

Phil(i)p 35.60
Poraz 8

6a C O R T A C H Y

Ramsay	62	Thomson	17-8
Reid	29	Tosh	17
Rob	12	Volome see Wollom	
Robbie	19.29.Notes	Walker	49
Robert	Notes	Watt	40-2
Robertson	Notes	Wheatley	11
Shaw	40.Notes	White, Whyte	14-5.Notes
Sime	61	Wilson	8
Smith	27.30.42	Winter	37.Notes
Soutar	Notes	Wollom	35.Notes
Steele	13	Young	3-4.12.23
Stewart	7.44		
Strachan	Notes		

The private walled burial ground in a field south of Turfachie (National Grid reference NO 420 580) had no surviving inscriptions when inspected in 1977.

6b G L E N P R O S E N

There is a quoad sacra church at Pitcarity to serve this detached part of Kirriemuir parish. The small churchyard is well kept.
National Grid reference: NO 328 657

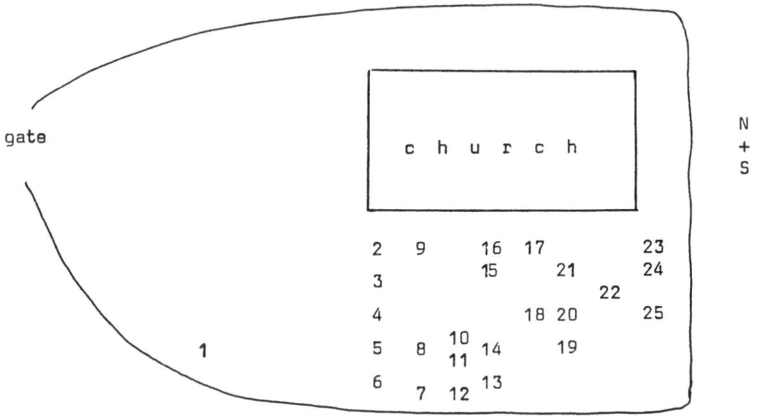

1 ob Thos shaw of Shawfield 28.12.1847 75, w Eliza Rattray 16.3.1852 74, da Amelia Ann MacLaren 2.1.1848 38 (wid of Jas MacLaren of Dalnabreck), da Mary Graham 9.9.1849 45, s Wm of Shawfield 2.8.1852 34; Thos Shaw MacLaren of Shawfield WS d Edinburgh 5.6.1907 65, w Isabella Davidson Smith d Peebles 21.1.1940 88; Thos Shaw of Shawfield, Dalrulzian etc fr Little Forter Glenisla where he d 20.11.1868 69; mrs Isabella I D Shaw of Shawfield d Shawfield 8.11.1888 69; Jas Maclaren of Dalnabreck, w Amelia Ann Shaw, da Cath Jessie d Kirriemuir 12.12.1924 78

2 John Donald sometime tent Burn End of E(dnau)ghty 25.4.1745 62, by w Jean Ogilvie & his bro Thos Donald & their chn David, John & Jean; plough; (west side) angel; 1745

3 by Jas Geekie greve at Balnaboth & w Helen Hanton imo s Walter 12.2.1836 10y8m, da Ann 8.5.1848 20; Jas Geekie 25.11.1864; Helen Hanton 28.7.1866

4 1845. Thos M Fergusson fr Milhall 16.1.1859 84, w Euphemia Mackenzie 3.3.1840 61, s John 1880, s Wm 1885, s Thos 1873, s Robt 1875, s Alex 1876, s David 1880, da Ann 6.12.1913 90

5 1852. Robt Marshall 7.3.1852 64, w Eliz Gordon d Inchmill 5.3.1852 81, s Wm 14.7.1842 26, by das Elis 31.7.1887 75 & Jean & Ann

6 1806. Wm Smart 20.11.1805 45, by w Elspat Low in Wester Inchbrathy. He left two chn Wm & Lea; (west side) cherub

7 Jas Milne 3.1835, w Jessie Gordon 27.4.1825, ss John, David & Jas, da Jane, by s Robt d Kirriemuir 15.2.1879 81

8 John Davidson d Woodend 6.1827 37, w Eliz McNicol d Delinch 6.1820 26, s Jas d at sea on board ship "Orwell" 27.1.1862 45 on his return passage to Australia, by only surviving s John residing in Victoria Australia

9 1810. Robt Hanton d in the Stron 20.3.1794, w Jean Lindsay 15.1.1807, s Jas who lays both within this church, s David 25.10.1807, by ss John & Robt

10 Jas Duncan d Wellhalt Cortachy 22.6.1899 83, w Betsy McNicoll d Wellhalt 22.4.1905 71, s Wm d Inchmill 26.1.1881 3

11 1813. by Jas Duncan tailor Carmoor par of Kirriemuir, da Margt 10.9.1812 4

12 1855. Dond McPherson d Buckwood Glenprosen 21.8.1833, w Jean Gordon d Dalinch Glenprosen 24.8.1834; John McPherson b 4.1.1790 d Glentarrie 26.7.1858; Annie Brown d Glenley 31.12.1873 78

13 Duncan McPherson b Glentarry 1.3.1830 25.9.1882, by chn John, Ann & Allan

14 CT by David How, Cormuir d Cormuir 28.3.1843 69, w Margt Edward 10.2.1835 61, eulogy; Elspeth How d Craiggmaig 9.1.1858 61

15 rev Arthur McArthur of Callendar b Balnaboth 1840; Wm Middleton of Balnaboth 12.8.1893 faithful servant for more than 20y to Donald Ogilvy of Clova & mrs Ogilvy

16 Wm Wilson fr Dalarin 1769, w Isabel Thom 1782, s John fr Ballentore 3.3.1812 52 (by w Barbara Gibson 19.9.1839 89, their surviving chn Jas, Wm 1866 79, Margt 1868 70), s Wm d London 1783, da Jane 1800

17 1787. Wm Holbert 15.11.1786 65 "an honest & trusty servant formerly in Pitcarity but he was a man", by Jas & Thos Holberts imo "there Uncel"

18 1806. by John Hanton & w Margt Ogilvy tent in Craig & Dodavo imo s Jas d Dodavo 27.8.1806 4, surviving chn David, Jean, John & Margt

19 1833. by Wm Findlay & w Helen Duncan farmers in Easterdelinch, s Wm 12.8.1830 17

20 1838. Thos Lindsay d Pitcarity 30.6.1823 50, w Jean McNicoll d Pitcarity 14.11.1845 78, s Wm d Montrose 3.1.1838 28, by s Jas & da Jean

21 Thos Philip of Cotgibbion 26.10.1842 97, w Euphemia Hendry 16.8.1843 73, s Thos late of Cotgibbion d Kirriemuir 17.3.1875 63, s John, s Wm, da Agnes all int here, da Margt 28.11.1881 72 int here

22 ID MG ; by John Duncan & w May Gall fr in Cormure imo s Wm 19.12.1771 32, deceased chn Chas, Isobel & Ranald, surviving chn John, Jas, Frederick, Martha, Betty & Samuel; (west side) square, saw, axe, ox-yoke &

plough; mantling; 1772; poem

23 John McNicoll 28.12.1880 83, w Betty Lindsay 12.8.1873 73, da Eliz 4.3. 1836 13, da Amelia 13.10.1879 52, s Walter 18.5.1844 19, da Jean McNicoll or Hendry d Lednathie cottage 2.1.1892 61 (da Betsy d East Baloch cottage 15.8.1923 63 (h Wm Morrison 27.8.1935 91, s Geo Lyell Stewart d 21 Victoria Street Kirriemuir 15.6.1937 43, s Wm 28.6.1947 59))

24 Jas McNicoll d Pitcarity 9.6.1837 67

25 Chas Fleming d West Mains of Auchterhouse 19.9.1865 89, w Jean Cameron d Shawfield 2.10.1847 64, s Thos d Shawfield 1836 10

Notes

Testaments from Glen Prosen were usually registered with the Commissariot of St. Andrews. The following is a selction:

Thos Edwards in Dillinch of Glen Prosen, 1737
Jas Hanton in Knows of Glenprosen, par of Forfar, 1720
Wm Hanton in Glenprossine, par of Kirriemuir, 1699
Robt Kendow in Glenorg, par of Kirriemuir, 1617
John Wright in Balnaboth, 1729

The following was recorded with the Commissariot of Edinburgh:
John Wilson in Glenwik (i.e. Glenuig), 1588

OPR with the Registrar General: see Kirriemuir notes

Index

Brown 12
Cameron 25
Davidson 8
Donald 2
Duncan 10-1.19.22
Edward(s) 14.Notes
Fergusson 4
Findlay 19
Fleming 25
Gall 22
Geekie 3
Gibson 16
Gordon 5.7.12
Hanton 3.9.18.Notes
Hendry 21.23
Holbert 17
How 14
Kendow Notes
Lindsay 9.20.23
Low 6
McArthur 15
Mackenzie 4
Maclaren 1
McNicol(l) 8.10.20.23-4
McPherson 12-3
Marshall 5
Middleton 15
Milne 7
Morrison 23
Ogilvie/y 2.15.18
Philip 21
Rattray 1
Shaw 1
Smart 6
Smith 1
Thom 16
Wilson 16.Notes
Wright Notes

7 DUN

This secluded graveyard beside the walled garden of the Dun estate is well-kept. The approach is a lane off the Bridge of Dun to Stracathro B road. National Grid reference: NO 667 598

The old church at its centre is now the mausoleum of the Erskines of Dun; it was dedicated to the Virgin Mary. (The present parish church and the modern cemetery are ¼ mile away.)

The parishes of Dun and Ecclesjohn were united in 1583. (Ecclesjohn was near Kirkhill at Nat. Grid ref: NO 689 604)

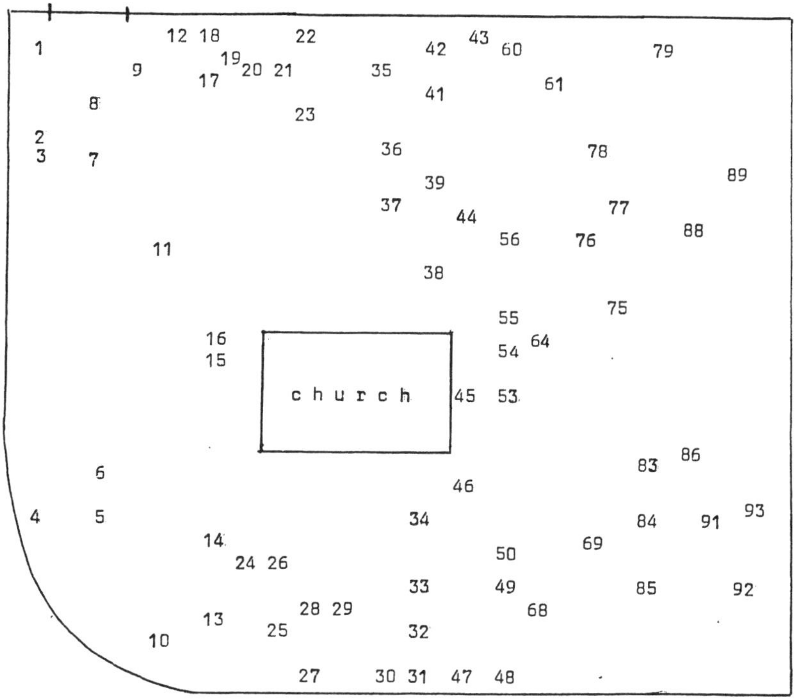

1 Geo Ross wright Dun 2.1.1905 93, chn B W 6.12.1848 3, C C 6.1.1849 7, child d inf, da sb 4.5.1855, Mary d Edinburgh 14.2.1880 20y8m int here, Alexy d Montrose 15.8.1883 35 (h Isaac Burgess of Hawden Chester), only s Jas b 14.9.1852 d Edinburgh 28.2.1887, w Jane Smith 11.5.1892 79

2 Robt McGregor d Old Montrose 31.12.1870 68, w Eliz Valentine 9.11.1871 69, chn Rebecca 22.11.1841 6, Agnes 5.4.1857 13

3 1788. by Robt Pirie & May Brechin naer Dun, s John 16.5.1784 8y11m; Alex Pirie d Honduras 14.8.1814 27y7m; Jas Pirie 22.8.1819 38y7m; (east side) above Robt Pirie 25.5.1825 83, w Marjorie Brecin 23.7.1828 82

4 17--; cherub; by - - - Scott & Jean (Lang)son & - -obb & (Elspet - -_) ison to their fa - - - - - - d 20.1.1769 48 (& his w Jannet Samsn 20.5.1764 35)

5 John Low wright Langley Park 14.8.1864 65, da Jane 28.1.1837 4, w Eliz Cloudsley 17.1.1890 90 (her sis Jane Cloudsley 15.12.1877 80)

6 TS Thos Crooks gardener Ecclesjohn then tent Roadside of Tayock b par Newbattle 29.3.1716 d 3.1.1798, w Christian Cormack b Bervie 1.11.1727 d 27.12.1802 both int here, s Wm d on his passage from Tobago to America 1802 38, by s Thos of Island of Tobago planter 21.12.1803 (Jervise "Epitaphs p 224 shows Wm as MD & the wife's name as Jean Cormack)

7 1803. Robt Clark 26.5.1797 78; David Clark, s Robt 3.5.1799 2y9m; Christian Clark 24.8.1802 4; also - - - - - - - - - - - aged 20, 3 & 18; (west side) 18--. Jas Smith - - - -

8 by Jas Gibson, da - - - (broken stone)

9 John Malcolm d at Woodside Balnillo 28.2.1895 72, w Christina McNicol 2.12.1900 81, s John FRCVS d Birmingham 23.9.1920 65, da Janet d at Gonan 4.7.1853 4; (west side) Alex Malcolm fr Woodside Balnillo 19.7.1867 72, w Jane Malcolm 21.10.1859 68

10 1780. by Jean White & John Murray imo her h Thos Stephen 26.5.1770 61 & of Margt Stephen their da & spouse to said John Murray who d 24.5.1778 29 & their da Jean Murray 12.4.1778 7m; also David, Geo & Thos ss to the said Thos Stephen & Jean White

11 Wm Milne d at Brechin 12.8.1891 87, w Ann Goudie d Crosshill 5.1.1888 86, chn Robt 1.8.1840 6, Wm 21.12.1842 11, Jas 29.12.1842 5

12 1866. by Wm Mitchell bootmaker Brechin, fa Jas 18.3.1862 68, mo Mary Stott 6.1.1826 33 int Maryton, stepmo Margt Ross 31.1.1881 85

13 FS "Under this ston does sweetly rest a woman pious vertous and chast..." in Latin. David Erskine in Ballachie, w Kath Fullarton 28.1.169(7) nearly 44y, five ss & das d inf ; poem (see Jervise "Epitaphs" p 223)

14 TS in Latin. A C 1733. Alex Cromar schoolmaster in Dun for 8y d 1733 27y (see Jervise "Epitaphs" p 224); emblems

15 1848. Sarah Erskine Eadie or Ross

16 1848. by John Eadie min Dun d at the Manse 29.9.1857 71 in 36th y of incumbency int here, w Helen Scott 20.11.1850 52, chn David d Glasgow 1846 18, John d at the Manse 1840 10, Sarah Erskine Eadie or Ross d Edinburgh 1847 22 (see Fasti v 389 for other details of family)

17 Wm McNeill & w Eliza McNeill 21.7.1854, by David Burgess who sincerely loved - - - - - - her

Stones no. 18-22 are set into the boundary wall:

18 - -es Young(husband to Margret Smith)d 27.2.1690 90 (illust: PSAS 1901-2 173)

19 Susana Scot(spouse to Thos Stevin)d 12.3.1693 50 (illust: PSAS 1901-2 fig 172

20 1737. J D , (J) P ; Tailor's scissors & goose

21 Here lyes an honest virgin Margret Simson d 16.3.1699 91 (but Jervise "Epitaphs" p 223 has: age 21y)

22 Robt Strachan younger d 10.10.1696 8; stag on shield

23 1851. Magdalene Cruikshanks 13.11.1875 82, s Alex Law 4.7.1845 23

24 FS Georg Steuart 8.2.1687 95, w Mary Erskin 13.1.1690 81; poem; emblems, death carrying an axe & a dart (see Jervise p 224)

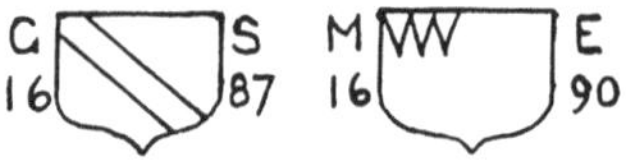

25 Alex Couley & Margt Lyell in Leis of Dun, chn John, another John, Alex, Isobel, Mary, Eliz; (west side) 1741. pincers, shoemakers knife & ? ; A C, M L ; I C, M C, K C

26 Alex Coully 17.6.1760

27 by Jas Coullie sometime wright at Dun to w Helen Falconer 1.7.1764 48, chn Jas, Alex, Jean, Margt, John, Helen & David Coullies all in time in 1773; (west side) 1773. shield with square, compasses, saw & axe

28 TS R P, M D; - P, - A; (R D, D O); Robt Paterson magistri de Dun qui obiit 16(90) aetatis suae 48, conjugis Margt - - - 169(9) (see SRO GD 1/559: a note by bailie Jas Low of Montrose "I am satisfied Robt Paterson was one schoolmaster of Dun, the fourth I have notes of, elected dominie on 25.8.1669 at a salary of 1/8 Scots for every plough on the parish. He was the successor of Walter Forsyth who was possessor of the charge in 1665. The only money that I can see that Paterson drew was 3 $\frac{3}{4}$ Scots. Of course he would have had the children's peat money or its equivalent." The same ms states that RP d 1606 48, & Margt de - - d 3.1690 17)

29 G M, E D ; by John Dores, s David sometime wright in Mentros 17.6.1742 27; (west side) J D, E J, 1744

30 FS in Latin. 1757. Geo Walker

31 TS Jas Paterson of Reidfield 15.10.1791 68, by sis Margt Paterson

32 TS John Paterson smith in Leys of Dun 7.1.1724 81 left the substance of the following line to be graven on his gravestone .. Poem ... w Jean Edeson 9.3.1704 59; crown, hammer, cherub; I P, I E (see Jervise "Epitaphs" p 223 for poem)

33 TS angel; R S, I L; Robt Strauchen in Beuillo, w Isobel Lindsay 29.11.170(3) 74 ... who left her chn to supply her stage; shield; emblems

34 John Pickeman & Jean Black irdwellers at Leadsid of Bruce mill, s John 23.7.1735 16; (west side) cherub; John Pickeman & Jean Black; shield with ?spade & pick?, I P, I B

35 John Jack 11.9.1843 79, w Ann Mathers 26.10.1841 79, by da Ann

36 Jas Beattie 6.6.1857 68, w Ann Catanoch 22.8.1853 68, chn Geo 6.1817 3½, Jane 4.1829 20, Agnes 11.1831 20, Helen Scott 1.11.1855 29, Jas 31.12. 1859 41

37 David Beattie d Shrewsbury 30.7.1862 46, w Margt Nicol 12.6.1859 39, da Agnes Mitchel 1.8.1856 12y9m, & two das d inf int here

38 1821. by David Forbes weaver Tayock, da Helen 3.4.1816 13, s David 2.11. 1821 27; (west side) David Forbes 29.4.1827 59

39 by Jas & Jean Webster, da Mary 27.10.1828 12, s Robt 22.8.1835 5

40 Jas Selby in Gate of Kinnaird 11.4.1844 77, w Elis Forbes 5.12.1841 73

41 Alex Selby d at Bridge of Dun 1.1.1889 52; (west side) Alfred Selby 28.1.1896 30

42 1867. by Isabella Colville 23.3.1882 81, h Thos Selby tailor Bridge of Dun 14.3.1848 51, chn And 1.6.1844 9.6.1844, Eliz 23.3.1829 21.11.1846, Thos 4.8.1841 8.2.1853, Jessie 3.10.1846 16.10.1866, Margt 10.3.1831 11.2.1870, Alex 2.8.1836 31.1.1889, Anne 4.9.1838 4.12.1889

43 by Wm Durie imo fa Thos Durie late fr Whitefield of Dun 7.1801 78, mo jean Thomson 5.1798 72, their family John 1.1800 43, Cath 1.1800 45, Jas 11.1801 34, Jean 2.1812 51, Agnes 4.1816 50, Mary 10.1830 72; (west side) Alex Durie 8.1844 81; Thos Durie 3.1845 85

44 by David Stratton imo bro Robt 25.8.1815 23, also near this stone lies their sis Jean; (west side) David Mill d Edinburgh 8.1.1860 45, only

child David Stratton d Montrose 8.1.1863 17, mo & gmo of the above d Momtrose 17.9.1864 78 int here

45 1840. Robt Smith 3.9.1776 15.7.1822, w Elis Ferrer 6.10.1778 4.5.1840

46 1757. share & coulter on shield, mantling; Jas Thomson late tent Mains of Dun 8.2.1719 36, w Isl Thomson 12.7.1742 58; Ia Thn, Is Th; Ro Th, Is Th; Robt Thomson, chn Eliz 28.10.1753 5, John 14.7.1756 1y (see Jervise "Epitaphs" i 345: inscriptions 46 & 51 relate to ancestors of a family named Thomson who were sometimes farmers at Leuchland, Arrat & Findowrie etc in the par Brechin & one of whom was long town-clerk of Montrose; see Brechin inscription no. 407)

47 FS David Lyel 16.12.1712 60, w Jean Strachan, chn D Ly, R Ly, E Ly, I Ly, A Ly; D L, J S; JoLy, Ro Ly, An Ly, Al Ly, Mare Ly, Je Ly; text ; I L, M W, 1714

48 TS by Jas Murey imo w Agnes Lyel 8.2.1732 48; Jas Murray sometime tent in Lielmil of Boroufild 20.6.1733; I M, A L, 1732; ox yoke; AM, RM, IM, IM, AM, EM, IM, DM, MM

49 TS in Latin. John Erskine sometime in Dunsmill, distinguished for his exemplary life d 15.4.1696 28, w Agnes Burn 1.5.1696 25 they lived like turtles & d together; two shields, 1696 I E, A B

50 in Latin. John (but Jervise has James) Burn 23.11.1706 59, w Janet Edison 18.3.1707 60 md for 37y; I B, I E

51 Jas Thomson late tent Balwylo 2.11.1735 53, da Margt 11.9.1721 2; (west side) share & coulter on shield; Ia Th, Ma Low; Io Th, An St (see no. 46 above)

52 TS by John Hill tent Mains of Dun, fa Thos sometime tent there 2.3.1852 73; T H, I L; T H, I H, 1757; I H, A M

53 1867. Jas Nicol fr East Leys of Dun 11.2.1861 69, w Agnes Mitchell 9.10.1865 77, by da Agnes

54 below 53. gs of the above, Geo Soutar esq MA BLitt b Leys of Dun 28.12.1864 d 9.2.1939, w Janet Aitken 10.7.1864 17.5.1944

55 Jas Mitchill blacksmith in the Leys of Dun 12.2.1790 41, w Eliz Baillie 5.6.1844 91y8m, chn John 1786, Elis 1788 both in childhood, by Jas Nicol

56 Robt Kirkland late smith Old Montrose 26.1.1790 35, w Agnes Mitchell & da Jean; 1791

57 by Mary Robert, fa Alex Robert mason Dun 8.4.1853 85, mo Susan Morrice 18.4.1842 80, sis Isabella 22.11.1822 23

58 by John McQuiver, fa Malcom McQuiver 24.2.1770 57; 1770. Malcm McQr, Kan All- -er; John McQr; Jas McQr

59 Robt Pickeman 6.10.1844 89, mo Ann Bertie 28.6.1782 59 (checked, Ed) by ss John, David & James Pickemans; (west side) 1813 (could his year of death have been 1811?)

60 1837. John Wyllie fr Links Montrose 18.8.1839 70, w Ann Ross 2.10.1821 39, 1da Mary d Glasgow 1.4.1858 41, 2s David member of medical profession d Glasgow 4.10.1866 50, 4s And druggist d Glasgow 19.3.1884 68

61 1770. by Kathrine Young to fa & mo; compasses & axe on shield; D Y, M W, J Y, M Y, K Y, H Y; (west side) David Young cooper 10.5.1770 70, w Margret Mil 6.7.1767 67

62 1837. by David Robb, w Helen Watt 12.6.1835 36, fa in law Alex Watt 24.3.1828 65

63 TS John Mather tent Balnillo 6.1.1737 80y6m, w Jean Thomson 28.12.1727 80, s Robt 29.9.1777 77 (w Margt Strachan 13.4.1772 58, chn Jas 16.1.1771 24, Chas 30.9.1771 19, Janet (15).8.1776 21, Mary 31.8.1775 17; share & coulter in shield, mantling; R M, M S; J M, G M, J M, J M, A M; J M, G M, C M, J M, J M; 1749

64 John Milne 21.5.1773 (3)0; Margt Milne 17.4.1770 25; (west side) 1773. JoM, E J; A M, R M, K M, MiM, My M

65 David Smith grocer Montrose 22.7.1867 54, w Helen Reid 17.7.1863 49, chn Jas 9.8.1852 7, Wm 18.9.1852 10, Geo 3.10.1865 18, Helen 9.3.1870 16, David 1.1.1871 20, Jessie Ann 19.2.1871 27, Susan 2.9.1876 17, Cath 24.9.1884 28

66 TS 1838. - - - - mson many y fr - - hland afterwards in Manis - - - - - - -nnithie & thereafter rest - - - - in Brechin -.8.1833 76, w M- - Ann Mitchell or Thomson 4.2.1820 55, chn Jean, Margt, David, John, David Carnegie & Robt all d inf, da Eliz Thomson 26.7.1838 54

67 TS - - - Thomson in parish of - - - - - - d Arrat 24.6.1781 70, wid - - - Strachan

68 TS by Francis Rober(tson) & - - Thomson in Househill of (Dunn) to s Alex 1765 25

69 by Jean Miln(e), h John Thomson sometime tent Glenskenno d here 2.8. 1--0 59, also - - nt Milne - - - (1860)

70 1782. by David Thomson blacksmith in Pathhead of Gomistown, fa Jas sometime residenter at Newbigin 9.1.1775 70

71 Alex Donaldson fr in the ground of Kinnaber 23.1.1747 63, w Margt Thomson 16.1.1747 63, s Alex 15.2.1770 43; A D, M T

72 1816. David Nicol mason Dun 9.3.1801 76, w Margt Japp 12.5.1771 34, da Margt 14.5.1793 22, s John mason d London 15.3.1815 45; setsquare & compasses; (west side) by John Orkney shipmaster & Magdalen Nicol for their friends

73 Jas Stevenson d at Dun's Green 9.7.1790 53, w Mary Hill, chn Ann, Jas, Robt, David, Alex

74 David Scott younger of Newton 12.2.1845 53, w Margt Gleig d Millfield 17.9.1874 82, 3s Jonathan D G, 28th regt Bengal Native Infantry 16.1. 1859 27, 1s David d Melbourne 1.7.1875 52

75 David Scott late of Newton 28.1.1846 90, w Helen Mitchell in Balwyllo 26.4.1824 59, s Alex 25.9.1791 3y2m (see Jervise "Epitaphs" i 345 notes that inscriptions 74, 75 & 77, three adjoining stones, relate to a family some of whose members were among the most enterprising agriculturists & stock raisers in Angus.)

76 1818. by Jas Spankie at Wood of Balnille to w Ann Tevendale 31.8.1817 73 (her fa John Tevendale 30.4.1794 91), da Margt 26.9.1776 14m, s David b 28.8.1773, da Margt b 8.7.1775, s Jas 2.3.1778, da Eliz 25.2.1781 da Jean 12.8.1784; Jas Spankie 8.3.1828 81

77 1855. Robt Scott - - - - - (see Jervise "Epitaphs" i 345: Robt had four ss & three das including David surgeon major Bengal Medical Service d Umballa 16.9.1867 42)

78 1850. Jean Jerves d Montrose 6.2.1850 59

79 Jas Christison d Montrose 4.10.1849 54, w Jean Knight d Montrose 9.10. 1849 52, chn Margt, two ss named John all d inf & int Rescobie, by chn W & D

80 Helen Forbes 27.3.1843 27.1.1849; Chas Forbes 29.6.1847 23.1.1849

81 Jas Moir d Burnside 8.8.1837 47, w Eliz Stool d Burnside 11.6.1880 80, chn Geo 25.9.1842 14, Jane 26.12.1848 11, Alex private K O B d Gibraltar 19.2.1859 23, Eliz 20.10.1912 78

82 Wm Cook 2.10.1890 75, w Jane Milne 18.2.1902 83, chn Christina 1859 6, Wm 1859 10m, David 1864 1y, Helen 1882 26

83 Geo Duncan 24.6.1877 77, w Agnes Carnegie 9.12.1860 53, chn Agnes 4.2.1848 5, Mary 15.1.1853 20, Geo drowned at sea 13.4.1859 in lat 36°40' south, long 0°10' west aged 19, Jessie 27.3.1895 57, Jane 7.1.1915 81, Wm d at West Pittendreich 6.10.1915 64

84 TS John Thomson 26.(1).1755 73, w Cath Jaap, s Jas 18.12.1727 15m, two chn John & Jean (see SRO:GD 1/559/1 notes: he was late tent in Fullertoun, s John d 12.12.1727)

85 TS (marginal) John Lindsay d in Fordess 8.5.1702 78, w Christan Edward (8.2.1697 or 170-) 7(3), s David tent Dunnsmill 22.5.173(7) 77 (w Margt Doors 25.8.1733 74;
I L, C E; D L, M D;
text, share & coulter
(SRO: GD 1/559/1 has
John L. d 5.1708)

86 by Jas Mackenzie mariner Montrose to w Margt Walker 5.8.1851 60, s Jas mariner 3.8.1853 35

87 1764. John Brichen 18.12.1763 29, w Agnes Norie, chn David 1784 22, John 1783 23

88 1827. by Joseph Petrie at Arratsmill to fa Joseph 20.5.1813 73, mo Cath Mill 25.12.1826 87, bro Benjamin 2.1800 15, 2w Isobell Morrison 21.8.1828 31

89 by Geo Eaton to fa G 3.1.1744 52, mo Isobal Fife 25.3.1756 50;
G E, M G, J E

90 by John Duncan, fa Jas d Mains of Dun 12.4.1792 73, mo Elspeth Norrie 13.6.1784 64

91 1776. by Alex & Jas to fa Jas Pulkace 20.4.1772 60,(w Margret Strachen) sis Isobella 30.8.1776 19; I P, M S, I P, A P, M P, I P

92 by Jas Lyell fr North Mains of Dun to w Eliz Smith 14.9.1850 44

93 Wm Petrie gardener at English Maldie, w Margt Dempster 24.11.1755 53; (east side) W P, M D; I P, C P, W P, K P; rake & spade; emblems

The following are noted in Jervise "Epitaphs" i and were not seen in 1977 - nos. 94-7 are in the old kirk which is locked, & 98-9 are in the walled garden:

94 FS I E M G 1703

95 coffin plate. Archd (Kennedy) marquis of Ailsa KT FRS 1846 76

96 coffin plate. Margt Erskine of Dun marchioness dowager of Ailsa 1848 76

97 coffin plate. Adolphus Kennedy d Montrose (yt child of lord Kennedy & Eleanor da of John Allardyce of Dunnottar)

98 lady Augusta Gordon Hallyburton 3.11.1803 8.12.1865

99 cross. hon John Kennedy-Erskine, w Augusta Fitzclarence, s Wm Henry of Dun 1.7.1828 15.9.1870 (by w Cath Kennedy-Erskine)

100 Alex Coulie, w Katren Stevenson 18.12.1672 42; John Jap, w Susanna Coulie 24.12.1692 35; poem

7 DUN

101 Wm Coulie miller, w Agnes Bertie 10.3.1697 55

102 TS John Erskine in Cottran, w Margt Gray 5.3.1702 70

103 David Cob 2.3.1698 75, w Margt Jamson

104 in Latin. Under this stone - - - full bros Alex & Jas; Alex Deas 12.4. 1613, bro Jas 1611, led a pious & honorable life (see also SRO: GD 1/559/1)

105 headstone built into dyke between nos. 21 & 22: Wm Findlow 29.5.1702 72, w Jean Milne; W F, I M, I F

The following are noted in SRO ms GD 1/559/1 and were not seen in 1977:

106 Hellen Machir 1.3.1750 57, chn Jas, Kath & Hellen & - - - - lying by her, h Alex Gearrie

107 cherub; Geo Young, w Jean Wat 4.5.1693 43; shield

108 Jas Edison 1789 80, chn Isobel 28.2.1730 3, David 1730; David Edeson 4.7.17(99), w Elis Edison 4.4.1794, two chn David - - - - ; two cherubs; shield with two ploughs

109 see Notes - SRO GD 1/559/1

Notes

Testaments from the parish of Dun are usually recorded with the Commissariot of St.Andrews - the following is a selection:

Helen Burn spouse to John Hill in Gleskenno, 1681
Alex Erskine of Dun, his spouse Margt Lindsay, 1635
David Erskine in Balylie, 1640
Geo Erskine cottar in Cottraw of Dune, 1596
John Erskine of Dune, 1593
John Erskine in Leys of Dun, 1618
John Erskine minister at Dun, 1621
Alexander Fyfe in Someshill, 1613
Alexander Fyfe in Fordes of Dun, 1617
Catherine Fyfe daughter to umquhile Alex Fyfe in Someshill, 1617
Janet Fyfe spouse to John Hill younger in Balwelo, 1617
Jane Hill widow in Leys of Dun, 1618
Margaret daughter to umquhile Jas Fyfe in Fordes of Dun, 1617
John Hill in Leys of Dun, 1614
John Hill subtenant in Fordyce par of Dun, 1774
John Hill in Bawilo par of Dinmuir, 1617
Robt Hill in Fordes par of Dun, 1617
William Lamb in Leys of Dun, 1617
Andrew Maden in Gleskennoch, 1619
Walter Maden, his relict Margaret Smyth, in Little Fordess, 1619
George Mader in Baluellie, 1674
Andrew Medden in Little Fordes, 1621 & relict Margaret Millar, 1621
Walter Medden in Cottoun of Fordes of Dun, 1614
James Reid in Leys of Dun, 1636
Christian Robertson spouse to John Anderson in Cottoun of Gleskenno, 1614
lieut general Jas Scott of Comistoun, 1747
colonel John Scott of Comiston, 1767
John Shepherd in Hill of Gleskennow, 1662
John Steel in Balwyllie, 1636
James Webster tenant in Leys of Dun, 1762

the following is a selection from the Commissariot Record of Edinburgh:
Richard Allan in Baluelie, 1606
Walter Arnot in Banitie, 1598

7 D U N

David Blewhoise in Somishill, 1591-2
John Blewass in Somishill, 1606
Andrew Carnegie in Banelie, 1596
Katherine Carnegie spouse to Wm Erskine at Myln of Dun, 1578-9
John Erskine of Dun, 1599
Thos Erskine of Quhytfield, 1579
William Erskine of Quhytfield, 1564
John Hill in Forderis, 1602
Alexander Mathew in Fordes, 1600
Katherine Wishart alias Myller spouse to Geo Erskine younger in Coitraw,1592

OPR with the Registrar General: 281 Dun — Births 1642-90, 1701-1854; Marriages 1646-90, 1701-1854; Deaths 1647-75, 1701-48, 1777-93, 1797-8, 1812-54; Kirk Session Minutes 1705-56

SRO Heritors' Records HR 180 minutes 1823 - accounts 1847-1929 etc

GD 1/559/1 in envelope: drawings of tombstones in Old Dun Kirkyard as far as 1860, about 18 elaborate quarto sketches including nos. 13-4, 18, 21-2, 24, 28, 30, 32-3, 49-50, 84-5, 102, 104, 106-8 & also 109 FS (marginal) Margt Beaty 1737 48, h Jas Napar, two chn; IN, MB; IN, IN, AN, IN, DN, CN, RN, MN, WN, AN; her h Jas Napier d 3.10.1771 90; share & coulter

These were deposited in 1970 by C Roy Hudleston FSA, 28 Church Street, Durham.

Andrew Jervise: "Epitaphs & Inscriptions ... in the North East of Scotland" vol i (1875) pp 221-6: some local history with inscriptions 6,13-4, 21, 24-5, 30-2, 35, 48, 50, 94-103; pp 344-5: inscriptions no. 21-2, 46, 51, 104-6; p 388 refers to the Erskines of Dun

Erskines of Dun: "Scottish Nation" ii 144-5
"The Lairds of Dun" (1931) by Violet Jacob
Spalding Club Miscellany v IV (1849) - "Papers from the Charter Chest at Dun 1451-1703"
Northern Notes & Queries vi (1892) pp 50-1 & iv (1890) p 116 - scattered sources of information.

Christison in PSAS 1901-2 refers, with illustrations, to inscriptions 18 & 19.

Fasti v 387 Ministers from 1567

I n d e x

A. 28
Ailsa 95-6
Aitken 54
All - - - 58
Allan Notes
Allardyce 54
Anderson Notes
Arnot Notes

Baillie 55
Beattie, Beaty 36-7.109
Bertie 59.101
Black 34
Blewhoise, Blewass Notes
Brechin, Brichen 3.87
Burgess 1.17
Burn 49-50.Notes

Carnegie 83.Notes
Catenoch 36
Christison 79
Clark 7
Cloudsley 5
Cob 103
Colville 42
Cook 82
Cormack 6
Coul(l)ie/y 25-7.100-1

Cromar	14
Crooks	6
Cruikshanks	23
D.	28
Deas	104
Dempster	93
Donaldson	71
Doors, Dores	29.85
Duncan	83.90
Durie	43
Eadie	15-6
Eaton	89
Edeson, Edison	32.50.108
Edward	85
Erskine	13.24.49.96.102. Notes
Falconer	27
Fife, Fyfe	89. Notes
Findlow	105
Fitzclarence	99
Forbes	39-40.80
Forsyth	28
Fullarton	13
Gearrie	106
Gibson	8
Gleig	75
Goudie	11
Gray	102
Hallyburton	105
Hill	52.73.Notes
J.	29.64
Jack	35
Jamson	103
Jaap,Jap(p)	72.84.100.
Jerves	78
Kennedy	95.97
Kennedy-Erskine	99
Kirkland	56
Knight	79
L.	52
Lamb	Notes
Langson	4
Law	23
Lindsay	33.85.Notes
Low	5.51
Lyall, Lyel(l)	25.47-8.92
M.	29.52
McGregor	2
Machir	106
Mackenzie	86
McNeill	17
McNicol	9
McQuiver	58
Maden	Notes
Mader, see Mather	Notes
Malcolm	9
Mather(s)	35.63
Mathew	Notes
Medden	Notes
Mill	44.61.88
Miller	Notes
Milne	11.64.69.82.105
Mitchel(l)	12.53-6.66.75
Mitchill	55
Moir	81
Morrice	57
Morrison	88
Murray	10.48
Napier	109
Nicol	37.53-5.72
Nor(r)ie	87.90
O.	28
Orkney	72
Paterson	28.31-2
Petrie	88.93
Pickeman	34.59
Pirie	3
Pulkace	91
Reid	65.Notes
Robb	62
Robert	57
Robertson	68
Ross	1.12.15-6.60.Notes
Samsn	4
Scot(t)	4.16.19.74-5.77.Notes
Selby	40-2
Shepherd	Notes
Simson	21
Smith	1.7.18.45.65.92
Soutar	54
Spankie	76
St- -	51
Steel	Notes
Stephen	10
Steuart	24
Stevenson	73.100
Stevin	19
Stool	81
Stott	12
Strachan/en	22.33.47.63.67.91
Stratton	44
Strauchen	33
Tevendale	76
Thomson	43.46.51.63.66-71.84
Valentine	2
W.	47
Walker	30.86
Wat(t)	62.107
Webster	39.Notes
White	10
Wishart	Notes
Wyllie	60
Young	18.107

8 D U N N I C H E N

The parish church was built in 1802 on the older foundation dedicated to St Constantine. The crowded burial ground is well kept.

National Grid reference: NO 510 487

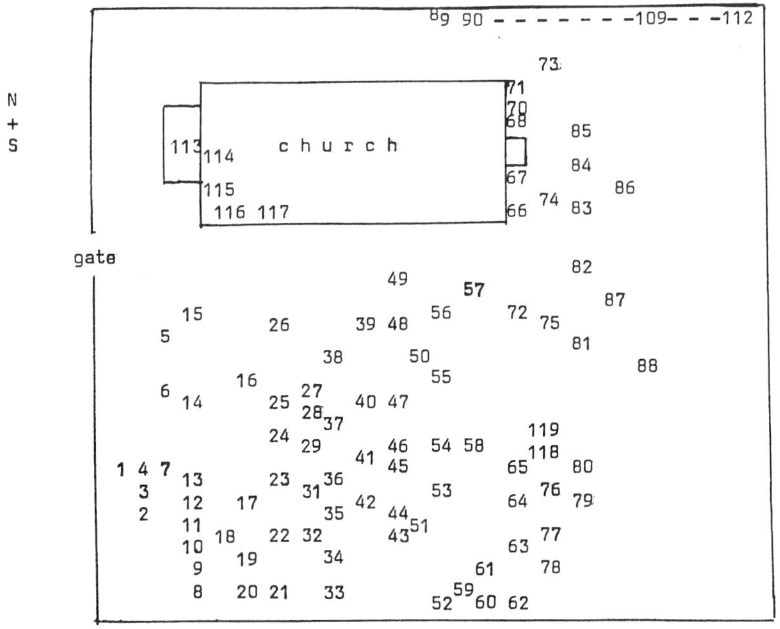

1 1854. by David Dalgity & w Jean Constable, ss d at Cotton of Lownie David 29.3.1834 5, Alex 6.6.1835 1y, Wm 1.4.1837 4w

2 1767. share & coulter; I O, I M; John Ormoand sometime fr in Ground Dod in Woodend 13.1.1757 45 having eleven chn Eliz, Jas, Jean, John, Isabel, David, Alex, Abraham, Thos, Patk & Thos, by w Isabel Mil & 1s John, Jas 2.3.1745 7, Eliz 23.4.1745 2, Thos 11.3.1755 1m; (west side) cherub; A O, I S, 1735; share & coulter; A O, I O, I O, I O, A O, M O, K O, A O; Alex Ormand sometime in Woodend of Dod 2.8.1731 51, w Jean Stevn; 1735 (see Notes - Lowson p 86 has resolved a few doubts in this inscription.)

3 by Robt Smith & Jean Mudie in Kirkden, twin das Barbara & Eliz, chn John, Margt, Barbara, Eliz & Robt; J S, M S, B S, E S, R S; maltman's brush & shovel, merchant's 4 sign with scales, tankard, quaich; (east side) 1748 R S M; two children holding flowers, helmet, emblems (see Notes - Lowson p 99 mentions only chn the twin das Barbara & Eliz & these were not seen in 1975)

4 cherub; David Dalgity - - - Cotton of Lownie, s Wm 26.5.1736 18; David Dalgity 28.2.1760 73; (west side) D D, J -, A -, W D, D D, A D, E D, I D

5 1867. Jas Lackie in Quarterburn 16.9.1855 63, w Margt Milne 12.4.1862, s David 14.7.1835 9m

6 1828. Frederick Thom late fr Craichie 29.1.1828 57, by w Mary Bo(a)th 7.10.1856 75, da Helen 9m, by da Mary; two horses & ploughman in top hat; (west side) da Susan d Forfar 27.2.1889 73 int here

7 1791. Geo Gray in Cotton of Lownie, w Jean Dalgety, s Geo (w Isobel Smith, s Wm 20.5.1789 5), s Wm, s John; (west side) G G, I D

8 1748. P W, M W in shield; M N, G F, M G; I W, E W, P W, A W, AgW, I W, A W, Patk Walace, to wives; poem (see Notes - Lowson p 102 suggests that Patk Wallace, apparently living with his 4th wife, has erected this stone to three previous wives & his children)

9 1867. by And & David Dick imo mrs Eliz Dalgety 19.12.1866 78 (h late And Dick fr Ascurry d Smallburn Carmyllie); above David Dick d by fall of earth at gold diggings New Zealand 31.3.1870 (41) int cem of Greymouth Westland NZ (see inscription no.59 infra)

10 1854. David Warden fr Cotton of Lownie 12.10.1880 81, w Jane Air 27.3.1873 69; to friends

11 ob Alex Warden solicitor Arbroath d Edinburgh 21.8.1874 42; Anne Lyon Robertson 4.12.1940 68 (wid of David W Ferrier); (west side) said David W Ferrier d Cotton of Lounie 15.8.1931 52; Geo Ferrier, wid Anne Warden d there 6.9.1919 69; Anna Air Ferrier d there 8.2.1911 30; (south side) And Warden d there 30.1.1915 66; Jessie Warden d Craichie 6.2.1918 80; Jas Warden d Timaru NZ 6.8.1926 86; (north side) David Warden mert Forfar 30.10.1892 62 int Forfar; Barbara Ferrier d Cotton of Lounie 13.11.1899 57; Wm Warden fr East Craichie 21.1.1900 65; Frank Warden in Cotton of Lounie 23.8.1904 58

12 1801. by David, Geo, Jas, Janet-Betty, fa David Stirling sometime Drummitdhen parish 15.3.179(5) 53 (w Janet Wallace 15.2.179(5) (51), da Jean 25.3.17(8- 23))

13 marble. Jas B Stirling d Letham 5.5.1905 39, w Jane S Cattanach 1.2.1933 65, da Winifred d Learig Trinity 26.8.1966 (h Jas Cleland)

14 John Cattanach 29.8.1914 84, w Mary Stirling 12.11.1914 80, da Ellen 25.1.1879 15, s Chas d Islay Alberta Canada 31.7.1930 76, da Mary 24.4.1943 83, Johanna 3.2.1944 73, Charlotte 6.4.1923 68 (h John Wilkie, USA) chn d inf, da Ellen 17.2.1950 71

15 1794. by Jas & Wm Glen, fa 28.2.1789 93, mo Eliz (Brewer) 31.5.1794 69; (west side) (J G, - -, W G, J G)

16 Geo Gray in Letham 27.1.1868 75, w Mary Stewart 13.11.1868 62, s And 7.1837 16m, s Robt 28.12.1871 27, John d Dundee 22.12.1894 62, Geo d Sydney 6.3.1896 57

17 1848. by John Soutar fr West Lownie, w Agnes Dick 19.4.1848 44, da Eliza 28.2.1835 2y6m, da Margt 10.8.1846 18 (see Inscription no. 19 infra)

18 John Wallace sometime tent Lownie of Dunechin 7.2.1772 (61), by w Margret Jarron & das Kath & Barbara; poem; (west side) 1773. two cherubs, helmet, shield; I W, M I; Io, M, K, B, Jam, M, Jean Wallaces; share & coulter)

19 ob John Soutar fr West Lownie 16.2.1863 74, w Agnes Dick 19.4.1848 44, by family, aunt Barbara Soutar 5.7.1875 87, uncle Thos Soutar 5.7.1878 83, da Agnes lived all her life in this par d Letham 3.3.1917 88; Alex Soutar d Clive House Letham 13.1.1921 76, w Betsy Robertson d there 13.10.

1925 83, yt s Alex D accidentally drowned in Sydney harbour NSW 25.1. 1914 50; Thos Soutar fr Auchrennie 1.9.1868 38

20 by Robt Soutar in Dykehead of Dod, chn Robt 12.5.1740 28, Anne 22.6. 1739 15; (west side) helmet, shield, crown, hammer, anvil, pincers; R S, K S; I S, M S, R S, F S, E S, A S

21 1849. by Geo Nicoll smith Ward of Turin & w Christina Fleming imo Alex Fleming 17.2.1845 81 (w Isabel Ogilvie 2.10.1811 42); Jessie Nicoll 21.7.1918 86

22 1760. W D ; by Wm Duncan, fa David 30.10.1757 73 sometime in Cotton of Lounie, mo Janet Lamb 16.3.1755 51, bro David 10.12.1755 27, sis Margt, bro Jas; (west side) three cherubs; shuttle & stretchers on shield

23 1774. David Espline formerly here d 12.2.1773 53, by wid Agnes Thomson, chn Agnes, Isobel, Helene, Anne, Margt, Jean, Elis; (west side) cherubs, joiner's tools; 1774 D E, A T

24 weeping willow. by Wm Shepherd, fa Jas d Newdyke 24.10.1894 75, mo Helen Davidson 23.8.1898 67

25 1756. W S, (J M); Wm Shepherd 6.10.1748 73 & Alex, Margt, Elspet - - - - - - - - & Jas her chn also Agnes, Eliz & Jas Shepherd - - - - - - - of Dunikan his eldest - - - - - - - Agnes & Cath - - - ; 1750 stretcher & shuttle; A S, M S, J S, W S, A S, M S, E S, J S, A S, S S, - S (Notes - Lowson p 85 whose rendering is: Wm Shepherd 6.7.1748 73, chn Alex, Margt, Elspet, Eliz & Jannet, 1s Wm - - - - - (by - - - - chn Jas, Eliz & Jas) 2s Alex (chn Agnes & Katherine) by w Isobel Moffet & Wm, Alex & Jas his chn)

26 1849. John Tarbat 21.9.1877 68, w Betsy Porter 21.2.1875 65, fa Alex Tarbat 23.1.1848 64, bros Wm 19.9.1836 15, David 15.5.1839 19, Jas 14.8. 1839 33, s Geo 12.7.1905 71

27 by John Peter tent Nether Tullos, w Margt Esplen 11.2.1823 62, chn Jas & Geo D

28 1799. And Maxwell sometime tent Crostown here 26.4.1780, w Jean Eilon 4.4.1799, by ss And & Jas

29 Jas Maxwell millwright Letham 20.10.1871 79, w Rachel Ogilvy d Forfar 23.9.1878 88, by family

30 David Maxwell JP fr d Panlathy mill Carnoustie 16.2.1924 84, w Betsy Ogilvie d there 13.1.1903 63, da Jane d Ascurry Mill 10.6.1875

31 David Maxwell for many yrs gamekeeper Pearsie d Newton Carmyllie 8.10. 1890 69, fa David d Ascurry Mill 5.12.1866 77, mo Helen Gray d there 8.3.1883 89

32 1823. by Alex White fr Drummiterment, fa David sometime manuf there d 23.9.1820 76, mo Jean Smith 20.9.1804 65; Alex White, w Helen Farquhar, s John 16.2.1805 inf; (west side) coat of arms (described by Lowson p 97 in detail)

33 1801. by Wm Ramzay in Drummiterment, w Margrat Lawrence 12.2.1799; WR, ML; W, Ia, Ie, An Ramzays; poem

34 Wm Constable fr Collerward 23.8.1853 46, by w Christina Stewart, chn Wm 14.11.1841 15m, Barbara 4.1.1848 5, Jane 5.1.1848 21m, Alex Ross 27.7.1874 24, Agnes Soutar 1.10.1875 28

35 by Peter Constable 9.6.1961 80, w Lizzie Gownie 19.3.1927 43

36 by Jas Constable junior 10.10.1947 89, w Mary Wilson 4.6.1927 70, da Jessie 21.10.1888 3w, Mary Ann 8.8.1959 77

37 And Constable d Letham 26.6.1936 66, w Jane Lesslie 20.3.1947 76

38 by John Young shoemaker Letham 9.10.1801 28.2.1898, fa John late feuar Létham 15.1.1850 73, mo Mary Young 17.8.1873 84, da Isabella 10.8.1878 23, Jane Ann 5.7.1885 25, w Helen Brand 1.10.1820 7.6.1907, ers John JP registrar here for 40y 25.5.1853 26.5.1933, yt da Helen Brand 19.8. 1864 19.5.1938

39 John Brand late slater Letham 29.9.1845 55, w Elspet Farquhar 30.11. 1870 78, das Jane d Letham 24.5.1887 60, Isabella 9.6.1900 71, by ss Chas & Wm

40 by Wm Brand slater & w Margt Samson, chn Eliz 2.5.1857 23.2.1865, Anne 6.3.1859 5.4.1865, Wm 8.11.1864 12.4.1865, Geo 29.9.1869 21.1.1880

41 ob 1866. Wm Ramsay late manuf Letham 5.10.1863 61, w Jean Lawrence 17.11. 1864 78, s Wm 2.1827 inf, by only surviving s Jas

42 Jas Ramsay 21.12.1868 45, w Mary Laing 13.4.1859 37, s Wm Jas 14.4.1851 5, Wm Jas 10.6.1857 3¼; Jas Laing d Bathurst Africa 5.11.1874 24

43 1757. by Alex Sturrock sometime tent Wester Balgavies & w Helen Binnie, s Alex 18.4.1755 17; poem; loom, AS, IS; "Here lyes a youth ane eldest ..

44 1763. two cherubs; shield with share & coulter; R P, A H; R, A, Io, Ia, E, M, A Peters; IoP,IsN; (east side) 1763. by Robt, John & Jas Peters to fa & mo who lived sometime in Crostoun of Dunnigton viz Agnes Hay 23.8.1733 39, Robt Peter 3.6.1734 56, also chn viz Agnes 11.1730 11, Margt & Agnes d nonage, Robt 6.1782 63; re-erected by Jas Fowlis joiner Letham & w Ann Couper to Robt Duncan late fr Crostoun here 1765 1850; Geo Duncan 1799 1855; Ann Whyte 1786 1863, da Ann Couper; Jas Fowlis, da Margt

45 Henry B Foulis 26.4.1928 85, w Jane Kennedy, da Bella inf

46 1853. And Ramsay 8.2.1850 63, w Isabell Wishart 20.2.1851 68; Jean Ramsay 11.5.1857 74; David Ramsay 9.11.1891 72, w Mary Hird 12.1.1901 72; Alex Ramsay 1.5.1905 79, w Mary Ramsay 9.4.1888 25 (da of David Ramsay)

47 by Wm Fettes manuf West of Lownie, w Harriet Donaldson d Kingsmuir 21.1. 1880 76, s Wm 18.5.1835 3½, da Agnes d America 21.2.1860 27; Wm Fettes 29.9.1861 85; Ann Fettes d Perth 5.12.1874 44

48 1861. by Robt Nicoll 7.8.1861 73, w Jane Ramsay 13.4.1864 79; Agnes Nicoll 7.8.1831 14; Geo 10.1.1840 27; Alex Nicoll mason Letham 7.9. 1896 81, w Betty Gray 18.9.1902 81, da Agnes 22.3.1856 3¾

49 1899. Joseph Nicoll builder Letham d Blair's Road Letham 7.1.1916 69, w Eliz Stevenson 8.3.1899 52, da Mary Jane 8.8.1898 20, s Jas Steven 23.9.1902 27, sapper Geo Robt RE fell in action France 7.12.1917 31 int Ribecourt cem near Cambrai, da Ann 3.11.1942 83; (west side) s Alex 11.8.1928 46 (w Barbara da of Joseph Smith); Alice Lowden Nicoll 8.11. 1968 78

50 Geo Sheriffs d Crachie 7.1.1817 86, w Agnes Esplen 2.1.1817, by s Henry tenant Unthank

51 1860. anchor; David Cant late feuar Letham 17.1.1841 85, w Mary Fair-weather 13.7.1828 66, chn Eliz d Tannadice 1791, Jean 1800 both inf, by s Alex Cant or Kent LLD paymaster in chief RN d London 16.4.1877 83; Isabella Cant 6.11.1879 75

52 by Jas Peter shoemaker Bowriefauld & w Katrine Fyfe, two ss Geo 10.4. 1837 1m & Jas 1.12.1848 6

53 Wm Christie drowned at sea 31.3.1850 33, w Sarah Allan 17.4.1880 57,

s Wm d Calcutta 16.7.1879 34, da Ann d Letham 8.2.1910 63

54 1858. David Allan late manuf Letham 7.12.1851 51, w Mary Young 21.10.1857 49, by chn David, Ann, Mary; David Allan junior 14.1.1868 39

55 1811. by Jas Adam mason Draffen, fa Jas sometime fr Draffen 1.1804 67, mo Isobel Ford 3.1781 36, chn Clement, Isobel & peter int here

56 by mrs Miller in Jamacia (sic), uncle rev Wm Lindsay for 38y pastor congregational church Letham min of Christ & laborious evangelist in many parts of Scotland 24.1.1841 80; (west side) 1845

57 Thos Smith fr Burnside of Tulloes 9.11.1872 66, w Sophia Speed 2.9.1900 74, s John 5.5.1850 6m, s David 14.9.1917 64, s Jas 24.7.1918 59, da Margt 25.11.1921 70

58 John Fairly fr Pikerton d here 30.1.1847, w Mary Langlands 1.6.1840

59 1818. by Alex Dick tent Tulloes & w Elspet Nicol, s Alex 7.3.1817 27, da Agnes 18.3.1862 63; (east side) re-erected by And Dick, fa Alex 12.2.1831 67, da Agnes 18.12.1832 13; Helen Dick 24.3.1835 13; And Dick late fr Ascurry d Smallburn Carmyllie 16.9.1865 80 (see no.9 ante)

60 by Jas Allan feuar Letham, w Margt Duthie 4.12.1804 34, da Elis 1804 inf; (west side) 1823. Jas Allan 20.11.1842 78, by s Wm postmaster Letham

61 David Allan d Drummeterment 20.4.1856 72, w Jean Dorward 20.5.1849 59, by s Jas (nephew David Melville 25.1.1845 5), da Margt 21.10.1877 57

62 leaning on wall. I B, K B, 1750; heart with flame; weaver's stretcher & shuttle; imo the just; blessed the seven and seven left; I B, M B, I B, IB, E B, D B, P B, I B, I B, W B; this stone was sett up by Jas Bouak & Cathren Baisler his spouse indwellers Drumeterment, deceased chn Agnes 28.1.1741 25, Patk 4.8.1745 18, also John & David d in nonage, at this date viz 1750 they have six living Magdalen, Jas, Eliz, Isobel, Jean & Wm ; dart & scythe, skull & bones

63 Peter Boyle late fr Drummieterment 21.9.1847 66, w Isabella Coutie 24.4.1860 63, two das Cathrine d inf, Ann 17.11.1835 15; John Ritchie da Mary 5.1848 inf; (west side) 1894. John Ritchie blacksmith Knowes d there 1.4.1903 82, mo Ann Burns 18.8.1868 79, fa John 17.1.1882 93, w Eliz Boyle 29.7.1894 74, chn Mary, Alex & Wm d inf, s Peter Boyle fr Freelands 22.10.1908 53, s And J fr Knowes 19.5.1924 67

64 by Patk Sturrock in Clocksbrigs, fa Wm tennant Wester Lownie 27.3.1675; 173(1). W S, P S, M W S, A S, P S, I E (see inscription no. 123 infra & Notes, Lowson pp 81-2 adds initials D S, I S, M S to the above & suggests that P S, I E are doubtless for Patk Sturrock & w Isabel Espline)

65 by mrs Pattillo in Craichie Mill, s David (24). 12.1848 (3 or 8)

66 Alex Young bleacher Vinny Den d Letham 23.12.1884 74, w Betsy Morris d Letham 21.5.1894 76, s Geo d London 5.2.1885 39, yt s Chas d London 3.12.1899 39 int here, 1da Mary d Letham 29.1.1914 69 (wid of David C B Adam of Newcastle on Tyne); Agnes Ann White 12.10.1944 82, wid of Chas Morris Young

67 by Alex Young & w Betsy Morris, his fa Jas 11.1816, his mo Ann Allan 3.4.1856, s John 6.2.1859 inf

68 1858. by Jean Farquharson 1.1.18(84), fa Robt Farquharson 27.8.1846 86, mo Eliz Geddes 17.5.18(44)(46), bro Jas 20.2.1823 (3), John 14.10.18(36 36)

69 Jean Japp 10.(8).1839 33; Wm Japp feuar Letham 5.2.1840 61; Jas Japp 22.5.1847 32; Duncan McInroy shoemaker Letham, chn Isabell 18.2.1844 &

Duncan 1.1.1850 both inf; Tibbie Norrie or Japp 8.6.1862 88

70 Wm Japp feuar Letham 13.4.1876 69, w Jane Thornton 15.3.1893 82, 3s Jas 13.11.1864 21, da Barbara 27.11.1927 88, by surviving family

71 Geo Japp late Letham 29.11.1910 65, 1w Annie Sturrock 4.1.1896 52, s David 25.7.1905 31, s Geo slater 9.2.1945 78 (w Annie Balfour 19.1.1939 65), da Annie Sturrock 26.9.1950 72

72 1821. crown, hammer, anvil, square & compasses; Wm Hood smith Bowdiefauld 1.10.1852 89, w Mary Ouchterlony 4.8.1820 68, s Geo 11.11.1861 72 (chn David 4.1825 9m, Rachel 3.1.1856 5m, Jessie 23.1.1875 16, wid Margt McWattie 2.1.1885 82, da Eliz 24.10.1909 67)

73 Jas Scott in Bowriefauld 20.5.1847 46, w Mary Anderson 4.7.1883 79, chn David 7.5.1843 14, Ann 11.6.1843 3, John 17.7.1853 18, Alex 2.3.1872 28, Jas 22.2.1890 58, Wm 29.9.1893 56, Margt 22.5.1894 64

74 Jas Burnett 3.10.1854 44, w Ann Scott 21.12.1886 71, chn Margt & Thos d inf, Thos 1.5.1855 1, s David d Monikie Mill 27.4.1926 79 (w Annie Gray Weir d Monikie Mill 29.9.1926 80)

75 by Jas & David Mordochs, fa Alex Mordoch 8.6.1754 68; (west side) two cherubs; A M, K S, 1755; A M ♡ A B on shield, mantling; Io, Ia, D, E, A, M Mordochs; poem

76 boulder stone. John Gray 1846 1934, w Mary Young 1842 1925, 3s sir Alex Gray CBE LLD 8.1.1882 17.2.1968 (Who's Who: professor of Political Economy, Edinburgh and poet)

77 1837. Wm Gray late feuar Letham 2.2.1837 82, w Helen Nicoll 5.12.1822 63, by das Margt, Helen & Eliz

78 John Young Gray undergraduate Edinburgh University b Hawick 13.4.1903 drowned in Montrose Bay 24.8.1923, mo Mary Ord Gray 20.6.1926

79 by Wm Forbes here & w Elis Miller, chn Elis 1.1790 7m, Chas 1.1792 4m, Ross 3.-.1792 5; (west side) cherub, text.

80 by Agnes Husband 2.12.1905 78, fa Jas Husband 3.1.1843 71, uncle Chas Ochterlonie 20.5.1869 71, mo Agnes Ochterlonie 20.11.1872 80

81 crown, hammer, two pincers above anvil; I O ♡ M S, 1741; A O, M O, H O, T O, I O, M O, I O, I O, I O, A O (ed. 10 chn); (west side) John Ouchterlony sometime hammerman Welltree 9.11.1738 73, w Margt Storock, ten chn And, Mrgret, Hellen, Thos, John, Mettie, Jannet, Isobel, Jas & Adam; above Margt Storock 19.4.1717 47; by And & Adam Ouchterlony, fa Jon & mo Margt Storock

82 1852. And Lawrence 16.2.1831 43, w Ann Miln 23.3.1827 38, by da Isabella C; Geo Hird 28.7.1845 72, w Mary Lawrence 6.12.1846 73, by s Geo & Jas; Jas Hird 28.3.1892 83 (west side) 1885. above Isabella Lawrence d Arbroath 26.12.1856 29 int Arbroath Abbey ground, h Wm Buick, by s John shipmaster

83 by David Cant in Letham, w Margt Taws 18.3.1848 59, s And 8.4.1841, da Margt 7.6.1847 20

84 1848. thistle; Dond Stewart in Letham 17.12.1847 65, w Elis Laing 14.12.1847 59, da Elis 1.6.1837 5, s David 7.4.1844 35, by surviving family; Jas Stewart 1.4.1833 15.12.1913

85 by Jas Hutchison schoolmaster Letham, fa David d Torrygourie 24.8.1823 33, mo Mary Malcolm 7.12.1846 63, bro David 18.10.1823 2, sis Mary 25.4.1831 5, sis Margt 6.4.1842 26, sis Betsy 20.4.1848 26

86 I B, I O; Mary d 10.1856, John, Jas d 29.11.18(47), Chas d 25.12.185(6), Geo d -.11.1789 4m, Robt, Helen, Betty; (west side). 1797. by John Boath tent in West (Lown), fa Jas sometime tent there d 10.6.1791 74

87 urn. Jas Boath late fr Craichie 12.11.1847 62, by w Eliz Hutton 2.12.1891 86, chn Isabel 30.11.1834 5, Jas 20.11.1847 2, John 14.2.1848 15, last surviving ch Ann B 17.11.1901 60

88 1767. by Wm & And Bowman in Drumeterment, fa Wm Reedmaker there 3.2.1764 66, five chn Margt, Hellen, John, Alex, Elspeth; W B, E E; A B, E F; (other side) W B, M S, 1767; D B, M B, W B, I B, M B, H B, I B, A B, A B, E B; restored by And Bowman in Langholm

89 - 112 have been stacked edge to edge along the north wall of the burial ground and in most cases the protected side is exceptionally well preserved:

89 large FS. shield flanked by A M, B D, D M; (marginal) Alex Mill in Murtovn Mil 2.2.16-- -- (see Notes - Lowson has 2.2.1676 32), w Bese Doig (see Notes - Davidson who has Dog in error); emblems

90 1801. by Wm (Steel), w - - - - - - - d 2(8). 3.1793 (2)9y - - - - - - - also s David - - - -

91 1791. Alex Masson sometime shoemaker Craichie 17.1.1790, by w Jean Thomson, only s Alex d inf; (other side inaccessible) cherub, but (see Notes) Lowson mentions shoe, hammer, nippers, cordiner's knife & elshin or awl

92 1752. D S ♡ I L; two cherubs; share & coulter on shield, mantling; emblems; David Steven sometime tent Broadlay 22.5.1751 48, by w Jean Langlands 27.1.1767 66; (on back) 1891. by Rennald Longland, fa sometime tent Craichiemill 24.1.1773 63 & mo Margt Bowman - - - - - 88y, bro - - - - -

93 FS (marginal) by David & Alex Walace, fa John in Ascury 20.11.1720 86, mo Eliz Gardin 22.6.---- 66 both int here (see Notes - Lowson p 105 has both fa & mo d 1725); 1754. I W, D W, A W, - W, -W

94 David Wishart late feuar Letham 23.8.1836 49, by w Eliz Watt

95 1787. John Fairweather tent Burnhead of Bractillo, w Eliz Cowel 1.3. 1788 88, da Jannet 24.6.1771 32, s Robt 8.8.1784 26, three chn Wm, Eliz, & Jane are survivors at this date (1787); John Fairweather 11.11.1789 66 (see Notes - Lowson p 85 has Jannet d 1776)

96 large FS. two cherubs; by Dougal Soutar here, w Eliz Wan & by their chn viz Chas, Eliz, John, Francis & Jean to their mo d 13.12.1743 70 & two chn John & Jas d in nonage; shield with D S ♡ E W, mantling; I S, C S, E S, I S, F S, I S, I S, 1745; axe

97 cherub; shield, mantling; emblems; (other side) loom, 1786, A M, M S; Alex Milne 25.3.1785 30, also May, Alex & May d inf, dedicated by fa Alex wiver & burges Forfar & mo May Stiurrock & surviving (family) And, Margt & May; text

98 FS - - - - - - - ; emblems

99 small, above 98. Geo & Alice Soüter,twin ss Geo & Edw 22.12.1937 inf

100 John Milne 17(75); Margt Sturrock; cherub, torches; shield with open book; 1775, I M, M S; emblems; M M, M M, M M, I M, AM, M M, E M, I M; (other side) I M, 1725, M S; by John Milne weaver Forfar & w Margt Sturrock 19.2.1775 68, s John formerly schoolmaster Aberlemno 20.1. 1774 21

101 FS I B, E D: skull & bones; Iams Boyl (see Notes - Lowson p 73 has John in error) sometyme indvelar in the tulloos 21.10.1648 51, wid Agnes Peter; W B, I B

103 cherub, shield & mantling, emblems; (other side) 1778. And Brown sometime tent Over Tullos of Guynd 19.1.1775 65, w Elspeth Gall 12.2.1776 84, by nephew And Brown tent Over Tullos; poem

102 1816. Geo Wallace - - - - E - - Wallace his spouse - - - - memory of their (fa Peter) Wallace (tent) in (Dunnichen) age (82), s Geo 20.2. in the same year 20m

103 see page 78 ante

104 small. 1746. by Robt Caird in the hilltoun of Dundie, w Bathia Brown 1.2.1744 23; poem, she d in childbirth; cherub, shield; R -, B B, A - (see Lowson p 101)

105 1850. Peter Brown 12.3.1880 74, w Jane Malcolm 26.4.1893 90, s Geo M 12.4.1841 5, da Jean 11.5.1842 3

106 And Hunter for 34y parochial schoolmaster here d Craichie 15.4.1849 74, w Margt Irons, chn Julius Caesar 4.6.1831 2, da Rose 22.12.1832 20, s Edw d Montreal 20.9.1847 28, s Geo Dempster 12.12.1848 31, s And d Edinburgh 17.5.1849 33, da Margt Hunter or Andrew d Dumfries 8.6.1851 29

107 FS (marginal) 

Heir lyes David Gibsone somtyme in Waster Lovnie 24.7.1657 & of his age 80 & (central) poem; Wm Gibson also rests heir; DG; angels trumpeting into ears of skull; A G, I A, E F

108 D M, A B, 1757; by David Mitchel tent Drumn, w Agnes Bennet 1722 27.6. 1756, chn Margt 1739 12.9.1742, Grisal 10.6.1744 1750, Agnes b 18.11. 1746, Isabel b 29.12.1748 9w; two cherubs; D M, A B, (A S) on shield, mantling; emblems

109 1838. by John Douglas imo w, das Ann 28.10.1837 3y8m, Isabel 1.11. 1837 5y7m

110 two cherubs; crown; oval with D F, M S; I E, C F, 1737; poem; (other side) David Findlou, w Margt Storock, da Cathrine 4.11.1736 going in 6y; poem

111 Jas Batchelor 19.2.1889 74, w Agnes Cant, s John 26.8.1853 3m, s Jas 2.12.1861 18, s David 15.4.1894 54 int Arbroath, da Margt (h Alex Cove, s Alex 15.4.1879 6m, da Margt Ann 22.5.1882 5), da Marjory 18.6. 1899 49, da Ann 4.7.1899 56

112 Wm Watt 6.7.1862 80, da Isabella 15.3.1845 14, da Jane 6.12.1852 40, s Geo 12.7.1856 21; by Alex Walker & w Ann Watt

113 portrait in vestry. rev Thos Masson DD min here 1788-1807 (Fasti v 283)

114 mural in church. Jas Whitshed Hawkins b 1797 & w Charlotte Dempster 1808 md 1830 both d 1841 int in one grave in Restennet priory, five chn of whom yt Gertrude Jemima Hawkins Dempster d Edinburgh 26.2.1870 the first of their chn to die

115 next 114. Charlotte Louisa Hawkins Dempster 10.4.1835 8.5.1913

116 mural in church. Jane Fergusson 5.5.1798 int Restenneth 11.5.1798, h John Hamilton Dempster of Polrossie, she was 1da of Chas Fergusson (2s of late sir Jas bart of Kilkerran)

117 mural in church. Jas Whitshed Hawkins & Charlotte Dempster, only s Geo Hawkins Dempster b Dunnichen 4.4.1836 d unm at Nice 2.12.1875 succeeded to the property on the death of his gmo mrs Hawkins Dempster 1.1855, da dame Kath Hawkins Dempster Metcalfe b Dunnichen 7.12.1830 md there on 26.8.1876 d London 17.12.1911 int Restennet priory on 4.1.1912 (h sir Theophilus John Metcalfe bart CB d Paris 8.11.1883)

118 D F, I F on shield; N F, A F, I F, D F; repaired by David Ford tent East Mains Craichie imo w Craford Pullar; farm implements;

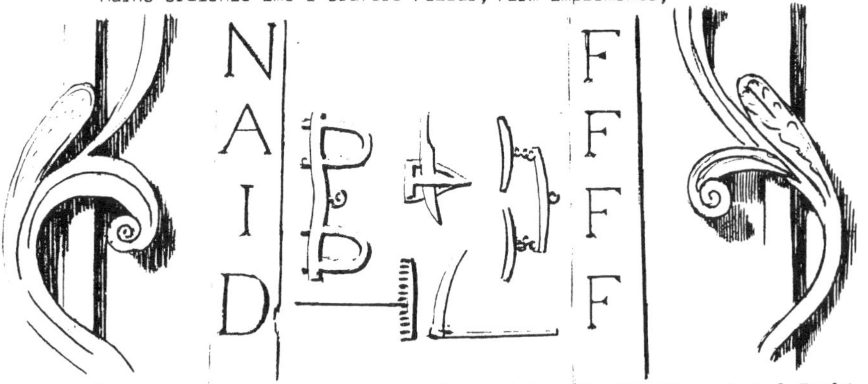

(west side) 1787. David Ford tent Dunnichen 12.1784 72, w Isabel Fauld 11.1783 69, by surviving chn Nicol & Ann, other two chn Isobel 4.1781 38 int here, David mert in Dundee 8.1783 34

119 David Ford, East Mains of Craichie 17.5.1861, w Crawford Pullar 3.6. 1848, by chn

The following are noted by Geo Lawson in the Transactions of Stirling Natural History & Archaeological Society 1920-1, and were not seen in 1975:

120 TS 1720. David Peter in Crache, w Isobel Strock 5.7.(1720) 55; Patk Peter 7.3.1701 7; Isobel Peter; D P, I S in shield; D P, I S; P P, I P; epitaph; emblems; W P, E M: D P, I K

121 John Pullar & w Agnes Soutar - - - 1782; initials of their ten chn

122 (marginal) John Ballo indveller Brodley, w Elis Mvrdo 16.6.1680 34; I B ♡ ♡ E M

123 1731. by Isebel Espline 4.12.1730 56, h Patk Sturrock, imo fa And Espline in East Lounie 1715 70; initials of surnames only E, R, E, E , E, S, S, E, E; (see Lowson:this stone had style identical to no.64 ante)

8 D U N N I C H E N

124 fragment by west wall of ground. 1739. by David Watt, sis Anna

125 small. John Skirling 1695; Agnes Dumbraik 1726; David Skirling 1740; Janet Guthrie 1750; emblems (see Brechin Testaments: Agnes Dumbraick relict of And Deuchar kirk officer at Dunnichen, 1728)

126 small. 1803. D A, D A, I A, A A (Lowson suggest the family of Airs in Cottown of Lownie)

127 1809. And Lawson weaver sometime in Letham 13.3.1807 62 int here, by w Margt Black & chn Jas, John, And, David, Jospeh, Mary, Isabel & Ann

128 rev Jas Headrick 1841 83 authority on geology & agriculture, w Kath M'Beth md 2.9.1804 (see Fasti v 282, Lowson's Forfar Notables pp 80-100 & 273, portrait, Warden's Angus iii 189, The Scottish Nation)

129 TS Thos Esplen in Mossyd of Lour d (1664) 99, w Magdalen (Bruce); shield with (T E, M B)

130 Ham: Dunn junior d Edinburgh 31.8.1790 d Dunhn 7.1.1795 (see Lowson p 100: he was s of a master of works at Dunnichen house)

131 1791. by John Wiseman ; poem

N o t e s

Lowson: this is an article by Geo Lowson LLD vice président of the Stirling Natural History & Archaeological Society at pp 68-108 of the Society's Transactions for 1920-21, "Churchyard Monuments of Dunnichen", reprinted in 1921 as a booklet. It has in full or in part the inscriptions numbered above as 2,3,6-8,18,20,22-3,25,32-3,41,43-4,56,62,64,75,77,79,81,88-9,91,93, 95-6,101,103-4,106-8,110,117-131. Many poems are quoted in full.

Davidson: Mrs Flora Davidson's "Inventory of 17th Century Tombstones in Angus" (1977) pp 25-6 details inscriptions no. 89, 101 & 107.

Dempster: George Dempster of Dunnichen MP founded the village of Letham on his estate in 1788. He was an ardent reformer & died 1818 & like some members of his family was buried at Restennet Priory. See DNB, Scottish Nation.

Fasti v 282: Ministers from 1567

Testaments: the parish came into the Commissariot of Brechin - the following is a small selection:
Alex Garland in Vindiage, 1598;
John Garland in Windeage of Dumbarrow, 1647, his spouse Margt Lamb, 1632
Henry Mudie in Careston, par of Dunnichen, 1622
Thos Ormond in Blairs, 1743
Margt Stewart spouse to Edw Gibson in Auchterlony, 1626
Agnes Sturrock spouse to John Dall sometime in Windiedge, 1668
Alex Sturrock in Draffine, 1647
Edw Sturrock in Draffin & spouse Margt Doun, 1667
John & David sons to Edw Sturrock in Draffine, 1700;
The following were seen in the Commissariot Register of Edinburgh:
Patk Bell late shoemaker in Dunnichen thereafter in Edinburgh, 1762
Jas Ferguson son of the late mr Griffith Ferguson minister of Dunnichen, 1800
Wm Young in Nethertoun of Tullois, spouse Beatrix Kay, 1607;
The following was seen in the Commissariot Register of St.Andrews:
Thos Finlay cotterman in Corstoune, par Dynnichin, 1606

OPR with the Registrar General: 283 Dunnichen
Births 1683-1708, 1747-58, 1760-1854
Marriages 1683-1854
Deaths 1848-55

8 D U N N I C H E N

Church Records in SRO: CH2/108 Dunnichen
CH2/936 Letham chapel
CH3/897 Dunnichen FC DC minutes 1844-94
baptisms 1857-81

Ewing ii 156: FC ministers from 1843

I n d e x

A.	107
Adam	55.66
Allan	53-4.60-1.67
Air	10.126
Anderson	73
Andrew	106
B.	75.86
Baisler	62
Balfour	71
Ballo	122
Batchelor	111
Bell	Notes
Bennet	108
Binnie	43
Black	127
Boath	6.86-7
Bouak	62
Bowman	88.92
Boyl(e)	63.101
Brand	38-40
Brewer	15
Brown	103-5
Bruce	129
Buick	82
Burnett	74
Burns	63
Caird	104
Cant	51.83.111
Cattanach	13-4
Christie	53
Cleland	13
Constable	1.34-7
Couper	44
Coutie	63
Cove	111
Cowel	95
D.	101
Dalgety	7.9
Dalgity	1.4
Dall	Notes
Davidson	24
Dempster	114-7. Notes
Deuchar	125
Dick	9.17.19.59
Doig	89
Donaldson	47
Dorward	61
Douglas	109
Doun	Notes
Dumbraik	125
Duncan	22.44
Dunn	130
Duthie	60
E.	88.110
Eilon	28
Esplen(e),	27.50.129
Espline	23.123
F.	8.88.107
Fairly	58
Fairweather	51.95
Farquhar	32.39
Farquharson	68
Fauld	118
Ferguson	Notes
Fergusson	116
Ferrier	11
Fettes	47
Findlou	110
Finlay	Notes
Fleming	21
Forbes	79
Ford	55.116-9
Foulis, Fowlis	44-5
Fyfe	52
G.	8
Gall	103
Gardin	93
Garland	Notes
Geddes	68
Gibson	107. Notes
Glen	15
Gownie	35
Gray	7.16.31.48.76-8
Guthrie	125
Hawkins	114.117
Hay	44
Headrick	128
Hird	46.82
Hood	72
Hunter	106
Husband	80
Hutchison	85
Hutton	87
Irons	106

Japp 69-71
Jarron 18

K. 120
Kay Notes
Kennedy 45
Kent 51

Lackie 5
Laing 42.84
Lamb 22. Notes
Langlands 58.92
Lawrence 33.41.82
Lawson 127
Lesslie 37
Lindsay 56
Longland 92

M. 120
M'Beth 128
McInroy 69
McWattie 72
Malcolm 85.105
Masson 91.113
Maxwell 28-31
Melville 61
Metcalfe 117
Mil(l) 2.89
Miller 56.79
Miln(e) 5.82.97.100
Mitchel 108
Moffet 25
Mordoch 75
Morris 66-7
Mudie 3.Notes
Murdo 122
Murdoch, see Mordoch

N. 8
Nicol(l) 21.48-9.59.77
Norrie 69

O. 86
Ochterlonie 80
Ogilvie/y 21.29-30
Ord 78
Ormand, Ormond 2.Notes
Ouchterlony 72.80-1

Pattillo 65
Peter 27.44.52.101.120
Porter 26
Pullar 118-9.121

Ramsay 33.41-2.46.48
Ritchie 63
Robertson 11.19

S. 20.88
Samson 40
Scott 73-4
Shepherd 24-5
Sheriffs 50
Skirling 125
Smith 3.7.32.49.57
Soutar, Souter 17.19-20.96.99.121
Speed 57
Steel 90
Stev(e)n 2.92
Stevenson 49
Stewart 16.34.84
Stirling 12-4
St(o)rock 81.110.120
Sturrock 43.64.71.97.100.123.Notes

Tarbat 26
Taws 83
Thom 6
Thomson 23.91
Thornton 70

W. 8
Walker 112
Wallace 8.12.18.93.102
Wan 96
Warden 10-1
Watt 94.112.124
Weir 74
White 32.66
Whyte 44
Wilkie 14
Wilson 36
Wiseman 131
Wishart 46.94

Young 38.54.66-7.76.Notes

9 EASSIE

The ancient church of Eassie, now roofless, was dedicated to St.Fergus. It stands on a high grassy knoll in its well-kept burial ground. In the SE corner of the ruin is an early Christian cross in the protection of the Dept of the environment.

The parishes of Eassie and Nevay were united on 21.3.1600

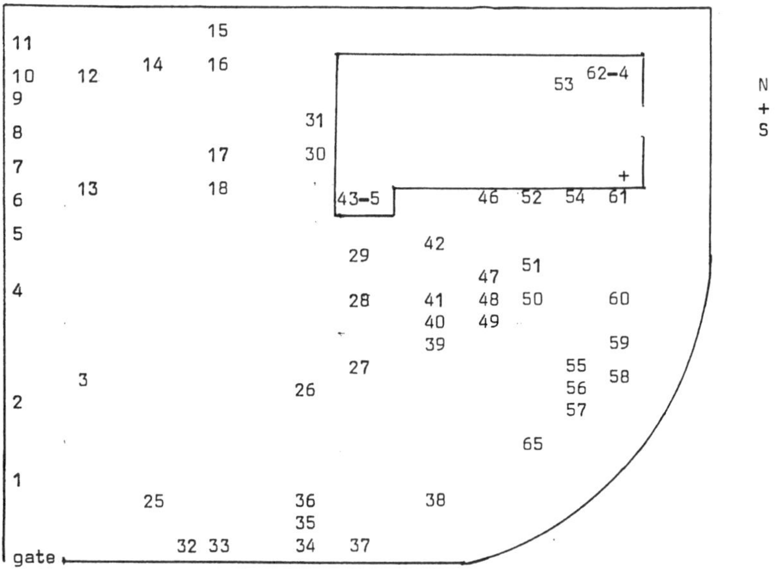

1 1846. Wm Forrester esq d Essie 27.7.1844, s of rev Jas min of Kilrenny Fife (see Fasti v 214: Wm b 25.10.1787)

2 A M ♡ I D; I M, I M ; And (<u>Mee</u>), w Jean Donaldson (by her niece); 1722

3 1773. John Young 2.3.1772 6(<u>1</u>) & w Elspat Ker 12.3.1772 68 lived some time in Castleton in par of Easie, by chn John, Joseph, Thos & Euphemia; (west side) cherub, shield with square & compasses; J Y, E C; emblems; I Y, I Y, T Y, E Y

4 cherub; by Alex Gibb in Kerrymuir, fa Wm sometime indweller Balkyrie 22.8.1730 80; Isobel Gibb 17.3.1737 55, h Wm Henderson in Englstoun; (west side) W G, 1737; epitaph, emblems

5 1857. by Wm Whamond in Balgownie Mill 26.10.1878 76, w Margt Clarke 20.3.1880 75, chn Jean 21.5.1840 3, Wm 31.5.1840 9m, Ann 28.6.1843 8, Joseph 6.3.1870 40, gs David 16.3.1859 6, gs Wm 18.7.1879 24

6 1834. by Geo Souter & w Ann Whyte, s Geo 30.12.1832 9m

7 Wm Watson 15.4.1923 77, 1w Margt Sydie 21.1.1877 33, 2w Jane Johnston 24.8.1929 80

8 John Watson smith Balkearrie 27.4.1905 86, w Ann Smith 23.6.1862, da Jemima 17.9.1854 7m

9 John Watson blacksmith Balkerrie 16.6.1957 81, w Jane Mitchell d there 29.1.1928 55

9 E A S S I E

10 Chas Watson blacksmith Eassie d there 10.1847 67, w Isabella Thomson 1.10.1835 48, s David 28.2.1817 4, s Robt 15.7.1822 2

11 1853. David Halkett esq late tent Dunkenny in Eassie par 4.12.1850 60, w Cath Guild d Edinburgh 28.7.1896 89, s Robt 4.2.1843 1, da Joanna Eliza 9.9.1848 8. s Patk d London 19.10.1886 49, da Cath 19.4.1901 56, da Isabella 10.2.1842 7.4.1920 (wid of John Halkett of Gualaquay Argentine Republic) da Helen Mackay 9.8.1835 23.1.1926, da Mary Jane 6.5.1846 23.7.1928

12 FS Janit Inchik spous to Wm Shiphart 1652; W S, I I; bare shield; emblems; (see St.Andrews Testaments: Agnes Craig sometime spouse to John Incheak ploughman to Jas Haliburton, of Kirktoun of Essie, 14.1.1600)

13 cross. 1866. by Chas Fairweather, w Bettsy Stewart 19.1.1845 31, s Jas 22.6.1858 18

14 T G, A M; text; emblems; (west side) cherub; 1734; shield with weaver's shuttle & stretcher; by And Gray weaver Longcot Town & w Mafgt Hardy & his sis (Je)an Gray, to fa Thos 7.5.1705 (54) & mo Anne Millar 23.1. 1733 75

15 by Margt Wilson, mrs John Sutar tent Balkirrie int 10.7.1825 80; 1828

16 by Wm Gall smith Balkirrie & w Agnes Hendry, s David 23.7.1826 8m; 1828

17 1801. by Wm Gall tuner smith in Pondfold, w Jean Farquharson 19.3.1801 30; (west side) cherub; crown & horseshoe

18 1790. by Alex Wilson in Englston, w Jean Rae 18.9.1781 69; (west side) shield with A W, J R

19 TS cherub; tailor's goose & scissors; 1756; emblems; by Thos, Archd & Agnes, to fa John Lyon 59y & mo Agnes Stei(l) 57y; T A, A L

20 TS two cherubs; shield; mantling; I F, I S; I F, D F, M F, A F, I F; open book with text; epitaph; (marginal) dedicated by Ioda & Alex Fullertons to fay^{r} Iam(es) Fullerton who having lived in ye Dungeon d 12.5.1711 42

21 TS W F, M(B); shield; by - - - - - tent in - - - - , w Margt Badenoch 10. 8.1780 (3)2, three ss, four das; (central) Kathrine, Jas, David, Geo, Jannet, Agnes & Eliz Fullertons; emblems

22 heir lyes Margret (Hay); Wwhom suppos is did this / this - - littl mon - - - / to stand up to hir - - - / somtim tho - in lived / into the house of Surewall and she loved our - - - who dron the best gal / departed this lif 1714"

23 by Alex Luke, mo Janet Duncan (1714), (chn John & Cirston Lukes)

24 A E 1747 K L ; emblems; text

25 Peter Roy fr Mains of Condie 23.6.1808 52 int Pathstruie, w Margt Robertson d Castleton 29.11.1849 83 int here

26 A A 1763 M M; (west side) two cherubs, star, loom; by - - - - - - - - - Allan - - - - sometime - - - - - -

27 1774. by Patk Ramsay in Englston, w Elspet Edward 1767, s David 1772, Patk 1770, Jannet 1748; (west side) cherub; emblems; shield; P R, E E; A R, D R, P R, J R, J R

28 Jas Barnet in Gatfold, s Jams 1714 7; (west side) 1718; I B, M R

29 TS (marginal) John Huntar somtyme induallez in Castleton 11.12.1693 71, w Eliz Jeali; shield with hunting horn; J H, E J, A N; by s And

30 FS (marginal) Tomas Hendri, w Girsel Tomson (15).12.1636 58; skull

31 TS tipped up. imo David Wightman - - - - - das viz - - - - - cherubs. (see Notes - Jervise "Epitaphs i 68: David Wightoun 1717 75)

32 1854. by David Grant & Betty Loudin 10.9.1879 62, chn Mary Ann 25.7.1851 4y9m, Wm 4.8.1851 3

33 1775. by Thos Piddy & w Elis Robertson, s David 22.10.1774 19; T P, E R

34 J T, J T; 1795. by Jas Thain tunier Balkirrie & Isabel Farquharson, s Jas 29.8.1787 11.8.1793

35 Robt Thain fr Bow of Ballinshoe par Kirriemuir b Balkirrie in united par Eassie & Nevay 22.11.1764 d 15.8.1836 int here 18.8.1836, by w Ann Mathew, two ss Thos & Jas; Matthew Thain proprietor Arthurbank & Sodmire in par Coupar Angus

36 by Alex Thain of Arthurbank, fa Jas late fr Balkirrie d Dragonhall 2.8.1811 68y5m, mo Isabella Farquharson d Dragonhall 17.4.1822 55y11m, bro David late fr Woodhead 9.11.1850 57y11m, niece Isabella Petrie d Arthurbank 3.10.1866 50

37 1771. by David Balharry, fa Jas 1770, mo Janet Nicol 1768; J B, J N

38 D T, I A; crown & hammer; (west side) John Anderson 8.3.1729 73, w Janet Kidd 8.5.1726 56

39 1828. by John Chaplin late fr Fofearty & w Margt Sinclair, only s Geo 27.5.1827; John Chaplin many y fr Fofarty & latterly for a considerable period in Cartershaugh d 7.8.1844 82 in 36th y of office as an elder in the KS of Kinnettles, tribute by wid "a sober, inoffensive, peaceable, pious & respectable man"

40 1767. by John & Jas Shingars to fa John 24.6.1762 76, mo Janet Gray 24.1.1763 72 leaving 5 chn

41 FS Ieames Crichtone sometime in the Hatone of Essie 3.5.1683 57, w Euphane Broune; emblems

42 TS (marginal) honest woman caled Janit Thomson 30.3.1652 6(2), w of Thos Mil in Haltoune of Esie; blank shield; emblems; T M, I T

43 Chas Laing mert London, 3s Chas Alex b Eltham near London 27.7.1808 d Newtyle 2.2.1847 (gs of And Dalgairns in Ingliston) sis Eliz b Ingliston 9.5.1803 d Edinburgh 28.2.1854

44 col Jas Dalgairns in HM Indian Madras army 30.12.1786 5.11.1875, sis Charlotte 7.12.1790 6.9.1877

45 And Dalgairns d Ingliston 4.2.1840 54 gifted with talents which qualified him for the more provincial posts of society, devoted himself in accordance with a revered fa's wishes to the peaceful pursuits of agriculture, wid Mary 6.11.1865 (da of the late Chas Greenhill esq)

46 cherub; 1797. Peter Low sometime tent Ascurry d 7.8.1797 62, chn And, Jno, Peter & Eliz, by s Peter fr Ascurry (& his w Eve Stubbles); monogram P L & E S; square & compasses, plough and heart

47 FS Jas Hostler d in Newmill 3.7.1667 63, w Isobel Strachan

48 TS (marginal) by And Hostler & Kathren Hill tents in (Dwniinil), their two das Jannet 11.3.1776 22 & Isobel 10.1780 23; shield with share & coulter, ox yoke; A(H), K H

49 TS 1801. by Jas Fenton tent Eassie, w Agnes Badenach 18.5.1800 58, six ss Jas inf, Alex, Jas, John, Peter & Wm & five das Cath, Isobel, Margt, Agnes & Betty

50 John Oastler d Ingliston 19.2.1921 90, w Jane Watson 6.8.1910 61, s Jas d Ingliston 12.2.1902 22, s rev John Watson min Forteviot d there 30.12.

1916 35 int there, Alex Smith d Vancouver BC 5.12.1953 69 (see Fasti v 213)

51 replaces a stone erected in 1894. Jas Oastler joiner Ingliston 23.6.1894 89, w Ann Roger 28.9.1887 93, s David inf, gchn Maggie Oastler 22.2. 1869 2, Mary Soutar Michie 12.4.1888 1, s Wm d Kobe Japan 22.9.1893 50, by family

52 FS tipped up. (marginal) Patk Chrystie 27.11.1650, w Agnes Jameson; (central) blank shield; P C, A I; emblems

53 pillar & urn. 1877. rev David Lindsay 33y min here b 19.5.1807 d 19.5.1877, w Janet Gow 7.3.1822 17.12.1889, s Robt Archd SSC Edinburgh 22.5.1861 29.6.1938 (w Christina Ann 18.4.1875 8.4.1944), Alex 19.5.1857 20.9. 1922 int Grange cem Edinburgh, Jas Aynsworth 31.1.1863 19.10.1928 int Liberton cem Edinburgh, David 30.6.1853 18.7.1938 int Grange cem Edinburgh, And Gow 13.3.1855 30.12.1939 at Eassie Sandyhills, s b & d 21.5. 1849, Jane Anne 7.9.1847 15.10.1854, Barbara Bruce 12.5.1850 5.11.1854, Marion Eliza Loudon 21.9.1851 11.4.1867, John Lawrenson Gow 21.5.1859 11.11.1868, Frederick 1.2.1868 12.11.1868, Janet Scott 22.2.1846 24.3. 1918 (see Fasti v 260)

54 large slab tipped against church wall. crown & hammer; 1649; A L, D L, B L

55 TS by Wm Osler & Ann Sharp, chn Ann & And who d 1786, Jean, Su, Wm, Alex, El, Ja Oslers all surviving 1786; emblems; share & coulter

56 Wm Ostler late of Murley Well d at Forfar 19.9.1872 71, tribute by wid Marjory Thain d Forfar 16.3.1876 76

57 by Wm Ostler & Marjory Thain late tents Murley Well, his fa Robt 2(1). 5.1827 61, his mo Janet Ostler 15.9.1833 55, his cousin David Ostler 15.1.1866 71

58 1861. Jas Hutcheson 3.1830 66, w Margt Lawson 2.1859 92, da Jannet 11. 1834 31, s Wm d Boston USA 3.1860 56, by family

59 1805. John Doig sometime wright Moor of Eassie, wid Jannet Dixon 22.6. 1804 38, leaving chn Nellie, Mary, Isobel & John; Jannet & David d nonage; (west side) cherub; 1805; J D, J D; square & compasses

60 FS bevelled edge. (marginal) by Margret Nicol/in Castleton imo her h Geo Ramsay who/died 10.4.1730 (3)2y; (central) shield with ox-yoke, share & coulter, M N, 1743; cherubs; J R, A R, A R, M R, W R, D R, T R, E R; And, Jas, (Alex), - - - , David, - - - - & - - - -

61 large slab tipped against church wall. J K; emblems; And Kea in the Englishtown of Essie, s Johne 14.12.1689 17; A K, I B, I K

62 broken fragment. (marginal) - - - - - 26 die mensis RIS FOL - - - - - - - - -; emblems

63 rev Adam Davidson min in the united parishes ord 24.12.1702 d 24.10. 1720 41 (see Fasti v 260)

64 in Latin. rev mr Alex Finlayson ord 20.9.1721 d 12.9.1731 40 (see Fasti v 260 has: ordained 23.8.1721; St Andrews Testaments appendix); shield with boar's head erased, two stars, lion; cherubs; emblems

65 cherub; by Jas Walls, fa John in Drum of Eassie 1.1.1737 68, w Janet Porter, s John 10.6.1708, das Agnes & Helen

9 E A S S I E

A previous recording of 1970 listed the following which were not seen in 1975:

66 Jas Stewart sometime tent at Newmill here 15.5.1837 65

67 by Jas Thomson & Euphemia Young, ss John 1770 & Thos

The following are recorded by Jervise "Epitaphs ...." i 68 and were not seen in 1975:

68 arms of Lamy & Forbes in ruins of the old church; John Lamee sometime of Dunkenny (Jervise notes that "the present laird" capt L'Amy was son of Jas L'Amy sheriff depute of Forfar who d 1854)

69 Thos White 1665; poem

70 1774. D Chisholm's mother

N o t e s

Testaments: the following is a selection from the Record of the Commissariot of St.Andrews:

David Bellie in Kirktoun, 1625; Grisall Bellie in Balgonnie, 1687
John Blair in Balkerie, 1615
Agnes Kerr spouse to Wm Watson in Balkirrie, 1617
mr John Lammie of Dunkenny, 1707
Andrew Ostlar in Inglishtoun, 1687
Thos Ramsay in Inglistoun, 1616
John Stewart at the Bridgend of Dunkeny, 1621
Geo Strachan in Cottoun of Inglistoune par Kinnettils, 1626

the following is a selection from the Record of the Commissariot of Edinburgh:

Margaret Broun spouse to umquhile Robt Kinneir in the Haltoun of Esse, 1582
Elspeth Christie, 1577 spouse to Andro Butschart in Castleton, 1597
Margt Currour spouse to Jas Osler at Newmylne of Esse, 1590
Helen Farar spouse to Robt Ker in Inglistoun-Essie, 1577
Helen Jack sometime spouse to Jas Osler at Newmylne, 1577
Elspeth Jack alias Anderson sometime spouse to Henry Louk in Cassiltoun,1577
Margt Melville relict of mr Sylvester Lamy minister at Eassie, 1732
Bessie Young spouse to Alex Wrycht in Dunkany, 1602
Margt Spottiswood relict of Geo Hereis of Eassie,indweller in Edinburgh, 161

OPR with the Registrar General: 284 Eassie & Nevay

Births	1728-1854
Marriages	1728-68, 1777-1813, 1837-54
Deaths	nil

SRO CH2/495 Eassie & Nevay church records
minutes & accounts 1721-59, 1802-06, 1829-41
accounts 1721-25, 1815-76
minutes 1841-1929
Church roll 1878-1906 proclamations 1873-1942

Fasti v 259 Eassie ministers from 1576 - the parish was united with Nevay 1600

SRO RH 16/1 D C Thomson "Genealogical chart of Jas Osler of Castleton of Eassie with Notes on Fentons, Spences, Eassons, Sinclairs & Coupers" (1924)

Davidson: "Inventory of 17th Century Tombstone Inscriptions in Angus" (1977) describes inscriptions nos. 12, 29-30, 41-2, 47, 52, 54 & 61

Alan Reid: "Royal Burgh of Forfar" (1902) notes the unmarked grave at Eassie of rev Jas Headrick 1841 82 (see Dunnichen inscription no 128)

9 E A S S I E

I n d e x

A.	19.26
Allan	26
Anderson	38.Notes
B.	61
Badenoch	21.49
Balharry	37
Barnet	28
Bellie	Notes
Blair	Notes
Broun(e)	41.Notes
Butschart	Notes
Chaplin	39
Chisholm	70
Chrystie	52.Notes
Clarke	5
Couper	Notes
Craig	Notes
Crichtone	41
Currour	Notes
Dalgairns	43-5
Davidson	63
Dixon	59
Doig	59
Donaldson	2
Duncan	23
E.	24
Easson	Notes
Edward	27
Fairweather	13
Farar	Notes
Farquharson	17.34.36
Fenton	49.Notes
Finlayson	64
Forbes	68
Forrester	1
Fullerton	20-1
Gall	16-7
Gibb	4
Gow	53
Grant	32
Gray	14.40
Greenhill	45
Guild	11
Haliburton	12
Halkett	11
Hardy	14
Hay	22
Headrick	Notes
Henderson	4
Hendry	16.30
Hereis	Notes
Hill	46
Hostler, see Ostler 47-8	
Huntar	29
Hutcheson	58
Inchik	12
Jack	Notes
Jameson	52
Jeali	29
Johnston	7
Kea	61
Ker(r)	3.Notes
Kidd	38
Kinneir	Notes
L.	24.54
Laing	43
Lammie, L'Amy	68.Notes
Lawson	58
Lindsay	53
Loudin	32
Louk, see Luke	
Low	46
Luke	23.Notes
Lyon	19
M.	22.26
Mathew	35
Mee	2
Melville	Notes
Michie	51
Mil	42
Millar	14
Mitchell	9
N.	29
Nicol	37.60
Oastler, Osler, Ostler, Hostler	47-8.50-1.55-7.Notes
Petrie	36
Piddy	33
Porter	65
R.	28
Rae	18
Ramsay	27.60.Notes
Robertson	25.33
Roger	51
Roy	25
S.	20
Sharp	55
Shingar	40
Shiphart	12
Sinclair	39.Notes
Smith	8
Souter	6.15
Spence	Notes
Spottiswood	Notes
Steil	19

9 E A S S I E

I n d e x

Stewart 13.66.Notes
Strachan 47.Notes
Stubbles 46
Sutar, see Souter 15
Sydie 7

T. 38
Thain 34-6.56-7
T(h)omson 10.30.42.67

Walls 65
Watson 7-10.50.Notes
Whamond 5
White, Whyte 6.69
Wightman 31
Wightoun 31
Wilson 15.18
Wrycht Notes

Young 3.67.Notes

10a E D Z E L L

The ruin of the pre-reformation parish church dedicated to St.Lawrence is 1 mile west of the church built in 1818 in Edzell (previously called Slateford). The burying ground remains in use to this day and is well kept.

National Grid reference: NO 583 687

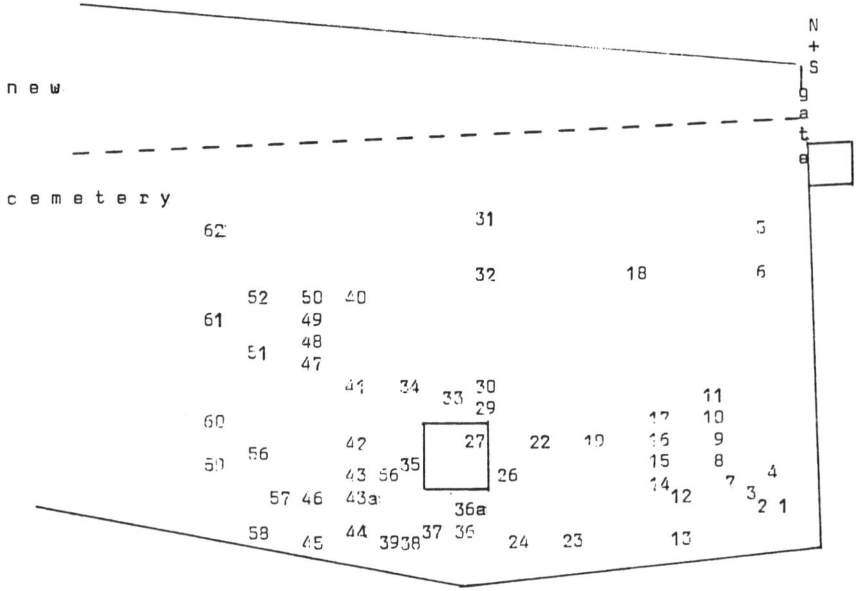

1 Geo Ferrier for 38y faithful servant of late rev Robt Inglis of Edzell, w Isobel Tindal b here 31.10.1821 d Montrose 2.4.1899 int here, yt da Eliz 17.10.1917 59 (s Robt 12th royal Scots killed in action 1.11.1917 36); by family of rev Robt Inglis

2 David Machir miller Mill of Invereskandy, w Margt Taylor 28.2.1751 48; (west side) D M, M T; I M, I M, K M, I M, E M; reversed torches; shield

with scales, two miller's picks and axe; helmet; mantling

3 John Smith feuar Edzell 5.2.1886 55, w Mary 26.6.1870 71 (da of John Will wright Slateford & Ann 7.2.1827 73 who was da of Jas Easton wright in Slateford), s Jas 26.3.1898 63; rest of that worthy family viz Isabell, Alex & Jas Easton all d in bloom of youth & lie here with their Fathers

4 Jas Caithness tent Duryhill & church elder 29.4.1830 63, w Jean Robertson 2.1.1859 85, s Jas & da Helen d early youth, Isobel 27.1.1832 18, s John 3.1837 28, s And 11.1848 44

5 Geo Cooper mert Slateford 29.11.1831 82y4m, w Jean Lindsay 19.4.1841 90, chn Geo 7.7.1800 21, Margt 22.5.1806 25, David 4.1.1818 40, Mary 12.6.1841 56, Jas 8.7.1881 90 (see Jervise "Epitaphs ...i"has Jane Lindsay in error, Geo Cooper left legacies)

6 David Low sometime tent Sandihillock 24.3.1748 35; (west side) by w Isobel Nedry; shield with D L, I N, share & coulter (see St Andrews Testaments: David Low tenant in Sandyhillock, 17.8.1748)

7 David Ogg baker Lau-Kirk (Laurencekirk) 1.8.1835 32, by w Eliz Craik

8 Jas Christison late tent Holmhead 10.12.1754 43, s Jas 2.2.1768 16, by w Margt Wallace; I C, M W, I C, A C

9 David Christison 1743 58, Jean Adam 26.9.1742 47, & their bairns Jean, (Alex) & John; angel & heart; potted flowers (Similar style to Menmuir no.3, Lethnot no.13, Stracathro nos.13 & 26, Newdosk no.15)

10 by David Archibald in Edzell, fa Joseph 25.10.1857 80, mo Janet Mitchell 27.8.1858 74, s Wm 18.3.1825 1½m, Joseph 22.10.1841 19, John 2.2.1850 33, Benjamin 17.2.1855 26

11 David Archibald mert here 25.7.1892 71, w Margt Caithness 9.2.1888 73

12 David Bertie miller Mill of Dalbog, s Chas 1.4.1757 19; (west side) D B, E K; E B, C B, A B, W B, H B, M B; shield with scales, axe & miller's picks; mantling

13 by Wm Willock, fa John late fr Bonfarry 4.1.1827 59, sis Ann 15.7.1821 9y

14 John High d Westhaugh here 17.6.1850 36, by w Ann Donald

15 Jas Low wright Arnhall 1854 77, sis Jane 1832 57, by da & family

16 David Low tent Meikle Tullo 25.5.1852 78, w Jean Jolly 15.3.1861 83, da Agnes 9.4.1814 1y3m, s John 27.12.1864 56, da Margt 30.1.1892 76, da Jean 31.1.1892 74 (see Jervise "Epitaphs i ": David was the last life-renter & occupant of his name in Meikle Tullo; John & Jas Low in Meikle Tullo in 1729 were like almost every tenant in the district found to be in arrears of rent to the York Buildings Co.; probably rev Geo Low of Birsay was of this race)

17 John Low late feuar Edzell village 21.1.1856 74, w Janet Jolly 15.8.

1868 86, s David 4.1.1893 76 at Mill of Balrownie

18 1870. John Jackson 25.7.1874 74, w Isabella Ley 16.4.1885 87, s Jas 14.5.1837 4½, chn And 13.12.1866 42 (s Chas 9.4.1869 3½, w Cath Law 31.3.1898 63), Hugh 15.9.1867 24, Chas 2.8.1868 34, Robt 25.4.1863 32, Wm 24.7.1887 49; Wm Jackson joiner here 2.9.1919 56, w Jean Sim Carnegie 17.9.1962 96

19 by ElizaThomson 11.4.1924 86, fa David Thomson 13.1.1844 52, mo Mary Taylor 24.1.1876 69

20 1880. Wm Cooper feuar here d Brechin 13.10.1880 79, w Eliz Mitchell 2.5.1878 71, da Eliz 19.9.1864 22, s Jas inf, da Jessie 6.10.1912 67, da Agnes 21.2.1915 67

21 Jas Caithness fr Blackhills Lochlee 3.4.1886 87, w Helen Grant 28.1.1884 75, da Mary 10.4.1848 9, s Jas 21.1.1932 88

22 David Caithness in Woodside of Hillock 4.5.1891 84, w Martha Duke 26.10.1899 84, da Agnes 13.1.1847 14, s David 4.7.1874 33, s Jas Ross 12.12.1852 6, s Wm Gold 27.11.1890 34, da Jane 12.11.1899 64, s John 6.3.1921 68, da Mary 21.1.1924 85, da Jessie Gold 6.1.1937 86, da Ann 9.4.1937 88

23 by David Smart tent Green Burn, w Jannet Christison 1740 36, da Anna 30.8.1756 18; John, David, Mary & Jean Smarts d inf; (west side) D S, M M, A S / J S, D S, E S, M S; shield with bird on tree

24 Jas Low late tent Shanno 11.9.1854 82, w Agnes Christison 18.2.1880 90, s Jas 12.2.1881 55, ss David & John inf, s Alex d Lawton Inverkeilor 3.12.1891 62

25 John Jolly 21.1.1877 57, w Mary Low 26.9.1913 90, s Jas 23.7.1941 81 (w Georgina Archer 17.10.1920) chn Agnes & Benjamin d inf, Mary Jane 21.12.1896 35; Robina Jolly 12.4.1942; Eliz Jolly 14.12.1944

26 1839. by Chas Strachan of Southampton Island of Jamaica, mo Eliz Smart 6.3.1831 81, fa Chas late tent Green-Cairn, bro David 17.11.1815 38

27 TS (marginal) Thos Don of Dalbog 1672 & w Agnes Steuard 1686, da Eliz 1661; (central) T D, A S, E D; poem (quoted by Reid PSAS xlix 295); in veneration by lineal descendants Wm Gerard Don, London; Jas Don, Brechin; & David Don, Natal in 11.1903

28 part of stone in vault. 20.8.1711

29 1831. Alex Robie tent Mill of Inveriscandy 20.3.1830 68, w Ann Lindsay 12.3.1845 75, 1s Jas 30.8.1881 79

30 John Milne fr Hole of Slateford 4.3.1863 83, fa Jas 1781 36, mo Eliz Carnegie 1844 94, w Jean Hood 8.11.1790 19.4.1875

31 Jas Duke tent Colmellie 18.5.1869 75, w Martha Edward, da Agnes, s David, by surviving family Wm, Edward & Helen

32 Richd Alexander fr Cowiehill 27.6.1868 85, w Eliz Gray 30.11.1850 66, gda Eliz G Alexander 9.2.1867 15, s John 12.7.1888 77, da Jean 3.4.1892 75

33 TS Thos Wyllie tent Mains of Edzell 21.5.1795 67, w Isobel Black 17.5.1790 Jervise has 1799) 61, by s Jas there; 1829; (other side) Wm Wyllie tent Mains of Edzell 11.8.1829 58, w Ann Mitchell 20.10.1836 61; (pink granite tablet on top) Jas Wyllie tent Mains of Edzell 18.3.1858 61; the farm has been in possession of mr Wyllie & his ancestors of upwards of 100y; Jas 5.4.1885 82; Eliz Scott Wyllie da of above d Brechin 31.12.1892 50; Jas Wyllie & Mary Rickard, chn Isabella 31.5.1835 29.12.1835, Jane Victoria 9.8.1839 9.11.1843 (see St.Andrews Testaments: Thos Wyllie fr in Mains of Edzell, 1795; Jervise "Epitaphs .."i 310)

34 1843. rev And Hutton min here for 53y d 5.5.1842 (see Fasti v 391)

35 1749. by David Bruce, fa Jas sometime tent Westsyde of Edzell 28.7. 1738 72, s Jas inf, Isobel, John, Agnes, Margt, Kath, David, Jean, Robt & Mary; (west side) cherub; reversed torches; mantling; I B, I M, plough; shrouded corpse; winged skull (style similar to Lethnot no.11, illustrated in Reid PSAS xlix 295 & Willsher & Hunter "Stones")

36 1797. David Christie tent Dalbog 25.12.1758 76, w Helen Gordon 8.3. 1764 55, s Peter tent Dalbog 27.7.1783 46, s Chas late tent Cowiehill 6.9.1788 52 (w Jane Brake 1812 84, s Peter 8.9.1841 73 (w Helen Carnegie 18.5.1843 67, da Isabella 10.8.1916 10))

36a Wm Christie, Cowiehill d 8.10.1890, w Cath Christie 12.5.1881 80

37 John Milne schoolmaster & Session clerk here for 21y d 21.5.1830 49

38 by David Hay 8.2.1844 70, fa Wm sometime tent Inveriscandy 17.2.1813 82, mo Mary Mitchell 30.10.1825 82, chn John, Alex, Chas, Jannet & Ann all d inf, Isabella 1801 35, Mary 1801 31, Geo 1835 36, Jas d Jamaica 1804 27

39 1776. by John Fitchet tent Blackymill, w Margt Valentine 19.6.1775 59, her chn by her 1h Wm Tindal also tent Blackymill: Anne, David & Isabel all survived their mo, her chn by John Fitchet: Martha, Margt & Cecilia all survived their mo, John, Jas & another Cecilia d before her; (west side) I F, M V, plough; A T, D T, I T; I, M, M, I, C, C Fitchet; "How still & peaceful is the grave, That silent bed how blest...."

40 Wm Smith innkeeper here 11.3.1861 69, w Jane Bennet 26.8.1873 77, da Mary 22.11.1840 1y3m, s Wm d Kirriemuir 30.10.1855 34, da Margt Robb 21.4.1884 60, Helen 22.7.1893 53; Jas Smith d Lochside farm here 30.1.1895 69, w Ann Cook 22.2.1924 83

41 by Mary Grant residing Edzell village, da Diana Stewart d there 3.3. 1853 28

42 CT Jas Duncan late of Wardhouse 13.1.1792 75, w Jean Michie 13.7.1795 63, Chn Margt, Eliz, Jean, Betty, Sophia, Alex, Jas int in vault of St Martins London, Jonathan governor Bombay from 1795 till d 11.8.1811 55 (see DNB), Mary 17.1.1836 75 int Arbroath Abbey (h rev Geo Gleig) (see Arbroath Abbey inscription no. 1463 & Fasti v 425; also Jervise "Land of the Lindsays"p 113 - Wardhouse is a small property near Montrose which governor Duncan bought for his parents who had farmed at Blairno)

43 Jas Alexander late tent Sheirstriped 18.5.1876 75, w Marjory Christie d here 25.12.1877 80, chn Betsy 6y, Chas 6y

43a cherub; reversed torches; mantling; I B, I D; M B, I B, I B, P B, E B, A B; scissors & tailor's goose; 1748; (west side) by John Bishop tent Slateford, w Janet Duncan 16.8.1747 53; revised 1874 by David Robertson d here 4.9.1890 83

44 Wm Carr 3.9.1853 72, w Eliz Machar 13.10.1885 95, family Margt, John, David, Jessie, Letitia & Mary Ann int here, Elis int Dalry Edinburgh, Jas int Kensal Green London, Anne int Buenos Ayres, Jane int Newry Ireland, Marjory int here, Ellen int Buenos Ayres, gda Eliz Machar Dempster int here

45 small. I D, 1712; (other side) 1712; I D; John Doroe indweller in Dilvhiper who departed this .... (under turf)

46 Jas Mitchell 29.4.1853 86, w Jean Kinnear 7.1.1885 87, da Louisa 1.7. 1914 89

47 Geo Lyall fr Little Tullo 5.11.1875 76, by w Isabella Lyall d Arbroath

12.6.1920 84

47a by Geo Lyall tent Burnsagard, w Ann Caithness 10.2.1853 52

48 John Lyall tent Burnsaugart 27.4.1826 77, w Violet Carnegie 22.4.1834 74½, chn Wm 1795 5, Helen 1797 3, Jas 1809 17, John 1814 19, Geo late tent Little Tullo 5.11.1875 76

49 Alex Lyall fr Ardo par Strathcathro d Ardo 25.2.1859 58, w Margt Ross d Ardo 2.12.1858 64, s John d Ardo 25.12.1848 14

50 1834. John Smith late tent Dalfooper 1813 79, w Isabella Molleson 1833 88, chn Janet 1824 49, David 1834 57, John late tent Dalfooper 1847 59 (w Jean Don 1870 .... (under turf)

51 Robt Stormont d Disclune Fettercairn 8.1884 82, w Eliza Smith 7.1888 76, s John 14.9.1889 40 int Tingwall Shetland (w Annie McAdam 16.2.1933 82 int Brechin, da Katie Eliza 12.5.1895 9 int here)

52 Alex Carr for 40y blacksmith here 9.7.1893 74, w Susan Graham 15.2.1905 82, chn Alex 10.3.1853 6m, Wm 22.2.1855 11m, Alex 15.8.1871 6, Jas 13.6.1893 44, John d NZ 9.10.1925, David d Laurencekirk 20.1.1927 71; Agnes Christison 28.12.1928 68

53 Robt Carr d here 22.10.1939 81; Frances Carr d here 13.12.1947 84

54 Jas Carr 28.7.1861 86½, w Ann Davidson 5.2.1854 72, s Jas 12.1834 20, da Eliz 24.4.1891 84, da Margt 19.4.1904 76

55 Wm Middleton fr Craigieshina 1839 60, 1w Mary Lindsay 1817 25, yrs Jas 1833 17; David Middleton MA LLD HM senior inspector of schools 17.6.1878 63, w Rhoda S Allan 2.6.1878 46; (other side) John Lindsay fr Auchmill 1872 85, w Betsy Mackie 22.10.1881 74, 2da Isabella 1859 26, 2s David d Rochester America 1875 35, Jane 13.8.1836 20.2.1909, Jas 7.3.1842 20.4.1915, John 1.6.1838 11.5.1915, Mary Ann 18.11.1834 29.1.1917, Betsy 20.9.1918 74

56 Robt Christison late fr Dalbog 21.5.1872 86, da Jean 3.7.1848 3w, w Ann Carr 26.3.1885 74

57 I D, E L, plough; mantling; 1748; two trumpeter angels (style similar to Maryton inscription no.60 also dated 1748); DaD, Jams D, AanaD, Sophia D, Jean D, Euphia D, Isabel D, Anne D, Alexr D; (west side) John Duray of that ilk, s Jas 13.2.1743 36 (see Jervise: "Land of the Lindsays" pp 329-330 app III "The Durays of that ilk, dempsters to the Lairds of Edzell", also p 51 for an account of their duties as pronouncers of "doom" or sentence of the court; Jervise "Epitaphs.."i 309 quotes the poem; St. Andrews Testaments, Euphemia Lyell relict of John Durie of Duriehill & Sophia & Jean Duries their daughters, par of Edzell, 1768, also David Durie of Duryhill, 1751)

58 FS A V I B; (marginal) Alex Walker indualler in Uackmiln of Corstonns d 12.-.1670 90, w Isobel Burn 17.2.1679 68; (central) Alex Walker induel-ler in Caepo 10.2.16-2 69, w Jannet Balfouer 14.2.1692 57; mantling & shield with (according to Davidson) two creels? one witha hooked handle & a large cloth finisher's shears for a waulkmiller, tongs, broom & two shovels for a maltman

59 1875. by Jas Dundas in Boston Mass USA d New York 16.1.1890 48 & Wm Dun-das of Boston Mass d 7.3.1902 86, to mo Isabel Smith 19.9.1854 38, fa Wm mason Edzell; Eliz d Boston Mass 12.3.1892 45

60 cherub; mantling with shield, spade & rake; W H, E M; C H, H H, I H, M H, L H, E H; (west side) by Wm Henderson gardener here & tent Slate-ford, da Mary 9.2.1765 8y5m3d, Lilly 1.1.1766 14m, Elis 16.1.1780 14

61 John Scott late tent Edzell village 26.6.1845 83, s John 6.1.1848 30

62 rev Robt Inglis MA 4.12.1803 19.1.1876 min Lochlee then Edzell from 5.6.1837 to 18.5.1843 then FC min here till death, s John Knox d of cholera Fyzabad India 3.8.1878 29, w Helen Brand 27.12.1810 9.10.1884, chn Wm Panmure 27.4.1841 27.2.1843, Robt 26.9.1835 8.3.1843, Cath 15. 5.1837 17.3.1843; Marion Welsh Vallentine d Corstorphine 20.3.1921 73 (h John Knox Inglis); sir Robt Wm Inglis 22.7.1843 10.4.1923; Thos Chalmers Inglis 23.10.1847 27.10.1893 int here; Wm Burnett Inglis 3.10. 1851 12.1.1888 int Wilcannie NSW (see Fasti v, Ewing: rev Robt was s of rev David of Lochlee; see Lochlee new burial ground inscription 22)

63 Alex Burness joiner here 14.11.1898 83, da Margt 3.2.1846 6½ at Dalbog, s Alex Low d Winnipeg Manitoba 19.1.1883 39, w Ann Falconer 4.4.1908 90, Eliza 13.2.1846 4y4m

64 by Jas Strachan, w Mary Lawrie 15.7.1896 75, da Mary 21.2.1845 13m; Jas Strachan 2.1.1909 89

65 by Jas Gold, w Betsy Valentine 24.6.1888 80, s Jas 25.2.1843 5, Robt d Highbury Ipolala South Africa 2.5.1891 (56); Jas Gold d here 1.11. 1893 84

66 FS 1675. (marginal) And (J)amie 16--, w Elspet Anderson 166- & Alex (J)amie 16-- (Jervise "Epitaphs.. i 309 has Iamie, mrs Davidson has Lamie, but in 1978 it was impossible to differentiate)

The following are noted by Jervise "Epitaphs.." i 307-10 but were not seen in 1978:

67 FS to south of Lindsay aisle. ... beneath this ston .... man Iames Donaldson ... mortal man ... soun lo laid ..... that to God vhos ever ... .. nd ivst heil pardon those that on him trvst Mankynd hath no repos bvt on

68 Lindsay arms. A L, W -; (in Latin) .... haec Joanes L..... er Germanus o.......oris ergo posui......

69 Jas Belly 20.8.1711, w Isobal Steurd

N o t e s

F Davidson: "Inventory of 17th century tombstones..." describes 27, 58, 66 (she has And Lamie d 1676, w Elspet Anderson 1665 & Alex Lam(y), & 68

Jervise: "Epitaphs ..." i 307-11 notes inscriptions 5,16, 27, 33-5, 39, 42-3, 57-8, 66-9; "Land of the Lindsays" (1853) appendix II has extracts from the rent book of Edzell & Lethnot 1672-1699

D H Edwards "Historical Guide to Edzell & Glenesk" 3rd ed.(1893) outlines local history.

OPR with Registrar General: 285 Edzell Births 1684-1703 1715-1854
Marriages 1641-52, 1665-80, 1684-1703, 1715-19, 1721-2, 1724-91, 1804-54
Deaths nil

SRO CH2/627 Edzell north: minutes 1706-73, 1837-1939
poors fund accounts 1801-34
male communicants 1837-42
heritors minutes 1843-5
minutes committeeof management of poor 1843-5

10a E D Z E L L

SRO CH3/543 Edzell FC minutes 1843-1924, D C minutes 1844-1935
private registration book baptisms, Marriages & burials of rev Robt Inglis: Edzell C of S 1841-3; Edzell FC 1843-75

HR 173 minutes 1859-1929

Episcopal church: rev David Rose's register of baptisms for Lochlee, Navar, Edzell & Stracathro from 1727, ms copy in Brechin Diocesan Library deposited at Dundee University library.

P D Morton: "Lindsay Family in Glenesk & Edzell" (Arbroath Guide dec.1922-Ap 1923

Fasti v 389 Ministers from 1567

Edinburgh Testaments. A selection from the Commissariot Record includes:
John Donaldson in the Sklaitfuird, 1605
mr Jas Fullertoun minister of Edzell, 1595

St.Andrews Testaments. A selection from the Commissariot Record includes:
Isobel Bellie spouse to Alex Smyth in Margie, 1620
John Carnegie at Coalmylie & Jas Carnegie at Mergie, 1769
Alex Durie in Slateford, 1777
Isobel Mitchell spouse to Alex Walker at Sklaitfuird, 1637
mr James Thomson minister at Edzell, 1729
John Walker at the Walk-milne of Edzell, 1620

I n d e x

Adam 9
Alexander 32.43
Allan 55
Anderson 66
Archer 25
Archibald 10-11

Balfouer 58
Belly 69. Notes
Bennet 40
Bertie 12
Bishop 43
Black 33
Brake 36
Brand 62
Bruce 35
Burn 58
Burness 63

Caithness 4.11.21-2.47a
Carnegie 18.30.36.48.Notes
Carr 44.52-4.56
Christie 36.36a.43
Christison 8-9.23-4.52.56
Cook 40
Cooper 5.20
Craik 7

D. 27
Davidson 54
Dempster 44
Dickson 42
Don 27.50
Donald 14
Donaldson 67.Notes
Doroe 45
Duke 22.31
Duncan 42-3
Dundas 59
Duray, Durie 57.Notes

Easton 3
Edward 31

Falconer 63
Ferrier 1
Fitchet 39
Fullertoun Notes

Gleig 42
Gold 65
Gordon 36
Graham 52
Grant 21.41
Gray 32

Hay 38
Henderson 60
High 14
Hood 30
Hutton 34

Inglis 1.62.Notes

Jackson 18
Jamie 66
Jolly 16-7.25

10a EDZELL

K. 12
Kinnear 46

L. 57
Lamie, Lamy 66
Lawrie 64
Law 18
Ley 18
Lindsay 5.29.55.68.Notes
Low 6.15-7.24-5
Lyall,Lyell 47-9.57

M. 23.35.60
McAdam 51
Machar,Machir 2.44
Mackie 55
Michie 42
Middleton 55
Milne 30.37
Mitchell 10.20.33.38.46.Notes
Molleson 50

Nedry 6

Ogg 7

Rickard 33
Robertson 4.43
Robie 29
Rose Notes
Ross 49

Scott 61
Smart 23.26
Smith 3.40.50-1.59.Notes
Steurd 69
Steward/t 27.41
Stormont 51
Strachan 26.64

Taylor 2.19
Thomson 19.Notes
Tindal 1.39

Val(l)entine 39.62.65

Walker 58.Notes
Wallace 8
Will 3
Willock 13
Wyllie 33

10b NEWDOSK

Although the small ancient burial ground of Newdosk, by Kirkton of Balfour, is in Kincardineshire, the parish of Newdosk was united with that of Edzell in 1658. No trace of the old church is visible, but the burial ground is still in use and is well kept. All inscriptions are listed below.

National Grid NO 602 735

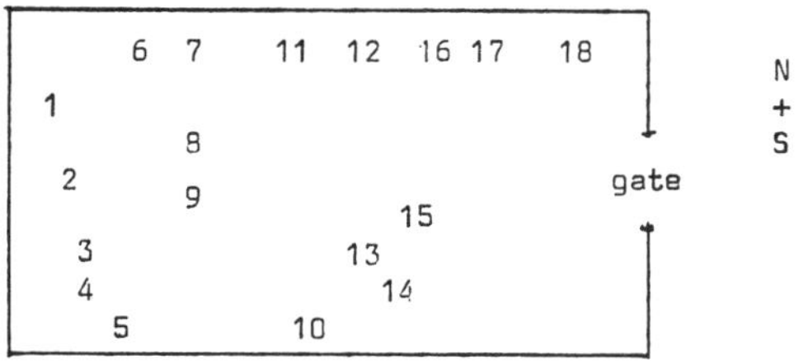

1 by Ann McDonald, h Alex McDonald 17.4.1817 58, da Ann 20.6.1825 20

2 Helen Dunn Smith 28.5.1828 5.11.1901; May Smith 16.8.1831 18.1.1902; John Smith late fr Steelstrath 5.9.1829 10.3.1906

3 1747. Wm Adam tent in Achmòl 9.5.1748 59, 1w Margt Dury d some time in 3.1735, 2w Margt Duncon b 1.1.1707 d 1740 33y; (east side) two nude figures holding a bearded head; reversed torches; shield with W A, M D, M D, I L, share & coulter; I A, D A, I A, I A, I A, I A, I A, A A; this monement is erected at the co of Wm Adam

4 Jas Adam 9.1870 90, w Margt Duncan 7.1852 62, da Agnes 7.1838 15, Jas London 6.1868 49

5 1846. by Jean & Helen Adam imo fa Wm Adam 12.2.1812 66, mo Agnes Low 1.12. 1844 81, bros Jas 4.2.1808 18, David 4.8.1819 21, Alex 14.1.1821 27, sis Mary 7.5.1818 18

6 Wm Valentine Lawie 15.2.1890 18.11.1947, w Margt Scott Duthie 4.2.1891 25.3.1973, s Wm Valentine 27.6.1922 21.3.1932

7 cross. Robt Matthew Lawie head gardener at the Burn 19.5.1858 14.5.1922, by family he faithfully served; w Betsy Valentine 27.3.1944 77; s Geo Deans d Calcutta 15.1.1939 42

8 Duff Weir d New Mill Arnhall 4.4.1906 85, w Jean Silver 1.2.1908 84

9 And Dow d West Woodtown The Burn 22.6.1891 83, w Christian Ross 24.5.1897 85; Barbara Dow 2.7.1911 74

10 by Chas Littleboy to mo Eliz Gibb 14.1.1844, gfa Jas Gibb, uncle Isaac Gibb

11 Robt Caw 26y gamekeeper on the Burn estate 7.3.1895 67, w Cath Campbell 26.8.1906 76, das Margt 21.3.1899 21 & Cath 13.8.1907 40

12 by Duncan McFadyen d Strathywell Fettercairn 13.7.1932 83, da Agnes Flora 7.6.1904 22

13 John Will tent Waggles 14.4.1881 80, w Helen Young 12.7.1858 58; John Bruce sometime tent Waggles 10.3.1890 84, w Mary Gold 13.2.1891 65

14 by Alex Gold senior Hillock 15.11.1835 89, w Janet Smart 18.3.1832, likewide his fa, mo, gfa & ggmo int here; Arthur Gold 19.11.1836 8m

15 Robt Carnegie in Fitnemo (Jervise "Epitaphs" i has Pitnemon), w Isabel Gold 30.9.1741 30 liewing behind her a son that she & her husband had betwixt them Alex his age 2y; (east side) 1742. by Robt Carnegie; cherub & heart; potted flowers; mantling with shield, Ro Ca, Is Go, share & coulter; emblems

16 cross. John Nicol fr Inch of Arnhall b Anguston Peterculter 15.12.1829 d Woodmyre cottage Edzell 31.3.1893

17 cross. Chas McInroy of the Burn 3.3.1838 4.2.1919

18 Wm McInroy of the Burn d there 29.4.1896 91, w Harrier Barbara d there 2.7.1890

Notes

Jervise "Epitaphs ..." i 127-30 & 312 notes inscriptions no 3.14,15

Testaments: the following were seen in the Commissariot Register of St Andrews - John Jamie in Banchrie, par Newdosk, 1625
Jas Stephen sometime at Kirktown of Newdosk, 1759

OPR with the Registrar General: see Edzell notes

Index

Adam	3-5	Duthie	6	McFadyen	12
Bruce	13	Gibb	10	McInroy	17-8
Campbell	11	Gold	13-5	Nicol	16
Carnegie	15	Jamie	Notes	Ross	9
Caw	11	Lawie	6-7	Silver	8
Dow	9	Littleboy	10	Smart	14
Duncan	3-4	Low	5	Smith	2
Dury	3	McDonald	1	Stephen	Notes
				Valentine	7
				Weir	8
				Will	13

11a FARNELL

The present parish church was built in 1806 beside the site of the medieval church dedicated to St Ninian. The incumbent was, as such, Dean of Brechin.
The well kept burying ground, still in use, is on a small eminence next the manse and sheltered by trees.
The parishes of Farnell and Kinnaird were united in 1772.

National Grid reference: NO 627 555

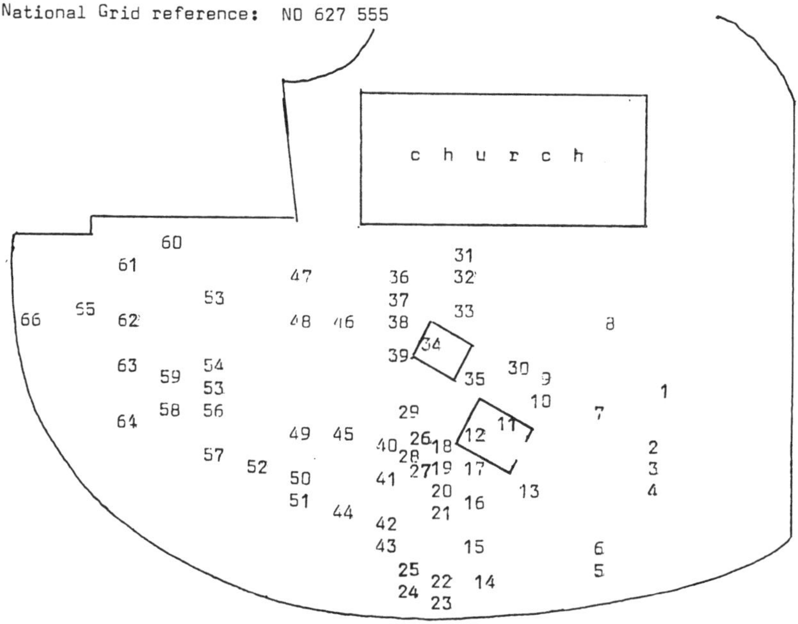

1 Wm Croall 18.8.1868 70, w Margt Croall 31.12.1875 66, s John 10.1840 2, s Jas 12.1848 13, s Jas 3.1855 8m, s Alex d Australia 1887 37, da Margt Hogg d Aberdeen 1893 51, s David d Australia 1893 53, s Wm 7.1.1905 67

2 1841. Wm Johnston 21.8.1836 81, w Agnes Bain 24.4.1831 56, by chn Wm, Jean & Margt, da Helen 6.12.1818 4, s Jas 16.3.1828 26, s Walter 5.6. 1831 20, da Cath 12.1.1831 30, s John 29.1.1832 26, da Margt 4.12.1842 34, s Wm 2.7.1844 39 (w Betsy Thomson d Brechin 19.3.1882 73); (west side) Wm Smart, w Jane Johnston d Andover Mass USA 1.9.1855 57, s Walter d Cuba West Indies 25.9.1853 30, das Cath & Fanny d inf

3 emblems; Arthur Hodge 23.3.1743 66, w Jean Layell 2.2.1739 66, two of their chn viz. Arthur 14.5.1732 21, John d inf, by da Janet; (west side) two cherubs; mantling with shield, A H, I L, share & coulter, 1757; I H, M H, R H, A H, I H

4 1807. by Eliz Bain, h Geo Coathill who lived happily in the married state 50y, tent Clushead of Farnell 23y, d 11.5.1804 77, s Geo d Jamaica 5.9.1802 45

5 Robt Law, w Magdalen Dalgety, s Jas 29.6.1851 58 (w Janet Hunter 16.5. 1883 92y5m, by s Alex blacksmith Brechin) all interred here

6 ob Wm Law d Greenlaw 3.12.1857, w Betty Ferrier 7.6.1830, 2w Annie Low 14.8.1862, by surviving ss Jas, Inellan & Wm, New York & Peter, Chicago in 1889; Hannah Law 1.5.1858; Jas S Law d Kirn 10.1897; Peter Law d USA 5.1898

7 by John Cobban shoemaker in Greenden & w Mary Coullie, only s Wm 1.1782 26 (see Jervise, "Epitaphs" i : has 1786 in error); (west side) crown & shoemaker's tools, 1782; mantling; cherub; I C, M C; W C; M, W, Ie, Ia Cobbans; "Death fierce is thy firie dart / No forester like thee / Wha cuts the Cyder whil it gros / And spars the withered tree"

8 John Gordon 15.4.1862 87, w Jannet Scott 23.8.1867 86, da Helen 1.9.1896 79; Eliz Stewart Christie 11.5.1849 5; David Gordon Johnston 16.5.1849 2y

9 John Mitchell blacksmith Fithie 7.3.1857, w Anne Fleming 21.12.1859 77, chn Janet 3.6.1833 18, Jas 14.7.1833 16, John 25.3.1852 28, da Annie 18.3.1865 47

10 unskillfully cut. 1840. by John Walker imo our parants;John Walker deyed 21.2.1823; Marget Peter deyed 1.8.18(20), both int her 5 of their chn;

M A			W
A L		1 7	W
J E	1817	2 4	W
(R) E	1823	eg 26	W
G O	1840		W

11 pediment surmounted by arms, collared eagle

..... anagramma ..... ompositum..... Davidi Carnegy ..... ramma ...... alia......Guidiac ..... (see Jervise "Epitaphs.." i 90: full inscription in Latin - mr David Carnegy of Craigo dean of Brechin & rector of this church, min Brechin 2y then min here 36y d 1672 76, 1w Helen Lindsay 18.7.1656 & ten of their chn int here - here follows an anagram composed by himself; dean Carnegy was descended from a laird of Cookston & Unthank, was founder of the Carnegys of Craigo; Helen Lindsay was 1da of bishop David Lindsay of Edimburgh (see Brechin Testaments: Helen Lindsay, 27.10.1656 & mr Robt son of mr David Carnegy dean of Brechin, 3.10.1679); see also Fasti v 393 which has their s David of Craigo physician, s Jas min Barry, s Robt, da Agnes (h Robt Paterson principal of Marischal College); Rogers ii 224; see also Logie-Montrose, Angus gravestone inscriptions)

12 mural. 1829. rev Jas Wilson min Farnell 18.10.1829 73 in 52ndy of ministry, two ss Jas d inf, & Geo d 21y, mo Ann Burnett, sisters Margt & Cath all int here (see Jervise "Epitaphs.."i 91: he was s of rev Geo Wilson min Kinnaird d 1787, he md a da of sir Wm Nicolson of Glenbervie, had 2 ss & 5 das of whom 1da md David Smith schoolmaster Farnell & another da md dr Badenach of Arthurhouse in Garvock; Fasti v 394 & 396)

13 periwigged cherub & ringed heart; R H, M L; Robt Hall 1706 40, three ss John 1696 1y, Robt 1697 4, Robt the 2 ... (under turf); (I)H, R H, R H, I P; sandglass, tailor's scissors & goose inscribed R H, bodkin, ring, rule, coffin; "All men And woman must depart / When dayes is spent on earth"

14 Alex Jameson who lived at Bridgend of Farnel 1687 52, 2w Christian Millne 1717 74; Agnes Jamieson 18.9.1750 67 spouse to Geo Scott sometime in Craneston; (west side) book; 4 4 ; scales; knife and  ; poems; A I, C M, 1734; A I, M I, E I, A I

15 John Addison farm servant d Kinnaber 31.8.1859 92, w Mary Anderson d Carcary 11.5.1803 30, 2w Isabell Addison d Howmuir 3.5.1850 87

16 David Oeikenhaid millor in Poymill, s John 1699 16, s Jas 1704 15, s Robt 1714 13; (west side)periwigged cherub & ringed heart; D O, E W, I O, IO, R O

17 David Sutter & Isobel Pyot, da Isobel 1.11.1734 6m; repaired & re-lettered 1896; (west side) "Stoop passenger for hear doth ly / a pleasant

Jeuel of sueet infancy / a harmless babe yt only came & cryd / in baptism to be washd from sin & dyed"

18 David Lyall esq of Gallery b East Carcary 2.1733 but who left Scotland & went to Gottenburgh in 1757 where he resided as a merchant till 1787 when he returned to his native country to enjoy the Fruits of his Industry and the Society of his Relations & Friends. He was much repested for his Integrity, Benevolence & Charity, d 29.12.1815 82 (see Jervise "Epitaphs" i 91 & 212: he have £250 scots in 1783 to the poor, d unm, & Gallery went to John Gibson a sister's son who took the name of Lyall; see inscription no 21 infra & Pert nos 67-70)

19 Jas Lyall fr Mains of Gallery 27.2.1808 72, w Susanna Burnes 16.6.1836 68, da Isabella 3.1.1815 10, 2 chn d inf int Pert, David 1797 & Harriet 1803, also Margt 14.6.1846 45 (see Pert inscription no.72)

20 David Lyall tent Arrat 30.5.1841 34, w Eliz Lyall d Arrat 26.3.1877 67

21 1818. Jas Gibson 22.3.1719 16.2.1817, w Margt Lyall 7.1731 8.1786, s David 1.4.1760 6 (see Jervise "Epitaphs" i 91: the fa of the above Jas Gibson also belonged to Farnell, went to Riga after the '45 in which he took part, was mert in Riga where he long resided & died - some members of his family also settled there; see inscription 18 above)

22 Joseph Ross auctioneer Brechin 26.12.1848 67, w Cath Young 12.10.1850 77

23 John Dundas tent White Myre of Aldbar 26.8.1864 77, w Mary Young 27.12.1853 68; David Young 27.11.1859 83

24 John Lamb, Elspat Daer; poem; (west side) 1776; loom flanked by bobbin frames; by John Lamb & Elspet Daer imo chn viz Mary 1747 1y6m, John 1750 1y6m, Mary 17(60) 9, (John) 177(6) 20

25 emblems; poem; (west side) Jas Matthie in Hauchs of Kinnaird, w Elis Ramsay 18.2.1734 36, here lyes 2 of their chn Jean & Ann d inf

26 ob Robt Lyall factor on estate of Southesk 1817-50 b Carcary 27.11.1778 d Arrat 13.1.1863, w Eliz Campbell 25.4.1832 52, 2w Mary Brown 11.6.1854 59; Chas Lyall b Carcary 10.8.1815 d Old Montrose 8.10.1888 factor on estate of Southesk 1850-78, w Anne Mustard b Leuchland 28.1.1823 d Old Montrose 13.6.1905, Edw 20.10.1860 6, Chas 23.7.1893 37, Frances 17.12.1885 33, Henry 10.7.1902 44; Robt Lyall b Carcary 20.12.1814 d 23.7.1900, w Mary Aitchison 31.5.1834 11.11.1927, Robt b Carcary 15.4.1854 d 23.10.1894, John 23.4.1855 30.4.1864, Mary Aitchison or Shearer 27.9.1856 27.11.1891, Eliz Campbell 16.2.1858 14.10.1924; Horace Lyall 15.6.1941 (see Jervise "Epitaphs" i 92: Robt Lyall 1778 1863 was son of Jas Lyall & Isobel Spence)

27 cross. Robt Chas Lyall 3.10.1894 40

28 David Ruxton tent Mains of Farnwell d there 8.2.1811 70, w Isabel Lyall 13.3.1790 54, also 7 of their family viz David 4.4.1774 11m, Eliz 13.5.1794 17, Jas d at sea 1794 25, s John sometime - - - - - - well d - - 18(33) 49y (s David 8.4.1826 10) (see Inverkeilor, Angus gravestone inscription no.112; Jervise "Epitaphs" i: David was son of Wm Ruxton of Myreside Inverkeilor & Marget Williamson)

29 crown & hammer; 1802. by Wm Scott blacksmith in Montrose imo fa Thos blacksmith sometime in Pittlegarcrie 1.6.1788 8(1) & Kathrine (Milne) 12.1790 87

30 Wm Dorward d Kinnaird 29.3.1839, w Margt Adam d Kinnaird 6.3.1825, by chn Jas H & Eliz

31 Thos Smith tent Haughs of Kinnaird 22.12.1835 67, w Helen Gray d

Cupar Fife 4.1.1858 83, chn Wm 21.9.1845 39, Jas d Moulmein India 2.3. 1854 47, Thos drowned at sea 7.1835 24, Robt drowned off Broughty Ferry 5.7.1849 32, Geo d London 8.11.1858 48, Eliz Mitchell d Edinburgh 23.2. 1880 72, Margt Brown d Edinburgh 27.12.1879 59, John d Woolley Berks 28.8.1888 75, Chas d Deal 24.11.1897 81, Helen (Landale) d Edinburgh 3.11.1899 87, Agnes d Edinburgh 9.1.1900 95, Jane Anne (Russell) d Edinburgh 16.6.1910 86

32 Jas Taylor 3.9.1832 55, w Margt Will 23.3.1862 83, s Alex 21.6.1858 50, s John 11.1.1841 26, da Ann 3.4.1847 25, da Grace 11.2.1875 67, by ss Jas & David

33 David Lindsay 6.8.1876 77, w Anne Steele 9.1.1841 37, s Jas 19.7.1843 9

34 sir Jas Carnegie bart of Southesk, wid dame Christian Doig 4.11.1820 91 (see Jervise "Epitaphs" i 90 for further notes - she was da of David Doig of Cookston near Brechin & Magdalene heiress of Symers of Balzeordie in Menmuir etc; Brechin Testaments under Symmer; Edwards "Guide to Brechin"3rd ed p 106; Jervise "Land of the Lindsays")

35 by rev And Fergusson min Maryton(see Ewing i 152), gfa rev David Fergusson admitted min Farnell 1716 d 1751, fa rev David Fergusson who succeeded him in 1751 d 1793, here also lie int their spouses Anna Russel & Janet Mitchell & some of their chn (Fasti v 393 & 407; Brechin Testaments)

36 Jas Sievewright late wright at Red-ford 20.9.1836 49, by s Wm d Woodend 21.6.1858 86 (w Isabella Strachan d Woodend 5.6.1904 91, da Margt b 26.5. d 29.10.1851, s Wm Smith 5.8.1853 26.8.1856, da Cath Smith 18.12.1847 28.9.1874

37 Wm Robertson d Farnell Mill 5.3.1877 83, w Ann Ducat 2.2.1898 86, s Peter 9.12.1877 29, s David b 17.5.1843 d Monifeith 30.11.1924

38 Wm Robertson miller Farnell, w Mary Bruce 3.11.1832 40, chn David 1.11. 1832 13, Adam 22.9.1837 6, Robt 28.9.1837 7, 2w Ann Ducat, chn And 2.1. 1838 6m, And 14.11.1842 1y, Susan 27.10.1845 5, Robt 11.6.1864 17, da Jane d Liverpool 11.2.1872 39 (s Wm Coutts 6.5.1858 1m)

39 Alex Robertson d Farnell Mill 14.11.1913 75, w Cath Davies 10.11.1917 75

40 mr John Ruxton, Mains of Farnell 5.1.1833 49, w mrs Anne Mustard 16.11. 1842 50, s David 8.4.1826 9, da Susan 28.6.1840 21, s Jas fr Powmill 18. 12.1844 26, s John distiller & mert Brechin 22.5.1847 24

41 Wm Ruxton fr Farnell 19.4.1877 63, w Cath Colville 22.4.1866 42, 1da Elizabeth-Anne 11.9.1858 8, ss John & Chas d inf

42 1835. Wm Johnston 13.3.1819 81, w Margt Williamson 12.4.1820 83, had nine chn of whom four d inf, da Jane & three of her chn lie here, s Jas d at sea, Mary, Chas & Janet survive this date, by da Janet (wid of Wm Thompson mert in Arbroath) as a tribute

43 John Dear sometime weaver in Ground of Bonytoune 9.11.1726 65, w Eliz Blaer, eight chn John, Eliz, David, Jannet, James, Alex, Mary & Mary - Alex & Mary being departed; (west side) cherub, loom, flaming heart; I D, E B, 1729; I D, D D, I D, M D, E D, I D, A D, M D; "My Days are swifter than a weaver's shuttle" Job the 7 & 6; "I have cut off like a weaver my life." Isaiah 38 & 12; "The Weaver's Art It is renowned so That rich nor poor Without it cannot go." Eliz Blaer (d 26.12.1736 73)

44 Alex Johnston, Muirside of Kinnell 11.8.1862 87, w Helen Steele 27.8. 1852 78, chn Alex 1803 5, Wm 1806 inf, Jas 1818 18, John 1819 18

45 1885. by Jas Kennedy of New York USA imo fa d 1847 51, bros David d USA

3.1851, John Stewart d USA 3.1871, above Jas d USA 10.1898

46 Jas Alexander 24.6.1852, w Eliz Low 28.2.1867 66, s Wm 17.1.1830 1y8m, da Annie 7.4.1845 22, s David 27.8.1864 26, s Jas 9.2.1871 45, da Christine 6.2.1872 39, da Emily 9.11.1901 69, da Eliz Alexander or Kenny 4.10.1921 87

47 Jas Whamond crofter Muirside of Kinnell 12.12.1860 73, w Betty Wilson 25.11.1856 58, 4s Wm 10.1847 16, 1s David d Philadelphia 30.4.1874 52, 1da Isabella d UF manse Lamlash Arran 3.1.1902 73 int Eastern Necropolis Dundee, by eight chn surviving in 1861

48 Wm Roberts miller Kinnairds Mill for 32y d 31.8.1849 68, w Eliz Guthrie 22.11.1847 65, s Jas d Perth 14.7.1832 22, s Wm d Glasgow 30.8.1844 38, by surviving family

49 Colin Dyker 6.8.1791 53, w Eliz Deuchar 15.1.1822 76, chn Mary 18.8.1792 21, John 8.10.1800 25, David 20.6.1804 26, Wm 27.3.1804 20, Jas 27.3.1815 28, Wm & David d inf, by da Ann

50 Peter Fife fr Egypt 20.9.1878 82, w Jannet Strachan 25.5.1880 77, s And 14.1.1865 25, gchn Alexina & Jennie d inf, s Jas 18.7.1900 68 (w Jean 30.11.1921 82) s Robt 24.7.1904 68 (w Mary Will 26.1.1898), da Mary 12.8.1934 91, s Alex 27.3.1919 73

51 Geo Fife tent Whandland 11.12.1813 68, w Jane Ferrier 18.7.1837 79, chn Jas 31.12.1787 11d, John 9.12.1806 22, Geo 24.3.1807 25, Margt 23.6.1809 28, Alex 4.7.1820 27, Robt tent Whandland 21.4.1839 53, by chn Wm esq of Slatefield & Peter tent Egypt & Janet (h And Ducat tent Barfauld)

52 1837. John Strachan sometime tent Greenlaw 19.3.1809 36, w Janet Ruxton 13.1.1837 62, ss Robt, David, Wm & John d young int here

53 Jas Reid & Meria Ward both d Farnell Castle he d 8.4.1852 73, she d 8.5.1853 67, by family

54 Robt Eston late tent Muirside of Balzordie 21.8.1856 64, s Jas 28.3.1851 30

55 by John Mathers, w Betty Ogilvy 2.2.1841 60, s David 4.9.1836 28

56 1846. Wm Nicol tent Willanyards 19.10.1839 85, w Isobel Wyllie 24.8.1842 80, by chn Ann, Alex, Jean & Wm, Alex 22.3.1867 78, Jean 15.9.1876 80, Wm 2.4.1877 79, Ann 19.9.1877 85

57 by John Ferrier sometime weaver in Greenden imo fa John Ferrier 1758 79, mo Eliz Gold d 67y, bro Alex d 31y; (west side) loom; 1764 IF EG; W, K, Ie, Io, Ia, R, A Ferriers (traces of paint: red on initials & black on the mantling)

58 1814. by Robt & Alex Smith imo mo Kath Forbes residenter in Moorside of Kinnell 19.11.1807 62y4m, fa Alex Smith d Hospital of Montrose 1812 he was put in by the par of Kinnel three different times, also sis Mary 19.6.1811 29 int here

59 1782. by Alex Lesslie & Isobel Renny in Paddockmyre imo his fa Alex Lesslie sometime in Cadgerglaik 26.2.1735 39, his mo Janet Shand 9.4.1766 63, chn Janet, Jean, Isobel, the above Alex, Mary & Eliz, of these Jean, Alex & Eliz was alive at this date (ie 1782)

60 And Chisholm 29.8.1866 75, w Betty Mann 21.8.1863 56, s Wm 28.2.1848 23, s Jas 19.12.1859 11y9m, s Robt d Liverpool 11.11.1862 32

61 Thos Spence late servant of the Honourable Family of Southesque 23.6.1764 78, s John 15.4.1740 6, 1w Helena Stephen with three of her chn

viz John 20y, David 20y, Margt 2y, by 2w Helena Matthew; Here lyes Isobel Anderson spuse was to Wm Spence, Woodside of Kinnaird, she d 28.1.1797 81; (west side) two cherubs; 1767 Thos Spence, Helena Matthew; St S, C S, A S; W S, T S, A S, E S; share & coulter

62 John Bremner 4.1.1791 75, by w Helen Smith; poem (see Jervise "Epitaphs" i 92, has Brimner in error)

63 John Smith in Greenlaw 4.12.1723 45, w Jannet Honey 12.5.1729 60, chn Alex 6.4.1730 21, Thos 11.4.1737 27, Elspet with Helen; "Under this monument of stone / Lies both the father & the son..."(poem quoted in full by Jervise "Epitaphs" i 351); (west side) 1738. I S, I H; share & coulter

64 1831. David Scott 25.3.1830 74, w Eliz Mill 27.1.1844 81, s John 26.1.1802 4, s David 8.5.1814 27, by s Gilbert

65 Wm Craig d Drum 19.12.1887 86, w Ann Maxwell d Kinnaird 2.4.1851 37, sis Margt d Drum 29.1.1886 76, family Margt Allison 30.6.1918, Jane Ann 19.1.1929, Alex 7.12.1931

66 Wm Grant 22.7.1875 74, w Betsy McCombie d Panmure 21.11.1887 83, da Betsy 18.8.1863 30, s Jas 7.4.1843 8, by chn Wm & Margt

67 Wm Robertson 12.11.1891 78, w Jane Hood 17.9.1868 54, s Wm 19.9.1854 6m

The following are noted in Jervise "Epitaphs & Inscriptions in Northeast Scotland" i pp 89-95 & 350-1 but were not seen in 1977:

68 - - - - - Agnes - - - - - - - Dais chil - - - - Iames Da- - - - Margarit Yo- - - in Carcary - - airted in - - - in - - - 1638 - - -

69 FS D E I S; David Enererity indweller Fithie, w Isobel Shilgreene 27.11.1675 70; poem; emblems ; 1676

70 FS Barbra Crichton 1717 53 w of Walter Tyler 1698 49 & w of And Andrson indweller in Villen Yeards; W T, A A, B C, I A (Jervise notes: And Anderson in Willanyards d 1729 was reported by the factor for the York Buildings Co to be "a right honest like man, pretty well upon it, and has the Town very well plenished.")

71 TS Robt Lyell 14.10.1707 43, chn Patk 24.6.1710 14, Robt 28.11.1706 ½, Ann 9.4.1701 2; poem; Jas Lyall sometime tent West Carcary & afterwards Mains of Gallery where he d 27.2.1808 71 (see Pert inscriptions 67-70 & 72)

72 TS Chas Lyall tent Carkary 28.3.1729 63, w Isobel Mitchell 12.4.1727 50, chn Robt 7.1707, Walter 3.1717, s John succeeded his fa in Carkary d 13.9.1736 34 (see Brechin Testaments) (w Margt Mudie 20.12.1761 59, da Margt 2y7m, s Jas succeeded his fa John tent Carcary d 14.5.1806 74 (w Isobel Spence d Brechin 26.1.1813 70)) (see Jervise i 92 & ii 362-3: Margt Mudie was da of the laird of Pitmuies; Isobel Spence belonged to a family that were notaries public & town clerks of Brechin for more than two centuries & she was mo of Robt Lyall factor of the Estate of Southesk 1778 1863; sir Chas Lyell bart the geologist (see DNB) was descended from Chas who d 1729, his gfa was bred a mert in Montrose, was purser in HM Navy during the American War of Independance & bought Kinnordy about 1780-3 (see Kirriemuir Old Episcopal churchyard inscriptions)

73 Chas Ferrier tent Fithie 4.1729, w Isobel Leith 5.1729; poem; John Ferrier wright Montrose 15.12.1860 86

74 John Crichton tent in Woodwrae, w Eliz Taylor 1747 61 "Espoused I was to a Husband dear / Liv'd with him 5 & 20 year / Now children four I left him have / I rest in hope God will them save"

11a F A R N E L L

75 David Cowllie shoemaker Karkrie 1734 40; poem

76 TS David Duquhare, East Fithie 1713 55, w Isobel Marnoch; poem

N o t e s

Testaments: Farnell was in the Commissariot of Brechin, but the following were noticed in the Register of the Commissariot of Edinburgh: James Ker in Carcary, 1601; John Ker in Carcarie, 1608; William Ker at Barnes of Farnell, 1601

OPR with the Registrar General: 286 Farnell
Births 1699-1714, 1716-1854
Marriages 1716-1854
Deaths 1752-95

SRO CH2/575 Farnell KS minutes 1716-9 (containing some proclamations & baptisms), 1743-50, 1796-1846
accounts 1751-, 1796-1894

Jervise "Epitaphs & Inscriptions .. in the North East of Scotland" i 89-95 &350-1 notes the inscriptions nos 7, 10-2, 18, 21, 26, 34-5, 43, 62-3, 68-76

Davidson "Inventory of 17th Century Tombstones .." describes nos 13 & 16

I n d e x

A.	10
Adam	30
Addison	15
Aikenhead	see Oiekenhead
Aitchison	26
Alexander	46
Allison	65
Anderson	15.61.70
Badenach	12
Bain	2.4
Blaer	43
Bremner	62
Brown	26.31
Bruce	38
Burnes	19
Burnett	12
Campbell	26
Carnegy/ie	11.34
Chisholm	60
Christie	8
Coathill	4
Cobban	7
Colville	41
Coullie	7.75
Coutts	38
Craig	65
Crichton	70.74
Croall	1
Daer	24.43
Dais	68
Dalgety	5
Davies	39
Dear	24.43
Deuchar	49.76
Doig	34
Dorward	30
Ducat	37-8.51
Dundas	23
Duquhare	76
Dyker	49
Enererity	69
Eston	54
Fergusson	35
Ferrier	6.51.57.73
Fife	50-1
Fleming	9
Forbes	58
Gibson	21
Gold	57
Gordon	8
Grant	66
Gray	31
Guthrie	48
Hall	13
Hodge	3

11a FARNELL

Hogg	1
Honey	63
Hood	67
Hunter	5
Inverarity	see 69
Jami(e)son	14
Johnston	2.8.42.44
Kennedy	45
Kerr	Notes
L.	10.13
Lamb	24
Landale	31
Law	5-6
Layell	3
Leith	73
Lesslie	59
Lindsay	11.33
Low	6.46
Lyall	18-21.26-8.71-2
Lyell	71-72
McCombie	66
Mann	60
Marnoch	76
Mathers	55
Matthie	25
Matthew	61
Maxwell	65
Mill	64
Millne	14.29
Mitchell	9.31.35.72
Mudie	32
Mustard	26.40
Nicol	56
Nicolson	12
O.	10
Ogilvy	55
Oiekenhead	16
P.	13
Paterson	11
Peter	10
Pyot	17
Ramsay	25
Reid	53
Renny	59
Roberts	48
Robertson	37-9.67
Ross	22
Russell	31
Ruxton	28.40-1.52
Scott	8.14.29.64
Shand	59
Shearer	26
Shilgreene	69
Sievewright	36
Smart	2
Smith	12.31.36.58.62-3
Spence	61.72
Steele	33.44
Stephen	61
Strachan	36.50.52
Sutter	17
Symers	34
Taylor	32.74
Thompson	42
Thomson	2
Tyler	70
W.	10.16
Walker	10
Ward	53
Whamond	47
Will	32.50
Williamson	42
Wilson	12.47
Wyllie	56
Yo- -	68
Young	22-3

11b KINNAIRD

There is now no trace of the 16th century parish church of Cuikston dedicated to St Romnald, after 1606 called Kinnaird, except for these ten gravestones in a small wood. The parishes of Kinnaird and Farnell were united in 1772.

National Grid refernce: NO 627 568. Access by permission of the Earl of Southe

1 FS tipped, half buried & upside down. Here lyes John Mathie 1699 16, Alexander Mathie 1703 13 two sons to John Mathie tennant - -rter in -er - - - - - - and - - - - - - -

2 Heir lyes Henrie Rait son to rev David Rait min here d 10.1669 18; H R ; Rait arms (see Fasti v 395: rev David Rait's fa was min of Mains, Dundee)

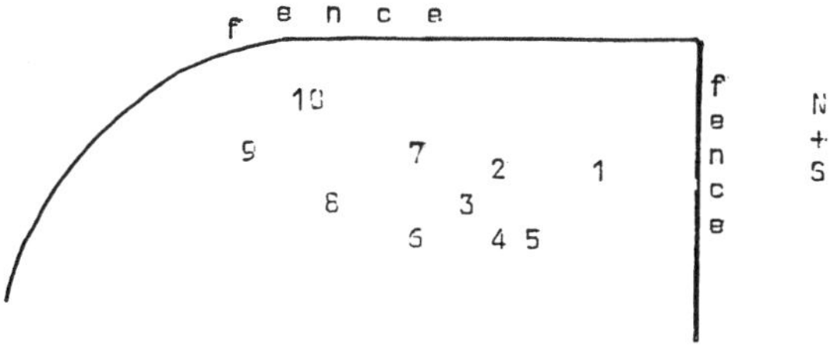

3 TS Wm M - gan the - - - - of Sevines - - - - April 1729 6(_6_)y, chn Margt S - - - William - - - - and - - - - - 1.(_7_).1742 (_5_)y; Here lyes Wm M-g-n son was to above named - - - - - - - d 20.10.1750 23; WM, AM, 1729

4 David Goodfeleov husband to Jain Jelitie. He d 10.3.1683 his age 70 and 6 and 11 months; open hand with fingers touching a very large key (see Brechin Testaments: David Goodfellow servitor to Earl of Southesk, and his spouse Janet Gelaty, 13.3.1683)

5 by Jas Millar imo fa Thos Millar & mo Margt Blair whose dust doth both lye heir. Thos Millar 19.6.1750 62, Margt Blar 5.10.1759 71, both lived together 37y, procreat Jas, Janet, John, Thos, Wm & Alex; text; (west side) shield & mantling

6 FS Jas Kar 8.3.1670, w Eouphan S(_i_)mpson. Hve doe not this for no uther end Bot that owr bvrell may be kend; (_I_)K, -S; cherub (see Brechin Testaments: Thos Carr in Tenements of Caldhame, 1667; Agnes Cobb spouse to Thos Car in Tenements of Caldhame, 1629)

7 Jas Fouller hammerman in the Nether Tenements of Caldham 21.7.1760 54, by w Isobell Steuart, two of their chn viz Mary 24.9.1759 20, Isobell d nonage; (west side) Jas Fouller; Isoble Stewart; crown, anvil, hammer & Tongs; Robt, Ann, Jas Foullers, 1761; "Her James lyes claid with a mournfull shade / Hath left his Friends & Loving Spouse sad / And now is gone above the stars to sing / Eternall prais to his imortall King" (see Jervise "Epitaphs" i 92 who has substituted Soutter for Fouller in error)

8 fragment of FS. (marginal) Esobel Wightoun sumetyme spous to Jas Jack & Robt Sampson who lived in Re(_sg n_) 2.12.1682 82; I I, R -, E W (see Davidson "Inventory" who notes that in ?1910 J Glow read "heir lyes Esobel Wightoun & lived in Re-sgrein"); (central) Here lyes Geo Mitchel sometime burges in Brechin husband was to Eliz Watt he d 19.3.1747 68 (see Brechin Testaments: Geo Mitchell burgess in Brechin, 25.2.1749; Geo Mitchell feuar in Nether Tenements of Caldhame, 4.10.1777)

9 1769. David Allan sometime in Br(_oom_)kno(_ve_) in the par Farnell, w Isobl Dorward 1762 57, 8 chn left six alive Robt, Thos, John, Isobel, Jas & Geo (see Jervise "Epitaphs" i 92 who has only: David Allan, Isoble, Zsobell Allan, Thos Allan, John Allan, Isoble Allan, Jas Allan, Geo Allan)

10 18th century fragment. Allaxander Dear, chn - - -, Alex, Wm, - - - -, Eliz, Margt & Patk

The following were noted in Jervise "Epitaphs" i 93-4 being in the Southesk family burial vault on rising ground to the south of Kinnaird castle:

11 in Latin. Robt earl of Southesk, w Ann (1da & heiress of Wm duke of Hamilton), s Chas earl of Southesk chief of Carnegie family b London 7.4.1661 d at his castle of Leuchars 9.3.1699 (by w Mary Maitland in 1704); arms of Southesk

11b KINNAIRD

12 Chas earl of Southesque & w lady Mary Maitland (2da of Chas earl of Lauderdale who was bro & heir to John duke of Lauderdale),s Jas now earl of Southesque, two das lady Anna & lady Mary whom he survived; 1704; Southesk & Lauderdale arms

13 marble mural on north wall. to the earl's father d 1849

14 marble mural on south wall. to the earl's mother d 1848

15 marble mural on north wall. the earl's 1w lady Cath Noel (2da of earl of Gainsborough) d 9.3.1855, leaving three das & a son

16 FS heir rest in the Lord a gentleman called Chas Carnegy 15.1.1655 60

Notes

Jervise "Epitaphs" i 92-4 has notes on inscriptions nos 2 (with poem), 6-7, 11-6

Davidson "Inventory on 17th century Gravestones in Angus" has detailed notes on inscriptions nos 1,2,4,6,8 & 16

OPR with the Registrar General, see 286 Farnell

Testaments Kinnaird was in the Commissariot of Brechin

Index

Allan	9	Kar	6
Blair	5	Maitland	11-12
Carnegy	11-16	Mathie	1
Car(r)	6	M--gan	3
Cobb	6	Miller	5
Dear	10	Mitchel	8
Dorward	9	Noel	15
Fouller	7	Rait	2
Gelaty	4	Sampson	8
Goodfellow	4	Simpson	6
Hamilton	11	Soutter	7
Jack	8	Stewart	7
Jelitie	4	Watt	8
		Wightoun	8

12 FERN

The original parish church in the den may have been founded about 666 AD by St Aidan. The present parish church was erected in 1883.
National Grid reference: NO 484 616

1 Jas Duncan in Glenley 8.11.1857 84, w Isabella Hebenton 2.6.1858 85, chn John d S Africa 11.11.1833 39, Jas 14.12.1863 64, Mary 25.4.1885 82, (H Thos Kinnear 9.10.1868), Chas 8.7.1885 78 (w Annie Crowe 25.5.1885 82), And 13.7.1888 74

2 TS David Taylour d Nethertoun of Melgund 13.5.1746 58, w (Margt Findlay) 11.17(53 57); D T M F

3 John Webster d Little Deuchar 2.1.1842 71, w Cath Webster d Noranside

5.4.1849 71, bro Jas d Burnhead 12.9.1828 59, sis Isobel d Burnhead 9.10. 1833 63, bro David d Burnhead 3.5.1837 81, gda Jane Traill 17.6.1849, da Mary 25.3.1851 36 (h Wm Cathro), erected in 1861 by chn rev David min Fetlar & North Yell in Shetland (see Fasti vii 297) & Isobel (h David Lyell in Kindrocket) & Ann (h Anthony Traill in Brechin)

4 1816. by Robt Carnegie, mo Elspeth Taylor 6.1795 38

5 John Baxter late in Craigie Bridge 8.4.1749 68, w Isobel Black 22.1.1751 60, s And 16.12.1720 18m; John Baxter younger, da Ann 20.9.1745 3

6 John Reid smith here for - y d 3.1702 70, w Margt (Ho)od d - - - - 65y, chn I R, I R, I R, M R, G R; (west side) emblems (see Jervise i 355 has Margt Hood d 9 November aged 64, and poem "Full sventy years he liv'd upon this earth,/ He livd to dye - the end of life is death -/ Here he was smith six lustres and three more,/ The third three wanted, it had but two before")

6a FS Ann M - - - - - - - - - - - Tindall - - - - - - - David, Patrick - - - - - - - - - - - -; A M, I T, - R, - - - - - P T, - - - -

7 Alex Wyllie late tent Warburton, da Eliz b 11.1.1787 d Brechin 21.6. 1836, da Isobell b 10.8.1787 d Brechin 19.2.1841 (sic)

8 1719. Here lyes David, Isobel, Agnus & Margt Duks & Agnus & And Duks twins all lawfull chn to John Duke & Janet Pickeman sometime indwellers in the parsih of Tannadice. The said chn d in the years viz 1687, 1697, 1703 & Margt & the forsaid twin in the year 1713; (west side) D D, K D, M D, I D, I D, A D, I D, H D, A D, A D, I D; poem

9 1796. David Lighton sometime tent Shanfoord 14.10.1794 72 (see Jervise "Epitaphs" i 355 has his age 92y), da Martha 15.1.1775 28 int in this kirk, also Isobel Lighton 30.6.1794 33 int in the Neither Kirkyard of Sinciras (i.e. St Cyrus), by w Isabel Thom

10 Wm Mackie d Deuchar 29.11.1872 71, s Jas 25.11.1848 6, w Jean Moonlight 6.1.1884 74, da Barbara d Edzell 25.6.1926 78

11 by David Tosh miller Finhaven 11.8.1885 67, chn Jane drowned 29.4.1850 3, David 19.1.1859 13m, Ann S 1.1.1863 13, w Margt Edgar d Plovermuir 15.9.1893 70, das Mary 22.9.1920 68 & Esther d California 18.1.1824 61 int Turlock cemetery

12 1845. Wm Mitchell tent Auchlochie 12.4.1854 72, w Janet Smart 21.10.1848 76, da Jean 4.4.1842 26, s John 8.9.1848.40, s David d Glenesk 1814 3

13 Alex Mitchell d Auchlochie 9.11.1891 78, w Barbara Stormont d Carnoustie 17.2.1921 91, da Barbara 22.9.1862 3, da Mary 27.4.1879 12, s Alex d Carnoustie 23.10.1926 56, da Betsy 7.8.1930 66, da Jessie 1.12.1942 70

14 FS

15 David Black late fr Barrelwell 2.7.1797 57, by w Eliz Webster, also two of their ss John 28.2.1789 26 & David 7.7.1799 28

16 window in church. by the misses Marnie, fa Jas Marnie of Deuchar 1849, mo Mary Ouchterlony 1856

17 1855. Chas Gall esq of Auchnacree 17.6.1837 75, w Ann Thomson 3.8.1849 65, chn Mary Ann 12.6.1824 8, John 29.10.1836 25, Betsy 11.12.1837 24

18 rev David Harris min Fearn 28.10.1867 92 in 65th y of ministry, w Grace Dow 22.2.1845 62, chn Mary Duncan 4.7.1813 24.6.1849, Geo b 18.1.1818 ord min & successor to his fa in 1853 d 20.6.1860, Grace 25.6.1819 5.4. 1842, Eliz Greenhill 18.1.1821 25.3.1840 (see Fasti v 397)

19 1826. by John Dalgety, w Margt Black 30.4.1822 62, da Elis 21.9.1811 17,

12 FERN

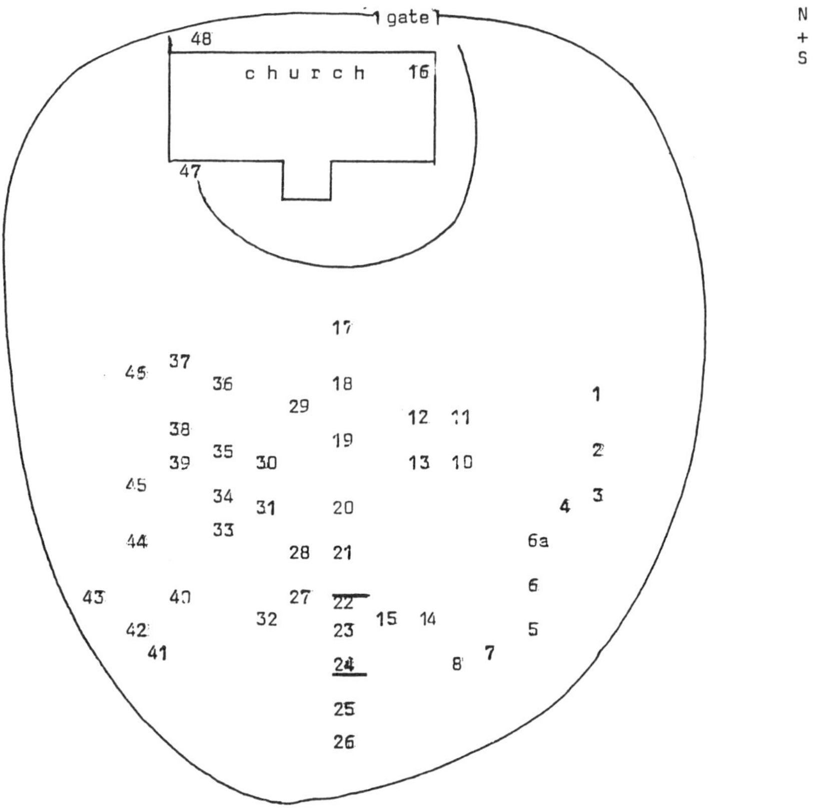

mo Ann Murison 16.5.1807 79

20 FS

21 David Dalgety late tent Muirton of Balrownie d there 19.8.1846 54, w Easter Proctor d Bangaton par Stracathro 1.10.1858 58, s Alex 19.3.1860 22, by chn John, David, Jas & Alex

22 Jas Mackie Black of Auchlishie 1.10.1826 19.4.1900

23 1871. John Black fr The Vane 18.10.1813 54, w Ann Thomson 15.10.1810 51, elder s David sometime fr The Vane 24.2.1861 69 (w Jane Rickard 18.3. 1841 45, 1s Jas 12.4.1829 7, 2s Wm SSC Edinburgh 27.8.1858 35 int Grange cem Edinburgh, 4s John 14.12.1879 44) yr s Jas sometime fr East Mains of Keithock 16.6.1832 38 (w Ann Mackie 12.9.1869 72, da Anne 28.4.1904 81, da Betsy 9.9.1900 70) all except Wm SSC int here (see Jervise "Epitaphs" i 268, these Blacks farmed in many parts of Fern for several generations; one of them, David, servant to rev mr Wemyss, became tent of part of Dub in 1731)

24 fallen. (west side) J B A T

25 John Hood, lawfull sone Robt 4.1714 4 (& his brethre & sesters Wm & Janne (west side) 1715. I H, E W; T H, H H, -H, -H, -H, -H; hammer & crown; poem (quoted in Jervise "Epitaphs" i 355)

26 by Jon, Ag^{s}, W^{m}, Ro^{t}, & Pa^{d} to fa Patk Grant sometime in Burnfoot 13.4. 1749 73 & their siss Mary, Jean, Mary & Eliz 1754; share & coulter; (west side) ♡ P G, A B

27 by Margt Bell, h John Black sometime in Windsore 25.12.1702 52, chn Jannet, John, David, Andreu, Cirsten, Jean, Isobel, Heu, Margret, Jas. This for the use of John Black younger & w Eliz Mather & their chn; (east side) I D, I B, D B, M D; H B, – B, – B, – B, – B; I B, M B, I –, E –; 1723 (but Jervise "Epitaphs" i 355 has John Black d 5.12.1709)

28 I B ♡ M B, 1723 on shield; (west side) by Margt Bell relict to the deceased John Black sometime in Windsore, to da Isobel Black 30.6.1717 15 (see Jervise "Epitaphs" i 268 & 355 for poem)

29 1826. by Jas Deuchar of Demarara, fa Geo Deuchar of Deuchar 20.1.1802 55, mo Elis Peter 27.2.1823 65 (see Jervise Epitaphs" i 269 says the Deuchars received the lands from which they took their name ... for service at the battle of Barry in 1010... Deuchars continued in possession of Deuchar until about 1815 when their male representative sold the property & went to New Zealand; Edinburgh Testaments: Jonet Strathoune relict of Wm Dewarche of that ilk par of Fairne, 1602; J C A Deuchar "The Deuchar Pedigree" (no date, copy in the Mitchell Library Glasgow); G F Black "The Surnames of Scotland"(1971))

30 FS Jannet Lyon 1687. Geo Craig, w Beatrice Black, chn Jeane & Margt int here; G C, B B; shield; two poems (quoted by Jervise "Epitaphs" i 268)

31 1812. by Alex Webster tent Farmerton, w Jean Scott 2.6.1811 40; (west side) 1812. A W, J S; J W, E W, I W, A W, M W, I W, A W

32 by John Bell, fa David Bell sometime in Wellford & mo Isobel Tendil d 5.1729; (west side) share & coulter

33 John Mill, w Eliz Lyel 1712 49

34 FS in latin. – – – – – – – – – & indweller of Ferne, s David Watson d 2.11. 16– – are int; As one house formerly held them so one holds them now; altho each had spent his life in another land they d in the place where they had been born; shield with IDW in monogram; D W (this reading is taken from mrs Davidson: "Inventory of 17th century Gravestones in Angus"; the stone is flanked by memorials of 18th & 19th century Watsons)

35 1837. Jas Watson 40y tent Balquhadlie d Ledmore par Menmuir 29.4.1835 80, he & his ancestors occupied that farm upwards of a century previous to 1821, w Mary Webster 14.6.1818 49, poem, s Jas tent Balrownie 24.11.1836 44, s David schoolmaster at Cortachy 31.3.1834 37, s Wm brewer in Arbroath 24.8.1832 32, s Robt brewer in Montrose 14.2.1836 34, s Alex cabinetmaker d Bartown Vandieman's Land 6.8.1832 29, da Jean 9.10.1834 26 (h Robt Scott in East Pittendrich) & May, Alex, Thos, Agnes & Mary d inf before 1809, by only survivor of family John (according to Jervise "Epitaphs" i 269 this John, lately fr at Ledmore, was author of poetry including "Whistling Tam" published in the 5th series of Whistle Binkie)

36 1826. by Peter Fenton schoolmaster Fearn, w Cathrine Hunter 6.9.1825 59, chn Charlotte 17.9.1801 1y5m, Peter 15.10.1807 4y11m. Eliz 27.3. 1832 26y5m

37 ob 1869. John Anderson tent Balquharn 9.7.1862, by w Charlotte Kennedy, chn Charlotte Mollison b 26.12.1852 d inf, John 2.3.1865 10y11m, Charlotte Kennedy 10.3.1865 4y9m

38 And Anderson late tent Balquharn 20.10.1846 90, by w Helen Thoms 5.5. 1865 91, das Helen 4.11.1842 37 & Ann 25.8.1849 42

39 A A Cruikshank late of Boston US formerly of Auchnacree d at Washingdales Inverarity 4.12.1877 32, sis Helen d Muirhouses Kirriemuir 3.1854 7

40 FS And Carnegy who dwelt sometime in Moortoun 21.2.1714 73, w Isobell Hood; A C, I H, A C, I C

41 Jas Scott sumtim husbandmon in Waterstoun mill 1701 94, his spous IIAEF Fordn dayed in the yer

42 1802. by Margt Hood 22.4.1827 64, h Joseph Robert sometime mert in Forfar 2.11.1800 36; (west side) J R, M H

43 W H I M; shield & monogram; W H, M H, B H, A H

44 1844. Geo Rickard 22.11.1840 90, nephew Jas Rickard sometime fr on Windsor 23.7.1842 48 "whose generous heart ever rejoiced to relieve the wants of the needy" (by wid Isabell Malcolm, s Geo 17.7.1841 7)

45 rough stone with modern metal plate. John Mackintosh, Ledenhendrie, hero of the raid of Fern (see Cortachy inscription no.37; D Harris "Leadenhendrie or the Chase of Fearn"(Brechin 1925) an account of the freebooters who terrorised the parish in 1707)

46 Thos Binny esq 5.3.1845 (see Jervise "Epitaphs" i 268: he d at his residence of Maulesden near Brechin, bought the barony of Fearn about 1836, which by marriage of his daughter Elizabeth came to hon Wm Maule third son of Lord Panmure)

47 two angels blowing trumpets (probably 18th century)

48 Death & Time; text (probably 18th century)

the following was not seen but Jervise "Epitaphs"i 355 notes two slabs built into the old manse:

49 17 M G T I R 47 (for mr Geo Tytler min Fern d 1785 89, w Janet Robertson)

N o t e s

OPR with the Registrar General: 287 Fern (Fearn)
Births 1762-74, 1776-1854
Marriages 1803-06, 1846-54
Deaths nil

SRO CH2/149 KSmin: 1739-
CH3/962 Fearn FC, Deacons Court minutes 1892-1915
HR 94 Fern (Angus) minutes 1853-1930

Kirriemuir District Council: ms Register of Interments 1832-
ms Fern churchyard register of lairs (no date)

Testaments: Fern was in the Commissariot of Brechin & the following is a selection from the Index to the Register till 1800:
John Anderson in Dubbitoun, 1595; Richd Anderson in Dubitoune 1578;
Christian Archibald spouse to John Scott in Doubtoune, 1599
Nicol Beddy at Balquharne, 1580
Robt Bell in Dubtoune & w Grissel Symmer par Brechin, 1629
Elspeth Lindsay spouse to Jas Lyell in Fermerton, 1659
Jas Symmer residenter in Dubtone, son of deceased Jas in Bogie, 1741
Jas Watson in Fermertoun, 1658;
David Webster sometime bedell at Kirk of Ferne, 1610;

Testaments (continued): the following were noticed in the Edinburgh Commissariot Register Index:
John Wilkie in Cristo, spouse Marjory Finlaysone, 1607
Jas How in Fermertoun, 1605

Jervise "Epitaphs & Inscriptions .. in the North East of Scotland" i 268-70 & 354-5 notes inscriptions nos 6,8,9,23(with poem),25,27-30,34-5,44-7 & 49

Davidson "Inventory of 17th Century Gravestones in Angus" (1977) has detailed descriptions of the stones bearing inscriptions 30 & 34

Index

Anderson 37-8.Notes
Archibald Notes

B. 26
Baxter 5
Beddy Notes
Bell 27-8.32.Notes
Binny 46
Black 5.15.19.22-4.27-8.30

Carnegie/y 4.40
Cathro 3
Craig 30
Crowe 1
Cruikshank 30

Dalgety 19.21
Deuchar 29
Dow 18
Duk(e) 8
Duncan 1.18

Edgar 11

Fenton 36
Findlay 2
Finlaysone Notes
Fordn 41

Gall 17
Grant 26
Greenhill 16

H. 43
Harris 18
Hebenton 1
Hood 6.25.40.42
How Notes
Hunter 36

Kennedy 37
Kinnear 1

Lighton 9
Lindsay Notes
Lyel(l) 3.33.Notes
Lyon 30

M. 6a.43
Mackie 10.22-3
Mackintosh 45
Malcolm 44
Marnie 16
Mather 27
Maule 46
Mill 33
Mitchell 12-3
Mollison 37
Moonlight 10
Murison 19

Ouchterlony 16

Peter 29
Pickeman 8
Proctor 21

R. 6a
Reid 6
Rickard 23.44
Robert 42
Robertson 49

Scott 31.35.41.Notes
Smart 12
Stormont 13
Stratoun 29
Symmer Notes

T. 24
Taylo(u)r 2.4
Tendil 6a.32
Thom 9
Thoms 38
Thomson 17.23
Tindall 6a.32
Tosh 11
Traill 3
Tytler 49

W. 25
Watson 34-5.Notes
Webster 3.15.31.35.Notes
Wemyss 23
Wilkie Notes
Wyllie 7

13a FORFAR PARISH CHURCH

The large parish church stands on an eminence on the south side of East High Street. The well-kept burial ground is on the steep slope to the south. After 1850 only close relatives of those already interred here could be buried here.

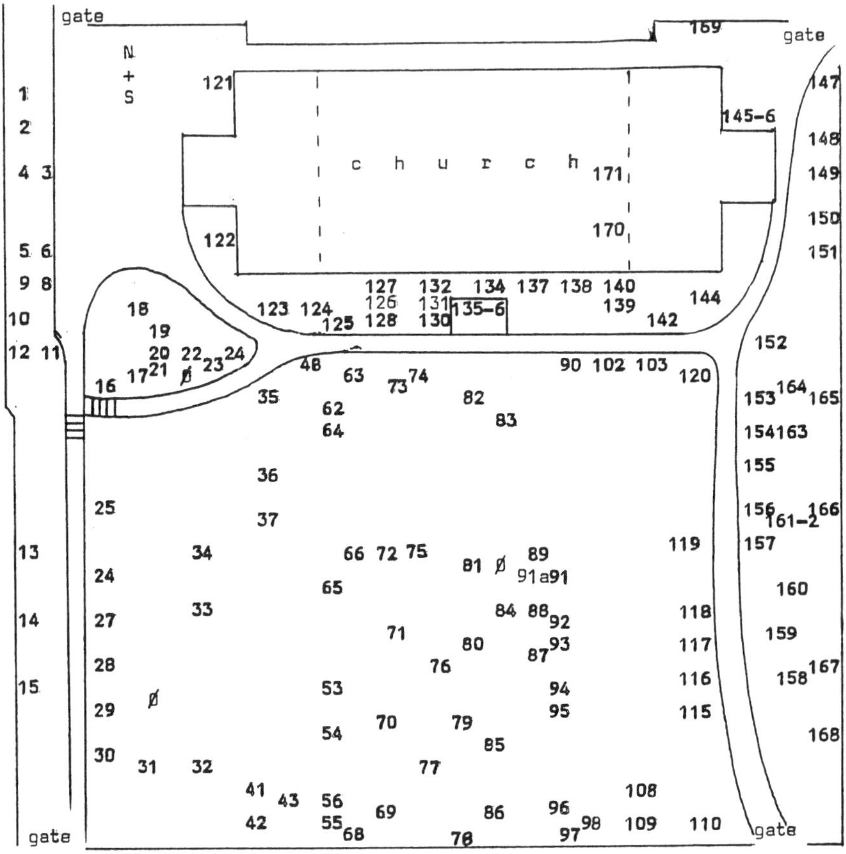

1 John Syme esq su(rgeon) here, by w mrs Eliz - - - - - - -

2 double marble tablet. patk Key esq physician here 29.4.1806 54, w Anne Binny 2.12.1832 65, da Isabella 26.10.1834 35, da Eliz Jackson 8.10.1843 38 (h John Guthrie fr Fletcherfield, da Emily 7.5.1835 2y11m)

3 John Robertson tailor here 11.11.1841 65, w Martha Anderson 15.1.1837 63, by da Martha (& h Robt Willis)

4 Patk Dickson of Slatefield 22.11.1801 29, w Isabella Steele 21.1.1838 63, da Susan 30.3.1825 25

5 Geo Webster of Westfield 29.4.1823, w Isobel Cock 22.1.1819, by Patk Webster; 1836 (see Jervise, SAS ms 530 p 807: Patk succeeded his uncle in Westfield & was son of a farmer at Barns of Craig near Montrose)

6 Isobel Binny 24.1.1782 21.6.——; David Sturrock 18.3.1819 1.4.18—;

Wm Binny 10.1.1780 10.12.18--; John Sturrock 13.1.1814 1.6.18(54); Eliz Cairns 13.8.1806 17.3.18(4)0

7 Patk Shedden formerly bailie Forfar 21.11.18(4)2 87, w Christian Mands 6.3.1841 86, by nephew - - Alex Shedden of Lo - - -

8 FS (Marginal) Wm Cuthbert - - - - Forfar, w Jean Pigot 7.5.1678 40, s - - 17.12.1679 24 (w Isobel who was da of Geo Wood late bailie Forfar) (but see Jervise SAS ms 530 p 802 who has in error: Wm Cuthill, w Jean Pigot, s 17.12.1679 (w Isobel who was da of Geo Wood late bailie here); (central) Geo Ramsay 1766 44, by s Chas reedmaker Forfar; 1832

9 1796. by Jas Williamson weaver Forfar; (west side) loom

10 Chas Adam esq d Dundee 6.2.1806 38, wid Ann Ure d Forfar 5.7.1829 58

11 John Livingston 20.12.1828 77, w Ann Donald 1.3.1833 73, by s Wm mert Carnoustie

12 clockface; Geo Ritchie 22.7.1806 64, w Cath Hair 15.5.1803 74, da Cath 9.1776 2y9m, s Jas d Hull 1815 38, s Archd 18.10.1829 50, by s Samuel watchmaker (chn Cath 24.3.1808 3, Janet 19.3.1814 11m, Margt 27.5.1817 3, one who d in nonage) (see John Smith "Old Scottish Clockmakers")

13 by - - - - irwedar weaver Muir of Forfar & w - - - Anderson, deceased s Jas Fairweder sometime mert Glammes 27.9.1759 37; (west side) J F, J B, (K W); - - - - chn Margt, Jas, Cath, Mary & Eliz

14 1823. by Thos Morris brewer Forfar 19.7.1830 63, w Anne Dowie 1814 40, das Isabella & Margt both d in nonage

15 Thos Morris brewer Forfar, 2w Mary Whitburne 13.5.1844 63, by s Jas weaver Forfar (s 28.10.1839 1y10m)

16 183(4). by Jas Kerr flesher Forfar & w Jean Tarbat 12.3.1845 31 (her fa Wm Tarbat 30.6.1827 37 & his chn May, Helen, Agnes, John & Wm) s Jas 11.4.1836 2

17 1841. by Alex Lindsay mert Benere East Indies imo mo Margt Beaton 30.12. 1822 49 & his - - Alex Lindsay 12.8.1839 68

18 - - - Ann - - - - imo Chas - - - - -

19 by Ann Paterson imo h John Roberts 27.11.1837 49, chn Ann 12.4.1837 19, John 1.1840 20

20 FS - - - - Margt Duncan & Rachell D - - - to Wm Binny - - - - - Edinburgh - - - and Isabel - - - - - Andrew

21 CT And Binny late stampmaster Forfar 5.6.1832 92, w Cath Binny 10.1.1844 74, da Clementina 5.12.1822 2(5)

22 loose stone. Wm Brew(er), Forfar & w Margt Paterson imo two das d nonage 1816

23 1777. by Wm Howe tailor Forfar & w Helen Mitchell, s Jas S 20.12.1776 20.12.1776 2y6w, s John 12.9.1784 1y; (west side) cherub; initials

24 repaired by - - - Ogilvy shoemaker - - - - & Ali(c)on R - - - imo - - Allo - - - (father) G - - - - - 17(3 or 8)5, his mo - - - - d - - - , Wm Ogilvy & - - - - der - - aged (3 or 5)6

25 1848. by lieut David Scott late Veteran Battalion imo w Janet Smith 21.3.1847 58, chn John 5.12.1805 2.9.1810, Jas 5.10.1808 7.1.1811, David 25.8.1814 15.2.1815, Bruce 16.6.1816 3.8.1821, David 4.6.1820 27.8. 1820, Thos 27.8.1833 15.2.1835

26 by Jas Lowson shoemaker Forfar & w Margt Cant, da Mary d 19.12.1821 19; (west side) crown & cordiner's knife

27 by Geo Hendry overseer at Inverighty & w Eliz Winter, 1w Margt Mc(R)eay 8.1790

28 by - - - - - wright Forfar & w Christian - - - -, chn Abram 1793 9m, Jean 1791 6m, Isabel 1799

29 1839. by Robt Ross wright Dundee & John Ross wright here & their bros imo departed friends

30 ob by David Fife slater here, - - - - - - - - - - - - - also departed 3.9. 1832 60, by surviving family & sorrowing friends

31 by Jas Malcom in Faire-Head & w Elis Mitchell & his mo Hellen Dand to his fa Jas Malcolm 6.12.1827 62 & their ss who d in nonage

32 by Ann Mathers, h David Malcom 20.10.1827 59, s Wm 12.6.1838 9, Alex d 27y, da Mary Ann d 3y; Ann Mathers d 53y

33 Wm Whyte 29.9.1836 62, w Cath Fyfe 12.18— - - - - - - - Wm 19.11.1814 5, Robt 2.1.1820 6, by das Jean, Ann & Agnes

34 1815. by (John Black)wood - - - - - - - - - - -, w Agnes M(udie) 19.5. 1798 39

35 - - - - - - - - - - - - -; Wm Snowie 16.3.1831 68

36 by capt John Laird, mo Helen Lowe 17.8.1790 75 (h Wm Laird manuf West Port of Forfar 2.3.1823 96) mourning figure; sailing ship; poem (quoted by Jervise SAS ms 530 p 819) (see also Forfar Cemetery inscription 134)

37 John Carle late tent Burnside of Dod 12.11.1831 76, w Agnes Duncan 23.1. 1844 87, ss John 21.9.1810 31, Alex 11.7.1818 38, Jas late tent Murthil-Mill 1.4.1842 60 (s Alexander 14.2.1844 22), David late fr Balbinny 14. 2.1844 55

38 David Kebel brewer Forfar 1783 60, w Lilias Dick 1780 52; Jean Kebel formerly in New Muir 1786 59; Jas Kebel in Willingyards, s Jas 1772 2; (west side) by Jas snior & junior, Robt, Alex, John & Thos Kebels; 1787

39 Thos Guthrie smith & farrier in Forfar, w Jean Hendry 16.5.1834 26; "With all a mother's hope she gave / Birth to her child; but found herself a grave" (see Jervise SAS ms 530 p 826: the poem was composed by Alex Laing of Brechin author of "Wayside Flowers")

40 - - - - - - their s John - - - - -

41 by And, John Charles & David Brown imo sis Jean 9.6.1825, fa David 14. 7.1826, Agnes Brown 18.12.1837, Jas Brown 26.12.1837

42 - - - - - - 1827 aged - - - - - - 10y - - - - - (Thos) Elder

43 Agnes Findlay 12.1797 - - - - by s David Findlay mert Forfar

44 1800. by John Crab & Isabel Wood, Forfar, imo chn Thos & Jas

45 - - - - - - - - - - aged 67y, - - - - - - - - their chn d nonage Eliz, Helen, Wm Waterstons - - - - alive are Mary, Elspet & Janet Waterstones

46 Peter Adamson, Forfar 23.4.1848 61, w Mary Loudon 12.2.1844 57

47 FS David Hariel 15.6.1680 42, da Agnes Heriel 21.4.16(7 or 9)8 20y

48 1803. Jas Masterton formerly butcher Forfar 31.10.1802 29, by wid Agnes Millar & chn Alex, Wm & Eliz

49 FS Heir lyes Isobell Wilson spouse to Alex Beanie burges of Forfar who d 1651; A ♡ B, H W; Alex Binny 20.6.1665 39; E B; emblems

50 1811. by Jas Milne stationer, mo Janet Grubb 2.5.1808, fa Patk Milne 5.2. 1849, w Mary Grig 28.11.1824

51 Alex Robert weaver in Forfar 17.2.1844 61, w Eliz Milne 22.5.1828 43, s Wm 17.6.1829 3, s David 4.5.1840 19

52 FS by Geo Nicoll litster in Forfar imo chn Jas inf & Eliz 31.12.1722 23; emblems. 1833. repaired by Peter Blair mert Forfar imo da Janet 19.9.1825 9m

53 - - - - - - - - John - - - weaver Forfar, w Agnes Wilson

54 by Wm Fyfe, Forfar d 29.10.1826 50, w Ann Fairweather 8.1.1824 41 (her fa John Fairweather late fr Balkemmock par Tealing), s Peter 21.5.1822 inf, three ss & two das survived to lament the loss of their father

55 against wall. by John Stiven baker Forfar & w Eliz Forsyth imo s John 15.7 in nonage & s John 22.11.18(5)1 2y; wheatsheaf

56 by David Hill in Caldhambank & w Agnes Allan imo chn Jas 1806 6m, Geo 1820 8m, Joseph 1826 nonage

57 1814. by Geo Key sawer in Forfar & w Janet Sorbel to da Janet 24.2.1814

58 by John Rob weaver Forfar, w Margt Mitchell 17.11.1777 55; poem (see Jervise SAS ms 530 p 805)

59 by John Sutherland messenger at arms Forfar & w Margt Stewart, imo chn Alex & Wm 1815 nonage int churchyard Airth, also Ann G 4.3.1818, Margt 22.3.1824 also in nonage int here

60 1797. by Geo Reid mert Forfar, w Strachan Morris 20.4.1796 - - -

61 FS Heir lyis Patk Suttie sumtym bailyie of Forfar 28.9.1655 77, his spouse Iannet Huntar wha deperted 19.9.1661 57; P S, I H (flanking shield with) depairtit / 15 Decem / 1669 agit / 37. D S. W S
David Suttie 3.1.1820 88 & w Isobel Reid 8.1.1780 52

62 - - - - - - Scot - - - - ouse to - - - R - - - - - - ie in Forfar - - - Decr. 18(3)1 aged - - eir daughter - - - beth Brown - - May 1813 16, their daughter Cathrine 4.5.18(2)1 21

63 Wm Law druggist Forfar, w Isabella Johnston 16.2.1849

64 - - - - - - d 24.2.1-5- - years - - (Will)iamson renued this imo his diesest father

65 by John Wm Laird, fa capt J Laird in White Hall cottage Forfar 5.3.1838 73; also Jean Fenton 24.3.1843 64 (h Wm Hill manuf)(see inscription no. 36 supra)

66 1839. by Mary Ann Donald, h Chas Donald taylor Forfar 13.3.1839 58, six of their family d inf & Cath & Christinia 5y

67 1816. by Alex Hurry of Glencoe & w Elsbeth Bower & their surviving chn John, Jean, Cath, to s Alex 22.2.1816 29; (west side) garden tools

68 - - - - - - - - - - - beth d 5.1730, viz Isobel upon 10th 5 & Allexr 19 age 9m also Jas Strachan his sister's son who d 2.1746 4, also his da Jean 22.2.1747 16; emblems

69 John Boath provost Forfar, w (e)liz Scott d 6.18(27) 25, also s Richd

70 1845. by John Cargill mason here imo fa Wm mert 6.10.1840 60, mo Magdaline Salmon 19.8.1843 55, bro Wm 30.6.1843 34

71 - - - - - - - weaver Wm Alexander d 1759 70

72 1800. by David Hird taylor Forfar & w Agnes Milne, chn David 3.3.1792 13m, Wm d September - - aged 3y, - - - - - - d nonage, also John 11.5.1809 21 (see Jervise SAS ms 530, extracts from the Register of Burials p 836 "21.(8).1809, John Hird laid in the mid grave died with a lump")

73 - - - - - - - - - -, fa Thos Webster 20.11.1807 & of his mo

74 TS Elizabeth - - - ay - - - - - - -

75 1831. by Jas - - - Alexander Tarb- - - - - - - to their - - Alex Tarbat d May - - - aged - -

76 1777. Geo Stark 1740 42, w Jean Rickart 1754 60, by Jas, Geo, Wm, Alex & David their sons; emblems

77 by Joseph Robi- - -, w Cath Burt- 26.8.18(51) 57

78 broken stone against wall. W C, M S

79 - - - - - - - Forfar - - - - to w Margret Gordon 27.6.1796 29 & four chn Elspet, Margt, Alex & Agnes Thomson, also his sis Margt Thomson 23.2. 1795 36

80 by Patk, Jas, John & Henry Samsons & their cousin David Samson to their parents John Samson formerly in West Craig 24.1.1769 85 & Jean Boath 15.9.1767 81 & their s Robt 15.4.1766 24; above Peter Samson, s Peter 2.8.1780 2; Jas Samson, chn Isobel, Eliz & Kath all d nonage; John Samson, w Jean Whyte 3.1770 35, da Elspeth 24.1.1773 7; Jas Samson 11.1772 18; Peter Samson 1764 66 & w Marg Lundie 1757 60 who were parents to said David; (west side) P S, I S, I S, H S, P S; emblems

81 1835. by Jas Anderson auctioneer Forfar & w Eliz Lindsay, chn John 7.1. 1823 1y, Eliz 11.1.1835 4

82 1782. by John Cobb taylor here to w Babie Duchars 20.6.1781 27

83 John Kerr esq of Pitruchie d Forfar 17.1.1838 78, w Ann Sturrock d here 20.4.1837 77, da Helen 2.2.1813 14, by nephew John Arnot (see Jervise SAS ms 530 p 820: mr Arnot fr Ingliston of Kinnettles succeeded to Pit-ruchie which after his death was sold to D Waterston innkeeper here)

84 1804. by David Suttie taylor here & w Eliz Adam, his fa John Suttie late tent in Heat- - - - - - - da Eliz Suttie 25.2.1801 12; (west side) cherub; D S, W S, E A

85 - - - - - - - - - - Findlay son - - - - Haltoun of Wes- - - 18.3.1724 aged - -, also by three ss Jo- - , Patk & David

86 by Jas Sievwright joiner here & w Betty Kenear, da Isabel 26.4.1824 15, s Robt 7.9.1826 19y7m

87 by Alex Leask mert Dundee, fa Jas 5.3.1839 66, mo Margt Calder 10.11. 1839 66, bros Thos & Jas, sis Margt d childhood; John Leask, ss Jas 3.4.1841 3y10m, Wm Strang 8.4.1841 1y10m

88 - - - - - - - - - - - - - - who d 8.8.1773 2y3m, s d nonage

89 1787. Wm Torn formerly mert here 28.12.1784 46, by s John also mert here

90 TS Chas Webster mert & provost Forfar, w Clementina Binny 1.4.1822 61, 2s Chas lieut EICS Bengal establishment d Saharunpore 4.11.1816 29, 6s Geo d Madras 30.6.1824, chn Alex & Isobel d young (taken from Jervise SAS ms 530 p 826)

91 by lieut John Thom 56th regt of - - , & w Eliz Clarke, s Wm 16.6.1822 21 David 2.1824 (8), gs David Thom 6.11.1831 8

91a FS under turf. (marginal) Here lyes Margt Crage 1715 36 (h Adam Simson baxter); (central) hourglass, skull & bones

92 1837. by Alex Hastings mason Forfar & w Ann Syme, chn Helen 24.8.1812 17d, Jean 17.4.1830 14

93 1795. by D – – – – – – to w – – – smith 9.9.1786 39, da Marjory Pigot 8.2.1795 29

94 1840. by Jas Ferrier to chn Geo & Ann

95 1828. John Hutchen 18.6.1827 54, da Mary 19.7.1802 4, by w Jean Doig

96 by Peter Thomson & Cath Duke, da Agnes 17.12.1823 18m

97 And Home 18.6.1825 45, by Margt Roberts, da Anne 20.9.1822 18m, s Wm 30.4.1826 17

98 ob by David Soutar mason Forfar 9.2.1835 83, w Elis Webster 23.6.1830 58

99 1828. by Geo Webster manuf, w Elspith Langlands 21.10.1827 63

100 1846. by John Stewart of Wellton of Auchter-Forfar & w Joan Steel, her mo Agnes Mann 1.1.1832 49, chn Ann 4.6.1835 7w & Margt 1.6.1844 5

101 quarter master John Allan of 46th regt d here 31.12.1845 52 while on visit to his native town for recovery of his health serving nearly 35y of which 23 he served abroad with his regt in the east & west Indies, Gibraltar & North America, by w Mary Ann Allan

102 Wm Butchart 12.6.1849 63, w Margt Willson 22.5.1837 73, by ss Jas & Wm

103 1849. Alex Smith 29.5.1845 70, w Elis Boath 1.8.1847 63, s David 29.6.1834 10, Agnes 26.11.1834 8, by s Chas

104 John Easton 23.1.1826 61, w Eliz Wallace 8.1803 32, da Eliz 17.4.1825 28, only surviving child Margt (by h David Mather of New Brunswick N America)

105 1828. by David Thornton & w Eliz Anderson, chn Mary & David d inf, also David 15.10.1826 6m

106 1836. by Geo Simpson mason here & w Ann Smith imo chn Janet 5.5.1818 4, Mary 18.3.1830 2m, Wm 17.2.1835 2

107 1837. by John Dunbar wright here

108 by David Roberts weaver here 4.6.1842 66, w Jean Lowson 24.4.1847 77, chn David 6.3.1802 7m, John 9.6.1813 2, Wm 22.5.1829 21

109 1856. (M A M, J W)

110 by Jas Wishart wright here, w Margt Morison 22.6.1823 42, s David K 14.1.1830 22

111 by Jas Kyd weaver here, w Jane Duthie 14.4.1829 41 & s Alex 21.3.1831 9

112 by John Webster mason here, w Margret Black 17.6.1823 48

113 by John Thomson, Quarrie-Bank to w Ann Philp 28.3.1829 52

114 1832. by mrs J Webster of Flemington, fa Robt Small late tent of the Mill in Kincaldrum 6.1822 72, also mo Margret Cowpar 28.11.1831 81

115 by John Glass tailor here, w Betty Larons 7.10.1798 27 & 2w Margret Craik 15.2.1829 62, da Janet 30.6.1808 20m

116 1841. by John Miller mason Whiteburn Dunnichen & w Jean McIntosh, s John 22.6.1831 19

117 1784. by Jas Anderson tailor here, w Kath Tarbat 9.12.1783 35, two chn d in nonage

118 fallen. (illegible) G Mills S

119 ob Geo Don botanist native of Forfarshire, resident here over 20y, d Doohillock 15.1.1814 "man of genius who with few educational advant-

ages raised himself to a high place in the ranks of the botanists of his day; he established a botanic garden here.... was superintendent 1802-6 Edinburgh Royal Botanic Gardens.... associate Linnean society of London ....; by public subscription through efforts of Forfar Field Club, John Knox schoolmaster here & Geo Claridge Bruce FLS by whom it was unveiled 1910 (see DNB, his ss Geo 1798 1856 & David 1800 1841 were also noted botanists)

120 1821. by John Ritchie & ss Wm & David - - -ers in Forfar to w Kath Cobb 26.1.1797 59y11m; (east side) 1821. Wm Ritchie & Margt Eston in Sparrowcroft, s Wm 6.6.1820 20, chn Betty, Cath, Isobel, Alex, Margt; J R, W R, I R, K, J, C, M, E, B, W ; shuttle & stretcher

121 Robt Paterson plasterer here, w Ann Wyllie 14.6.1839 57, da Eliz 2.6. 1820 4

122 fragment on top of eroded TS. David - - - - - 13.12.1821 -y10m

123 loom & shuttle; John Lowson in Muirsnook of Lower 21.1.1763 83, w Cath Boutchart 10.1748 76, by her ss David, John, Patk & Alex & by his last w Matilda Burns; (west side) 1763. (see Jervise SAS ms 530 p 803: these were ancestors of the manufacturers Lowson or Lawson in Forfar, Arbroath & Dundee, often chief magistrates in Forfar; see Forfar cemetery inscriptions no. 96, 119, 134)

124 FS Jas Gall shoemaker here 1781 41, w Ann Cuthbert 26.2.1826 84, by s Robt manuf here

125 And Stirling 8.9.1796 68, by s Chas at Carsebank, da Eliz 23.4.1784 16

126 Jas Byars dyer here 2.2.1837 74, w Janet Bain 28.1.1822 52, three chn d inf, by surviving chn

127 Patk Whyte 29.1.1847 88, s Thos 29.1.1849 49, s in law Wm Whyte 22.4. 1813 28, gda Margt Whyte 8.5.1813 1y3m

128 FS (marginal) Heir lyes - - - - - -si ane faithfvl one:whom God hes blest to sie his - - - -; (central) shield with: erected by - - Miln taylor in Forfar imo his spous Christina Miln 5.(5).1776 aged --y; 1645; emblems & cordiner's knife; Alexr Quhytlawe who departed this - - - - - - - ; A Q, - T, - Q

129 FS (marginal) heir lyes Jas Wood cordiner & burges in Forfar d 1607, 1s David 6.11.1647 78; (central) shield with - W, D W; shield with tree; heir lyes Robt Hv- - - - - - - - Wood his spous - - - - - - bel - - - st - - - - - amd elizabeth - - - his spous; Isobel Hvntar spous to Jas Wood; Eupham Cuthbert spous to David Wood

130 1801. John Ritchie esq RN provost Forfar 31.3.1809 87, w mrs Mary Bower 6.4.1800 75

131 TS John Binny esq of Forneth sometime mert Madras b here d Brechin 15.9. 1841 61 int here (see Jervise SAS ms 530 p 803: mr Binny was succeeded in Forneth & Cluny in Perthshire by his bro in law Jas Speid sometime a writer & provost Brechin whose fa was farmer at Windton in Fearn)

132 neo-gothic. by John Milne builder, w Isabella Ramsay, s Geo Ramsay 12.1845 17, s John 1.12.1846 21

133 FS heir lyes Wiliam Guthrie maltman burges Forfar 13.7.1648 -- & w Cath Dicksone 1628 - - - - Cath Dickesone - - - - Chas & John Milne - - -s Christie - - - - gloria - - - or inferni - - - datibi; emblems; four shields

134 FS resembling 133. heir lyes Geo Wood bu(rges of Forfar) d 2.16(4)- - - - - - - - - departed (this lyf) 29.4.16-- (see Jervise SAS ms 530 p 802

. notes that this stone "presents curious carvings of the Woods of Bonnington & Craig, with supporters, & a figure of Death, an angel on each side holding a trumpet to the ear of a skeleton"; Davidson "Inventory" notes that Geo Wood d 2.1642)

135 TS Patk Watson Carnegy esq of Lower & Turin d Lower 3.9.1838 46, w mrs Rachel Ann Forbes d Edinburgh 16.11.1852 50 int here, s Jas Forbes d Hurstmonceaux 1.5.1855 17 int here (see The Scots Peerage, earl of Northesk p 490)

136 Chas Carnegy 22.3.1874 66, w Sophia Bell 10.7.1886 74, da Rachel Anne Forbes 22.7.1841 9w, s Patk Thos 21.1.1878 39 int Cholochat Assam, s Chas Wm 9.4.1905 65 int Puebla Mexico, s Jas Souter 8.9.1915 68 int Puebla, da Williamina Sophia 8.11.1915 62, da Margt Anne Ogilvy 5.3.1922, da Alison Ann 5.8.1929 78

137 sarcophagus. rev John Bruce b 24.7.1758 admitted here 24th birthday d 19.1.1817, w Mary Fergusson 1844 85, four chn d inf & early childhood, s David 20.4.1806 12, da Margt 13.2.1864 67, by s rev John DD min Guthrie then in Edinburgh d 4.8.1880 85 int St Cuthbert's Edinburgh, only surviving gda Agnes Bruce; 1882 (Fasti v 286 & i 89; Ewing i 106)

138 Wm Hobb 15.5.1815 61, w Margt Winter 21.12.1816 62, by da Janet (h Alex Mitchell) & s John; David Hobb 21.2.1812 (21)

139 Wm Boath sometime tent Weltoun 18.1.1773 65, 1w Jean Foord 14.4.1752, 2w Ann Ormand 4.3.1762, four chn d nonage, Kathren 19y11m, s Jas 4.1.1778 18y9m, by ss Wm tent Weltoun (w Jean Gowrie 7.11.1777 32y1m17d who was da of Geo Gowrie in Mosside of Lowr, s Geo 3.10.1777 1y); (west side) cherub; 1778; by Wm, John, David & Alex; our eldest bro's wife & his young son

140 by Wm Boath w(riter) 14.4.1826 52, w Margt Wallace - - - -, da May 5.2.1823 (6y10m), s Jas 27.10.1826 1-y11m, da Ann Jane 1.183(1 38)

141 1848. Wm Steele d here 11.5.1833 67, w Eliz Sampson d here 15.5.1837 72, by ss Wm & Geo (s Wm 3.9.1830 14m)

142 1823. Wm Neish 7.1847, by nephew John Spence manuf in Forfar

143 TS David Dickson late kirk treasurer here 15.5.1840 66, w Helen Peter 9.8.1843 66, da Mary 6.10.1825 19

144 1803. by John Milln weaver here, w Agnes Spence 14.12.1801

145 by - - - - -A - - - -, her da Margt - - - - -

146 Wm Fraser road contractor of this town, w Cath Rattray 2.4.1833, da Ann 14.5.1809 11, by s Wm mert Kingston Jamaica in 1835

147 by Graham Bower tailor here 29.3.1833 29, w Betty Glass 3.5.1875 74, s John 7.5.1830 nonage; (east side) Geo Bower d China 1861 29

148 TS Thos Spence late tent Garth 9.6.1841 83, w Ann Peter 3.7.1808, 1s Jas drowned near Carnoustie 8.8.1831, das Ann & Mary int New Cemetery & Chas int Kersal churchyard near Manchester

149 David Fenton 6.4.182060, w Martha Hamilton 6.3.1841 79, by s Jas cooper here, two das & four ss also deceased

150 1818. by Alex Wallace tent in par Dunnichen, w Helen Peter 1.11.1837 74, da Agnes 7.1793 6m, da Jean 5.1798 4, s Alex 3.1800 14w, da Janet 9.1803 2, s Jas 10.1803 9w

151 by David Ker weaver here & w Eliz Samson, da Jean 1.8.1762 19, s John 1.2.1752, da Janet - - - nonage

152 1833. Wm Adam 1.6.1805, by da Elspeth (h Alex Moilison turner here)

153 TS Jas Mitchell supervisor of excise Dundee 7.2.1815 73, w Eliz Watt 1815, chn Eliz (1).9.1820 (36)(h Jas Hendry mert Glasgow), s Jas esq surgeon EICS 9.8.1839 (52)

154 J M E S ; thistle; eulogy; (west side) John Milln fr 16.(5).1771 83y 6m, w Eliz Suttie 22.4.1773 76, surviving chn John, Wm, Alex & Jas, David, Robt, Martha & Eliz

155 by Alex - - - shoemaker here, w Isobel Simpson 31.8.1--- 47y

156 TS Geo Fyfe 9.12.1836 83, w Cath Brown 13.6.1838 72, s Geo 18.9.1846 37

157 FS emblems; J ♡ G, 17 EN 50; - G, - G, - G, - G, - G, -G, D G, J G, G G, (T)G, C G, A G, - G

158 FS Jas Gordon mert here 20.3.1804 29.12.1869, w Clementina Jarron 9.7.1807 21.5.1862, 2s John Jarron 9.10.1836 1

159 sarcophagus. John Brand innkeeper Drumlithie d here 6.1836 7(3), w Mary Brand d Dundee 1.1831 5(3), s John cabinet maker d here 18(48) 34 (w Esther Tosh d Kirriemuir 9.12.18(47); (north side) John & Jas Brand int here; Mary Brand int Dundee; Esther Tosh int churchyard Glamis

160 FS Robt Bell 24.3.1835 (3)y9m, by granduncle Robt Gall & gfa Jas Gall

161 Graham Henderson, gs David Millar 5.7.1881 18

162 FS 1839. Graham Henderson 28.5.1875 71, w Helen Peddie 15.8.1873 66, s Wm 8.1.1834 21m, s Geo 12.12.1834 3w, Alex 2.1849 6

163 pillar. - - - - -11 - - - - - - Forfar who - - - - - 1837

164 TS Patk Barry mert here (13).9.1833, w Ann Dick 8.5.1834, da Cath 26.3. 18(45), Jas fr West Carsebank 28.4.1849, by survivors Eliz & Isabella Barry

165 1817. John Morgan blacksmith here 1816 61, s Jas 2.7.1790 3, da May 10.6.1792 1y4m; (west side) crown over 4 horse shoes & hand holding hammer

166 John Clark d Orchardbank 5.2.1834 45, by ss David & Alex farmers; said Alex, da Jemima 21.12.1859 2

167 mural. John - - - d 26.-.1845 5-, w Jessie Ba- - d - - - age 6-y, their - - - - - - - - - - -

168 by Wm Wilson weaver here - - - - , w Kathrine Wood 4.7.18--

169 FS Erected 1846 imo Jas Irons who d - - - 8(4)y, (Elspo)t Duncan who d - - - 80y, da Jean 10.1825 - -, s Jas 3.183(1) aged --y, also da Elspot 3.1839 -y

170 mural in church, in Latin. Patk Carnegy esq of Lower b 11.1720 succeeded on death of his fa d 11.1799, w Margt (da of sir Alex Bower of Kingaldrum) eight ss & four das, by Patk Carnegy of Lower on 20.9.1820 (ie.xiii Kal Sept) ; Patk Carnegy esq of Lower 11.11.1720 (ie.iii Id Nov) d 12.11. 1799 (ie. Prid Id Nov), "pronepotis" of David 2nd earl of Northesk

171 mural in church, probably dating from 1750-1800. maj general David Kerr of Jamaica, fa Wm Kerr esq provost in Forfar, mo Eliz Ballingall (da of capt Ballingall esq of - - - -), their chn Wm, Thos, Alex, Helen, Cath, Jas, Margt, David, John, Patk, Chas, Eliz, Robt & Agnes

The following inscriptions were npted by Jervise, Society of Antiquaries for Scotland ms 530 pp 799-807 and were not seen in 1976:

172 mural. Jas Wyllie writer here & commissary Brechin 12.12.1800 45, w Margt

Webster 1829 76, 2s Thos surgeon EICS d Bacdalla Ceylon 5.11.1818 36

173 mural. mr Wm Webster sometime mert Dundee d Edinburgh 13.11.1801 58 son of late bailie Webster here, by siss Agnes (wid of late bailie Watt of Meathie) & Helen (h mr David Adam mert here)

174 mural. 1800. John Watt 1765 72 acquired estates of Meathie & Kinneries, s David 1797 78 chief magistrate here & councillor for 50y & succeeded to his father's estates(by s John Watt late provost Forfar)

175 1815. bailie David Watt of Meathie, w mrs Agnes White 20.9.181- 83, s John of Meathie provost here 20.8.181(4) 64, twelve ss & das who d at home & abroad, their mo surviving to see all of them buried except two, by da Margt

176 FS John Adam esq late surgeon H M 13th regt Foot d here 13.1.1831 74, w Margt Ure d here 5.7.1837 68, chn Margt 21.2.1831 40, Isabella 29.12.1830 17

177 Jas Dall, w Euphemia Milne 1777 60; poem

178 from west wall. rev John Skinner here, w mrs Eliz Ure 12.5.1820 43, chn who predeceased her Margt inf, Mary Robertson 14y, Alex 4y, by family (note: she was da of mr John Ure the first episcopalian provost here after removal of civil disabilities in 1792, s Geo Ure d of yellow fever at Aspinall Panama 9.1.1867 62 crossed Atlantic 39 times, an enthusiastic botanist, when in central Asia as a merchant collected many plants especially orchids; see Forfar St John's inscription no. 29)

179 from east wall. 1794. Wm Kerr esq of Dumbarrow 11.3.1794 63, w mrs Jean Gray 14.3.1793 57, by chn Kath, Jean, Eliz, Agnes & Janet

180 John Barclay esq writer here killed by fall from his gig 10.11.1831 40, by w Eliz Petre (bro Wm Petre d from effects of same accident 11.12.1831 46)

181 Jas Craik manuf here 21.7.1843 67, w Isobella Steele 22.3.1855 76 (note: were parents of provost Craik who d 1872 55)

182 Chas Mill builder & sculptor here 28.2.1837 66 (note: he was the carver of most of the tombstones erected here in his day)

183 TS Chas Grant 1820 56 "an honest man through labouring gained his bread", chn; poem; by friends

184 mural. Francis Ross of Auchlessan, w Anne Carnegy (da of Alex Carnegy & Ann Blair of Kinfauns), da Eliz 2.10.1705 7.12.1732; by her mo & step fa Wm Lyon of Carse (see St Andrews Testaments, dame Anna Blair spouse to mr Robt Carnegie fiar in Kinfauns, 1688; mr Alex Carnegy of Kinfauns par Errol 1692, 1706; Anna Blair spouse to Alex Carnegie of Kinfauns, 1693; see also Chas Rogers "Monumental Inscriptions" ii 227)

185 two bells inscribed. Wm Strang & w Margt Pattillo in Stockholm, 1660.
186 Robt Strang native of Forfar d Stockholm 21.4.1651, made by Gerot Meyer 1656.

Fasti v 284 Forfar & Restennet mentions a tombstone inscribed to:
187 rev John Ker b Roxburghshire about 1715 d 15.12.1781, w Agnes Burton 15.3.1788

Jervise SAS ms 350 pp 835-7 also notes extracts from the Register of Burials kept by the beadle - - Neave:

188 15.9.1808 Christian Young's son d about the middle of the brae;
189 2.9.1809 Jas Stuart's son d of a host
190 15.12.1811 Thos Doig d with a swelling

191	9.9.1812	Eliz Downie's child laid at Margt Kidd's feet, her partner denying the child
192	16.3.1813	Chas Wood's miscarriage
193	28.9.1814	(John) Allan d with belf
194	6.2.1815	Jn Dalgety d of old age or burnt in the fire
195	22.5.1820	Alex Strachan laid straight with the blind widow in David Rodger's house, near the kirkstile died of a night's illness or we may say of old age - shoemaker
196	2.4.1821	A laddie from the Hatton of Carse laid 2 graves south from Alex Nevay's stone, d of getting his thigh bone broken with a ride
197	9.1.1821	Thos Bruce laid at the north corner of the Cobbles stone being a friend - d of an asthma
198	24.8.1820	Patk (Johnston)'s child laid in the Cubbles place its mother a Cabble d in the same month
199	27.2.18(20)	David Hillocks laid on the south side of Alex Low's stone d of a decay being a (friend)
200	3.-.1820	David Webster's stillborn child laid on his goodmother's feet in the north grave at Alex Webster's stone d in old age
201	19.2.1809	Alex Milne wright who was killed of a (plank) with Jas Brown laid at his feet at a tree betwixt the middle of the brae
202	21.(8).1809	John Hird laid in the midgrave d with a lump
203	7.7.1812	John Murison's stillborn child laid above that one
204	8.2.1814	Widow Bowman laid straight with her own stone on the north side of Wm Laird's stone d in a moment - shoemaker
205	1.4.1816	Chas Hill's da laid on the south side of bailie Sands with his head at Jas Rock's stone on 4 pillars 2 graves length from the West Dick d in a decay
206	6.10.1816	Alex Alexander laid two graves south from blind John Alexander's stone d in old age
207	3.1.1817	John Cameron's wife laid on the south of Patk Guthrie good father look up to the 26 of last month from Killeemore poor
208	10.4.1817	- a child from the Back(yard), a bell ringer's son
209	9.(8).1817	Robt Welsh's son had a child laid on Frederick's feet
210	3.6.1817	Robt Smith's child laid in the north grave of John Findlay's place d in the as with (himself)
211	17.5.1817	A woman named Sturrock from Dr Milne's laid in the Big Tree Howff 4 trees from the east dick and 6 from the west near the road that leads to the east stile - d in poor old age
212	13.1.1820	Patk Mackie laid in the south grave of the Cabbles place being a good brother d in old age. (Jerrieance) Walker's daughter's child d in a decay on the north side of Wm Farquhar's stone 4 graves north. John Smith's wife laid on the north grave of the Boath's Place d in a decay from Patk Bell's - - - - -

N o t e s

A Jervise, ms 530 in the library of the Society of Antiquaries of Scotland, Edinburgh, has a valuable collection of inscriptions compiled about 1873; he observed that many of the inscriptions were much eroded & much further erosion has occurred since. He mentions inscriptions no. 4,5,8,31,38,40,47,49,58,61,83,90,123,128-31,133-5,170,172-86

F Davidson, "Inventory of 17th Century Tombstones in Angus" gives detailed descriptions of nos.8,47,49,61,128-9,133-4

Testaments. Forfar was in the Commissariot of St Andrews and the following is a selection from the Index to the Register 1549-1800 which includes

13a FORFAR PARISH CHURCH

over 70 names of Forfar citizens:
Helen Carnegie da of deceased Robt of Lauchland Forfar, 1662
Eupham Cuthbert spouse to John Symson in Wester Dod in Forfar, 1683
Wm Cuthbert late bailie Forfar, 1695, 1720
Wm Cuthbert shoemaker Forfar, 1704
Bessie Hunter spouse to Patk Beny burges of Forfar, 1620
Bessie Hunter da to deceased Wm Hunter skinner burges Forfar, 1640
Geo Hunter s of And provost Forfar & w Euphemia Beny, 1629
Janet Hunter spouse to Patk Suttie burges Forfar, 1618
Margt Hunter spouse to Geo Bellie burges of Forfar, 1618
Thos Hunter wright in Forfar, widow Jean Binny, 1752
Margt da of Thos Mylne in Lower, 1725
Isobel Sturrock spouse to John Frisley shoemaker, 1675
Margt Thornton spouse to Jas Thom burges of Forfar, 1687
Wm Ure bailie, spouse Eliz Lindsay, 1736
David Watt weaver in Forfar, spouse Margt Brandon, 1681
Eliz Wood spouse to Christopher Ranny par of Forfar, 1674
Geo Wood burges of Forfar, spouse Mary Mathie, 1681
Helen Wood widow of Archd Anderson burges of Forfar, 1620
Isobel Wood w of Gilbert Ramsay sometime bailie Forfar & s Jas, 1722

The following were noticed among the Edinburgh Testaments:
Jas Barrie cordiner burgess Forfar, 1608
Wm Dickson yr s to deceased Chas of Connonsyth late provost of Forfar, 1735
John Dog in Myresyde, 30.10.1598
Jas Dysert alias Laird burgess of Forfar, 1593
Wm Kid burgess of Forfar, 1606
Alex Sympson in Cloksbriggs, 1607

John Smith "Old Scottish Clockmakers": located in Forfar were Robt Keith fl 1819-37, Samuel Ritchie fl 1800-37, Patk Young d 18.1.1811, Wm Nevay in Castle Street 1837, Chas Davidson fl 1798-1815

Index

Adam 10.84.152.173.176
Adamson 46
Alexander 71.206
Allan 56.101.193
Anderson 3.13.81.105.117.Notes
Arnot 83

B. 13
Ba- - 167
Bain 126
Ballingall 171
Barclay 180
Barry/ie 164.Notes
Beanie 49
Beaton 17
Bell 136.160.212
Bellie Notes
Ben(n)y Notes
Binny 2.6.20-1.49.90.131.Notes
Black 112
Blackwood 34
Blair 52.184
Boath 69.80.103.139-40.212
B(o)utchart 102.123
Bower 67.130.147.170
Bowman 204
Brand 159
Brandon Notes
Brewer 22
Brown 41.62.156.201
Bruce 119.137.197
Burns 123
Burt 77
Burton 187
Butchart 102.123
Byars 125

C. 78
Cabble, see Kebel 197-8.212.Notes
Cairns 6
Calder 87
Cameron 207
Cant 26
Cargill 70
Carle 37

Carnegy 135-6.171.184.Notes
Christie 133
Clark(e) 91.166
Cobb 82.120
Cobble 197-8.212.Notes
Cock 5
Cowpar 114
Crab 44
Crage 91a
Craik 115.181
Cubble, see Cabble, Kebel
Cuthbert 8.24.129.Notes
Cuthill 8

Dalgety 194
Dall 177
Dand 31
Davidson Notes
Dick 38.164
Dick(e)son(e) 4.133.143.Notes
Dog, Doig 95.190.Notes
Don 119
Donald 11.66
Dowie 14
Downie 191
Duchars 82
Duke 96
Dunbar 107
Duncan 20.37.169
Duthie 111
Dysert Notes

Easton 104.120
Elder 42
Eston 104.120

Fairweather/weder 13.54
Fenton 65.149
Gergusson 137
Ferrier 94
Fife, Fyfe 30.33.54.156
Findlay 43.85.210
Foord 139
Forbes 135
Forsyth 55
Fraser 146
Frisley Notes
Fyfe, Fife 30.33.54.156

G. 157
Gall 124.160
Glass 115.147
Gordon 79.158
Gowrie 139
Grant 183
Gray 179
Grig 50
Grubb 50
Guthrie 2.39.133.207

H. 171
Hair 12
Hamilton 149
Hariel 47
Hastings 92
Henderson 161-2
Hendry 27.39.153
Heriel 47
Hill 56.65.205
Hillocks 199
Hird 72.202
Hobb 138
Home 97
Howe 23
Huntar/er 61.129.Notes
Hurry 67
Hutchen 95

Irons 169

Jarron 158
Johnston 63.198

Kebel, see Cabble 38
Kenear 86
Keith Notes
Ker(r) 16.83.151.171.179.187
Key 2.57
Kid(d),Kyd 111.191.Notes
Knox 119
Kyd, see Kid 111

Laird 36.65.204.Notes
Langlands 99
Larons (?Lawrence) 115
Law 63
Lawson 123
Leask 87
Lindsay 17.81.Notes
Livingston 11
Loudon 46
Low(e) 36.199
Lowson 26.108.123
Lundie 80
Lyon 184

M. 109
McIntosh 116
Mackie 212
Mc(R)eay 27
Malcom 31-2
Mands 7
Mann 100
Masterton 48
Mather 104
Mathers 32
Mathie Notes
Mill 182
Millar/er 48.116.161
Milln, see Milne 144.154

Mills 118
Milne, Miln 50-1.72.128.132-3 144.154.177.201.211. Notes
Mitchell 23.31.58.138.153
Mollison 152
Morgan 165
Morison 110
Morris 14-5.60
Mudie 34
Murison 203

N. 157
Neish 142
Nevay 196.Notes
Nicoll 52
Northesk 170

Ogilvy 24
Ormand 139

Paterson 19.22.121
Pattillo 185
Peddie 162
Peter 143.148.150
Petre 180
Philp 113
pigot 8.93

Quhytlaw 128

Ramsay 8.132.Notes
Ranny Notes
Rattray 146
Reid 60-1
Rickart 76
Ritchie 12.120.130.Notes
Rob 58
Robert 51
Roberts 19.97.108
Robertson 3
Robi- - - 77
Rock 205
Rodger 195
Ross 29.184

S. 78.171
Salmon 17
Sampson 141
samson 80.151
Sands 205
Scot- - - 62
Scott 25.69
Shedden 7
Sievewright 86
Sim(p)son 91a.106.155.Notes
Skinner 178
Small 114
Smith 25.93.103.106.210.212
Snowie 35
Sorbel 57
Soutar 98
Speid 131
Spence 142.144.148
Stark 76
Steel(e) 4.100.141.181
Stewart 59.100.189
Stirling 125
Stiven 55
Strachan 68.195
Strang 185-6
Stuart 189
Sturrock 6.83.211.Notes
Sutherland 59
Suttie 61.84.154.Notes
Syme 1.92

Tarbat 16.75.117
Thom 91.Notes
Thomson 79.96.113
Thornton 105.Notes
Torn 89
Tosh 159

Ure 10.176.178.Notes

W. 49.109
Wallace 104.140.150
Walker 212
Waterston 45.83
Watt 153.173-5.Notes
Webster 5.73.90.98-9.112.114.172-3 200
Welsh 209
Whitburns 15
White 175
Whyte 33.80.127
Whytelaw 128
Williamson 9.64
Willis 3
Wil(l)son 49.53.102.168
Winter 27.138
Wishart 110
Wood 8.44.129.134.168.192.Notes
Wyllie 121.172

Young 188.Notes

13b FORFAR CEMETERY

The cemetery at Newmonthill was landscaped by George Henderson of the Den Nurseries, Brechin. It was opened for burials in November 1849. At the top of the slope is the monument to sir Robert Peel and the Repeal of the Corn Laws, erected in 1851 by public subscription.

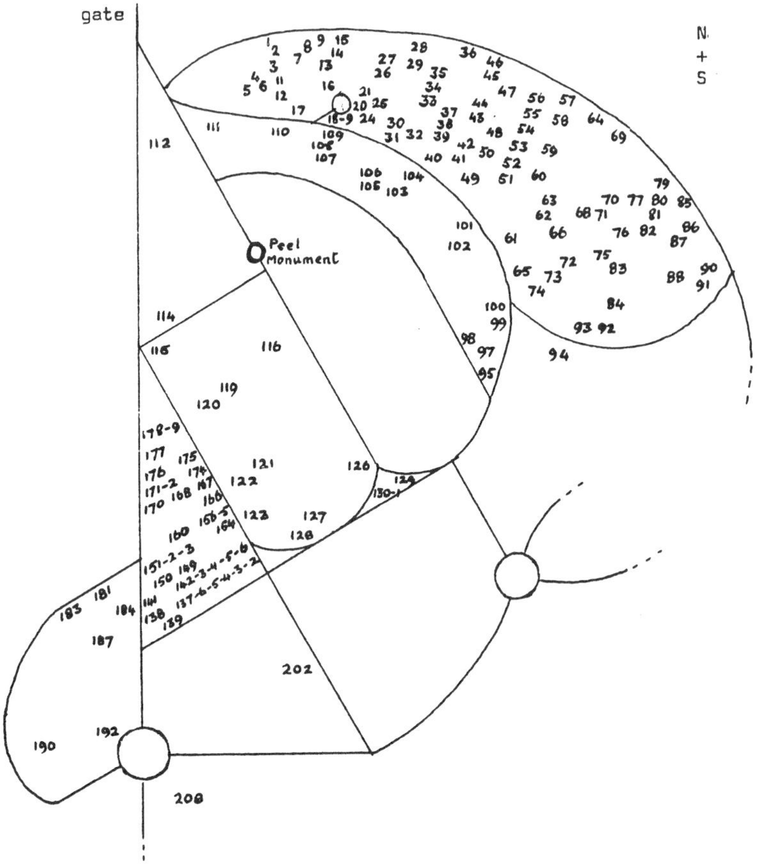

1 Donal Gordon innkeeper here 24.9.1886 83, w Jane Symon 22.9.1857 45, chn Jas 13.3.1842 6, Peter 1.12.1848 8, Margt 10.1.1860 10, Wm 10.9. 1871 26, John d Melbourne 25.4.1890 53, Frank 30.12.1908 66

2 David Milne 1.8.1857 41, by w Mary McKinzie, s Jas 3.3.1844 6m

3 David Milne 13.8.1860 47, w Isabella Guthrie 6.3.1878 63, da Jane 8.7. 1848 6, s in law Peter McIntosh 9.2.1898

4 Wm Samson 23.2.1891 85, nephew David Ogilvie 11.6.1854 19, nephew Wm Ogilvie 18.5.1858 18, mo Eliz Boath 29.3.1862 85, sis Agnes Samson or Ogilvie 1.7.1883 74, w Agnes Smith 8.7.1912 98

5 David Soutar mason Forfar 9.2.1835 83, s David 27.9.1865 64; John Soutar 22.12.1885 79, w Eliz Leys 7.9.1884 77; John Soutar junior mason 3.2.1899 66, w Isabella McKinnon 12.1904 78

6 by David Fife, ss Wm 31.7.1852 9m, David 31.7.1857 21 & Wm 15.2.1834

2; Cath Liveston 17.4.1886 81; David Fife 28.8.1900 88; Margt Fyfe (sic) 13.2.1912 72

7 by Agness Chaplain 21.9.1899 83, mo Agnes Robb 4.12.1847, nephew David Hill 19.2.1855, aunt Ann Chaplain 15.3.1855, fa David Chaplain 8.11.1855

8 Chas Wilson quarrier 29.1.1854 75, w Eliz Nevay 10.6.1869 91, da Agnes 21.10.1890 86, s Chas 18.4.1873 64 (w Eliz Walker 16.4.1896 84)

9 by David Webster, da Jean 6.6.1854 16, s Jas 6.8.1863 19

10 1894. by Jas Dickson 20.6.1819 8.11.1900, w Euphemia Barrie 18.8.1818 1.1.1894, fa John 5.2.1856 84, mo Jean Horn 16.1.1847 69, bro John 3.4.1836 20

11 Wm Smith fr Lochhead 7.10.1870 65, w Magdeline Walker 15.8.1893 86, da Eliz d Lochhead 5.7.1916 85; (west side) Jas Smith fr Lochhead 26.5.1816 40, w Betty Andrew 20.2.1858 78

12 Jas Langlands 24.4.1856 47, w Elis Roderick 7.3.1853 38, da Rose 30.6.1845 11m; Betsy Jane Langlands 4.3.1857 6y6m; Wm Langlands 15.9.1859 84

13 John Keith 12.3.1845 78, w Eliz Millar 20.12.1853 72, chn And 10.10.1813 7, Jas 18.5.1822 9, Ann 18.5.1823 4, John 24.5.1823 2, Isabello (sic) 16.4.1827 4, Janet 21.6.1849 38, by surviving chn Wm, David & Margt who d 25.1.1855 47, foresaid Wm, 24 Canmore Street Forfar 26.4.1889 79

14 by Alex Farmer 18.1.1899 78, s Jas 27.5.1854 3y6m, w Agnes Grierson 3.3.1888 72, da Margt 13.8.1934 80

15 Adam Sutherland 7.4.1880 84, w Marjory Bruce 8.8.1853 49, s Adam 19.8.1849 2, da Cath 9.9.1925 82 (h Wm Crockatt 1.8.1931 86)

16 by John Turnbull & Ann Bell, da Margt Ireland d Kirkton of Aberlemno of diphtheria 22.2.1864 7, parents Wm Turnbull 19.11.1854 73 & Helen Jamieson 5.6.1856 81; Wm Turnbull junior 9.3.1879 69, w Ann Anderson 16.3.1868 58

17 Wm Laird manuf Forfar 9.12.1859 68, w Cath Leighton 3.1.1823 28 int Old Churchyard; John Laird, mo in law Sarah Grant 17.5.1852 59; John Laird manuf Forfar, chn Wm 23.11.1851 5m, Eliz Ann Wells 27.4.1859 6½, Wm 16.6.1860 3m, Jas Reid d Genoa Italy 16.5.1877 23 int here 6.6.1877; Annie Ellis many y servant in the family 10.1851 71; Jas S Orchar, w Mary Laird 30.4.1892 34; John Laird manuf 27.12.1904 87, w Mary Milne 22.7.1923 92; Alfred Ward Laird 1893 23; Geo Milne Laird 1906 50, w Cath Kyd Laird 1942 (see Jervise SAS ms 530 p 822)

18 David Easson tobacconist 7.6.1866 48, fa John 7.4.1842 47, mo Isobel Ness 12.8.1852 68, s John 30.1.1849 7, s Chas 26.5.1854 13m, da Isabella 17.4.1856 4, s Wm 2.7.1856 14m, 1w Margt Bremner 4.7.1857 39, 2w Betsy Barry 24.4.1864 41

19 by Jas Nicoll cattle dealer, w Mary Copland, chn Mary Ann 3.10.1852 4m, And 1.5.1857 6m, Jamima 24.4.1858 14d, Patk Miller 3.5.1868 14m

20 ob Jas Moncur china mert 12.4.1860 50, w Ann Touch 15.4.1860 50, s Jas 30.9.1854 2, da Jessie Ann 24.9.1860 10

21 Alex Nicol gardener 18.3.1876 77, by w Jane Milne, s David 20.1.1847 2

22 1852. George Smith

23 1853. G McK

24 John Kinnear 18.1.1848 65, w Mary Gilchrist 4.9.1862 77, s in law Jas Thom 29.11.1852 32; Geo Porter wright Forfar, w Ann Kinnear 10.7.1872 56

25 by sergt Stewart Pert 92nd highlanders, parents Wm 25.1.1847 61, & Mary Traill 1.10.1853 57, bros Wm 27.6.1847 28, Jas 15.3.1857 17 & Robt 23.1.1857 23

26 by John Adamson, fa Chas late shoemaker Forfar 29.4.1854 50, mo Jean Ross 10.11.1836 31

27 by Wm Eadie & Mary Meldrum, s Wm 14.1.1854 14m

28 by John Milne, Forfar, w Agnes Food 8.6.1859 66, da Ann 24.3.1836 2, s Thos 25.12.1839 20

29 Alex Macklagan professor of dancing b Mullion 1778 d Forfar 4.4.1861

30 Geo Thornton 14.5.1855 96, w Isabella Fyfe 10.10.1847 73, s Geo 25.11.1877 76, da Agnes 13.2.1853 54, da Jane 4.8.1861 65, da Isabella 28.2.1872 67, s John 18.1.1876 65

31 David Miller baker & Ann Craik, s John 22.6.1854 25, da Margt d Newcastle on Tyne 8.7.1900 72 (h Alex Inverarity 25.11.1869 36); Wm Whitton tinsmith 13.4.1862 60, w Jean Craik 10.4.1877 75

32 1857. by Betsy, Clementine & Mary Ann, fa Alex Moffat manuf 18.3.1841 57, mo Agnes Sturrock d Arbroath 13.6.1857 74; Jas Inverarity warehouseman 30.4.1883 78, w Betsy Moffat 4.12.1884 77, s Jas carpenter 25.3.1865 27, da Betsy 21.9.1886 41

33 Jas Fyfe 28.10.1896 74, w M A Chaplin 15.10.1898 76, aunt Isabella Strachan 8.5.1855 59, da Eliz 20.2.1882 28 (h Geo Nicoll), da Agnes d Denver Colorado 11.5.1882 30 int there (h A R Cuthbert), da Jane Duffus 25.1.1908 60, 1s Wm d Berkeley California 13.8.1930 82, 3s David 1.4.1931 75, 2s Jas 13.2.1937 87 (da Agnes Chaplin 6.10.1956 79)

34 by John Miller mason's labourer, fa Geo 5.2.1854 79

35 Jas Guthrie mason 3.5.1877 69, by w Barbara Peacock, chn Jas 12.12.1853 16m, John 22.8.1859 5, Mary 11.10.1868 5, Margt 1.12.1891 41; Barbara Peacock d Carnoustie 19.6.1899

36 David Robbie 4.11.1853 33, w Jessie Mitchell 3.3.1888 61

37 by Jas Ogilvy, s Alex 14.9.1854 1y

38 1856. Geo Winter 17.6.1871 79, w Cath Donald 23.2.1855 66, chn David 11.5.1828 7, Geo 13.4.1838 11m, da Ann 2.3.1887 64 (h Alex Robertson 11.1.1864 43, s Geo 18.8.1925 67)

39 by David Nicol slater, w Jean Marshall 26.5.1855 52, chn Wm 1830 7w, Agnes 1835 12m, Janet 1838 7m, Jas 1840 11m, Alex 15.7.1859 2, Ann 18.5.1861 22

40 by Jas Milne councillor magistrate Forfar 18.5.1908 73, w Isabella Duthie 21.5.1864 27 (da of Alex Duthie 11.4.1844 55), sis Ann 7.7.1856 16, sis Jessie 14.7.1849 17, fa Jas Milne 11.10.1887 82, mo Mary Mann 7.11.1868 65, w (sic) Mary Mann 21.4.1870 27, s Jas 16.1.1869 7, da Isabella 5.3.1871 10m

41 by John Forsyth blacksmith here 21.6.1861 63, w Agnes Brand 20.5.1856 58, chn Margt 28.3.1820 2, John 6.3.1821 18m, Margt 13.12.1834 6, John 27.12.1834 4, Agnes 13.7.1855 29, Wm 31.12.1859 27, John d at sea 2.1.1869 28

42 Jas Barry 13.8.1882 69, w Ann Doig 1.3.1896 81, chn John 14.1.1848 11, Mary Ann 15.1.1848 11m, Alex 22.1.1848 3, Helen 2.9.1854 10m, John 8.2.1862 1m, David 25.9.1863 25, Jas 17.10.1882 46

43 1856. David Nicoll 10.11.1864 84, w Eliz Hendry 28.2.1855 72, chn Margt 1823 4, Jas 1.1.1833 16, Alex 6.10.1854 39

44 by Jas Reid engine driver Forfar & w Ann Hendry, chn Jas 21.2.1854 9w, Robt 2.10.1854 8, David 5.10.1854 7

45 1872. David Milne 25.6.1877 61, w Barbara Milne 1.1.1878 66, chn Eliz Dow 7.1.1843 20m, Jeannie 31.3.1847 21m, Jeannie 21.2.1871 23, Geo Webster engineer drowned at sea on SS Delfina in S America 15.10.1874 24, Jas C d Talca S America 8.3.1883 28, 1s Alex of Callao Peru d Valparaiso 24.1.1919 75

46 1853. J M

47 by David Ferrier 4.3.1887 79, s Jas 16.4.1841 5, parents Jas Ferrier & Cath Ramsay d in mature age, w Janet Hobart 6.3.1874 73

48 1854. Thos Edward d Mill of Lower 7.3.1854 68, w Margt Mitchell d Mill of Lower 22.10.1859 70, s Thos d there 7.7.1870 58

49 by Wm Burnett accidentally killed at Tain 7.7.1863 36, fa Alex 13.1.1838 36, uncle Geo Burnett 9.6.1856 50, two chn d inf, da Nancy 6.3.1886 23, da Jessie 8.7.1891 35, w Margt Smith 3.7.1909 76

50 Geo Sturrock 23.3.1855 82, w Margt Doig 2.3.1860 84, s Jas 14.5.1866 60 (w Eliz Wilkie 1.1.1867 72, s Jas 5.12.1861 24, da Margt mrs Dollan 14.9.1866 43, by s Alex builder Melbourne Australia

51 by Jas Soutar accidentally killed on railway 19.9.1882 57, w Agnes Webster 4.6.1891 66 (da of Jas Webster 1.1.1846 62 & Agnes Simpson 19.8.1855 62), s Wm 16.7.1859 7, da Jean 23.3.1932 83 (h Alex Craik 10.6.1873 27)

52 by Jas & Wm Morris, sis Isabella 5.11.1854 27, fa Wm Morris 4.2.1865 62, mo Margt Milne 21.11.1880 76, bro Alex 23.11.1902 58, sis Ann 6.5.1901 75 (mrs Leighton), sis Mary Ann 5.6.1908 67

53 by A Cuthbert, s David 16.3.1854 3

54 1853. Jas Allan 24.4.1870 56, w Ann Hastings 23.5.1853 39, 2w Eliz Jolly 14.4.1891, s Alex 29.3.1894 63 (w Mary Porter 14.1.1914 77)

55 by trustees, Chas Boath warper Northlon 25.7.1854 69, sis Margt 12.2.1858 69

56 1853. John Boath 13.5.1853 70, by w Eliz Inverarity; Thos Thornton 29.1.1931 83, w Isabella Cable 24.7.1923 69

57 1861. by John Douglas, s Chas 3.1853 7, fa Chas 30.3.1855 64

58 by And Milne 13.11.1893 70, parents John 30.1.1869 81 & Elspet Miller 1.10.1853 66, w Barbara Lighton 5.4.1860 26, w Betsy Herald 16.10.1906 79

59 by David Sturrock, w Janet Clarke 3.4.1853 31

60 by Wm Cable 2.9.1893 66, mo Jean Torbat 20.12.1854 62, chn Jean 12.11.1854 11m, Wm 9.8.1857 1y9m, Alex 1.6.1859 1y, David 1.12.1867 18m, Hellen 3.1870 13m, w Barbara Nicoll 16.2.1873 47, s Jas 1902, da Isabella

61 Alex Rennie mert Forfar 22.3.1861 45, w Mary Ann Robb d Edinburgh 21.1.1872 58, chn Mary Ann 20.3.1847 2½, Susan 24.4.1853 6m, Mary Ann 9.2.1861 10y6m

62 Jas Japp fr Oathlaw 1770, Wm Japp cabinetmaker Forfar 14.7.1813, Jas Japp manuf Forfar 9.6.1835, Isabella Japp 28.9.1855, Agnes Japp 16.1.1863 being four generations; Jas Japp, w Jean Black 27.2.1844; Agnes Buchan or Black 9.10.1847; Eliz Black 29.6.1890 90

63 Alex Peter 23.7.1882 62, w Johan Brown 20.3.1883 65, chn Allan 30.3.1854 1y, Hellen 31.3.1854 3, Betsy 24.2.1863 14

64 1862. by Alex Brown, w Hanna Duncan 8.1.1857 52 (her mo Ann Jack 22.1.1853 76), gchn Wm 21.4.1857 5m, Alex 10.5.1858 6

65 by Ann Ramsay 6.3.1863 58, h Geo Scott 28.9.1862 70, fa Alex Ramsay 19.3.1843 72, mo Janet Nicol 24.7.1828 65; Jas Scott 20.4.1878 62, w Ann Smith 10.3.1897 84, s Geo mason 5.6.1902 (w Jessie Strang 25.5.1931 87)

66 by Wm Nicoll, w Helen Hendry 1.12.1854 58

67 by Wm Warden draper, w Jane 4.7.1867 28 (da of John Jamieson 18.3.1863 73 & Janet Torry 17.10.1855 52, sisters Jessie 29.9.1826 2, Eliz 23.8.1834 5, Margt 7.9.1834 8, Isabella 31.3.1862 35; Wm 18.12.1878 9

68 1855. by Margt, Mary & Eliz, fa Joseph Wilson 1854 83, mo Eliz Sturrock 1846 77, bro John 1853 49; Chas Roberts 8.1.1870 64, w Margt Wilson 27.1.1881 80; David Milne 2.6.1925 67, w Jane Stewart 1.11.1911 53; John Wilson 3.3.1912 68

69 1854. by Jas Addison, mo Eliz Gamley 16.9.1852 60

70 John Moffat 30.7.1894 78, s Wm 13.5.1868 25, da Agnes 26.5.1859 5, bro in law Wm Rae 18.10.1852 37, fa Peter 21.12.1856 73, mo Isabella Lowson 7.4.1863 78, w Agnes Rae 19.2.1893 80

71 by And McKay contractor Greymouth New Zealand, fa Jas 5.10.1892 77, mo Ann Moffat 2.7.1894 76, aunt Mary Moffat 17.8.1880 51

72 by Jas Moncur baker St Cyrus, s John 12.7.1848 3, fa Jas 19.12.1854 77, mo Margt Smart 20.11.1864 82, s Jas 7.4.1856 5, da Ann 1.7.1863 2, Mary Ann 9.9.1869 30, w Annie Cargill 8.4.1880 64, sis Mary Ann

73 David Adamson 24.4.1872 75, w Janet Gardener Neave 1.6.1880 72, chn David 1.6.1835 5, Jean 20.6.1835 3, s Jas (chn Eliz 13.4.1859 4, Annie 28.5.1870 3, David 27.12.1880 28)

74 Wm Lyon & Jean Robertson, yt da Jessie 24.1.1857 15y6m, s Jas imperial military school of medicine Koomberhana Constantinople, 1st class surgeon imperial Ottoman army d 4.3.1864 39y3m int here, two bros & three siss predeceased Jas of whom Wm suffocated buried alive under a sandbank along with two older boys 10.11.1826 4y5m, Ann 29.5.1831 3y8m, Edw 11.8.1833 7m & the others at birth

75 by Geo Lowson 14.6.1880 71, w Cecilia Morrison 3.1.1875 65, chn Mary Ann 10.12.1841 2, Chas 17.12.1841 4, Ann 1.8.1852 3, John 10.10.1873 43, Geo 24.12.1874 24

76 Chas Roberts 7.11.1854 77, w Kath Thornton 14.9.1853 63, s Wm 20.5.1874 65 (w Eliz Ferrier 22.3.1855 46, s Wm 10.11.1864 21)

77 1853. P S

78 Wm McKenzie 1.3.1908 58, w Eliz Ogilvie 17.8.1904 55, s Thos Crichton 21.8.1899 19, fa Wm 13.6.1867 52, mo Jane Petrie 28.6.1874 54, bro David 24.9.1852 4

79 by Jas Byars dyer Forfar 6.9.1892 84, w Margt Anderson 1.2.1879 73, chn Margt 15.9.1835 20m, Isabella 31.8.1847 5m, Eliz 22.4.1852 5, Jas 20.6.1857 25, And Home 16.4.1863 26, David 3.12.1888 40

80 by John Nicol & w Mary Binny, s Alex 5.3.1846 4, da Isabella 14.9.1866 20, s Ramsay Scott 16.12.1867 18

81 by David Caird, s Wm 22.5.1853 8m

82 John Low 13.5.1852 58, w Margt Sinclair 16.12.1889 93 (her mo Marthew (sic) Jack 8.1.1855 81)

83 ob by John McLeish late of California, mo Jane Butchart 28.2.1862 73 wid of

John McLeish manuf

84 David Fenton 20.2.1857 55, w Agnes McLean 3.3.1871 66 (fa Roderick McLean 15.7.1854 92), chn Amelia 4y, Eliz 7y, Margt 1y, David 4y, Jas 11y; Chas Gregory, s Geo 4.10.1866 3y

85 by Mary Malloch, s Chas Cook 27.2.1852 19

86 by Alex Findlay, royal artillery, fa Jas 25.2.1853 52

87 1854. John Crichton 31.8.1845 64, w Mary Ann Davidson 10.12.1853 68, da Jane 28.7.1827 3, by s Chas 12.9.1866 54

88 1878. Wm Rae 11.6.1872 71, w Jean Keir 19.5.1898 81, chn Mary Ann 23.11.1846 2, Jas 16.7.1852 5, John 24.5.1859 7, Betsy 13.5.1883 26 at Adelaide South Australia (h John Hall)

89 1853. D Tasker

90 Wm Bremner 19.1.1859 69, w Margt Jack 26.10.1876 73, s Chas 14.3.1852 7, gs Robt Lowson 10.5.1854 3, s And of Scots fusileers d at sea on passage from Crimea 17.3.1855 23 as a consequence of wounds received at the battle of the Alma on 20.9.1854, s Jas 21.9.1902 67, da Isabella 6.11.1915 87

91 by Wm Tosh 2.1924 91, mo Jane Mitchell 10.2.1853 54, das Jane 22.10.1859, Janet 12.6.1867, fa Alex 12.10.1882 83, s Jas McIntosh 31.5.1891 21, da Agnes Mitchell McIntosh 5.3.1896 24, w Janet Smith McIntosh 1917 83

92 Joseph Bissett 26.12.1853 54, w Eliz McRitchie 15.8.1869 69, s Thos b 1830 d London 3.1879, by da Eliz Bissett or Roberts, s Geo b 1840

93 Jane Roberts 5.10.1915 77, bro Joseph d Bowrisfauld 18.5.1923 80

94 John Smith writer Forfar, w Eliz Fish, chn John, Isabella, Eliz all int Old Church Yard Forfar, da Marjory 29.8.1859 60, by last survivor Jean 3.7.1872 78

95 broken column. Peter Hutton fr Craighie Mill 7.9.1810 40, w Ann Butchart 1858 77, chn Alex 1812 9, John 1810 17m, Peter 1810 9m; Jas Robb session clerk Forfar 30.12.1855 57; Jas Boath fr Craichie, wid Eliz Hutton 2.12.1897 86 (her sis Isabella Hutton 8.12.1891 84), da Ann 17.11.1901 66

96 Wm Christie writer Forfar d Jersey 11.5.1851 35, w Marianne Lowson 23.8.1904 80, chn Wm Lyell 10.4.1859 10, John 13.8.1861 14, And 24.4.1883 32; John Lowson Forfar provost 2.1.1875 88, w Ann Webster 14.1.1865 78; Peter Lowson, 1w Margt Home 15.1.1838 21, 2w Janet Ramsay, chn And 6.4.1841 22m, Isabella 4.8.1854 6m, John 3.9.1862 12; Jas Lowson junior manuf provost 27.11.1883 68, w Agnes Barrie 20.11.1881 68, chn John 26.2.1838 4, Francis 16.10.1852 17m, Mary Ann 18.12.1863 21, s Francis d Bournemouth 1886 33, s And 30.1.1887 51, s John L 6.4.1910; Francis Barrie 3.1.1854 81, w Euphemia Morrison 26.10.1852 73

97 Wm Nicoll cattle dealer Forfar 28.7.1843 53, w Isabella Cairns d Flemington 17.9.1875 84, da Margt 31.10.1880 61, Isabella, Thos & Joseph d inf

98 David Cable fr Balbinny, by w Agnes Morgan 18.9.1874 77; David Cable 9.11.1854 11

99 John Findlay manuf Forfar 7.6.1812 43, w Agnes Wilson 18.2.1843 69, chn Agnes & Margt d inf, Isabell 6.7.1824 23, Betty 6.11.1845 38, Jospeh manuf 21.9.1868 72 (w Isabell Thain 19.1.1840 39, s John 16.11.1857 18); (west side) Alex Watt house factor Forfar 15.2.1879 68; Agnes Findlay

1.4.1810 7.1.1892 (h Peter Reid junior confectioner); Peter Reid senior 2.1827, w Agnes Findlay 1838 both int Inverarity, s Wm 30.9.1801 11.5.1865, da Margt 16.8.1796 11.9.1868

100 Wm Boath manuf Wellton, w Margt Wallace 14.9.1850 77, da Barbara 30.10.1861 53; Wm Thoms fr Auchterforfar 27.12.1865 66, w Margt Boath 26.3.1884 80; Jane I Boath 28.3.1895 84; Cath Boath 20.9.1900 80; Wm Thoms fr Auchterforfar 14.5.1905 62

101 And Home seedsman 13.7.1852 41, by w Agnes Whyte, chn Wm 20m, Chas 4m, Jas 17m, And 1890 45, Eliz 1915 76, Jane 24.2.1919 75; (west side) Jane Whyte 19.1.1856 51

102 Jas Watt d Zoar 30.9.1857 81, w Eliz Davidson 24.12.1841 54, by das Eliz 26.2.1889 72 & Ann 3.2.1892 69; Mary Watt or Hutton 7.10.1880 73; David Ramsay fr Lochhead 21.2.1906 74, w Cath McKenzie 16.4.1905 73, da Mary Watt 16.6.1938 69

103 Walter Stewart d Lochlee Glenesk 6.6.1820 45, w Isabella Inverdale 6.1.1853 69, by s bailie Stewart, Forfar (w Annie Gall d after long illness 28.11.1870 49, s Jas 6.11.1848 1y5m); Jas Stewart 26.1.1879 62

104 Geo Nicoll mason 29.5.1882, w Margt Wallace 7.7.1847 51, da Jane 24.5.1863 62 (h David Hebenton hosier 11.3.1890 60); Alex Spence teacher Forfar 11.1.1938 74, w Milly J Brown 20.10.1921 56

105 Alex Anderson printer 21.3.1848 56, w Margt Webster 12.3.1848 46, chn John 26.1.1835 9m, Helen Watt 26.12.1839 10, John Alex 11.3.1850 7, Jas 21.2.1869 31, Isabella 9.7.1882 46, Janet Yeaman 30.4.1908 75, Margt 20.4.1921 93, Helen 18.2.1847 11m

106 John Anderson auctioneer 29.3.1860 72, w Eliz Lindsay 82y, ss John, Wm, David all d in Australia, da Ann d Kirriemuir

107 Wm Littlejohn hosier 16.8.1858 66, w Ann Coupar 2.2.1863 73, da Eliz 22.12.1838 7; (west side) Wm Law chemist b Dunfermline 1810 d Forfar 15.10.1867, w Mary Littlejohn b Forfar 8.1.1827 d Forfar 7.1.1912, 1s Geo MA LLB advocate Edinburgh

108 urn Wm Waterston 10.2.1852 77, w Martha Suttie 22.12.1842 69; Geo Ross Fowler 13.4.1912 52; (west side) Wm Waterston, Union Hotel Forfar 13.5.1879 60, sis Eliz 7.12.1893 80; John Sim, wid Eliz M H W Girvan 13.2.1923 76

109 John Morison innkeeper 30.7.1850 67, w Eliz Gibson 8.5.1854 71, da Mary Ann 26.8.1823 18m; Jas 26.10.1849 29; Eliza 11.4.1890 76

110 rev Wm Lowe here, w Jessie Campbell 10.3.1857 60, 1da Jessie McLaren 11.1.1846 23, 1s Wm 3.9.1854 32

111 Wm Gibson fr Baldardo 23.4.1855 50, w Eliz Fairweather 4.3.1894 78, s Wm in Kinnettles 26.1.1845 4, s David d Sydney 30.6.1866 16½, gda Margt W Scott d Forfar 7.2.1867 5m

112 ob Jas Craik junior provost of Forfar d Manor Place 29.3.1872 55, w Cath Fyfe 18.4.1902 85

113 by Jas Craik junior manuf Forfar, bro in law Wm Fyfe fr Mains of Dunnichen 9.6.1850 30, step s Peter Coupar fr Newton of Affleck 4.4.1865 31 (da Anne Batchelor 24.6.1866 2, w Mary Batchelor 11.1.1890 54, yr s Jas Craik 2.12.1896 34, 1s Francis Batchelor 6.1.1937 75)

Many more recent Craik family stones surround nos. 112 & 113

114 pillar. 1861. by David Barry builder Forfar, fa David d Forfar 16.6.1844 84, mo Jean Lockhart d Forfar 5.5.1852 72

115 And Cook fr Blairyfeddon 5.2.1860 76, by w Margt Nicoll 31.3.1868 80, chn John, And & Jas d nonage, Jane 15.2.1835 5, David 25.2.1835 15m, Wm 3.6.1864 48; And Cook retired grain mert 13.6.1902 77; (west side) Robt Cook fr Blairyfedden 23.5.1903 84, w Mary Aitken 19.8.1874 34

116 large pillar. Wm Meffan esq writer & provost here 12.3.1829, w Jane Low 8.3.1837; Wm Meffan 8.6.1814; Margt 10.8.1822; Agnes 7.6.1842; Helen 30.9.1854; Jane Meffan 18.6.1879; s Patk esq writer & provost here 11.8.1863

117 John Liveston cattle dealer & w Annie Grant, s Robt 12.3.1844 20m

118 Jas Grant manuf, fa Jas 30.8.1846 64, mo Elspeth Roger 17.7.1852 70

119 Geo Lowson manuf Forfar 4.4.1861 71, w Eliz Ritchie 10.7.1863 72, chn Peter 12.12.1829 16, Jospeh 8.12.1838 3, Alex 14.5.1847 24, And 29.5.1859 42, Isobell 12.11.1902 87 (h David Johnston fr Lochmill 16.1.1893 88)

120 by Jas Taylor, w Jean Low 20.2.1868 59, chn Peter 5.11.1833 2, Eliz 5.6.1851 18, Wm 7.9.1851 10, Alex 19.10.1858 7

121 by Robt Watt & Jane Crabb, da Eliz 11.1847 10, Marjory 6.1853 - - - (behind holly tree) - -; (west side) & Margt 5.7.1877 36, Eliz 11.4.1890 41 (h Jas Lawson)

122 Wm Dyce 6.2.1866 85, w Isabella Stirling d Spittleburn 4.4.1853 68; John Dyce 22.5.1892 72, w Janet Grant 15.4.1909 92, s David 19.5.1871 17

123 Wm Sturrock manuf Forfar 1889 80, 1w Eliz Cairns 1840 33, chn Wm 1843 8, Jas 1895 56, Eliz 1910 73, 2w Jean Duncan 1901 83, chn David 1849 inf, Margt 1860 15, Joseph Hume 1862 9, Richd Cobden 1872 25, John 1919 69

124 Wm Ogilvie 9.12.1886 71, w Isabella Fitzhard 8.8.1879 65, chn Jas 2.9.1845 2, John 10.8.1849 3, Wm 18.8.1849 12, Agnes 9.7.1872

125 Wm Clark 4.10.1892 77, w Eliz Roberts 11.12.186- 56, chn Ann 5.18-- 22m, Margt 21.5.1859 11

126 Joseph Kinnear 14.10.1865 75, w Jane Meldrum 21.1.1862 71, chn Jane 2.5.1812 2, Ann 4.12.1826 1, David 25.9.1849 21

Several other Kinnear stones of a later date are nearby no.126

127 Peter Caird 14.6.1879 49, fa John 2.6.1860 78, mo Isabella Burnett 29.8.1838 54, relative Jane Kydd Caird 15.3.1954 80

128 Wm Porter d Gars barracks 1876 74, w Betsy Kerr 22.11.1858 56, chn Jas 10.1.1830 17m, Agnes 16.4.1835 5, Wm 8.1.1849 16, Mary Ann 18.12.1844 14m, Jas 6.8.1846 7m

129 ob John Finlay fr Baggerton 24.4.1850, w Martha Milne 10.9.1852, s Wm 22.10.1834

130 Jas Anderson mert 28.3.1883 83, w Mary Potter 23.7.1900 89, chn Eliz 22.3.1844 2, Isobel 23.6.1846 7, Mary 13.9.1852 15

131 Robt Campbell tobacconist Forfar, by 1s Jas & da Jean imo da Janet 10.8.1782 23.11.1852 (wid of Jas Marshall fr East Carsebank)

132 Peter Malcolm 5.5.1860 79, w Isabella Butchart 27.4.1850 72, da Isabella 27.2.1866 50 (h David Kidd 22.2.1855 49, chn Ann, Jean & Mary d inf int Old Rattray), da Ann 3.11.1906 86. Burying ground of David Kidd brewer Forfar

133 David Steele 14.3.1879 82, w Ann Barry 16.12.1869 77, chn Mary 1844

2, Margt 1847 7m, Betsy 1850 16, Alex 1854 2, Cath 1863 19, Wm 1875 21; Pat M Steele d Ruatangata New Zealnd 1.2.1893 36; Isabella 10.2. 1908 71

134 Alex Lowson manuf 21.3.1860 76, w Cath Allan 4.1.1793 26.6.1878, chn Agnes 3.1823 4, And 3.1823 9m, Isabella 1.1835 2, Cath 5.1850 26

135 Jas Watt 27.5.1853 73, w Jean Butchart 26.6.1868 82, chn Robt 7.5.1842 40, Jannet 18.3.1850 31, Margt 24.9.1861 51, by s in law Jas Forsyth 23.8.1878 73 (w Eliz Watt 12.5.1879 66, s Robt Coupar 4.4.1854 3) & by s in law Jas Dick; Jas Forsyth, da Ann 4.4.1886 42, s David 10.11. 1908 59, s Alex d Sydney Australia 4.2.1921 67; Jas Forsyth d Rydalmere Australia 7.5.1917 75; Wm Forsyth d Forfar 6.4.1915 71

136 Chas Beattie 5.5.1862 44, w Jane Rennie 16.8.1869 55 (sis Elspeth Rennie 5.9.1865 44), s Wm 26.3.1852 11, s Jas 17.6.1876 29

137 Walter Stewart 2.8.1870 75, w Mary Hill d Ballindurg 14.2.1863 72, chn Jane 23.4.1834 11, Walter 4.4.1836 6, Chas 20.7.1843 21, Joseph 1.9. 1845 14, Margt mrs Nicoll 21.3.1878 51, 1s Alex d Colorado Springs USA 17.4.1884 66

138 1866. by Wm, Geo, David & Jas, fa Wm Greig 31.3.1848 48, mo Jean Brown 21.6.1865 64; Mary Martin 30.12.1902 68, da Mary Roberts 14.1.1939 73

139 by John Welsh 28.5.1905 59, fa Alex 2.1865 73 (wid Isabella Kennedy 7.12.1877 77); Chas 26.11.1830 2; John 4.1.1834 13; Isabella 6.1. 1834 2; w Mary Ann Milne 25.9.1910 63

140 John Donald 15.3.1851 46, w Madglane Allerdice 7.1.1884 81

141 Jas Laird 30.1.1789 6.8.1878, w Mary Cownie 22.11.1852 66, chn Wm 14. 1.1829 7, Margt 4.2.1831 7, Mary 11.5.1830 10m, Eliz 19.9.1834 14

142 by Jas Kennedy esq, Ceylon, mo Helen Millar 16.4.1862 85, fa John 1812 34 int Cortachy

143 Jas Rea stonebreaker 19.11.1881 78, mo Margt Lyon 16.12.1850 81

144 Wm Piggott 23.4.1892 83, w Eliz Dewars 20.2.1849 42, da Mary 7.10.1848 18, Isabella 7.1.1850 16, Jane 19.2.1867 24, da Cath 30.11.1873 27, sis Mary 18.11.1887 80, da Jessie 1.5.1917 83

145 John Adamson 9.9.1859 81, w Agness Webester 30.1.1839 62, by s Jas 30. 12.1891 84 (s Jas 8.10.1849 5); Jean Hillocks 12.10.1896 85

146 next 145. Wm Halkney 14.2.1855 (56), by w Jean Adamson, s John 6.1857 22

147 And Gray mason 15.2.1850 55

148 by Geo Bruce, s David 22.7.1850 22

149 Hay Adamson 18.11.1891 80, w Ellen Samson 17.12.1894 82, chn Binny 6. 11.1836 2, Ann 27.10.1846 8, Alex 16.3.1863 2½

150 urn by Alex Kinnear 2.6.1839 19.12.1870, sis Helen 20.10.1844 2, sis Ann 16.12.1868 19, mo Janet Rea 13.6.1888 72, fa Robert 30.7.1891 82

151 by Peter Scott 2.5.1872 71, w Jane Landale 9.5.1889 80, da Jane 19.5. 1846 2, Helen 1.10.1863 21

152 1873. by John Sinclair, fa sergt Alex 25.6.1851 68, mo Agnes Crighton 23.2.1872 85, bro David 22.4.1832 4; Agnes d Dundee 3.9.1880; John C Sinclair d Cutramundra New South Wales 27.9.1884

153 Wm Milne b Montrose 12.6.1802 d here 19.4.1860, chn Jean 1.5.1843 3y3m, Mary 28.4.1844 1y2m, David 10.5.1851 6, Jas 19.8.1867 29, w Mary Roberts 10.2.1892 80, gs Wm Nicol Milne Doig 31.1.1882 2y1m; Wm Nicoll Milne d Forfar 30.5.1890 44

154 ob by David Soutar, fa Alex 11.9.1843 45, mo Margt Paterson 29.12.1846 49, sis Mary 23.3.1851 23, chn David & Jean d inf, Alex 11.9.1871 23; David Soutar 11.5.1877 54, gchn Eliz & David d inf

155 Wm Ritchie in Sparrowcroft Forfar 17.3.1850 83, da Cath 8.6.1869 77, da Margt 3.12.1871 65

156 Alex Findlay 17.8.1837, w Matilda Lowson 13.1.1837, s Alex 13.2.1844 45, da Jean 14.1.1860 63, da in law Eliz McDonald 30.7.1878 77 (s Jas joiner 2.1.1909 67, da Matilda 16.11.1909 80), by da Eliz 13.8. 1873 71

157 by Alex Hutcheon, w Eliz Esplin 13.6.1851 48

158 Peter Smith grieve Pitscandly d Chapel of Kirkbuddo Guthrie 13.5.1881, w Ann Mitchell 12.11.1851 29

159 by John Samson in Myreside d Dundee 10.1.1892 75, da Helen 22.7.1851 2, w Margt Boyle 12.1896 77

160 by Thos Kinnear, fa Geo many yrs foreman Forfar Gasworks d Letham 17. 7.1872 57, bros Wm 27.1.1838 3, Geo 26.12.1862 15, Thos 20.1.1838 1y, mo Margt Robertson d Clatterhall Oathlaw 8.9.1883 73, gfa Jas Robertson 5.7.1851 65, gmo Margt Williamson 2.1.1856 73, da Maggie 8.1.1885 18

161 And Roberts 30.5.1851 50, by w Eliz Dunbar

162 by Geo Henderson, chn Ann 23.2.1849 1y, John 27.2.1849 3, David 24.8. 1850 7m

163 Alex Tarbet 7.3.1857 62, w Ceclia (sic) Henderson 7.12.1839 55

164 David Allan 29.6.1896 73, w Mary Adamson 26.6.1851 28

165 1850. W Black

166 by John Craig manuf, da Eliz 24.7.1835 5, s John 14.5.1847 18, David 3.3.1850 22, w Isobel Fyfe 6.11.1852 54

167 Thos Thornton shoemaker Forfar 29.10.1883 60, w Eliz Petrie 20.12. 1893 71, chn Jane Marr 21.6.1850 4, Ann 6.1.1858 18m, John 2.4.1859 6, Will Adamson 14.4.1862 18m, Clementina Black 13.1.1902 51 (h Wm Morrison 21.3.1902 51), yt s Peter 11.5.1908 44, sis Ann 28.9.1908 93

168 David Hendry 10.9.1891 68, w Betsy Milne 5.1.1860 38, da Ann 20.3.1851 3, Mary 15.3.1852 1¾, Betsy & Cath d inf, w Jane Addie 20.4.1886 48

169 1853. J Adam

170 ob Wm Petrie manuf 22.12.1851 75, w Helen Shepherd 15.5.1861 83, s Thos 15.11.1890 76 (w Margory Milne 17.1.1871, s Geo Lowson 12y); Ernest John Petrie d Rochester New York 3.3.1925 24; Agnes Petrie 30.10.1963 92 (h late Ormond Stewart); Isabella Mason Petrie 2.5.1917 48, h John Douglas Petrie 3.2.1950 79

171 Alex Tarbat 13.12.1870 70, s Wm 11.6.1851 20, s Alex 7.12.1879 33

172 Alex Wighton 9.2.1869 74, w Jean Mill 22.6.1851 56, s David 1828 7m, da Jane 5.6.1890 65

173 by Peter Watt, w Eliz Ramsay 5.5.1851 70

174 Jas Inverwick in Forfar 15.8.1867 77, w Ann Thomson 6.12.1890 80, chn Ann 6.6.1839 4, Wm, Helen & Eliz d inf, David d Meerut India 23.11. 1868 31, Wm royal horse artillery d Glasgow 21.4.1906 62, Mary Ann d Forfar 21.3.1912 73, Chas d Forfar 24.11.1923 72

175 1862. by Geo Barrie mason 16.12.1862 64, w Clementina Erskine 19.5.

1863 63, chn Jas 9.12.1834 4, Margt 4.1.1840 4, Jas 26.12.1848 8; Geo Barrie junior cattle dealer Letham 16.7.1874 41, w Jane Cathro 16.1.1868 33

176 David Arnot mert Dundee, mo Agnes Milne 23.1.1880 62, sis Agnes 17.2.1851 6m, bro Jas 8.3.1854 5, fa David Arnott 15.3.1882 65; Alex Arnot 20.12.1889 33

177 Jas Kyd in Newmonthill 10.11.1853 60, w Betty Mann 14.1.1851 50, da Jean 27.10.1853

178 by Geo Keay, da Eliza 2.10.1850 7; Geo Keay 28.12.1875 74, w Helen Milne 25.12.1876 72, also Jas Fraser d Allitown Australia 4.9.1878 49; Geo Keay, w Eliz Milne 16.2.1881 80

179 ob by rev John Milne 3.7.1886 67 of Holburn Church Aberdeen, fa Jas 19.4.1851 71, mo Eliz Proctor 28.4.1858 74

180 Mary McDougall 10.12.1885 78, sis Betsie d Padanarga 24.12.1847 2

181 Jas Mitchell fr Quilkoe 21.9.1909 82, fa Alex 20.10.1848 67 int Kirriemuir, mo Margt Ritchie 27.5.1879 80, bro Wm 13.5.1875 44; Allan Calder banker 26.5.1927 66, w Jessie Reid Cargill 28.8.1940 77

182 rev Wm Geo Shaw, w Eliz Wulfynmie Clarke 13.12.1827

183 Chas Souter 29.12.1853 int Dunnichen, w Helen Christie 15.6.1876 98, s Wm sometime fr Forehill Carmyllie, afterwards draper Forfar 26.11.1873 55, s Jas 22.6.1849 38, s Geo 7.3.1890 84, da Jane 13.12.1893 85, da Agnes 27.12.1906 85, da Isabella 20.3.1907 85

184 Wm Reid fr West Muir of Lownie 9.1.1880 71, w Isabella Smith 9.2.1871 60, s Wm Smith 17.5.1836 4½, da Clementina 30.6.1873 36; And Reid 26.1.1920 86, w Isabella Elder 1.6.1913 75

185 Peter Ogilvie 9.11.1865 58, by w Mary Campbell, ss Jas 3.1842 2, John 1.2.1851 16, Wm 13.7.1859 5

186 Geo Thornton 14.5.1874 71, w Helen Sherriff 19.4.1862 69, chn Alex 3y, Jessie 11y, Jas 7y

187 ob Chas Crabb 25.4.1874 75, w Agness Bisset 15.1.1874 71, da Helen 26.5.1853 16, s Alex 19.10.1844 18.3.1928 last survivor of the family

188 David Grant fr Mosside of Lour 18.3.1878 74, s John 18.5.1848 6, w Sarah Crabb 1.5.1890 86

189 by Wm McIntosh & w Marjorie Petrie, s Wm 1.7.1843 19

190 Chas Allardice 4.1.1889 75, w Elspeth Aldie 25.2.1898 83, s Robt 6.1838 & s Wm 1.1864 int Glamis, s Chas 17.7.1905 57, da Isabella 10.8.1908 68

191 by Margt Esplin, fa John 21.6.1859 64, mo Agnes Livie 27.8.1869 88, aunt Ann Livie 8.9.1865 86; Alex Livie 15.10.1913 85, w Margt Esplin 13.12.1882 59, 2w Helen Scott 13.1.1917 78

192 John Chaplin 23.12.1898 85, w Jean Hurry 19.6.1880 71, da Jean Hurry 21.5.1848 2y8m, s David 14.2.1876 27, da Agnes 20.2.1919 78, da Mary 27.10.1925 73 (h Jas W Hunter)

193 Jas Lyall 18.12.1882 74, w Wimes Reed 18.3.1853 50

194 by David Fyfe, fa John 17.9.1849 48, mo Ann Bell

195 Francis Fairweather 3.8.1862 63, w Martha Murray 22.2.1880 80, da Agnes 22.11.1845 3

196 Geo Anderson 22.5.1854 31, by w Margt Forbes

197 Wm Robertson d here 22.9.1875 75, bro Jas d here 14.6.1897 78; Isabella

Robertson 3.3.1902 87

198 by Jas Yates & w Marjory Carr 27.11.1882 75 (fa Thos Carr 14.4.1833 59, mo Marjory Dawson 4.7.1828 55), s Thos Carr 8.7.1855 18, s Jas 8.7.1855 16

199 by Robt Laird, family Mary 29.3.1842 9, Cath 6.7.1855 1y, Charlotte 12.11.1836 2, Lavina 26.8.1848 1y

200 Harry Mathieson Mann 11.1.1848

201 Jas Addison 6.7.1857 46, by w Helen Coutts, chn Eliz 8.2.1851 2, David 1.11.1868 22, Robt 17.6.1873 33

202 by Chas Webster 2.12.1891 79, fa Wm auctioneer & corncaster 8.1.1847 74, mo Eliz Kerr 1.10.1873 84; Jas P Mason hairdresser 21.12.1912 22; David Mason 2.11.1926 64, w Eliz Peters 4.3.1948 86

203 Geo Webster 13.7.1853 80, by w Isabella Adamson (mo Jean Hall 31.12.1849 79)

204 Wm Stewart 12.1.1850 49, by w Eliza Powers

205 Wm Brown 26.9.1853 71, w Eliz Blair 31.3.1877 66, s Jas 16.2.1843 3w, da Eliz 27.12.1923 71

206 Jas Guthrie 31.1.1851 41

207 Chas Mill mason here, w Agnes Millar 8.11.1806 32

208 Thos Esplin shoemaker 16.12.1857 50, w Marjory Leckie 4.11.1856 47, by s Thos B 15.9.1842 7.6.1925 (w Isabella Barrie 8.5.1840 30.4.1915), s Jas 10.5.1848 3, s Peter d inf, s Geo 28.11.1893 53, s John teacher St John's College Untata South Africa 1.3.1848 25.11.1911

Notes

Jervise ms 530 p 830 in the library of the Society of Antiquaries, Scotland, notes the inscriptions nos. 17, 90, 96, 114 & 116

Angus District Parks & Cemetaries Office, Forfar: Register of burials from 14.5.1850 along with lair books, available for inspection.

Index

Adam 169
Adamson 26.73.145-6.149.164 167.203
Addison 69.201
Aitken 115
Aldie 190
Allan 54.134.164
Allardice 190
Allerdice 140
Anderson 16.79.105-6.130.196
Andrew 11
Arnot(t) 176

Barrie 10.96.175.208
Barry 18.42.114.133
Batchelor 113
Beattie 136
Bell 194
Binny 80
Bisset(t) 92.187
Black 62.165.167
Blair 205
Boath 4.55-6.95.100
Boyle 159
Brand 41
Bremner 18.90
Brown 63-4.104.138.205
Bruce 15.148
Buchan 62
Burnett 49.127
Butchart 83.95.132.135
Byars 79

Cable 56.60.98
Caird 81.127
Cairns 97.123
Calder 181
Campbell 110.131.185

13b FORFAR CEMETERY

Cargill 72.181
Carr 198
Cathro 175
Chapl(a)in 7.33.192
Christie 96.183
Clark(e) 59.125.182
Cook 85.115
Copland 19
Coupar 107.113.135
Coutts 201
Cownie 141
Crabb 121.187-8
Craig 166
Craik 31.51.112-3
Crichton 78.87.152
Crockett 15
Cuthbert 33.53

Davidson 87.102
Dawson 198
Dewars 144
Dick 135
Dickson 10
Doig 42.50.153
Dollan 50
Donald 38.140
Douglas 57
Dow 45
Duffus 33
Dunbar 161
Duncan 60.64.123
Duthie 40
Dyce 122

Eadie 27
Easson 18
Edward 48
Elder 184
Ellis 17
Erskine 175
Esplin 157.191.208

Fairweather 111.195
Farmer 14
Fenton 84
Ferrier 47.76
Fife 6. see Fyfe
Findlay 86.99.156
Finlay 129
Fish 94
Fitzhard 124
Food 28
Forbes 196
Forsyth 41.135
Fowler 108
Fraser 178
Fyfe 6.30.33.112-3.166.194

Gall 103
Gamley 69
Gardener 73
Gibson 109.111
Gilchrist 24
Girvan 108
Gordon 1
Grant 17.117-8.122.188
Gray 147
Gregory 84
Greig 138
Grierson 14
Guthrie 3.35.206

Halkney 146
Hall 88.203
Hastings 54
Hebenton 104
Henderson 162-3
Hendry 43-4.66.168
Herald 58
Hill 7.137
Hillocks 145
Hobart 47
Home 96.101
Horn 10
Hunter 192
Hurry 192
Hutcheon 157
Hutton 95.102

Inverarity 31-2.56
Inverdale 103
Inverwick 174
Ireland 16

Jack 64.82.90
Jamieson 16.67
Japp 62
Johnston 119
Jolly 54

Keay 178
Keir 88
Keith 13
Kennedy 139.142
Kerr 128.202
Kidd 132. see Kydd
Kinnear 24.126.150.160
Kyd(d) 127.177. see Kidd

Laird 17.141.199
Landale 151
Langlands 12
Law 107
Lawson 121
Leckie 208
Leys 5
Leighton 17.52
Lighton 58
Lindsay 106
Littlejohn 107
Liveston 6.117
Livie 191

Lockhart	114
Low(e)	82.110.116
Lowson	70.75.90.96.119.134.156.170
Lyall, Lyell	96.193
Lyon	74.143
M.	46
McDonald	156
McDougall	180
McIntosh	3.91.189
McK.	23
McKay	71
McKenzie	78.102
McKinnon	5
McKinzie	2
Macklagan	29
McLaren	110
McLean	84
McLeish	83
McRitchie	92
Malcolm	132
Malloch	85
Mann	40.177.200
Marr	167
Marshall	39.131
Martin	138
Mason	170.202
Meffan	116
Meldrum	27.126
Mill	172.207
Millar	142.207
Miller	13.19.31.34.58
Milne	2-3.17.21.28.40.45.52.58.68 129.139.153.168.170.176.178 179
Mitchell	36.48.91.158.181
Moffat	32.70-1
Moncur	20.72
Morgan	98
Morison	109
Morris	52
Morrison	75.96.167
Murray	195
Neave	73
Ness	18
Nevay	8
Nicol(l)	19.21.33.39.43.60.65-6.80. 97.104.115.137.153
Ogilvie	4.78.124.185
Ogilvy	37
Orchar	17
Paterson	154
Peacock	35
Pert	25
Peter	63
Peters	202
Petrie	78.167.170.189
Piggott	144
Porter	24.54.128
Potter	130
Powers	204
Proctor	179
Rae	70.88
Ramsay	47.65.96.102.173.
Rea	143.150
Reed	193
Reid	17.44.99.184
Rennie	61.136
Ritchie	119.155.181
Robb	7.61.95
Robbie	36
Roberts	68.76.92-3.125.138.153. 161
Robertson	38.74.160.197
Roderick	12
Roger	118
Ross	26
S.	77
Samson	4.149.159
Scott	65.80.111.151.191
Shepherd	170
Shaw	182
Sherriff	186
Sim	108
Simpson	51
Sinclair	82.152
Smart	72
Smith	4.11.22.49.65.91.94.158 184
Soutar	5.51.154.183
Spence	104
Steele	133
Stewart	68.103.137.170.204
Stirling	122
Strachan	33
Strang	65
Sturrock	32.50.59.68.123
Sutherland	15
Suttie	108
Symon	1
Tarbat	171. see Torbat
Tarbet	163
Tasker	89
Taylor	120
Thain	99
Thom	24
Thomson	174
Thornton	30.56.76.167.186
Torbat	60.see Tarbat, Tarbet
Torry	67
Tosh	91
Touch	20
Traill	25
Turnbull	16

13b FORFAR CEMETERY

Wallace	100.104	Whitton	31
Walker	8.11	Whyte	101
Ward	17	Wighton	172
Warden	67	Wilkie	50
Waterston	108	Williamson	160
Watt	99.102.105.121.135.173	Wilson	8.68.99
Webster	9.45.51.96.105.145.202-3	Winter	38
Wells	17	Yates	198
Welsh	139	Yeaman	105

13c FORFAR ST. JOHN'S

The Episcopal church in East High Street was built in 1824 on an older site. The small locked burial ground at the rear is kept locked (keys with the rector). National Grid reference: NO 457 506

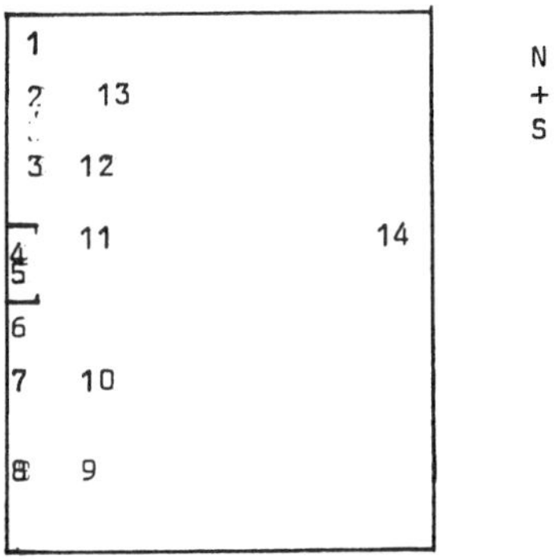

1 by David Scott late plumber here 20.8.1855 44 & w Charlotte Malcom, da Charlotte 3.3.1839 1.4.1840, yt s Walter d in Gl- - - 20.3.18-- 20y

2 John Steele mert 10.4.1807 21.11.1878, w Helen Maclean 13.7.1809 13.12.1847, chn John b 19.11.1835 d Kellewatte Ceylon 5.3.1875, Thos Duncan b 25.5.1837 d Culross 4.10.1872 int here, Hector McLean b 30.11.1847 lost in wreck of SS Dandenong off Jervis Bay Australia 11.9.1876, Jas d Malta 18.4.1894

3 Wm Whyte esq writer & Bank Agent here 9.9.1849 56, w Margt Campbell Adam 21.7.1893 91, yt s Chas 12.1.1843 5m (see inscriptions 15 & 16)

4 FS Jas Scott of Westby House 14.7.1849 72, w Isobel Wyllie 17.1.1852 68, s Alex Binny 11.1.1821 4.9.1865 (see Jervise ms 530 SAS p 810: Jas Scott was a mert in Forfar who made a fortune by trade in Ceylon)

5 FS David Scott 11.4.1839 58

6 capt Jas Nash late 26th regt foot 11.5.1838 82, w mrs Janet Ritchie 31.8.1846 77

7 marble tablet out of frame against wall, nearly worn away. Thos(Carnegy) clerk of L- - - - - - - - - - - - -

8 FS Jas Wyllie 4.9.1780 17.8.1833; tribute

9 by Jas Edward MD here & w Margt Lunan, s Robt Lunan 27.2.1846 inf; Ann Blair domestic servant 8.12.1859 20

10 Chas Thornton 21.1.1833 76 first person int here, w Jane Wood 12.1836 74, 1s John 16.10.1846 60 (w Betty Mitchell 26.6.1842 53); Peter Thornton 28.2.1880, w Jean Cramond 9.7.1856; Chas Thornton, chn Chas 10.4.1879 8m & Geo 6.5.1889 18

11 ob Patk Barry esq mert here, da Eliz 20.9.1852, da Isabella 19.3.1868 (h Jas Burns 15.6.1878)

12 Jas Steelr fr Ingliston 28.8.1813 17.1.1851, w Margt Anderson 7.9.1813 12.1.1903, chn Cath 23.11.1842 16.2.1848, Jas 31.7.1844 23.2.1848, Wm 11.10.1847 23.2.1848

13 - - - - - - - - illegible - - -

14 And Robertson sheriff substitute Forfarshire 1.12.1848 68, w Nancy Matilda Murray d Edinburgh 23.2.1867 78, das Mary-Ann 11.1823, Margt 2.2.1857 47, Jemima Murray d Herne Bay Kent 21.4.1865 41, Nancy d Aberdeen 17.1.1879 63, Matilda Jane d Aberdeen 24.4.1910 81

15 16 window. Wm Whyte & Margt Campbell Adam, by das Eliz Whyte & Margt K Shaw

17 window. Eliz Whyte 4.6.1924 84

18 window. John Steele 71y & Helen McLean 38y

19 window. John Sturrock of Pitreuchie who gave site of this church erected after the '45, by gs Archd Sturrock in 1884

20 brass tablet. Patk Thos Carnegy esq deputy commissioner & political officer Naga Hills Assam d Samaguting 21.1.1878 39

21 in porch. col sir Wm Douglas KCB d Valenciennes France 23.8.1818 42, by brother officers of 91st or Argyllshire regt (see Jervise SAS ms 830 p 811: he was son of Douglas of Brigton in Kinnettles whose ancestors bought that estate in 1748 & are descended from James,2s of Archd Douglas of Glen(bervy) & half bro of 18th earl of Angus)

22 in porch. col Balfour-Ogilvy d Balaclava 12.7.1855 44, gallant conduct on the Danube & in Crimea, memorial by brother officers in Valley of the Tchernaya (see Jervise SAS ms 530 p 811: he md the heiress of dr Chas Ogilvy of Tannadyce who was b 1759, made money in the EICS & on returning built the house of Tannadyce, & who was bro to Jean countess of Airlie b 1762)

23 in porch. John Adam esq surgeon here, da Emily Ure b here 16.6.1807 d Portobello 17.7.1856 (h Thos Key esq surgeon EICS)

24 in porch, in Latin. John Guthrie of Guthrie esq 12.11.1845 82, w Ann Douglas 2.12.1845 75 (see Jervise SAS ms 530 p 809: she was da of Douglas of Brigton)

25 Wm Gray of Carse Gray esq 17.2.1861 37 (see Jervise SAS ms 530 p 809: he was s of Hunter of Burnside & assumed name of Gray on marrying the heiress of Carse Gray; poet)

26 Alex Binny Scott d London 4.9.1865 44, by sis in law Margt Scott (see inscription no. 4)

27 mural in church. Jas Scott esq 14.7.1849 73, w Isobel Wyllie 17.1.1852 68,

chn Jas d Madras 29.4.1842 33, Margt 30.9.1818 20, Wm Thos 10.2.1833 20, Thos Wyllie d at sea off Mauritius 6.6.1836 20, Isabella Wyllie 20.8.1825 8, 5s David d at sea near Mauritius 9.3.1855 36, by surviving members of family (see inscriptions no. 4 & 26)

28 next 27. Wm Binny native this town d 27.5.1788 60, w Margt Sturrock 17.8.1843 95, by surviving das; 1844

29 brass wall tablet. John Skinner AM dean of Dunkeld & pastor this parish for 44y b 20.8.1769 d 2.9.1841, by congregation in 1853 (see Jervise SAS ms 530 p 810: he was s of dr John Skinner bishop of Aberdeen d 1816 & gs of rev John Skinner author of "Tullochgorum" 1721 1807, the latter being s of mr Skinner sbhoolmaster Birse; Jervise "Epitaphs" i 98 & ii 45; Chas Rogers, "Monuments" ii 227; "Scottish Nation" iii 474; DNB)

Notes.

Jervise: ms 530 in the library of the Society of Antiquaries, Scotland, pp 808-17 relate to St.John's Episcopal church. A press cutting mentions some early incumbents: 1688 rev mr Small, followed by his s in law rev mr Seaton, followed by mr Skene d 1799, one of the Skenes of Careston. He included some extracts from the Congregational Register:-

6.2.1756 baptism of a da of Patk Carnegy of Lower
16.7.1758 bapt. Wm Nicoll 1s of 2nd marriage of John Nicol in Drumgley & Eliz Hill being formerly sprinkled by a presby. min^r.
19.7.1758 D^r. Ogilvy had a da baptised Mary
25.11.1759 bap. a son to Dr Ogilvy named Charles (after of Tannadyce)
5.4.1761 Dr Ogilvy had a da Margt
16.6.1762 bap. a da of Dr Ogilvy named Jean (afterwards countess of Aitlie)
10.7.1763 Dr Ogilvy had a s Walter
27.2.1767 Lower's son was baptised Patk
11.11.1798 baptised a son to Patk Dickson slater

The Congregational Register ms: baptisms from 5.9.1754 & deaths or burials from 6.2.1825, both until 1854. These are now (1978) deposited in the Brechin Diocesan Library at Dundee University Library

The Scots Peerage: vol i p 129 - Earl of Airlie, Walter Ogilvy of Clova b 1733 advocate & titular earl of Airlie d Cortachy 10.4.1819, 2w md 12.11.1780 Jean (fa John Ogilvy of Murkle physician in Forfar) she d Cortachy 11.6.1818 56

Index.

Adam 3.15.23
Airlie 22.Notes
Anderson 12

Balfour-Ogilvy 22
Barry 11
Binny 4.26.28
Blair 9
Burns 11

Carnegy 7.20.Notes
Cramond 10

Dickson Notes
Douglas 21.24

Edward 9

Gray 25
Guthrie 24

Hill Notes
Hunter 25

Key 23

Lunan 9

13c FORFAR ST. JOHN'S

Mac/McLean	2.18	Shaw	15
Malcom	1	Skene	Notes
Mitchell	10	Skinner	29
Murray	14	Small	Notes
Nash	6	Steele	2.12.18
Nicol(l)	Notes	Sturrock	19.28
Ogilvy	22.Notes	Thornton	10
Ritchie	6	Ure	23
Robertson	14	Whyte	3.15.17
Scott	1.4-5.26-7	Wood	10
Seaton	Notes	Wyllie	4.8.27

13d FORFAR, RESTENNET

The ruined chancel of the priory church dedicated to St Peter in 1243 stands on a rural eminence which was once a peninsular. John son of King Robert Bruce was buried here, but latterly it has been the burial place of the Dempsters of Dunnichen and the Hunters of Burnside. It is in the care of the Dept. of the Environment. All inscriptions are listed below.

National Grid reference: NO 482 516

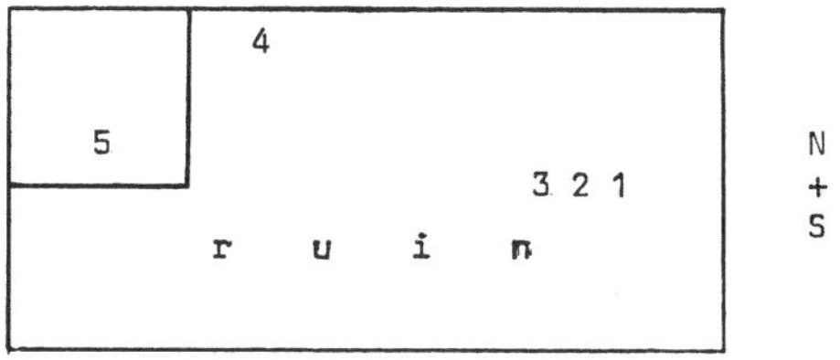

1 FS the Hunters of Restennet, Burnside of Dod, from 16th century

2 FS cross

3 FS V R M CI 1585 ; skull

4 dame Kath Dempster Metcalfe 19.12.1830 7.12.1911 (wid of Theophilus John Metcalfe bart) (see Dunnichen inscriptions nos. 114-7)

5 in wall of tower. cross; figure

rev Chas Rogers, "Monuments & Monumental Inscriptions" ii 229, notes the burial in west of chancel of:

6 Geo Dempster of Dunnichen MP 13.2.1818 86 (see DNB; Scottish Nation ii)

Jervise, SAS ms 530 p 832 notes a slab "now at Dunnichen House":

7 John Hamilton Dempster of Polrossie, w Jean 5.5.1798 (1da of Chas Fergusson who was 2s of late sir Jas Fergusson of Kilkerran bart)

but he notes "there were at one time five Dempster monuments in their portion of the church - traces of the framework only remain"

13d FORFAR, RESTENNET

Notes.

Dempster of Dunnichen: see The Scottish Nation ii 29; Fasti v 362 for rev John Dempster min of Monifeith; The Faculty of Advocates in Scotland 1532-1943 (Scott.Record Society) for two John Dempsters & Jas White-head Hawkins; Jervise, "Memerials of Angus & Mearns" ii 217-8 & Appendix xxxiii 335-6 & "Epitaphs & Inscriptions" ii 407

Hunter of Burnside, or the land & barony of Dod: The Scottish Nation ii 511 - gen David Hunter of Burnside md a da of Wm Duncan of Brigton Forfar-shire who d 1846, their s maj Wm d in Scinde when ADC to his uncle gen Geo Hunter & was succeeded by his s David who d Isle of Man 1847 26 leaving a s Wm Geo b 1847 in Isle of Man

Testaments: The Index of the Commissariot Record of Brechin includes
John Dempster of Dünnichen, 1760
David Hunter of Burnside deceased, da Katherine, 1707
" " " " , 2s Andrew, 1707
" " " " , w Catherine Campbell, 1659
The Index of the Edinburgh Commissariot includes
Adam Brounhill in Nether Craig par of Restennet, 26.6.1598

Index.

Brounhill	Notes	Hamilton	7
Campbell	Notes	Hawkins	Notes
Dempster	4.6-7.Notes	Hunter	1.Notes
Ferguson	7	Metcalfe	4
		R.	3

Notes
Forfar & Restennet

OPR with the Registrar General: 288 Forfar

Births	1633-4, 1636-8, 1659-1854
Marriages	1659-1701, 1705-12, 1714-5, 1718-1854
Deaths	1826-54 (burials carelessly kept by beadle)

Church Records in SRO: CH2 for Forfar parish - nil
CH2/159 Forfar Presbytery
CH3/493 Forfar East FC, minutes 1845-57, 1856-86
HR 415 Forfar - buildings 1717-1930 etc

Fasti v 284 Forfar & Restennet were united early in the 17th century; ministers from 1566.

v 287 St.James - services were held from 1836 in an old episcopal chapel & the parish was disjoined from Forfar in 1872; ministers from 1838

Ewing ii 156 First Church from 1843; East Church from 1851

Small i 81 Forfar Antiburgher congregation disjoined from Dumbarrow (4 miles to the east) in 1778

Alexr. Lowson, "Forfar Notables" (Forfar 1891)

Alan Reid, "The Royal Burgh of Forfar" (Paisley 1902)

13 FORFAR

Angus District Parks & Cemeteries Office, Forfar: ms Burial records for the Old Parish Chorchyard, Forfar, dating 1733-60 & 1770-84, in a rather frail condition but available for inspection.

14 GLAMIS

A celtic community was founded here in the 6th century by St Fergus. The present foundation was dedicated in 1242, and the present church was built in 1792. The burial ground is sheltered by trees and is very well-kept.
National Grid reference: NO 386 468

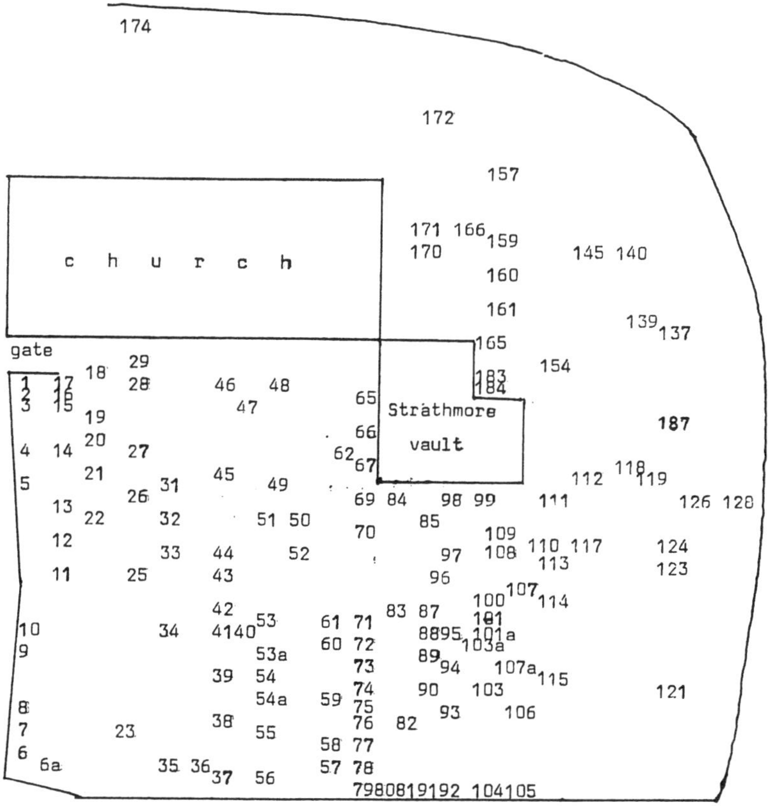

1 Jas Sturrock, the Mill Glamis, w Frances High & family Tom, Jas, Stewart, Maggie, Jane & Mary all int here & Lizzie & Jessie int Ontario Canada (no date, probably 20th century)

2 1874. by Thos Dick mason, gfa Thos Sturrock joiner 10.9.1871 77,(w Jane McFarlane 18.2.1837 46)

3 Wm Sturrock 13.10.1894 72, w Mary Guild 3.5.1887 67

4 1870. by Margt A Ross or Croll, gfa Robt Ross 2.1857, gmo in law Mary Kerr 11.1846

5 David Irons 22.10.1846 62, w Elspeth Robertson 4.10.1875 86, das Mary & Betsy d childhood, da Susan 13.1.1917 86 (h Geo Elliott 31.3.1897 69, only child Jeannie d Calcutta 22.11.1878 24 (baby da 13.3.1877 int here, h capt John Robertson d Rio de Janeiro 3.8.1892 45))

6a loom, stretchers, shuttle; J M, J L, J M, B M (probably 18th century)

6 1781. by Geo (Cabel) & Christian All(an) imo da Elspet Cabel - - - d 17(6)7 - - - -

7 1777. by Jas Donaldson in Glammis & Peter Donaldson in Nevay imo their fa also by Agnes Gray in Glammis imo her h John Donaldson 1727 63. David Donaldson 1773 73. Peter Donaldson 1750 45. (other side) mantling; crown & shoemaker's knife

8 John McFarlane 4.6.1884 75, w Margt Rea 13.3.1898 86, s Wm 1848 7, s Henry 28.8.1903 67, s Jas 2.8.1921 86, da Betsy 14.6.1923 75, da Annie 23.3. 1925 72

9 1823. by Jas Whyte grieve at Mains of S - - - - -s & w Margt Cuthbert, da Henrietta 5.12.1816 22

10 1764. Here lyes John, Jas, John, David Gilless who d young; (other side) I G, A L; M G, I G, A G, I G, I G, I G, P G, W G, D G

11 1855. by John Stewart, Wetherleys, s Wm 27.11.1848 5y4m, da Susan 27.8. 1854 3½

12 1777. D K, A G

13 1824. by David Smith weaver Grass-houses 24.3.1833 49, w Margret Glenday 26.8.1824 38, s Jas 7.2.1850 23, da Eliz 14.7.1855 21, s David d New York 20.1.1856 36

14 FS David Stormont 7.5.1805 6.2.1887 parish beadle for 66y, by rev John Stevenson LL.D imo faithful service. The enclosed stone formed the seat at the door of his cottage.

15 by Helen Paterson, fa Walter Paterson 10.4.1860 38, siss Isabella & Barbara d inf, gmo Margt McLean 13.12.1851 69, gfa Chas Paterson 8.3.1861 82, gmo Jane Martin 3.4.1831 53, gfa David Gibson 19.4.1872 94, mo Margt Gibson 25.11.1901 82. 1899

16 late John Raphael, London, yt s Emilius 28.8.1844 11.9.1909, w Jeannie Mudie Lyon 7.8.1859 26.12.1886

17 Joseph Lyon fr Muckle Kilmundie 14.12.1900 88, w Marjory Reich 27.9.1900 82, s Wm Reich 1.5.1845 20m, s David drowned at Klang in the China Seas 29.5.1883 35, da Mary d at Drumgley 23.10.1905 84

18 by Alex Ostler, Plans of Thornton, fa John 29.6.1862 86, mo Elis Miller 25.7.1865 80, da Mary Adam 11.8.1873 2y4m

19 1876. And Rough 10.7.1842 53, w Cath Moncur 11.9.1851 62, by family

20 And Rough, Plans of Thornton 22.2.1887 74, w Ann Drummond 30.4.1890 70, da Ann 23.10.1867, gs Wm Rough McLean d at Plans of Thornton 17.7.1878 4

21 I O, J O, - O, - O; (west side) A O 1753 J^O^M; crown, hammer & shears; ; by Alex Orchartson imo w Mary 1751 49, also a son dayed Jan, a son d 8.1749

22 1803. by Wm Low imo fa Alex 13.6.1802 64, mo Janet Farqurson 14.5.1803 66;

(west side) A L, J T their chn Agnes, Hellen, Wm, Jean, Isobel, Margt

23 cross. Forbes Mitchell d at Woodend 28.4.1854 78 & Wm Small fr Woodend 4. 12.1884 79 & his w Margt Roberts 15.10.1887 88

24 David Gillies quarrier Charleston 2.8.1815 15.10.1897, w Cath Rodger 24.5.1815 8.1.1897, s Robt 4.5.1853 4m, da Cath Steven 15.8.1868 18

25 1848. by Samuel Mortimer, Arnie foul d 5.1.1865 82, w Isabella Coupar 15.5.1847 68, s John 23.5.1842 23, da Agnes 19.5.1834 24

26 by W (R or M) (H)ay, w Janet Elder 4.8.18-- 63, s Chas 30.12.1838 -y, da Maggie 15.6.1848 (3)y

27 1850. by David Pickard & w Jane Chisholm, s Jas 5.7.1836 2m, her parents Jas 18.1.1849 66 & Jane Elder 29.3.1849 75; (other side) Jas Chisholm sawmiller Glamis d at Newton Glamis 11.11.1885 76, w Isabella Taylor 19.7.1909 96, da Isabella 6.5.1849, da Eliz 11.1.1869, s David 19.1. 1877, 1da Jean 7.8.1923 88

28 1810. by Alex Bower, fa Alex fr in Miltown in Glen of Ogilvy d 23.9. 1795 71, mo Matilda Steven 24.12.1808 85, s David 2.6.1772 7, Ann 20. 9.1775 10, Robt 14.7.1800 40

29 September 1879. by Wm & Margt Gibson imo her bro Jas Bower 23.3.1848 19

30 R S, A G; by mr Robt Smith present schoolmaster of Glamis & Agnes Guild his spouse, s John "a very engaging sweet tempered child"; (west side) sandglass, skull & crossbones

31 by John Tindal slater Lochee, mo Margt Meldrum 8.1.1842 59, s Wm 20.12. 1871 33, his friend Jas Lindsay 28.2.1838 15; John Tindal 14.12.1875 73, w Barbara Fyfe 16.2.1889 77; David Tindal 16.5.1922, w Jessie Brodie Mollison Tindal 11.3.1928 83, s David 16.5.1889 12

32 1774. by David McKiddy & Mary Ramsay in Newtoun of Glammiss, chn John, Elisbith & Elspet int here. Jane McKiddie 12.2.1893 90
(other side) DMK, M R; David McKiddie b 14.6.1741 d 2(5).12.1790

33 by Jas & John Adam, fa Jas Adam mason 23.10.1857 53, mo Margt Thomson 25.7.1835 31, gmo Jane Anderson 20.3.1846 72, uncle Thos Adam 10.12. 1860 53; (west side) by John Adam ship carpenter & rev Jas Adam MA of Sydney imo aunt Ann Adam 25.7.1864 55; Jas (s of above John) d 28.10. 1870 3

34 by W & David Davidson, fa Thos Davidson 5.10.1786 15.1.1864, mo Agnes Valentine 4.7.1795 8.2.1877. Above David Davidson d USA 4.9.1887 47; their sis Amelia Davidson 20.4.1836 5.8.1889 at Douglastown; bro Jas V Davidson 17.6.1820 26.12.1866 in USA, sis Jane 6.7.1822 d Edinburgh 15.3.1851, sis Margery 17.3.1829 d USA 11.6.1885

35 1851. And Meldrum & Janet Easson, s Jas late miller Mills of Finhaven 26.7.1849 63,(by w Eliz Fyfe d Arbroath 26.3.1886 74)

36 FS (marginal) by Patk Mollison late millar in GlenOgilvy imo w Margt Fleming 11.7.1758 50; (central) - - - - - 1760; - M, M F (see Jervise i 182 for poem:"This stone is set to celebrate/ This worthy woman's praise;/ Whose equal you will hardly find / For candour nowadays....")

37 by Jas Johnston, fa Wm mason 29.6.1878 74, mo Jean Webster 20.1.1890 74, bro Geo 9.1854 3; above Jas Johnston 21.1.1904 61

38 1777. by Alex, Thos & John, fa Thos Farquharson mason in Balindarg d 17.3.1765 65, mo Grissal Brown 13.4.1752 45 leaving issue; (west side) mantling; three castles, square, dividers, chisels, mallet, builders trowel; A F, T F, H F, B F, M F, A F, I F, E F

39 1771. David Wightman 22.5.1760 65, w Jannet Sturrock 27.11.1770 79, by ss Jas & John in Rochelhill; said Jas, w Isobel Mitchell 8.3.1767 32, chn Gorge, Agnes & Elspet; (west side) mantling; J W, loom & shuttle; DW, IS

40 FS Margt Wilkie 2.5.1688 23, h And Fairweather at the Barnes of Glamiss (see F Davidson:"Inventory of 17th Centery Tombstones in Angus")

41 next 40. 1885. by Wm Fairweather, fa Jas Fairweather, Nether Bow 8.8.1877 63, gmo Margt McIntosh 14.10.1860 76, uncle John Fairweather 2.5.1859 50, uncle Wm Fairweather 14.4.1871 54, mo Eliz High 19.5.1885 69

42 1826. by John Robertson junior Glamis, s John 19.4.1825 4y7m, bro Wm 2.2.1791 16, sis Jean 16.9.1812 27, das Mary Anne 29.4.1831 22m, da Isabel 12.4.1840 6, s Wm 16.3.1845 26, s John 19.12.1845 18, fa John 12.8.1830 87, mo Margt Learmonth 26.2.1837 86, da Jane 2.3.1851 28, s Edwin 1.5.1855 23; (other side) John Robertson erector of this stone d 14.12.1857 65, w Agnes Johnston 30.1.1869 77, da Helen Robertson or Kinnear 13.9.1907 84

43 by Jas Young registrar Dundee 23.10.1894 78, w Margt Gracie Robertson 12.3.1868 52, s Jas Barrie 16.10.1855 12, s Robt Hutchison 22.11.1859 17m, s Edwin Robertson 16.9.1874 19, das Agnes, Isabella & Margt all d inf; John R Young solicitor 3.11.1883 41 int Allenvale cem Aberdeen; Wm E R Young solicitor 25.5.1888 41 int Western cem Dundee

44 R M, E C ; 1775; by Robt Miln in Hottmiln & w Euphin Crystie, ss Wm & Robt int here; Robt Milne 29.1.1783 55; Euphen Chrystie 9.6.1794 56, da Jean 22.11.1790 24

45 Robt Turnbull sometime baker in London d Dundee 22.8.1825 94, by bro David d Dundee 10.9.1829 86 (w Margt Low 8.12.1839 77)

46 rev Jas Lyon min of Glamiss, da Margt 9.7.1808 15 & da Jane 10.7.1808 5 both of scarlet fever

47 by Alex Davidson tent in Haltown of Glen, fa Robt 1.3.1751 85; mantling; oxyoke, share & coulter; (other side) 1752; R D, E A; AnD, AlD, RoD, JaD, ThD, IsD, MaD, JeD, MayD

48 very rev principal Playfair's da Margt d 18.8.1810 35 (niece of rev dr Lyon (see Jervise "Epitaphs" i 181: principal Playfair md a sister of dr Lyon; see Fasti; DNB)

49 1819. by Alex Rattray tent Miltown of Craigie & w Janet Taylor, s David 9.7.1818 10y7m, s Alex 17.11.1818 16½

50 1816. John Hall 6.1813 66, w Eliz Stewart 11.1803 54; Jas Hall 27.2.1846 70; Jas A Taylor 7.1.1853 22

51 IM IN; 1787; J M, J N; Jas Mann stamp master in Glammiss, chn Mary, Jannet, Elis, Geo all d in childhhod

52 G S, I M; by Geo S- ar in Philipstown imo w Isobel Mores 12.5.1733 68 having left behind her sons & on (daughter)

53 1829. by Jas Low fr Wardmill, fa John & mo Jean Ostler, w Margt Currier & three of his bros, s John 9.1833, s Walter 2.1846; (other side) Jas Low who erected this stone d 4.1849, da Margt 3.1852, s Jas 8.1875, da Ann 8.7.1878 (h John Lakie 21.5.1893 68), da Agnes 16.7.1878; John Lakie, w Christina Campbell 7.12.1885

53a Samuel Mortimer mason Charlestown 3.3.1870 65, w Lilias Glenday 17.1.1876 68, s Samuel d USA 15.7.1859 24

54 1769. by Jannet Nicol at Glammiss, h Geo Glenday 9.7.1763 59; (west side) G G, J N; oxyoke, share & coulter

54a Jas Suttie 1.9.1867 67, w Eliz Glenday d Grangemill Inverarity 11.10.1893 88

55 1753. T D, A(V); W D, H D, A D, I D, M D, T D; (west side) - - - - - (Dug)uid & Agnes - - - - - - in Mostown imo their chn & Helen both which d very young

56 1738. F B, K S; (west side) by Fraderick Bruce weaver in Mostown & w Catrin Smith imo their chn Agnes, Alex & Margt d inf; I B, A B, A B; E B, M B, T B

57 Jas Hill 6.10.1837 45, w Jane Young 18.12.1897 100y3m

58 1734. R R, I N; A R, I R, E R, R R, I R, I R, M R; John his son d 28.4.1742 22; (other side) by Ro Ross in Balnaimoon & w Isobel Neel imo chn Isobel 29.1.1730 20m, Jean 4.2.1730 4, Margt 1.1733 2

59 Jas Doig formerly brewer in Glammiss & feuar of Wood-Fold b 1723 d 12.5.1777, by da Jean (& h David Proctor fr in Inglestown; (west side) 1778; brewer's shovels (see St Andrews Testaments: Jas Doig late feuar at Woodfolds, 12.5.1779)

60 Peter Duff 14.2.1841, w Ann Watt 10.1831, ss Peter 1.1805 12, Thos 23.12.1853 62, by da Isabella 23.5.1886 87

61 FS Patrik Philp quha depairtit this lyfe in May - - day the Zeir of God 1637 and of his aige 62y husband to Isobel Vright (see F Davidson: Inventory to 17th Century Tombstones in Angus)

62 And Wood 24.5.1829 72, w Lucy Wood 13.11.1817 50; eulogy

63 by parishioners of Glamis, late rev John Tannoch DD, chn Mary Jane 6.9.1855 17m, John 19.7.1863 11, Geo McPherson 29.8.1863 6, Margt 1.9.1863 18, Anne 9.3.1875 25, Jane d Salonica 21.12.1877 31, his mo in law Margt McPherson d Broughty Ferry 4.3.1873 78, his w Anna 18.11.1907 86; Sarah Mackintosh Cummings 3da d 12.4.1929 80

64 Wm Henderson esq late of Rochelhill 2.9.1860 44, by wid Helen Chrystal Henderson

65 mural. by Esther Proctor Alexander, fa Patk Proctor 50y factor Glamis Estate d 8.7.1819 75, bro John fr Mains of Glamis, bro Robt WS Edinburgh, bro Geo, Bengal Medical Staff, bro Thos, Bombay army, bro Wm David 40y factor on Glamis estate d Glamis 3.12.1860 74, bro David EIC home service, bro Patk royal Navy, sis Jane d St Andrews 18.4.1865 (see Jervise "Epitaphs" i 184: Esther was wife of dr And Alexander professor of Greek at St Andrews & her fa came from Morayshire)

66 mural. Patk Proctor factor for Earl of Strathmore, w Esther Hamilton 28.6.1802 54

67 Christopher Proctor 6.3.1850, w Annabella Newall 17.9.1847, 1s Wm Geo b 20.5.1839 d Kandy 3.5.1875; Jane Proctor d St Andrews 27.9.1885

68 mural. Hugh M Alexander, w Amelia Smith d Denoon 28.1.1857 29

69 by Richd Doig, fa John late of Bridgend 19.7.1841 60

70 FS erected by Youphan - - - imo her spouse Geo Doig: crown & shoemaker's knife; by Geo & Jas Doig in Glammis, (fa) - - - Doig shoemaker th(ere) - - - - May 1777 ag- - - Margt Doig - - - - - - - and of - - - - - - who d - - - (see St Andrews Testaments: Geo Doig shoemaker in Glamis, 31.3.1783 & 25.8.1784)

71 FS I B A W ; "..My name was James, my surname Brvce,/Exasperat against each abuse...." (see Jervise "Epitaphs"i 182 for acrostic & note that he "had been a retainer of the noble family of Glamis," & dates it 1680)

72 FS Isobell Roch(da to John Roch) 17.12.1675 3; skull & crossed bones; I R, I B (see F Davidson,"Inventory ...")

73 by John Craig 3.2.1905 89, w Eliz Coventry 24.4.1878 53, s Wm 5.7.1850 5w, s John 6.12.1851 6m, David 24.9.1878 23, da Mary d Dundee 21.1.1887 34 (h Alex Petrie)

74 1731. I K, M W ; by Jas Kilgour brewer in Glammiss, w Margt Whiteburn 4.1731 52, left four chn Jo, Eliz, Hel, & Margt, the rest two James's & two Margrets, Phil, Jean & Kath d in infancy

75 1874. David Stormont 15.12.1845 67, w Isabella Stewart 5.12.1851 74, da Margret 25.8.1854 37, by s John, Thornton d 19.2.1875 63, da Ann 12.7. 1889 80

76 I S, M M; miller's pick; by John Stocks, w Margt Milne 3.1732 40, chn Agnes - - - - - - - - - -; (west side) loom, shuttle, stretcher; I S, R S; M S, I R; by Ro Stocks & Ja (Rodgr) imo chn Agnes 4.6.1712 1y, Pat 8.1714 2y, with concurrence of John Stocks & Jas Stocks & Marg Daa

77 Dond Reich cattle dealer Glammiss 26.9.1850 72, w Margt Davidson 1.1.1859 71, s John 5.3.1810 6, by s David d Scroggarfield 21.12.1893 65 (w Mary Johnston 5.1.1895 62, s Wm Elder 10.5.1868 14, 3s Geo Johnston d Ballindarg 14.10.1921 56)

78 fallen. I McK ; weaver's emblems (Inscription will be underneath)

79 1768. by David Wat tent in Netherhalldyck, 1w Isobel Scot 1763 42, 2w Mary Duff 1766 37; eulogy to both wives; (other side) loom & shuttle; oxyoke, crosstree & coulter; H, I, D, I, K, I, T, A, M, I, I Watt

80 1852. John Campbell

81 Jas Shepherd 1837 66, w Ann Kyd 26.5.1856 77, s Geo 1818 11m, da Jane 1820 3, s Wm 1837 33, s John 1847 35, by s Alex shoemaker Glammiss 14. 12.1895 86 (w Bessie Harris 25.5.1890 75, s Jas 30.4.1861 2)

82 TS (marginal) by Patk Husband fr in Thorntown, w Elspet Marishal 17.2.1724 56; (central) 1738. P H, E M; P H, A H, I H, A H; This Patk d 28.4.17(57) (89), 1s by first marriage Robert succeeds owner of this stone with his w Jean Hendry

83 1849. by And Nicol fr Nether Middleton, w Jean Fergusson 27.11.1833 45, fa And 15.7.1840 83, mo Elis Crabb 17.1.1809 46, s Wm Proctor 1.9.1857 25. And Nicol 1.10.1879 89, s John 9.10.1902 76 (w Janet Smith 25.12. 1854 25), twin das Eliz 9.5.1906 85 & Margt 20.5.1906 85

84 1855. John Stivens 26.11.1847 74, w Eliz Marshall 3.12.1854 74, by s John mert Charleston 29.3.1902 85 (w Edith Blackadder 8.1.1896 77, da Eliz 1.11.1920 62, 2da Anne Blackadder 16.5.1939)

85 Jas Watson fr Knockenny 23.11.1841 69, w Margt Doig 4.2.1828 56, chn Jean 16.6.1817 7, David 28.9.1822 7, Esther 11.9.1840 23, Janet 15.9.1845 33, Jas 29.12.1854 49, John 17.7.1861 53, Geo 7.4.1864 59, Cath 28.4.1873 73, Margt 10.7.1873 71, Anne 16.6.1878 77

86 plate on coffin. Thos Geo Bowes Lyon 12th earl of Strathmore & Kinghorne viscount Lyon, baron Glamis, Tannadice, Sidlaw & Strathdichtie d 13.9. 1865 42

87 I K, E D; by And Kid weaver in Upper Arnafoul & Agnes Meek his spouse with the concurrence of Thos Guild weaver also there to ye memory of Thos Kid eldest son d 13.2.1725 16; T G, A K, A M, T K, A K, I K; (west side) loom, stretcher, shuttle; T -, J K M; I K, F D

88 FS (marginal) by Patk Fife tent in Berrielock imo w Isobel White 19.11.1759

70 having born eight ss & four das

89 FS (marginal) Jeanett Langlands spouse to John Blair in - - hill 7.1691 77; (central) John Blair weaver in Blakhill 9.10.1693 75; poem; 1736, W N, M B; I B, I L; W G, I B (see F Davidson "Inventory...")

90 by Jas Simpson, fa Alex 12.1847, mo Margt Martin 11.1885 100

91 1827. by Ann Watson, h Peter Couty 20.11.1824 62

92 by Wilhelmina Adam 16.12.1884 54, h David Davidson 15.5.1866 46, s Thos 1854 22m, da Mary Ann 1856 3w, s Alex 1857 7

93 FS Barbra How 6.12.1729 99, h John Mortomer in Knowhead of Glamis 5.4. 1738 99, s Alex(& w Jean Robbie) indwellers in the said Knowhead

94 FS (marginal) here lyes John Blaer in the Thorntown 23.11.1687 53; (central) & his spouse Agnes Mur(e) 12.11.1689 52; I B, A M; I B, (H)B, E B, P B, A B, M B, M B, I B (see F Davidson, "Inventory...")

95 G A, I S; A A, D A, A A, W A, R A (18th century)

96 1765. by John Nicol fr Mill of Arnefoul, w Margt Couty 28.2.1765 33, leaving four chn Jean, John, Margt & David

97 John Gibson fr Chamberwells 8.8.1855 84, w Helen White 29.11.1873 91 (her sis Jean White 13.2.1875 85), s John 9.8.1846 31, Jas 13.9.1844 23, s Alex 13.5.1873 55 (w Christina Lundie 1.5.1854 32)

98 by Wm Whitton wright Glen of Ogelvie & w Elsphet Meek, da Ann 25.5. 1841 18, Margt Jane 26.11.1864 10m3w, s Wm 2.11.1865 9d

99 1848. Alex Donald 9.4.1864 78, w Janet Ramsay 1.8.1859 73, chn Dempster 18.8.1823 6, Eliz 13.5.1837 21, Jas 16.5.1837 15

100 FS A C, I S; And Cathro fr Wetherlays 27.(11).1778 70, w Isabel Shaw 2.12.1791 83, by two of their ss Alex & Thos in 1796

101 FS (marginal) Alex Cathrou 24.7.16(7)3 81; (central) A C, H B, I C (see F Davidson, "Inventory....")

101a TS - - - - - - - - - - - to - - -gritt Falconer - - - 20.1732 50y

102 by Jas Cathro fr Berryhillock, w Helen Wyllie 16.1.1855 28, s Alex 30.5.1849 15m, da Helen 29.3.1856 15m. Jas Cathro 19.8.1902 86, w Mary Fenton 18.4.1907 89

103 by Thos Cathro tent Inglestoun of Kinnettles, w Jean Proctor 26.5. 1761 30; (west side) square & dividers, oxyoke, plough

103a 1745. A C, A H; by Alex Cathrou tent Brockhols & w Agnes Hu - lo, chn Jas 17(2)2 21, Eliz 1730 18, Kethren 1738 17; Agnes Cathrow 25.1. 1746 29; Alex Cathrou & w Agnes Huntr, s Alex

104 by Charlotte Deuchars, John Deuchars shoemaker Glamiss 1785 63, his - - - - - Donaldson 10.1783, also other bros & siss John 8.1786 int Oathlaw, And 2.1840 51 int Newtyle, Peter 9.1785 18 int Oathlaw, Isobel 11.1783 32 int here, Margt 1784 33, Agnes - - -

105 1839. Alex Robertson, Plans of Cossans d 9.1852 66, w Helen Mortimer 14.6.1866 78, s Alex 8.12.1822 4, da Isabel 12.12.1822 6, da Eliz 13.5.1826 6, da Helen 18.5.1826 2w, s sb 4.8.1827, s David 3. 1840 17, da Mary Buchan 23.1.1884 53 (h Wm Clark, Arbroath)

106 1850. David Malcom 1813 1878, w Elspeth Doig 1816 1898, s Geo 9.3. 1848 8, s Robt Doig b 1843 d Belle Fourche South Dakota USA 1909 (s Robt Mortimer 1867 1895)

107a W N, E D; by Wm Neil cooper in Glamis imo da Margt 7.179(3) 1y

107 W R, H G, 1734; by Wm Rhind shoemaker in Glammis & w Helen Gray, s Jas 14.2.1734 1y6m2w, Alex 12.5.1734 (3)y. The said Wm d 27.7.1744 40; crown, pincers, shoemakers knife

108 by Alex Gray tent in Folsorty, da Janet 7.1.1742; poem

109 by Wm Urquhart nurseryman in Dundee, fa Daniel d Glammis Castle 19.6.1798 69, mo Marion Wilkie d Dundee 4.8.1811 80, Robt & Margt two of their chn int near this place

110 1769. by David Lindsay mason in Glamiss & w Jean Ramsay, da Jean 24.11.1766 22

111 1870. by Alex & David Nicoll, fa David 27.4.1843 54, mo Helen Wilkie 16.5.1867 72, sis Betsy 11.10.1839 23. Wm, s of above David Nicoll, 21.1.1868 17. David Nicoll 19.6.1882 70, da Helen 3.5.1874 37 (h Robt Bell), s John 19.12.1874 41, w Isabella Gibson 20.5.1886 73. David Nicoll 13.7.1890 54. Mary Nicoll 2.8.1894 86. Above Alex Nicoll 9.3.1900 69

112 January 28 1728. by Agnes Hood, h John Dalgety hammerman in Glammis 24.6.1727 41, surviving chn Mary & John. Jas, David & Jean d young. Jas Baxter hammerman in Glammis, w Agnas Hood 18.1.1734 40 having left behind her one s to foresaid Jas also called Jas Baxter; crown & hammer; "O dear John Dalgety! who can / Thy praises all express?/Amost expert artificer/ In iron and in brass./Discreet was't thou to ev'ry one,/ Obliging, just and kind;/And still thy tongue ingenuous spoke/ The language of thy mind..." (see Jervise "Epitaphs.." i 183)

113 1862. Alex Fairweather mert Glamis 2.1861 86, w Isabel Barrie 5.1855 79, da Isabel 11.1828 26, s John 2.1845 39 int Aberdeen, da Margt 8.1857 50, da Mary 6.1841 30 int Arbroath (h Hammack, da Rose 7.1848 9), s David 12.1874 56, s Thos 12.1874 54 int London, Jane 9.11.1884 85, Eliz 27.9.1886 72, Helen 25.3.1897 80

114 1863. Alex Barry, Newton of Glamis 16.9.1859 74, w Anne Guthrie 29.8.1836 41, chn Jannet 18.1.1816 31.7.1828, Agnes 5.10.1817 19.12.1899, Thos 15.11.1819 6.3.1823, Wm 2.2.1821 26.2.1823, David 2.2.1821 13.3.1823, Jas 27.7.1823 13.2.1852, Anne 22.10.1825 6.7.1905, Eliz 4.3.1828 23.10.1894, John 12.4.1830 11.7.1865, Jane 30.12.1832 21.1.1908

115 1849. by Wm McDonald, Glammiss, w Isabel Cay 29.8.1848 71, s Jas 12.8.1828 18, s Wm 21.7.1835 31. Wm McDonald 29.9.1868 84, s John 12.3.1889 75(w Elis Greenhill 16.7.1846 32)

116 by John Tindal slater Charleston, s John 25.2.1840 4, fa serjt John Tindal late of H E I Company's artillery 6.8.1869 86

117 1852. by Alex Brown, fa in law Wm Donaldson late fr East Drumglie 13.12.1851 79, his wife Barbra Guthrie 11.12.1847 79

118 1850. David Hendry 3.2.1826 41, w Isabel Smith 27.2.1836 56, s Alex 1821 4, da Margt 11.1822 11, da Isabel 2.1818 1y, by da Helen Rose innkeeper Glammiss (h Robt Adamson Ross 8.2.1847 26, s Alex 28.12.1841 3, s Robt Adamson 8.7.1847 4, s David 30.12.1875 33)

119 1853. Alex Rattray fr Templebank 23.1.1851 58, by w Margt Gray 23.3.1869 78, s Alex 5.11.1847 27, da Sarah 8.1823 11m, da Janet 21.10.1843 24, da Margt 22.5.1849 22, s John fr Templebank 13.10.1887 68 (w Eliz Suttie 3.10.1912 77)

120 Wm Gellatley d Airneyfoul 21.11.1868 76, w Agnes Crabb d Airneyfoul 2.12.1877 86, da Agnes d Lara cottage 19.2.1916 82 (h John Johnston d Airneyfoul 19.5.1910 79, da Janet d inf, da Agnes Crabb d 1 Lammerton terrace Dundee 17.8.1948 76 (wid of And Pellow)). Eliza Margt Helen Johnston d 1 Lammerton terrace Dundee 21.3.1957 82

121 1829. by Daniel, Wm & Jas imo fa Wm Geddes 9.10.1816 42. (east side) Robt Macdonald, Kinnettles d 28.2.1867 66, w Jane Anderson d Glamis 27.11.1847 40, chn Cath 15.10.1833 24.2.1838, Robt 7.10. 1835 15.12.1839, Jas 7.10.1835 12.7.1844, Eliz 25.8.1843 4.2.1845, Wm 20.7.1839 20.11.1845, John 24.1.1828 29.10.1846, Ann 11.3.1831 10.12. 1846, Helen 11.1845 9.4.1847, Janet 17.9.1837 27.4.1849, Alex 10.9. 1829 22.5.1852, Geo (w Ann Gordon 13.11.1874 25)

122 And Ralston 53y factor on Glamis estates d 17.7.1914 83, w Jane Wallace 4.3.1871 31, da Jane 10.6.1864 23m, s Claude Lyon WS Glamis d 6. 10.1928 61, s Gavin MMO 37y factor on Glamis estates d 25.3.1951 81

123 CT Jas Horn at Bridgend of Glammys 20.5.1773 57, w Kath Shepherd 18.12. 1793 86 who were distinguished in their time for being very liberal to the poor (see St Andrews Testaments: Kath Shepherd residenter in Glamis, relict of Jas Horn sometime blacksmith at Bridgend of Glamis, 13.1.1794)

124 fallen. Jas Horn hammerman in the town, w Margt 30.12.1676 28; skull & bones (see F Davidson, "Inventory..")

125 (marginal) John Budworth & Anna Lee indwellers, da Helen 1714 1y4m; (central) - B, A L; John Budworth 24.4.1718 39 (see Jervise, "Epitaphs .." i 183:"Here lyes John Budworth, English born /Whose life these fortunes did adorn -/ He was both curteous, kynd & just /A friend whom on might firmly trust;/With other gifts both rare & fyne /Tho' lodged but in a crazy shrine,/Death smot the pott, thus sadly rent,/ And here to ly, the shells has sent.")

126 TS (marginal) Wm Lov sometyme hammerman & indweller in Glammis who d ------ of his age --y, his spouse Christian Burn "a good & vertuos fruitful vif"; W L, C B; crown & hammer; emblems (17th century, see F Davidson, "Inventory.."p 40)

127 1876. Robt Suttie d Airnifoul 14.12.1874 65, da Annie d inf, by w Ann Edward d Forfar 8.2.1885 82

128 1846. by John Johnston mason 3.12.1848 53, w Jannet Alexander 30.9. 1843 42, fa John 1809 43, mo Isabell Gibson 1814 45

128a ob Jas Johnston, Woodfaulds 1889 60, da Louie d Southampton 1908 37 (h John Reid), w Eliza Jeffrey Trotter 1913 80

129 1780. by - - & Thos Mudies, fa - - - - - - - - 65y June - - viz - - - - -

130 1868. John Johnston 21.2.1881 83, w Jannet Waddell 5.5.1893 87, chn Jean 24.5.1837 2y7m, Agnes Brodie 31.3.1848 1y3m, Wm Waddell 5.5. 1860 29, John Cunningham 27.9.1861 24, Adam 6.9.1865 22, Jane 12.11. 1873 41 (h Wm Orem), Jas Lyon 16.11.1873 45. Mary Johnston 8.7. 1897 58

131 David Johnston 1.2.1864 55, s Wm 23.1.1853 18, w Barbra Mortmer 25.6. 1875 65

132 Wm Abbot 3.8.1850 42, s John 19.8.1838 8m, s Jas 17.11.1846 1y, s Wm 24.3.1855 21, s Alex 6.4.1866 25, da Susan 1.1.1872 33, w Jemima Otman 5.5.1887 74; Margt Abbot 5.1.1892 61; Jane Abbot 28.7.1902 55

133 by Jas T Davie & w Jane McIntyre (her fa Jas McIntyre 15.2.1837 31, her bro Alex 31.10.1856 20), chn Geo O 29.12.1869 11m, Betsy 3.9.1871 17; Jas T Davie - - - - (covered by bricks) - - -

134 1876. Jas Alexander fr Ballindarg 4.5.1873 76, w Betsy Johnston 5.4. 1882 62, da Eliza 6.6.1835 6, da Margt 13.3.1847 21, da Agnes 17.10.

1847 15, das Jane & Betsy d inf, by s John fr Ballindarg 16.8.1901 65, da Mary Ann d Ballindarg 4.10.1907 78

135 1788. by John Hagart, fa Thos 10.2.1788, mo Isabel Lyon 13.5.1779. By Thos Mitchell & Thos - - - - - their sons in law

136 1868. Jas Young, Leys of Cossans 17.12.1850 66, w Ann Smart 28.11.1867 80, da Jean 8.11.1846 33 (s Jas Lindsay 19.9.1862 28), da Margt 20.4. 1878 63 (h Jas Crabb 18.2.1892 79); John Young, Leys of Cossans 23.5. 1909 85, w Jean Donald 13.5.1895 66, da Agnes 19.3.1870 2y8m

137 by Eliz Duncan, h Peter Laird mason Glamis 1.11.1841 32, da Mary 6.12. 1843 20m

138 1815. John Johnston mert Glamis, w Jane Anderson 8.1809 41, two ss Alex 4.1813 17, Chas 4.1815 23, Ann d inf; (west side) John Johnston 24.6. 1842 78, w Margt Gibson 9.1.1867 89, da Jane 22.11.1843 40 (h Jas Ramsay), da Mary 18.11.1846 31, da Margt 17.12.1910 93

139 1803. Jas Young weaver in Latch 16.5.1820 81 int here, w Jean Milne 5.5.1801 70 leaving issue Jas & Isabel

139a 1921. David Young d Latch 16.3.1920 73, by w Mary Watson d Glamis 14. 5.1929 81

140 FS Heir lyis Helen & Cathrine Luke who departed the yeir of God 1650 (see F Davidson, "Inventory..")

141 John Hogg d Charleston 9.9.1884 78, w Cath Kidd d Airlie 18.9.1846 38, s Wm clothier Glamis 10.1.1911 67 (s d 15.5.1876 inf, 1da Jessie Murray 28.8.1921 50, w Christina Allan 27.1.1922 76, s Wm mert tailor Glamis 9.12.1931 49 int Glamis cem, s Robt Allan d Northfield cottage Brechin 9.1.1937 62, s Gavin Murray 4.1.1939 51, da Annie Hogg Mudie 17.12.1940 62, s John Allan 6.4.1942 70, s Jas 15.2.1954 69, da Christina Hogg Edward 21.11.1963 84)

142 FS Andreu Taylor somtym indweller (Killmundie) 1.8.1690 39, w Janet Blair 15.2.1686 48; I T, M T, W T, A T, A T, E T, I T, D T, I T, I T, E T, A T; A T, I C; emblems (see F Davidson, "Inventory .." p 40)

143 FS (marginal) by And Fife brewer Glamis imo w Helen Gwthrie 3. 4.17-- 55, leaving four hopefwl chn Eliz, Janet, Geo & Wm; (central) A F, H G on hub of cross; angel; "Below this monument a jewel/ Of womankind doth ly;/Who night & day was exercis'd/ In acts of piety... (for complete poem see Jervise "Epitaphs.." i 184; Willsher & Hunter, "Stones" fig.9)

144 Geo Fullerton in Knockennie, w Janet Mitchelson 2.2.1687; G F, I M (see F Davidson, "Inventory...")

145 FS broken. Heir lyis Agnes Volvm spovs to Williame Lyon in Clippithils vha depairted 1 of May 1650 her age vas 62 yeirs (see F Davidson, "Inventory.."; also Jervise i 182 who notes that Clippithils is now called Mossend of Glamis)

146 FS David Kid in Thornton som tym in Chapelton. Here lyes David Kid lawfoul son to David Kid in Thornton d 1679 24; (see Davidson, "Inventory..")

147 FS (poem quoted in full by Jervise "Epitaphs.."i 183: the acrostic reads as follows:) David Kid elder G (for Glamis); D K E G

147a by Wm Kyd labourer in Plans of Thorntoun 12.2.1855 79, & w Ann Tosh 1.9.1864 83, chn Jas 23.11.1805 1y, Ann 28.5.1813 3, Agnes 17.7.1823 8, Jean 15.5.1826 3w; Betsy Kyd 23.5.1885 74

148 1849. Jas McIntosh 7.7.1844 82, w Eliz Rattray 19.10.1848 78, by da Grace 15.1.1880 71 (chn Ann Gibson 9.7.1841 4, Eliz Gibson 16.2.1849 19)

149 1851. by John Milne, s John 1.7.1848 5, da Jannet 15.7.1848 3

150 1767. Geo Nevay in Newtown, w Marg Milne 35y leaving issue Is:, Jean & Chs Nevay

151 1807. by Thos Neave & w Janet Gray sometime resident in the par of Glammiss imo s Thos - - - - - - - - - - (under turf) - -

152 by Jas Baxter smith in Glammis, w Margt Honie 21.11.1772 36 leaving issue five ss & two das David, Margt, Jas, John, Robt, Patk & Jean

153 Alex Couper 1821 48, w Janet Osler 1812 30, s Alex 1815 8, da Margt 1821 7m, da Agnes 1836 10, s Robt 1839 28, 2w Agnes Osler 1855 73, by s David 2.12.1882 74 fr Hatton, Glen of Ogilvy (w Isobel Sinclair d West Scryne 27.11.1896 85, da Jessie d West Scryne 18.8.1895 58, s Jas Davidson fr West Scryne Carnoustie d there 5.3.1927 84)

154 1873. by Geo Johnston, Loanhead d 10.6.1899 93, s Alex 6.1834 9m, s John 11.10.1872 33, w Mary Stormont 23.7.1881 74, da Betsy 1.3.1921 89 (west side) & our friend lieut Jas Davidson quartermaster 41st regt of foot b Dundee 10.2.1787 d Carnoustie 22.1.1861. He had seen much active service & when in the Guards gained his medal at the Battle of Waterloo

155 1823. by John McLean tent Foffarty, spouse Lillias Morton 29.12.1821 66

156 by Laur. Macfarlane, s John 7.5.1842 25

157 1818. by Daniel & John McLeod, mo Jean McIntosh 16.3.1818 63

158 FS I H A B
P H

159 John Bennet tent Balgray of Pearsie 15.1.1872 73, w Margt Roberts 26.7.1871 68, ss John, Wm & Thos all d young, s Jas 18.11.1880 43

160 1838. by Rae M Davidson millmaster Glammis, w Janet Young 9.10.1837 38, fa Alex Davidson 6.1.1832 75

161 by David Hood, Hatton of Essie, fa And tent in Wester Denoon 9.2.1826, s Jas John McKay 23.8.1847 10. David Hood 14.5.1861 71, s And 6.8.1861 35, s Stewart Thos Mitchell 22.7.1863 31, wid Jane Ogilvy 20.1.1865 60, s David 2.6.1867 36, s Wm 13.5.1868 32

162 beside 161. late David Hood, Hatton of Eassie, ss Arthur d Calcutta 17.1.1888 35, lieut col Geo, Lincoln regt d Edinburgh 3.6.1885 41,(by sisters)

163 ob John Smith factor on the Douglas estate Forfarshire d Broughty Ferry 14.1.1862 73, w Jessie Halket d there 24.9.1868, chn John 30.8.1834 6m, Francis Nicoll 31.1.1835 5, Margt 14.2.1835 7, Amelia 28.1.1857 30 (h Hugh M Alexander), Joan 22.7.1858 18, Wm Proctor 2.2.1865 30

164 1801. by Alex Davidson & Jane Proctor in Loanhead, s Alex 13.6.1799 16

165 Alex Stevenson surgeon Glammis who practised there for 15y d 21.5.1844 36

166 1848. Wm Blackadder civil engineer Glammiss b East Blanerne Berwickshire d Glamis 20.10.1860 71, w Betty Baillie d Dundee 18.12.1870, chn John 16.6.1825, John Alexander 19.1.1828 both in inf, Anne 1.8.1832 15 being their whole family

167 ob by Jas Reid fr Kilmundie, w Jeanie Kermath 30.6.1867 27. Jas Reid 18.3.1905 88, wid Ann Cathro 21.4.1919 67, fa Thos Reid 29.11.1862 71, mo Helen Ireland 19.2.1870 69, bro David 20.1.1845 9m, uncle David Reid d Kilmundie 28.3.1858 75, sis Jane Mudie Reid 16.3.1906 69, da Helen Wyllie Ireland 1.3.1911 35; Jas C Reid 1.4.1963

168 1868. Archd McDonald 20.11.1822 71, w Marjory Robertson 29.9.1834 71, by da Ann (h Alex Kidd 20.12.1856 71, s David 8.4.1831 4, s Jas 17.9.1834 21), s John 9.10.1867 78, a relative Eliza Kidd 18.6.1859 10

169 David Guild, home farm of Burnside Rescobie 3.5.1883 61, s David d Omaha USA 3.3.1886 36, w Christina Dunbar d Carnoustie 19.4.1911 87; Margt Clark d Haughs of Cossans 9.11.1843 58, h John Dunbar d Haughs of Cossans 7.6.1864 85

170 by Wm Cable, Forfar, w Mary Buchan 19.5.1844 28

171 by Mary Campbell, h Alex Buchan 7.12.1833 44. John Buchan d Charleston 29.8.1897 74

172 urn. Geo Dove fr West Rochilhill 29.12.1905 75, w Jean Johnston 7.12.1891 64, s Alex Grieve 23.10.1867 14½, da Helen Robertson 14.2.1887 27, gda Maud Dove Ellson d Beaufort Australia 20.9.1907 25 (h John Nicol), gs John Dove Ellson d at sea 25.7.1919 36; Annie Dove Ellson 20.12.1922 65; (south side) their (i.e.A G & H R Dove's) gfas Jas Grieve 25.12.1834 65 & Geo Dove 31.3.1852 82; Samuel Dove fr Manorwater house Co Fermanagh Ireland, w Georgina Dempster 27.10.1871 int churchyard of Maguire's bridge Fermanagh (see inscription no. 183)

173 Jas Langlands 20.6.1885 78, w Marion Miller d at Hayston 13.7.1874 75, chn Robt 15.12.1833 10m, David 27.4.1837 2m, Isabella 29.9.1838 1m, da Helen d Hatton of Eassie 16.12.1903 75 int Glenprosen churchyard (h Wm Whyte)

174 David Hutchon tailor Charlston 3.12.1873 63, w Janet Kinmond 21.4.1884 81, da Jane 27.4.1838 1m, s David 20.10.1848 1y11m, da Isabella 6.4.1866 29

175 FS Jas Chalmers musician to noble family of Strathmore 3.3.1770; poem "...He played with such dexterity,/ By all it is confest,/ That in this grave interred is /Of violists the best." (quoted in full by Jervise, "Epitaphs.."i 184)

176 1778. by Chas Allan in Glammis & w Jean Moodie imo da Margrat 7.12.1776 1y

177 mural in church. rev Jas Lyon DD min par Glamis, w Agnes L'Amy, da Margt 9.7.1808 15, da Jane Playfair 10.7.1808 5, s Jas 17.2.1815 24, da Ann Dempster 20.3.1815 20, da Agnes 30.7.1816 29 (h rev W Roger min Rescobie), da Barbara Cath 23.11.1823 23, s Wm min Union Chapel Aberdeen 4.7.1828 30, s Stewart 25.9.1830 25, da Janet 30.6.1834 37, s Geo d Stirling 9.1.1859 69

178 mural in church. rev Jas Lyon DD 3.4.1838 79 in 58th y of ministry in par of Glamis, w Agnes L'Amy 14.9.1840 78(see Fasti v 290 & Jervise,"Epitaphs.."i 181: his fa was min at Longforgan, his gfa was min at Airlie, his ggfa was min at Tannadice; she was sis of Jas L'Amy of Dunkenny sheriff depute of Forfar)

179 by Thos Mitchell baker Glammis & w Christian Bell (no date, probably early 18th century); baker's peles with scones

180 Alex Gray in Glamis, da Eliz 9.7.1714 (Dr Stirton, "Glamis" has 7.6.)

181 John Bruce & Barbara Ferguson in Glammis, da Mary 19.-.1730 2y8m; M B

182 by (Iso)bel Spaldon in Glamis, h Geo Tailor 1760 while miller there 54y

183 1836. by Alex Dove, chn Eliz 10.8.1832 5, Samuel 17.2.1832 2, Mary 22.7.1835 2, fa in law Jas Grieve 25.12.1834 65 (see inscription 172, also D Whyte, "Introducing Scottish Genealogical Research" for a family tree)

183a 1766. by Euphen Dryburns imo h Jas Baillie late gardiner at Castle of Glammis d 64y leaving Geo, Thos, Jean & Mary

184 mrs Margt Davidson 17.4.1793 76

185 The burial place of Ihon Low valkar in Glamis & his family obit 1603; an 1607, W L, A L; I L, waulker's shears (see F Davidson, "Inventory ..")

186 behind 185. T B, E D; (reverse) - - -(inaccessible)

187 Alex Thornton 22.1.1652 60, w Helen Balbirny 12.1652 70; A T, H B, G T (see F Davidson, "Inventory...")

188 FS Thos Tailyour 18.2.1649 60, w Agnis Philp 26.2.1663 57 somtym in Haystoun with their chn (see F Davidson, "Inventory..")

189 Wm Adam in the Meltown of the Glean (ie Glen of Ogilvy) 28.4.1684 57 (see F Davidson, "Inventory..", also Jervise "Epitaphs.." i 182)

190 small stone leaning against south dyke. I S, I H, 1706

The following are listed in Jervise, "Epitaphs.." i and/or in Stirton, "Glamis", but were not seen in 1978:

191 Jas Badenach, w Agnes Low 1755 58; "Good, sober, pious, frugal, chaste, She wade through trouble, till at last / The ghastly tyrant struck the blow /And laid her bones this stone below."

192 Iohne Watt in Dunkennie, w Janet Smith 18.5.1677 73

193 Wm Cruickshank tailor 1731 61 (but Stirton & Chas Rogers "Monuments.." have 1718); poem (quoted in full by Jervise)

194 Andrew Steven, wife d 1741; poem (quoted in full by Jervise)

195 Jas Rhynd 1734 1y5m; "Here lies a sweet & loving child,/ Ah, cover'd o'er with mud; Resembling well the lillie fair, Cropt in the very bud. .... (poem quoted in full by Jervise)

196 TS in Strathmore aisle, in Latin. (marginal) sir Patk Lyon lord of Glamis 21.3.1459, w Isobella Ogilvy 12.1.1484 and

197 FS (John 3rd lord Glamis 1.)4.1497, his lady Eliz Scrymgeour (of Dudhope)

198 enclosure on east side of Strathmore aisle with no monument. mr Laing-Meason of Lindertis, one of his six children

199 triangular stone built in west dyke. 1672, Alexr Nisbet, Hellen Wood; armorial bearings

200 panel over door at Cossins. 1627, mr John Lyon, mrs Jean Young; armorial bearings; latin inscription (quoted in full by Jervise)

14 G L A M I S

N o t e s

Jervise, "Epitaphs & Inscriptions .. in the Northeast of Scotland" vol i notes the above inscriptions 36,48,63-7,71,89,94,112,123,125-6,140,143,145-6,175, 178,187-200

F Davidson, "Inventory of 17th Century Tombstones in Angus" has detailed descriptions of the stones above indexed as 40,61,71-2,89,94,101,124,126,140,142, 144-6,185,187-190

Chas Rogers, "Monuments & Monumental Inscriptions in Scotland" notes inscriptions 30,65,71,112,147,175,193 & 196

rev dr John Stirton, "Glamis, a Parish History" (1913)

Testaments: The Index to the Commissariot Register of Edinburgh includes the following - Geo Fithie (Fethie) in Newtoun of Glammis, 1602
Alexr Fullartoun of Denune, 1603
Sara Fullartoun in Tarbray spouse to Thos Ogilvie, 1608

and the following is a small selection from the Index to the Commiasariot Register of St Andrews -
John Allan younger in Denhead of Ogilvie, 1619
Silvester Allardyce in Glamis, 1718; Thos Allardyce in Glamis 1625
And Blackie in Glen of Ogilvie, 1614, spouse Isobel Ferguson
John Blair cotterman in Chappelfuird, 1600
John Blair in Kilmundie, 1615; John Cathro in Dryburnes, 1638
Robt Fairweather in Chaippelmoss in Glen of Ogilvie, 1619
Geo Luke, 1637; John Fleming & w Isobel Luke, 1652
Jas Kid, spouse Bessie Shepherd, 1616
Jas Mitchell in Haystoun, 1797
Helen Nicoll spouse to John Blair in Raits, 1619
John Rhind in Balnamoir, 1723
John Roch cottarman sometime in Kilmundie, 1600
Jas Samson in Crawsnest of Glen of Ogilvie, spouse Christian Deuchars, 1628; Bessie Soutar sometime spouse to John Mitchelson brabener in Cottoun of Easter Dynnown, 1605
Elspet Thornton spouse to Jas Wat, in Haystoun, 1617
Gilbert Thornton of that ilk, 1618
John Thornton younger, spouse to Alison Butter, 1616
John Thornton ground officer in the lordship of Glamis, 1777

OPR with the Registrar General: 289 Glamis (Glammis)
Births 1699-1737, 1739-1854
Marriages 1699-1715, 1834-54
Deaths (mortcloth dues) 1685-1715
KS minutes 1684-1715

Church records in SRO: CH2/170 KS minutes 1719-47, 1780-1874
HR 760 Glamis 1926-8

Fasti v 289- ministers from 1567

I n d e x

A.	47.95	B.	70.72.101.158.186
Abbot	132	Badenach	191
Adam	18.33.92.189	Baillie	166.183a
Adamson	118	Balbirny	187
Alexander	65.68.128.134.163.166	Barrie/y	43.113-4
Allan	6.141.176.Notes	Baxter	112.152
Allardyce	Notes	Bell	111.179
Anderson	33.121.138	Bennet	159

14 G L A M I S

Blackadder 84.166
Blackie Notes
Blair/Blear 89.94.142.Notes
Bower 28-9
Bowes Lyon 86
Brodie 31.130
Brown 38.117
Bruce 56.71.181
Buchan 105.170-1
Budworth 125
Burn 126
Butter Notes

C. 142
Cabel,Cable 6.170
Campbell 53.80.171
Cathro/u 100-3a.167.Notes
Cay 115
Chalmers 175
Chisholm 27
Chrystal 64
Chrystie 44
Clark 105.169
Coupar/er 25.153
Couty 91.96
Coventry 73
Crabb 83.120.136
Craig 73
Croll 4
Cruickshank 193
Crystie, see Chrystie
Cummings 63
Cunningham 130
Currier 53
Cuthbert 9

D. 87.107a.186
Daa 76
Dalgety 112
Davidson 34.47.77.92.153-4.160 164.184
Davie 133
Dempster 172.177
Deuchars 104.Notes
Dick 2
Doig 59.69-70.85.106
Donald 99.136
Donaldson 7.104.117
Dove 172.183
Drummond 20
Dryburns 183a
Duff 60,79
Duguid 55
Dunbar 169
Duncan 137

Easson 35
Edward 127.141
Elder 26-7.77
Elliott 5
Ellson 172

Fairweather 40-1.113.Notes
Falconer 101a
Farquharson 22.38
Fenton 102
Fergus(s)on 83.181.Notes
Fethie Notes
Fife 88.143.see Fyfe
Fithie Notes
Fleming 36.Notes
Fullerton 144.Notes
Fyfe,Fife 31.35.88.143

G. 12.89
Geddes 121
Gellatley 120
Gibson 15.29.97.111.128.138.148
Gill(i)es 10.24
Glenday 13.53a-54a
Gordon 121
Gracie 43
Gray 7.107-8.119.151.180
Greenhill 115
Grieve 172.183
Guild 3.30.87.169
Guthrie 114.117.143

H. 158.190
Hagart 135
Halket 163
Hall 50
Hamilton 66
Hammack 113
Harris 81
Hay 26
Henderson 64
Hendry 82.118
High 1.41
Hill 57
Hogg 141
Honie 152
Hood 112.161-2
Horn 123-4
How 93
Husband 82
Hunter 103a
Hu- - lo 103a
Hutchen 174
Hutchison 43

Ireland 167
Irons 5

Jeffrey 128a
Johnston 37.42.77.120.128a.130-1 134.138.154.172

K. 12
Kermath 167
Kerr 4
Kid(d), Kyd 81.87.141.146-147a.168 Notes
Kilgour 74

Kinmond	174
Kinnear	42
Kyd, see Kid	
L.	6a.10.89
Laing-Meason	198
Laird	137
Lakie	53
L'Amy	177-8
Langlands	89.173
Learmonth	42
Lee	125
Lindsay	31.110.136
Low	22.45.53.126.185.191
Luke	140.Notes
Lundie	97
Lyon	16-7.46.48.135.145.177-8 196-7.200
M.	6a.21.87
Malcom/Malcolm	106
Mann	51
Marishal	82
Marshall	84
Martin	15.90
Meek	87.98
Meldrum	31.35
Miller	18.173
Miln(e)	44.76.139.149-50
Mitchell	23.39.135.161.179.Notes
Mitchelson	144.Notes
Mollison	31.36
Moncur	19
Moodie	176
Mores	52
Mortimer/Mortomer	25.53a.93.105-6.131
Morton	155
Mudie	16.129.141.167
Mure	94
Murray	141
McDonald	115.121.168
McFarlane	2.8.156
McIntosh	41.63.148.157
McIntyre	133
McKay	161
McKiddy/ie	32
Mackintosh	63.see McIntosh
McLean	15.20.155
McLeod	157
McPherson	63
N.	51.89.185
Neave	151
Neel, Neil	58.107a
Nevay	150
Newall	67
Nicol(l)	54.83.96.111.163.172.Notes
Nisbet	199
Ogilvy	161.196.Notes
Orem	130
Ortchartson	21
Os(t)ler	18.53.153
Otman	132
Paterson	15
Pellow	120
Petrie	73
Philp	61.188
Pickard	27
Playfair	48.177
Proctor	59.65-7.83.103.163-4
Ralston	122
Ramsay/ey	32.99.110.138
Raphael	16
Rattray	49.119.148
Rea	8
Reich	17.77
Reid	128a.167
Rhind/Rhynd	107.195.Notes
Robbie	93
Roberts	23.159
Robertson	5.42-3.105.168.172
Roch	72.Notes
Rodger,Roger	24.76.177
Ross	4.58.118
Rough	19-20
S.	95.190
S- -ar	52
Samson	Notes
Scot	79
Scrymgeour	197
Shaw	100
Shepherd	81.123.Notes
Simpson	90
Sinclair	153
Small	23
Smart	136
Smith	13.30.56.83.118.163.192
Soutar	Notes
Spaldon	182
Steven	24.28.194
Stevenson	14.165
Stewart	11.50.75
Stivens	84
Stocks	76
Stormont	14.75.154
Sturrock	1-3.39
Suttie	54a.119.127
Tannoch	63
Tailor,Taylor	27.49-50.142,182,188
Thomson	33
Thornton	187.Notes
Tindal	31.116
Tosh	147a
Trotter	128a
Turnbull	45
Urquhart	109

14 G L A M I S

V.	55
Valentine	34
Volum	145
W.	71
Waddell	130
Wallace	122
Watson	85.91.139a
Wat(t)	60.79.192.Notes
Webster	37
White	88.97.see Whyte
Whiteburn	74
Whitton	98
Whyte	9.173.see White
Wightman	39
Wilkie	40.109.111
Wood	62.199
Wright	61
Wyllie	102.167
Young	43.57.136.139-a.160.200

15 G L E N I S L A

A church was founded here before 1200, was rebuilt soon after 1469 and dedicated to the Blessed Virgin. The present church was built 1821-9 on the site of the original church. The burial ground is well-kept but there are evidently a large number of flat stones under the turf.
National Grid reference: NO 214 604

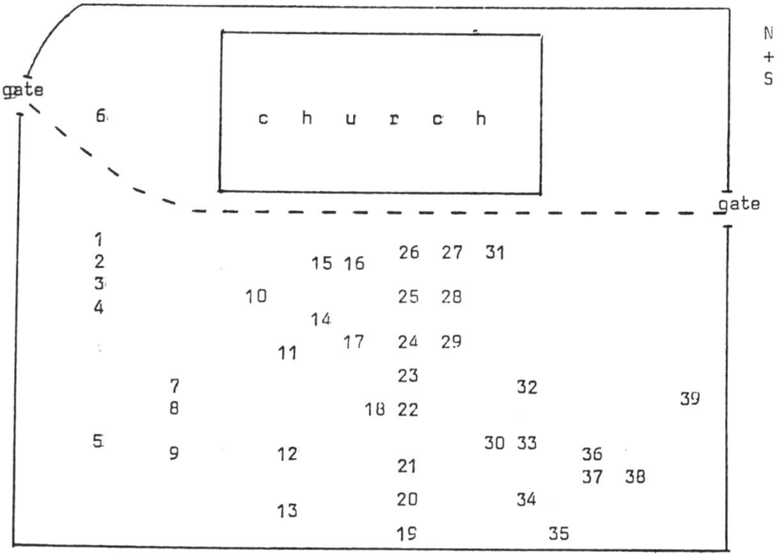

1 book. John Grewar d Dalnamer 7.3.1898 84, s John inf, w Janet McFarlane d Kirkmichael 2.7.1915 77, da Janet 5.1933

2 Peter Brodie 12.3.1832 33, w Susan Grewar 7.9.1859 63, da Cath inf, s John 20.12.1910 79 int Erith cem Kent

3 David Steel Grewar FSAScot & author of "The Story of Glenisla" anti-

quarian & naturalist Folda 8.10.1945 79, gfa Wm Grewar d Dalnasnaucht 30.11.1885 86, gmo Helen McIntosh d Dalnasnaucht 22.2.1872 72, aunt Janet Grewar d Dalnasnauchton 1.7.1918 86

4 book. Jas Grewar d Balloch result of accident 19.4.1910 39, s inf; Jane Robertson d Williamstone Kirkmichael 2.3.1920 56

5 1852. Angus Morgan d Wester Doltby here 14.9.1834 39, s Thos 12.1.1840 5, s John 15.1.1840 10, da Jane 22.1.1840 16

6 Jas Stewart fr Craighead 1.10.1873 80, da Mary 1839 6, s Jas 1834 5w, s John 1848 6, s Alex 1878 47, w Martha Jack 1881 77, s And 23.1.1925 81 (s Jas 10.4.1883 7m, w Anne McAndrew d Islabank 31.3.1947 88, only da Jean 10.3.1953, s And 21.2.1956 (w Mat 12.5.1965))

7 by John Stewart at Folda, w Christian Charles 22.3.1818 72; (west side) 1826; square & dividers

8 J McD. J McN. by John McDougal in Kirkton of Glenisla, s Chas 25.3.1828 11, fa Colin 2.1819 71, mo Eliz McKenzie 3.1821 77 (her s Dond d abroad, da Jean d 8y); (west side) man in naval uniform; 1826; hand holding dagger; "Brevis hominum vita"; poem (quoted by Jervise, "Epitaphs.." ii 254)

9 replica of celtic cross of Farnell. 1870. by Peter McDougall 6.8.1889 75, fa Wm 1.6.1848 55, mo Jean Grant 10.4.1836 42, sis Ann 2.1835 15; John 1.1845 19

10 by Jas Stewart at Dalvanie, two bros Wm & Donald, mo Eliz Mitchell 12.9.1823 52, fa Chas 11.1851 88, sis Mary 10.1860 60; revised; (west side) 1830; "Aspera juvant"; thistle; by Dond Stewart, das Agnes 6.1845 2m & Elspeth 1.1865 12; Jas Stewart d Easter Balgeddie Kinross-shire 19.9.1877

11 1766. share & coulter, ox yoke, sheaf; by Thos Dounie fr Gobertoun Glenisla, w Margt Paton 14.2.1748 33, leaving chn Margt & Thos, chn Elspeth & Isobel d young; revised 1829; (west side) cherub; T D, M P; poem (quoted by Jervise "Epitaphs" ii 254; see Brechin Testaments: Thos Downie tent in Gobintore, 1.12.1785)

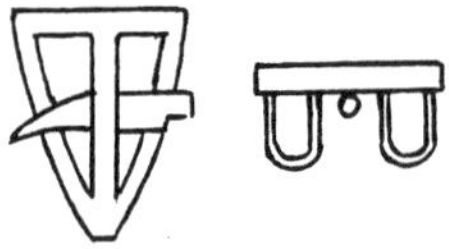

12 urn. David McDonald fr Mains of Crochies, imo fa Thos d Needs Lintrathen 9.7.1850 66 & mo Cath Robertson 9.9.1856 82

13 Alex Lyon d Drumheads Kilry 10.3.1906 70, w Cath McDonald d there 1.1.1914 70, s David killed in action France 4.10.1918 34, 1s Wm d Rosebank Coupar Angus 17.1.1960 76 (w Annie Milne d Rosebank 6.6.1962 68)

14 by Wm Phillips, fa John late fr East Mill of Glenisla 12.1804 60, mo Janet Ogilvie 3.1826 73, bro Thos 1.1796 22, siss Mergery, Helen & Eliz d inf, surviving chn Wm, David, Ann, Janet, Isabel; (north side) share & coulter; by Ann Phillips, h And Soutar d Edinburgh 26.6.1825 37 int Greyfriars Edinburgh (see Edinburgh Testaments: Alexr Ogilvie late of East Milns of Glenisla & surgeon lately outward bound on board the merchant ship "Chance" capt Chicoman commander, 20.12.1771)

15 John Wanless of Auchenlish, mo Jannet Cargill 2.1826 61, uncle John Cargill 9.1827 67, aunt Isabell 3.1817 51; (other side) 1828; text

16 by Wm McKenzie in Craig-head, s Thos 9.1817 2; (other side) 1828

17 ob John McKenzie fr Loups Tannadice 24.3.1868 80, w Isobel Jack d there 0.6.1851 56

18 John Reid late fr Kilry this par 1.11.1850 38, bro Thos 6.10.1818 20m, sis Elis 22.10.1824 3, fa Wm 20.10.1860 82, mo Janet Whitson 28.1.1869 78; poem (quoted by Jervise "Epitaphs" ii 255)

19 1888. David Spence d Bellaty 25.6.1888 81, w Cath Robertson d there 11. 7.1888 81, chn Agnes 1840 2, Alex 1871 17, 4s David b Bellaty 17.6.1846 d Letham 3.12.1929, Thos d Easter Needs 23.6.1914 82 (w Eliz Alexander d (Ley Backwater) 5.5.1902 64)

20 late Thos Spence of Easter Neids, da Margt 10.5.1952 85, s Thos d Meigle Hospital 10.5.1952 76

21 1851. Wm Edwards fr Kirkhillocks d Birchhill 2.5.1864 88, w Ann Gibson 5.6.1851 76; poem (quoted by Jervise "Epitaphs.." ii 254 who notes Ann Gibson was a relative of the laird of Drumhead & maid to the "Little Lady" of Kirkhillock)

22 Thos Robertson fr Bellaty 3.8.1848 85, w Agnes Robertson 9.1.1868 84, da Susan 26.4.1833 (23), s John late fr Bellaty 26.4.1886 74 (w Margt Farquharson 13.2.1898 47), da Agnes 28.12.1889 73

23 Thos Clark 12.1847 72, w Jane Mitchell 6.1836 32, by s Jas in Loanhead 9.12.1919 87 (w Agnes Henderson 25.6.1931 91, s Jas 6.1.1885 4, da Mary Jane 7.4.1887 8)

24 David Thomson d Powderswells 13.12.1900 80, w Ann Clark d Bridgend Ruthven 20.4.1881 60, s Peter d Loanhead Glenisla 9.4.1857 3, by family

25 John Robertson in Meikle Dounie 1885 72, w Margt Cameron 1905 88, chn John 1841 1843, Wm 1843 1848, David 1848 1858, Chas 1844 1860, Margt 1857 1875, Peter 1846 1890, Alex 1840 1911, Mary 1855 1926

26 Chas Robertson in Reelatches 31.10.1863 48, w Betty Farquharson 8.3. 1899 81, s Wm 27.1.1915 56 int Alyth

27 David Shaw of Auchenleish WS b 6.1835 d Little Forter 3.1921; by Mackenzie Smith Shaw WS of Little Forter & Auchenleish b Finegand 27.8. 1875 d Little Forter 30.5.1942 int Glenshee

28 cross. Alex Shaw b Glenconglass Banffshire 3.10.1824 d Bollieyell Glenisla 12.4.1876, w Helen Gordon b Tulloch Abernethy Inverness-shire 9.2. 1840 d Dundee 10.12.1906; (east side) da Elspeth b Bollieyell 28.7. 1863 d Ballhall Menmuir 15.3.1892 int Menmuir (h Alex Anderson); (north side) s Alex d Eassie Angus 15.8.1938 (w Mary Brough 4.1.1971)

29 Thos Shaw d Dundee 18.8.1927 62, s Alex Jack 2nd lieut Argyll & Sutherland highlanders killed in France 12.10.1916 19, s Thos Gordon lieut royal flying corps killed in France 17.3.1917 19, s David d Dundee 7. 9.1915 14, w Mary Jack b Tulloch 6.5.1867 d Newcastle Staffordshire 18.8.1957

30 by Betty Mitchell, mo Isobel Murray d East Mill 1.1.1824 72; 1828

31 1825. Wm Robertson in Faulds 27.10.1823 65, da Margt 27.9.1823 24, da Susan 16.2.1824 27, by ss Jas, John & Wm

32 David Storrier d Ley 7.8.1854 78, w Janet McKenzie 28.8.1865 84, s Wm 4.1862 44, by ss Chas, John & Andrew

33 cherub; ox yoke, share & coulter; I M, M L, 1750; - M, - M, - M, - M, - M; by Robt McInnis, fa John sometime in Clachnocter 15.1.1743; (other side) emblems, epitaph

34 by Alex Ballantyne, fa Jas d Dyke-ends Lintrathen 15.10.1872 72

35 by Thos Ballantyne 23.5.1888 78, w Jean Stewart 26.3.1873 66, bro John 5.2.1870 73, fa & mo & others of their family the dates of whose deaths are unrecorded

36 1831. by Alex Rattray, fa And d East Mill 3.1804 60, mo Janet Robert-

son 8.1812 63, bro John 6.1811 23, sis Isobel May 1805 20; (other side) cherub; hand holding axe; emblems; couplet (quoted by Jervise "Epitaphs .." ii 255)

37 Robt McKenzie d Craigmiky 28.1.1825 77, w Ann Robertson d Glenoig 27.12.1839 81, da Cath d Dalhallie 27.10.1795 15, s John d there 17.5.1817 33, by ss Wm, Robt, Stewart & Alexander

38 TS rev And Burns 1.3.1823 49 in 17th y of ministry in this par (see Fasti v 262; Jervise, "Epitaphs.." ii 255 has his death in 1822)

39 Jas Mitchell in Loanhead 29.7.1892 84, w Janet Lamond 4.11.1850 41, bro rev Wm Lamb Mitchell d Aberdeen 15.5.1880 78 (see Fasti & Ewing)

40 Francis Rattray d Bridge of Allan 9.2.1856 10 only child of Thos Rattray of Kirkhillocks d Bridge of Allan 19.2.1856 51 & w Agnes Rattray (according to Jervise "Epitaphs.." ii 255 Francis & Thomas were gs & s of the following whose stone is at Glenisla FC - National Grid ref: NO 214 606:

41 Jas Rattray of Kirkhillocks 19.9.1771 22.3.1853, w Johan Rattray 17.1.1781 17.12.1813, da Margt 11.11.1801 17.2.1811 (see Jervise, "Epitaphs.." ii 255: he was a successful cattle dealer & grazier who acquired Kirkhillocks from the Ogilvies & he paid for the building of the Free Church)

41-42 are noted by Jervise, "Epitaphs.." ii 252:

41 unmarked grave at east end of church. Duncan Shaw of Crandart (son of Crathienaird) d 1722 73, 2w - Farquharson of Coldrach, seven ss & three das (but the family burial place was at Drumfork)

42 stone at Crandart old house. I M, K C, 1660 (for John McComie & w Kath Campbell (da of the laird of Denhead); see Epitaphs i 227, ii 252, Memorials of Angus & the Mearns 33)

N o t e s

Jervise "Epitaphs.." ii 252 notes that according to tradition the resident heritors had their burial places within the church and among them were the M'Combies of Forthar, Shaws of Crandart & Ogilvys of East Miln (see also "The Scottish Nation" ii 237 for the murder of Thos Ogilvy of East Miln.

Testaments - the following is a selection from the Brechin Commissariot:
Helen Elliot w of David Barnet in Lytill Derrie Glennyllay, 1614
Beatrix Adam in Meikle Davie, 1659
mr Jas Fleming minister Glenylla, 1724 (Fasti v 262)
John Fenton in Bellemenay Glenyla & w Janet Frisell, 1662
Kath Findlay w of Wm Beg in Freuchie par Glenylla, 1629
Findlo Grewar feuar of Auchtene par Wester Inneraritie & w Janet Kanzow parish Glenylay, 1610
Isobel Grewar wid of John Fleming late in Meikle Downie, 1752
Margt Grewar w of Wm McNicoll in Easter Innerartie, 1664
Robt Grewar in Hillhead of East Mill, 1742;
and the following is a selection from the Edinburgh Commissariot Register:
Andro Adam in Litill-Darye 1.2.1581-2
capt David Crichton of Eister-Craig, 21.7.1586
Jas Crichton of Eister Craig, 1581
Isobel Laing relict of Andro Adam in Darie, 1591

OPR with the Registrar General: 290 Glenisla Births 1719-23, 1741-1854
Marriages 1719-23, 1741-1854
Deaths 1748-55, 1792-3

15 G L E N I S L A

Church Records in the SRO: CH2/568 KS minutes 1723-1929
CH3/512 Glenisla FC, UP, C of S minutes 1850-1941
Deacons Court minutes 1853-1940
baptisms 1860-1942, marriages 1937-41
CR 1849-1941
HR 338 minutes 1789, 1812, 1814, 1826, 1844-1932, buildings 1790-
GD 16/46 & 49 (Airlie muniments) church, manse & school 1764-1874

Fasti v 261 ministers from 1567

Ewing ii 155 ministers from 1843

Index

Adam	Notes
Alexander	19
Anderson	28
Ballantyne	34-5
Barnet	Notes
Beg	Notes
Brodie	2
Brough	28
Burns	38
C.	40
Cameron	25
Campbell	42
Cargill	15
Charles	7
Clark	23-4
Crichton	Notes
Dounie	11
Edwards	21
Elliot	Notes
Farquharson	22.26.41
Fenton	Notes
Fleming	Notes
Gibson	21
Gordon	28
Grant	9
Grewar	1-4.Notes
Henderson	23
Jack	6.17.29
Kanzow	Notes
L.	33
Laing	Notes
Lamb	39
Lamond	39
Lyon	13
M.	40
McAndrew	6
McCom(b)ie	42.Notes
McDonald	12-3
McDougal(l)	9.12-3
McFarlane	1
McInnis	33
McIntosh	3
McKenzie	8.16-7.32.37
McN.	8
McNicoll	Notes
Milne	13
Mitchell	10.23.30.39
Morgan	5
Murray	30
Ogilvie	14
Paton	11
Phillips	14
Rattray	36.40-1
Reid	18
Robertson	4.12.19.22.25-6.31.36-7
Shaw	27-9.41.Notes
Soutar	14
Spence	19-20
Stewart	6-7.10.35
Steel	3
Storrier	32
Thomson	24
Wanless	15
Whitson	18

16a GUTHRIE

The church may have been a Culdee foundation, but was certainly founded before 1178. A fine collegiate church was built in 1479, but this was demolished and replaced by the present structure in 1826, the south transept being retained as the Guthrie aisle. The burial ground is sheltered and well-kept.

National Grid reference: NO 567 505

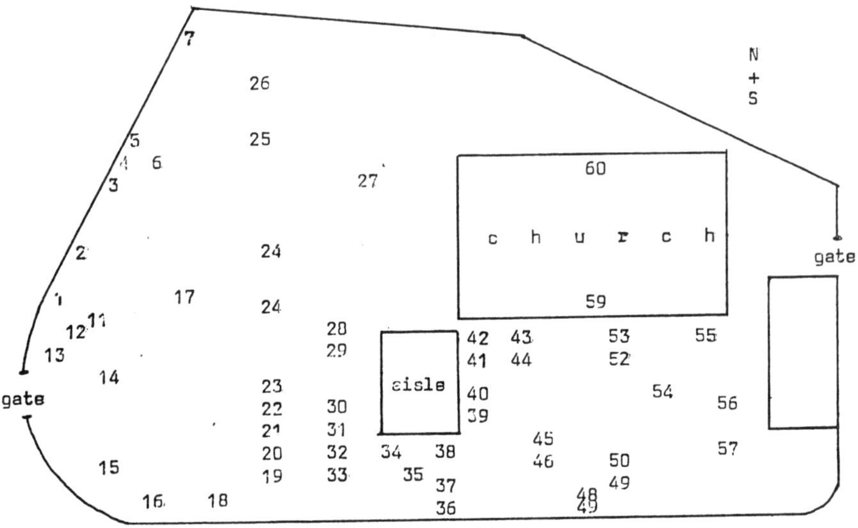

1 1763. David Iaron 10.3.1742 62 sometime tent Ground of Co(un)side, w Magdalen Taws 15.2.1756 65, da Elesbeth 20.7.1761 35, by s Will; (west side) D I, M T, 1763; DI II EI II EI WI AI

2 1877. by Wm Bruce in Cotton of Guthrie 19.12.1881 67, w Mary Stephen 22.5.1871 57, da Mary 20.12.1849 3m

3 fragment in the dyke. a lion

4 fragment in the dyke. M H G (probably mr Henry Guthrie min here who d 1676 aged about 76y as bishop of Dunkeld; see Fasti v 253, Jervise, "Epitaphs .." ii 144, DNB, & his own Memoirs published 1702, 1747, 1748)

5 by Jas Webster - - - - - - - - - Cottoun of G - - - - - he d 14.5.17(5)4 56y

6 Geo Ritchie 27.3.1851 63, by w Eliz McKenzie 14.10.1866 72, da Marjory 14.10.1855 27, four gchn d inf, da Jessie 13.12.1881 48

7 rev Jas Whitson min Guthrie 1.1.1840 46, two ss John & David who predeceased him d inf (see Fasti v 438: s John 22.3.1828 13.12.1838, s David 10.11.1836 19.12.1839)

8 Robt Cooper stationmaster Friockheim for 35y d 2.8.1885 67, da Eliza Rachel 28.3.1854 18m, da Agnes Salmon 13.8.1879 25, w Margt Cameron 27.5.1899 86, da Mary Margt d Edinburgh 22.9.1938

9 Thos Nicoll 5.4.1879 82, w Eliz Moagn 27.10.1877 83, da Helen 7.12.1842 19, by family

10 Wm Air 12.11.1631 63, w Besse Scrymgeour 2.4.1628 6(1) (see F Davidson, "Inventory..." notes this as being in the Guthrie aisle)

11 broken. - - - - - imo his w - -- - -ll d 2.1814, s - - - (Fa)irweather d 1802

12 Alex Anderson sometime in - nnin(s- - who d 4.1720 7(6), w Jean Do - -

13 by - - H(ain) pickyman at Guthrie Mill & w Margt Ker imo s Alex 25.12.1763 19m; (east side) cherub;1765; InH, RH, AH, MH; mantling; miller's picks & axe on shield; emblems

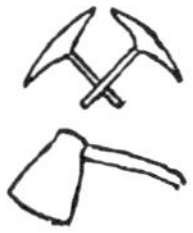

14 by Alex Nicoll & w Helen Lyall sometime tent in Milltoun of Guthrie, da Agnes 26.1.1765 18y6m; (west side) cherub; 1765; text; ArN, MN, AsN, IN; mantling; ploughshare; skulls

15 - - - - - - - - - (Cock) imo her (moth)er Isobel Bertie 22.-.1757 21y

16 by Joseph Murray railway contractor Friockheim & w Eliz, da Hannah 7.12.1845 7

17 John Anderson overseer Pitmouies 28.8.1782 66, by w Ann Lawson; cherub

18 1764. by Jas Renny & w Isobel Black tent Bridgend of Pitmouies, s Robt 19.12.1763 3; (west side) M R, E R, H R, I R, R R; shield with I R, I B; axe & setsquare; poem

19 1815. Geo Thom brewer Kirktown of Guthrie 12.1814 50, by w Eliz Rough (see Jervise, "Epitaphs" ii 148 who notes the stone then was near the churchyard gate)

20 1776. Robt Irvine 18.2.177(5) 65, by w Ann Watson, his chn John, Robt, & John, Kathrin, Margt, Isobel, Thos, Jean, Agnes, Jas, Ann were all aliven here; (west side) cherub; torches; poem (quoted by Jervise "Epitaphs" ii 148); emblems

21 David Reid 27.1.1900 82, w Mary Anne Menelaws 21.8.1899 85, da Mary Ann 20.9.1844 2, s John 9.8.1864 22, by sisters

22 And Hay sometime in Pickertoun of Guthrie 20.2.1724 44, w Jannet Adam; (west side) mantling; shield with A H, I A, axe, ox yoke & ?plough, 1724; flanked by I H, I H, IaH, M H, E H, IaH, IsH, - H (see Brechin Testaments: Janet Tulloch spouse to John Adam at Pykertoun of Guthrie, 22.7.1686)

23 1810. mr Wm Ireland land surveyor d Forfar 7.8.1808 61 int here, by sisters mrs Taylor & mrs Wallace

24 1824. Jas Dickson in Pickerton of Turin 1.1.1822 81, by surviving chn (their mo Janet Boyle 19.12.1827 87); David Dickson 27.9.1868 85, w Betsy Fairweather 18(6)1, da Betsy 18.6.1891 6(8)

25 erected 1835 by John Brown wright Bridgend of Pitmuies 26.10.1847 68 & w Jean Middleton, s John 2.8.1830 7y7m, da Mary Mudie 26.2.1848 20

26 by Jas Hebeton & Margt Carnagie residing at Bridge of Dumbarrow imo chn David 17.8.1808 9w, Mary 29.3.1813 4, Magdalene 2.9.1826 10, Ann 16.7.1834 17, Geo 3.5.1838 18

27 Jas Watson late fr Ouchterony 4.5.1857 82, by w Margt Forbes 28.9.1859 86, s David 9.5.1833 18, s Henderson 6.12.1852 35, 1da Ann 4.10.1869 68

28 rev Wm Nicol min Kirtlebridge Dumfriesshire d at Cotton of Gardyne 14.12.1851 43 (Fasti ii 252)

29 John Nicol in Cotton of Gardyne 6.8.1851 73, w Isabel Mann 24.6.1842 66; Ann Nicol 30.11.1872 62; Jas Nicol 2.9.1879 68; Matilda Nicol 10. 12.1883 68

30 skull. Alex Scot sometime in Mains of Ballmadies 28.4.1719 75, w Elis Smith 5.1711, by s Jas; (east side) two cherubs; shield with A S, A R, (T)S, - S; "Heauen keeps the soul,/Bot heir the body lyes:/ They liud on earth both just / Kind, vertuos, and wise."

31 David Strachan 19.1.1872 55, by wid Isobella Nicol d at Manse of Clova 2.6.1892 81, s Wm 17.3.1867 28, da Helen 2.7.1853 5y6m (see Fasti v 281 rev John Strachan b 14.2.1857 son of Jas Strachan & Isobel Nicol, min of Clova in 1892)

32 David Esplin 23.12.1860 80, w Margt Gordon 6.6.1859 84, by family

33 Jas Windrem in Hiltoun of Guthrie 25.2.173- 5(4), by w Cicilia Langlands 7.4.1761 70, also David Windrem 28.1.1755 33; (east side) cherub; - -, M W; - W, - W, - W, - W, - W, - W; mantling; shield with IW, CL, 1730, and ploughshare

I ♡ W
C L
1730

34 1821. by Wm Nicoll at Baldardie, mo Ann Hendry 4.6.1799 47, gfa Wm Nicoll late schoolmaster Guthrie 30.9.1786 78, gmo Isabel Howe 22.4.1754 46 (h said Wm Nicoll); (east side) Thos Nicoll 19.7.1828 82, s Wm (the erector of this stone) killed by a flash of lightning on the farm of Baldardie 30.7.1830 47

35 1756. I E ♡ I B; Jas Esplen sometime kirk & ground officer Guthrie d 15.1.1630 95, s & successor in office Jas 16.2.1680 103 (s & successor in office Jas 27.3.1717 53 whose w Jean Petrie 16.4.1706 38 & whose s Jas succeeded in aforesaid offices d 16.2.1755 59); this last Jas, w Jean Allon 1.2.1739 41; Jas Esplen sometime one of the gardeners at Panmuir d 9.5.1783 by fall from tree aged 25, fa Jas sometime kirk & ground officer Guthrie d 16.2.1793 73; (west side) 1756. H E ♡ H B; Henry Esplen ground officer Guthrie d 17.9.17(4)6 83, w Isobel Webster 20.4. 1721 52; Allison, Frances & Geo Esplens all buried here.
Thos Esplin kirk & ground officer 1774 1859, w Isobel Balfour 1774 1856, chn Jane 1817 1875, Margt 1812 1883, Thos b 1807 d Forfar 1857 (w Marjory Leckie b 1809 d Forfar 1856, restored in 1892 by s Thos B Esplin baker Forfar d Forfar 7.6.1925 82) (according to letter dated 1977 from miss A I M Esplin "Thos Balfour Esplin had three sons & two das of whom only the 2s John had issue viz two das Anne Isabel Mary & Marjorie Jean McKenzie last of the line")

36 Thos Milne tent Pool 8.3.1840 61; Margt Milne 13.2.1840 59, by surviving sisters Eliz 13.3.1852 88 & Ann 17.1.1841 75

37 1760. Patk Millne tent Kirktoun of Guthrie 4.2.1769 86, w Eliz Findlay 17.9.1757 71; And Milne & Margt Scote, three of their chn Margt 2.1.1763 10m, Jas 3.1.1764 3y9m, Geo 4.1.1770 16m; (west side) two cherubs; HM, IM; AlxM, IoM, IaM, HeM, IeM, M M; P F, plough, E F; A M, M S; PM, AM, RM, IoM, TM, AndM; "Here Lizbeth lyes dade, with a mournfull shade / Hath left her friends & loving husband sad /And now is gone above the stars to sing /Eternall praise to her immortal king...." (see Jervise "Epitaphs" ii 147 for full poem)

38 crudely cut & leaning against wall. by David Mill in Cottoun of Pitmouies imo - - - - - - -; - M, - G, - M, - M, - M, - M, - M, - M; Jas Kelie who depairted this life the - - - - , w Jean Wat d - April - -, chn depairted Agnes, Eliz, Wm & Jas Kellies; & Jas Kellie d 12.2.1725 & w Alison Kelli(e) - - - 1781 aged - - - they had - - - John, Jas, - - Elspeth, Robt, Ja - - - - - - - - both dead 17- -; IK, IK; AK, EK, W(K); -K,(J)W,25

39 Jas Langlands 18.6.177(8) 81, w Jean S(mall) 14.3.17(6)4 (64), by ss John fr in K- - hill of Panbride & Jas fr East (Idvie) & David fr in Pickertoun of Dunichen

40 I W, 1761, IT ; by John Watson in Ground of Garden imo gfa John Watson & gmo Jannet Smith sometime lived in Hewchhead of Guthrie 1679 aged about 40y, & his fa viz John Watson 22.12.1753 74 & mo Maren Walker 7.11.1754 68 who sometime lived in Ground of Gardyn, also their chn viz Kathren, Jas, Jannet, Eliz, Margret all int here & John survives in Ground of Gardyn with w Jean Tyrie & their da Jean; (east side) cherub; tailor's goose, scissors & bodkin; 1761; - W, - S; K W, I W, M W, I W, E W, I W

41 1854. Alex Smith tent flour mills Milden of Ouchterlony 2.10.1847 78, by das Margt & Mary, gs Alex Doig 7.2.1878 52 (w Margt Nicoll 19.4.1918 82)

42 loose stone. David Cristy, w Agnes Wach 5.1720 41

43 John Dorwart indweller Ground of Balmadies 4.1727 75, s Robt 30.3.1750 27, da Isobel 25.10.1750 36, by Jean & Helen imo foresaid sister; by Jean (Christie) imo her parents Jas Christie & Jean Dorward who are int in this place; (west side) two cherubs; "Below this stone a lovely maid doth lye / Whom God did take in her virginity / She was virtuous, godly & sincere,/ A (pleasure to) her masters here /But now she serves her God she did adore /In praising her Redeemer ever more;/Its better than an earthly prince's wife, /Her hire is now a lasting crown of life" (poem similar to inscription 70 & Kinnell inscription 55)

44 1855. Alex Matthew tent Leanmonth Carmyllie for 46y d 2.6.18--

45 1807. by John Black smith Kirkton of Guthrie 8.12.1811 58, s Jas d a child 1782, s John 1788 6, s Geo 1805 21, w Jean Thornton & the following family Margt, Andrew, Wm, Jean & Eliz survive 1811

46 Geo Black blacksmith Guthrie d Letham 8.8.1912 89, w Agnes Darling 25.10.1891 69, da Mary 4.3.1862 7, s Robt 9.5.1865 2, da Jessie 23.8.1927 72

47 by Alex Clark imo fa Wm sometime indweller Ground of Balgavies & his w Margt Potter 22.7.1762 93, also three of their chn Cecilia, John & David; (west side) 1762; two cherubs; mantling, shield with shovel, bill hook, ox yoke & plough; CiC, IaC, WiC, IoC, DaC, BeC, A C

48 1820. John Potter weaver in Balmadies 11.5.1819 58, w Jean Hendry 27.1.1827 6(6), s Alex 17.10.1817 27 in Island of St Lucia, chn Jas & Jean d inf, da Mary 11.10.1842 53; inscribed by Geo & David Potter as a tribute of respect; (west side) by John Potter, mo Ann Potter 21.1.1852 61y

49 John Potter sometime Piccarton of Guthrie 29.9.1702 8.6.1760, s And 18.9.1737 17.12.1763, s John 17.9.1738 10.12.1741, by w Margt Duncan & s in law Wm Ritchie; 17 WR MD 67; (west side) two cherubs; mantling, shield with loom & shuttle with A P, I P, M P; poem

50 David Smith 15.1.1766 86, w Isobel Gemlo 11.1752 80 they lived Houehead of Guthrie for 48y, s David 2.2.1753 43; John Peter 74y, w Margt Smith 66y, s And 21y, by Geo & David Peter in 1776; Alex Neish & Agnes (Smith) - - - - - inscription covered by another stone - - - -; G P, G P, D P, A P, A N, A N; (east side) two cherubs; 17 DS 53; mantling, shield with DS IG; M S, D S, A S, S S; elegy

51 David Paton in Bridgend Pitmuies 10.12.1864 62, w Jane Peters 13.1.1882 71, chn Alex 1.3.1850 2m, Ann 27.2.1854 6½

52 ob capt Robt Mill accidentally drowned Grangemouth 4.12.1866 31, by wid Anne Mill d Edinburgh 25.4.1882

53 Geo Mill blacksmith 4.2.1881 74, w Mary Milne 5.4.1870 59, chn Robt 17.3.1844 4, Margt 28.11.1854 16, Geo 8.11.1907 55, Isabella d Bentmore Carnoustie 9.11.1918 68, Eliz Hay d Bentmore Carnoustie 14.10.1919 74

54 by Wm Leitch mert in Glasgow, fa Alex 4.11.1781 27.10.1854, mo Eliz Petrie 21.3.1783 28.10.1846, bro David 29.6.1813 1824 int Arbroath, sis Jane 10.2.1817 11.3.1863 int Laurencekirk (h Thos Wilkie); above Wm Leitch d Montreal Canada 14.2.1876 59, bro Jas d Damside Aberlemno 6. 1889

55 Jas Graw late gardener Pitmuies 15.4.1838 81; (west side) - - - - their da Eliz Graw 24.11.181- 27, s Alex 31.1.18-- 25

56 Robt Simpson 7.8.1851, (w Jean Alexander 20.2.1872 33), ss Peter 2y & John 25y all int here, by s Jas d Melbourne 28.10.1897 76

57 by Jean Bell, fa Alex Strachan 14.2.1864 83, mo Janet Graham 29.12.1839 50, bro Jas 6.1835 18; Alex 8.1837 18

The following 58-60 are inside the church:

58 Jane Guthrie b here 7.4.1809 d Dundee 19.4.1891 last of her line, int in the aisle which was restored by her in 1881

59 rev Wm Ramsay AM min here 1844-50 d here 6.1.1850 30 (see Fasti v 438)

60 rev Jas Will, 14y min Ruthven, 19y min Guthrie d 3.5.1818 58 (see Fasti v 438 & Jervise "Epitaphs" i & ii: his fa was mert in Dundee & his mo was da of Wise of Lunan, she had four ss & two das, Peter d before 1818, John of Lucea Jamaica (s who was fa of John Shiress Will of the Middle Temple London, da (h Wm Shiress solicitor in Brechin)), And lieut 92nd regt, Isabella (h dr David Ogilvy of Rosehill Brechin), Christina d unm, &rev Jas md 16.4.1810 Susan Imlach who d 24.10.1823(wid of Jas Lamb surgeon))

The following is inside the Guthrie aisle, as recorded by F Davidson in 1977:

61 mural tablet now set in the floor. mr Geo Strachan min 6.12.1692 60 & w Janet Thomson 2.12.1691 50; M G S, J T; matrimonial achievement of Strachan & Thomson (see Fasti v 437; F Davidson "Inventory ..")

The following were not seen in 1973-7 but are listed by Jervise "Epitaphs.." ii 145-51:

62 slab at north door of aisle. 1629

63 slab at north door of aisle. G 1747

64 slab at west door of aisle. D - I G 1670 ; shield

65 slab. Heir lyes ane - - - - - - - - - - - - 1663 and - - - - - - - -

66 Jean Brown 14.9.1801 70; the other half of this stone stands in the churchyard of Ruthven to the memory of Wm Kandow her husband who was schoolmaster of the par of Ruthven for 36y, he d 14.12.1798, by only surviving child Jas Kandow schoolmaster Guthrie (see Ruthven inscription 25)

67 near Guthrie aisle. by John Guthrie esq of Guthrie to an old & faithful servant Eliz Morison who nursed him in infancy & consistently resided 49y in the House of Guthrie where she d 21.11.1812

68 near southeast corner of church. by David Spence elder sometime in Houghhead of Guthrie 27.11.1719 81, w Margt Miller 1.2.1674 30, 2w Margt Cuthell; David Spence & Jean Miln, chn; tailor's goose, bodkin & scissors;

(west side) setsquare, sheaf of corn & stick with measuring line

69 1774. by Robt Spence in Muirside of Kinnel, ground officer to South Esk & sis Helen to their forefathers, & his 1w Jean Blacklaw, chn, 2w Jean Donaldson; "Beside this stone lie many Spences / Who in their life did no offences /And where they lived, if that ye speir /In Guthrie's ground four hunder year." (see also Chas Rogers, "Monuments" ii 236)

70 Isobel Lourance, daughter d about 1738; "Below this stone a lovely maid doth ly......"

71 David Jaron d 1773 25; "I in the bloom of hopeful youth,/ Resign my mortal trust; And at the age of twenty-five /Did haistely drop to dust."

72 John Langlands imo his w & two chn (a son & another); 1778; poem (quoted in full)

73 lintel of gate. -G BG 1639 (for Guthrie of that ilk see "The Scottish Nation" ii 386)

N o t e s

A window in the present church was presented by the family of Victor Lowel Guthrie in memory of Guthrie family pioneers who settled in Yolo County California USA.

F. Davidson, "Inventory of 17th Century Tombstones in Angus" details inscriptions 10 & 61

A.Jervise, "Epitaphs..." ii 145-151 notes inscriptions 4,7,19-20,24,28,30,34, 37,43,60,62-73

D C Guthrie of Craigie, "The Guthrie Family 1178-1900" (Northampton 1906)

Testaments: the following is a selection from the Register of the Commissariot of Brechin - Elspet Buchan spouse to And Esplin on Lonhead of Guthrie,1637
David Esplin in Hiltoune of Guthrie, 1583
Patk Esplin in Heughead of Guthrie, 1686
Nicholas Guthrie spouse to John Fentoun at the Mylne of Guthrie, 1598
Alex Langlands schoolmaster at the Kirk of Guthrie, w Bethia Pyott, 1686
mr Patk Lyall late min Guthrie & spouse Barbara Dirow, 1662
Patk Mann in Pykertoune of Hiltoune, w Isobel Watchman,1614
Thos Strachan in Eastertoun of Guthrie, w Elspet Mill, 1665

OPR with the Registrar General - 291 Guthrie: Births 1664-1854
Marriages 1663-1728, 1730-1854
Deaths 1748-55, 1783-94 (note - an amendment to the OPR bookmentions that a letter of 1913 says "a record of burials made up from tombstone inscriptions is in "the custody of the KS: the record contains many additional en- "tries to the above"; in 1978 this was not with the KS but may be the following

Angus District Cemeteries office, Forfar: refernces to pre-1855 burials.

SRO CH2/535 Minutes & accounts 1663-1737; minutes 1737-1912
Collections & disbursements 1737-1800; accounts 1801-41
KS accounts 1842-60
HR 193 Guthrie minutes 1861-1927

Small i 65 Dumbarrow Anti-burgher ministers from 1740

16a GUTHRIE

Index

Adam	22
Air	10
Alexander	56
Allon	35
Anderson	12.17
Balfour	35
Bell	57
Bertie	15
Black	18.45-6
Blacklaw	69
Boyle	24
Brown	25.66
Bruce	2
Buchan	Notes
Cameron	8
Carnegie	26
Christie	43
Clark	47
Cock	15
Cooper	8
Cristy	42
Cuthell	68
Darling	46
Dickson	24
Dirow	Notes
Do- -	12
Doig	41
Dorward/t	43
Donaldson	69
Duncan	49
Esplen/in	32.35.Notes
Fairweather	11.24
Fentoun	Notes
Findlay	37
Forbes	27
G.	38.63-4.73
Gemie	50
Gordon	32
Graham	57
Grew	55
Guthrie	4.58.67.Notes
Hain	13
Hay	22.53
Hebeton	26
Hendry	34.48
Howe	34
Iaron	1.71
Imlach	60
Ireland	23
Irvine	20
Jaron	1.71
Kandow	66
Kel(l)ie	38
Ker	13
Lamb	60
Langlands	33.39.72.Notes
Lawson	17
Leckie	35
Leitch	54
Lourance	70
Lyall	14.Notes
McKenzie	6
Mann	29.Notes
Matthew	44
Menelaws	21
Middleton	25
Mill	38.52-3.Notes
Miller	68
Miln/e	36-7.53.68
Moagn (?Morgan)	9
Morison	67
Mudie	25
Murray	16
Neish	50
Nicol(l)	9.14.28-9.31.34.41
Ogilvy	60
Paton	51
Peter/s	50-1
Petrie	35.54
Potter	47-9
Pyott	Notes
Ramsay	59
Reid	21
Renny	18
Ritchie	6.49
Rough	19
Salmon	8
Scot(e)	30.37
Scrymgeour	10
Shiress	60
Simpson	56
Small	39
Smith	30.40-1.50
Spence	68-9
Stephen	2
Strachan	31.57.61.Notes
Taws	1
Taylor	23
Thom	19
Thomson	61
Thornton	45
Tulloch	22
Tyrie	40

16a GUTHRIE

Wach	42	Webster	5.35
Walker	40	Whitson	7
Wallace	23	Wilkie	54
Wat	38	Will	60
Watchman	Notes	Windrem	33
Watson	20.27.40	Wise	60

16b KIRKBUDDO, GUTHRIE

The church of Crebyauch or Carbuddo was dedicated to St Buit before 1275 & was ruinous before 1682. The ruin and the manse were demolished in 1822. Although 7 miles away, it has long been attached to the parish of Guthrie. The small burial ground at the site of the church is reached by bridle paths. An ancient beech tree is at its centre & in its shade it is not overgrown with weeds.

National Grid reference: NO 493 432

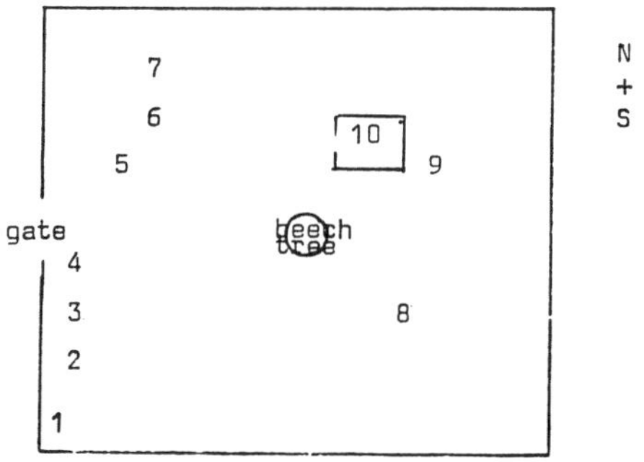

1 TS Geo Ogilvy esq of Kirkbuddo d Edinburgh 17.3.1848 65 (see Jervise, "Epitaphs.." ii 152: he was nephew & heir of lieut col Francis Erskine)

2 1847. by Leonard Black imo w Mary Anderson 23.6.1846 68

3 Hendery Petrie maltman in Arbroath & w Isabel Keard imo his fa Jas Petrie sometime fr in Ground of Kirkbuddo 3.5.1735 41, two of his chn procreat betwixt him & Jean Brodie his spous viz Jas & Jean; "We wait ye trumpet & its solemn sound." (West side) 1760. Jas Petrie; fork & spade; Jean Brodie

4 1850. Peter Smith fr Drowndubbs 18.4.1831 78, w Cath Mudie 9.2.1850 72, by family

5 1862. Jas Taylor late tent Ward of Kirkbuddo 23.4.1862 78, w Ann Taylor 5.3.1862 68, "they were kind & loving in life & in death they were not divided", by family, s And d Blairnavaid par Drymen Stirlingshire 17.11.1865 28; Wm Taylor fr Middle Brighty 7.2.1891 63

6 1853. Jas Taylor, w Jessie Weir 14.9.1859 33, da Eliza 14.8.1853 10m, da Mary Ann 15.11.1872 16 (poem quoted by Jervise, "Epitaphs.." ii 152)

7 Alex Nairn 28.7.1905 86, w Barbara Taylor 25.10.1900 78, by s Wm

8 And Secundus Cuthbert schoolmaster Kirkbuddo 18.2.1900 63, w Jane Bell 27.9.1896 60, yt s Jas d Chicago USA 9.8.1896 29

9 John Spark 7.3.1801 28.6.1866, w Margt Smith 28.2.1806 15.12.1876, s John 20.6.1839 11.2.1853, da Margt 13.2.1842 16.12.1870

10 enclosure dated 1822. Erskine of Kirkbuddo: John 1615; Geo 1647; David 1691; Francis 1724; Francis 1746; Francis 1776, w Jean Guthrie 1815, s colonel Francis 1833, gda Jane Ogilvy 1848.
col Francis Erskine, nephew Geo Ogilvy 1848 (g nephew maj gen Wm Jackson 1912 int Folkestone, g nephew surgeon general Jas R Jackson 1887 (s maj Geo Erskine Jackson OBE MD 2.8.1945 73, da Alice Mabel Erskine Jackson OBE JP 26.2.1948 74)) (see Jervise, "Epitaphs.." ii 152; also "An Appreciation of maj G Erskine Jackson 1872-1945" in Forfar Public Library)

Jervise also notes the following which was not seen in 1974:

11 TS (defaced) Francis Erskine of Carbuddo lieut col 50th regt d 1833 unm(sis was w of Geo Ogilvy of Baikie & other sis was w of mr Molison (& mo of mr F Molison mert Dundee latterly of Errol Park)

N o t e s

OPR with the Registrar General - see notes for Guthrie on p 173

Jervise, "Epitaphs..." ii 151-2 notes inscriptions 1,3,6,11

Testaments: the following is a selection from the Commissariot of Brechin -
Janet Bell spouse to John Mudie in Ward of Kirkbuddo, 1723
Jas Esplin in Kirkbuddo, 1722

I n d e x

Anderson 2
Bell 8.Notes
Black 2
Brodie 3
Cuthbert 8
Erskine 10-11
Esplin Notes
Guthrie 10
Jackson 10
Keard 3
Molison 11
Mudie 4.Notes
Nairn 7
Ogilvy 1.10-11
Petrie 3
Smith 4.9
Spark 9
Taylor 5-7
Weir 6

17a INVERARITY

Inverarity parish church was dedicated in 1243 at the confluence of the Arity and the Corbie burns, now in the Fothringham estate. In 1754 a new (present) church was built farther west and the old burying ground was gradually cleared of stones, many of them transferred to the present ground which is still in use, and in excellent condition.
The parishes of Inverarity and Meathie-Lour were united in 1612.

National Grid reference: NO 452 443

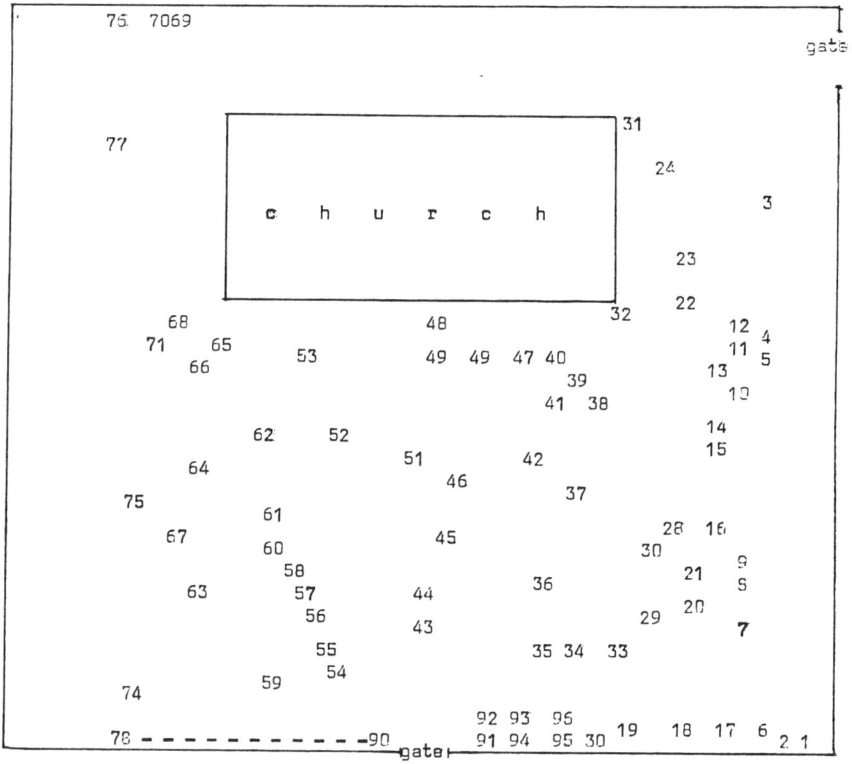

1 1780. John Bennet in Seggyden, w Mettilda Watson 10.12.1778 40; poem (quoted by Jervise, "Epitaphs"ii 300: he notes Burnet in error)

2 1807. John Morton, w Ann Robertson, by ss David tent Slatery Mill & Thos miller Inverarity; David Morton, w Jean Wighton, chn John, Eliz & Adam all d inf

3 by John Key weaver & w Isabel Barrie, s And 21.1.1823 1y

4 Sylvester Gleig 28.8.1877 84, w Ann Jolly 12.8.1894 89, s John 22.5. 1835 2, da Mary 11.5.1843 12, s Alex 6.9.1854 6

5 1845. Wm Malcolm 17.11.1868 92, w Agnes Laird 4.1.1844 59, s David drowned in Tay 11.6.1829 21, s Jas 6.11.1834 14

6 David Myles 5.1804 91, w Janet Wilkie 1814 76, by s Jas servant Fothringham (& w Agnes Fraser, da Margt 1.7.1821 30, da Anne 3.1793 1m)

7 ob Jas Mitchell fr Carrot d Australia 2.1883, w Annie Batchelor 1.9.1860 21, s Jas d Australia 11.9.1932

8 ob Jas Smith fr Little Lour 17.10.1840 47, w Jane Mollison Salmon d Blairgowrie 10.4.1871 52, da Margt d Bridge of Allan 1.10.1897 59

9 Alex Smith fr Carrot 10.6.1825 76, w Margt Stiven 1.1.1850 88, s Alex 20.4.1820 33, da Cath 16.6.1794 5, s Wm 20.3.1805 7, da Cath 18.-.1805 2m, s David 24.4.1806 5, by s John fr Carrot (s Peter 10.12.1851 25); Jas Smith fr Little Lower 17.10.1840 47; Jas Mitchell fr Ovenstone 28.12.1861 78, w Jane Smith d Carnoustie 2.1.1873 81 int here, their bro John Smith fr Carrot 17.2.1851 55; Eliz Mitchell 9.7.1858 32, h Peter Keer fr Easter Braikie

10 Jas Taylor 4.12.1874 76, w Ann 25.5.1877 80, da Agnes 14.4.1850, da Jane 18.4.1865, da Mary 11.11.1874, s Alex 21.7.1913 77, da Isabella 13.3.1917 75

11 Jas Taylor fr East Mains of Lour 24.8.1906 84, w Ann Grant 15.6.1916 81, s Geo 6.4.1876 4, 1da Ann 3.6.1920 46

12 John Taylor tent & cooper Whigstreet 12.4.1814 45, w Alison Airth 12.1.1820 58, s Peter 14.7.1814 22, s Wm 8.1.1819 13, s David 16.3.1824 (21), by ss Jas & John

13 John Salmon fr Newton of Fothringham 1.2.1866 77, w Margt Mitchell 8.12.1881 94, s David 30.8.1823 12, da Eliz 13.6.1850 23

14 Peter Salmon fr Little Lower 7.2.1816 9.9.1879, w Janet McLaren 29.11.1826 6.10.1894, da Margt 25.2.1854 8.2.1913, s Thos 28.6.1862 18.6.1913, chn d of scarlatina in March 1870: Mary on 19th 11y, Chas on 24th 6y4m, Charlotte on 28th 9y10m, Isabella 30th 2y10m, Jane 17.7.1903 47

15 lieut Jas Begbie RN 20.10.1820 49, mo in law Mary Counsell 18.5.1824 72; anchor & cable; eulogy (quoted by Jervise, "Epitaphs" ii 300 who notes he was s ofthe grieve at Fothringham later tent Ovenstone of Inverarity)

16 John Hume fr West Mains of Kincaldrum 3.12.1846 57, w Isabella Elder d Mersehead Kirkbean Kirkcudbrightshire 4.10.1861 int there, da Isabella d Rossie 10.7.1888 66, s Wm fr Rossie Dunning Perthshire 16.8.1883 62,(w Eliz McLaren d Mersehead 22.4.1860 36 int Kirkbean, da Mary 24.2.1925 66, da Isabella d Glenrossie Dunning 21.2.1911 54)

17 1769. Jas Fairweather 24.3.1768 55 sometime mert Mosside of Lower, by wid Helen Watt

18 1826. by John Mungo, w Ann Anderson 1818 47, da Ann 1818 17, s John 1820 10

19 by Thos Benet weaver Gallafauld, w Eliz Heemin 16.4.1742 16.10.1770 (da of Jas Heemin in Cotton Kincaldrum & Maisdry Kid), s John 11.7.1767 2.10.1770, da Margt 8.3.1769 8.4.1769, they md 23.7.1766 & lived in the honourable bond of matrimony 4y2m "for her price is far above rubies..."; (west side) mantling with shield

20 David Gibson d Cotton of Ovenstone 10.2.1890 85, w Annie Strachan 24.2.1908 93, da Isabella 8.1.1844 4, da Jessie 3.8.1874 23, da Helen 17.8.1925 81, s Jas 27.11.1927 79, da Ann 3.9.1929 83

21 1831. Jas Gibson who lately resided at Reskingie in Ground of Kirkbuddo 7.2.1827 60, w Isobel Dryden 12.10.1817 46, by ss Alex & Thos

22 Robt McLaren fr Lackaway par Kinnettles 23.1.1843 64, w Isabella Crighton 15.5.1863 79, sis in law Margt Crichton 13.6.1853 77, s David 9.9.1823 7¾, s John 15.6.1853 35, da Margt 7.5.1873 59, da Ann 15.5.1874 52

23 1872. John McLaren fr Leckaway d Woodville Rattray 21.9.1910 91, w Isabella McLaren d there 24.10.1905 81, s John d Tilton Grange Leicestershire 14.3.1868 7¼, da Isabella d Leckaway 7.9.1869 10½

24 Thos McLaren fr Seggieden d Magdalen Bank, Craigie Perth 15.9.1904 82, w Margt Salmon 18.3.1863 36, s David 24.2.1862 4m, s Peter 12.3.1863 25, das Margt & Mary Elizabeth 15.3.1863 9½ & 3¾y, s John d Pert Logiepert 6.3.1900 44

25 1780. by Wm, David, Robt & John imo fa Wm Ramsay tent Cotton of Kincaldrum 1.5.1773 84, 1w Agnes Dick 1746 49, her four chn d nonage, 2w Margt Dempster 9.5.1773 69 surviving him 8 days, s Wm (w Agnes Alexander, s Wm 11.12.1779 24); "Here lyes our loving parents dear;/ They were parents of great care,/ They never faild, when in their Healths,/ For ther family to prepare." (see Jervise, "Epitaphs" ii 299: he has Agnes Dick's age at death as 42y, & Wm Ramsay as weaver not tenant.)

26 1852. Thos Milne 6.12.1847 76, w Susan Myles 5.3.1851 71, s Thos fr Kincrech 2.11.1873 66, s Jas 2.6.1850 26, s Wm d Kincrech 18.1.1897 77

27 Alex Grant fr Hillhead of Hedderwick near Montrose 15.12.1875 62, w Mary Ann Wilson 28.10.1887 68 (her fa David Wilson 72y, her mo Euphemia Drummond 65y, her sis Jessie d inf, her bro Thos 9y, her bro David 9y, her bro Jas 2y all int here)

28 TS Alex Nicoll smith & tent Hatton of Inverarity 26.1.1787 77, w Margt Thain 26.8.1786 67, ten chn: John, Alex, Jas, Eliz & Peter all alive in 1790, Margt, Helen, Elspeth, Wm & Robt d before their parents

29 Peter Alexander 13.6.1879 82, w Agnes Strachan 24.4.1893 92, s David 15.2.1837 3½, da Susan 10.2.1853 15, s Wm 15.1.1916 82, da Mary 22.9.1926 88, da Ann 16.2.1931 87

30 FS (marginal) revised here by Isobel Kenner imo h John Spalding late wright Galafould 10.5.1768 68, brought here from the old churchyard, chn Jannet, John, Ann, Alex, Jas; (central) 1701; I S, I S, I M, K R, T S; setsquare, axe/adze, dividers

31 Peter Grant 1.2.1874 84, w Annie Smith 28.1.1875 86, s John 28.5.1847 23, da Betsy d Dundee 23.5.1917 90

32 1772. by David Ramsay watchmaker Forfar, sis Margt 25.1.1772 41y2m2w; Jas Patterson 9.5.1872 47; Cath Jolly 17.12.1881 81; Eliz Lowson 2.9.1904 67; (west side) two cherubs, scrolls, torches, flowers, mantling with shield bearing a hand & seven watchmaking tools; emblems (see Willsher & Hunter, "Stones" p 65)

33 John Norrie d Cotton of Ovenstone 30.11.1891 79, w Margt Alexander 4.8.1848 42, 2w Mary Ann Batchelor 31.12.1878 54, da Mary 19.2.1893 53 (h Alex Young d Chicago 18.7.1872 28); Wm Norrie 16.8.1842 27.4.1923, w Annie Robertson 15.7.1844 4.2.1904

34 Thos Smith fr Holl Mill 19.4.1845, w Mary Paterson Smith 5.5.1841, s Jas 31.2.1844, by s Peter, Natal South Africa

35 1742. by David Thom gairdiner Lowr & w Margt BreMar, s Patk 6.11.1741 22; poem (quoted by Jervise, "Epitaphs" ii 299); (west side) cherub; mantling, shield with tailor's scissors & goose

36 TS Thos Mill tent Corbiemill 5.9.1785 50, wid Eliz Bower & a son & two das surviving him; poem (quoted by Jervise, "Epitaphs" ii 299: he has the year of death as 1765)

37 Geo Laird, Cotton of Ovenstone 9.1.1888 86, w Margt Grant 26.11.1883 82, da Kath Ann 1834 6, s Alex fr Downiebank 26.4.1895 56 by an accident

38 Geo Bennet 17.11.1874 72, w Agnes Dick 5.3.1885 82, s Geo 11.1835 1y8m, by s Jas fr New Zealand

39 TS by John Smith tent Hatoun of Invererity imo w Bety Car 23.5.1737 41 mo to ni hopeful chn, five ss & four das; said John Smith his spous with four chn ly the Old Kirk Yard, s Wm lys here 2.3.1759 24; J S, B C; A S, H S, E S, M S, I S, T S, I S, W S, A S; two angel trumpeters & skeleton; crown & hammer, tu ox yokes, plough; emblems or mortality

40 TS I D 1756 M P; Christian Dick 4.1755 27. Thos Dick fr Kinnettles 1831 78, w Eliz Dick 1803 45; hourglass, coffin on poles, bell, skull, bones

41 1866. Geo Henderson, w Jean Fleming, da Helen 26.7.1862 60, da Ann 6.3.1882 gda Ann 13.10.1893 69

42 Robt Dron overseer Fothringham 6.3.1906 72, 1w Grace Marshall 6.3.1886 52, 2 Innes Kay 23.10.1892 32, Walter 30.6.1871 3, Eliz b 20.10.1862 d Australia, Thos b 16.8.1891 d Johannesburg South Africa 16.6.1933, Annie Bruce b 7.4.18 d Sherbrooke Quebec 21.3.1937, Henry b 18.10.1868 d Edinburgh 24.3.1942, Jar b 3.10.1864 d Edinburgh 22.4.1942

43 Geo McLaren, Gallowfauld 17.4.1876 63, w Helen Mitchell 19.3.1875 $58\frac{1}{4}$, da Ma 19.1.1842 $2\frac{1}{2}$, s son 24.7.1860 inf, s Thos 1.12.1873 $23\frac{3}{4}$, da Jan 25.1.1877 3 int Monikie (h Jas Constable), s Jas 15.1.1878 34

44 Wm Adam fr Wester Meathie 1.2.1852 51, w Helen Reid 1.3.1875 69, s Jas d Wes Indies 1862 23, s Wm d Wester Meathie 9.10.1891 54

45 Robt Kerr 8.5.1853 95, w Eliz Hay 2.7.1868 86; Thos Ogilvie 5.11.1869 71, Barbara Kerr 7.2.1889 80, da Jane 30.3.1840 12, da Mary 12.10.1856 27, da Jessy 17.10.1856 9; Geo Kerr 79y

46 Jas Jolly fr Hatton of Fothringham 21.2.1800 6.8.1853, wid Cath Lowson, s David 15.2.1845 25.10.1848

47 TS by Jas Cowper, w Kath Tindal 26.3.1758 63; "This modst ston / What feu vain marbls can / May trewly say /Her lays ane onast woman".

48 Thos Kerr tent Littleower 16.9.1823 44, by wid Margt Walles & da Eliz

49 TS by Robt Hume & w Helene Kerr tents Haystone, s Jas 21.2.1772 11; wright's tools; R H 1775 H K; poem (quoted by Jervise, "Epitaphs" ii 300)

50 (John Ker) 2.6.1759 59, by s John

51 TS (marginal) Wm Ker in Carrot 8.1768 78, he buried two of his ss here viz. Alex 11.1758 27, David 9.1767 3; (central) Wm Ker ♡ Hellen Scot; two cherubs; medallion with oxyoke & plough; emblems (illustrated on p 176)

52 1834. Jas Millar fr New Grange Inverarity d Apoplexy 14.7.1826 52, by wid & mo, 1s Jas d croup at Douglastown 1.2.1833 11 (Jervise "Epitaphs" ii 300 notes 17y in error), surviving chn Jean & John; poem

53 Jas Smith hammerman Kincrich 28.3.1765 56, w Jean Brown 7.1.1765 58, by ss Alex & Jas, also surviving da Margt; Jas Smith fr Kinreich 24.7.1842 67, w Caroline Dingwall 6.9.1856 84

54 Thos Craig, Preston of Kincaldrum, by w Agnes Kidd, s John 12.6.1767 33; John Craig; "For dust thou art and /Unto dust shalt thou return"; 1769, T C, A K; emblems; (west side) cherub; mantling with shield, pincers, hammer, shuttle & shoemaker's knife

55 My mo Margt Hill d Tarbrax 19.5.1919 72; Wm Hill 7.9.1930 75; David Hill 2.5.1885 74, w Ann Adie 24.4.1898 83, s David 10.1.1857 5

56 Jas Adie, Tarbrax 26.1.1829 44, w Margt Alexander 5.9.1871 85, two ss d inf, by s Geo mason, s Chas 11.4.1892 81, gda Hannah Adie 8.8.1842 3,

gda Margt Adie 7.7.1862 18

57 1865. David Stirling quarrier Forfar 8.9.1846 30, w Margt Smith 20.4.1868 51, da Mary 3.3.1847 10m, s John 20.12.1852 7, da Eliz 5.11.1864 23, by s Jas, Dundee

58 by, Jas & Wm Whyt, Wm Whyt, w Mary Jarren 178-; Jas Whyt 1774, by s Wm

59 1789. Wm Maxwell tent Mill of Kincaldrum 18.10.1779 62, w Eliz Bower 2.8.1783 78, they had seven chn: Alex, Cath, Eliz, Wm, Margt, Geo & Mary; (west side) torches; mantling; W M 1773 E B; share & coulter, millstone, rhind & two picks; by Wm Maxwell fr Mill of Kincaldrum, da Mary 1757 inf, da Kath 20.3.1772 25, s Wm 1753 inf, da Eliz 1753 inf, da Margt 1754 inf, last three int in the old churchyard at Fothringham; Kath Maxwell - poetic eulogy (quoted by Jervise "Epitaphs" ii 299)

60 1915. Wm Nicoll d Luthrie Fife 27.10.1903 65, w Margt Lowson 17.12.1900 53, s David 7y, da Margt inf, s Chas inf, s John killed Dardanelles 6.1915 29, da Isabella McKenzie d 27 Logie St Lochee 1.9.1949 73

61 1829. by Alex Nicoll fr Newton of Kirkbuddo, w Mary Dawson 22.3.1776 18.6.1820; Margt Nicoll 2.2.1802 23.9.1821; Peter Nicoll 14.6.1800 8.10.1824

62 1775. Jas Fleming shoemaker Cotton of Kincaldrum, w Marjory Kydd 6.6.1774 63, by s John

63 Ann Robertson d Windyloanings Kincaldrum 4.1850 44, by s J MacGregor sculptor, Great Western Road Aberdeen

64 John Kinnear fr Muirfaulds 4.12.1852 74, w Ann Blair 1.2.1853 71, by s John (w Cath Brown)

65 Peter Smith fr Leyshade 30.6.1857 71, w Janet Smith d Grange of Monifeith 19.7.1878 82, da Eliz d Leyshade 11.3.1829 4y8m, s Jas 23.7.1833 inf, s Peter 1.4.1840 7, s Thos fr Grange of Monifeith 4.5.1879 50, da Jane d Murroes 12.5.1904, s David fr Murroes 23.6.1912 87, by surviving family; David Smith fr Leyshade 17.9.1838 90, w Eliz Laing 2.10.1825 82, s Wm 1776 inf, s Jas 1.12.1792 12, da Eliz 29.12.1792 10, da Margt 17.3.1797 22, s David 24.3.1807 23, da Jean 15.12.1848 69

66 Hugh Fraser, North Meathie 15.8.1850 85, w Janet McQuattie 1.5.1848 78, da Ann 11.4.1864 60 (h Wm Mitchell 1.5.1849 58, gda Ann Mitchell 11.1.1854 1y, gda Ann Fraser Mitchell 14.2.1871 ½y, gs Jas Mitchell 9.6.1867 ½y)

67 Geo Sadler 2.1.1837 66, w Isabella Sturrock 7.1847 79, da Margt 8.5.1867 67

68 Jas Hendry tent Mury-fauld Ground of Invereighty, w Ann Hill 11.11.1818 56, s Chas 25.9.1801 15y10m, s David 12.12.1812 21y4m

69 by David Dingwall fr Govels, s David 9.3.1795 30; David Dingwall 4.7.1818 75, w Margt Rhind 14.2.1818 82, gs Alex Bower Smith 13.10.1843 38, gda Caroline Dingwall Smith 26.7.1850 32, gda Barbara Dingwall Smith 16.8.1891 80

70 rev Geo Loudon ordained min Lintrathen in 1819, translated to Inverarity in 1831, d 1867 75, w Mary Montgomerie 1838 43; M L, E L, 1869, J E, D M C (see Fasti v 293)

71 David McLaren fr Kinpurney Newtyle 13.10.1897 82, w Eliz McFarlane Louden 11.6.1922 89, s David d Senekal South Africa 16.8.1911; Frances McLaren 16.8.1913

72 John Duff d Hosenat Kincaldrum 8.1.1853 63, w Margt Orrock 27.6.1868 71, sis Janet 2.4.1860 71, s David 9.10.1857 25, s Wm 6.3.1875 50, da Isabella 8.2.1884 49, gs Alex McGilvray 5.6.1861 1y10m, by members of family

73 by Alex Kerr, St John New Brunswick imo Betty Couttie d Invereighty 10.9.1873 77 (h Alex Smith)

74 1815. Peter Brown weaver Gallowfauld, w Susan Smith 2.3.1811 72, by ss Jas maltman Dundee & Alex serjt royal artillery

75 Jas Thow d Meathie 10.4.1879 63, w Mary Brown d Forfar 7.11.1906 78

76 Jas Paterson fr Knellock, 35y elder here d 19.1.1859 75, w Helen Low 10.7.1856 72, da Isabella 14.1.1830 15, s Jas, Kinnettles manuf Dundee b Knellock 25.6.1819 d Dundee 17.3.1882

77 Jas Grant fr Ovenstone 14.2.1906 85, w Margt Paterson 17.1.1886 63

Stones 78 - 91, 94 - 95 are loose, leaning against the south dyke:

78 by David Smith fr Leyshade, w Eliz Laing 2.10.1825 82, s Wm 12.1776 inf, s Jas 1.12.1792 12, da Eliz 29.12.1792 10, da Margt 17.3.1797 22, s David 24.3.1807 23; Peter Smith fr Leyshade, w Jannet Smith, da Eliz 11.3.1829 4y8m

79 by Wm, Eliz & John Scott imo their friends May Booth 6.1809 54 (h Wm Scott); John Urquhart 16.10.1823 32, w Eliz Scott, s Wm 1821; John Scott w Margt Neish 14.10.1824 46, s Robt 11.10.1813

80 Wm Rae fr Ingetside, da Jannet 1749 1y, s Jas 1772 21, da Margt 1771 17, s Wm 1773 17, da Hellen 1769 inf; W R 1775 M W; HR, MR, AR, IR, JR; AR, WR, IR, - - - ; (west side) 1804. miller's rhynd with share & coulter; John Rae 15.4.1804 52

81 David Duncan toll keeper Tarbrax 31.5.1845 60, w Martha Linn 25.4.1876 79

82 Peter Hunter 30.11.1817 48, w Ann Bruce 1.1.1837 57, s Peter 1.4.1832 16, by ss Robt, John, Wm & Geo

83 1813. David Orem late miller in Kincaldrum 4.7.1812 72, by s John

84 1808. John Manuel tent Braehiller, w Christian Ammer, chn deceased Robt & Maren 8.5.1777 9d, Cirston 25.2.1789 4, David 12.9.1789 4, survived 1808 Elis, John, Alex, Wm & David also Margt

85 1739. J H, M C; (T)H, JH, AH. by John Heckno imo s Thos 15.10.1738 22; this stone was brought from the old churchyard by John & Alex Hackney imo mo Margt Cobe 25.2.1768 77; (other side) loom & lay

86 1782. by Jas Henderson fr Mill of Ki(n)rich, w Katrin Ballie 10.8.1782 58; Jan, Jas, Isab, Wm, Agnes

87 1777. A B, A W, J B; by Alex Browster aometime mert Kincaldrum & w Ann Wilkie, da Agnes 17.10.1776 9

88 1768. Jas Allan tent Walkmill of Glenboy 28.11.1780 58, w Eliz Scot 2.1.1770 62, da Janet "after a tedious & painful distress which she suffered with the patience and magnanimity of a Christian" d 3.4.1766 16; I A, E S, A M

89 by Geo - - - - - - mert in Dundee imo - - Jean Smith 11.1757 77; (west side) loom; D A, - -; D-, G-, A-, Y-, B-, Je-, D-

90 by Thos Yong & w Margt Ramsay, s Thos 20.4.1759 10

91 FS broken in two parts. (marginal) Est tumulo honorabilis vir Jacobus Ramisaeus qui singulari et spectata probitate vitae que integritate - - - desiderio faeliciter fatis concessit anno humanae salutis 1646 die 3

mensis - - - -; (central)Monumentum hoc posuit dilecta eius uxor Margaretae Kynnard. i.e. Jas Ramsay 3.(6).1646 6-, by w Margt Kynhard (illustrated in Christison, PSAS 1901-2 fig 169, also F Davidson, "Inventory of 17th Century Tombstones in Angus")

92 by David & Eliz Dick imo bro Wm late weaver Draffon 10.2.1758 39; John Dick sometime in Ground of Lour, 1w Kath Scott, chn David & Eliz, 2w Agnes Goodle, chn John, Wm, Alex & John

93 (Don)ald Anderson fr, s Geo 18(10) 6y

94 David Anderson, w Margt Blair, da Jean late tenementer in Carrot 31.5.1729 6.2.1782

95 1739. W A, A D; W A, B S; by Wm Anderson & Barbara Sand imo her husband Wm Anderson 3.12.1738 27; George 23.3.1762 46; R A, W A, G A, A A, A A, loom & shuttle

96 1761. by Jas Walker in Boddymire, s David 31.1.1761 28 tent in Boddymire (wid Eliz Dick, 1s Jas surviving him); poem (quoted by Jervise, "Epitaphs.." ii 300)

The following were not seen 1953-75 but are mentioned by Jervise, "Epitaphs":

97 FS (Marginal) David Davidson 4.8.1732 45, h of Elspet Stiven, sometime in Corbiemill

98 Wm Morrison par schoolmaster Inverarity d 29.4.1829 29, bro of Alex weaver in Kirriemuir (see Kirriemuir par churchyard inscription 42)

N o t e s

Jervise, "Epitaphs & Inscriptions..." ii 298-304 notes the above inscriptions 1,15,25,30,35-6,47,49,52,59,85,91,96-8

Testaments: the following were noticed in the Index to the Register of the Commissariot of Edinburgh - Alex Lindsay of Bonytoune, 1569
David Lindsay min Inneraritie, 1581
David Lindsay in Bonytoun of Inneraritie, 1592

and the following are a few selected from the Commissariot of St Andrews -
David Bellie in Quhischit-grein of Ounstoun, 1619
Janet Mitchelson spous to John Gibson flesher in Gallofauld, 1625
Matild Mitchelson spous to John Butter in Balgirshe, 1621
Janet Halkney spous to Wm Wilson in Easter Methie, 1614
Thos Rae in Happas sometime in Balgirscho, 1634

I n d e x

A.	89
Adam	44
Adie	55-6
Airth	12
Alexander	25.29.33.56
Allan	88
Ammer	84
Anderson	18.93-5
Ballie	86
Barrie	3
Batchelor	3.33
Begbie	15
Bellie	Notes
Ben(n)et	1.19.38
Blair	64.94
Booth	79
Bower	36.59.69
Bremar	35
Brown	53.64.74-5
Browster	87
Bruce	82
Butter	Notes

17a INVERARITY

C. 70
Car (see Kerr) 39
Cobe 85
Constable 43
Counsell 15
Couttie 73
Cowper 47
Craig 54
Crighton 22

D. 95
Davidson 97
Dawson 61
Dempster 25
Dick 25.38.40.92.96
Dingwall 53.69
Dron 42
Drummond 27
Dryden 21
Duff 72
Duncan 81

E. 70
Elder 16

Fairweather 17
Fleming 41.62
Fraser 6.66

Gibson 20-1.Notes
Gleig 4
Goodle 92
Grant 11.27.31.37.77

Hackney, Heckno 85
Halkney Notes
Heemin 19
Henderson 41.86
Hendry 68
Hill 55.68
Hume 16.49
Hunter 82

Jarren 58
Jolly 3.32.46

Kay 42
Keer, see Car 9
Ker(r) 45.48-51.73
Kenner 30
Kid(d),Kyd 19.54.62
Kinnear, see Kenner 64
Kynnard 91

Laing 65.78
Laird 5.37
Lindsay Notes
Linn 81
Longair 76
Louden 70-1
Low 76
Lowson 32.46.60

M. 30.88
McFarlane 71
McGilvray 72
MacGregor 63
McLaren 14.16.22-3.43.71
McQuattie 66
Malcolm 5
Manuel 84
Marshall 42
Maxwell 59
Mill 36
Millar 52
Milne 26
Mitchell 7.9.13.43.66
Mitchelson Notes
Montgomerie 70
Morrison 98
Morton 2
Mungo 18
Myles 6.26

Neish 79
Nicoll 28.60-1
Norrie 33

Ogilvie 45
Orrock 72
Orem 83

P. 40
Pat(t)erson 32.34.76-7

R. 30
Rae 80.Notes
Ramsay 25.32.90-1
Reid 44
Rhind 69
Robertson 2.33.63

Sadler 67
Salmon 8.13-4
Sand 95
Scot(t) 51.79.88.92
Smith 8-9.31.34.39.53.57.65.69.73-4.78.89
Spalding 30
Stirling 57
Stiven 9.97
Strachan 20.29
Sturrock 67

Taylor 10-2
Thain 28
Thom 35
Thow 75
Tindal 47

W. 80
Walker 96
Walles 40
Watson 1

17a INVERARITY

Watt	17	Wilkie	6.87
Weaver	3	Wilson	27.Notes
Whyt	58	Yo(u)ng	33.90
Wighton	2		

17b MEATHIE, INVERARITY

The foundations, and a decorated aumbry, are all that remain of the parish church of Meathie-Lour high up on the north slope of Fothringham hill. As Machynlur it was dedicated in 1243, but the church was ruinous by 1682. In 1612 the main part of the parish was united with Inverarity, and the Lour part to the parish of Forfar. Many stones are reputed to have been taken for the building of Lour House & neighbouring farms. The approach is across rough grazing.
National Grid reference: NO 465 462

1 mural. "In this ancient graveyard lie the bones of the family of Bower of Kincaldrum, Kinnettles & Meathie including those of Alex Bower who d 1740 of injuries inflicted on him by Hessian dragoons & of his w Margt St Clair who d from the shock caused by her husband's death. R.I.P. When Easter Meathie passed in 1771 from the ownership of Alex Bower of Kincaldrum son of the above, this chapel yard was reserved in perpetuity. In 1926 the sacrament house was found during the course of excavation & set up in the wall." (see Jervise,"Epitaphs" ii 301-3)

2 FS shattered. (marginal) (Heir) lyes Alexander Waighe portioner of the Half of Glenboy w(ho - - - - - - -)yf Ivn 21 1644 his age 80;
(central) A.W. IS (so)NE
A.W. IS OYE (his grandson presumably)
(see F.Davidson, "Inventory.." addendum for details.)

Notes

Testaments: the following were noticed in the Commissariot Register of Edinburgh - John Butschart portioner of Mylne of Kincreich par of Meathrie, 1597
Adam Waugh in Glenwoye, 1565

The following is a selection from the Register of the Commissariot of St.Andrews - Jas Bower of Meathie, 1738. Patk Bower of Kinnettles, 1687
John Daes in Gaitsyde of Kintreith, par of Methie, 1600
Bessie Milne spous to umquhile Patk Trest in Newtoune of Methie, 1627
John Milne in Aidgertoun, 1617
Walter Mitchelson portioner East Grange of Kincreith, 1635, spouse Christian Walker, 1595, spouse Euphaim Ker, 1614
John Nevay of that ilk, spouse Margt Hay, par of Methie, 1615
Christian Steven spouse to Wm Ritchardsoune now in Arnahall par Methie-lour, 1624. And Steven in Kincreich, 1616
Patk Waugh in Glenboy, 1597-8

Dame Nellie Melba, born Nellie Porter Mitchell in 1861, was third child of David Mitchell and Isabella Dron who left Meathie parish for Australia.

Fasti v 294, Meathie ministers from 1574-1612

17b M E A T H I E , I N V E R A R I T Y

I n d e x

Bower	1.Notes	Nevay	Notes
Butschart	Notes	Porter	Notes
Daes	Notes	Ritchardsoune	Notes
Dron	Notes	St Clair	1
Hay	Notes	Steven	Notes
Ker	Notes	Trest	Notes
Melba	Notes	Waighe	2
Milne	Notes	Waugh	Notes
Mitchell	Notes	Walker	Notes
Mitchelson	Notes		

Notes: Inverarity & Meathie

OPR with Registrar General: 292 Inverarity & Methie -Births 1710-1854
Marriages 1710-1854
Deaths (mortcloth dues) 1716-1819

Church Records in SRO: CH2/381 Inverarity KS minutes 1714-1882
other matters 1710-1947

Fasti v 292 - Inverarity & Meathie ministers from 1560

"The Scottish Nation" has article about Archd Bower d 1766 80y (also in Scottish Biographical Dictionary & DNB)

18 K E T T I N S

The parish church was dedicated to St Bridget in 1249. The present church, on the same site,was built in 1768 and since enlarged. The burial ground beside the church, the manse and the burn is well-kept and still in use.
National Grid refernce: NO 238 390

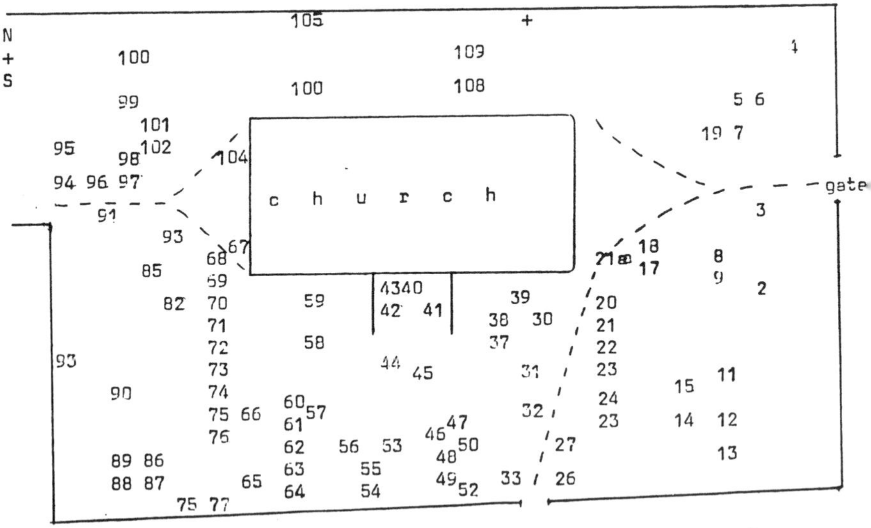

18 K E T T I N S

1 1825. by Thos Kid gunner 5th battallion royal artillery imo mo Isabella Hackney 18(02) (55)y; Patk Galletly 29.3.1822 75, w Jen Kid

2 Robt Robertson in Gask, w Eliz Rollo 10.4.1748 (5 or 3)5y

3 Robt Robertson 10.6.1741 59, by s John in Gask (imo w Cath Baillie 10.3.1748 35, chn Eliz, John, Isable); (west side) I R plough; I R, I R, H R, M R, E R, D R

4 Lockhart Gordon esq d Beechwood villa 30.10.1837 62, w Sarah Ogilvy Hay d Beechwood villa 18.5.1875 88; Geo Goodlet esq mert Leith, wid Mary Hay d Linnkeith Blairgowrie 4.3.1876 75, da Mary Georgina d Abbeyhill 12.9.1858 14, da Marion Joanna Gordon d Hastings 5.3.1860 19, da Jane Hay d Links Place Leith 21.7.1868; John Gordon esq d South Corstoun 15.3.1840 85, sis Jessie d Beechwood villa 23.10.1855 88 (see Jervise, "Epitaphs.." ii 96: he notes that Lockhart Gordon was cousin to Lord Hallyburton, md a da of mr Hay wine mert Leith to whom the misses Goodlet were related; John Gordon was factor for the property of Hallyburton)

5 Wm Shaw of Newhall imo da Mary Ann 17.5.1841 20

6 Wm Shaw esq of Newhall 17.9.1860 79, w Ann Watt 28.2.1862 81, 2da Susanna-Miller 27.11.1851 33 (h John Adamson of Ericht Side house Blairgowrie), da Mary Ann 17.5.1841 20 (see Jervise, "Epitaphs.." ii for many notes: his other two das were mrs Alex Geekie of Baldowrie & mrs Bishop, Edinburgh; John Adamson (son of capt Adamson of the whaler "Horn" of Dundee) was later proprietor of Careston & had an only son etc)

7 John Arthur 14.8.1873 77, w Ann Bruce 4.4.1872 76, da Jessie 13.2.1851 21, by ss Jas & Wm in 1852

8 1761. David Robertson, w Magdalene Herauld in Tillebackert, two chn d unbaptised, s Patk 18.2.1760 3; E R, P R, E R, M R

9 1814. by Joshua Tosh fr Doctormill & w Agnes Craigie, imo s Peter 19.5.1809 14

10 by John Gilray, w Elis Cochran 16.10.1812 63

11 1834. C C , I S

11a Margt Stevenson 21.9.1891 84

12 Jas Weir 23.6.1847 82, w Janet Huntly 18.11.1848 62, s John 15.4.1858 42 (w Margt Smart 1.3.1882 55)

13 by Jas Weir & Janet Huntly in 1832 imo da Mary 23.2.1831 21, da Jean 4.3.1824 inf

14 Wm Blair Hill 7.9.1880 49, w Isabella Dick 24.1.1922 86, da Mary Blair 31.10.1886 21, da Agnes Cook 18.8.1936 (h David Philp), s Wm Dick 9.4.1896 32; And Blair Hill 12.3.1940

15 TS 1838. by Jas Blair fr North Ballo, fa Wm 7.5.1826 89 & mo Elspet Ramsay 11.12.1837 90; Jas Hill 25.12.1853 50, s Wm Blair 7.9.1880 49 (da Mary Blair 31.10.1886 21, his uncle the above Jas Blair 20.3.1856 71)

16 1848. Jannet Gillespie 4.4.1844 83, s Wm Sidey 4.12.1842 41 (yda Margt d Kettins Cross 22.4.1859 19) s David Sidey, Coupar Angus (1da Jessie d Kettins Cross 28.2.1872 31, wid Margt McLeish d Millhaugh 22.3.1891 81)

17 1787. John Angus 18.4.1773 63, w Isabel Balneaves 15.2.1782 79, by s Patk in Easter Greenburns

18 Alex Reid forester Hallyburton 8.12.1853 57, w Jean McIntosh 3.3.1874, s Wm 1.7.1839 8, s Jas 20.11.1848 10, s Robt 13.1.1855 14

19 Louis Pedrana 29.4.1844 91, by ss & da

20 1856. by surviving family, Peter Haggart tent Ardlar Mill Kettins, w Christina Miller bpth int here

21 Wm Soot 3.2.1763 80, by s Alex, Campmoor

21a 1753. D L, M S

22 David Soot b Coupar Angus 9.10.1807 d Kinpurnie 22.12.1875, w Margt Clark b Balbrogie 10.3.1809 d Auchtertyre 5.12.1890 - - - - two das d inf

23 1812. by David Adams teacher Dundee imo fa in law Alex Heron late brewer Inchture & Forgan 15.4.1811 75 (w Margt Smith 12.1791 47, s Jas 2.8. aged 1y, da Margt 1792 5); (west side) cherub; shield with two sheaves, shovel, fire-hook (ie weedock) & maltman's slatted shovel

24 large. David Mills 19.12.183- 45, w Agnes Morrison 1.7.1845 54, da Jane 20.3.1827, s John 20.5.1819, s Geo 30.10.1823, s Wm d Otago 1868, s Jas 21.4.1876, da Agnes 19.3.1888, by s Robt mert Coupar Angus 17.1. 1906 (w Mary Brough 11.7.1897, ys David 17.1.1887 34), fa Jas fr Ardlar 1.12.1796 48, mo Helen Rodger 6.2.1824 78

25 David Rattray in Kettins, w Jean Robertson 26.6.1736 33; Magdalene Patullo 28.8.1718 48; Agnes Patullo 12.11.1736 74; (west side) tailor's shears & goose

26 FS And Rattray & w Agnes Patullo lie here, also s Thos a gardiner served in England 52y & acquired £218 sterling which he brought here August last 1772. A few days after he came he sickened & d aged 6/74. His money he legate to his bro David & his chn with orders to erect this monument; T R, A R, A P, 1773; rake, line & spade; latin verse quoted by Jervise, "Epitaphs.." ii

27 Alex Conacher 12.1828 78, w Eliz Dysart 11.1846 85, da Helen 12.1851 68. (s Jas Ireland, Ley of Hallyburton 15.4.1878 69), da Margt 7.1858 64, da Annie 2.1859 73

28 1812. by Jas Gou in Lawton imo w Agnes Craig 26.1.1811 59, six of their chn lie here: Jas, Thos, Wm, Agnes, Bell & Alex

29 1776. Patk Robertson 2.(9).1774 87, w Elspet Musterd 22.9.1773 90, by s Patk (w Marin Robertson)

30 1834. Robt McLachlan 20.11.1835 72, w Jean Black 13.5.1801 37

31 1838. by Alex Dunn tent Mill of Pitcur imo two ss David 7.5.1834 1y, Alex 15.4.1836 4

32 1807. Wm Sim fr in Patie 19.5.1799 81, w May Galloway 27.7.1761 31, s Jas 7.1805 44, by ss John & Wm

33 rev David Symers 16.7.1842 64 for 41y min Kettins parish (see Fasti v 264; Jervise, "Epitaphs.." ii 94 -he was succeeded in the property of Eassie Angus & Kettle Fife by his bro John, British Linen Bank Dundee who d 1866)

34 1796. by Thos Duncan fr imo - - Emilia Anderson 1794 44, - - - - David & Jas both d in 1st year of life (see inscription 50, probably the same)

35 1737. by Wm Soutar maltman & brewer Kettins & w Grissal Baxter, da Christian 10.2.1732 14d (but see inscription 47, probably the same stone)

36 Jas Hunter fr Knollhead 26.8.1871 70, w Margt McKenzie 26.8.1863 59, s Wm 18.10.1851 14, s John 10.7.1863 19, s Jas 11.1.1891 58, s Alex 18.6. 1895 55, da Agnes 18.9.1891 56 (h Jas Stewart)

37 1834. Peter Bruce of Couston, w Jean Constable, chn Alex, Wm & Eliz, by das Margt, Jean & Janet, bro Wm 30.11.1834 89

38 Jas Marshall parochial teacher, w Eliz Shepherd, chn Agnes, Thos, John, Wm, Eliz & David, chn Agnes & Joan int at Collace, by only surviving member of family in 1838

39 TS John Geekie 16.2.1784 77, by s John tent N Ballunie d at Nether Ballunie 13.5.1814 77 bequeathed £100 sterling to kirk session for education of the poor in Kettins; I G & M S intertwined; I G, P G, I G, A G, I G, M G, M G, C G, W G; 1785

40 mural. Alex Geekie of Baldowrie 21.10.1811 14.9.1889, w Janet Shaw 13.4. 1817 21.10.1893 (see inscription 6), s Wm 20.12.1839 28.6.1848, da Janet Shaw 8.2.1848 7.1.1914, s Robt of Baldowrie & Rosemount 10.8.1920, da Isabella Shaw 21.4.1923, da Susanna Mary Miller 5.5.1937; Alex Wm Geekie of Baldowrie b 2.1873 d Torquay 23.3.1966, w Mabel Adelaide Crane b 11.6.1875 d Torquay 13.9.1957 (1s Alex Stuart Grace 25.3.1970 69) (see Jervise, "Epitaphs.." ii 94 where Alex Geekie of Easter Baldowrie is noted as eldest in error, really youngest bro of the three lairds of Easter Baldowrie, Balbrogie & Rosemount)

41 FS John Geckie 22.6.1720 77, w Janet Smith 14.2.1721 71 indwellers Kingoughtrey; heire lys John Geekie son to P G in Kingoughtray; I, M, I Geekies

42 FS Here lys ane wirtous prudent discreet pious & honest man Wm Geekie of Baldovrie 15.4.1701 73, w Elspit Crichtone (see F Davidson, "Inventory")

42a sarcophagus originally in Kettins was brought to the Howff Dundee (see Angus gravestones, Dundee Howff no 87b) on 13.9.1851 by John Steill son of Jas Steill: Wm Geekie of Easter Baldourie, 3s David 10.8.173(6) 72; John Steill of Parkhead & Baldourie 12.2.1792 62, w Agnes Geekie 22.7. 1785 42, 1s John 19.4.1815 51, by s Jas; side panels depicting St George & the dragon, man clasping a tree etc

43 mural. Robt Geekie of Rosemount 25.10.1772 14.9.1858, w Margt Rutherford 19.8.1782 15.1.1843, s Jas 1.1807 2.1808

44 FS Wm Geekie elder in Baldowrey 27.12.1683 73; latin eulogy (quoted & translated by Jervise, "Epitaphs.." ii 93); W G M A E; Wm Geekie in Easter Keilor 16.2.1728 67, w Isabel Gray; Alex Geekie of Wester Baldowrie 10. 2.1751 70, w Isoble Johnson (see F Davidson, "Inventory.."; Warden, "Angus or Forfarshire" iv has an account of the Geekie family; Jervise, "Epitaphs.." ii 93 notes that Wm G in Easter Baldowrie & Alex G surgeon in London were sons of Wm G & Marjory Adam, Alex being b 4.7.1655 at Baldowrie & left a bequest to Kettins school)

45 TS And Tasker 14.3.1842 93, w Mary Hunter 25.4.1844 92 who were b in this par & d at Hatton of Cargill, only da Eliz d inf. "They enjoyed conjugal happiness for a period little short of 64y"

46 And Geekie fr Tauldsley 5.2.1828 68, wid Jean Baxter, by s Wm

47 John Balardie sometime tailor Foord of Pitcur 18.8.1735 70, w Helen Stubbles 3.1734 64, by s Jas miller Kettins; (west side) W S, G B, 1737, E S, G S; by Wm Soutar maltman & brewer Kettins & w Grissal Baxter imo da Christian 10.2.1752 14d (but see inscription 35, probably the same stone)

48 – – – – – – agh of – – – – who departed this l– – (October)1712 & age – – He left behind him a son Jas & spous Agnes (K)e

49 capt John Martin 29.11.1843, w Amelia Nucator 15.9.1864, by da Eliz, Dundee

50 -- - - - - - - - - - - - - - Anderson - - - - - David Anderson both dyd in - - - - - - - (but see inscription 34, probably the same stone)

51 FS - - - - - - - - - - -

52 FS by John Low, w Jean Stewart 11.5.1801 28

53 179(1)by Henry Mood & w Kath Tindle residenters in boarlands bleachfields in the grounds of - - - - - - - imo s Henry 28.(8).1789 7; (west side) setsquare

54 FS Richard Wandless late indweller in Newtoun 10.3.1678 70, w Lyllas Hay 13.3.1678 62; Richard Wandless indweller in the Newtoun 14.5.1732 76, w Elspet Whittet 20.5.1704 40; R W, L H; R W, E W (see F Davidson, "Inventory.."; Jervise "Epitaphs.." ii 95

55 FS Geo Roch smith in Balgllo & w Ellieson Thain, s Geo 23.3.1669 20; G R, E T; hammer & crown, wire drawer & pincers; "O fatil death, O crvel death,/ What meaveth the to rage;/ For to cvt of young tender plants / And pas by crvket age." (see F Davidson, "Inventory..")

56 TS Hir lyes Jean Whitet 2.2.172(1) 67 spvs to Robt Gregory at Mill of Halabvrton; R G, I W, W G; setsquare, compasses, adze etc

57 Jas Halket sometime w- - - in K(ettins)d 5.170- (47)y, w Jean (Jack) 14.-.1709 55, by da Isabel (h John Kay in Kettins); (west side) I H, 1713

58 Geo Jack 10.1811 84, w Eliz Scott 1.12.1819 70, by ss Alex, Balgone,& Geo; renewed by Alex Jack we(av)er in Bardinnie, s Peter 19.6.18(25) 3

59 John Hutton esq capt HM 88th regt of foot & formerly of 31st regt, da Matilda Whitaker 4.7.1854 31

60 TS David Halket fr Ballunie 20.1.1795 75, w Jean Thomson 2.12.1803 75, by chn Jas, Patk, Robt & Jean; 1847 revised by David Halkett, Dunkenny & mrs C Morris in lower Canada imo David Halkett 5.2.1805 12 (son of above Robt Halkett 22.5.1831 72); also Charlotte Strachin 18.7.1818 58 (da of Robt Halkett); Patk Halkett, s Robt 7.12.1823 25, da Margt 3.1838 35

61 1781. T S, A P; Thos Souttar portioner in - - - & w Agnes Petrie imo his fa Thos Souttar fr in - - - d 1.1727 51, also Isabel Smith 1.1746 67, das Agnes & Isabel Souttars

62 1737. I T, H M ; (west side) W T, I T, T T; - - - - - - - -

63 FS Patk Robertson indweller Petie (28).3.1678 55, w Ian Strachn, by Jas Semon imo ggmo Ievfance Smal - - - - (Andre)w Semon 1756 (see F Davidson, "Inventory..")

64 FS - - - - - - - - - - - -

65 1805. John Small, w Jean Toad, by s Alex (w Ann Allan); A Small 1825 85; A Allan 1828 91; John Robertson 1842 70; Jean Small 1845 70; revised by Alex Robertson bootmaker Lochie in 1869

66 1782. Chas - - - , w Agnes So- - she had six chn by her h Chas: firstborn Chas 26.12.1756 28.1.1780, Kathrine 27.9.1758 4.2.1767, Jean b 3.176(4), Helen b 4.1761, Jane b 23.2.1766, John b 6.11.1767

67 mural. 1777. Geo Ramsay wright 13.7.1763 51, w Agnes Bruce in Chappel of South Corstoun, chn Elspet, Margt, Isobel, Jas, John & Agnes, two last here int, by s Jas 29.7.181(9) 71 (w Janet Gardiner 4.7.1836 84)

68 by Jas Waddel, w Henrietta Spalding 15.1.1842 31

69 Jas Martin 25.10.1822 65, w Margt Duncan 27.4.1858 90, da Agnes 13.4.1877 84 (h John Smart fr Wester Leys 10.8.1863 71, s David 1.11.1857 33, s Jas 17.3.1901 77 (w Eliz Strang 25.10.1902 78))

70 Agnes Martin Smart late of Wester Leys 18.9.1948 88

71 1812. by Alex Duncan proprietor in Coupar Angus, w Agnes Hunter 7.1811 64, s Peter 1781, s John Newtound- - - - 19y

72 John Hall Hindmarsh teacher of elocution late of Perth d 24.7.1856 70, w Sarah Hindmarsh d Coupar Angus 7.2.1853 67, long eulogy (quoted in full by Jervise, "Epitaphs.." ii 98) da Antoinette Nesbitt d suddenly in the Manse of Kettins 4.4.1853 13 (da of Abercromby Nesbitt late of Alnwick); (west side) principal Tulloch of St Andrews, s Chas Jas 17.5.1858 4½m (see Fasti v 264: mr Tulloch was s in law of John H Hindmarsh)

73 1831. by John Millar, s John 1.10.1800, s Jas 6.8.1813, s David 26.8.1813, da Margt 24.6.1826, da Jannet 9.9.1828; Alexander Millar

74 next 73. John Millar manuf Coupar Angus 21.1.1859 73, w Jannet Millar 3.3.1865 80, by da Agnes

75 1885. Peter Morris, Market hill 19.5.1870 63, w Christina Pullar 4.8.1847 35, by ss Peter & Jas; Ratchel Morris 2.11.1885 48

76 1840. by Wm Spalding, w Jane Alexander 13.5.1839 40

77 John Spalding 3.1849 78, w Henrietta Bruce 23.12.1845 77, by ss Wm C, Robt & Jas

78 FS ii 95 covered by other stones probably that noted by Jervise, "Epitaphs.." ii 95 as follows: David Dick indweller in Killer 12.1.1699 57, w Janet Bruce; poem (but see Davidson, "Inventory": in 1977 the date seemed to be 1692)

79 FS Wm Coupar d Pitcur 26.12.1794 70, by ss John & Robt

80 Wm Anderson miller d Newtyle 29.7.1851 72, w Janet Brown d Newtyle 2.1860 75, by da Margt in 1860

81 1778. - - - Forbes, w Eliz O(ch) d 6.-.1774 69, six chn viz. Rachel, Janet, Patk, Eliz, Margt of which Jane & Eliz are also here int, by s Patk in N- -chiry

82 FS Patk Eyevlo 8.11.1699 65, w Elspit Dwchirs whose chn were indwellers at the Millen of Pette, he & his forefathers lived two hundrith y by Con; poem (quoted by Jervise), s David yevlo 13.4.1727 55, (w Isabel Haaket, five chn David, And, Pitier, Christan & Christan indwellers at the Millen of Petie (see Jervise, "Epitaphs.." ii Appendix pp 419-422 for many extracts from the Kettins KS records concerning the Yoolow family; Elspet Deuchars d 18.12.1716; also lawsuit March 1837, Peter Duncan v. legatees of David Yoolow)

83 1846. by Jas Morris, da Ann d Pitcur 13.4.1842 17, s Peter 21.5.1843 23

84 David Keay 24.3.1811 82

85 TS - - - Blair sometime in North Ballo 12.17(2)0 66 & (Jean) - - - - their son who d October 17-- (28)y; rev Chas Blair 21.11.1870

86 TS Chas Hood bleacher at Borland Field imo s Chas 9.7.1806 5y6m

87 FS Thos Bruse d Ford of Pitcur 29.1.1667 90, w Margt Cristie; by Geo Bruse in Balgove & w Grasol Bruse in 1760 imo their disest childs; Alex Bruce fr Balgoun 5.4.1800 (57), w Margt Petrie 12.1802 54, by s Jas

88 FS Jas Fyfe in Miln of Ardlar, w Elspet Jack 4.3.1684 38, also here int seven hopeful chn procreat betwixt them; poem (see Jervise, "Epitaphs.." ii 95, also F Davidson, "Inventory..")

89 FS Anton Ramsay, Bogsyde of Couper 3.12.1700 69, w Janet Small; poem (see Jervise, "Epitaphs.." ii 97, also F Davidson, "Inventory..")

90 John Smith, Meiklour, s Wm 11.17(97) 44, da Jean 17.2.180(4) 44, s Peter 9.5.1811 4(9)

91 Androw Walker 17(1)4 50, w Sarah (Wilkie) d last day of A(ugust) 1741 77

92 by Isabella (Rorer) imo her fa Jho Mo- - -

93 Geo Bruce, Kettins 8.6.1783 20.4.1859, w Eliz Stewart 5.2.1804 4.6.1886, er s Geo d Lyttelton NZ 7.10.1910 80 (w Margt Pitcaithly d Christchurch NZ 26.5.1876 49), da Isabella 26.10.1832 2.10.1833, 1da Susan 3.12.1828 3.2.1909, 2s Jas Gibb (presumably named after the parochial schoolmaster , Ed.) 22.10.1834 15.10.1909; Eliz Bruce 10.1.1925 84

94 1832. Archd Macdonald d Ford of Pitcur 12.8.1820 68, w Elspeth Macdonald d Ford of Pitcur 6.1.1831 72, das Kath & Janet int here, by ss Jas & John; Jas McDonald, s John d Rosebank Dundee 29.11.1847 17

95 - - - - - - - - - - - - - - - - ; (west side) 1737. gardener's tools

96 1839. G Burns

97 Stewart Saunders, Mill of Lintrose 13.1.1809 69, w Janet Trotter b Kelso 2.8.1752 d 4.1813 (da of Geo Trotter & Isabel Purvis)

98 TS 1782. A G, (M E), M G; - - - - - - - in Campmuir and - - - - - - - imo fa Jas Blair 9.1763 & w Jean Geekie 17.4.176(1), six chn viz Jas, David, Wm, Marjory, Elspet & Christian

99 Joseph Steven 1.10.1850 66, w Margrie Ritchie 6.3.1846 61, s Jas (w Isabella Smith 19.9.1868 63)

100 1879. Roderick C Mackenzie teacher Mosfield Rosshire d Coupar Angus 12.9.1882 80, s Dond Fraser b Rogart Sutherland 30.6.1840 d Glasgow 22.5.1877, s Lewis Andrew b Rogart 31.10.1831 d Bareilly East Indies 18.6.1858 da Margt d Morris cottage Coupar Angus 9.8.1906, 4da Alice d Alness Rosshire 21.8.1913

101 David Robertson 24.7.1869 78, w Susan McIntosh 1829 28, da Ann 1820 1y, w Agnes Barrie 1.10.1859 69, da Sarah d inf

102 1837. Jas Watson fr Mudhall, w Jean Lauder d Baldinnie 21.5.1827 53

103 John McDougall cooper Markethill Kettins imo da Margt 6.8.1797 14

104 mural in latin. mr Jas Gray min Kinloch for 20y5m, min Kettins 26y4m, twice md, d 17.3.1743 72, by wid Christian Arbuthnot who was childless, & by only da Eliz (h Wm Morison of Naughton) (see Fasti v 264, also rev dr Campbell, "Balmerino & its Abbey"" for reference to Wm Morison)

105 large murals. John Murray esq of Lintrose, wid Anne Murray d Woodside 3.11.1846 69, 2s John Gray 4.12.1802 10.3.1866, 1s Mungo esq of Lintrose 14.12.1890 88 (w Anne 11.7.1893 87), yt s Mackenzie 8.2.1810 11.2.1876; Mungo Murray esq of Lintrose, s Mungo esq d Dunkeld 25.12.1843 71 (see Jervise, "Epitaphs.." ii 96 notes a monument in St Cuthberts Edinburgh: capt Wm Murray, HM Excise 26.12.1809, w mrs Jessie Neil M'Arthur 10.3.1808 (niece of Archd Campbell of Jura); John Murray esq of Lintrose, 3s Wm d Edinburgh 23.4.1810 4½y) (Ed. Lintrose was formerly called Foderanc

106 1835. John Nicoll brewer Dundee 7.1834 28, by wid Janet Robertson

107 Daniel Stewart, Ballunie par Kettins 26.11.1830 69, w Eliz Robertson 2.9

1834 59, da Charlotte 16.7.1831 20, s Thos 27.4.1837 28, da Susan 20.2.1802 20.1.1884, by s Wm; Isabella Stewart 2.12.1891

108 Wm Nicoll fr Cottward 18.7.1855 79, w Helen Thom 7.4.1863 73, s Peter 16.12.1841 15, s Thos 11.12.1885, s John fr d South Auchry 18.3.1895 80

109 John Leys 21.10.1877 79, w Jean Farquharson 15.10.1855 52, da Margt 14.7.1854 25, da Mary 27.4.1856 23

110 mural. Jas Hutton schoolmaster here 40y d 2.5.1801 62, by scholars

The following was noted by Jervise, "Epitaphs.." ii 94 but was not seen in 1974 "upon the west side of the church."

111 FS Alex Giekie 10.2.170- 68, w Margt Cargill 13.2.1701 67 indwellers in Balgov; "The king of terrors who dare withstand Who hath the glass & dart in hand."

The following was noted by Mrs F Davidson, "Inventory.."

112 small. Margt Petre umqhyl spouse to Patirk Ta- - -

Notes

Six chapels were attached to the medieval church of Kettins i.e. Pettie, South Corstoun, Pitcur, Mairyfaulds, Denhead and one on the south side of Kettins village - most of which had burial grounds.

A Jervise, "Epitaphs & Inscriptions in North east Scotland"" ii 90-100 & 419-22 has notes on inscriptions 4,6,26,33,39,41,42,42a,44,54-5,67,72,82, 87-9,104-5,110-111 and also on the Yoolow family.

F Davidson, "Inventory of 17th century Tombstones in Angus"" (1977) has details of inscriptions 42,44,54-5,63,78,82,87-9 & 112

Testaments: a few indexed for the Register of the Commissariot of Edinburgh include - Katrene Bell relict of mr Thos Halyburton in Kethynns, 1597
John Blair of Bagillo, 1597
Thos Clark in Kethynns, 1586,
Isobel Gib relict of Bohn Ferguson, 1586-7
Wm Geikie in Kethynnis, 1608

and the following is a selction of those in the Commissariot of St Andrews
David & John Dougatt sons to umquhile David Dougatt in Balgoiff, 1625
Jas Haliburton of Fodderance, 1743
Euphame Ductor spouse to Geo Haliburton in Kynnochtrie, 1721
Margt Myles spoyse to Alex Geikie of Balderone, 1733
Thos Watson in Peattie & spouse Janet Slidder, 1636 & 1637
Thos Soutar in Midle Taith of Kinochtry, 1729
Jas Steill at Miln of Kinochtry, 1730

OPR with the Registrar General - 294 Kettins Births 1650-1717, 1719-1854
Marriages 1618-47,1652-82,1685-1854
Deaths 1685-1716, 1750-1854

Church Records in SRO: CH2/518 minutes 1682-1791, 1801-75
collections 1718-28
accounts 1750-64 (but Jervise ii 420 notes that in 1837 the KS minutes began in 1622 & were with the Session clerk)
HR 10 Kettins minutes 1766-1928
accounts 1829-1928

Fasti v 263 Ministers from 1567

18 KETTINS

Index

Adam	44
Adams	23
Adamson	6
Alexander	76
Allan	65
Anderson	34.50.80
Angus	17
Arbuthnot	104
Arthur	7
Baillie	3
Balardie	47
Balneaves	17
Barrie	101
Baxter	35.46-7
Bell	Notes
Bishop	6
Black	30
Blair	14-5.85.98.Notes
Brough	24
Brown	80
Bruce	7.37.67.77-8.87.93
Burns	96
C.	11
Campbell of Jura	105
Cargill	111
Christie see Cristie	
Clark	22.Notes
Cochran	10
Conacher	27
Constable	37
Cook	14
Couper	79
Craig	28
Craigie	9
Crane	40
Crichtone	42
Cristie	87
Deuchars	82
Dick	14.78
Dougatt	Notes
Ductor	Notes
Duncan	34.69.71
Dunn	31
Dwchirs	82
Dysart	27
Eyevlo, see Yoolow	
Farquharson	109
Ferguson	Notes
Forbes	81
Fraser	100
Fyfe	88
Galletly	1
Galloway	32
Gardiner	67
Geekie	6.39-44.46.98.Notes
Gibb	93.Notes
Gillespie	16
Gilray	10
Goodlet	4
Gordon	4
Gou	28
Grace	40
Gray	44.104-5
Gregory	56
Haaket see Halket	
Hackney	1
Haggart	20
Halket	57.60.82
Hall	72
Hallyburton	4.Notes
Hay	4.54
Herauld	8
Heron	23
Hill	14-5
Hindmarsh	72
Hood	86
Hunter	36.45.71
Huntly	12-3
Hutton	59.110
Ireland	27
Jack	57-8.88
Jobson	44
Kay, Ke, Keay	48.57.84
Kid	1
L.	21a
Lauder	102
Leys	109
Low	52
M'Arthur	105
Macdonald	94
McDougall	103
McIntosh	18.101
McKenzie	36.100
McLachlan	30
McLeish	16
M.	62
Marshall	38
Martin	49.69.70
Millar	73-4
Miller	6.20.40
Mills	24
Mo- -	92
Mood	53
Morison	104
Morris	60.75.83
Morrison	24

18 KETTINS

Murray	105
Musterd	29
Myles	Notes
Nesbitt	72
Nicoll	106.108
Nucatar	49
O(ch)	81
Ogilvy	4
Patullo	25-6
Pedrana	19
Petre	112
Petrie	61.87
Philp	14
Pitkaithly	93
Pullar	75
Ramsay	15.67.89
Rattray	25-6
Reid	18
Ritchie	99
Robertson	2-3.8.25.29.63.65.101 106-7
Roch	55
Rodger	24
Rollo	2
Rorer	92
Rutherford	43
S.	11.21a.39
Saunders	97
Scott	58
Semon	63
Shaw	5-6.40
Shepherd	38
Sidey	16
Sim	32
Slidder	Notes
Smal(l)	63.65.89
Smart	12.70
Smith	23.41.61.90.99
So- -	66
Soot	21-2
Soutar	35.47.61.Notes
Spalding	68.76-7
Steill	42a.Notes
Steven	99
Stevenson	11a
Stewart	36.52.93.107
Strach(i)n	60.63
Stubbles	47
Symers	33
T.	62
Ta- - -	112
Tasker	45
Thain	55
Thom	108
Thomson	60
Tindle	53
Toad	65
Tosh	9
Trotter	97
Tulloch	72
Waddel	68
Waker	91
Wandless	54
Watson	102.Notes
Watt	6
Weir	12-3
Whitaker	59
Whitet	54.56
Wilkie	91
Yevlo, Yoolow	82

19 KINGOLDRUM

The present parish church was built on or near the site of the pre-Reformation church on the steep slope above the Cromie burn. The burial ground is well-kept, but a large number of flat stones are covered by a shallow layer of turf and there are many open spaces between stones.

National Grid reference: NO 335 549

1 mural outside the Farquharson mausoleum. "Tollat Quotidie". John Farquharson of Baldovie, w Eliz Ramsay, chn Eliz 4.1.1768 18.6.1855, Agnes 26.3.1769 inf, Thos magistrate & deputy lieut Forfarshire 3.10.1770 21.11.1860 last male representative of the Farquharsons of Broch Dearg in lineal descent from chieftain Finla Mor royal standard bearer who fell in defence of his country at Pinkey 10.9.1547 & int in neighbouring cem of Inveresk (see rev C Rogers, "Monuments.."ii 329 & A Jervise, "Epitaphs.." i 163: capt Mitchell cousin & heir of Thos Farquharson bequeath-

ed £50,000 for the support of aged priests of the catholic church & d 1865
84 unmd)

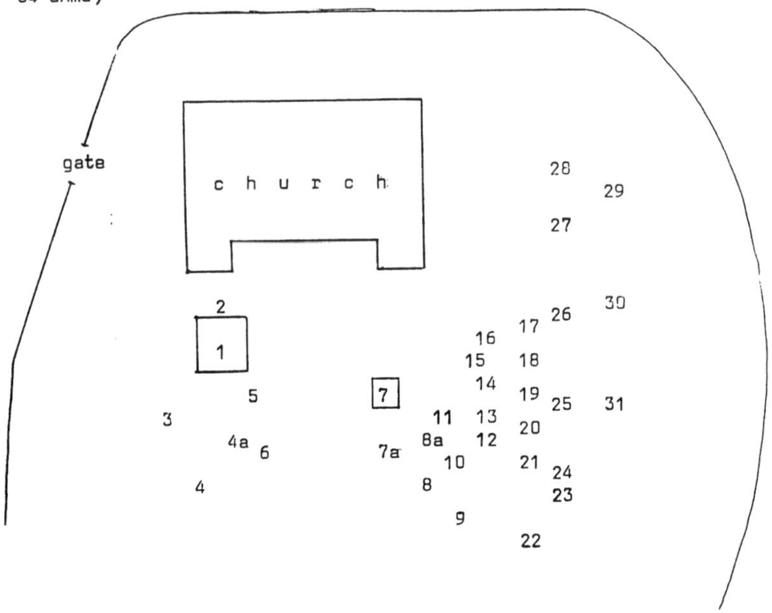

2 Wm Ogilvy of Glenure d Kenny 1825 75, w Eliz Ogilvy 1826 72

3 - (T), (A)C, A B J C; share & coulter; - - - - - - - - - -

3a by Wm Barrie, w Ann Rood 1753 45; (west side) also int here John, Wm, Thos & And Barrie

4 1843. Wm Miller d Bickenhillock 31.1.1829 69, w Euphans Wilson 5.7.1842 76, by chn Chas int here, David int here (s Chas 24.2.1839 5) & Jas int here

4a FS (marginal) David M(y- - -) d 5.12.16(89), w Agnes Nickol; D M, A N

5 by Jean Young Adam, uncle Am Edward surgeon b Over Ascreavie d Letham 6.8.1889 72, mo Ann Edward Young, gparents Peter Edward & Janet Ramsay, uncles & aunt Jas & David both surgeons Forfar, Thos & Jean all int here (see Forfar St John's Episoopal churchyard insoription 9)

6 cross. Thos Lindsay in Kirkstyle here d Over Ascreavie 18.3.1913 93, w Ann Couper 2.3.1877 52, s Wm 9.5.1875 13, da Susan 23.5.1878 28, mo Margt Farguson 28.8.1843 61, fa Geo Lindsay 15.10.1856 71

7 cross in railed enclosure. Jas Ogilvy of Ascreavie 20.4.1787 28, only ch James Catharine 25.1.1871 83 (wid of col Keith Young) (see Brechin Testaments: David Ogilvy of Ascreavie, 1787)

7a by David Lackie, Montrose & his sisters, fa John d Lun- - Airlie 3.9.1832 52, mo Janet Walker 24.5.1865 85

8 Thos Low late in Mill of Queech 8.1.1779 49, chn Agnes 1759 20w & Thos 8.1783 8, by w Margt Finlay

8a TS two cherubs; shield with -S, -F, 1731, E S

9 1838. Chas Adam miller here 10.1.1837 65, by w Janet Thom, chn Janet 9.9.1818 10, Jas 14.9.1819 8m, John F 24.7.1824 23m, Susan 7.2.1837 25, Betty 13.2.1842 21

10 TS 1728. T E, I E, I E, D E, A E, - E; emblems; (Allex) Edward sometime in Wester (Persie) d (27).12.1727 age - - - - - Isobel Ogilvy - - - - - - - - -; helmet, shield with A E, I O, 1728

11 TS collapsed. two cherubs, man, woman & child; helmet, shield with T S, I H, 1717; (on supporting sides) daughters - - - - Stormont - - - -; M S, A S, B -; here lyes Margt Stormont 15.5.1716 14y

12 1749. shield with ox yoke, share & coulter; I D, H D, A D, C D; Jas Duncan d 8.17-9, by wid Elspeth Edward; (west side) large heart; J D, E E; emblems; poem (quoted in Willsher & Hunter, "Stones" p 19, A Jervise, "Epitaphs" i 164 & Rogers "Monuments" ii 239 who all have the date 1742 in error.)

13 fallen & broken. 1823. John Fenton late HM 72nd regt foot served king etc in all quarters of the world for 24y & returning to his native place erected this monument to fa Thos fr Ballantore 6.11.1781 33, bros Peter d St Vincent 9.7.1794 18 & Wm d C(olauk) 8.8.1799 23

13a FS under turf. Catharin Roger - - spouse to - - - Smal (yo)unger quha d Februar 16(34); - C R H N T (see Brechin Testaments: Oliver Small younger in Kirktoun of Kincoldrum & w Kath Roger in par Kincoldrum, 3.3.1634, also Cath Roger widow of Oliver Small younger in Kingoldrum, 15.1.1650)

14 FS (marginal) an honest woman called Isobel Wright d 1.16-4 age -3y spouse of Olifer Smal in Kingorthervm; John (Smal) here in Sln- - - & he - - - - Isob - - - - -

15 by Wm Jack & Elis Fordell, fa Robt Jack 27.5.1697 74, mo Eliz Ogilby 2.10.1696 62 (their s Jas 12.10.1703 53); by Thos Eduard & w Agnes Eduard, fa Thos 83y & mo Helen Jack 76y; (west side) shield with axe, compasses & setsquare; emblems

16 W O, J O, 1739; by Wm Ogilvy & w & by Jas Ogilvy (& his w Margt McNicol) & by Patk Ogilvy to their fa Wm 18.2.1724 (62) & mo Jannet Smith 24.7.1718 38

17 cenotaph in railed enclosure. rev Wm Haldane for 34y min here d 1836, w Ann Roberts 1835; (south side) rev Jas O Haldane for 55y min here d 1891 (see Fasti v 267: rev Jas was 4s of rev W Haldane)

18 TS (marginal) John Fenton in Kirktoun of Kingoldrum, w Helen Blair; (central) emblems; I F, shield, H F, H B; P B, K W; 27 December 1703 (see Brechin Testaments: John Fenton in Kirkton of Kingoldrum & w Helen Blair, 1698)

19 TS (marginal) Jas Watson at the Mill of Kingoldrum 1.1.1719 95; 1728 I W, E W; emblems

20 next 19. Alex Reid fr tent Auchindorie for 46y d 8.1.1856 67, w Margt Bower 23.6.1871 74, chn Wm 12.7.1866, Janet Reid Neill 29.8.1871, Jas 13.11.1886, Alex 3.4.1898, s & two das d inf

21 next 20. Alex Reid tent Auchindorie for 40y d 8.1.1856 67, two das & s inf

22 Thos Edwards bootmaker Lintrathen 1903 72, w Betsy Murray 19.8.1929 77, s Thos 16.4.1896 21, fa Thos 15.12.1886 86, mo Barbara Adam 12.3.1862, bro John 12.8.1842 20, bro Geo 15.11.1862 26, sis Susan 2.5.1872 36

23 Alex Duncan d here 4.5.1911 87, w Sarah Herald 12.1.1915 90, s Jas inf

24 next 23. David O Downie 8.8.1938 85, w Susan Duncan 15.6.1961 95, gda Susan inf

25 by John Cairncroft, uncle Thos Cairncroft fr (Brone) of Baldovie d 23.10.1746 63; shield with ox yoke & monogram (D C)

26 by Jas Smart & w Clara Craig, his fa John Smart 12.6.1719 55, his mo Margt Jack & deceased wives Jannet Pyett & Euphon Webster, & chn Jo & W & Ja & Mt & El & Je

27 TS (Marginal) by John Dick fr Over Ascreavie, w Margt Bunch 4.4.1748 62; (central) I D I O; shield with ox yoke, share & coulter; poem; John Dick 27.3.1767 83, das Betty & Janet (see Jervise, "Epitaphs" i 163 who quotes the poem, but has Janet Buchan in error instead of Margt Bunch)

28 J O, E B; by John Ogilvy & Eliz Black (w of Alex Black 13.8.1739)

29 And Anderson weaver Kirriemuir 24.3.1809 68, w Helen Young 16.3.1819 76, three chn Alex 3.1785 3, David 12.1789 20, Eliz inf, by four surviving chn John, And, Eliz & Margt in testimony of esteem

30 John Duncan d Crief 29.7.1819 57, w Jane Culbert 13.10.1839 73, da Margt d America 1822 29, da Julia 18.8.1830 29, s Jas 20.12.1834 37, da Betty 27.4.1841 31, s Wm late fr Crief 5.2.1853 61, by Isabella Duncan tent Crief par Kirriemuir only survivor of the family & Margt Brown wid of their s Jas

31 by John Edward fr Kinclun, w Elspeth Hepburn 6.1.1748 59, da Isobel 3. 11.1740 18; JtE, DdE, JoE, KnE, 1749; shield with share, coulter & oxen yoke

32 maj W B Young of Ascreavie, w Lilias Blackwell 13.6.1807

33 fallen. "Animum homini sunt in meritate sed corpora pulveram redeunt"

34 FS broken. John Red 1639. David Reid in Drumf- - - , da Margt 2.1711 17y

N o t e s

A Jervise, "Epitaphs & Inscriptions.." i has inscriptions 1 (with brief biography), 12,14,19,28

C Rogers, Monuments & Monumental Inscriptions" ii 239 has inscription 1

Testaments: Kingoldrum was in the Commissariot of Brechin and the following are selected from the Index to the pre-1801 Index:

Walter Adeson, w Isobel Duncan in Mur-Persie, 1621
Alex Duncan in Kincoldrum par & w Agnes Bruce, 1621
Alex Duncan in Mourepersie & w Margt Malcolm, 1666
David Edward in Mildad, yt s of Thos sometime Muirperse, 1712
David Edward sometime Easter Pearcy, 2s of John of Pearcy, 1721
John Myll in Balgray, w Euphemia Adam, 1621
Abrahame Mylne in Bagray, w Christian Smart, 1625
Alex Mylne in Wester Persie, w Kath Duncan, 1624
Jas Ogilvy of Balfour & w Helen Clepan, 1613
Olipher Ogilvy in Kirktoun of Kingoldrum, w Chritian Scrymgeour, 1629
John Smart in Bagray, w Elspet Gray, 1614
Richd Reid in par Kingoldrum, w Margt Lorimer, 1581
John Young in Auchquiroche, 1610

Fasti v 265 Ministers from 1567

19 K I N G O L D R U M

OPR with the Registrar General – 295 Kingoldrum:
Births 1700–23, 1725–1854
Marriages 1743–94, 1797–1818, 1820–54
Deaths 1747–92, 1798–1804, 1820–54

Church Records in the SRO :

CH2/220 KS minutes 1758–1813, 1820–1928
accounts 1756–1823
poor's fund accounts 1820–51
burials register 1855–1927
minutes of heritors & KS 1823 & others post 1881

HR 385 Kingoldrum buildings 1840–77
stipend 1811–1927, minutes 1863–1922

GD 1/46/70 poor's fund accounts

GD 16/46 & 49 (Airlie Muniments) church matters 1802–23
church, manse & school 1731–1872

Index

Adam 5.9.22.Notes
Adeson Notes
Anderson 29

B. 3
Barrie 3a
Black 28
Blackwell 32
Blair 18
Bower 20
Brown 30
Bruce Notes
Bunch 27

C. 3
Cairncroft 25
Clepan Notes
Couper 6
Craig 26
Culbert 30

Dick 27
Downie 24
Duncan 12.23–4.30.Notes

Edward 5.10.12.15.31.Notes
Edwards 22

F. 8a
Farguson 6
Farquharson 1
Fenton 13.18
Finlay 8
Fordell 15

Gray Notes

H. 11
Haldane 17
Hepburn 31
Herald 23
Hood 11

Jack 15.26
Lackie 7a
Lindsay 6
Lorimer Notes
Low 8

McNicoll 16
Malcolm Notes
Mill Notes
Miller 4
Mitchell 1
Murray 22
Mylne Notes
My– – 4a

Neill 20
Nickol 4a

O. 27
Ogilvy 2.7.10.15–6.28.Notes

Pyett 26

Ramsay 1.5
Red, Reid 20–1.34.Notes
Roberts 17
Roger 13a
Rood 3a

Scrymgeour Notes
Smal(l) 13a.14
Smart, Smairt 26.Notes
Smith 16
Stormont 11

T. 13a
Thom 9

W. 18
Walker 7a
Watson 19
Webster 26

Wilson	4		
Wright	14	Young	5.7.29.32.Notes

20a K I N N E L L

The pre-Reformation church dedicated to St Malrubh was replaced in 1855 by the present large church disused since 1967 (keys with the minister at Friockheim manse). The burial ground is still in use and in excellent condition.

National Grid reference: NO 609 503

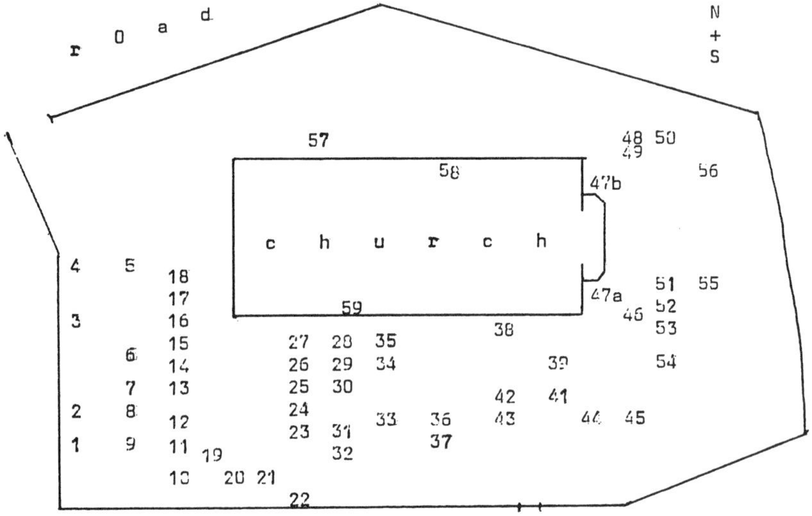

1 John Broun sometime tent in Ha(ll)on 1725 42, w Ann Eslo 17.5.1758 77, by s Jas in Million of Guthrie (w Jean Ruehie 19.7.1771 60); (west side) A B, J B, J B, - B, - B, - B; revised by Jean Milne in Kirktoun of Guthrie imo h John Brown 26.11.1776 35, chn Isobel, Jean, Margt, Robt all alive when this stone was set up

2 1755. by Robt Brown tent in Bolshean, w Christian Duncan 23.7.1754 29, only s John 12.3.1752 9m; (west side) R B, C D; "Possess'd of Accomplishments /That grace a female Mind /She, ripe for heav'n Tho' young in days To God her Soul resign'd." (see Jervise, "Epitaphs.." ii 39 for notes on the family)

3 1765. by Christian Urquhart imo bros John 27.2.1763 27, Colin 7.7.1764 21 both wrights sometime in Rennysmiln; (west side) M U, I U, I U, C U, C U, M U; 1765; shield with axe & setsquare, mantling

4 John Bruce tent Holemill 31.12.1834 73, w Isabella Duncan 30.3.1866 95, da Ann 12.3.1866 55, da Isabella 2.10.1878 74, s John tent Holemill 1.4.1882 74 (w Jane Forbes 4.8.1875 70), s Jas tent Bonharry 26.5.1882 72 (w Helen Forbes 6.10.1852 42); Robt Bruce fr Woodfield 22.5.1889 76

5 John Esplin 23.6.1894 88, w Eliz Falconer 9.12.1891 87, da Mary Ann 15.2.1852 21, da Jane 29.12.1855 11

6 John White 10.4.1766 61, w Elspeth Bouden 11.2.1773 58 sometime tents Moorside of Kinnell, by chn Jas, Elis, John, David, Chas, Wm, And & Agnes, Alex & Jean, forenamed Chas, John, Agnes & Alex int here;
(west side) I W E B
1 7 7 4

7 Alex Alexander tent Newtown of Boysack 6.8.1803 76, w Iscbel Brown 3.3. 1838 80, by four surviving members of family out of thirteen viz. And, Margt, Jean & Mary, the others being all int here except John & Wm who d India; Jean 4.10.1847 65, And 25.11.1853 74, Margt 9.4.1860 79

8 TS John Broun, w Jane Walker who lived in Mureside of Bolleshan 3.1.1701 54, also two chn Jas & Margt; by And, Wm & Robt imo fa And Broun tent in Bolleshan 1.1.1753 76 & mo Elis Fairweather 13.3.1766 78. Restored by Robt Wemyss Brown of Lochton, Wm Francis Brown bishop of Pella, Chas Francis Brown late RE, Jas Norman Methven of St Martins in 1937

9 CT by Margt Jameson imo h Wm Brown tent in Kin - y - - he d - - - 4.(8). 1769 45. He left behind a widow & eight chn viz. John, And, Robt, Jas, Margt, Wm, Mary, Eliz; above Wm Brown, w Margt Jamieson, lawfull s Wm 18.3.177(1) 13

10 by Wm Strachan sometime in this par imo w Margt Cobban 17.10.1790 35y6m, they had three chn, John, Maryann & Jas all d inf

11 Alex Harris 28.4.1890 53; And Harris 29.12.1894 81, w Nickles Rennie 20. 4.1861 65; Margt Harris 12.5.1912 77, h Jas Scrimgeour, Dubton of Turin

12 Alex Harris d West Mains of Collieston 26.12.1865 70, w Isabella Ross 23.10.1857 74, by s John

13 by Wm Harris 17.2.1874 85, w Isabella Mackay 16.9.1877 85, s Jas 8.9. 1843 24, da Ann d Edinburgh 20.8.1871 48, s Alex (w Isabella Gray 8.8. 1853 31)

14 by David Blyth, Muirside of Kinnell 8.4.1890 87, w Martha Cuthbert 7.1. 1894 85, da Marjory 16.7.1835 1y, das Agnes & Eliz d 1852 inf, da Ann 24.1.1855 19, s Jas d Invercargill New Zealand 30.11.1892 52, s Wm d Christchurch New Zealand 1898 69, s David d Liverpool 28.9.1899 57, s Alex d Winton New Zealand 9.3.1901 69

15 Jas Brown, w Margt Harris d Kintore 1.10.1814 50, ss Alex, David, & And all lie here, by s Robt vintner in Arbroath (&w Janet Strachan) on 1.10.1833; "..Who children fair did bear on earth eleven,/ Then firm in hope resign'd her soul to heaven."(of Margaret Harris, quoted in full by Jervise, "Epitaphs" ii 40

16 TS with inscription below. John Whyte, Muirside of Kinnell, w Jean Scott 21.6.18(0)6 71

17 Jas Whyte 1.1.1864 59, w Mary Wright 11.2.1889 84, s Wm inf, da Annie d Broughty Ferry 1.6.1887

18 by Jas Bowden & Isobel Rennie in Muirside who had chn: Margt 25.2.1731 6m, Ion 8.11.1735 5m, Heln 15.8.1741 5, Ar 8.6.1746 1y, Ja d Ma- - - (broken)- - ; (west side) Jas Bo./ Isob. Ren / 1757; mantling, shield with tailor's goose & scissors; I B, M B, A B, I B, I B; poem

19 David Smith resided in Ground of Beauchamp d 5.11.1763 66, w Helen White 5.7.17-- 61, three chn John, Jean & Wm here int, four remaining David, Alex, Helen & - - -, by ss David & Alex on 3.1772

20 Robt Ferrier 30.10.1772 41, w Jean Donaldson, his fa Wm Ferrier marshand in Braco, his bro John in Old Cotton was empowered by him to set this stone up; (west side) Tailor's goose & scissors; R F, I D

21 1852. by Wm Grubb & w Eliz Forbes at Hatton Mill, da Jean 30.11.1847 2y9m

22 FS leaning against wall with inaccessible, but clear, inscription. - - - - - - 1758 - - - - - 20 day of - - - - -

23 T S, 1746; Here lyeth the bodies of Wm Scot sometime tent Lawtoun d 19.7.1743 79, w Elis Strachan 24.8.1746 71, by s Thos 2.7.1773 56 (w Jean Dorward 4.8.1767 41); (west side)
Methinks I see the humble aged sire
Pass swiftly by, with feet unapt to tire;
Upon his head an hourglass he wears,
And in his wrinkled hand a sythe he bears -
Both instruments to take the lives from men
The on sheweth with what, the other when.

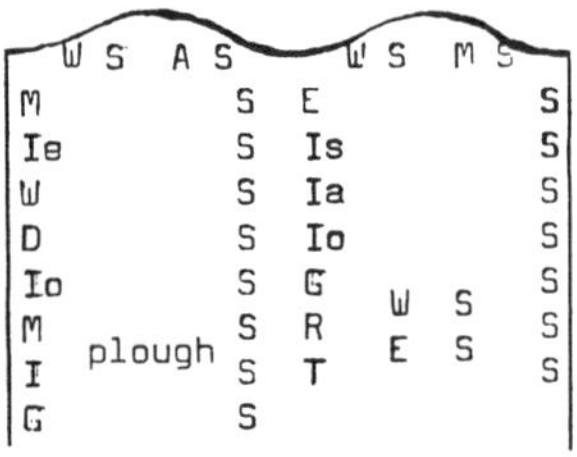

24 dr Alex Skair, London, da Eliza d Boysick Mills 15.8.1819 19

25 Thos Skair 21.1.1767, w Margt Scot 22.11.1764 70, da Margt 25.12.1742 21; (west side) T S, M S, 1746; plough; IoS, W S, M S, IeS, T S, AnS, IsS (see Jervise, "Epitaphs.." ii 41 who notes Thos Skair was tent of West Miln of Boysack); "When death doth come in his full rage /He spares not young nor old /But cuts down many of every age /He'll not be brib'd with gold./ Take warning then ye that may see /And read this passing by /And learn so to live as you /May not be afraid to die"

26 Thos Skair tent Boysackmills, w Eliz Duncan, ss Thos, David & Jas & unm sissHelen, Betsy, Ann, Agnes, Eliz & Jean all int here, by ss John of Lunan Bank & Alex surgeon London d Camden Town 27.10.1846 71 int Kensal Green cem

27 John Skair of Lunan Bank sometime tent Boysack-Mills d Arbroath 9.7.1856 82, w Isabella Anderson d Park-Conon 18.5.1811 26, s John d inf all int here

28 Jas Molleson tent Hatton of Brakie 15.8.1793 74, w Jean Skirling 12.2.1798 79, chn Jas 1761 17, Jean 26.8.1757 7, Mary 27.5.1764 11, by surviving chn Patk min of - - -ton & Alex min of Mon- - -

29 Robt Colville fr Balnabreich 21.4.1841 81, w Betsy Low 19.3.1826 34, by chn Robt, Eliz, Margt & Cath; eulogy

30 TS Thos Colville tent Boysick 7.4.1808 54, by w Ann Stiven, three chn Margt int here, Ann (h Robt Scott in North Mains of Turin) & Mary (h David Lowson town clerk Arbroath) (see Angus Gravestones, Arbroath nos.1203-8)

31 Jas Ferrier 5.7.1846 72, w Beattie Wylie 15.12.1847 52, s Jas 15.5.1837 10, s Wm 22.9.1868 33, by surviving family

32 John Scott & Mary Fairweather tent in Gilchorn, lawful da procreat betwixt them Margt, also four of hir bros & three of hir sisters David, John Mary, Wm, Eliz, David & Eliz here int; poem

33 John Scot tent Gilchorn, w Mary Fairweather 12.3.1735 40 brought forth to him twelve chn of which eight are departed viz. Margt, David, John, Mary, Wm, Elis, David & Elisebeth & four are alive John, Isobel, Jas & Robt; "Here lyes the bones of eight and one,/ Whose souls are to the heavens agone,/ This matron with her children dear /Before their Saviour to appear..."; (west side) two cherubs; M S, D S, I S, I S, I S, M S; W S, I S, R S, E S, D S, E S; "A good wife she is from the Lord..." (see Jervise, "Epitaphs.." ii 39 for both poems in full)

34 TS - - - - Raitt of (-ien)field d 10.1.1826 69

35 CT two cherubs; crown; Jas Raitt; Elisebeth Low; 1756; Here lyes the dust of Jas Raitt sometime tent in Chappeltown of Boysock & h to Elis Low by whom he had seven chn Elis & David here int, John, Jean, Kath, Jas & - - - alive at this date. He d 21.2.1755 66 (Ed. carving similar to Angus, Panbride no. 31)

36 1862. Jas Petrie tent Waulkmill of Boysack 7.11.1839 70, w Isabella Young 3.8.1862 89, chn Wm 1836 42, Ann 22.6.1842 30, Mary 13.6.1848 40, gda Isabella Tosh 12.8.1840 7, s Jas 17.4.1836 25, by dau Isabella Eliz & Jane 21.1.1890 68

37 by Jas Campbell sometime tent West Brakie, w Jean Man 17.11.1789 50, they had three chn viz. Jas, Wm & Jean 20.7.1785 6

38 leaning against church. by John Gowans & Helen Ireland imo da Ann 11.2. 1767 17y(<u>2</u> or 1<u>0</u>)m, they had these surviving chn at that time viz. Dohn, Janet, Jas,Eliz & Jean; merchant's mark; (other side) - - - - -; mottos in latin.(see Fasti v 446 for rev John Gowans)

39 TS in latin. Wm Dall 8.11.1696 48, w Eliz Mare(<u>ham</u>) (see Jervise"Epitaphs" ii 38 has Marechan). T W, M M, 1758; Thos Webster sometime tent Newbigging of Letham 10.4.1757 48, w Mary Mollison, chn Jas, Thos, Isobel, Mary, David, Anne who survived him & Eliz who d young

40 FS broken under 39.

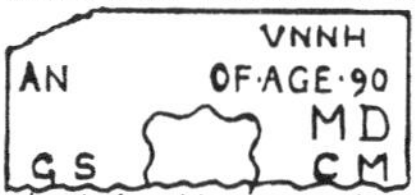

41 TS This stone was erected on the remains of John Gowans d 1.6.1787 74, w Helen Ireland 19.11.1780 60, by honest industry in the mercantile line & the profits of a small farm - a portion of Pitmikie - he reared a family of six chn besides two who d prematurely, gave their two sons a liberal education & for their rank in life left their four daughters in easy circumstances; poem (see Jervise, "Epitaphs" ii 40: s John sometime schoolmaster St Vigeans, later min of Glenisla then Lunan, s David physician d West Indies, da Janet (h Robt Cairncross blacksmith Bolshan) da Eliz (h Jas Ferrier fr Broadmyre near Brechin), da Helen (h Wm Simson draper Arbroath, da Jean (h Peter Laing tanner Brechin)

42 by rev David Milne min Gilcomston par Aberdeen imo beloved mo Jane Cairncross 21.10.1835 56, sis Jessie 17.2.1839 27, w Eliza Wright 20. 12.1874 59

43 urn. rev David Milne min Gilcomston 7.8.1879 71

44 by Jean Wilson imo h Alex Scrymsour sometime tent Milton of Guthrie 6. 4.1772 69, also his 1w Alison Esplén & two of their chn Alex & Thos, four of his chn by his 2w viz. Elspeth, Wm, Jas & Mary were all alive at this date 1773; (west side) cherub; Alexr Scrymsour; Jean Wilson; E S, W S, I S, M S

45 (marginal) - - - Androw Mal(<u>l</u>)/ Sw - - - - - / the year - - - - - (central) Here lies Helen - - - - ea - - - - - "Whose soul is to the heavenly mansions gone." (east side) (marginal) This monument imo his fa in law - - - - - -

46 1840. Jas Mill sometime tent & cattledealer on the Ground of Colliston par St Vigeans d 2.5.1837 47 int here, by w Jean Mill; (west side) Jas & Jean Mill, s Wm 10.6.1852 18, da Barbara 31.3.1856 25, s David 5.5. 1856 24, da Isabella 22.9.1856 20, s Jas 17.5.1858 29 all int here

47a mural. I F M W; 1719; R F, I F, M F, (<u>I</u>)F,(<u>E</u>)F, K F,(<u>M</u>)F, A F (see Jervise, "Epitaphs.." ii 38 who suggests the surname Fraser)

47b mural. Mr I T, K O; (in Latin) mr Jas Thomson junior pastor, w Cath

Ouchterlonie (da of the min of Aberlemno), only son int near his father. He d 1681 33. A true priest. Reader, learn how to die. (see Fasti v; F Davidson, "Inventory"; Jervise "Epitaphs.." i 36)

48 1842. Jas Patterson late residenter in Muirside of Kinnell 23.2.1842 75 int here, by wid Jean Gothill & surviving family viz. Thos, John, Francis, Jas, Jean, David, Alex, Geo & Wm; said Jean Gothill 4.8.1843 71; above Wm Patterson of Muirside Kinnell 3.3.1902 85, w Eliz Harris d Muirside 7.9.1903 82; (west side) "Weep not for me my Wife & Family Dear Though my body's dead and lying here./ Death is a debt to Nature due. I've paid that debt and so must you."

49 Jas Aitken, Margt Spence, M A, H A, 1761; by Jas Aitken & Margt Spence imo chn Alex 31.5.1755 31, Jas 1.5.1753 32, David 1760 30, Isobel 6.4. 1756 22, Wm 1754, gs John Rough 1735 10 who lies at the wo- - of this stone with Wm, Alex & John Aitken; (west side) three cherubs; poem

50 1767. by David Hill in Lochlaw, w Jean Scot 28.2.1763 67, s mr Andrew late schoolmaster in Dundee 2.11.1764 27 with the rest of their chn deceased viz. Elspet 23.3.1751 23, Margt, Jean, Janet, Wm, Margt, John & Helen all d inf; "At sides and foot of the tombstone /Lies the mother & her children nine/ In hopes one day to soar on high /With Christ our King to reign." (west side) D I [shield: A M H] H S

M H, G H, I H, I H, I H, W H, E H, M H, I H, D H, H H; mr And Hill late student of Divinity was Gradeuat in King's Coledge auld Aberdeen 12.4. 1760; John xi vers 25

51 1760. by John & David imo fa Wm Addison sometime in Cotoun of Bws d 30. 4.1759 63, his w Jean Hutchen 27.3.1744 44, their da Isobel 1.1750 28, their s Wm 6.1750 20; (west side) cherub; Wm Addison, Jean Hutchen; I A M F; loom & shuttle; D A, - -; I A, I A, W A, I A, A A, D A

52 by Jas Donaldson tent Kinnells Mill d there 1.4.1876 76, w Mary Jamieson 15.6.1841 32; David Donaldson 26.8.1864 26

53 urn. by Robt Donaldson d East Newton 9.2.1925 95, w Jane Ann Bell d East Newton 13.2.1899 46, s Peter Bell sometime of East Newton d Richmond Yorkshire 16.12.1957 78, da Helen Buchanan d East Newton 28.11.1875 2m; Louisa Rowe d East Newton 13.5.1904 23

54 by Margt (Begg) in Damside of Pitmouies imo h David Brown 3.4.17(59) 60, s David 8.1762 30, s Jas d 7y, da Mary d 1y both int here; (west side) cherub; shoemaker's tools - hammer, pliers, shoe; -B, -B, AB, JoB; AB, MB, MB, SB, MB, AB, KB

55 1760. by Geo Roger & w Margt Hutchen sometime in Wester Brackie imo da Margt 22.1.1752 20; (west side) cherub; mantling, shield with G R, M H; M R, I R, D R, I R, M R; "Below this stone a lovely maid doth lye /Whom God did take in her virginity./ She was - - godly and sincere,/A pleasure to her parents here /But now she serves her God she did adore /It's better then on earth - - - " (see Angus, Guthrie inscription no. 43)

56 And Scott tent Redcastle 23.6.1809 72, w Mary Jamieson 26.1.1(8-0) 75

57 leaning against church. by Wm Clark & Flora Dargie imo chn who d at Williamyards, Chas 8.10.1850 3y10m, Mary Ann 22.12.1854 2y2m, Alex 15.8.1860 2y9m, Jean Nicoll 16.8.1860 7m

58 mural inside church, in latin. mr Jas Thomson senior min here for 50y d 13.12.1690 84, w Margt Colace, three ss & seven das, succeeded by yt s David (see Fasti v 441) ; arms; M I T, M C, 1690 (see F Davidson)

59 mural in church. arms; "by Industry we prosper"; Alex Gavin mert in Mont-

rose d 59y md 23.6.1713 Eliz (da of John Jameson in Hawkhill), chn Alex, David, Joseph, Benjamin, John, Ogilvie, Mary, Marjy, Eliz & Cath - Iosh d 4y, Eliz d 6y, Ion d 13y, Mary d 25y on 21.11.1751, w Agnas d 1753 50 (da of Ion Ogilvy), md 11.1753 Isobel (da of rev Patk Lyon min Rescobie (see Fasti v 302)), Ogilvie midshipman d Plymouth 4.1756 19, md Janet (da of Wm Baillie & gda of provost Baillie both magistrates & merts of Brechin) (see Jervise, "Epitaphs" ii 37-8 & 419 for many further details: OPRs have births of the eldest chn at Petloch, others at Denhead & of Cath the youngest at Braeheads in Lunan, all chn of Eliz Jameson - Alex Gavin md four wives, his 2w was "mrs Hood alias Agnes Ogilvie indweller Cowpar md 1750", his 1da Mary md Jas Ritchie in par Farnell on 17.8.1743, his 2s David of easter Brakie & Langton Berwickshire md lady Eliz Maitland(1da of earl of Lauderdale) in 1770; (see also Jervise "Epitaphs" i 243; St Andrews Testaments - Alex Gavin senior at Milntown of Braikie, 1776)

The following inscriptions nos. 60-64 are listed by A Jervise, "Epitaphs.." ii 35-42 but were not seen in 1977:

60 TS Thos Crichton indweller Whanlon 24.11.1719 34, by w Elspet Ferrier; poem quoted

61 TS John Hall indweller Douglas Muir 6.8.1720 80, w Helen Makie 10.12.1725 79; poem quoted in full ...."Sometime in Gardnerie he serv'd,/ And from the truth he never swervd;/And with his work did well Agree,/ He father was of many A tree./Att Knock-Millie-hill where he did dwell,/His produck there it Looketh well,/Now when he is dead its to be known;/Likewayes one his Children shown/ With spade & Raik he Wrought his life,/ The snading ax & pruning knife./All these he wrought but any thraw, /With shouel fin and cutting saw,/The truth of All if you will ken, /He still was loved of honest men." garden implements

62 TS by Wm Ritchie marchand Muirside of Kinel & w Margret Grige, s Wm 1.3.1728

63 1731. by John Wrquhart wright in Renny's Mill imo fa John Wrquhart wright 2.2.1729 63; "If you would know who lues below this stone/ A mechanick Faber Lignarius, he was one;/Who in his day, for Science was exceling,/Yet with the worms he's taken up his dwelling...."

64 TS next 41. by Alex imo fa Alex Smith many years factor for the Panmure Estate d at his house near Middelton 9.7.1815 84; eulogy

N o t e s

A Jervise, "Epitaphs & Inscriptions" ii 35-42 notes inscriptions 2,15,23,25, 33,39,47a & b,50,58-64

F Davidson, "Inventory of 17th Century Tombstones in Angus"" has details of inscriptions 47b & 58 at pp 53-55

Duncan Fraser, "Land of the Ogilvys" (1964) p 82 notes that the 1st & 2nd lords Ogilvy were buried in the aisle of the kirk of Kinnell with their ancestors including sir Walter d 1440 & his son d 1489

Testaments - the following is a selection from the Index of the Commissariot of St Andrews:
Alex Daw in Haltoune-Kinnell & his spouse Agnes Paton, 1605 & 1606
Patk Henry wobster in Garlait, 1592
Alex Johnstone in Wester Brakie, 1617
Isobel Marshall spouse to David Fyfe in Muirsyde-Ballischun, 1606
Christian Vallance spouse to And Bowak in Muirsyd of Loschoun, 1605

20a KINNELL

Rosehill Cemetery, Montrose, inscription no. 60 is: And Gardyne 9.10.1846 84, w Margt Brown 1808 40 whose remains lie at Kinnell, by s Jas shipowner Arbroath.

Geo. Lowson, Transactions of the Stirling Natural History Society, 1920-1, has notes on inscription no. 23

OPR with the Registrar General - 296 Kinnell:
Births 1657-1723, 1725-1854
Marriages 1657-1759, 1761-65, 1770-1854
Deaths 1657-63, 1814-54

Church Records in the SRO: CH2/574 minutes 1657-1720, 1725-1880
proclamations 1855-65
miscellaneous
HR 575 after 1924
GD 45/13 church matters 1766

Fasti v 441: ministers from 1543

Small i 606: Kinnell Antiburgher, 1747

Ewing ii 169: Friockheim FC ministers from 1843

Index

Addison	51
Aitken	49
Alexander	7
Anderson	27
Baillie	59
Begg	54
Bell	53
Blyth	14
Bouden	6.18
Bowak	Notes
Brown	1-2.7-9.15.54.Notes
Bruce	4
Buchanan	53
Cairncross	41-2
Campbell	37
Clark	57
Cobban	10
Colace	58
Colville	29-30
Crichton	60
Cuthbert	14
D.	40
Dall	39
Dargie	57
Daw	Notes
Donaldson	20.52-3
Dorward	23
Duncan	2.4.26
Eslo	1
Esplin/en	5.44
F.	47a.51
Fairweather	8.32-3
Falconer	5
Ferrier	20.31.41.60
Forbes	4.21
Fraser	47a
Fyfe	Notes
Gardyne	Notes
Gavin	59
Gothill	48
Gowans	38.41
Gray	13
Grige	62
Grubb	21
Hall	61
Harris	11-3.15.48
Henry	Notes
Hill	50
Hood	59
Hutchen	51.55
Ireland	38.41
Jamieson	9.52.56.59
Johnstone	Notes
Laing	41
Low	29.35
Lowson	30
Lyon	59
M.	40
Mackay	13
Makie	61
Mal(l)- -	45
Man	37
Marechan/Mareham	39
Marshall	Notes

20a K I N N E L L

Methven	8	Skair	24-7
Mill	46	Skirling	28
Milne	1.42-3	Smith	19.64
Molleson	28.39	Spence	49
Nicoll	57	Stiven	30
Ogilvie/y	59.Notes	Strachan	10.15.23
Ouchterlonie	47	Thomson	47b.58
Paton	Notes	Tosh	36
Patterson	48	Urquhart	3.63
Petrie	36	Vallance	Notes
Raitt	34-5	W.	47a
Rennie	11.18	Walker	8
Ritchie	59.62	Webster	39
Roger	55	White	6.19
Ross	12	Whyte	16-7
Rough	49	Wilson	44
Rowe	53	Wright	17.42
Ruehie	1	Wylie	31
S.	40	Young	36
Scot(t)	16.23.25.30.32-3.50.56		
Scrymgeour	11		
Scrymsour	44		
Simson	41		

20b K I N N E L L , F R I O C K H E I M

Friockheim is now a quoad sacra parish. The town was founded in 1824 at the junction of Kinnell, Guthrie and Inverkeilor parishes on the site of Friock Feus. The well-kept cemetery was opened about 1858.
National Grid reference: NO 598 496

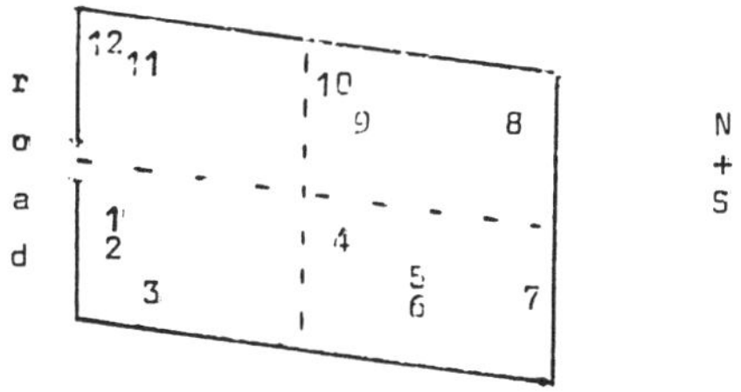

1 Alex Donaldson forrester estate of Middleton for 34y d 25.10.1855 67 int Guthrie, w Ann Ritchie 4.2.1859 70, da Agnes 1.3.1850 20; Jas Fyfe & Elis Donaldson, chn Mary Ann 28.12.1840 20m, Jas 16.3.1849 20m

2 Jas Fyfe 30.1.1896 84, w Eliz Donaldson 2.4.1874 56, da Eliz 31.7.1896 49, s Geo (w Ann Petrie, da Annie 24.1.1871 5w, s Jas 6.1.1873 14m int Port Glasgow)

3 Robt Mackay 28.12.1852 64, w Mary Gordon 25.1.1887 84, da Jessie 28.2.1860 20, by gs Robt Mackay

20b KINNELL, FRIOCKHEIM

4 David Mann 24.1.1874, w Eliz Mather 2.1878 76, da Amelia 16.7.1849 6 int Carmyllie, gs David Stephen 9.7.1864 3y9m

5 Robt Leisk 27.9.1893 70, w Eliz Dempster 28.12.1886 65, s Alex Edward seaman d Demerara West Indies of yellow fever 8.5.1867 23, da Eliz d Friockheim 19.3.1868 5y6m, gda Ruby Wallace 12.5.1896 5w

6 David Dundas 27.3.1865 60, w Magdalen Strachan 2.3.1864 57, da Mary d Inverkeilor 3.5.1836 6w, da Jessie 22.12.1846 5y5m, s Geo 24.2.1849 16.1.1876

7 Alex Garrie 4.6.1847 32 int Guthrie, w Margt Anderson 13.6.1874 58

8 ob John Fairweather d Friockheim 27.3.1903 83, w Cath Falconer 21.10.1850 30; J Fairweather, 2w Ann Ferrier 27.11.1887 55, da Jane 14.3.1864 1y2m

9 Wm Fyfe 22.11.1882 75, s Jane Young 30.12.1885 84, da Helen 21.2.1841 6m, da Susan 14.9.1844 6, s Wm 1.7.1851 **1y7m** int Kinnell, Jessie 29.9.1869 32 (h Jas Mill, her two chn Wm & Jane d inf int Sighthill Glasgow), (see bel

10 ob John Young 64y fr Pitmuies Mill 18.11.1872 92, w Margt Nicoll 24.6.1854 61 int Carmyllie, da Grace 14.12.1887, da Mary d Alehousehill 25.9.1891; Hector Young fr Pitmuies Mill d Alehousehill 23.2.1889, da Emma 30.12.1914

11 ob John Edward 21.2.1847 59 int Arbroath, w Jean Edward 2.12.1863 69 int here, by s Jas Hill mert Friockheim 12.8.1877 63 (w Helen Runcie 23.7.1865 50, s Wm 21.2.1843 12m, da Jane 2.8.1851 7m int Kinnell, da Mary 7.5.1859 8m int here, da Eliz 20.1.1869 25, da Christine 22.1.1874 19, s John d Scone 29.6.1916 75)

12 ob 1871. David Ritchie 15.2.1819 9.12.1856, w Mary Rew b 25.11.1819 d 19.5.1849 int Kinnell, by s Jas mason Broughty Ferry; Barbara Ritchie, h Jas Mason bootmaker Friockheim, s Colin 9.4.1855 9.10.1857, da Ann 16.10.1858 2.3.1861, da Jean 9.10.1861 1.12.1862, s Jas 29.6.1863 8.3.1873; Barbara Mason 22.11.1868 28.1.1878; Ann Petrie 26.5.1783 17.4.1879

9 continued. , s David d New York after two hours illness 19.8.1872 31 int New York Bay cemetery

Index

Anderson 7
Dempster 5
Donaldson 1-2
Dundas 6
Edward 5.11
Fairweather 8
Falconer 8
Ferrier 8
Fyfe 1-2.9
Garrie 7
Gordon 3
Hill 11
Leisk 5
Mackay 3
Mann 4
Mason 12
Mather 4
Mill 9
Nicoll 10
Petrie 2.12
Rew 12
Ritchie 1.12
Runcie 11
Stephen 4
Strachan 6
Wallace 5
Young 9-10

21 KINNETTLES

This church was among those dedicated by Bishop de Bernham in 1241 The burial ground is well-kept, though many old flat stones have been tipped up against the east dyke (nos. 28,29,31,33,36,37,40,41,43,44)
National Grid reference: NO 422 465

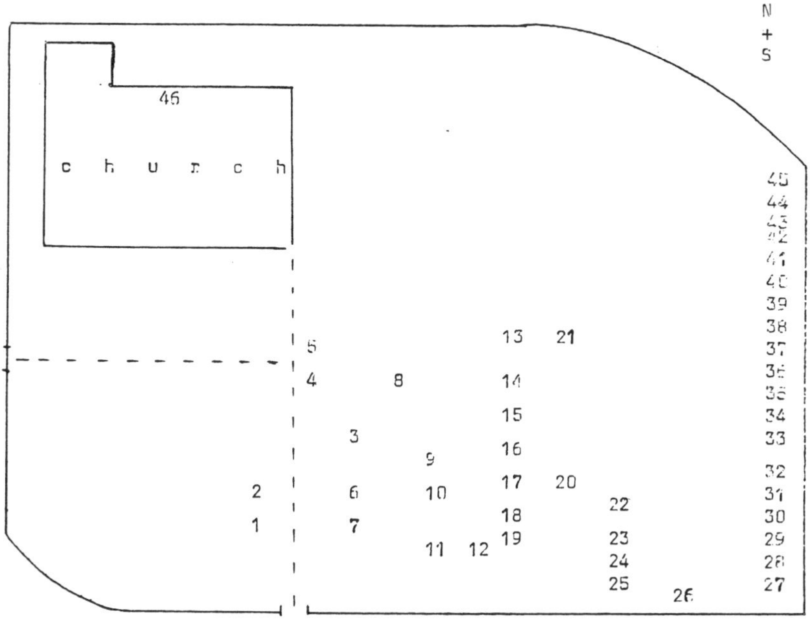

1 railed enclosure. by Jas, And, Wm, Barbara & Margt Melvin, mo Margt Kinnear 23.2.1838 62, bro John mert Forfar 3.6.1838 30, above Wm 24.5.1846 35 (s Jas 27.1.1847 5m, s And d Dawlish Devonshire 21.12.1867 29 int there); (west side) fa And Melvin mert Glasgow d 2.1813 37 int there (1da Barbara d Forfar 22.4.1879 75 int here); above Wm, wid Eliz Johnston 11.11.1887 76; above And, yt da Margt d Forfar 18.7.1900 89 int here

2 next 1. cherub; tree with three grafted branches, crossed rake & spade, saw, pruning knife; emblems; (west side) by Jas Proctor, fa John gardener 28.2.1743 56

3 ob 1819. by Jas Easson mason, w Jean Thom 6.6.1816 20

4 1867. by surviving family, fa Robt Stewart 13.9.1865 late tent Kinnettles Mill, mo Mary Ogilvie 16.5.1864, bro Wm 13.8.1865, bros David, Jas & John & sis Elis inf

5 1840. by Jas Rae fr North Mains of Kinnettles,to friends; (east side) the erector of this stone an elder of this parish d 19.4.1876 79

6 1838. by Daniel Robertson schoolmaster here 29.7.1863, w Mary Augusta Duke 13.6.1837 45, s Joseph inf, da Ann 19.12.1863 9, 2w Eliz Sime 8.3.1872 54

7 next 6. Geo Robertson 26.2.1956 78, w Esther Findlay 29.8.1931 53, 2w Alexina Joiner 30.3.1955 67

8 FS Eliz Eleanor Wiggen Harvey b 7.11.1807 d Chittagong Bengal 21.2.1832 int here, by adoring husband John Inglis Harvey esq of Kinnettles accountant general Bengal establishment EICS 3.11.1804 17.2.1869

9 ob Jas Lindsay 5.1821 82, w Eliz Gibson 1821 68, da Anne 3.1797 19, da Eliz 1.1819 37, Jean 12.5.1861 74, s David fr Ingliston d there 4.9.1869 75, by David Lindsay's trustees in terms of his settlement

10 by Alex Lindsay tent Inglistoun, s Alex 21.2.1761 25; (west side) A L, 1761; shield with loom, shuttle, stretcher, share & coulter (Ed. for fr and weaver); emblems; two cherubs

11 casket. 1851. Thos Dick fr Easter Meathie 23.11.1850 55, w Isabella Lindsay d Sydney Place Laurelbank Dundee 19.11.1872 78

12 1869. John Duff 8.1835 49, w Agnes Wighton 6.1851 73, by da Margt

13 1892. Alex Morton 18,5.1887 80, s Alex 12.1848 1y, da Jane 30.10.1874 31, w Jane Martin 13.1.1903 95

14 ob Jas Arnot esq of Drumshade 22.9.1863 80, w Margt Doig 3.1824, da Cath 9.1826,2w Eliz Smith 7.1860, by his thirtyseven nieces & nephews

15 ob Jas Arnott sometime tent Ingliston 2.12.1831 79, by w Helen Kerr 2.7. 18(45)(Jervise, SAS library ms 530, has 1848) 93y, gda Helen d Carnoustie 12.12.1891 88 (1da of John Arnot of Ingliston & w of Sylvester Kerr)

16 ob John Arnot esq of Pitreuchie & fr Ingliston 31.8.1866 71, da Mary Ann 3.2.1843 5, s John 22.2.1843 3, w Margt Bell 7.10.1903 94

17 Thos Guthrie fr Ewnie Glamis 10.9.1859 62, w Isobel Fairweather 13.3.1849 chn Anne b (sic) 26.5.1838, Wm d 1844 7, Anne Fairweather 8.3.1849 14.3. 1849, Agnes Barclay 24.3.1870 35 int Nellfield cem Abdrdeen, Thos 20.6. 1892 61 int Southdown cem Liverpool, John d Edinburgh 11.4.1910 68; Isabella Guthrie or Nicol d Forfar 10.3.1917 73; Eliz Barry Clark 14.9. 1847 7.5.1931

18 next 17. 1781. by Jean Cathro in Scrogarfield imo h John Guthrie 18.3.1773 65, seven chn Helen, Thos, David, Wm, Jean, Anne & John; Wm d 7.6.1772 before his fa; John 24.3.1780 19; (west side) cherub; square & compasses, saw, axe & mallet (see Alan Reid, "Royal Burgh of Forfar" p 146: a lawsuit followed the removal of this stone by the schoolmaster of Kinnettles to be a hearth stone.)

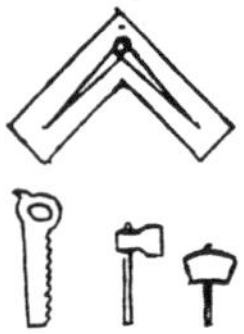

19 1832. by Wm & Jas Ramsay, mo Jean Anderson 1.3.1832 63

20 Robt Guthrie 15.7.1850 79, w Martha Fleming 8.7.1845 65, da Eliz 15.9. 1884 60, Cath 5.5.1887 72, da Easter 29.1.1893 76, s Jas 22.7.1894 74, s Peter in Foffarty 20.8.1894 82

21 rev Robt Lunan d here 9.4.1850 71 in 43rd y of ministry, 1w Isabella Smith b 178(3) md 1808 d 1841 having issue b in the following order, Helen, Margt, Robt, Eliz & Wm, 2w Eliz Bell d Newtyle 10.4.1880 75; above Helen 18.4.1842 33; eulogies (see Fasti v 295)

22 John Robbie d Dalnaclar 12.12.1917 93, w Jane Nicol d Foffarty 26.3.1888 57 (sis Ann Nicol d Foffarty 27.12.1888 58)

23 next 22. Robt Nicoll in Foffarty, w Elspet Doig 13.7.1861 64

24 next 23. by Jas Smith, w Isobel Doig 10.1.1819 28

25 next 24. Jas Smith d Eassie 9.8.1867 79, w Jean Anderson 6.9.1871 88

26 Thos Soutar late joiner Gateside Kincaldrum 5.1.1912 86, fa, mo, two bros

int here

27 David Brown sometime lived in the Fruchment of Kinnettles 6.3.1731 75, by w Christian Boutchard; D B, C B, 1731

28 FS David Brown indweller in the Mi(l)toun of Kincaldrum 30.3.1729 61, leaving w (Griz) Ro- - - & six das Christ, Barb, Mary, Eliz, Isob & Griz; cherubs; shield; & Jo, Mary, Jas, (Alex) and - - - d before him; shield with (D B)

29 FS Jas Watt in Brigtown to w Margrat Garland 35y; J W, M G; emblems

30 broken. rev Dd Ferney min here, s Wm Douglas 11.1794 18; eulogy (see Fasti v 295 for rev David Ferney 1738 20.4.1806)

31 FS John Skirling in Inglistoune, w Margret Lyon 19.6.1657 26; emblems

32 1769. by John Lawson weaver Ground of Kincaldrum, w Helen Walker 11.5.1769 33, two ss b the preceding day survived about one hour, da Helen 30.12.1767 1y, left behind her two ss Jas & John; (other side) loom & shuttle; J L; emblems; J, J & H Lawson

33 FS And Robrt in Knoppy Knows 22.4.1703 54, w Margt Reid; A R, M R, K B, A R, D R

34 1826. Jas Ramsay 8.5.1825 60, by wid Eliz Reid, s Wm 13.2.1826 15

35 1812. by John Mackay, chn Douglas 6.8.1804 14m, Euphemia 20.9.1807 6w

36 FS (marginal) Jas Lyon in Inglistoun of Brigtown, w Isabel Talbert 6.1.1660 56; (central) shield with lion rampant for Lyon; 1741

37 FS (marginal in latin) Christian Lon- - - - - Marg, Jo, Agn; two cherubs; shield; Rob, Will, Eliz Skirling

38 1738. by Androw & Patk Stirling, to bro David late tent Pool Falds 4.4.1737 61 (Ed. perhaps originally cut as Skirling then recut as Stirling); (other side) oxenyoke, share & coulter; D S, A G

39 1818. by Mary Davidson, sis Maudlin 12.2.1814 61

40 FS (marginal) - - - - honest man called Thom- - - - - in Kinka(drum)- - - - - (see F Davidson, "Inventory" p 56, has the place as Kineatle)

41 TS slab. (marginal) Georg Horn hamberman 1643 34, w Margrat Young 20.8.1661 57; (central) G H, M Y, M H, B H; crown & hammer; emblems

42 1779; cherub; weaver's tools; by Alex Laird & w Christian Robson, John Laird 1751 12; Wm Laird in Muir of Forfar & w Christian Ormond, chn Jas & John d inf; W L ♡ C O , 1779

43 FS (marginal) Alex Mil at the Mill, late Issobel Gwild 8.10.1626 42; (central) David Dick in Blackhill, w Eliz Mil int here 2.3.1763 68; shields & emblems; D D, E M; I B, 1764, H M

44 FS (marginal) - -er Carnagie sometimes spous to David Fovler of Litilmil who departed the 29th of Avgvst 1657

45 FS Margrat Riche spous to Iohne (Bowie) (smith Knowe) Wright(on) who departit - - - - s - - - B (Ed. 17th century)

46 mural. 1810. col Wm Paterson FRS member Asiatic Society & Linnean Society, lieut col 102nd regt for many yrs, lieut governor New South Wales served 30y in army 25 of which in East India & in New South Wales, twice

circumnavigated the globe, travelled from Cape of Good Hope into the interior of Africa etc etc, b this parish 10.8.1755 d 21.6.1810 on voyage home from New South Wales, by wid (see DNB which does not mention place of birth or parentage, md about 1789, arrived NSW with wife in 1791, FRS 1798; see Jervise SAS library ms 530 p 840 notes he was son of a gardener at Bridgton, was educated & patronised by lady Mary Lyon of Glamis; in 1975 the occupant of Kinnettles house said there was a memorial in the grounds to an indian woman who died there, supposed wife of colonel Paterson, but with no inscription.)

N o t e s

A.Jervise, ms 530 in the Library of the Society of Antiquaries, Scotland has notes on inscriptions 2,8,10,14-6,21,30-1,33,36,41,43-4,46 and also on Robt Douglas who bought Bridgton from Chas Lyon in 1743.

F Davidson, "Inventory of 17th Century Tombstones in Angus",pp 55-7 has details of inscriptions 29,31,33,36,40-1,43-4

Testaments: the following are selected from the Index to the Commissariot of Edinburgh - Isobel Arbuthnott spous to Alex Strachan of Brigtoun, 1587-8
Janet Butchart spouse to John Forrest in Inglistoun, 1577
Jas Butchart in Inglistoun, spouse Janet Furde, 1577-8

and the following are in the Index of the Commissariot of St Andrews -
Janet Henderson spouse to David Skirling in Kirkton, 1619
Geo Kid cotter Innerritchie, spouse Eupham Milne, 1617 & 1624
Elspeth Kyd spouse to Jas Lyon in Kinnetles, 1686
Geo Lindsay in Invereighty, 1725
Patk Rae in Inglestoun of Kinnettles, 1728 etc. etc

OPR with the Registrar General - 297 Kinnettles
Births 1696-1715, 1717-1854
Marriages 1709-43, 1753-92, 1804-54
Deaths 1718-1805, 1820-54

Church Records in SRO: CH2/221 minutes 1710-35 (with gaps), 1807-25 & -1846, also 1736-60, 1774-5
loose financial documents 1782-1806

Fasti v 294 ministers from 1596

Ewing ii 156 FC minister 1845-95: revT J Petteson

I n d e x

Anderson	19.25	Clark	17
Arbuthnott	Notes	Davidson	39
Arnot(t)	14-6	Dick	11.43
B.	33	Doig	14.23-4
Barclay	17	Douglas	30.Notes
Bell	16.21	Duff	12
Boutchard	27.Notes	Duke	6
Bowie	45	Easson	3
Brown	27-8	Fairweather	17
Butchart	27.Notes	Ferney	30
Carnagie	44	Findlay	7
Cathro	18	Fleming	20

21 K I N N E T T L E S

Forrest	Notes	Nicol(l)	17.22-3
Fowler	44	Ogilvie	4
Furde	Notes	Ormond	42
G.	38	Paterson	46
Garland	29	Proctor	2
Gibson	9	Rae	5.Notes
Guild	43	Ramsay	19.34
Guthrie	17-8.20	Reid	33-4
Harvey	8	Riche	45
Henderson	Notes	Ro- -	28
Horn	41	Robbie	22
Johnston	1	Robertson	6-7
Joiner	7	Robrt	33
Kerr	15	Robson	42
Kinnear	1	Sime	6
Kid,Kyd	Notes	Skirling	31.37-8.Notes
Laird	42	Smith	14.21.24-5
Lawson	32	Soutar	26
Lindsay	9-11.Notes	Stewart	4
Lon- -	37	Stirling	38
Lunan	21	Strachan	Notes
Lyon	31.36.Notes	Talbert	36
Mackay	35	Thom	3
Martin	13	Walker	32
Melvin	1	Watt	29
Mil	43	Wiggen	8
Milne	Notes	Wighton	12
Morton	13	Young	41

22 K I R K D E N

The medieval parish church of Idvie was dedicated in 1243 on a site in the den of the Vinny, possibly in a field now called Kirk-shed in the lands of Gask whence it may have been moved to its present position in the early 18th century. The church was completely re-built in 1825 and is now roofless. The burial ground is well-kept, but the congregation has moved to a newer church in Letham.
National Grid reference: NO 532 486

1 TS - - - - - - - - - spous to (Andre)w Alexander (Tenant) in Gairn who d (23.7.)1722 29y & her son (David) - - - - - - - - - -

	A A	♡	A H	
I S	I A		R A	
	E A		I A	

coulter

2 TS R A, I S, 1739 (Ed. a very worn & flaked stone, probably that noted by Jervise, "Epitaphs" i 34 as: Here lyis the dust of Robt Alexander sometime tent in Parconon, late h to Isobel Scot betwixt whom were procreate six chn viz. Wm, Jean, Isobel, Robt, John & Thos. He d 19.6.1738 43; poem (quoted in full by Jervise) "..An old clay chimney that downfell Kill'd both his servant and himsell.."

22 K I R K D E N

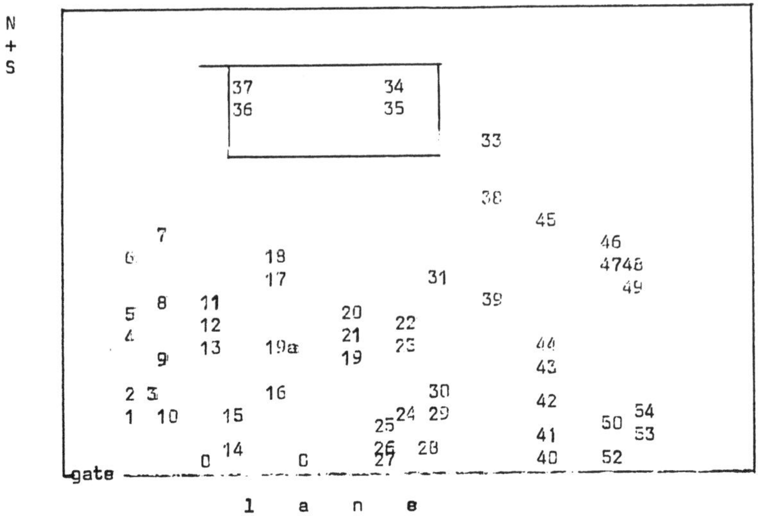

3 1755. John Broun sometime - - - of Pressock 2.(6.)1755 61, 1w Elspeth Hodge (12).6.1721 (33), 2w Margt Thomson -.-.1740 47 - - - - - (ed. under turf)

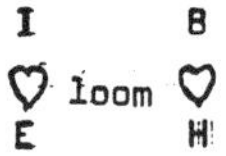

4 FS tipped. Heir lyis Robt Dvthie sometyme in Balmadie 12.1667 47, w Evphane Gvdlet; 1668; hourglass, skull & crossed bones; "I rest in hope/ and shal Aryse/ To reigne with Christ/ above the Skyes."

5 FS David Austin sometime weaver Moss-side of Towk 1723 63, his chn were David, Isobell, Francis who are - - - -, John, (Wm), Jannet, - - , Eliz

6 1824. Geo Farquhar fr Letham 16.3.1811 58, w Isabella Mann 20.8.1821 67, by chn Geo, Alex, And, Wm, Helen & Elspet, chn Eliz, Margt & Wm, Ann & Betty int here

7 1824. by David Thomson & w Betty Coullie resident at Letham, s Geo 26.4. 1822 6m

8 Alex Webster fr Dumis-Holes, w Jean Ramsay 5.9.1828 34, she had born nine chn of whom six survive this date, Eliz, Jas, Matilda, Alex & Sarah

9 1835. Wm Watson & w Agnes Lumgair indwellers Ballmuir of Gardyne, s Wm 4.6.1834 10

10 R A, M B, K B; Alex Brouster sometime indweller in Grounds of Idvie 2.3. 1755 71, w Margret Reid 3.1736 aged - - - - (ed. under turf)

11 1780. John Ritchie who lived sometime in the Cotton of - - side d (9).11. 1757 42, w (Jeane) Adam 29.(5).1768 50, chn John & Kath, Jas & Robt, by da Jeane

12 David Philp - - - - setteth this stone up here - - - De(clare) that this Spot is the burying place that doth belong - - - - - - - - - - -; scales & merchants mark; D P, H D; T P, I G, 1741; (west side, inscription divided vertically) Here lys the dust of Thomeis Palmor sometime in ground of (Gask) who d 20.3.1734 48, w Isobel

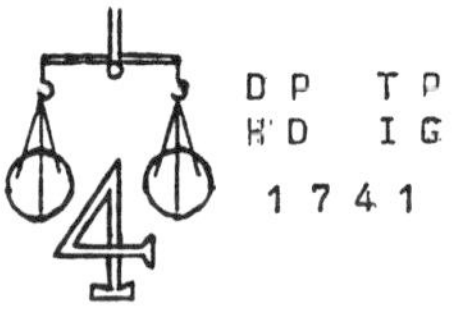

G(ray)- - - -, chn - - - - - - - - - - - - - - 1736 52y; Here lys the dust of (Jannet Dorward) who was spous to David Philp sometime in ground of Gard(ee) who brought forth three chn viz. David, (Eliz & John) - - 18.3.17(11) 27y

13 John Middleton late smith at Ballmuir 1.1818 63, w Ann Ormond 9.1.1818 61, two chn Alex & Ann d inf; (east side) I M 1819 A O; they procreat betwixt them Jane, David, John, Jas & Elesabeth who survive 1819 & erected this stone

14 1849. Wm Cameron 22.3.1833 71, w Elspeth Wilson 28.11.1847 64, by s Jas fr Bracktullo, s John 29.6.1829 11, four ss int elsewhere

15 1851. by Wm Patterson, w Margt Cowie 25.8.1851 24, s Jas inf

16 by Jas Petrie taylor in Moore of Gairn, Hellen D(uncan) 9.6.1782 62, eight chn Isobel, And, Jas, Alex,Wm, David, Barbara & John who all survive

17 David Robb fewer at Bourie Cauld 31.1.1852 68, w Mary Ritchie 24.6.1867 75, da Mary 30.6.1869 44 (only daughter)

18 by Alex Gray in Cott(ertoun) of (Middeltoun) imo w Giles Brown d 26.3. 1764 58, also s John 6.1747 15; (west side) I G, M G, H G, T G, A G, I G, 1771; Alex Gray; Giles Brown

19 TS Robt Scott tent Chappelton of Balmadies 30.12.1780 74, by wid Eliz Brown in 1781, chn Eliza, Mary, Mary, Ann, Robt, Marjory & Kath, Isabel, Jas, Wm, Jean, Geo / Marjory & Geo d nonage & rest survive this date

19a FS under turf. John Da(le) sometime in Gairn 24.4.1667 6(3), w Agnes S- - - brok 11.1668 50; I D A S (see Jervise, "Epitaphs.." i 34 simply notes "another slab with the name Agnes Dall is dated 1668")

20 David Salmond, Gurden Mill 11.1782 1.1865, da Anne drowned by accident in the Vinney at the Corn Mill Bridge while going to school 23.1.1831 7y, by s John

21 Wm Salmond contractor Letham 11.5.1859 63, w Eliz Mathew 7.4.1877 78, chn John & Margt d inf, s Geo 20.3.1866 35

22 David Colv(ill) sometime tent West B(all)gate, w Isobel Scott 31.12. 1748 34; (west side) I C, W C, D C, P C, - C, - C

23 by John Robertson tent in Knockhells of Middltoun & w Isobel Colvill in 1774 imo chn viz. Isobel 28.5.1768 21, John 23.6.1773 19, Chas survives; (west side) said Chas Roberts, s Alex fr Corston Dunnichen 14. 12.1863 80 (w Ann Pritchard 21.2.1859 75, gs Alex Roberts town clerk of Dumbarton renovated this stone)

24 TS 1773. David Scott sometime tent Milden 19.9.1772 57, w Kath Brown 9. 12.1809 93, three ss & seven das d inf, John, Ann, Mary, Eliz, Margt, Mary, Isab, Da, Ge, Elis; Margt Scott 16.2.1812 63

25 Frank Malcolm d Maryfield Letham 29.11.1951 70

26 Alex Malcolm 17.1.1845 68, by w Cath Milln 19.1.1847 63, gs Wm Malcom 9.3.1846 3

27 David Smith 25.10.1942 76, w Janet Malcolm d Maybank Letham 12.7.1935 76

28 (Donald) - - - - - Green - - A- - - imo w Elizabeth 20.(6).1766 58

29 John Anderson - - - - - - - - - 1780 64, by w Margt Ritchie, loving chn - - - , - - - , Jean, John, Robt, David, Geo all alive; (west side) J A, M R, merchant's scales

30 David Dorward feuar Drummietermont, w Jane Cant, chn John 28.2.1870 40, David 28.8.1843 9, Bella 8.9.1843 6, gs Jas Dorward 5.9.1873 22

31 1795. by Thos Herald tent in Bra(ctila) & w Jean Young imo his fa John late tent Bra(ctila) 10.11.1774 65, da Jean 29.11.1790 2y2m, Mary, Ann, John, And, Isbeal, Wm, Janet, Jean surviving; (west side) Thos Herald brewer Forfar 20.3.1849 53, w Agnes Nicol 3.12.1851 49; Jean 5.1792 2; Jane 4.1855 61; Mary 11.1848 68; Andrew 9.1858 73; Janet 8.1865 73

32 Jas Barrie 26.2.1844 73, da Jean 1.5.1865 62 (by h Wm Fairweather fr Gask, s Wm 24.8.1836 inf, da Betsy 24.4.1844 13, da Jane mrs Hood 17.5.1864 24)

33 1815. by John Smith blacksmith in Milldens imo w Isable Mollison 10.12.1805 51, deceased chn Isable 24.11.1792, Eliz 4.9.179(4), (Jannet) - - - -, Jas - - 1799 (17)y, John 12.10.1809 19; (west side) Hellen Smith 7.8.1843 68, s John Coulie; Robt Smith blacksmith Douglastown 21.5.1850 76

34 Alex Lyell esq of Gardyne 11.1852 68, w Eliz Gibb 1795 1861, chn Thos 11.1821 6m, Chas 6.1825 6, And 8.1842 11, Jane 12.1842 13, dr Robt who unfortunately lost his life on the night of 3.7.1857 31 while quelling the insurrection at Patna during the rebellion in India

35 Thos Lyell 2nd of Gardyne 1705 1800, w Marjory Renny of Usan 1705 1788; Alex Lyell 1st of Gardyne 1745 1789 (see St Andrews Testaments), 1w Jean Renny of Seatown 1745 1767, 2w Eliz Renny of Montrose 1752 1812.
Alex Lyell 3rd of Gardyne 4.8.1819 11.2.1887, da Helen 30.10.1868 5.11.1868, s Thos 1857 1863, da Margt 5.11.1870 18.7.1874, da Marjory 22.2.1863 21.7.1874

36 Alex Lyell 5th of Gardyne 23.9.1882 27.12.1958, w Isobel Joan Yeaman 16.7.1881 24.4.1955

37 Alex Lyell 6th of Gardyne 13.5.1915 8.2.1963

38 1826. Alex Tod in Dykehead of Bur- - - imo w Ann Young 4.1.1826 44, chn Mary, Ann & Jas all d inf

39 Jas Nicol fr Kirkton of Inverkeilor, w Ann Paterson 17.5.1854 55, s Wm 3.1.1835 6, s Thos 1.1.1869 31; above Jas Nicol 19.11.1879 86

40 by - - Carrie, w Isobel Wat 1712, his fa Robt Carrie 1739, his gfa John Carrie 6.1720; (west side) J C, K H; A C, I C, M C, C C

41 Robt Kerrie 31.5.1760 28, by w Christian Ferrier, two chn Robt & Ann survive 1769; (west side) John Kerrie d 79y, s Robt 15.4.1739 54 (ss John & Jas alive in 1769)

42 W L 1771 I L; I L, W L, I L, D L, J L, K L, I L; Wm Longlands sometime in Dru(m)head 1.1729, w Agnes Arnet 20.2.1762 77, by chn Wm & Kathrine; (west side) 1771. Wm Longlands, w Jean Longlands, s John 25.10.1761 24 hours, da Jean 5.1767 10m, da Katharine 1.3.1769 19m

43 Jas Findlay, w Eliz Ritchie 12.1829 (34), chn Helen & Eliz d inf

44 1850. David Ritchie fr Cairnconan 31.5.1827 37, w Christina Sim 5.5.1850 53, by chn David, Alex, Robt, Wm & Jas; David Ritchie fr Cairnconan 23.7.1861 60, w Ann Ferrier 15.2.1882 79; Alex d St Vigeans 26.7.1872 70, w Eliz Welsh d St Vigeans 2.12.1875 70

45 1845. Jas Lowson, w Mary Paterson 28.6.1842 23, s Jas 26.2.1843 8m; (west side) Jas Lowson 12.12.1846 79, w Margt Maxwell 8.2.1832 71, by s Jas flesher in Arbroath

46 Robt Taylor tent in Old Cottoune of Gairn 29.5.1745 71, w Margt Petrie

2(4).12.1744 71, by ss Robt tent in Backboath & David tent in Oldcot-toune of Gairn; R T, M P, 1753; W T,(R)T, D T, I T, - T, M T, E T

47 Robt Taylor sometime fr Backboath 2.1772 65, by w Margt Fife, had six chn Wm, Margt, Robt, John, Jean, Barbara /alive at the date is Wm, John & Barbara; "Deus dedit, Deus abstulit; Benedictum sit nomen Dei."

48 FS Wm Taylor tent Hillhead of Ascurey 9.5.1800 67, by wid Jannet Ireland & her chn, da Barbara 19.11.1788 18

49 FS John Taylor fr Backboath 24.3.1807 65, w Kath Taylor 10.2.1813 61, da Janet 21.2.1821 (h David Logan civil engineer erected this stone in 1821); Patk Logan architect 1.8.1815 63

50 Alex Robertson tent Netherwood of Dumbarrow 6.5.1830 75, da Mary 1.1831 18, s John 25.2.1831 26, by ss Wm, John & Jas

51 rev Jas Mor ord min on 30.4.1735 d 28.1.1753; (west side) rev mr Jas Moir min Kirkden, w Margt Walker, da Kath 1.1754 9 (see Fasti v 444)

52 rev David Carruthers min here 21.11.1846 61, by niece Margt Carruthers in grateful remembrance (see Fasti v 445)

53 John Carrie tent Knockhill 16.2.1795 72, w Helen Carr 8.8.1794 51, by s John tent Knockhill, s Wm 12.5.1772 13m, da Eliz 28.6.1799 26, chn surviving Ann, John, Jas, Alex, David, Isaac, Boseph, Robt, Isabella, Agnes & Henry; John Carrie tent Knockhill 1847, bros Henry, Alex, Joseph, Isaac & Robt, siss Ann & Agnes all int here, also several nephews and nieces

54 John Carrie, Carnoustie, da Isabella Agatha 19.2.1898, da Janet Caroline Margt 12.3.1913, da Eliza Gordon 27.7.1924, da Mary Jane 18.12.1950; John Carrie 18.2.1819 10.12.1893

55 by Robt Philip, w Agnes Morton 4.8.1852 26 (her fa Wm Morton 24.3.1839 54, her mo Mary Ritchie 1.9.1830 42

56 Jas Wishart blacksmith Letham 12.1871 79, w Jean Mitchell 9.1850 61, s Geo 9.1840 12

57 FS rev Wm Milligan min Kirkden 15.11.1823 89, by Wm, Jas, Elizabeth & Mary Cowie & Eliz & Grizel Knox (see Fasti v 445: b at Balmaghie)

58 mural tablet, in latin. John Baxter of Idvie, Thos Gardyne of Middleton, Alex Lyell of Gardyne, Jas Mudie of Pitmuies & John Watt of Kinneries proprietors of lands in this parish caused this church to be rebuilt in 1825, the rev David Carruthers being minister & D Paterson & J Carrie, elders. And Spence architect. Don.Mackay. Jas Milne & Geo Fyfe artificers

The following inscriptions nos 59-65 are from A Jervise, "Epitaphs" i 34-5 are were not seen in 1975:

59 in church. I G E A (arms of John Gardyne of Lawton md 1643 Eliz (da of sir John Arbuthnott of that ilk, had four ss & twenty das, int Inverkeilor)

60 next 19a. - - lliam Stevinsone h to Beatrix Stu - - - - Novr. & of age 59 - - -

61 by Jas Lesly imo w; "Ane Epteaf to spik thy praisee this svfes thov vas a vyef vertovs and vyes of children carfovl and to thy neghbovrs kynd. Ane honast voman and of a libral mynd."

62 Wm Mill, w Janet Greig; 1730; poem (quoted in full)

63 next 2. by Wm Scott blacksmith, w Isabella Clark, thirteen chn of whom seven are deceased; fire tongs, shovel, broom, rose & thistle

64 broken slab. John Hay in Easter Idvie, w Janet Roy 6.11.1716, six chn ss David & John, four das Margt, Issobel, Jannet & Agnes; I H, I R; Justice & Faith flanking a poem (quoted)

65 David Hay & Margt Morgan, 1s John 1744 16 (poem quoted), s David 1746 5 "of sons the last" (poem quoted)

N o t e s

A Jervise, "Epitaphs & Inscriptions" i 32-5 notes nos.2,4,34,47,51-2,,& 57-65 also some genealogical notes on the Lyells of Gardyne.

F Davidson, "Inventory of 17th Tombstones in Angus" p 57 describes stone no.4

Testaments - the following are a small selection from the Index to the Commissariot of St Andrews:
Archd Annan in Cottoun of Gardun, par of Idvie, 1682
David Both sometime in Cottoun of Gardin & Jonet Deuchars his spouse, par of Idvie, 1606; Robt Deuchars in Old Cotton of Garden par Kirkden, 1747
Jas Lyell of Gairdine, par Cardoan, 1715
John Morgan in Milton of Ascurrie, par Kirkden, 1730
David Scott in Kineres, par of Kirkden, 1728
Cath Strachan sp to Walter Berty cotterman in Cottertoun of Ascurrie, 1600
Helen Stuill spouse to John Lawdor in Braktullo, par Idvie, 1606
David Windram merchant at Idvie, 1737

OPR with the Registrar General - 298 Kirkden, of old Idvie

Births	1650-90, 1735-1854
Marriages	1650-90, 1735-1802, 1810-54
Deaths	1749-52, 1789

Church Records in the SRO: CH2/227

minutes & accounts	1735-1827
baptismal register	1855-94
marriage register	1856-63
accounts	1824-46

Fasti v 444-5 ministers from 16-

Ewing ii Letham was the site of the Dunnichen FC from 1843

National Register of Archives: 0056 Lyell of Gardyne papers
0022 Bruce-Gardyne papers

Small i 108 Letham secession ministers from 1797

I n d e x

A. 10
Adam 11
Alexander 1-2
Anderson 29
Annan Notes
Arbuthnott 59
Arnet 42
Austin 5

Barrie 32
Baxter 58
Berty Notes
Both Notes
Brouster 10
Brown 3.18-9.24
Bruce-Gardyne Notes

Cameron 14
Cant 30
Carr 53
Carrie 40.53-4.58.61
Carruthers 52.58
Clark 63
Colvill 22-3

22 KIRKDEN

Coul(l)ie 7.33
Cowie 15.57

D. 12
Dall 19a
Deuchars Notes
Dorward 12.30
Duncan 16
Duthie 4

Fairweather 32
Farquhar 6
Ferrier 41.44
Fife, Fyfe 47.58
Findlay 43

Gardyne 58-9.Notes
Gibb 34
Gray 12.18
Greig 62
Gudlet 4

H. 1.40
Hay 64-5
Herald 31
Hodge 3
Hood 32

Kerrie, see Carrie 41
Knox 57

Lawdor Notes
Lesly 61
Logan 49
Longlands 42
Lowson 45
Lumgair 9
Lyell 34-7.58.Notes

M. 57
Mackay 58
Malco(l)m 25-7
Mann 6
Mathew 21
Maxwell 45
Middleton 13
Mill 62
Milligan 57
Milln, Milne 26.58
Mitchell 56
Moir, Mor 51
Mollison 33
Morgan 65.Notes
Morton 55
Mudie 58

Nicol 31.39

Ormond 13

Palmor 12
Pat(t)erson 15.39.45.58
Petrie 16.46
Philip 55
Philp 12
Pritchard 23

Ramsay 8
Reid 10
Renny 35
Ritchie 11.17.29.43-4.55
Robb 17
Roberts 23.50
Robertson 23
Roy 64

S. 1
Salmond 20-1
Scott 2.19.22.24.63.Notes
Sim 44
Smith 27.33
Spence 58
Stevinsone 60
Strachan Notes
Stu- - 60
Stuill Notes
S- - brok 19a

Taylor 46-9
Thomson 3.7
Tod 38

Walker 51
Wat(t) 40.58
Watson 9
Webster 8
Welsh 44
Wilson 14
Windram Notes
Wishart 56

Yeaman 36
Young 31.38

23a KIRRIEMUIR PARISH CHURCH

The medieval church dedicated to the Virgin Mary on this site was replaced in 1787 by the present building. The burial ground was closed for interments in 1858 and many of the stones have been destroyed. Once named the Barony church. National Grid reference: NO 385 538

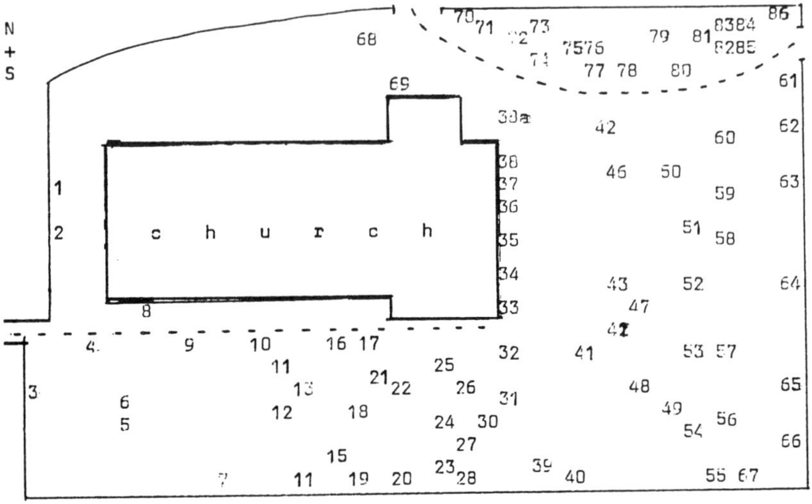

1 1846. Wm Osler tent Newmill 25.12.1849 83, w Jean Spence 28.1.1846 78, s Jas fr Kinnearis 6.4.1848 44

2 by Wm Young & w Margt Miller, da Margt d Kinnordy 17.10.1848 15; Helen Hunter Young d Canaan Park Edinburgh 24.2.1835 12d

3 1841. Thos Robb 27.7.1817 38, by w Ann Hodd, da Helen 27.2.1806 3, s Chas 3.12.1840 25

4 1849. John McNicoll late fr Ballnagara 1826 51, w Jean Douglas 1848 69, s Thos 1825 21, da Mary 1828 8, s Jas surgeon d abroad 1834 24, by surviving members of family; Jas McNicoll writer Edinburgh d Ballnagarrow 1838 49

5 Geo Webster - - - - - - - -, w (Agnes) G- - - - d 3.5.18(60)(51), (chn Wm - - - - - - - -)

6 next 5. by Geo Webster manuf Kirriemuir 21.6.1852 43; Jas Webster manuf here, w Isabella Louden 21.5.1853 33; Jas Lawson & Margt Webster, das Mary 1.11.1840 3, Jane Ann 21.7.1854 12, Mary 26.4.1855 14m

7 1827. Wm Stevens feuar & barber here 2.5.1842 59, w Agnes Glenday 1.4.1843 66, fa Chas Stevens 15.6.1819 70, mo Helen Low 26.12.1822 80, da Isabel 30.9.1812 4; Wm Low tent Cottershade 6.10.1836 87, w Cath Barclay 7.3.1826 81, chn Jas 15.3.1783 3, Cath d nonage both int Dundee

8 slab tipped up against wall. David Walker burgess 15.12.1655 64, w Agnes Smith; D W, A S, I W

9 FS (marginal) Alex Hutcheon maltman in Kirrimure, w Janet Cudbert 27.9.1655 60; monogram A H/I C; shovel & sheaf

10 1846. Jas Mitchell shoemaker here 3.10.1844 87, w Isabella Dundas 11.4.

1845 75, s John capt EICS latterly indigo planter Tirhoot d at sea in Bay of Bengal on his return to Europe 4.10.1843 48, s Alex formerly officer on ship Shawinshaw latterly indigo planter Tirhoot d at Rajai factory 22.4.1843 37, da Margt 1.1818 16, by s Geo in Tirhoot, da Isabella 6.12.1854 45, s Chas Dundas surgeon d Calcutta 27.4.1847 36, da Marjery 1.1813 16

11 1839. by Thos Baxter fr Muir-houses & w Margt Anderson, ss John 16.9.1835 10, Thos 26.9.1835 14m, da Margt 8.9.1841 17m

12 1834. by John Tyrie blacksmith Bogside, fa Jas 4.5.1822 72, sis Jean 6.1800 21; by Jas & John, mo Eliz Stormonth 19.3.1845 89

13 by Geo Lindsay quarrier, bro Jas mason 1819 29, two siss Agnes 1803 1y, & Margt 1807 20, fa Jas 2.1827 82, sis Isabel 7.1827 27; Jannet Lamb 8.8.1833 76, h Jas Lindsay; moon, square & compasses, sun

14 by David Stewart slater here, imo friends; 1856

15 (1759). - - - - - - - Jas & John - - - - to - -er Jas & Agnis - - - - ing their mo, their fa d 31.5.1756, their mo d 8.4.1735 50

16 by Alex baker in Kirriemuir & John baker in London imo fa John Adamson 2.1.1819 59, sis Jean d nonage, bro Wm 3.1799 3, mo Elis Bennet 12.11.1799 37, step mo Cecelia Scrimger 2.12.1820 64; Janet Adamson d London 1860 68; John Adamson, wid Margt Jones d London 1870 73; Margt Adamson d here 1883 84; (west side) Elis Smith 19.4.1821 35 (late w of Alex Adamson); Alex Adamson 19.2.1837 50; John Adamson baker at 20 Lime Street City of London 21.7.1844 54; Eliz Adamson 24.11.1850 63; Eliz Adamson d London 9.4.1851 38 (da of late Alex Adamson)

17 1853. by Jas Gibson fr Drumglay, mo Margt Wyllie 25.6.1805 37, sis Helen 28.1.1807 7, fa Alex 11.1.1838 76, uncle Jas Gibson 14.2.1847 77

18 FS under turf. (marginal) Wm Doig maltman in - - - 5.1686 46, w Helen Adamson - - - - - - 45y

19 1837. Chas Low late dyer & tanner here 21.11.1831 (51), w Isobel Smith 28.11.1813 - -, four das Janet, Emily, Agnes & Margt, by surviving family

20 Robt Myles life tent of Hillend & Redhall 27.8.1826 72, w Cath Ramsay 29.8.1838 72, ss Geo 1825 22, Jas 1826 33, Thos 1856 56, John 1859 65

21 - - - - - - - - - - - - (Smith) - - - -

22 Agnes Dickson or Robb 14.6.1844 36, David Robb July 18-6 49, their s Chas 1.1.1837 2; Wm Beharrie Robb d Cincinnati USA 18.4.1853 (2)1

23 Wm Cruikshank for 21y a private in 92nd regt & latterly out pensioner Chelsea Hospital 21.11.1850 71, chn Wm 4.11.1821 inf, Euphemia 16.8.1822 inf, John 29.10.1825 inf, Jas 15.12.1828 inf, by wid & rev Frederick only survivor of his chn, min of Navar & Lethnot (see Fasti v 400: Wm Cruikshank was a weaver & his w was Janet Muir)

24 - - - - - - -

25 coped FS. (marginal) Alex Wood shoomaker in Brokhols burges of Forfar 14.12.1666 78, w Margt Adam 3.5.1668 74; Androw Wood cordiner Kirriemuir 13.5.1679 55; (central) A W, M A; A W, E F; two shields, one with ?a last? over a cordiner's knife (see F Davidson, "Inventory" for sketch)

26 1812. by Chas Robb fr Nether Migbie, fa Jas 22.11.1790 61, mo Jean Young 26.12.1811 74

27 Eliz Bu- - - - - n Gibson aged (5 or 5- - - - n or m)es Ricka- - aged - - -

28 - Jean - - - - -

29 Jas Forrest, w Elis Wilkie 18.2.1841 57; Thos Bell fr Ballinshoe, w Isabella W Forrest 24.3.1854 29; 1859; by Jas Forrest of Easter Ogil to fa, mo, w & da; Wm Forrest clothier here 3.2.1819 71, w Margt Hood 9.5.1809 48

30 Robt Wilkie of New Barns 7.1.1837 79, w mrs Jean Johnston 6.7.1848 85 (see Jervise, "Epitaphs.." ii 362: he was mert in Montrose, his bro a mert in Dundee bought Auchlishie, his s major Jas held lucrative appointment of army clothier & left a son who d childhood & two das etc)

31 1827. by Geo Riccard, w Jean Glenday 21.11.1825 70

32 Wm Whitburn 18.4.1855 58, w Mary Lindsay 7.7.1834 36, chn Wm 3m, Eliz 11y, Robt 9y, 2w Isabella Fife 11.1845 48

33 by Jas Don imo mo's bro Jas Thomson d in Cossacks 16.11.1744 71; (west side) two cherubs

34 under turf. Geo - - - , Betty & James

35 - - - - - - who d - - - age - - - - also his twin bro still(born)

36 Jas Webster wright Kilrie 3.12.1848 40, by w Janet Crabb

37 1836. by David & Jannet, fa And Low late tent Plivermuir ground of Logie 15.2.1827 73 (w Margt Philp 6.7.1833 89); Jannet Low 7.11.1838 58

38 Geo Johnston of Herdhill 2.12.1846 93, sis Helen 3.10.1848 100y9m

38a 1853. Thos Rattray manuf 22.2.1858 69, w Agnes Grant 9.12.1850 57, s Jas Doig 25.12.1838 4, s David 6.8.1848 22; John Rattray 8.6.1879 50; Jean Rattray 8.8.1890 75;both int New cemetery

39 Thos Adam "of unsullied deportment" formerly in Hatton of Carse d - - - - 51y, by wid - - Anderson & M - - - - - - - - - - his chn; (west side) cherub; shield with share & coulter; T A, I A; poem (quoted by Jervise "Epitaphs.." ii 361)

40 - - - - - - ; (west side)

41 Jas Duncan & w Jean Mitcheton, by s Jas (& w Helen Souter); (west side) cherub

42 1831.Alex Morrison weaver here 8.10.1828 77, w Euphemia Fife 12.4.1803 42, s Wm Morrison par schoolmaster Inverarity 29.4.1829 29, by das Agnes & Elspith

43 1839. by Alex Lawson fr Sandyford, da Margt 22.8.1838 1y, s Alex 15.1.1835 3, bro John fr Kilnhill, bro Jas 19.10.1812 10, sis Elspit 6.3.1813 16, sis Marjory 13.3.1813 22, sis Margt 2.10.1834 42, mo Isobel Grewar 17.3.1836 73, gfa Alex Lawson 23.12.1831 96

44 by John Crawforn china mert here, s Jas

45 by Wm Stewart manuf here, 1s David surgeon 31.1.1835 35 (da Isabella 13.12.1834 3y3m, da Mary-Ann 20.12.1834 20m & Mary-Ann 2nd 14.3.1836 1y); (west side) Wm Stewart manuf 6.12.1767 17.9.1845, w Agnes Dalgity 19.10.1772 1.2.1827

46 by Robt S Cowie wright at Cortachy, w Mary Clayton 1.8.1831 29, s John d in nonage

47 Alex Menderson carrier in Forfar 3.8.1849 55, w Marion Prophet 29.4.1853

48 Alex McBain 4.11.1834 54, by John Kinloch esq of Kilrie as a mark of esteem to deceased who had faithfully served his family for part of three generations.

49 Geo Scrymgeour 19.12.1850 48, w Margt Reid 22.11.1847 45, by das Isabella & Agnes

50 Joseph Stewart 16.5.185(3 or 5) 12

51 rev Jas Lyall episcopal clergyman here 15.2.1794 83 (see Jervise, "Epitaphs.." ii 361 notes he was uncle of Chas Lyell of Kinnordy esq who d 1796; see inscriptions at Kirriemuir St Mary's & at Fearnell)

52 1828. by Jas Barrie here, fa Wm 17.3.1827 75, mo Jean Stevenson 5.3.1831 83

53 1851. by David Ross, w Eliz Sampson 3.5.1851 68

54 by Jas Colvill fr Knowhead, w Jannet Wilson 12.5.1848, da Ann 11.18-- 3y

55 1827. by Wm McKillop mason here, w Jane Kiell 13.11.1824 62

56 John Sandison fr Nether Migvie 25.10.1841 54, w Betty Robbie 6.8.1857 65, s David 22.7.1847 18, s Jas 9.5.185(4) 29

57 TS John Soutar late in - - - of Ballinsho 27.12.1832 39, 3s of Geo (in Balmonth) North in par of Tealing, by bro Patk

58 small. A W

59 - - - - -

60 1858. by John Buttar smith Ballenshoe, w Janet Dougles 20.2.1847 70 & two ss & one da int here

61 (by) Mary Dick- - - - - - - - John - - - sur(geon) - - - - - (n)avy

62 Chas Dickson surgeon RN 4.12.1834 32, Chas & Eliz Dickson, 1s Chas Henry 29.12.1834 (1 or 4)y9m, yt da Mary Eliz Duff 19.7.1832 18y5m

63 mural. Jas Nicoll d Ballindarg 29.11.1826 75, w Margt Glenday d Lochside of Balfour 4.9.1815 59, s capt David late commander of ship Merope of Calcutta killed in massacre at Manilla 9.10.1820 25, da Jane d Ballindarg 21.4.1834 52, s capt Jas of EICS d Ballindarg 4.5.1838 58, s John late fr Greenbank 29.5.1850 61

64 mural. rev John Buchan for about 40y episcopal clergyman here d Elgin 14.5.1851 84, w Janet Ritchie d here 8.5.1828 43, chn Chas d here 13.10.1822 1½y, David 30.8.1829 17, John d London 14.9.1829 21, Jas d here 12.2.1833 19, Geo 4.10.1844 20, Clementina d Elgin 29.12.1845 18

65 urn. 1842. Margt Forrester 21.1.1824 56, by ss Jas F Clark agriculturist Ireland & Thos Clark mason Forfar

66 fallen mural. Jas Jafferson late tent Newmill of Craigeassie 12.12.182(3) 86, w Jane Smith 4.11.1833 88

67 rev Jas Aitken senior min of Congregational Original Seceders here 24.9.1834 77 in 56th y of ministry, by congregation, mrs Aitken d 1822 60, Eliz Aitken d 1788 5; Isabella 1791 6; rev John Aitken, s Jas AM licensed on 16.10.1844 min Original Seceders here but seized with fever passing through Dundee d there 28.12.1844 22, da Isabella Ferguson d Aberdeen 1831 12 (see Jervise, "Epitaphs.." ii 361: "old Aitken was a man of great energy of character etc."

68 mural. 1850. Robt Brown sometime fr Usan par Craig d 31.5.1847 74, s Peter d India 3.3.1849 31, by w Ann Aymer

69 mural, in vestry. Thos Goodlet 20.1.1837 67, w Ann Black 24.7.1810 32, chn Helen 10.1818 5, Thos Duncan 10.1818 1y, Anne 8.7.1843 28, by gchn

70 1839. Wm Wylie late tent Balbridie & Hirdhill 2.9.1838 54, by wid Ann Osler d Balbridie 3.-.1852 54, da Jean 5.1826 3

71 John Reid late schoolmaster this parish d 24.2.1837 75 after incumbency of 47y, w Jean Milne 27.10.1834 53, s Joseph inf, by family

72 by Alex Duthie weaver Knowhead, bro & sis Ann 4.6.1806 16, Wm 10.4.1819 19, Jean 14.4.1829 41

73 1855. Geo Alexander fr Longbank 20.4.1854 70, by w Margt Ogilvy, chn Geo 12.6.1822 2, Wm 13.3.1832 5, Margt 14.10.1835 7

74 Chas Lyon d Shielhill 10.1.1836 65, w Isabella Lyon (her sis Margt d here (21).4.1821 (4)2

75 David Watson 30.5.1831 52, w Jean Bowman 26.10.1822 47, s John 19.10. 1807, da Betty 12.8.1809, s David 21.6.181-, s Alex (da Ann d nonage)

76 Jas Stormonth esq of Lednathie 20.10.1817 86; Jas Stormonth Darling esq of Lednathie WS, chn Eliz Ann Moir Tod 16.9.1826 inf, Robt 3.3.1836 inf, And Tod 9.12.1838 inf (see Jervise, "Epitaphs.." ii 359, notes Jas Stormonth lawyer in Edinburgh d unm 1817, succeeded by yr bro's gs Jas Stormonth Darling 9.2.1799 12.8.1866 int Kelso abbey; also notes a stone at old Lednathie house with 1688 J S ♡ J L, for Jas Stormonth & w Jean Lyell)

77 Wm Howe - - - in Kirriemuir & - - - Addison his wife imo their - - - (Jane or Anne) d - - - - 4y

78 1823. Alex Grant fr in Kintyrie 25.4.1834 74, w Mary Grant, ss Peter 16.6.1822 14, John 16.7.1822 12; poem (quoted in Jervise "Epitaphs" ii)

79 1852. by Geo Duke & w Ann Couts, da Ann M (17).5.1851 (11)y

80 Jas Palmer d Littleinch 28.4.1832 83, w Eliz Fenton 24.2.1835 77, da Isabel 25.5.1806 14, by das Barbara & Elspeth (s Jas Douglas Lamond saddler 12.4.1840 19)

81 urn. Alex Grant mert here d 8.18(4)3 75, w Isabella Mackay 30.8.1841 66, da Janet 28.12.1822 14

82 Peter Mudie tent Ladywell 7.1837 64, by only child Jas

83 John Donaldson 19.4.1840 49, by w Janet Baxter

84 Thos Yeats for 25y (overs)eer at Kinnordy to the - - - Chas Lyell esq, w J., da Marianne 22.7.1830 12; epitaph

85 by Jas McGrigor 19.7.1838 72, w Elis Hindy a native of St Austell Cornwall 13.6.1833 56; Helen Ross 9.8.1832 40

86 1853. John Roddick late gamekeeper Lindertis 18.9.1852 74

The following are noted in A Jervise, "Epitaphs & Inscriptions" ii 360-2 but were not seen in 1976:

87 - - - - -roun, spovs to Alexander Strachon qha depairted - - - -

88 - - - - - - - -Lyndsay qva - - - - - - - -

89 Heir lyis Alexander H - - - - - -ho lived in Kil- - - - -

90 - - - - Iohn Anderson - - - - 1669

91 - - - - - - - - Bve hvsband to Evphan Pal- - - vho departed vpon the 18 - - - - - - - - - Ivn - - - - - -

92 - - lyis Agnes Beattie spovs to Androv Dvgal wright vha - - - - - - - depairtit the 21 of Apryl 1654

93 FS in latin. David Cromb, w Margt Tamson 4.2.1613 72, by s & husband for mo w & himself.

94 FS Thos Wobster in Balingara 12.4.1675 75, w Eleebeth Leang

95 Alex Cudbert cordiner Garlobank 26.3.1674 60, w Janet Samson

96 John Nicoll in Burnside Dersie, da Isabella d here 1753 57

97 John Chalmers, w Mary; elegy; 1810

98 FS John Adamson shoemaker here 10.4.1681 59; shoe, skull, bones

99 FS Wm Care in Eist- - - - - , s Wm 13.12.1656

100 in quire of the previous parish church, in latin. Anna Ogilvy 2.1605 31, da of sir John Ogilvy of Inverquharity & w of rev Alex Kyninmonth min Kirriemuir

101 removed from its place in the burial ground & set up against the back wall of a house on the NE side of the kirkyard. rev Thos Ogilvy min here 6.4.1802 44 in 17th y of ministry, da Ann 17.9.1800, da Jane 4.10.1800 both in childhood, s Walter surgeon EICS d Nagpore Madras 30.9.1818 22 (see Fasti v 297)

Notes

A Jervise, "Epitaphs & Inscriptions" ii 357-365 refers to inscriptions above 8-10,18,25,27,29-30,35,39,48,51,64,66,76,85 & 87-101, with brief histories of the families of Ogilvy, Stormonth, Lyell

F Davidson, "Inventory of 17th Century Tombstones in Angus" details stones no 8,9 & 25 & she mentions that a large number of recumbent slabs were lifted in 1970 and stacked in piles to avoid damage to the motor mower.

Index

Adam 25.39
Adamson 16.18.98
Addison 77
Aitken 67
Alexander 73
Anderson 11.39.90
Aymer 68

Barclay 7
Barrie 52
Baxter 11.83
Beattie 92
Bell 29
Bennet 16
Black 69
Bowman 75
Brown 68.?87
Bu- - 27
Buchan 64
Bue 91
Buttar 60
Care (?Carrie) 99
Chalmers 97
Clark 65
Clayton 46
Couts 79
Cowie 46
Crabb 36
Crawforn 44
Cromb 93
Cruikshank 23
Cudbert 9.95

Dalgity 45
Darling 76
Dick- - 61
Dickson 22.62
Doig 18
Don 33
Donaldson 83
Douglas 4
Dougles 70
Duke 79
Duncan 41
Dundas 10
Duthie 72
Dugal 92

F. 25
Fenton 80
Fife 32.42
Forrest 29
Forrester 65

Gibson 17.27
Glenday 7.31.63
Goodlet 69
Grant 38a.78.81
Grewar 43

H. 89
Henderson 47
Hindy 85
Hood 13.29.100
Howe 77
Hutcheon 9

Jafferson 66
Johnston 30.38
Jones 16

Kiell 55
Kinloch 48
Kyninmonth 100

Lamb 13
Lamond 80
Lawson 6.43
Leang 94
Lindsay 13.32.88
Louden 6
Low 7.19.37

23a KIRRIEMUIR PARISH CHURCH

Lyall, Lyell	51.76.85
Lyndsay	88
Lyon	74
McBain	48
McGrigor	85
Mackay	81
McKillop	55
McNicoll	4
Miller	2
Milne	71
Mitchell	10
Mitcheton	41
Morrison	42
Mudie	82
Muir	23
Myles	20
Nicoll	63.96
Ogilvy	73.100-1
Osler	1.70
Pal- -	91
Palmer	80
Philp	37
Prophet	47
Ramsay	20
Rattray	38a
Reid	49.71
Riccard	31
Rick- -	27
Ritchie	64
Robb	3.22.26
Robbie	56
Roddick	86
Ross	53.85
Sam(p)son	53.95
Sandison	56
Scrymge(ou)r	16.49
Smith	8.16.19.21.66
Soutar/er	41.57
Spence	1
Stevens	7
Stevenson	52
Stewart	14.45.50
Stormonth	12.76
Strachon	87
Tamson	93
Thomas	39
Thomson	33.93
Tod	76
Tyrie	12
Walker	8
Watson	75
Webster	5-6.36
Whitburn	32
Wilkie	29-30
Wilson	54
Wobster	94
Wood	25
Wyl(l)ie	17.70
Yeats	84
Young	2.26

23b KIRRIEMUIR EPISCOPAL CHURCH

On the site of old St Mary's Episcopal chapel which was erected by Chas Lyell of Kinnordy about 1790 there is a small neglected burial ground, in parts reverted to jungle. Access is through the Masonic Lodge car park behind the Roods.
National Grid reference: NO 385 541

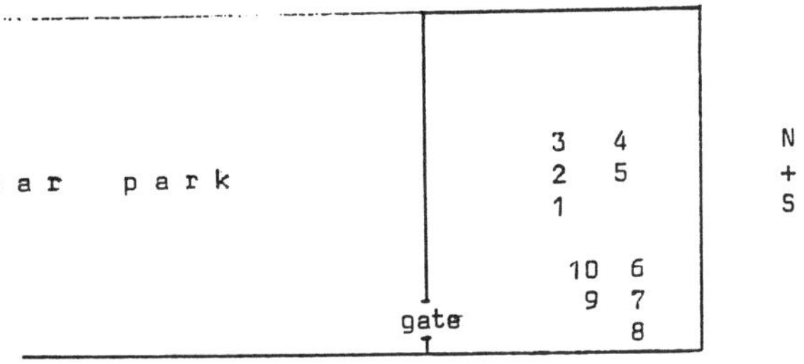

1 coped stone. Sophia Georgina Lyell 18.10.1897 85

2 massive sarcophagus. Chas Lyell esq of Kinnordy 19.1.1796 62

3 massive sarcophagus. Mary Lyell 16.5.1843 71 wid of Chas Lyell esq of Kinordy

4 Chas Lyell esq, wid Frances 4.3.1850 (65) (see DNB, her fa Thos Smith)

5 sarcophagus. Chas Lyell esq of Kinnordy 8.11.1849 80 (see DNB, botanist)

6 sarcophagus. Eleanor Lyell 3.10.1866 60

23b KIRRIEMUIR EPISCOPAL CHURCH

7 Gilbert Lyell Heathcote 11.2.1845 13m

8 (Eliz) Lyell 5.10.1835 21

9 coped stone. Frances Lyell 17.10.1783 73

10 coped stone. Thos Lyell 25.6.1871 72

Notes

A Jervise, "Epitaphs & Inscriptions" ii 362-3 & i 92 relates to this family: Chas Lyell was one of several bros in Carcary, Farnell, was bred a mert in Montrose, was purser on several ships during the rebellion in America, amassed a fortune, bought Kinnordy 1780-3, md Mary Beale from West Loce Cornwall

The Scottish Nation ii 704: Chas Lyell of Kinnordy d 1849 was discoverer of many British plants including the genus Lyellia, editor of Dante's works.

Encyclopaedia Brittanica 14th ed & DNB: sir Chas Lyell of Kinnordy, geologist, int Westminster Abbey

23c KIRRIEMUIR CEMETERY

The new cemetery was opened in 1858, including the site of a quarry. The Celtic carvings found in the foundations of the old parish church are sheltered in a wooden hut at the summit of the steep slope of the cemetery. National Grid reference: NO 389 545

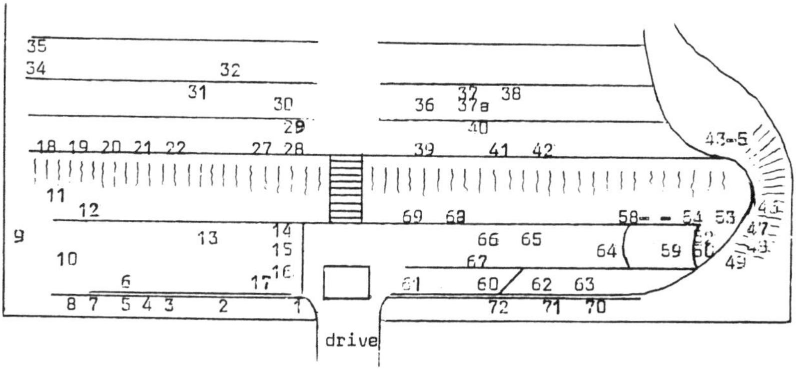

1 Maurice Heggie 9.6.1871 63, w Margt Langlands 15.7.1847 46, chn Wm 15.10.1853 20, Margt 24.6.1846 9; Jas Niven killed Gallipoli 8.8.1915 33; And Niven junior 25.5.1928 37

2 John Davidson 9.11.1867 58, w Helen Crabb 24.12.1877 68, s Wm Crabb 18.11.1854 5, by das Ann 11.4.1912 69 & Jessie 22.9.1921 77; Jas Davidson Duke 10.3.1939 71, w Annie Watson Mitchell 28.12.1948 75, s in law Geo Anderson Machan 19.6.1951 44

3 urn. Jas Robb mason 1.2.1861 41 int Western cem Dundee, w Annie Ramsay 1848 31 int Kirriemuir old churchyard (her mo Mary Lyall 30.1.1862 75), by da Euphemia 17.7.1909 62

23c KIRRIEMUIR CEMETERY

4 1865. by Jas & Wm Robbie now in Australia to parents Chas Robbie & Eliz McKenzie both d Southmuir of Kirriemuir, sis Anne 11.6.1865 (h Thos Donald, Southmuir)

5 David Phillips mason Northmuir 1860 67, w Betsy Lindsay 1854 57, das Betsy 1916 73, Jane 1918 82

6 John Ogilvy fr Glaslet 22.2.1853 76, w Jane Lindsay 22.5.1859 73, by da Jane 18.2.1883; Margt Ogilvy 21.1.1910 72, h Geo Gracie 15.1.1915 74

7 ob 1861. Alex Low 1843 60, w Charlotte Cuthbert 1859 74, s Alex 1813 4m, da Helen 1820 22m; David Low 25.1.1823 15.3.1899; Ann wid of Jas Lindsay d 11.10.1865 51; Jas 4.8.1868 42; Isabella 1.5.1875 54 (h John Mustard); Wm 17.11.1883 54; Jane Low 27.2.1894 78; our parents Marjory Duke 25.9. 1897, David Low 15.3.1899

8 ob Wm Brown 29.9.1849 52, w Ann Lyon 9.8.1878 74, chn Alex, David, Geo d inf, Helen 1836 1844, Jane 1839 1847

9 by Geo Duke manuf here 3.12.1885 79, mo Eliz Spence 16.11.1839 65, fa Geo 29.9.1859 88, w Ann Coutts 2.8.1881 76, da Eliz S 2.9.1917 76

10 1864. by Wm Gray 15.5.1868 54, imo ss Wm 18.9.1849 20m, Chas 31.5.1851 5, int old churchyard, David 13.9.1855 8, w Ann Mann 28.4.1911 89, Ann 20.12. 1912 55 (h Wm E Lothian)

11 1873. John Malloch surgeon RN b Burnside Methven Perthshire 31.3.1788 d 1.1.1872, w Helen Simpson b Littleton par of Airlie 31.3.1791 18.9.1848, chn John Simpson d inf, Wm S surgeon here d here 11.4.1867 42, Francis Henderson d Dunedin NZ 28.8.1870 39, Susan d here 6.5.1896 73, Peter S, SSC Edinburgh d Edinburgh 20.2.1897 69, Agnes last of family d here 22. 9.1901 82

12 Robt Moir flaxspinner Newmill 1.1850, w Eliz Stewart 15.6.1867 (her sis Ann 28.11.1870), s Wm cloth mert here 30.8.1885 51 (w Esther Maiden 30. 1.1863 28, two of their chn John & Geo d inf), da Betsy 25.9.1929 87

13 1881. Geo Peter 3.3.1881 68, s Geo 14.5.1863 18, w Julia Rattray 25.5. 1850 int churchyard, wid Ann Robertson 13.6.1892 70

14 1874. by John Mann contractor d Southmuir 20.3.1892 72, fa David contractor d Gaskhillock 1.4.1859 78, mo Elspeth Fenton d Gaskhillock 19.9. 1859 76, bro Wm d Bridge of Prosen 29.6.1835 10, w Isabella Cameron d 45 Forfar Road 30.1.1919 76, da Mary 28.6.1958 (h Thos Muir 18.6.1948)

15 Chas Robb, Northmuir 11.9.1886 79, s Jas 29.8.1840 4, John 16.10.1854 14, da Annie 29.6.1884 41, da Susan 15.12.1889 56, w Isabella Myles 14.5.1894 87, by da Jane

16 Jas Reid, Northmuir 26.5.1889 84, w Janet McDonald 3.3.1898 85, chn Sophia 29.10.1839 2, David 25.11.1847 6, Jas 2.12.1847 4, Jane 23.3.1855 1y, Margt 20.12.1860 3, gda Janet Reid 20.4.1881 6, s Wm 4.6.1899 63

17 Alex Whyte 21.2.1860 63, w Isabella Fairweather 26.4.1873 83, s Jas 17. 7.1835 10, David Lamont 12.3.1882 51, David 19.3.1897 73,

18 by John Herald of firm of Davidson & Herald joiners here d 25.8.1882 81, w Isabella Gowans 2.5.1862 54, chn Jas Davidson 7.6.1842 11m, Helen 14.7. 1848 13m, John Lawson 2.6.1865 18, Jane Reid 18.3.1928 83, Isabella Osler 2.12.1928 76 (h Jas Walker)

19 by Peter Haggart tent Crieff & w Eliz Don imo da Isabell inf (no date)

20 John Barrie late fr Pluckerstone d Barnhill 26.11.1897 78, w Agnes Brown d Barnhill 16.9.1879 54, chn John 26.1.1855 15m, Wm Brown 10.10.1861 12, Agnes 13.4.1863 2, 2da Bessie Lindsay d Southampton 29.10.1927 68 (wid of John Glass)

21 cross next 20. rev David Ogilvy DD min Dalziel FC Motherwell b here 4.11. 1822 d there 25.8.1904, niece & adopted da Sara Mitchell Barrie b here 3.6.1854 d there 1.11.1905 (see Ewing i 285: he md 1859 Jane Bridges)

22 David Barrie 26.6.1902 87, w Margt Ogilvy 6.9.1819 3.9.1895, da Jane Adamson 12.3.1847 31.8.1895, da Eliz How 12.3.1849 2.4.1851, Agnes Matthew 23.12.1850 1.1851, s David Ogilvy 30.1.1853 29.1.1867, s Jas Matthew 9.5.1860 19.6.1937; Ethel Margt Barrie 14.10.1878 25.12.1967, h rev canon J A Philip (for J M Barrie see DNB etc)

23 cross next 22. Alex Ogilvy Barrie HM Inspector of schools b here 26.3. 1842 d here 16.7.1914, w Mary Cowan 8.2.1856 19.2.1928; Mary Cowan Barrie 4.12.1890 10.5.1939; Eliza Dorothy Barrie or Smart 10.1.1948 int Alderley Cheshire; Lilian Knight Barrie 11.6.1878 13.8.1953 int Fort William

24 urn. 1869. by Jane Skinner 6.3.1875 60, h Jas Hood baker Dundee 30.12. 1864 48, fa John Skinner builder here 29.1.1842 81, mo Mary Forbes 6. 4.1853 81, sis Margt 10.8.1830 18, uncle Jas Skinner 13.4.1849 79

25 next 24. by John Hood spirit dealer here & w Jane Kidd, her sis Margory Kidd 22.12.1863 75; John Hood 22.1.1870 85; Jane Kidd 17.11.1877 75

26 by Mary J Rattray, fa John Rattray sergt d Arbroath 28.12.1852 62 int Abbey burying ground, mo Jane Barty McLaren d here 10.11.1861 63 int here, bro Robt McLaren Webster late min Chalmers church Hobart Tasmania 12.8.1890 63 int Sandy Bay cem (see Ewing i 353: Webster, Robt Maclaren, b Perthshire 1826, studied at the Universities Aberdeen, St Andrews & Edinburgh, ordained at Garvald in 1861, translated to Sprouston in 1867, md 1872 Eliz S Jacob, settled 1875 at Hobart d 1890), cousin Mary G Thomson d Arbroath 17.12.1887 56 int here

27 David Lindsay in West Roods 24.5.1879 66, w Ann Lindsay 17.11.1893 74

28 by Wm Lindsay, fa Robt 29.2.1864 81, mo Jean Lindsay 25.9.1852 (ed. altered from 1848) 64, (bro) Jas d New York 18.8.1848 33, Chas d Glasgow 5.10.1856 31, Sophia 26.4.1857 40, Jannet 1830 20, Geo, Robt, Richard & Helen d inf

29 Alex Donaldson d Liverpool, w Hanby Smith 1873, da Margt McNicoll d Tulchan Lodge Glenisla 17.10.1899 (by da Cath Hanby Donaldson), s Alex d Ayra India 1868, da Janet 2.3.1878, Thos 30.4.1900

30 John Milne shoemaker 27.2.1868 70, w Isabella Lindsay 3.5.1873 63, chn David & Margt d inf, s Thos 13.1.1866 18, s Geo d Orient USA 14.2.1904 70, s Jas Angus d Cupar Fife 16.3.1914 75, by da Mary S d Dundee 23.9. 1917 81 int Western cem Dundee

31 Geo Deuchar 23.1.1839 30 int Invergowrie, w Ann Nicoll 2.12.1875 71, s Jas 5.3.1875 37, da Margt 18.1.1920 85

32 John Wills, Northmuir 22.9.1849 49, w Janet Burns 6.6.1883 75, s Chas 10.7.1838 11m; Wm Carrie 17.5.1932 93, w Jessie Will 17.1.1923 78, s Allan Henderson 11.3.1901 19, da Jemima 4.5.1935 55

33 Alex Webster LFPS 46y surgeon in Kirriemuir b 2.3.1811 d 26.5.1879, w Ann Webster d Glasgow 3.7.1900 83, da Eliza 9.1841 inf, da Jane Ann Webster or Niven d Stonehaven 24.9.1900 61

34 Jas Kirkland 23.9.1878 70, w Margt Scott 12.6.1897 88, s Jas 9.6.1845 2m, da Jean 15.6.1906 63

35 David Lowe 1851, w Jane Wallace 1895, s Chas Duff 9.1891, s David 3 1899 both merts Dundee, by da Annie 11.4.1907

36 John Kermack mason 16.12.1884 80, w Minnie Findlay 30.11.1863 59, chn Annie, Jessie & Alick d inf, da Mary 1.10.1892 52, da Eliz 13.6.1909 75, da Margt 22.2.1914 77

37 Alex Low, Forfar Rd 30.4.1888 80, w Mary Whyte 2.7.1897 87, da Annie 15.10.1848 4, s Jas 25.3.1851 10, s Wm 13.12.1920 81

37a Wm Low 16.1.1894 81, w Margt Mathers 2.1.1894 79, da Annie 9.7.1851 6, da Mary 8.11.1854 2, s Jas 7.4.1855 inf, da Jane 11.4.1915 73 (h Jas Mathers sergt major Gordon highlanders 13.12.1907 70); Jessie Low 4.8. 1928 75

38 1850. imo Jas Lees, w Elspit Jamieson 10.2.1883 78, by s Alex d Mill of Allardice near Bervie 3.1.1886 43

39 John Brand baker here 10.7.1877 74, w Eliz Ivory 26.12.1878 72, chn Mary 19.6.1839 11m, Wm 7.6.1842 2, gs John Brand 26.11.1868 10m; David Brand 25.12.1881 40, w Margt Hume Smith 13.9.1889 42

40 ob by Jas Hood, mo Annie Nicoll 10.12.1877 70, fa Robt Hood 3.1837 int old churchyard; David Hume 25.2.1901 82, w Mary Hood 26.6.1902 72

41 Alex Irons Lackie, Fernbank Balbeggie Perthshire 10.2.1957 72, by wife

42 next 41. Alex Lakie (sic) 4.1.1869 71, w Elspeth Bearn 9.1831 32, w Isabella Stewart 25.4.1855 52, s David 24.7.1879 52, da Jane 4.2.1905 66; David Lakie, w Margt Anderson d Whitewell Tannadice 27.11.1909 78; Wm Lakie, w Helen Farquharson Hay d Brahan Ross-shire 6.2.1912 57; Wm Lakie d Brahan Estate Office Ross-shire 5.3.1930 77, da Christina Campbell d Forfar 14.3.1945

43 And Scrymgeour 15.7.1970 91, w Christina Brown 26.12.1962 89

44 next 43, gothic, ivy, cross & crown. Alex C Brown d Easter Balloch 30.9. 1896 39, w Betsy Rattray d there 2.3.1907 76, da Jane Brown Hick d West Balloch 4.10.1914 52, s Alex 4.2.1943 74, da Margt 15.4.1958 85

45 next 44. by Janet Crabb to mrs Jas Brown d Easter Balloch 14.11.1875 59, fa Alex Crabb 1.1854 76, mo Jane Crabb 1.1869 84; above Janet Crabb d 3.6.1897 77

46 1896. by Helen Robb to mrs David Baxter 26.6.1889 73, Helen 13.6.1906 90, s Wm 20.2.1865 4, Alex 26.10.1870 7, Jas 11.8.1900 48, David 9.4. 1911 58, And 6.4.1917 62, gda Georgina Caird 11.7.1895 13

47 Jas Robb 1826 1910, w Ann Dear 1829 1900, chn David 1850 1916, Fanny 1851 1877, Peter 1853 1864, Jane W 1856 1923, Margt A 1858 1930, Mary 1860 1890, Isabella 1862 1938

48 1873. Peter Robb 28.7.1867 75, w Charlotte Adamson 22.2.1872 74, chn Peter 14.7.1840 5, Susan 10.6.1859 26, Thos 14.10.1865 24; Wm Adamson, w Mary Ann Robb 26.8.1900 58, by Mary Ann Robb

49 Ewan Macpherson 3.1827 56, w Eliz Macpherson 17.9.1849 73, s John 22.10. 1846 30, das Margt 29.12.1852 40, Ann 28.7.1886 76 (wid of Jas Stewart), by s Jas 3.5.1882 62

50 by Alex Grant tailor & clothier here imo family Janet 28.12.1822 14, Jane 19.3.1871 67, Abigail 18.1.1874 73, Eliz 15.1.1875 79, Isabella 9.12.1886 84, Barbara 28.4.1887 77

51 by Jas Kennedy mert Southmuir 6.5.1908 84, mo Margt Spalding 14.5.1877 87, fa Adam 18.1.1879 87, da Maggie S 6.6.1854 4, s John d Redwood City Cal USA 20.4.1890 42, w Janet Clark 15.9.1891 68, sis Margt 13.5.1913 84 (wid of Wm Guthrie), s Chas d Hilo Hawaiia 9.1.1919 71

52 ob 1861. Geo Adamson 1.3.1856 67, w Betsey Cuthbert 3.5.1868, chn Eliz 18.

10.1867 39, Helen & Margt d inf

53 by mrs Mary Grant or McPherson imo mrs Duncan McPherson mert here 15.6.1858 65, s Jas 1826 3; John McPherson surgeon in Brechin 5.9.1852 32; Robt G McPherson surgeon Bristol d Australia 1854 39; David Grant McPherson surgeon Bristol d there 26.5.1865 40; Mary Grant or McPherson d Kirriemuir 19.7.1877 94y3m

54 by Sarah Alexander & Ann Ogilvie imo fa Alex Grant fr Kintyrie 25.4.1834 74, mo Mary Grant 6.9.1864 83; Ann Grant 1888, h Jas Ogilvie 1892, da Sarah A 1882

55 cross. David Wilkie JP Ardmore provost here for many yrs d 24.12.1914 69, w Margt Louson Mill d Ardmore 16.10.1938 93, da Elsie Bowman MD d Naples 3.3.1912 31, s David Percival Dalbreck Kt OBE FRCS professor of surgery Edinburgh university d 28.8.1938 55 (see DNB)

56 David Wilkie linen manuf here 1813 1885, w Elspeth Bowman 1813 1867

57 next 56. Jas Bowman manuf here 14.3.1857 77, w Binia Nicoll 26.6.1859 74, da Mary 4.12.1808 6m, da Esther 18.3.1850 29, s Jas junior manuf here 2.7.1892 82; Alex Millar 9.8.1867 52, w Binia Bowman 28.9.1904 86, da Jessie 8.12.1857 6m, da Binia Nicoll 22.6.1858 11

58 ob by family to fa John Donaldson 19.4.1840 49, mo Janet Baxter 1.7.1878 74, step fa John Patterson 5.11.1871 59, sis Margt A 3.3.1858 22.3.1890 (ie Margt A Donaldson)

59 David Lindsay 3.12.1866 74, w Margt Lindsay 10.1838 43, by s Jas, Southmuir 6.4.1899 66 (w Betsey Low Colville 28.6.1873 38, da Helen d inf, da Margt Wilson 19.1.1925 63 (wid of Wm Anderson builder, s Jas killed Ypres 20.8.1916 23), da Jessie Wilson 16.9.1867 3y8m)

60 angel. 1880. by Jas Milne mert Dundee d Newport on Tay 10.2.1898 int here, w Margt Chalmers Dand 7.10.1829 13.4.1880, s Robt inf, mo Agnes Fenton 27.11.1859 61, aunt Ann Fenton 27.7.1860 69

61 Wm Webster d at Park View 7.6.1887 81, w Eliz Findlay 27.3.1876 69, da Janet 29.3.1842 2

62 by Eliz Cownie, Belliesbrae Kirriemuir 5.4.1878 84, imo mrs Thos Webster 28.1.1855 67 & three chn d inf, also her sis Betty Cownie 14.7.1860 70

63 Wm Matthew 19.2.1842 52, w Helen Robertson 29.2.1871 81; 1861. by Micah Matthew 3.5.1896 76, w Charlotte Euphina McHardie 7.8.1883 67, da Jane 20.6.1859 3y10m, da Ann 31.12.1862 11y6m, s Geo 12.1.1904 59, da Helen 16.3.1916 75

64 sarcophagus. by Wm Forrest imo fa Jas Forrest of Easter Aylort 9.1787 5.1862; Robt Wilkie, 1da Eliz 8.1783 7.1841

65 David Ewan shoemaker here 19.1.1837 38, w Margory Duncan 28.5.1842 40, chn David 27.8.1838 8, Geo 15.4.1838 4, Betsy 29.5.1840 2, Wm 24.7.1863 35, John saddler & harness maker 29.10.1864 33

66 Mary Winifred Philip 29.12.1955 46

67 next 66. Frederick Philip 1.1837 48, w Susan Dunbar 7.1.1877 78, s Wm 19.7.1877 37, by s Frederick 15.6.1901 69 (w Mary Ann Dunbar 24.3.1912 81, da Mary 11.8.1884 18,s Wm 18.7.1864 3, s Chas d Edinburgh 28.4.1891 20, s Frederick 21.1.1924 60 (w Annie Clark 18.11.1940 89)

68 by Jas Moncrieff builder 8.3.1874 73, w Jane Wilkie 6.2.1890 83, chn Jas 1835 9, Wm 1836 3, David 1840 10, Joseph 1842 4, Agnes 16.11.1869 41, Ann 18.5.1902 62

23c KIRRIEMUIR CEMETERY

69 ob 1868. by John & Mary Brown & Isabella Cameron imo fa Wm Cameron 6.3.1854 62 & mo Isabella Findlay 13.2.1866 (62 or 69)

70 by Frederick Cruickshank AM min of Navar & Lethnot (see Fasti v 409)

71 John Low, Southmuir 18.6.1868, w Isabella Edward 10.3.1855, da Annie 21.6.1898, da Mary 19.10.1900, da Jane 27.12.1916, by grandsons

72 ob G Glenday, w Janet Milne 3.3.1861 55, s David 4.1878, s P- - - - , da - - - - - - ; chn Jas 4.1837 1y-m, J- - - 4.1848 3y10m, Ro - - - - - 1854 - -

Index

Adamson 22.48.52
Alexander 54
Anderson 2.42.59

Barrie 20-3
Barty 26
Baxter 46.58
Bearn 42
Bowman 55-7
Brand 39
Bridges 21
Brown 8.20.43-5.69
Burns 32

Caird 46
Cameron 14.69
Campbell 42
Carrie 32
Chalmers 60
Clark 51.67
Colville 59
Coutts 9
Cownie 62
Crabb 2.45
Cruickshank 70
Cuthbert 7.52

Dalbreck 55
Dand 60
Davidson 2.18
Dear 47
Deuchar 31
Don 19
Donald 4
Donaldson 29.58
Duff 35
Duke 2.7.9
Dunbar 67
Duncan 65

Edward 71
Ewan 65

Fairweather 17
Farquharson 42
Fenton 14.60
Findlay 36.61.69

Forbes 24
Forrest 64

Glenday 72
Gowans 18
Gracie 6
Grant 50.53-4
Gray 10
Guthrie 51

Haggart 19
Hay 42
Heggie 1
Henderson 11.32
Herald 18
Hick 44
Hood 24-5.40
How 22
Hume 39-40

Irons 41
Ivory 39

Jacob 26
Jamieson 38

Kennedy 51
Kermack 36
Kidd 25
Kirkland 34
Knight 23

Lackie 41-2
Langlands 1
Lawson 18
Lees 38
Lindsay 5-7.20.27-8 30.59

Lothian 10
Louson 55
Low 7.37.59.70
Lowe 35
Lyall 3
Lyon 8

McDonald 16
Machan 2
McHardie 63

McKenzie 4
McLaren 26
McNicoll 29
Macpherson 49.53
Maiden 12
Malloch 11
Mann 10.14
Mathers 37a
Matthew 22.63
Mill 55
Millar 57
Milne 30.60.72
Mitchell 2.21
Moir 12
Moncrieff 68
Muir 14
Mustard 7
Myles 15

Nicoll 31.40.57
Niven 33

Ogilvie 54
Ogilvy 6.21-3
Osler 18

Patterson 58
Peter 13
Philip 22.66-7
Phillips 5

Ramsay 3
Rattray 13.26.44
Reid 16.18
Robb 3.15.46-8
Robbie 4
Robertson 13.63

Scott 34
Scrymgeour 43
Simpson 11
Skinner 24
Smart 23
Smith 39
Spalding 51
Stewart 12.42.49
Spence 9

23c KIRRIEMUIR CEMETERY

Thomson	26	Webster	26.33.61-2
Walker	18	Whyte	17.37
Wallace	35	Wilkie	55-6.64.68
Watson	2	Will(s)	32
		Wilson	59

23d KINLOCH MAUSOLEUM

This private burial ground with imposing temple is on a mound surrounded by a wall too high to look over with a locked gate on the west side through which the inscriptions 1-5 were read. It may be there are other stones. National Grid reference: NO 382 512 off the road A 928, 2 miles S of Kirriemuir.

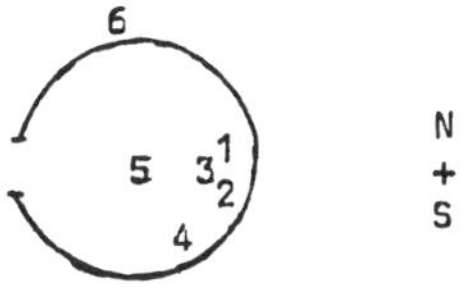

1 Thos Kinloch esq of Kilrie 24.4.1759 17.5.1824, w Ann Morley 1856 77

2 John Kinloch esq 1798 74

3 maj general A A A Kinloch CB, w Constance Mary 27.1.1916 86, s Frank 21.6.1915 33

4 Thos Kinloch of Kilrie & w Anne Morley, da Anne b Logie 14.3.1809 d Chittagong 5.12.1841 (h Jas B Ogilvy esq HEICS)

5 cross. Francis Garden Kinloch lieut Bengal staff corps, adjutant 5th Bengal cavalry & late 92nd Highlanders killed Afghanistan 29.9.1879 27 int at Thal; Ronald Kinloch 1873 1955, 2s of maj gen A A A Kinloch of Logie, w Mary Eva Channer 1880 1949; John And Kinloch 1886 45; col John Grant Kinloch 1894 86, w Agnes Garden 1860 43

6 outside the enclosure. Nelly Scrymgeour

Notes

A Jervise, "Epitaphs & Inscriptions" ii 266-8 concerns Kinloch chapel in Meigle, Perthshire and the Kinlochs of Kinloch & a younger son James a physician who md a Fothringham of Powrie & bought the estate of Kilrie & was succeeded in it by 1s David "ancestor of the present colonel Kinloch of Kilrie & Logie."

Brechin Commissariot Testaments: David Kinloch of Kilry, 1755

Index

Channer	5	Morley	1.4
Garden	5	Ogilvy	4
Kinloch	1-5.Notes	Scrymgeour	6
Fothringham	Notes		

23 K I R R I E M U I R

N o t e s

Glen Prosen, being in a detached part of Kirriemuir parish, has been included in this volume after Cortachy as 6b.

Kirriemuir parish in medieval times included chapels at Muirhouse (St Colm's), Chapelton of Kintyrie, Kilhill, Aberneathen near Kinnordy,& Ballinshoe. That at Ballinshoe is now a walled square in a field of Fletcherfield farm,was the burial ground of the Fletchers of Ballinshoe,but no inscriptions were seen in 1977.

Alan Reid, "The Regality of Kirriemuir" (1909) is a useful reference book; appendix x lists 58 rebels from Kirriemuir involved in the '45.

John A Philp "The Church in Kirriemuir from 1560- ". (1909)
"The United Free Church in Kirriemuir 1773-1923" (1923)

John Smith,"Old Scottish Clockmakers" mentions John Bower, Kirriemuir, 1802 & John Low, St Malcolm's Lane, 1837

Testaments: the following was noted in the Index of the Edinburgh Commissariot - Bessie Watson spouse to Wm Newton in Ballindarg, 1589;
the following are a small selection from the St Andrews Index:
Eliz Easson spouse to John Wauche in Kirriemuir, 1626
Euphemia Fyfe spouse to And Steill mert in Kirriemuir, 1737
Geo Fife shoemaker in Kirriemuir, 1742
And Hunter sometime of Restennet & Margt Hunter relict of John Campbell stampmaster at Kirriemuir, 1764
Janet Murray spouse to John Brechen in Gask, 1616
Alex Ogilvie late shipmaster Rotterdam then residenter Kirriemuir, 1765
Christian Wallace spouse to Robt Green in Muirhouse, 1615
Jas Webster mert Kirriemuir & w Jean Chaplain da of decd John Chaplain in Lochniglo, 1715
Cath Wood & Alex Laing in Shilhill, 1662
Grissell Wood spouse to Robt Cowll in Balmuckelie, 1637
Margt Wood da to umquhile And Wood cordiner in Kirriemuir, 1683

OPR with the Registrar General - 299 Kirriemuir Births 1716-1854
Marriages 1821-1854
Deaths 1830-1854

Church Records in the SRO:
CH3/899 Kirriemuir South FC, UF, Livingstone C of S
minutes 1873-1936; baptisms 1849-55, 1860, 1869-1960
HR 479 minutes 1839-1932
accounts 1843-1927
church, manse, glebe, churchyard, hall 1782-1928
printed valuation Forfar county 1822
appendix Kirriemuir church manse, school 1784-1873
cess rolls & assessments 1817-54
division of Muir of Kirriemuir 1808-35
GD 16/46 & 49 Airlie Muniments

Episcopal Church Records with the Brechin Diocesan Library deposited at Dundee University Library - Births 1797-1860 (baptisms)
Marriages 1840-56
Deaths 1835-61

Fasti v 296 ministers from 1567
Ewing ii 157 ministers North Church from 1844
South Church from 1843 (see also Memus)
Small i 319 Kirriemuir Antiburgher from 1778
324-5 Kirriemuir Relief, 1793 Bank Street Relief, 1831

24 L E T H N O T

The spacious burial ground surrounds the church, now roofless, built in 1827, but the site is medieval. Tha parishes of Lethnot and Navar were united in 1723 when the bridge over the Westwater was first built.
National Grid reference: NO 542 683

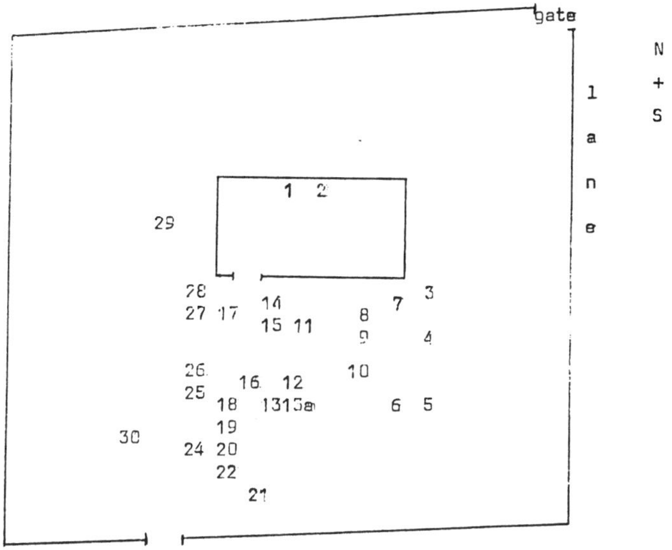

1 mural. mr Wm Davidson min Navar & Lethnot & w Janet Farries, s Geo finished first session at college etc d 16.8.1760 15, s Alex b 6.11.1746 & coming from Riga a sailor d 23.7.1763 16 int Woulosound burial place (see Fasti v 399: rev Wm Davidson b 1702 d 12.3.1775; Jervise, "Epitaphs.." i 294 has Ferrier in error for Farries; see Brechin Testaments)

2 mural. 1747. mr John Row min Navar 5y then in Lethnot & Navar 22y, d 24.12.1745 "while the Nation was distracted with Civil Wars, but had the pleasure to see his People adhering to their religion & liberties...", w Eliz Young who had lived 43y md with him d 8.9.1746 int here (see Fasti v 399; Brechin Testaments 1.4.1746 & 9.10.1746 - Mrs Row bequeathed £10 towards the support of the bridge of Lethnot)

3 1840. by Alex Stewart blacksmith Montrose, w Jean Carnigie 10.8.1840 20

4 Jas Ramsay late tent Newbigging 1771 1850, w Agnes Carnegie 1776 1832, da Martha b 1798 d inf, s Alex draper Alresford Hants 1803 1850, s John fr Newbigging 1.1799 9.1878 (w Margt Christison d Edzell 29.12.1883 75)

5 small. Jn.D.

6 Francis Christison 17.3.1889 78, fa Jas fr Finnochie 12.4.1847 78, mo Jane Stewart 13.7.1835 61, bro David 8.4.1843 37

7 1858. John Carnegie late tent Milton 1768 23.5.1829, w Betty Duncan 1774 23.12.1865

8 David Rickard fr Bogton 18.7.1880 73, da Margt 12.9.1852 4, w Betsy Christison 13.6.1813 30.1.1851, s Jas 28.1.1846 14.11.1893

9 1839. by Alex Smith tent Tillydovie, bro Jas sometime tent there 15.12.1826 31

10 David Smart 30.11.1770 64, by w Kathren Tulloa, he was ploughman in Drumcairn for 44y, they lived in a married life 36y in Dykehead of Drumcairn & had no chn; (west side) D S 1771 K T; mantling, shield with plough, flail & cross tree; David Tulloa, square, dividers, hammer & rule

11 And Smart late tent Achurie 12.3.1740, w Jean Milne 26.4.1748 68, by ss And, David, Thos, John & Alex; 1750; (west side) mantling, shield with plough; A S, D S, T S, I S, A S; (on top) two nude figures (ed. similar design to Angus, Edzell no 35)

12 a virtous man callit And Arsbald who sometime lived in (Ballfild) in par Lethnot departed, deceased w Janet Talbert, chn Geo, Margt, Alex, Janet (ed. late 17th or early 18th century)

13 Jas Laing in Drumcairn par Lethnot, w Anne Gibb 1.1737 48, left chn John, Jas, David, Wm & das Ann & Margt; potted flowers, angel & heart; (west side) potted flowers, angel & heart; poem; mantling, shield with plough (ed. similar design to Angus Menmuir no 3, Edzell no 9 & Stracathro no 26

13a by Geo Tullo, w Jean Enderdeal 12.5.1773 60, s Geo 18.5.1772 29, chn were David, Kath, Geo, John, Alex, Jas; poem; (west side) May 25 1774; G T, J E; mantling, shield with axe, saw, rule, dividers

14 David Smart late tent Townhead 4.7.1771 65, 1w Ann Alexander int Edzell, her s David 12.8.1748 19, s Thos, da Margt 3.4.1765 29, by 2w Agnas Grant, only s John 23.5.1769 28, her das Ann inf & Mary; (west side) mantling, shield with D S, A A, A G, plough

15 David Smart late tent Polburn 2.8.1753 53, w Ann Tosh 1759 58, da Ann 9.1755 18, s John 3.1757 28, chn And, Thos & Jean d inf, their chn were Margt, David, And, John, Isabel, Alex, Agnes, And, Ann, Joseph, Margt, Thos & Jean; (west side) mantling, shield with plough

15 CT (marginal) by Jas Black tent Wood par of Edzell of age 68y, w Jannet Wallas 6.6.1745 65; (central) Jas Black b Mill of Lethnot d 24.10.1750 at Wood of Dalbog, chiefly built the Bridge of Gannochy & doted ... for other Bridges & pious uses viz. for a schoolmr at Tillibardin & to building a Bridge at Balrownie & to the poor of Fettercairn. "No Bridge on Earth can be a Pass for Heav'n,/ To generous deeds Let yet due Praise be given." 1746 (see A Jervise, "Epitaphs"i 295 & "Land of the Lindsays" 108; Rogers ii 242; Duncan Fraser "Glen of the Rowan Trees"pp 43 & 78; Brechin Testaments, Janet da of decd Jas Black at Mill of Lethnot, 27.1.1743)

17 1750. A G, T G; by David Gib, fa John sometime tent Argeeth 11.1747 50, & his w Janet Low 11.1746 64 int Edzell; John Gibb 1789 9.11.1864; (west side) mantling, shield with I G, I L, crosstree & coulter

18 Jas Leighton sometime tent Drumcairn 1.1.1795 65, w Janet Black 2.8.1783 36, s Robt tent Drumcairn 3.5.1798 27; by Alex Leighton in Drumcairn 26.6.1857 78, s Jas surgeon EICS d Kirriemuir 17.4.1840 33, da Eliza Martha 10.7.1810 2, da Louisa Cath 28.4.1824 3, s Alex 23.11.1824 13, w Cath Smart 29.7.1855 77

19 Robt Leighton d Blairgowrie 31.8.1876 66, w Eliza Smart Davis d Cupar Fife 4.12.1892 83 int Cupar cem, da Georgiana 12.3.1851 4, da Eliza 1.11.1854 10, s Alex Robt 30.6.1859 19

20 David Stewart tent Clochie 4.8.1845 75, w Janet Smith 12.4.1824 49, da Eliz 4.12.1834 35, by das Isabella & Helen

20a Alex Smith tent Clochie 11.10.1880 88, w Isabella Stewart 28.1.1875 73

21 Alex Mitchell fr Townhead Newbigging & Traffat 9.8.1913 86, w Agnes Mollison 14.3.1911 83, 1s Jas d St Brides Edzell 23.3.1932 77, 2da Mary Ann d Eastbank Brechin 27.2.1938, Agnes Mollison d there 8.3.1941 84, John R d Los Angeles 27.9.1940, Betsy d Arbeith Brechin 5.7.1945 84, David S d Portland Oregon 9.6.1947 78, Wm d McCall Idaho 3.1949 84

22 Robt Black tent Clochie, w Isabel Webster 1743 38, chn alive Alex, Davis, Isobel, Chritian & Eliz, s John 1741 4, Alex 1745 17, s called Jas d inf int Menmuir; (west side) 1745. I B, A B, D B, I B, I B / C B, E B; mantling, shield with plough

23 Alex Dunbar 21.3.1900 84, w Eliz Stewart 20.1.1867 50, chn David & Eleson d inf, w Rachel Duncan 19.1.1913 80

24 TS

25 Chas Will fr Tillybardin 10.3.1828 85, w Eliz Bowman 26.9.1823 44, by da Isabella Farquharson d Edinburgh 18.6.1883 (wid of Francis Hogg in Edinburgh)

26 by Wm Law, w Jane Stewart 6.5.1878 28

27 cross. Chas Will tent Tillybardines 22.12.1868, w Betsy Milne 16.1.1897, s Chas also tent there 12.11.1904, s David inf, by members of family at home & abroad; (north side) Alex Will sometime tent Tillybardines & w Ann Jolly

28 1901. rev Jas Mitchell MA schoolmaster Lethnot 11.6.1879 80, David Mitchell 15.1.1855 40, their sis Mary Mitchell 12.2.1901 91

29 urn. rev Alex Symers min Navar & Lethnot 33y d 9.5.1842 76, w Clementina Carnegy 14.2.1851 83 (da of late Jas Carnegy of Balmachie Panbride), chn David Lyell 6.5.1821 19, Alex commander of Haidee lost in Indian Ocean 1838 33 with all on board, John Peter 2.6.1821 17, Clementina Lyell 24.8.1824 18, Margt 6.1820 11, Patricia Alison Carnegy 1.1817 2 (see Fasti v 399 which spells it Symmers; Jervise, "Epitaphs" i 295 notes mr Symers was previously schoolmaster at Barry, the monument was erected by two of his ss Geo surgeon RN & Stewart Lyell mert Tranent who changed the spelling of his name to Seymour)

30 1814. by Francies Stewart in Dalbreak, uncle Wm Stewart tent Waterhead d Mill of Inveriscondy 20.10.1809 61, only s Jas d Brechin 31.7.1813 10; Wm Stewart, w Helen Robie d Invereskandye 12.6.1850 87

The following are noted in Jervise, "Epitaphs" i 294-5 but were not seen in 1975:

31 ms note in rev mr Symers papers. David Rose episcopal clergyman .. of Lethnot & Lochlee d 1758 63 int kirk of Lethnot, w Margt Rose 1785 80, by his 1w had four chn all d at an early age, by 2w had five chn of whom two only survive - the hon Geo & da Margt by whom this marble is erected (she d unm in Montrose about 1820 & int St Peter's cem there) (see DNB for Geo Rose 17.6.1744 13.1.1818 int Christchurch minster, statesman; also Jervise, "Memorials of Angus & Mearns"ii; also Brechin Diocesan Library deposited at Dundee University, for rev David Rose's register of Baptisms from 9.7.1727 to cover Lethnot, Lochlee, Navar, Edzell & Stracathro; also Jervise "Epitaphs" i 382 & 129)

32 CT John Leitch tent Bonnington, ss David 22y & John 20y perished in the West Water 7.10.1757; epitaph composed by dr Beattie - the bros being upon one horse attempted to cross the river during a flood

24 L E T H N O T

N o t e s

A Jervise, "Epitaphs & Inscriptions" i 294-5 notes inscriptions 1-2,13,16,31-2
"Land of the Lindsays" 104-110 & 326-9 has several anecdotes about Lethnot natives & Appenix II has extracts from the rent-book for Edzell & Lethnot for 1672 & 1699.

F Cruickshank, "History of Navar & Lethnot" (Brechin 1899)

D H Edwards, "Historical Guide to Edzell & Glenesk" (3rd ed.1893)

Testaments: the following were noticed in the Index of the Commissariot of Edinburgh - Alex Lindsay only lawful s of decd Geo Lindsay of Lethnot & sometime sailor, 1727
Margt Smart spouse to Patk Hutcheone in Eglismaquhen in Wester Water of Esk, 1580-1 ;
The following is a small selection from the Index of the Commissariot of Brechin - David Low in Argeith & w Janet Black, 1641
Margt Duncan wid of John Lindsay late tent Tulliebardin, 1742
Isobel Mair w of Alex Gibb in Dykehead of Drumcarne, 1611
Jas Mair in Hunthill of Glenesk & w Kath Brek, par Lethnot, 1624
Isobel Smart wid of Wm Niddrie in Balnakattell & last w of David Lyell in Cottoun of Margie par Lethnot, 1614
Isobel Smart spouse to And Archibald in Pitmuidie, 1656
Agnes Will spouse to John Paterson in Tillebarns, 1637
Agnes Will spouse to Robt Gibb in Old Town of Lethnot, 1688

OPR with the Registrar General - 300 Lethnot & Navar
Births 1728-40, 1743-1854
Marriages 1751-99, 1824-54
Deaths 1750-1854

Church Records in the SRO: CH2/628 minutes & accounts 1746-1808
heritors minutes 1829-61
minutes 1811-1944
poors' fund & minutes 1775-1825
list of male heads of families 1834-42
communion roll 1856-1906
baptismal register 1893-1952
GD45/13 (Dalhousie muniments) glebe 1774-1791

Brechin Diocesan Library deposited in Dundee University library:
Episcopal church register of baptisms made by rev David Rose from 9.7. 1727 (to 1758?) covering Lethnot, Navar, Lochlee, Edzell & Stracathro

Fasti v 398 - Lethnot & Navar ministers from 1567
v 460 - Navar ministers from 1587 to 1723

I n d e x

Alexander 14
Archibald Notes
Arsbald 12

Black 16.18.22.Notes
Bowman 25

Carnegie/y 3-4.7.29
Christison 4.6.8

Davidson 1
Davie 19

Dunbar 23
Duncan 7.23.Notes

Enderdeal 13a

Farries 1
Farquharson 25

Gib(b) 13.17.Notes
Grant 14

Hogg 25
Hutcheone Notes

24 LETHNOT

Jolly	27
Laing	13
Law	26
Leighton	18-19
Leitch	32
Limdsay	Notes
Low	17.Notes
Lyell	29.Notes
Mair	11.27
Milne	11.27
Mitchell	21.28
Mollison	21
Niddrie	Notes
Paterson	Notes
Ramsay	4
Rickard	8
Robie	30
Rose	31.Notes
Row	2
Seymour	29
Smart	10-11.14-15.18-19.Notes
Smith	9.20.20a
Stewart	3.6.20.20a.23.26.30
Sym(m)ers	29
Talbert	12
Tosh	15
Tullo(a)	10.13a
Wallas	16
Webster	22
Will	25.27.Notes
Young	2

25 LINTRATHEN

The medieval church was dedicated to St Meddan and on or near its site, the steep and sheltered brae above the Melgam, the present parish church was built in 1803. The burial ground is well-kept.
National Grid reference: NO 285 545

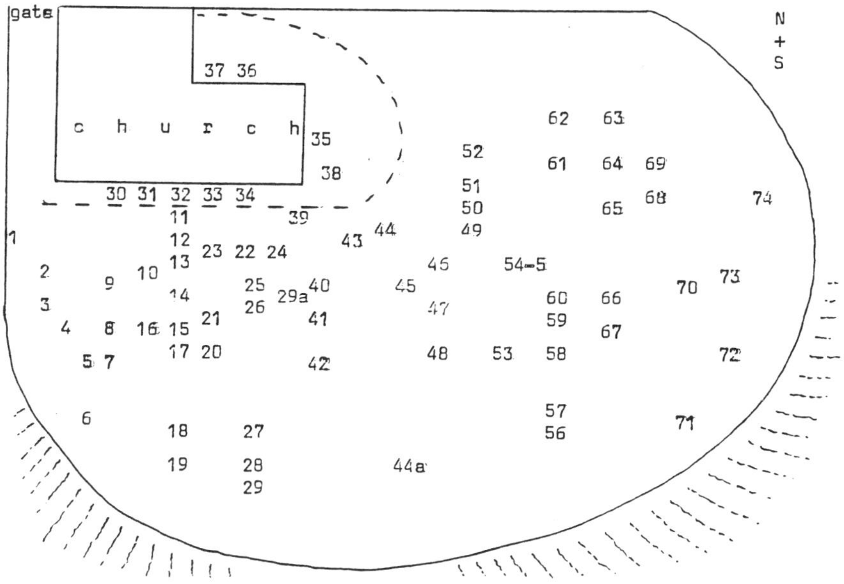

1 John Annand, w Ann Fenton, s Geo fr Middleton d there 3.11.1886 75 (w Margt Reid 5.8.1870)

2 1834. by Alex Wallace, w Helen Chaplain 12.12.1833 72

3 Geo Mitchell fr Mid Derry Kilry 17.2.1940 76, w Christina Helen MacDougall 3.3.1890 26, da Jessie Wallace MacDougall 16.9.1956 68, w Cath Ann McInnes 5.2.1927 70; Thos Wallace of Craigieloch 11.11.1892 90, w Eliz Esplin 3.10.1891 86, da Janet 30.7.1901 86, s John Wilson 9.11.1927 76

4 1828. John Thoms tent Kirkton of Nevay 12.7.1840 77, w Helen Warden d Wednesday 27.9.1826 53, chn Charlotte, Wm & Jas int here, s Edward d London int Hackney churchyard

5 FS (marginal) Androv Wright who lived in Wester Camsie departed in Iun the - 16(1)0 his age was 68y. Heir lyes Ihone Wright his son 16(2)9 21y; A W ♡ I W; I W, H W, I W; emblems (see Davidson, "Inventory" p 63, has 1699 for 1629)

6 FS (marginal) John Dickson who lived in Litl Kenie 5.11.1695 84, w Janet Wright; I D ♡ I W; I D AG 47 ◇ I D; skull;  (ed. which may be a cordiner's knife, or a T, or a millrhind & pick)

7 John Eduart in Neather Sheithens, w Elis Smairt 27.12.1713 36; emblems; (incised later) J E, E S

8 by Agnes Edward imo h Alex Lindsay late of Loanhead d Cauldswell 12.9.1911 59

9 1831. by Alex Edward fr at Standing Stone Bourn of Kilrie & w Gelles Ogilvie imo s John 3.3.1824 22

10 FS (marginal) And Ogilwi 12.11.1701 74, w Janet Gi(b)in

11 "Lait my soule liv and it shall prais the"; A O ♡ I G; A O, I O; emblems; (white marble inlay) Isabella Adam Clark 24.3.1951 83, h Wm Brown also int here, da Isabel 26.11.1936

12 next 11. Thos Adam fr Clintlaw 11.5.1865 80, w Ellen Adam 9.7.1875 77, s John 12.2.1889 67, s David d Morris City Manitoba 15.1.1886 54, s Thos fr Shanley 5.6.1901 75, da Isabella 6.4.1903 69, da Margt 8.12.1903 75

13 next 12. Jas Adam late fr Balnakilly 15.2.1852 58, w Euphemia Galloway 21.3.1866 64, s Jas fr Brairestone Meigle 12.8.1910 65

14 next 13. Mary Annand 1.8.1886 49, h John Adam of Castleton Eassie, he d at Bolshan Friockheim 29.9.1920 80

15 Jeanie Annand Hunter d Meikle Kenny 14.11.1906 28. John Hunter fr at Meikle Kenny 25.7.1915 77, w Euphemia Adam d Boyne Inchture 18.7.1935 94, da Eliz Jane d Boyne Inchture 19.4.1958 83

16 FS (marginal) - - - - (John Cams) - - - - - - - - -
(central) (S)ayers ; shield; emblems

17 1837. John Ogilvy

18 Jas Adam Hunter of Inchmartine d there 31.7.1932 62, w Margt Euphemia Annand 20.1.1928 49, da Morna Annand 6.11.1916 2½

19 next 18. Jas & Margt Hunter, Inchmartine Inchture, yt s Colin Ross killed on active service Lowestoft 13.6.1941 24

20 1799. by Elspeth (da of David Ogilvy sometime in Tarrybuckle), h Robt Peter smith in Pitmudie 20.12.1798 55y6m; (west side) mantling, shield with crown; emblems; R P, E O

21 by Thos H Wilson, Eaton Colorado USA, fa John fr Bridgend 1805 1869, mo Margt Hood 1820 1908, bro & siss Margt, Cath, Mary & John

22 FS (marginal) - - - called John Creech - - - ; (central) emblems

23 fallen next 22. (probably 18th century)

24 David Ogilvie fr Scithie 21.11.1889 81, w Betsy Falconer 17.3.1883 64, das Annie 10.1841 3, Jane 17.2.1884 40, Margt 25.8.1836 15.4.1895, Hellen 20.11.1925 82, Lizzie 18.10.1942 84

25 1845. David Ogilvy of Rosebank 27.10.1844 80, sis Helen 21.10.1845 71, by s Walter

26 FS Alex Ogilvy, 1w Margt Lawson, 2w Jannet Davie, nine of his chn Jo, He, Js, Tho, And, Wm, Alex, - -, & Ja (ed. perhaps late 17th century)

27 small. T (B or R)

28 by Alex Dunn miller at Pitcur par Kettins imo mo Anne Stewart int here 2.5.1833 66

29 FS John Dens, w Isabel Macher 21.1.1713 38; J D, I M

29a 1852. by ss & das of Jas Wilson b Brae of Auldallan 1756, moved to Hilton 1806 d 10.1830, his w Ann Smith 8.1830 62, gparents And Wilson & Helen Smart & other relatives laid here, s (of above Jas) Archd d Hilton 8.2.1855 54y10m, da (of Jas) Eliz d Hilton 17.12.1873 62

30 Alspit Adam(w of Alex Newttoun da to John Adam & Isabel Gibbin) d in Clintley (6).2.1701 24; emblems; I A ♡ I G; - A E A, F A (ed. see Airlie inscription no 13)

31 1732. John Gourie sometime miller at Bridgend 14.7.1716 58, w Euphan McNab, chn Geo, Tho, Mar, Eliz, Kat & Jean, by John; (other side) mill rhind, two mill picks & brush

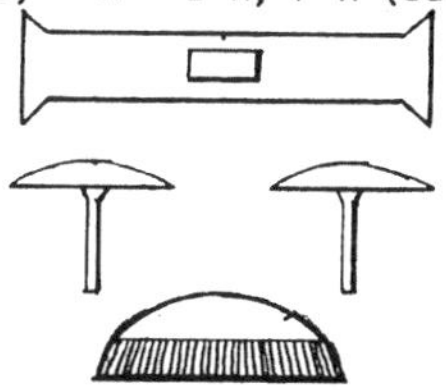

32 John Alexander fr Bridgend, w Helen Spalding, s Jas fr Bridgend (w Rachel Galloway 16.2.1905 91, da Jessie 3.8.1893, da Mary 26.8.1900) das Janet, Mary & Helen, by da Jean 30.8.1886

33 John Dickson d Needs here 24.7.1867 60, w Agnes McDonald d Needs 16.10.1876 64, s Thos d Needs 13.2.1848 11, by ss Wm d Craiglea Rattray 25.1.1929 87 & David d Muswell Hill London 29.1.1918 69

34 FS broken (marginal) - - - et Thomson who lived in Wester Coull - - - (ed. this is probably the other part of 43 infra in which I T would be for Janet Thomson w of David Smart - both parts are red sandstone)

35 FS by David Ramsay & Eliz Millar in Geivels; D R, A R, I R, 1774; 1647, emblems; - - - called John - - -

36 Jas Grant late miller Inzion 24.4.1861 64, s Thos 14.2.1848 13, s Wm in Shreveport America 5.11.1853 25, by s David

37 broken. - - John & Jas Wilkies - - - - th Ogilvy & Elspt McNicoll - - - d 8.10.171(8) - -4, Jas d 7.3.170(0) - - - Eliz d (6.7.1690) - - - - Elspet d 7.10.1727 - - - sometime in Ballanlo - - -; shield; (AW, IW)

38 Thos Garvack - - - Bridgend of - - - - & spouse Eliz - - - imo chn John, Kath & Thos; Jas & David d inf; cherub; helmet over shield with scales & symbol 4 for merchant; (T)G, E P; (west side) 1762; emblems "These three alas - - - - - into the world - - - - - - -

39 FS (marginal) by David Duncan in (Nether) Drumhead of - - - - & w Janet Craik, chn Thos 12.6.173(6) aged 25, Lilias, Geo yong chn; (central) share & coulter; emblems

40 FS And Alexander in Nevtovn, w Margt (H)all, by ss John, Jas & Wm in 1759

41 by Ann Stewart 13.9.1848 73, h John Low 28.9.1836 70

42 1804. by Dond Brown fr Dryburgh & w Jean Farquharson, da Susan 10.1. 1804 17

43 FS (marginal) David Smart h to - - - - - - 23.6.1724 aged 8(1 or 4); DS, IT; DS, AS, GS (see inscription 34 supra - the wife is probably Janet Thomson)

44 FS - - -- the body - - - - of Yur - - - - - - - derson - - - Robt - - - departed - - - 1736

44a 1869. by Jessie Warden 7.2.1872 64, nephew John Adam manuf Alyth 27.4. 1868 27 (mo Marjory Warden in Broadmuir 22.11.1841 32)

45 cherub; mantling, shield with I K, I D, R K; emblems; (west side) Jas Kandow, twin s Robt 1785 48 (by twin bro Patk); Jean Kennedy 5.3.1880 77

46 David Robertson late fr Middleton 5.11.1839 62, w Margt Ramsay 17.6. 1843 67, ss Wm, John & Alex d inf, by ss Jas & David; (west side) 1s Jas 11.3.1853 45

47 cherub; I S, E H; shield with oxen yoke, share & coulter; (west side) Thos Steel sometime in Inchaen 12.6.1746, w 2.1729, by s David

48 FS David Stil in Fornitie 5.12.1705 58, w Janet Wright; D S, I W

49 Abram Milne in Northmuir Kirriemuir 5.1.1882 74, w Eliz Lamond d Wester Coul 29.1.1900 84, gs Abram Milne Lowson d Darmali Soudan 26.7.1898 22, da Mary d West Coul 6.2.1912 60, s David d Beech Cottage Northmuir 7.3. 1929 77

50 next 49. Thos Milne d Middle Coul 7.9.1903, w Isabella Duff 17.7.1904, s Thos 14.11.1918, s Geo 13.8.1907, sister in law Margt Duff 11.7.1904

51 next 50. David Milne late fr Middle Coull 11.8.1867 86, w Mary Lighton 21. 2.1861 83, s Jas 17.1.1854 33; Wm Milne 13.11.1854 50; Helen Milne 19. 11.1862 48; David Milne 15.4.1863 58

52 1777. David London in Cole of Cortachy, w Margt Doug(ell) 22.9.1774 34; Wm London & Jean Miller his fa & mo; (west side) D L, M D

53 by David Smith & w Agnes Peter, s John 1816 32 & by ss Wm, Robt & Thos

54 John Ogilvy in Little Kenny 1828, w Jane Small 1811, only s John d Little Kenny 3.12.1856 49, by das Eliz d Hatton 31.3.1866 65 & Jane (h David Hood in Hatton of Eassie)

55 FS under turf, next 54. (marginal) Jas Ogilvie - - ved in Litl Kilrie 16. (4 or 8).1719 26 (see Jervise, "Epitaphs" i 280 has August)

56 1857. David Fenton & w Helen Ramsay d Dalwhirr par Glenisla, ss David, Jas & Thos & Peter all int here, by surviving s John fr Scruobleth par Glenisla (& w Janet Cargill)

57 Thos Fenton fr Foldend 28.10.1916 91, w Eliz Adam 8.3.1926 96, s Thos d Puerto Gabello 19.12.1882 21, da Eliz Adam 25.7.1957 85 (h John Smith in Alyth d Dunedin NZ 1932 62)

58 TS (marginal) Jas Fenton in Purgavie 11.8.1742 55, w Chirston Johnston 5.8. 1746 52; (central) 1747. two cherubs; I F, (C)I; Io F, I F, Ia F, T F,

I F, (W)F, Al F, An F, Ch F; helmet, shield with oxen yoke, share & coulter; emblems; "Below this tomb are laid the bones / Of a good virtuous pair; Both scholars, pious & discreet, Accomplishments most rare. Whose knowledge serv'd not to puff up,/ But for a nobler end; That lowlyness might them prepare,/ A glorious life to spend."

59 Thos Craik fr Cairnhall 26.11.1871 42, w Stewart Mitchell Adam 17.4.1910 79, s Alex 15.12.1890 30 (w Isabella Kinnear 9.3.1888 27), s in law Jas Nicol d Titaghur Calcutta 5.5.1898 28, s Wm 25.1.1921 51, s Jas Adam d Pitcrocknie Alyth 20.8.1938 73 (s Alex Samson 26.2.1941 50, s Wm Thos 24.3.1946 60, w Magdalena Samson 15.7.1952 87)

60 TS next 59. (marginal) by Jas Craick, fa John fr Breay(s) of Old Allan 1.3.1740 71, mo Margret Davidson - - - ; "...He snatched of the virtuous wife,/ The husband fond doth mourn;/ But death his days it soon did cut -/ Here his beseide her urn." shield with oxen yoke, share & coulter (as sketched above, similar stone to 58); I C, I (F); emblems

61 David Annand late tent farm Inzion 14.7.1854 61, w Mary Milne d Inzion 30.12.1902 91, da Helen 30.4.1864 20, da Susan 9.11.1878 32, s David d Bridgend of Ruthven 22.12.1913 75 (w Helen Annand 10.4.1935 85)

62 next 61. Thos Annand fr Wellton 30.12.1908 72, w Jane Adam 16.4.1911 74, s David 23.11.1925 61, da Mary Milne 26.12.1934 66; David Annand, w Betsy C McKay 19.2.1942 74

63 Thos McKay late fr Wester Auldallon 25.12.1854 81, w Jean Ramsay 9.6.1869 80, by s Peter & s Thos; Peter McKay 29.10.1856 28; Thos McKay 28.3.1913 87, w Margt Hill 27.11.1915 86

64 next 63. John McKay fr Knowhead Auld Allan 15.6.1947 82, w Margt Jane Addison 24.3.1940 71 (sis Jane Addison 19.6.1924 54), s Jas 26.11.1901 1y, da Betty 29.5.1906 15, da Mary 29.4.1913 4

65 urn, next 64. Jas McKay fr Auldallan 8.10.1799 17.4.1889, w Marjory Annand 8.5.1801 18.6.1887, da Jane 17.7.1842 27.3.1870 (h Jas Wylie), s Thos 6.3.1829 14.4.1882, s Jas 10.7.1837 30.10.1906, s Wm 28.12.1830 1.10.1910; Jas McKay Wylie late of Auldallan d Edmonton Canada 17.3.19(53), w Annie Duncan

66 David Doig millwright Kingoldrum 3.11.1885 84, w Janet Mitchell 31.5.1887 90

67 next 66. 1837. by And Doig wright Shanly, w Girzel Gellatly 24.4.1836 59, tribute, chn Girzell 4.2.1823 1y, Geo 14.2.1823 3, Thos 16.2.1823 7, da Hellen 21.3.1823 24 (h Thos Douglas 21.6.1833 43), s And 19.4.1836 29, s David (s Jas 21.3.1823 1y, s David 26.6.1831 1y), s John (s John 28.11.1828 4, s David 11.4.1832 12d, s Jas 29.4.1834 5m)

68 small. Jas Thomson d Dykend 22.8.1914 76, w Margt McGregor d Newtyle 28.6.1933 77 (mo Cath McGregor 7.11.1912 98) by chn

69 next 68. 1869. rev Alex Thomson min here d in Manse 2.4.1813 (see Fasti v 268; also North Perthshire Blairgowrie churchyard inscriptions 86 & 87; also Jervise, "Epitaphs.." i 281 - he was gs of Ross author of the poem "Helenore" published Dundee 1812 with biographical notice of the author)

25 L I N T R A T H E N

70 1879. Jas McHardie 29.1.1899 73, w Helen Adam 22.7.1895 65, five ss d inf, da Jessie 17.7.1864 10, s Steward Adam 21.10.1878 6, s John 5.8. 1910 59 (w Sarah Reid Yule)

71 Rodrick Kennedy d Cupar Fife 11.3.1852 46 int there, w Janet Lamond d Lochee 4.2.1884 83 int Liff, sis Cath Kennedy d Stephaugh 14.4.1886 86 (h Wm Mitchell s Stephaugh 16.11.1887 88), by da Cath d Myreside Meigle 14.10.1910 68; Thos Wighton tailor d Stephaugh 8.2.1907 90

72 David Stewart 12.11.1859 63, w Fanny Farquharson 28.8.1845 34, da Bettsy 6.1848 22

73 1846. Chas Stewart 12.3.1841 42, by w Isabella Nicoll 19.11.1872 77, s Thos 9.1.1823 11m, s Daniel 12.1.1823 3, s David 1.3.1839 4, s Wm 31. 8.1862 24

74 next yewtree. by Jas Edward, fa Thos d Padanaram 1.2.1886 76, mo Betsy Duncan d Meikle Kenny 11.1848 36, uncle Jas Edward d Newton Moss 24.11.1883 83, sis Susan 3.7.1932 93 (h Alex Fyfe 3.8.1916 83, da Betsy Fyfe Stewart 26.11.1909 38, s Edw 2.5.1970 89)

The following are from Jervise, "Epitaphs & Inscriptions" i 280 & 364 & were not seen in 1976:

75 Andrew Hay, daughter; 1759; verse quoted

76 John Deuchars hammerman Burnside of Kinclune, w Janet Candow 26.9.1721, chn John & Robt d inf; poem quoted

N o t e s

A Jervise, "Epitaphs & Inscriptions" i pp 279-81 & 364 notes inscriptions 6-7, 26,29,55,58,60,75-6

F Davidson, "Inventory of 17th Century Tombstones in Angus" has detailed descriptions at pp 62-3 of nos. 5,6,30,35 & 48

Craig burial ground, a small walled enclosure in a field near Reekie Linn, was neglected with no gravestones visible in 1976. Ghosts of a laird of Lochblair & an Ogilvy of Cluny are reputed to haunt it (see Duncan Fraser, "The Land of the Ogilvies" p 69)

Testaments: The Index to the Register of the Commissariot of Angus includes -
Wm Adam in Bottom, 1799
Thos Blair & Janet his sister chn of Geo Blair at Bridgend, 1731 & 1744
Wm Cairncross in Scheill of Cleuchlaw par Lantrathauchin, 1613
Wm Farquharson yt s of decd Dond Farquharson in Balnakeillie, 1761
Archd Glenny in Blakdykis, 1620; Jas Kandow in Roughhaugh, 1793
Margt M'Nicoll spouse to John Smairt in Sechie, 1617; John Smart in Schethie, 1624; John Valentine in Longdrum, 1769
Janet Wilkie spouse to John Bruce in Bray of Glenquharitie, 1616
Geils Williamson spouse to Thos Edward in Ley of Lintrathen, 1619
John & Alex Wright sons to John Wright, 1731

OPR with the Registrar General - 302 Lintrathen
Births 1717-62, 1773-1854
Marriages 1717-8, 1720-46, 1773-93, 1796-1854
Deaths 1717-72, 1830-54

Church Records in the SRO: CH2/ 243 marriages 1798-1802;
minutes 1664-1716, 1772-8, 1794-1812, 1814-1938;
account book 1813-42;
baptismal register 1863-96

25 LINTRATHEN

Church records in SRO continued: **GD 16/46 & 49** (Airlie Muniments), church, manse & school 17th century - 1879
HR 120 papers re church sittings 1859

Fasti v 267 ministers from 1571 (including Jas Edward schoolmaster Aberlemno ordained min here in 1772, d 11.7.1793, St Andrews Testaments 1793, Scots Magazine xxxiii-iv)

Index

Adam	11-5,30.44a.57.59.62.70
Addison	64
Alexander	32.40
Annand	1.14-5.18.61-2.65
Blair	Notes
Brown	11.42
Bruce	Notes
Cairncross	Notes
Cams- - -	16
Candow, see Kandow	76
Cargill	56
Chaplain	2
Clark	11
Crai(c)k	39.59-60
Creech	22
Davidson	60
Davie	26
Dens	29
Deuchars	76
Dickson	6.33
Doig	66-7
Douglas	67
Dougell	52
Duff	50
Duncan	39.65.74
Dunn	28
Edward	8-9.74.Notes
Edvart	7
Esplin	3
F.	60
Falconer	24
Farquharson	42.72.Notes
Fenton	1.56-8
Fyfe	74
G.	11
Galloway	13.32
Garvack	38
Gellatly	67
Gib(b)in	10.30
Glenny	Notes
Gourie	31
Grant	36
H.	47
Hall	40
Hay	75
Hill	63
Hood	21.54
Hunter	15.18-9
I.	59
Johnston	58
Kandow, see Candow	45.Notes
Kennedy	45.71
Kinnear	59
Lamond	49.71
Lawson	28
Lighton	51
Lindsay	8
London	52
Low	41
Lowson	49
McDonald	33
Macdougall	3
McGregor	68
McHardie	70
Macher	29
McInnes	3
McKay	62-5
McNab	31
McNicoll	37.Notes
Millar/er	35.52
Milne	49-51.61
Mitchell	3.66.71
Newttoun	30
Nicol(l)	59.73
O.	11.45
Ogilvie/y	9-10.17.20.24-6.37.54-5.Notes
P.	38
Peter	20.53
Ramsay	35.46.56.63
Reid	1
Robertson	46
S.	47
Samson	59
Sayers	16
Small	54
Sma(i)rt	7.29a.34.43.Notes
Smith	29a.53.57

25 LINTRATHEN

Spalding	32
Steel, Stil	47-8
Stewart	28.41.72-4
Stil, Steel	47-8
Thoms	4
Thomson	34.43.68-9
Valentine	Notes
W.	5
Wallace	2-3
Warden	4.44a
Wighton	71
Wilkie	37.Notes
Williamson	Notes
Wilson	21.29a
Wright	5-6.48.Notes
Wylie	65
Yule	70

26a LOCHLEE OLD CHURCHYARD

The church was founded by St Drostan beside the loch about 800. The ruins are approached by a mile of cart track from Invermark castle.

National Grid reference: NO 431 802

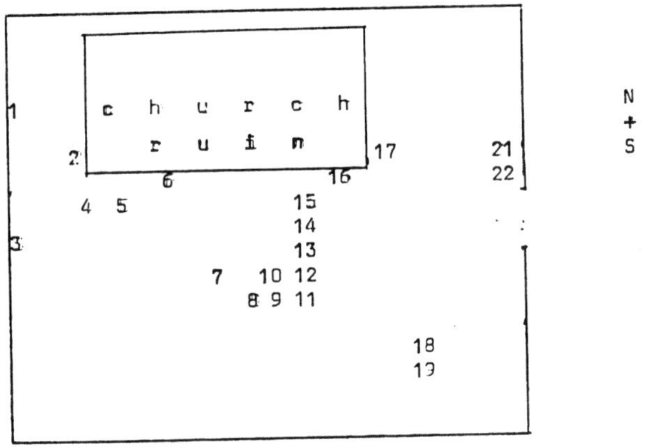

1 1800. Dond Nicol 9.10.1799 85, s David 11.8.1798 52; (east side)emblems

2 leaning against church. (I C, - -); I C, (I)N; A C, - - flanking cherub; (other side) - - - - - - - - (Christian or Chisholme) - - - - -

3 by rev Peter Jolly 57y episcopal clergyman Lochlee, s Jas 14.3.1798 10, w Jean Dieack 12.5.1809 56 (see Jervise, "Epitaphs.." i 129: rev Peter Jolly d Brechin 1845 82, his da md bishop Moir of Brechin)

4 Margt Campble 5.9.1794 24, h David Couts in Drowstie, his mo Jean Gibb 18.3.1794 65

5 1846. John Milne of Glencatt 2.9.1818 50, w Susan Farquharson 2.9.1843 75, they left two das Magdalene & Agnes, by Magdalene to parents

6 David Christison fr Auchronie 20.12.1761 61, he left chn John, David, Chas, Hugh, Jean & Magdalene by w Helen Mill; (east side) David Christison late tent Auchronie, w Helen Miln 19.12.1775 64;"a Man of Integrit .... & charitably disposed to the indigent." (see Brechin Testaments:

Thos Chrystison tent in Wester Acbrony, 8.2.1744)

7 Dan Christison 4.6.1751 36 (see Jervise "Epitaphs" i 128:"he was accidentally burnt to death among a quantity of heather"); (east side) I C M K I C I W; poem

8 & 9 two small headstones re-erected back to back, no.8 illegible.

9 I N, - -; W(N), A -; S - flanking cherub

10 Al Broun;hear lys; A M, f B, f B; emblems & cherub/heart; (east side) A B 1732; dart, dividers; emblems

11 pillar & urn. by Wm Innes fr Arsallary 27.5.1926 81, w Christina Innes 21.5.1934 73; Jas Ian Innes, Chartered Bank of India killed in action Givenchy France 3.1.1915 21; David W Innes of Mains of Fordoun 1.4.1950 72; Alex Innes, Blackcraig 14.10.1958 61; John Innes, Arsallary 23.4.1915 88, bro Jas late tent there 27.3.1917 87, sis Martha C d there 15.10.1919 81

12 Jas Coutts, Whitestone Lochee 15.3.1856 65

13 by Jean, Mary, Ann & Eliz Innes of Kirnie to parents Chas d Kirnie 12.1.1856 59 & Mary Dunbar 3.11.1871 76 & bros John 2.7.1865 40, David 15.6.1879 52

14 David Innes fr Arsallary 2.9.1865 (6)9, s Edw clerk Royal Bank of Scotland 7.8.1880 31, s Robt 29.6.1889 47, w Martha Christison 7.2.1894 88; Johana Innes 12.10.1899 18; Alice H Innes 30.11.1901 25, h John McArthur gamekeeper Ganochy

15 by David Innes, mo Margt Edward 28.6.1823 60, fa John Innes 7.11.1838 84, da Mary 28.4.1837 11, s David 11.11.1849 18

16 Her lays Dond M'Donel, Margt Dufs, John MDonel, Margt Tohou; (east side) May the 21 1733; knife & ? D MD, M D, I MD, M T flanking a cherub/ heart; bones & gravedigger's shovel & spade

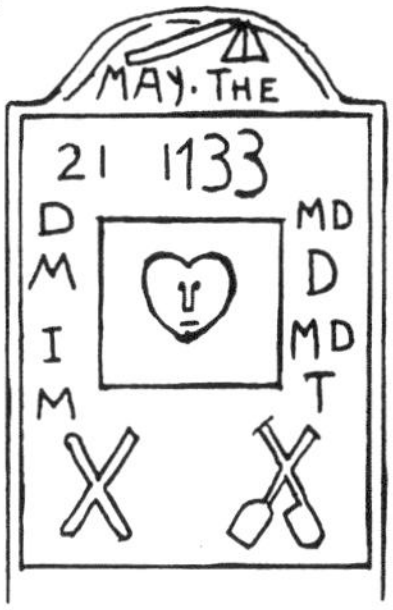

17 Alex Ross AM schoolmaster of Lochlee author of "Lindy & Nory" and other poems in the Scottish dialect b April 1699 d 29.5.1784; poem (see Jervise, "Epitaphs"i: his school & house lie ruined next the church; see inscription no.22; see DNB, "The Scottish Nation"iii)

18 in railed enclosure with 19. And Welsh fr Gleneffock 27.2.1814 7(4), w Ann Murray 25.1.1825 (4)8, s Jas 1806 22, s Alex surgeon d S America 1821 22 during the Chilean war under lord Cochrane, s Murray officer of Inland Revenue d Langholm Clova 29.11.1855 49, s Robt fr Aucharn Clova d Tillytoghills 10.1.1879 8-, da Isabella 13.5.1824 36, da Mary d Tillytoghills 8.11.1869 67, also int here s And fr Kirktown 9.12.1826 40 (w Cath Pitie 25.11.1822 44, s And student of divinity 1840 (2)0)

19 with 18. John Welsh tent Gleniffock 7.12.1845 55, by w Mary Falconer 15.12.1859 56

26a LOCHLEE OLD CHURCHYARD

20 FS Chas Garden of Bellastreen gent 22.11.1761 aged above 90y, 1da mrs Margt Garden aged above 60y; "....Of stature handsome, front erect & fair,/Of dauntless brow, yet mild & debonair./The camp engaged his youth & would his age /Had cares domestic not recalled his stage,/By claim of blood, to represent a line,/That but for him was ready to decline..." (see Jervise "Epitaphs" i 128 for notes on the family)

21 mural in latin. John Garden esq of Midstrath d at Invermark 26.4.1745 73, md on 29.10.1696 Cath Farquharson 24.11.1738 63; poem; erected by s Robt min St Fergus; poem (see Jervise, "Epitaphs.."i 126 & A.&J.Tayler, "Cess Roll of Aberdeenshire 1715 pp48,64 for Garden of Migstrath)

22 mural. by mr Alex Ross schoolmaster Lochlee, w Jean Catanach 5.5.1779 77 int here (see inscription 17, Jervise i 127, Rogers ii 245, Edwards "Historical Guide to Edzell & Glenesk pp 125-36: he was a native of Kincardine O'Neil & she was a da of a farmer in Logie-Coldstone)

Notes

A Jervise, "Epitaphs & Inscriptions.." i 127-9 notes inscriptions 1,4-8,11-19, 21-2; "The Land of the Lindsays" pp 69 & 73 also refers to Alex Ross.

Testaments indexed for the Commissariot of Brechin include -
John Christison in Assailzie, 1627
Margt Christison spouse to Wm Low in Glentennet, 1627
Kath Campbell spouse to Wm Nicoll in Migvie, 1627
Alex Nicoll servant to John Nicoll in Keeny, 1751

Index

Broun(e)	10
C.	2
Campble/ell	4.Notes
Catanach	22
Chisolm	2
Christison	6-7.14.Notes
Cout(t)s	4.12
Dieack	3
Dufs	16
Dunbar	13
Edward	15
Falconer	19
Farquharson	5.21
Garden	20-1
Gibb	4
Innes	11.13-15
Jolly	3
K.	7
Low	Notes
M.	10
McArthur	14
McDonel	16
MK.	7
Mill	6
Miln(e)	5-6
Moir	3
Murray	18
N.	2.9
Nicol(l)	1.Notes
Pirie	18
Ross	17.22.Notes
Tohou	16
W.	7
Welsh	18-19

26b LOCHLEE NEW CHURCHYARD

The new parish church was built in 1803, but the first burial there was in 1808
National Grid reference: NO 446 804

1 1840. by Chas Mitchell tent Auchintoul imo s Alex 16.5.1838 23y10m12d

2 1844. by John Stephen, Cutleheugh imo ss Alex 29.7.1837 1y, Wm 29.3.1844 10y4m

26b LOCHLEE NEW CHURCHYARD

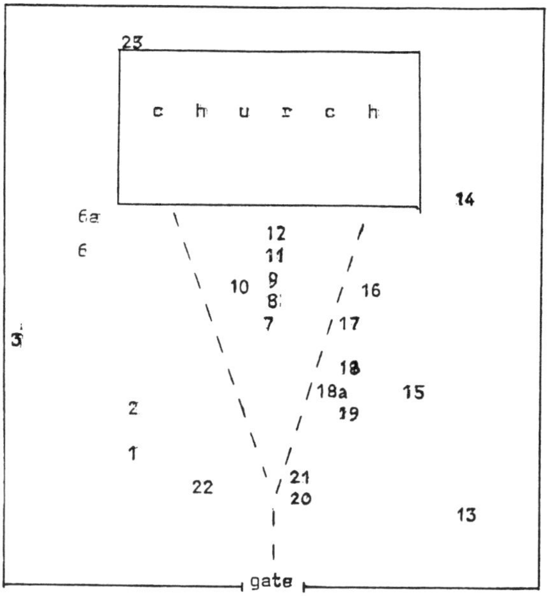

3 by Jas Kinnear tent on West Bank imo fa John 21.12.1842 67, mo Ann Bowman 22.2.1857 70

4 Chas Will mason Dykenook Lochlee 14.10.1854 81

5 in latin. David 27y & Archd 18y both perished in the Mark 27.10.1820, by fa Jas Whyte (translation by their bro rev John Whyte min of Lethnot & Navar printed in Jervise, "Epitaphs" i 130 & "Land of the Lindsays" 74: accidental drowning during a snowstorm while the brothers were collecting their father's sheep)

6 1854. by Mary Grant d Glentennet 5.8.1875 77, imo h Wm Stewart late tent Dalbrack 3.11.1853 68, s Wm 29.2.1832 inf

6a by Margt Clark, h John Gall late tent Stony-Well 23.2.1855 80

7 Wm Duke tent West Migvie 9.5.1884 73, da Elis 22.12.1851 4, s David d inf, wid Elis Caithness 26.3.1896 87; Jane 15.11.1835 29.8.1877, h David Lord; Ann Duke 18.12.1896 53; Alex S Duke 19.2.1905 64; Mary Duke 24.9.1922 77; Martha Duke 6.1.1925 87; Agnes Duke 4.10.1926 77; by W Duke in 1861.

8 1849. Alex Watt mert Tarfside 4.6.1848 59, da Jane 7.10.1829 4, s Alex 30.4.1837 3, da Helen 1.6.1848 16, s John 10.6.1853 22, Eliz 26.7.1855 28, s David 15.9.1860 20, da Margt 21.5.1863 20, da Mary Ann 21.4.1865 29, s Robt 3.3.1883 36, w Jane Caithness 26.10.1802 8.1.1893, 1s Jas 13.12.1828 8.5.1896, gchn Jane G Donald 7.2.1861 9 & Jas Smith 12.3.1889 26

9 ob by rev David Inglis min Lochlee imo mo Christian Inglis 15.7.1808 72. rev David Inglis, Lochlee 18.1.1837 65 in 31st y of ministry, w Cath Collier d Montrose 30.1.1861 91; Jane Inglis 11.9.1811 2y10m; Wm Burnet

26b LOCHLEE NEW CHURCHYARD

Inglis 12.9.1815 4y11m; last survivor of the family of rev David Inglis, Jane Christina 14.7.1893 81, restored in 1902 by his gchn David Inglis esq of the Baillies Lochlee & rev Robt Inglis MA of Edzell (see Fasti v)

10 by family, John Mitchell late fr Turnabrain 26.2.1840 61, w Agnes Kinnear 14.3.1871 89, da Jessie 7.1.1814 8m, da Eliz 5.2.1820 11, Isabella 26.1.1837 23; Margt Mitchell 21.12.1898 77; Agnes Mitchell 16.1.1901 79

11 general Hart of Doe castle of Kilderry Ireland, s Edw d manse of Lochlee 1.5.1836 25

12 by David Gall imo fa Joseph 24.4.1850 92

13 pillar. rev Walter Low 48y min Lochlee d Carnoustie 22.3.1887 85, w Marjory Malcolm 8.1.1853 48, da Jane Jamieson 7.10.1846 21, s Robt Thomson d at Wairaw New Zealand 2.9.1858 27

14 1815. by John Middleton in Middlefoord imo w Eliz Coutts 31.5.1809 32

15 1878. John Tasker, w Eliz Stephen 14.9.1852 50

16 David Laing 11.1.1835 83, w Martha Edwards 11.4.1853 both d at Wester Auchintoul, s Chas d Easter Auchintoul 4.10.1836 39, by s Peter d Trinity village Brechin 7.7.1888 75

17 Geo Duncan d at Baillies 1852 29, w Betsy Birse d East Migvie 6.10.1903 81, da Mary d London 5.1867 23, by s Robt, East Migvie d 28.11.1928 82

18 David Birse sometime tent in Auchronie 22.2.1851 40, gs Chas Skene drowned in the Forth 30.6.1893 19

18a mr & mrs Chas Skene, Turnabrane, 2da Margt A d 14.12.1963 87

19 1841. Chas Clark d Excellry 23.10.1839 68, w Rachel Findlay 18.1.1856 75, by chn.

20 Frances Davis, Tygwynne Pembrokeshire, 11.1854, h rev And McIlwraith FC Lochlee (see Ewing 1 231: rev A McIlwraith b Ayr 1811, ordained Lochlee in 1847 - at first he suffered great hardships from the opposition of the proprietor to the FC, he was twice md his 2w being Janet Thomson Gray, he d 1886)

21 1811. by Wm Reid shoemaker in Aberdeen imo s Geo who perished among the snow about the end of 1.1810 29 within the bounds of this par

22 David Christison fr Milton 1.2.1890 80, ss Jas 3.3.1853 5, Chas 9.10.1863 20, John 1.4.1866 22, gs colour segt David Christison, Argyll & Sutherland Highlanders killed Magersfontein 11.12.1899 30, w Isobel Ingram 22.7.1912 92, da Mary 15.4.1931 84

23 by rev David Inglis min Lochlee imo mo Christian Inglis 15.7.1808 72

Notes

A Jervise, "Epitaphs.." i 129-30 refers to inscriptions 5,9,11 & 21

D H Edwards, "Guide to Glenesk & Lochlee" (1876) & "Historical Guide to Edzell & Glenesk"

Glenesk Folk Museum at The Retreat, Tarfside: ms Episcopal records of Lochlee 1856-1883 ; ms miscellaneous letters of Glenesk people 1844-1970; M F Michie, "Studies of Glenesk"

OPR with the Registrar General (the parish was united with Lethnot 1618-1723)
- 303 Lochlee: Births 1731-1854
Marriages 1783-1854
Deaths 1783-92, 1808, 1810-54

26b LOCHLEE

Church Records in the SRO: CH2/455 minutes & a/cs 1775–1840
minutes 1834–1932
management committe minutes 1825–1975
accounts 1836–1932
communion rolls 1879–1932

CH3/218 Lochlee FC, UP, Maule Memorial, Tarfside, C of S
minutes & a/cs 1848–1932
see Edzell CH3/543 for Lochlee McKenzie
HR glebe 1831

Episcopal church records deposited by the Brechin Diocesan Library in Dundee University Library: rev David Rose's register of Baptisms from 7.1727 in Lochlee, Lethnot, Navar, Edzell & Stracathro.
(The New Spalding Club Miscellany i 313 (1890) mentions episcopal records of Lochlee – Births from 1766 & Marriages & Deaths from 1840, but these were not traceable in 1966)

Index

Birse 17–18
Bowman 3
Burnet 9

Caithness 7–8
Christison 22
Clark 6a.19
Collier 9
Coutts 14

Davis 20
Donald 8
Duke 7
Duncan 17

Edwards 16

Findlay 19

Gall 6a.12
Grant 6
Gray 20

Hart 11

Inglis 9.23
Ingram 22

Jamieson 13

Kinnear 3.10

Laing 16
Lord 7
Low 13

McIlwraith 20
Malcolm 13

Middleton 14
Mitchell 1.10

Reid 21

Skene 18.18a
Smith 8
Stephen 2.15
Stewart 6
Stormonth 9

Tasker 15
Thomson 13

Watt 8
Whyte 5
Will 4

27a LOGIEPERT

The parishes of Logie-Montrose & Pert were united in 1661, but the two kirk buildings were maintained (probably with altereating services) until 1775 when Logiepert church was built halfway between. It was rebuilt in 1840 & no burials have taken place there. National Grid ref: NO 665 643

27b LOGIE-MONTROSE

The church of Logie Cuthill was dedicated to St Martin in 1243. The pre-Reformation building became ruinous & was replaced in 1857 by a memorial chapel for the Carnegys of Craigo, which lies secluded below the farm of Mains of Logie.

National Grid reference: NO 706 635

27b LOGIE-MONTROSE

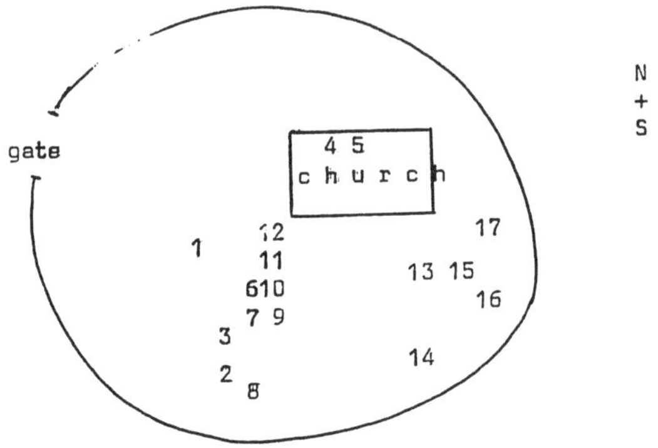

1 FS (marginal) Jas Croll in the Lau of Craigo, s Jas 18.12.1728 21; (central) shield with I C, (C)W; I C; bible; poem (quoted by Jervise, "Epitaphs" i 210:"...Hers moistie bons & broken skuls,/And graves all over green.

2 Alex Thomson 5.11.1847 68, w Jane Norrie 27.3.1862 84, chn John 19.2.1850 41, Wm 11.1.1855 46 int Magherahamlet Ireland, Jane 5.11.1860 55, Mary 23 3.1871 62 (relict of Alex Clark, by s Adam, Belfast)

3 I D plough C P; I D, C C, John, Catherne, Jas, Marget, Elis, Allex & Jas Doneltson children 1727

4 mural. Thos Carnegy of Craigo esq 9.6.1793 64, w Mary 20.11.1815 65, by 2da Eliz (h hon Lord Gillies); eulogy (see Jervise, "Epitaphs.."i 209: Mary was 2da of Jas Gardyne of Middleton - a flat stone in NE corner of the aisle covers the graves of her son & his wife, a sister of sir Geo M Grant of Ballindalloch; see inscription 18 infra)

5 empty mural panel.

6 1823. Alex Vallentine resided Hill of Craigo d 18.5.1794 60, w Janet Cai d Montrose 18.4.1823 92 with chn John, Elis, Helen are int here, by s in law Jas Jolly carter Montrose; (west side) Jas Jolly 18.2.1827 56

7 Wm Galdie mason 22.6.1817 60, by w Eliz Milne

8 Wm Thomson smith at Craigo 12.1797, w Mary, s Robt, da Anne

9 John Miln lived sometime at Craigie d 4.4.1730 72, w Margt Nuckle; (west side) mantling, shield with 1748, square, axe, rule, dividers; J M, M N; C M, J M, J M, A M

10 two cherubs & flowers; mantling with shield, R F, M R, share & crosstree; W F, R F, M F, E F, D F, J F, 1746; (west side) Robt Findlay lived in Tolmants 1742 60, by w Margt Read, da Margt 1720 1y; poem (quoted by Jervise, "Epitaphs" i 210; east side illustrated in Willsher & Hunter, "Stones" p 45 no 38)

11 1849. by Isaac Mackenzie at Logie Works, w Elis Forbes 2.2.1849 46 leaving one s & four das (her mo Elis Niddrie 11.10.1838 75, her fa John Forbes 13.9.1839 73)

12 Wm Niddrie tent Hill of Craigo 25.12.1837 79, w Jean Lakie 21.8.1835 62, da Mary 11.

11.4.1837 34 (h Alex Alexander fr East Hill of Craigo 9.11.1884 77, his w Jane McPherson 25.12.1891 81, ss Jas 1.11.1867 22, John 20.7.1904 54); (west side) mantling, shield with share & crosstree, 1748; J R, J C; ER, WR, RR, MR

13 by Jospeh Taylor tent at the Mill of Hedderwick, w Mary Taviotdale (13). 3.176(3), also three chn; I T, M T, 1765

14 1851. Robt Murray d Logie 30.6.1855, w Jane Cooper d Montrose 24.12.1873 72, chn John d Montrose 26.4.1857 22, Joseph d Logie 31.8.1854 10y6m, Robt d Logie 6.12.1848 7y6m, Edw d Logie 9.12.1848 2y6m, Jas d Vicenza Italy 9.3.1876 44

15 Robt Graham tent Boat of Craigo 22.10.1847 57, by w Mary Bowan 30.5.1881 90, s David 17.9.1846 23, da Ann 23.7.1909 76

16 1859. David Duncan 4.3.1853 51, w Jean Davidson 5.5.1859 70, by family

17 1851. Robt Davidson 28.3.1838 92, w Ann Sime 28.12.1825 78, by s Chas 9.12.1862 72 (w Ann Carter 23.6.1851 56, da Barbara 26.12.1907 75, ss Jas 7.4.1862 43 (w Eliz Croll 15.5.1899 80), Robt 27.1.1879 45, gda Barbara 6.9.1904 52)

The following were not seen in 1978 and presumably are buried under the rubble of the chapel, but they are detailed in Jervise, "Epitaphs" i 210:

18 FS David Carnegy of Craigo 9.3.1776 10.11.1845; mrs Carnegy of Craigo 9. 1779 24.9.1856 (see no.4)

19 FS David Carnegy of Craigo, 2da Mary 4.5.1811 23.2.1847

20 FS Thos Carnegy of Craigo 9.3.1804 12.6.1856 (according to Jervise he was the last male descendant of David Carnegy of Craigo min of Farnell - he left Craigo to his cousin Thos Grant WS of Edinburgh, son of sir Geo Macpherson-Grant of Ballindalloch (see Speyside Gravestones, Inveraven inscription 90); two shields with the Carnegy and the Macpehrson & Grant arms were built over the chapel door when it was restored in 1857)

N o t e s

A Jervise, "Epitaphs & Inscriptions" i 209-10 notes inscriptions 1,6,10,18-20

J G Low, "Galraw: Home of the Fullartons" (Montrese, 1937)

Testaments: the following were noticed in the Register of the Commissariot of Edinburgh - Henry Fullertoun portioner of Craigow, 1582-3
Wm Fullertoun of Cragow, 1581
Christian Strachan sometime spouse to Alex Fullerton portioner of Craigo, 1590;
The following are a small selection from the Commissariot of St Andrews:
Margt Cockpen, h Thos Low in Cottertoun of Logie-Montrose, 1627
Elspet Jap, h John Joy in Three Lawes, 1640
David Joy in Laws of Toments, 1662; Walter Joy in Three Laws of Dun, 1618
Isobel Ked spouse to Robt Myln in Hill of Craigo, 1662
Elspet Grub spouse to Jas Fairweather in Mains of Craigo, 1675
Janet Cob spouse to John Milne in Galraw, 1606
John Greig in Lundin of Gallery, 1774
Isobel Shepherd in Den of Midgate spouse to John Graham,par Logie, 1676
Janet Will spouse to John Miln in the Hill of Craigo, 1662

A Jervise, "Memorials of Angus & the Mearns" ii 230 for Logie-Montrose kirk

J D Gilruth, "Ancient Churches on the Northesk", Scottish Ecclesiology Socy. Transactions 12 1936/7 41-59

27b L O G I E - M O N T R O S E

I n d e x

Alexander	12
Bowan	15
C.	3.12
Caird	6
Carnegy	4.18-20
Carter	17
Clark	2
Cob	Notes
Cockpen	Notes
Cooper	14
Croll	1.17
Davidson	16-17
Doneltson	3
Duncan	16
Fairweather	Notes
Fin(d)lay	10.Notes
Forbes	11
Fullertoun	Notes
Galdie	7
Gardyne	4
Gillies	4
Graham	15.Notes
Grant	20
Greig	Notes
Grub	Notes
Jap	Notes
Jolly	6
Joy	Notes
Ked	Notes
Lakie	12
Low	Notes
Mackenzie	11
Macpherson	12
Macpherson-Grant	4.20
Miln(e),Myln	7.9.Notes
Murray	14
Nicol	see Nuckle
Niddrie	11-12
Nuckle	9
P.	3
R.	12
Shepherd	Notes
Sime	17
Strachan	Notes
Taviotdale	13
Taylor	13
Thomson	2.8
Vallentine	6
W.	1
Will	Notes

27c P E R T

Some of the best-preserved stones of the folk baroque school of masons which flourished in Strathmore from 1730-50 are to be seen in this quiet ground above the main road. The church has been roofless since at least 1775. The old parish was also called Over Inchbrayock.

National Grid reference: NO 650 661

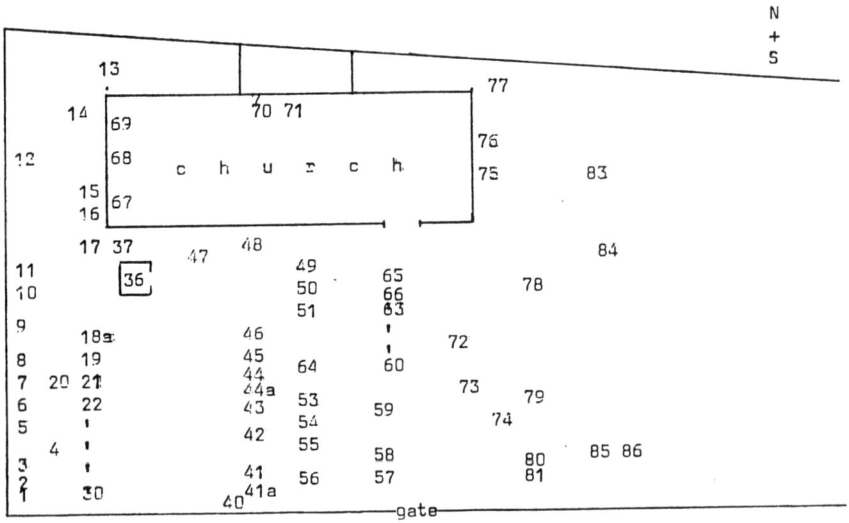

1 Eliz Ogilvy 16.3.1804 63, 50y in the service of Jas Macdonald esq Inglismaldie, by his only da Mary Macdonald

2 by Ann Lunan, bro rev mr Alex Lunan presbyter of the Episcopal church of Scotland first at Blairdaff & last at Rosehill d 29.9.1769 66 (see Jervise "Epitaphs.."i 212 & 375: rev Alex Lunan of Kintore, w Jean (fa sir Wm Forbes of Monymusk) s Wm (w Barbara da of Alex Gordon of Merdrum in Rhynie, md 24.12.1663, s Wm (md Isobella Thain of Blakhall in the Garioch on 4.10.1691, 7ch rev Alex (above) b 1703, 10ch Ann (h N Cruickshank of Aberdeen)))

3 Jas Bromley 9.1809 73, 30y esteemed servant in the family of Jas Macdonald esq Inglismaldie, by Mary mrs Ogilvy (only da of Jas Macdonald)

4 TS Jas Hodgston 12.10.1702 (Jervise "Epitaphs"i 212 has 1720 in error) & s Wm & w Janet Fulerton; monogram W H F; I H, W H, I F, I H; M H, A H, M H, K H, E H, I H, W H, I H, D H; (central part illegible)

5 by Thos Durie tent Capo & w Margt Middleton, da Isobel 1.8.1791 14, s Alex d inf

6 Chas Durie fr Dalladies & Capo 2.1.1862 72 (see Jervise "Epitaphs" i 375: he was s of Thos & Margt Middleton & was auctioneer remarkable for .. integrity ... & good humour), his family Cath 22.12.1855 27, Thos 10.11.1858 23, Isobel 31.10.1860 33, Chas who succeeded his fa on Dalladies & Capo d 10.11.1870 39, Alex brewer North Port Brechin (Jervise: where his maternal ancestors had conducted same trade for 200y) 23.3.1872 39, w Jean Durie 4.11.1878 80, s John tent Dalladies 14.2.1880 41, da Jane d Edzell 23.12.1890 66, 1da Margt 5.11.1910 87 (h Geo Knowles)

7 rev Thos Hill d Manse of Logie Pert 1.1.1864 in 40th y of ministry (see Fasti v 404)

8 Geo McGhonachie schoolmaster LogiePert 18.11.1844, w Helen Rennie 16.9.1846, s Alex d London 27.8.1830, s John d Honduras 13.9.1832, da Helen 18.11.1859, da Janet 6.12.1861, s Geo 27.2.1867, da Ann 4.7.1886

9 by UP congregation of Muirton imo rev Jas Renwick 22.10.1845 59 for 23y 7m pastor of that congregation. "A workman that needeth not be ashamed"; rev Wm Arnot Mitchell 28.11.1916 min of Muirton congregation since 21.5.1879, w Jane Ann Duthie 30.9.1915

10 David Meek sometime min Luthermuir, w Eliza Ferguson 24.1.1820 62

11 Joseph Willocks 9.4.1865 79, by Margt Jolly

12 mural. David Lyall esq residing at Balmakewan, da Isabella Jane 1.5.1845 inf 10m7d, eldest bro And 7.1797 inf

13 John Balfour d Hillside Esslie 21.5.1898 82, w Agness S Simpson d Hillside, Esslie 4.8.1890 66, by chn

14 1852. John Balfour blacksmith North Water Bridge 9.1.1852 42, w Helen Gillespie 6.12.1843 37, s Jas d inf, s Wm mert North Water Bridge 3.8.1860 26, w Agnes Ross 24.7.1888, s Robt Ross 27.3.1923

15 Benjamin Gibson, Brae of Pert 23.12.1875 76, w Jean Brane 18.10.1871 66; Jean Gibson 20.11.1866 34, h John Hood; Isabella Gibson 26.2.1890 61, h Jas Crocket; Mary Gibson 26.5.1891 63

16 Adam & Eve; flowers in pots; John Prestack 1742 72 who lived sum tim in muirton of Ballache, w Margt Scot 1.1732 56

17 1828. John Balfour 27.2.1828 81, w Eliz Paterson 28.1.1823 76, yts David 15.7.1800 15, also two gchn Mitchell Stevenson 15.7.1823 18 & Helen Stevenson 13.8.1824 17

18 by Alex Whitetent Mill of Woodston, s Wm 18.2.1816 22, w Ann Milne 26.1. 1826 73. Alex White 22.11.1836 88

18a FS Thos Robertson in Easter Ballachie, s Johne 13.12.1665 44

19 FS Beneath this stone covered is the body of Bone (Jervise, "Epitaphs" i 211 has Ihone in error) Robertsone "That part which beter is away to Haven is gone etc"; Wm Robertson - - - (see Christison, PSAS 1901-2 p 306 for illustration, he has d 1646 46y, s Jas d 1664); W R, I R; (central) 1810, Millne

20 FS (marginal) 1688. Chas Renny s to David Renny & Isobel Strachan he d 4.1. 1688 18; (central) sun, moon, stars, cherub; "Mors certa est..."; Alex Renny 10.11.1739 75y9m, w Isobel Crystie 20.2.1694 26

21 FS (marginal) Ain fames youth s to John Smith somtym goodman in Garrov d (2).2.1666 27; I S; yoke, spades, hourglass, skull, bell & bone; poem (quoted by Jervise "Epitaphs" i 374 who has Galrow for Barrov; illustrated by Christison, PSAS 1901-2 p 308)

22 TS - - - - - - get Smith his spouse 28.3.1719 36, Andrew(her son) 9.6.1701 (21)y; spades, shield, crown & hammer, anvil; A M, M S, A M, M M, I M

23 FS Jas Stevenson sometime tent Craigo 10.1.1721 70 with two of his chn viz. Alex & Jean (h Peter Fettus freeholder in Montrose); I S, M S; A S, I S; I S, I E

24 FS I S, 1662; Jannet Gorme sumtym spous to Jas Strahauchn d 28.12.1637; I G (illustrated by Christison, PSAS 1901-2 fig 23a; St Andrews Testaments - Margt Gorme spouse to Jas Strachan in Over Peart, 1638)

25 FS Johne Purvise sometyme in Lighton Hill 31.2.1683 70, w Isobel Scot 3-.12. 1666 43; I P, I S, 1683; greek & latin texts

26 FS hexagonal. Here rests in hope of the blessed resurrection Elspeit Fulerton da to Robt Fulerton in Balachie a pious & virteous damisell 10.8. 1667 19; R F, I W, E F (see Christison, PSAS 1901-2 fig 23b & p 305)

27 FS (marginal) - - - in the Lord John Fullarton h to - - Wilson he d - - - his age 70y & his da E(ilspit) 6.1693 40; (central) Margrat Willson - - - r to (Jo)hn Fullarton - - - 1703 73y; M F; R F, J F, A(P), J F, I F, - -, - F, J F, M F, A F

28 TS Jean Mores 20.9.1717 50, h David Murra late tent Mill of Bar(ns) 16.11. 1737 77; John Murray in Mill of Barns sometime tent (Barrie) 27.2.1768 72, erected by him imo his parents; A M, W M, D M, J M, A M; J M, M C; M M, J M, K M, his da Ann 16.7.180(6) 59, s Jas late tent in - - - te Mondyns 16.2.1805 56, w Margt Christie 16.9.1807 95

29 FS Charlis Murr(a)y d 25.- - mber 16(36) & w M(ergret)St(ra)w(chn) d 4.2. 164(6) & Androw Murray 24.4.16(5)4; shield of arms (see F Davidson, "Inventory" p 64)

30 TS (marginal) Here lies the bodies of Robt Fullerton & Janet Fullerton his/wife who departed this life/ May the 13 1741 aged ab(out) (70)y. Unto whose just and honest memory the /To - - - -

31 Geo Sherratt fr Muirton 29.3.1862 72, w Isobel Wright 22.1.1854 72

32 John Kirkland tent East Ballochy 21.12.1848 74, w Jane Kirkland d Newbigging 6.8.1861 76, s Alex student of medicine 16.9.1822 19, sis Ann d Laurencekirk 20.7.1878 74; poem (quoted by Jervise "Epitaphs" i 212)

33 1808. by Ann Farquhar, h Geo Kirkland late tent Lunden 14.12.1802 66, da Elis 1784 1½y, s Jas 29.1.1792 22

34 Wm Greig shoemaker Northwater Bridge 13.8.1857 82, w May Mill 13.1. 1837 60, by family; Wm Greig junior 13.12.1879 68; Jas Greig 28.6.1892 86 (ed. she was sister of Jas Mill philosopher 1773 1836, see DNB, & da of Jas Mill shoemaker Northwater Bridge & Isobel Fenton)

35 FS David Landsay. I sobel Lindsay - - - - -

36 Eliz Fife 6.5.1737 55, h John Buchanan late tent in Bridge 8.8.1751 70, s John 1803 73 (w Mary Middleton 1814 87, s John 1845 84 (w Agnes Bell 1835 54, s John 1828 5, da Ann 28.10.1818 14.7.1892 int Old Churchyard Brechin beside her h dr Robt Douglas of St Anns)); cherubs; angel blowing trumpet in skeleton's ear (see Willsher & Hunter, "Stones" fig 3 & 3a; also Christison PSAS 1901-2 p 311-2); (west side) 1751. "I do ring, I did ring, I once rang, I shall ring" (ed.ring= reign) wheel of time (see Willsher & Hunter"Stones" p 4); a child Mary Buchanan d 9.3.1761 15m; J B, M M, A B, M B, M B, J B; M B, W B, M B, E B

37 TS by And Anderson tent Ballin(snow), w Kathrin Fullerton 15.5.1759 55

38 by Jas, David, John & Eliz, fa David Crabb 3.12.18(03) 66, mo Isobel Brechin -.-.1799 62

39 Colin Gillie 1824 36, w Ann Spankie 1838 54, da Jean 4y, da Margt 59y, da Ann 11.1883 69 (h Peter Douglas mason), s Colin 4.1884 60, by s Wm 12.1891 78 & da Marjory d Montrose 17.5.1897 75

40 FS Robt Wilack 10.8.1705 67 & Margt Smith & Isabel Strachen his spouses; R W, A B; M S, D C; I S, K S; shield with loom & shuttle; "And Robt Wilox dwelt at Pearth /As just a weaver as on earth..." (see F Davidson, "Inventory" p 63)

41a Jas Foreman d Commieston St Cyrus 14.12.1882 70, w Helen Poustie 25. 12.1882 70

41 1798. by Jas, Alex & Robt Foreman imo mo Isobel Dekars 28.4.1797 78; (J)F, M G, R F, E S; (other side) I F, R F, D F, I F, M F, I F

42 by Margret Greg, h David Robb sometime weaver in Dun d 2.5. 1767 56 who left one son David; mantling, shield with two shuttles, stretchers, loom with heddle; D R, M G, D R, W R; (west side) poem

43 1822. by And Lyall & Isabel Miller, her parents Jas Miller & Isoble Clark

44a Wm Millar 24.11.1914 65, w Ellen Nicoll 27.3.1899 59

44 J 1760 G; mason's tools; (west side) by Robt Gray in Bridgmiln, w Isobel Cargill 10.8.1749 45, s John 31.5.1755 20, da Christian 22.2. 1800 64 (h David Miller), da Ann d inf

45 John Millar mason Inglismaldie 26.10.1827 59, w Margt Garvie 5.1.1854 75, chn John, Jas, David, Helen, Sophia,& Christina; Robt Wallace & w Mary Millar, one da d 2.1838 inf, da Margt 16.3.1841 1w; Jean Millar, da Mary Ann Mill 19.3.1853 13; Margt Millar 30.10.1872 69; Jean Millar 22.12.1873 54

46 Alex Millar 20.9.1879 66, w Mary Caithness 25.9.1893 80, s Jas 2.6. 1843 3, gs Alex Millar Durie 31.7.1878 10, s Alex 21.5.1893 57

47 Geo Touns sometime tent Dobtoun of Pert 1763 83, his wives Janet Clark, Elspet Wiley, Margt Toun, Elis Nokel & chn Geo, Isbel, Janet, John, Anne, Isbel, Alex; Wille Herue & w Elis Touns; David Tpuns, w Janet Glen & Jean Touns; cherub; flowers in pots; plough; G T, E (N) (see Christison PSAS 1901-2 fig 26f; one David Touns was int 26.7.1789)

48 FS John Jame (2.1.)1708 86y2d, w Margrat F(uller)ton 1702 84; I I, M F; D I, I P; I I,M G; (central) here lyes David Jamie & Jaen (sic) Pitcarns and - - - - - - - - spouses; monogram I M G (see Jervise, "Epitaphs" i 374 who has "Here lys David Iamie & Iohn Iamie and Iean Pitcarnes and Margrat Gleag ther spouses")

49 by And Couper, Brae of Pert, w Marianne Wylie 28.8.1881 45, da Margt Jane 7.12.1872 7m. And Couper 14.11.1906 73

50 Agnes Jape 26.7.174(3) 4(9), Jean & Isabell Davidson their chn who d young; poem; (east side) M, A, T, A, A, I, I D(for Davidson); cherub & flower in pot

51 FS - - - - - - - - - - - - - - 16(2)9 - - - - - -

52 1822. by Rachel Cree 17.1.1842 78, h And Low plough & cart wright at Langley Park 27.5.1819 68, s And 21.11.1804 16, s David 27.3.1827 23, s John d Calcutta 1828 30, s Lauchlan d Liverpool 16.8.1840 46; (other side) Alex Low sometime tent Nether Pert 4.1779 69, w Elis Findlay 10.6.1789 70, da Margt b 30.11.1757

53 by John Spankie, fa Wm Spankie fr Brae of Pert 1829 74, mo Ann Low 1838 75, bros Robt 1837 37, Wm 1866 76

54 1798. David McKay tent in Connonie, fa David McKay late tent there 24.8.1795 75, mo Isobel Taylor 14.12.1786 67

55 by Jas Mitchell at East Mills Brechin d 16.4.1874 63, s David 11.2.1842 3y9m, bro David SSC d Morningside Edinburgh 22.4.1844 27 int here, bro Francis d at sea on his passage to N Zealand 2.1848 25, w Margt Hood 23.6.1868 52, s Wm 5.4.1864 4½

56 1827. by Francis Mitchell tent Hillhead of Craigo, w Margt Mill d 5.12.1822 40, da Elis 24.1.1822 2

57 David Laing fr Muirshed Logie, s David d at Lummington 2.5.1838 (widow Rachael Robertson d Inverkeilor 15.1.1873 int here)

58 1842. Jas Milne late tent Woodside of Craigo 7.1.1837 46, by w Elis Cowie 12.10.1886 86, s Alex 30.11.1837 3m, s Jas 18.10.1838 9, s Hugh 18.12.1841 11, s John 27.3.1852 17, last surviving s And 26.12.1892 59

59 1851. revised by Jas Miller & Wm Wishart imo departed relatives Ann, Geo & Colin Millar, Ann & Mary Wishart & Jas Lamb

60 1829. by Jas Millar mason Bush, fa Chas 19.5.1815 67, mo Jean Cadenhead 3.5.1798 45, bro David 1839, sisters Ann, Jane, Susan & May all d inf

61 by John Durward tent Ardo, in 1804, imo relations & family; poem

62 1808. Jas Caird 1755, w Jean Low 1766, da Jean 1774 & their relations Christian Caird 1719, Jean Caird 1740, Jas Caird 1765, Jean Cloudslie 1770, by ss John & Jas

63 Adam & Eve with flower in pot (see cover of this book, also Christison, PSAS 1901-2 p 313, Willsher & Hunter "Stones" p 10); Anna Annandal 1.5.1743 20, two chn d young Robt & Isabell Annandall, also three chn laying at Fordon John, Elis & Margret, their fa Jas Annandal 29.7.1754 65; I V elder; I V younger; (west side) mantling with shield I A, M R, mason's tools; cherub; E A, M A, I A, I A, A A, I A, R A, M A

64 FS - - - - - - - - - - -

65 FS Here lyes in the lord Jas Fettes 1681 57 with his spouse Isobell Findlow 1688 68; I F, H F, D F; A F, I F, M F; I M P P F I S; I F, M F, D F, I F, I F; shield with I F, I F, I F, M F, share & coulter

66 FS Jas Fettes in the Hill of Perte 1697 51 with Margt Low his spouse & chn John, Jas & Isabell

67 Jas Lyall of Gallery, 2s Jas 21.10.1827 2.2.1909

68 Jas Lyall esq of Gallery 20.3.1851 87, w Margt Simpson d Montrose 7.7.1889 83, yt da Matilda d Heidelberg 18.1.1862 19 int there, 3da Mary Anne 15.12.1911

69 Jas Lyall of Gallery, 1s David 11.2.1826 25.1.1911

70 Jas Lyall of Gallery, s Robt Lyall of Bannety Fifeshire 6.6.1829 26.6.1900 (wid Maria Jane MacKenzie 29.11.1838 8.4.1919, only s Jas Wm d Edinburgh 19.5.1891 19, yt da Edith Elis d Bannety 24.4.1892 17, 2da Louisa MacKenzie 14.11.1869 12.2.1930 (wid of Wm Ed Lawrence), 1da Ella Matilda 5.6.1867 1.3.1947

71 mural. Jas Allardice esq of that Ilk in the Mearns (according to Jervise "Epitaphs" i 211 his w was a Milne of Balwyllo), da Mary d Inglismaldie 4.1.1801 74(md 42y to Jas Macdonald esq long sheriff substitute as his 2w, only s of Thos Macdonald advocate Aberdeen, he d 23.8.1809 82, by only da & only surviving of six chn Mary (h Chas Ogilvy esq of Tannadice, da Margt 25.10.1805 3w)) (see Jervise, "Epitaphs" i 375: dr Chas Ogilvy,son of the laird of Murthill, made money as medical officer in EICS, bought the lands of Tannadice & built a mansion there, his son was an army officer d 1845-6, 1da was mrs Balfour-Ogilvy - see Forfar St John's Episcopal church inscription 22)

72 by Elis Burness, h mr Jas Lyall in Mill of Gallery 27.2.1808 70 int churchyard of Farnell, fa Wm Burness 1788, mo Mary George 1802 77, chn David & Hariet d inf (see Farnell inscriptions 19 & 71)

73 I S, K B, 1742. John Spark dyer in Craigo, w Kath Burnet 31.1.1742 37, da Anna 23.8.1741 7, David Spark 9.8.1760 24, mo Marget Stephenson d at Craigo 23.5.1732 70, fa Robt Spark d Glenbervie 24.6.1737 73 int there

74 David Machir snuff box maker at North Water Bridge 24.2.1836 53, w Susan Ley, three of their chn Eliz 7.1828 18, Margt 1.1829 17, John d inf; (west side) David Machir mert Northwater bridge 1813 84, w Agnes Birnie 1834 95, chn Jean 3.8.1774 3y3m, - - - d 17-7 - - - - - -

75 by Robt Findlay wright Gallery, w Elis Hogg 22.3.1842, da Jean d inf, fa Robt Findlay 23.11.1846

76 1849. Jas Dures wright at the Northwater Bridge 11.2.1845 51, by w Sarah Neilson d Brechin 13.11.1884 88, da Sarah d 6y, da Eliz d 2y, 1s Jas 13.6.1903 83 (w Jane Fearn 19.5.1868 47, 2w Isabella Grieve 17.10.1907 80)

77 rev Jas Landreth min par of Logie Pert from 1884-1934 d 22.2.1934 83, w Eliz Stewart 24.9.1890 30)see Fasti v 405)

78 Alex Fairweather weiver who lived some-time in The Links of Montrose d 2.2.1798 73, 1w Kath Bruce 27.1.1791 73, by 2w Eliz Findlay, s Alex 3.1.1795 14.4.1795 aged 14w3d

79 Jas Wallace som-tim weaver in Ballachie 26.2.1742; Robt Wallace d 6y; Janet Wallace 1733 17; shuttles & loom (see Christison, PSAS 1901-2 fig 26b); (west side) Adam & Eve & cherub

80 John Nicol at Rosehill (ed in 1830) d Bogburn par Fordoun 30.4.1855 66¼, w Bettie Don 9.2.1830 43, 1da Ann 8.5.1822 7, 1s Thos (s of Helen Graham) d Brechin 16.1.1877, w Helen Graham 6.6.1891

81 by David Balfour, Inglismaldie, w Jean Nicol (da of John Nicol - see inscription 80 supra) d Laurencekirk 4.6.1861 41, s David draper d Greenock 10.6.1872 21

82 Alex Russell 19.12.1873 63, w Rachel Paterson 14.8.1899 88, das Eliz & Margt d inf, da Rachel 29.1.1931 85 (h Geo Petrie mert St Cyrus d 2.2. 1933 86, yt da Mary 6.3.1935 58)

83 Chas Watson 24.10.1849 78, w Rachel Sim 2.2.1848 63, by da Isabella

84 1863. by Wm Prott, fa Wm Prott 26.5.1854 36, sis Hellen 31.10.1853 1y10m, bro Alex 31.3.1867 19, mo Eliz Barnett 11.1.1889 72

85 Wm Huggans 16.12.1826 86, w Jannet Reddell 7.11.1821 84, da Jannet 18.9. 1824 54, by surviving das

86 TS by David Smith, w Jean Hoggen 9.5.1841 68. David Smith 23.7.1846 58

The following are noted in A Jervise, "Epiatphs & Inscriptions" i 210-4 but were not seen in 1974:

87 John Falconer bishop of Brechin from 1709, a cadet of the noble family of Halkerton, d Inglismaldie 6.7.1723; "a good & grave man & very modest, tall, black and stooping."

88 Robt Grey, s John 1755 20; poem

N o t e s

A Jervise, "Epitaphs & Inscriptions" i 210-4 & 374-5 notes inscriptions 6,9, 18a,19-21,24,32,36,40,48,61 & 71

F Davidson, "Inventory of 17th Century Tombstones in Angus" p 63-5 details 4,19-20,21,24-7,29,40

Christison, Proceedings of Society of Antiquaries, Scotland, 1901-2, describes the carvings of 19,21,24,26,36,47,63 & 79

Testaments: the following were noticed in the Index to the Commissariot Register of Edinburgh -
Kath Carnegy spouse to Wm Carnegy in Connonie, 1598
Robt Lindsay in Netherpert, 1589-90
& the following is a small selection from the St Andrews Commissariot -
Cath Simpson spouse to Allan Townes in Perth par Pert, 1620
John Strachan in Over Pearth par Inchbreak, 1613
John Strachan tent Over Pearth, 1685
John Strachan in Over Perth par Pert, 1696

OPR with the Registrar General - 304 Logie-Pert
Births 1717-1854
Marriages 1717-40, 1775-1854
Deaths 1717-39, 1771-1801

Church Records in the SRO: CH2/248 Logie Pert KS minutes 1717-1935
accounts 1770-1801, 1825-1923
proclamations 1855-1944
baptisms 1855-1923
communion rolls 1859-1948
CH3/443 Logie-Pert FC, UP, St Martins C of S
KS minutes & cash 1843-1942

27c P E R T

<u>Fasti</u> v 405 Pert or Over Inchbrayock ministers 1567-1616
403 Logie-Pert ministers from 1563

<u>Ewing</u> ii 165 Logie-Pert ministers from 1845

I n d e x

Allardice 71
Anderson 37
Annandal(l) 63

B. 40
Balfour 13-4.17.81
Balfour-Ogilvy 71
Barnett 84
Bell 36
Birnie 74
Brane 15
Brechin 38
Bromley 3
Bruce 78
Buchanan 36
Burness 72
Burnet 73

Cadenhead 60
Caird 62
Caithness 46
Cargill 44
Carnegy Notes
Christie 20.28
Clark 43.47
Cloudslie 62
Couper 49
Cowie 58
Crabb 38
Cree 52
Crocket 15
Cruickshank 2
Crystie 20

Davidson 50
Dekars 41
Don 80
Douglas 36½39
Dures 76
Durie 5-6
Durward 61
Duthie 9

E. 23

Fairweather 78
Falconer 87
Farquhar 33
Fearn 76
Fenton 34
Ferguson 10
Fettes/us 23.65-6
Fife 36
Findlay/ow 52.65.75.78
Forbes 2
Foreman 41.41a
Fullerton 4.26-7.30.37.48

G. 41
Garvie 45
George 72
Gibson 15
Gillespie 14
Gillie 39
Gleag 48
Glen 47
Gordon 2
Gorme 24
Graham 80
Gray,Grey 44.88
Gre(i)g 34.42
Grieve 76

Halkerton 87
Herue 47
Hill 7
Hodgston 4
Hogg 75
Hoggen 86
Hood 15.55
Huggans 85

Jam(i)e 48
Jape 50
Jolly 11

Kirkland 32-3
Knowles 6

Laing 57
Lamb 59
Landreth 77
Landsay 35
Lawrence 70
Ley 74
Lindsay 35.Notes
Low 52-3.62.66
Lunan 2
Lyall 12.43.67-70.72

M. 22
Macdonald 1.3.71
McGhonachie 8
Machir 74
McKay 54

27c P E R T

Mackenzie	70
Meek	10
Middleton	5-6.36
Mill	34.45.56
Millar/er	44-6.59-60
Mil(l)ne	18-19.58.71
Mitchell	9.55-6
Mores	28
Murra(y)	28-9
Neilson	76
Nicol	44a.80-1
Nokel	47
Ogilvy	1.71
Paterson	17.82
Petrie	82
Pitcarns	48
Poustie	41a
Prestack	16
Prott	84
Purvise	25
R.	63
Reddell	85
Rennie/y	8.20
Renwick	9
Robb	42
Robertson	18a.19.57
Ross	14
Russell	82
S.	41
Scot	16.25
Sherratt	31
Sim	83
Simpson	13.68.Notes
Smith	21-2.40.86
Spankie	39.53
Spark	73
Stephenson	73
Stevenson	17.23
Stewart	77
Strachan/en	20.24.40.Notes
Taylor	54
Thain	2
Toun(s)	47.Notes
V.	63
W.	26
Wallace	45.79
Watson	83
Weir	22
White	18
Wilack/ox	11.40
Wiley, Wylie	47.49
Willocks	11.40
Willson	27
Wishart	59
Wright	31
Wylie, Wiley	47.49

28 M E N M U I R

The medieval church was dedicated to St Aidan. When it was replaced in 1767 by a new building the burial aisle of the Collace and Carnegy families was preserved. The present spare building was erected in 1842 on the same high terrace above the manse. This high terrace wall was probably built by mr Walter Leslie in the early 16th century and it contains the crowded burial ground shaded by a large gean.
National Grid reference: NO 535 644

1 mural. 1717. four panels of interlaced initials; by Alex Fairweather in Little Crowack, Geo Fairweather in Milltoun of Ballhall (Jervise, "Epitaphs" ii 340 has Blackhall in error), Jas Don att the Mill of Blackhall & Alex Smith in Teaugertoun imo their Ancestors, Residenters in this par & for themselves, wives & chn & their posterity: opposite lies Thos Don wright Duninald d Brechin 9.10.1809 85; poem

2 FS leaning against wall. (marginal) - - - (Ge)org Hill d 1(7--) with Geo, John, Magdalen, John & Isobel - - - ; (central) G H, M H; arms supported by swans

3 Geo Webster 17(32), w Isobel Boack in (Wester) Bogton; (west side) cherub;

28 MENMUIR

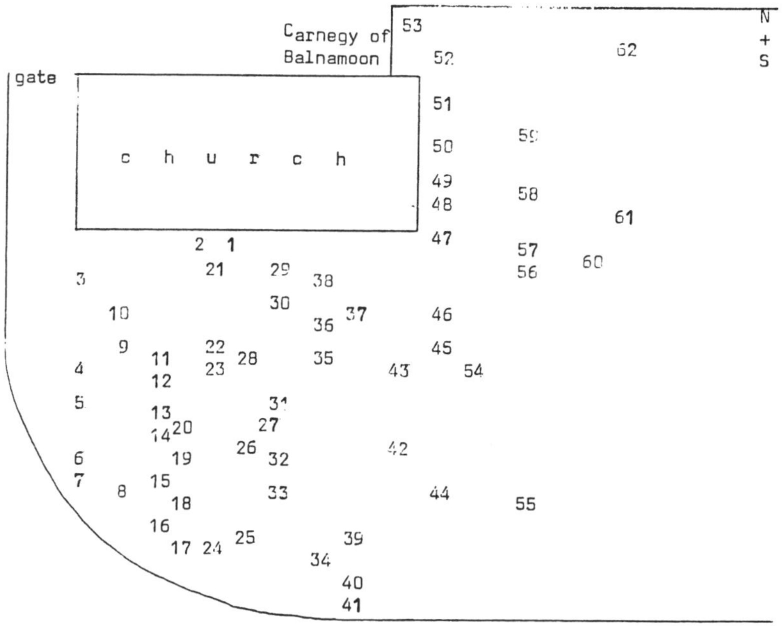

flowers in pots (style similar to inscriptions Edzell no 9, Lethnot no 13, Stracathro nos 13 & 26); G (W), I -

4 by Jas Farquhar 9.3.1899 68, w Mary Ann Young 14.11.1884 57, s Jas 2. 4.1863 8

5 1750. And Wyllie 20.3.1737 31, w Isabel Skair 15.7.1750 44, by chn Thos, And, Alex, Margrat & Isobel; Poem (quoted in Jervise, "Epitaphs" ii 340)

6 by John Young in Lochty & ss John & Jas & David imo w Isobel Young 20. 3.1754 74, his fa (Wm)Young sometime tent Birkhill (w Agnes Webster 12. 12.1714 75; Jas Young 4.1751 (4)0, w Margt Smart; M Y, Io Y, Ia Y, I Y, D Y

7 And Young fr West Muirside Menmuir 16.4.1946, w Isabella Reid 28.2.1944 by da Ethel P Watson

8 Jas Fettes tent Leadmore 11.1.1784 83, w Kathren Mitchel 22.5.1771 45, s Geo 19.3.1786 25, by ss David & Chas; I F, K M, 1788, mantling

9 Robt Thomson, Rosebank 9.1844 63, w Elis Cuthbert 3.7.1873 78, da Elis d inf

10 Jas Watson d Balrownie 23.11.1836 44, w Eliz Guthrie d Forfar 26.10. 1899 93, da Kath Ann 28.12.1836 10m, da Jane d Melbourne Australia 21. 4.1876 46, by s Jas mert Singapore d West Ferry 8.5.1882 50

11 FS two cherubs; mantling, shield; - - - - - - - - - ; emblems

12 by Alex Guthrie tent Balhall, w Jean Wyllie 16.8.1792 nearly 72y, chn Isoble, Alex (see Jervise, "Epitaphs" ii 427: he became fr Coull Tan-

nadice, md 1774 Barbara Suttie, s Chas b 1781 etc etc), Margt, David, Ann & John who all survive 1793; (west side) mantling, shield with two sheaves, share & coulter; skull, bone, dart, scythe, coffin; poem (quoted in Rogers ii 253 & Jervise "Epitaphs" ii 339)

13 1829. John Guthrie tent Balfour 27.2.1826 68, w Jean Wyllie 21.5.1829 68, s Jas 16.3.1815 22 (Jervise, "Epitaphs" ii 339 notes another s John mert & magistrate Montrose d 1875)

14 Alex Guthrie proprietor of Burnside (see Jervise, "Epitaphs" ii 338: s of David Guthrie & Ann Skair of inscription no 16) sometime tent Leadmore d 20.11.1836 89, md upwards of 60y to Margt Guthrie 26.10.1839 84, s David 11.12.1834 56, s Jas 6.2.1830 42, s Thos 30.9.1841 49, da Margt 6.6.1841 64, chn Betty, Isobel, Alex & Helen all d inf, Jas & Margt are int churchyard Brechin, others int here, by s Alex mert Singapore

15 Jane Guthrie d Arbroath 5.9.1889 72, h Geo Campbell d Arbroath 8.1.1874 60

16 Alex Skair once in Burnside 12.7.1751 67, by w Margt Wedderburn, four chn int here viz. Isable 16.11.1722 4, Thos 19.3.1724 3, Alex 16.2.1731 8, Isable 4m; (west side) two cherubs; mantling with shield, A S, M W, 1753; IS / M S, I S / I S, A S, A S, E S / A G, M G; David Guthrie of Burnside 3.3.1781 64, w Ann Skair 28.10.1801 77 (Jervise, "Epitaphs" ii 337: Alex Skair succeeded his fa David as tent & became proprietor of Burnside about 1743; his fa (probably a bro of Thos tent of Boysack) had seizin of Balconnel in 1740 but in 1749 sold it to a Dundee family Murison; his da Ann brought Burnside to the Guthries through her marriage to David)

17 Alex Guthrie of Burnside, s David 11.12.1832 56 (w Cath Grant 14.4.1869 89, s Alex 13.12.1834 22, by s Jas mert Singapore) (Jervise, "Epitaphs" ii 338 notes Jas mert Singapore md a da of mr Scott, Balwyllo who d young leaving one s & two das the yr of whom md mr John Shiell solicitor Dundee)

18 by Stewart Guthrie imo her (sic) da Georgina Bell Campbell 14.4.1854 29.4.1867; above Stewart Guthrie d Dalhousie cottage Brechin 16.12.1904 80 (h Jas Mair)

19 Geo Bell late of Balconnal 25.11.1885 66, w Mary Guthrie 5.4.1887 76

20 John Guthrie tent Knowhead 1.10.1820 (Jervise ii 338 has 1824) 87y, w Helen Wyllie 12.1.1821 85 md 60y (Jervise has 66y), chn d before them Isabel 1767 childhood, Thos mert Dundee 1794, Robt cattle dealer 1802, Geo tent Pitmoodie 1817 (Jervise notes a reference to Forfeited Estates & York Building Co)

21 A S; cherub; Alex Smith, w Keatren Fearwather 29.9.1702 40, chn Alex, John & Isabell; John Smith, w Margt Fairveather d 2.- - - - - - - -; (east side) K F; cherub; "Remember all who passeth by /That thou most die as weel as I /Deaths Sumonds, non escape it can /Remember therfor mortal man/ Daylie thy sins to mortifie/ That thou mayest live eternelie"; crown, anvil, hammer & tongs with shield & mantling

22 Jas Fairweather sometime fr Balzeordie thereafter distiller in Brechin b 7.4.1788 28.7.1870, w Ann Black b Vane Fearn 11.7.1789 d 10.3.1876

23 CT 1825. Thos Leighton, w Ann Fairweather, by s col David CB adjutant general at Presidency of Bombay (Jervise, "Epitaphs" ii 340: later general sir David Leighton d Cheltenham 1860 86; "Land of the Lindsays" 244: their forebears are in the parish register back to 1683 when Wm Leighton died & 1698 when David Leighton md Jean Mathers)

24 Jas Milne sometime tent Balyordie 8.1.1754 85, w Elis Moleson 25.(1).1754 63, chn Jas, Isobel, - - , David, Wm & Margt; (west side) armorial; M E, M I, E I, M I, M K, M -, M -, M -, M -, O -, M -

25 mantling, shield with E M 1714; A G, G B, M G, I G, I G; (east side) poem; angel blowing trumpet into ear of unshrouded skeleton. (ed. top section of stone missing, was pegged with two pegs; but Jervise "Epitaphs" ii 341 has: And Gowrlay sometime wiver Chancein, chn Magdalen 1710 23, John 1713 21, Jean 1699 3y)

26 David Lighton sometime tent Balrownie 9.11.1753 48, w Anne Skair d Little Pitforthie 1774 61, yt s Wm fr Blackhall 15.7.1828 76 (w Margt Wyllie 15.4.1850 91); also And Lighton tent Knowhead 20.5.1745 35, w Ann Findleson 20.2.1748 38, s John 8.4.1754 17; (west side) mantling, shield with D L, A S, plough; D,T, Is, A, A, A, E, I, W Lightons; I L, D L, A L, A L; poem; (at top) A L ♡ A F, 1755 (see Jervise, "Epitaphs" ii 340: And Leighton md 4.1705 Jean Birnie (session records), s David (w Ann Skair, s David fr Burnhed, s Thos wheelwright Brechin (only s gen sir David, 2da md Geo Fairweather fr Brathinch), And fr Syde of Stracathro, s John factor for mr Scott of Dunninald (s of 1st marriage David of Bearehill nr Brechin, ss of 2nd marriage lieut col Thos & Jas town clerk of Montrose) & s Wm fr Blackhall & several das; see also "Memorials of the Leightons of Ulishaven" in Antiquaries Library, Edinburgh p 121 photograph of the stone)

27 FS David Lighton & w Janet Davidson sometime in Easterton, da Agnes 20.10. 1727 (h - - - - - Mil in Dunlapie) - - - - - by chn (according to "Memorials of the Leightons" pp 116 & 118 her h was (Geo)Birnie tent in Dunlappie); G B, A L; G B, I B, D B

28 Jas Clyne schoolmaster Menmuir from 1787 d 1817 "his attention to the improvement of his pupils was general & especially ... in the scriptures.. & taught many poor children gratis; a native of Strichen Aberdeenshire received his education there & at Marischal College Aberdeen; one word from him always commanded silence" (quoted in full by Jervise "Epitaphs"ii 341); (west side) Wm Clyne d Tigerton 25.4.1932 84, w Isabella Keith 25.1.1929 78, s Wm 8.4.1952 73

29 1795. Jas Webster, Mains of Balrownie, w Eliz Scott 11.10.1793 59, fourteen chn ten of whom survive viz. Robt, Eliz, Jas, Alex, David, May, Wm, John, Thos & Mary; (west side) cherub; 1847; - -, E S; Jas Webster in Mains of Balrownie 12.2.1812 84

30 David Webster fr Mill of Balrownie 4.1.1850 83, w Jean Don 1.3.1854 77, chn Janet 8.11.1809 5, Eliz 3.4.1822 13, Wm tent Mill of Balrownie 8. 3.1858 42, David tent Blackhall afterwards of Mill of Balrownie 8.7. 1872 68, Jas, factor to duke of Hamilton d 3.1.1875 75, s Alex tent East Muirside Balzeordie 21.12.1879 78, Ann d Annfield Brechin 1.1. 1910 96

31 1811. by David Webster tent Belliehill imo da Eliz 14.9.1810 20

32 Hugh Irvin scoolmaster Menmuir for 40y d 28.1.1784 71, by wid Agnes Fairweather; (west side) shield with H I, A F, 1784

33 1852. Geo Fairweather tent Brathinch 9.10.1848 84, w Margt Leighton 26.5.1851 80 (see notes to inscription 26 supra)

34 1817. by Alex Scott, Balconnel & Birkhill, d Cookston Brechin 1.1831, w Eliz Black 16.7.1817 68, s Alex fr Milton (w Jean Guthrie 17.3.1846, two chn Jane d Benholm Villa Hillside Montrose 19.11.1895 75 & Eliz d Benholm Villa 19.10.1898 82), w Ann Cobb d Edinburgh 22.6.1857 68 int there

35 mantling with shield, A C, A R; And C, Ia C, (W)C, - C, Da C, W C; (west side) Alex Coob 23.3.1727, s Alex 23.12.1750 27, by s And

36 1803. by And Rickard & w Margt Low formerly in Blackhall & par Menmuir imo chn Alex 25.7.1763, Margt d London 1798 35y9m, David d Brechin 1801 34, John b 2.1769, Jas 1798 27y8m, Wm 1772 8m, Wm b 11.4.1776, Chas 1802 24; poem (quoted by Jervise, "Epitaphs" ii 340)

37 TS John Rickard late in Blackhall 17.4.1816 47, w Mary Wyllie 23.9.1829 64, by s David late of St Vincent, da Janet 4.1806 18m, ss Jas 4.1810 10, s Wm d in the island of Tobago 1.1820 25, da Jane b 22.11.1798 d St James Park Brechin 24.6.1891

38 1822. Thos Webster in Balrownie, w Isabell Thomson 26.9.1822 31 leaving six chn viz. Jas, Alex, Ann, Elis, Margt & Isabell; (west side) Thos Webster sometime in Balrownie, after in Balfour d 25.8.1846 65, w Isobell Black 6.5.1844 55 leaving two ss Wm & John

39 Jas Sime 20.5.1862 58, w Susan Low 28.4.1898 94, chn John & Jane d inf, Alex 12.3.1843 9, Jas 7.6.1850 22, by da Susan 7.11.1940 90

40 Alex Davidson tent Knowhead 27.7.1860 63, s Wm 15.3.1837 5

41 Alex Milln tent Knowhead formerly of Ladywell 31.12.1831 76, w Jean Duncan 30.5.1839 81. Rev. xiv & 13

42 175-. two cherubs; mantling, shield with D A, A L, plough; D, A, I, A, I, M, A Allans; (west side) David Allan 28.2.1735 38, chn Alex & Margt d inf, Agnes 20.2.1749 20, David 22.6.1752 28 int in F- -en, by ss John & And

43 Hugh Baird d Tigerton 2.7.1888 84, by w Helen Pearson d Gungeon 10.2.1904 92, da Jessie 9.9.1846 5

44 John Davidson mert Brechin afterwards tent West Ballochy par Dun d 26.1.1837 36, sis Ann d Murlingden 5.1822 20

45 1843. John Mollison fr Chapelton of Menmuir 14.7.1841 86, 1w Jane Mollison, their family Jane, John, Jas, David & Thos all deceased, of his 2nd family Jane 3.1814 12m, Ann 10.1817 2, Wm 27.11.1836 11, 2w Isabella Walker 18.1.1856 70, s John 4.11.1858 49; Isabella 14.8.1810 21.5.1891; Margt 22.11.1818 17.7.1899

46 Jas Stewart tent Balhall 31.8.1826 63, by w Margt Stewart 12.6.1845 78, da Margt 7.11.1823 35 int here, Robt 27.5.1799 5, Francis 11.6.1799 7, David 12.6.1799 2 int Lethnot, surviving chn are John tent Bellfield, Jas tent Balhall & Francis tent Candy; (west side) 1830. Jas Stewart tent Balhall 5.7.1844 43, nephew Jas Stewart d 21y (fa John Stewart fr Bellfield)

47 Geo Anderson, Belliehill 1879 74,w Eliz Carnegie, da Jane 1874 30

48 Robt Carnegie fr Mill of Cruick 20.9.1875 71, w Eliz Mitchell 2.7.1909 86

49 Jas Carnegie d Mill of Cruick 1823 57, w Jean Fairweather 3.1851 71, s John 5.1834 26, by da Annie d Brechin 24.3.1900 81

50 CT rev Jas Somerville episcopal clergyman at Brechin d Brechin 19.2.1812 63 in 42nd y of ministry, s Alex 19.3.1796 2, by wid Margt Campbell d Brechin 21.7.1846 91 int here (see Fasti ii 52 & 64: he was nephew of rev Robt Somerville min Hutton 1756 71; see Jervise, "Epitaphs" ii 337:

Margt Campbell was da of the farmer of Broombank in Glenbervie, s Alex studied for the church, d Fettercairn 4.1872, two das md merchants in Liverpool)

51 TS by Frances Eliz Gregory imo h rev John Waugh 41y min Menmuir 9.1.1756 7.7.1824 68 (see Fasti v 408: she d 28.5.1827 without issue), sis Dorothea Gregory 1831 71

52 1837. by And Thomson, w Mary May 12.5.1830 63, s John 21.1.1830 30, s And 6.3.1826 21

53 Jas Sime, Cotton of Balnamoon 26.5.1862 58; John 12.9.1839 4m; Jane 11.3.1843 22m; Alex 2.3.1843 9; Jas 5.6.1850 22

54 1802. by Jas Mearns overseer Balnamoon imo w Anne Rait 9.6.1801 57, fa David formerly overseer there d 6.6.1777 71, mo Agnes Neish 9.5.177(2) 69

55 miller's rhynd & pick; bridled head (ed. for psalm xxxix?); this ston was erected at the charge of Margt Tylior imo h David Bean sometim miller at the Mill of Carraldston 7.6.1743 61, chn D B, A B, I B, I B, A B, M B, A B, E B, M B, R B, D B, C B, W B & the said Wm B; poem (see Willsher & Hunter, "Stones" p 31); (west side) two cherubs; reversed torches; mantling, shield with bones; D B ♡ M T, 1743

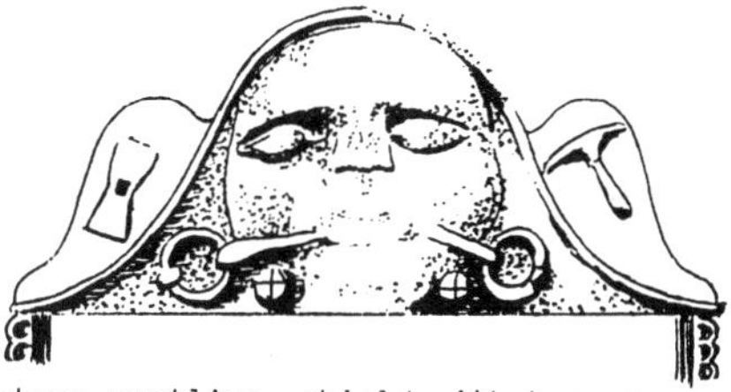

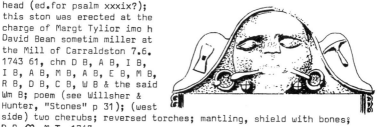

56 1859. Joseph Low 25.9.1876 81, w Mary Wishart d Burnside of Balzeordie 17.1.1858 66, s David 21.12.1888 59, by s Jas, Lachine, Canada East

57 1861. John Walker, Friendly Park d 27.9.1860 94, w Sarah Towns 23.1.1848 79, s Joseph, Friendly Park d Glasgow 4.6.1890 83 int here

58 John Nicoll d Teiggerton 10.3.1835 72y6m, w Anne Tosh 5.5.1833 73, by ss John, Thos & Jas

59 Wm Moir 27.10.1832 41, w Betsy Mitchell 29.5.1874 79, s Jas 23.10.1823 3, by s Wm mert Montrose

60 1858. David Christison tent in Castle 31.12.1852 82, w Jean Jolly 14.10.1853 72, chn Agnes 29.7.1841 14, Margt 22.6.1856 32, two ss d inf

61 by J T Sturrock, Estcourt Natal imo fa Alex 30.8.1871 67, mo Eliz Mowatt 22.3.1863 45

62 1823. John Guthrie & Helen Wyllie, surviving chn Alex late tent Findaurrie now in Brechin, John tent Balfour (see inscription 13 supra), David mert Brechin, Jas tent Maisondieu & East Town Dunlappie, Chas late tent Cookston now Fiddes, Margt (h Alex Guthrie of Burnside (see inscription 14 supra)) & Jean residing Kirkton (see Jervise, "Epitaphs" ii 338 for further details of this family)

63 mural in church. Alex Guthrie of Burnside, yt s Alex left this country early in life, many y resident Singapore afterwards at 8 Upper Wimpole St London where he d 12.3.1865 68 int Kensal Green cem. "Successful merchant, a kind friend, & always took a warm interest in this his native parish

The Carnegy enclosure is locked, but detailed in Jervise "Epitaphs" ii 336 as follows:

64a panel. 1639, S A C/D G B for sir Alex Carnegy of Balnamoon & w dame Giles

Blair of the family of Balthayock near Perth

64b mural. Jas Carnegy-Arbuthnott esq 23.12.1788 12.4.1871

64c mural. his w Mary Anne 12.11.1854 69 (fa David Hunter of Blackness), chn David Wm d Port Natal 18.3.1852 39, Eliz Gibson 16.5.1831 17, And Knox 9.6.1832 11, Jas d Ventnot Isle of Wight 18.10.1832 17, yt s Thos Hunter d Australia 6.1858

64d Anne Carnegy-Arbuthnott 31.8.1817 16.11.1872 (Jervise notes (before 1878) that the only survivors of the family are miss Helen & her sisters, wives of mr A B Capel mert London & rev mr Johnson rector Oaksey Wilts)

Notes

A Jervise, "Epitaphs & Inscriptions" ii 335-41 & 427 notes inscriptions 1,5, 12-14,16,20,23,26,28,36,50-1,62-4

W G Don ed. "Fairweathers of Menmuir" by Alex Fairweather (London 1898)

Testaments: Menmuir was in the Commissariot of Brechin, but the following is a randon selection from the Register of the Commissariot of Edinburgh:
John Bellie in Balconnall, 1600
Chas Dempster of Balrowney, 1602
Christian Dempster sometime spouse to Thos Arnot in Balrowney, 1606
Eliz Erskine spouse to John Collace young laird of Balnamoon, 1589
John Fairwedder at Kirk of Menmuir 1576-7, spouse Katherine Archibald
John Ordie in Boigtoun, 1607

OPR with the Registrar General: 309 - Menmuir
Births 1701-08, 1711-33, 1758-1854
Marriages 1704-82, 1848-51
Deaths nil KS minutes 1701-08

Church Records in the SRO: CH2/264 minutes & collections 1622-1701, 1709-33, 1762-1902
cash 1845-1900
communion roll 1868-80
CH3/230 Menmuir FC, UF: KS minutes 1844-1923
DC minutes 1849-1906
cash book 1844-95
seat rent book 1852-1907
HR 565 Menmuir, minutes etc 1826-1928
a/cs 1844-1928
buildings 1767-1916
Statute labour roads 1852

Fasti v 407 ministers from 1568

Ewing ii 165 ministers from 1847

Index

Allan	42	Bean	55	Campbell	15.18.50
Anderson	47	Bell	18-9	Capel	64d
Arbuthnott	64	Bellie	Notes	Carnegie/y	47-9.64a
Archibald	Notes	Birnie	26-7	Carnegy-Arbuthnott	64
Arnot	Notes	Blair	64a	Christison	60
B.	25	Black	22.34.38	Clyne	28
Baird	43	Boack	3	Cobb	34

28 M E N M U I R

Collace	Notes
Coob	35
Cuthbert	9
Davidson	27.40.44
Dempster	Notes
Don	1.30
Duncan	41
E.	24
Erskine	Notes
Fairweather	1.21-3.26.32.49.Notes
Farquhar	4
Fettes	8
Findleson	26
G.	25
Gibson	64c
Gowrlay	25
Grant	17
Gregory	51
Guthrie	10.12-20.34.62-3
Hill	2
Hunter	64c
I.	24
Irvin	32
Johnson	64d
Jolly	60
K.	24
Keith	28
Knox	64c
L.	42
L(e)ighton	23.26-7
Low	36.39.56
M.	14.25
Mair	18
Mathers	23
May	52
Mearns	54
Milne	24.41
Mitchell	8.48.59
Moir	59
Moleson	24
Mollison	45
Mowatt	61
Murison	16
Neish	54
Nicoll	58
Ordie	Notes
Pearson	43
R.	35
Rait	54
Reid	7
Rickard	36-7
Scott	17.29.34
Shiell	17
Sime	39.53
Skair	5.14.16.26
Smart	6
Smith	1.21
Somerville	50
Stewart	46
Sturrock	61
Thomson	9.38.52
Tosh	58
Towns	57
Tylior	55
Walker	45.57
Watson	7.10
Waugh	51
Webster	3.6.29-31.38
Wedderburn	16
Wishart	56
Wyllie	5.12-3.20.26.37.62
Young	4.6.7

29 N A V A R

This isolated and neglected burial ground lies at the end of a cart track down from Lightnie in a cluster of trees. Only the bell tower and eight stones in the walled area show that this was the parish church until 1723. National Grid reference: NO 529 676

1 by John Davidson tailor & residenter at West Side, w Jean Buchan 16.4. 1784 57, of six chn two d inf & Agnes, Jas, Isobel & Margt survive 1791 ; (west side) 1791. tailor's goose & scissors

2 cherub; by Wm Jolly in Slateford, chn Alex 29.9.1797 inf, Wm 1798 inf, Ane 22.10.1803 2y3m, Frances 25.10.1804 10m, Wm 10.12.1809 3y8m, Wm

29 N A V A R

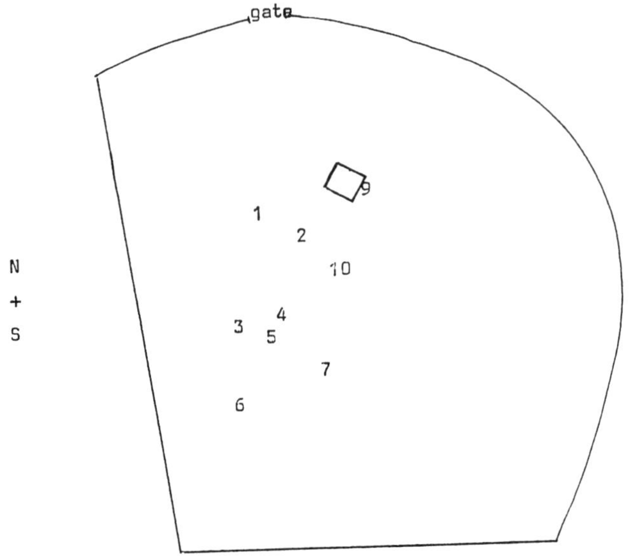

3.1810 inf, surviving sons in 1811 David, Jas, John; W J, J B

3 1792. by Geo Cobb presently in Scarborough Yorkshire, fa Jas sometime in Newbigging 10.10.1791 66, mo Margt High 8.3.1782 57, sis Mary 1767 1y, sis Betty 1770 1y, Eliz & Jean's bodies are here buried; Jas Cobb, chn surviving in 1792: Geo, Isobel, Agnes, Elspet, Margt & Anne

4 Thos Gordon fr Leightnie 18.6.1886 87, w Betsy Ramsay 15.11.1902 89, da Mary Ann 1.3.1866 18, s Alex 15.1.1871 29, da Agnes 10.8.1874 33, s John 11.6.1876 32, s Wm 29.11.1891 39, s Jas 6.2.1904 64

5 1849. Jas Gordon sometime tent Leightnie 5.2.1848 87, w Helen Christison 7.7.1834 60, s Robt 1.1813 inf, da Ann 7.1818 inf, s Alex 2.5.1838 28, da Helen 6.9.1839 23, s Chas 8.8.1864 50

6 by Jas Alexander tent Ledmore, w Agnes Gordon 10.8.1874 86, da Lizzie 28.6.1874 20.10.1877; Jas Alexander 11.1.1895 72, s Jas d Cradock Cape Colony 10.9.1897 24

7 1771. by Wm - - - imo chn - - - - - 11.176-, ss Wm & John, 2w Margt Cobb 17.12.1770 & two chn Jas - - - Jean 3.1768 lie here

8 not seen in 1975, but noted in Jervise, "Epitaphs" i 296: a very honest woman Margt Fyfe sometime spouse to Jas Molison in Craigendowie who cheerfully left this life in hope of a better 25.11.1712 69; poem (quoted, also in Rogers ii 342; see also Brechin Testaments, Margt Fyfe spouse to Jas Molison in Craigendowie, 1717 -Jas Molison in Craigendowie, 1717 - Margt Webster spouse to Jas Molison in Craigendowie, 1675 - Alex Durwart in Craigendowie & Margt Webster his wife, 1668)

9 leaning against bell tower, defaced, but completed from Jervise, "Epitaphs" i 296 & "Land of the Lindsays" 111: Ann Wylie in Westside omitted. This bell house was built 1773 at the expense of the following

mr Alex Gold tent Argeith;
Frances Stewart in Nathrow;
Ja. Lighton in Drumcairn;
Jas Cobb in Ledbreakie;
Jas Molison in Craigendowy;
John Molison in Oldtown;

29 N A V A R

Alexr Jolly in Witton; Will Speid in Blarno;
Thos.Gordon in Lightney; Da. Wyllie in Tillyarblet;
Jon & Andr Cobbs in Tilliebirnie; Geo Cobb in Achfearey;
John Cobb in Room.

10 by David Molison in Old Town imo fa John 11.1.1783 71, w Isbel Wishart 3.1.1792 62, also chn Jean, Isobel, Joseph & A(lex d inf), Jean, Jas, - - - survives at this date

N o t e s

A Jervise, "Epitaphs & Inscriptions" i 296-7 notes inacriptions 8 & 9, also notes Jonathan Duncan sometime Governor of Bombay b Blairno 1756 & his parents int Edzell (see Edzell inscription 42); also Jock Gudefellow a vagrant d Tillyarblet 11.1810 where "he was taken care of .. by David Wyllie & his mother"; also inscription on Stonyford bridge - built 1787 (by) John Spence esq commissary Brechin, John Taylor min Lethnot, Thos Molison tent Craigendowie, Chas Will, Tilliebardines, John Will at Mill of Glascory, John Smart at Auchourie, John Wyllie at Ballindairg, foundation stone laid by John Smart, Hunthill, keystone driven by Geo Molisen shoemaker Craigendowie.

Testaments: the following was noticed among the Edinburgh Commissariot indices
John Duncan in Tilliarbetis, 1603

Fasti v 398 ministers 1567-1723 when the parish united with Lethnot

OPR & Church Records etc etc see notes for Lethnot.

I n d e x

Alexander	6	Jolly	2.9
B.	2	Lighton	9
Buchan	1	Molison	8-10. Notes
Christison	5	Ramsay	4
Cobb	3.7.9	Smart	Notes
Davidson	1	Speid	9
Duncan	Notes	Spence	Notes
Durwart	8	Stewart	9
Fyfe	8	Taylor	Notes
Gold	9	Webster	8
Gordon	4-6.9	Will	Notes
Gudefellow	Notes	Wishart	10
High	3	Wyllie	9.Notes

30 N E V A Y

The roofless church tops a steep knoll rimmed by a few cottages. The burial ground is well kept, on the kirk inch itself. The medieval church was reputed to have been dedicated to St Nevydd; the parish was often called St Ringans. It was united with Eassie in the early 17th century, but it appears the church remained in use as the lintel is dated 1695.(The present parish church was built about 1840 halfway between Eassie and Nevay, with no burial ground.)
National Grid reference: NO 313 441

30 N E V A Y

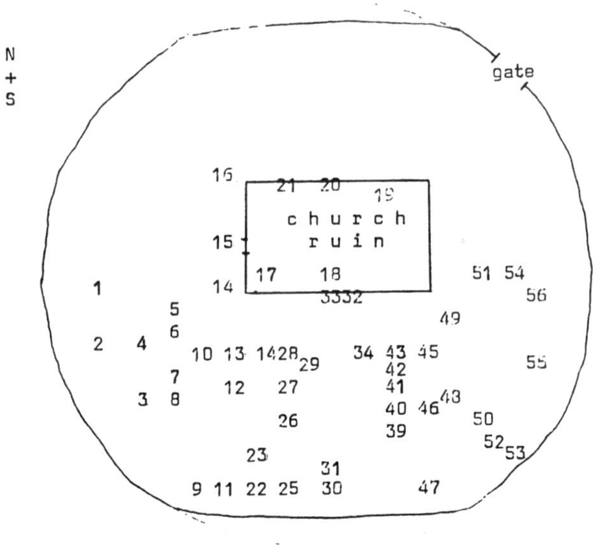

1 1854. by John Donaldson at Toll of Eassie & w Ann Taylor 23.3.1861 45, Thos 12.9.1838 15m, s Wm 6.12.1921 72

2 1844. by Geo Winter, Kirkinch, w Cicillia Barrie, da Janet 12.1839 3

3 1769. by Jas & Wm, fa Jas Barry sometime in par Newtyle d 9.11.1764 77, mo Agnes Grahame 20.4.1740 47 leaving issue; (west side) shield, 1769, share & coulter; Jas Barry; G B, W B, A G, B –; emblems

4 Alex Barrie d Claypots Glamis 28.5.1886 76, w Mary Mackay d Strathview Kirriemuir 27.10.1890 75, only da Jane Lockhart d Carnoustie 20.7.1921 69, 1s David d Arbroath 28.9.1924 80

5 John Black mert Leith 2.7.1852 58, w Margt Aikman 29.10.1855 44, chn Barbara Simpson 14.6.1850 16, s Wm 24.6.1854 6; Hutchison Aikman d Christchurch 15.2.1867 21

6 by Helen Mitchel, h Wm Black weaver in Padock-hall d 15.1.1805 42 having issue Margt & a female child d noneage; (west side) 1806. cherub; W B, H M; stretcher, shuttle & wool-winder

7 1784. by Hellen Smith in Drum of Eassie imo h David Doig sometime tent Drum of Eassie 19.9.1783 50 leaving issue John, Agnes, And & Geo; (east side) cherub; emblems

8 17♡2(9). David Low & Jean Doige in Craghead, s John 4.12.1728 2; (west side) shield with pincers, hammer, mallet

9 FS – – – – – – –

10 1898. by Thos Mitchell 5.12.1937 82, w Eliz Wyse 2.1.1909 60 (her mo Betsy Doig 17.5.1898 85), s And Thos & Cath Jane d inf, s David Meldrum contractor here 21.12.1930 45, da Eliz Wyse 2.1.1964 76

11 TS (marginal) by David Farquharson in Balkirie, w Jean Petrson 3.3.1776 44, (central) leaving Eshou, David, Alex, Agnes, Isobel, Wm, Jean & Margt;

1776; elaborate carving of shield with square & compasses & three castles for a mason.

12 J D, A C; shield with loom, shuttle & weaver's tools; I D, A B; John Doig indweller here 18.9.1780 71, w Agnes Christie; (east side) cherub; heart & arrows

13 next 12. Peter Doig lived in Kirkinch d 28.2.1813 33, da Agnes 15.3.1813 11m, by w Eliz Anderson; (west side) P D, E A, 1815; - - - - -

14 TS (marginal) by Wm Black, fa David sometime fr Templeton 16.2.1751 63; (central) two cherubs; & his chn d young Wm, David, Jean & Mary Black; D B, M T; A B, W B, D B, J B, M B; shield with 1754. 1801. Alex Black present tent North Navey farme renewed this stone imo deceased relatives herein named also imo gfa Alex Black late fr Kirkton of Navey, also Wm, JasAndThos & Alex Black his uncles & Margt Black his aunt; emblems

15 TS by Eliz Murray imo h Robt Anderson tent North Nevay 2.4.1801 38, she had chn by him John d inf, Margt, And, Janet & Robt; Eliz Murray d New Scone 14.7.18(3 or 5)5; And Anderson d New Scone 28.10.1862

16 by David Walker 3.4.1908 79, & w Jean Butchart 10.10.1918 87 both d Meigle int here, fa John slater Meigle d 1830, mo Ann Hutcheson 1839 52 both int Meigle; also Alex Martin d Carsegray 8.6.1899 40 int here

17 FS tipped up. Here lyis ane honest man Iohne Iake in Balkery 30.8.1597 60; (central) - - - (see F Davidson, "Inventory" p 77: describes escutcheon for Jack; see also St Andrews Testaments, Grissell Watson relict of John Jack in Balkirie, 20.4.1615)

18 A D, I W; I D, I D, H B; Heir lyas Jas Doog lavfvl s to Androw Doog & Jean Wardroper indwellers in Gatsid of Ballgrugo who dayed 1715 29; emblems; poem (quoted by Jervise, "Epitaphs" i 372)

19 heir lyis Alex Neave X Jean Storach; woman's head backed by bearded man's head; emblems

20 FS topping ruined wall. Heir lyes ane honest woman Margt Ha- - -tun of (age 55 yeares); I B, M H (see F Davidson, "Inventory" p 77 no 3 describes escutcheons for Blair & Halyburton)

21 topping wall. Heir layes John, Jas, Mary & Ann chn of Gilbert Dugat & Eliz Scot in Templetowne their ages are 20 days - - - - 10.11.16-7 - - - - - 2.1678. (Jervise "Epitaphs" & Davidson "Inventory" have 10.11.1667 but Davidson omits Mary). Beneath this stone lys John Adam sometime in - - - - - spouse - - - - 1735 - - - John & Elspat Adams

22 FS Heir lyis ane honest man John Wardroper in Templtun (d 11.)1645, w Margt Broun; I W, M B; emblems

23 D R, M R; 1759; by Jean Ross in Wester Keilor, bro David Ross sometime fr Egliston of Kinnetles 24.12.1757 47, h Patk Hill; (west side) cherub; shield with 1759, oxen yoke & share & coulter

24 1818. Peter Hutchison tent Mireside of Nevay 14.2.1816 69, by wid Jean Gray, chn Janet, Jean, Cath, Alex, Anne, Eliz, Peter; (west side)cherub

25 Christina Stratton 14.3.1914 78, h Robt Kidd blacksmith Kirkinch 9.3.1922 86, das Margt 14.5.1949 75, Mary 29.1.1951 87, Christina Kidd Benzie 10.12.1969 93

26 Geo Simpson 9.9.1946 76, w Helen Kidd 20.3.1958 87

27 by Jas Kidd blacksmith Kirkinch d Dundee R Infirmary 15.3.1952 86, w Agnes Young Simpson 27.2.1945 83

28 1877. by Geo Simpson in Kirkinch 8.8.1903 89, fa Chas 28.4.1863 91, mo Ann Mawer 21.12.1867 91, bro And 23.12.1853 42, s Chas 1.6.1843 18, w Agnes Young 29.4.1907 86

29 1774. by Henry, John, Jean, Margorie & Janet Spalden imo fa Sylvester 9.6.1771 81, mo Elspet Morice 4.17(6 or 7)2 79; (west side) S S, E M

30 next 31. Alex Martin 13.4.1907; Ann Barclay Martin 22.2.1909; Alex Martin Cuthill 16.10;1935; Geo Peter Cuthill 14.9.1938; Ann Anderson Cuthill 20.3.1944; Isabella Martin 5.10.1962

31 1843. by Peter Martin tent Kirkinch, fa David 1818 57, mo Margt Martin 1825 65, w Margt Stewart 13.6.1844 45; Peter Martin 12.7.1880 83

32 tipped up. (marginal) Janet (but Jervise "Epitaphs" i 372 has Jean) Pullar 7.4.1755, h John Anderson lived in Nevay; (central) cherub; shield with share & coulter; emblems; I A, I P; Ian. Elis. Mar. Iea. & Ian Anderson is dead; Iohn, Iam & Ann Andersons

33 lintel over church door. 16 D N 95

34 FS Heir lyes ane honest man Iohn - - - - - - - (could this be no.57?)

35 in railed enclosure with nos.36-38. 1820. by Wm & Robt, fa Jas Butchart mason Get-side of Nevay 5.3.1793 55, mo Agnes Farquharson 8.1797 54, also by their sis Jean (h Robt Robertson d Ingliston 30.5.1820 52); (west side) cherub; mantling, helmet, shield with square, compasees, & level

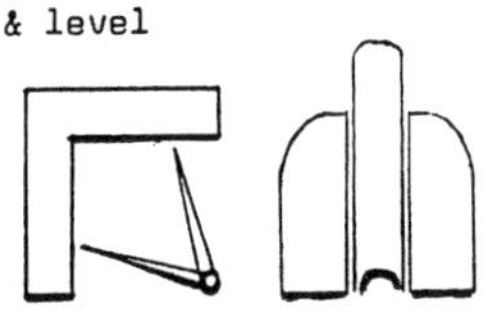

36 cherub. by Jas Sanders, parents lived in Nevay Jas 15.5.1731 68 & Barbray Mill 23.11.1733 71, chn dead Elspath, Agnes, Ann & Chirston & Wm & David d 11y; (west side) cherub; shield with sheaf & crossed shovels; I S, B M

37 by Patk Ogilvy tent Balkiry, w Barbara Storier 29.10.1752 33, chn Henry, Jean, Jas, Margt & Elspat surviving; shield with oxen yoke & plough;1753

38 Robt Butchart 1858 71, w Margt Martin 1891 90, s Robt 1863 29, gda Joan Smith 1874 21

39 1871. by Chas, Alex, Wm & Thos imo fa Thos Wilkie 22.11.1870 78, bro Jas 2.6.1836 6½, bro And 3.6.1836 4½

40 FS - - - - - - - - - -

41 crown; D B I S each in oval rope coil; two hearts; 1733;"Here are repos'd two godly youths/ Which loving brothers were....."(quoted in full by Jervise "Epitaphs" i 69); (west side) cherub; A B, A B; helmet over shield with hammer, shoemakers tools ; by David Barron shoemaker & w Jean Scot, their two eldest ss Alex 6.1732 21 & And - - -17-- 14y

42 next 43. And Barron 1.8.1851 82, w Mary Smith 16.6.1826 55, by da Margt (h Chas Clark of Princeland, Coupar-Angus)

43 anchor in rope oval; 1827. David Barron lieut HM RN, w Margt Barron 29.5.1824 54 (see Jervise "Epitaphs" i 69 has 1827 age 55 for 1824 age 54, & quotes the poem)

44 tipped up. (marginal) Thos Tyrie sumtym indvelar in Nevay (s to deceased David Tyrie & h to Janet Veilant) d 10.10.1651 3(7 or 3); (central)"..he

vas both vertuvs cynd & wyse"; shield; emblems

45 1835. Wm Brown late fr Mains of Fullerton 15.6.1822 56, w Elis Low 8.9. 1859 81

46 next 45. Wm Brown d Balkerrie 4.10.1861 65, w Janet Robertson 15.3.1891 79, s Jas 16.2.1899 56 (s Wm inf, w Ann Simpson d Willowbank Forfar 24.8.1909 57) da Margt d Balkirrie 2.6.1922 84

47 FS - - - - - - - - -

48 Alex Mitchell 18.1.184(3 or 5), by w Mary Watt

49 FS Here lyes an honest man Wm Watsone in Balkeire & w Elspeth Smith d 12. 5.1667 he aged 77y & she aged 54y, md 36y; W W, E S; emblems

50 1873. by John & Jane Butchart, da Margret 19.12.1847 nearly 2y

51 1843. by Alex & Wm, mo Agnes Crichton 1814 68, fa Wm Crichton sometime tent Kirkinch 1.1821 75

52 1851. by Margt Mitchel Crichton, h John Crichton 25.3.1851 60, s Jas 26.7.1851 16, her sis in law Elspet Crichton 14.5.1845 56

53 1855. by Alex McKay d Mains Auchterhouse 6.10.1893 73 & Mary Whitton 10.10.1886 60, da Betsy 3.7.1854

54 casket. John McIntosh in Balkerrie 21.2.1879 82, w Cath Millar 14.11.1878 71, s And 15.6.1840 8w, da Isabella 29.8.1843 5, gda Cath Cooper 25.1. 1890 36, Agnes 27.9.1918 84, s David 18.4.1926 79

55 next 56. Chas Neave 27.12.1891 80, w Annie Hawtyn 25.2.1879 68, chn David 5.8.1853 20, Willie 12.2.1866 15, Chas 1.6.1868 30, Jas 29.12.1887 38, Annie, Henrietta, Geo & Wm - - -

56 by Chas Nevay wright in Balkirrie & w Henrietta Doig, da Agnes Steel 13.2.1815 2; (west side) square & compasses; C N,1815

The following 57-60 are from Jervise, "Epitaphs & Inscriptions" i 68 & 371 and were not seen in 1975:

57 FS John Riven (or Rynd?) in Navey - - - w Elspet - - - March - - - - - ; I R, E W, M I, 1645 (but see F davidson, "Inventory" p 78 no 7: John Nivin in Navey d 4.1.(16)4(5) & his tvo vifs Elspet (Vat) & Mar - - -)

58 FS at west end of ruin. shield charged in pale a chevron between three roundels, possibly for Moreton of Cambo & a St Andrews cross possibly for Maxwell

59 in latin. And Baron mert 12.10.1714, w Margt Fairweather d Easter 1692

60 multilateral inside the ruin. - - - - yries in N - - - e Follous (all that remained of an inscription reputed to read "Here ly the Tyries in Navay honest men & brave fellows" - proprietors of Drumkilbo, one was killed 1581 by Crichton of Ruthven; sir Thos Tyrie of Drumkilbo was at Aberdeen with Montrose in 1644)

N o t e s

See 9 Eassie, notes

Jervise, "Epitaphs & Inscriptions" i 68 & 372 notes inscriptions 2,33,41,43, 60 & 18-22, 32,42,44,57-9

F Davidson, "Inventory of 17th Century Tombstones in Angus" pp 77-8 describes inscriptions 17,19-20,22,44,49 & 57

And.Tyrie, "The Tyries of Drumkilbo Perthshire, Dunnideer Aberdeenshire &

Lunan Forfarshire" (Glasgow 1893)

Scottish Record Office: E 763 Forfeited Estate papers, Kinloch & Nevay 1747-56

Testaments: the following were noticed in the Index to the Register of the
Commissariot of Edinburgh: David Abercrombie in Nevay, 1608
John Annerdaill in Bogischallow, 1602
Grissell Arbuthnott spouse to David Watson in Balkerie, 1577
Christian Auchinleck relict of Andro Donaldson in the Templetown of Nevay, 1591
Andro Donaldson in Tempiltoun in Balgrugo, 1580-1
John Jack alias Anderson in Balkerie, 1577
Elspeth Forrester widow in Nevay, 1608
and the following are a random selection from the Commissariot of St Andrews: Patk Dog in Loan-end of Dalgrigo par Nevye, 1681
Jas Flowris in Nevay, 1605; Robt Flowris cotterman par St Tringans, 1599
John Kyd mert traveller in Angus, par Nevoy, 1707
And Vallentine cotterman in Nevay par St Ringane, 1599

Index

Abercrombie Notes
Adam 21
Aikman 5
Anderson 13.15.30.32.Notes
Annerdaill Notes
Arbuthnott Notes
Auchinleck Notes

B. 12.18
Barclay 30
Barrie 2.4
Barron, Baron 41-3.59
Barry 3
Benzie 25
Black 5-6.14
Blair 20.Notes
Brown 22.45-6
Butchart 16.35.38.50.Notes

Christie 12
Clark 42
Cooper 54
Crichton 51-2.60
Cuthill 30

Dog,Doig,Doog 7-8.10.12-3.18.56.Notes
Donaldson 1. Notes
Dugat 21

Fairweather 59
Farquharson 11.35
Flowris Notes
Forrester Notes

Grahame 3
Gray 24

Halyburton 20
Hawtyn 55
Hill 23
Hutcheson/ison 16.24

Jack, Jake 17.Notes

Kidd, Kyd 25-7.Notes

Lockhart 4
Low 8.45
Louk(Luke) Notes

McIntosh 54
MacKay 4.53
Martin 16.30-1.38
Mawer 28
Maxwell 58
Mill 36
Millar 54
Mitchel(l) 6.10.48.52
Morice 29
Moreton 58
Murray 15

N. 33
Neave 19.55
Nevay, Nevoy 56.60
Nivin 57

Ogilvy 37

Petrson 11
Pullar 32

Reidie 60
Riven 57
Robertson 35.46
Ross 23
Rynd 57

Sanders 36
Scot 21.41
Simpson 26-8.46
Smith 7.38.42.49
Spalden 29
Steel 56

30 N E V A Y

Stewart	31	Vallentine	Notes	Whitton	53
Storach	19	Veilant	44	Wilkie	39
Storier	37	W.	57	Winter	2
Stratton	25	Walker	16	Wyse	10
T.	14	Wardroper	18.22	Young	29
Taylor	1	Watson(e)	17.49.Notes		
Tyrie	44.60.Notes	Wat(t)	48.57		

31 N E W T Y L E

The medieval church was dedicated in 1242 and was replaced in 1767. This church was taken down in 1870 to make room for the present building, impos- at the west end of the gridiron village. Several old stones were taken from the burial ground to make pavements and gateposts but (except for 117) were broken up in the 1960's.

National Grid reference: NO 296 411

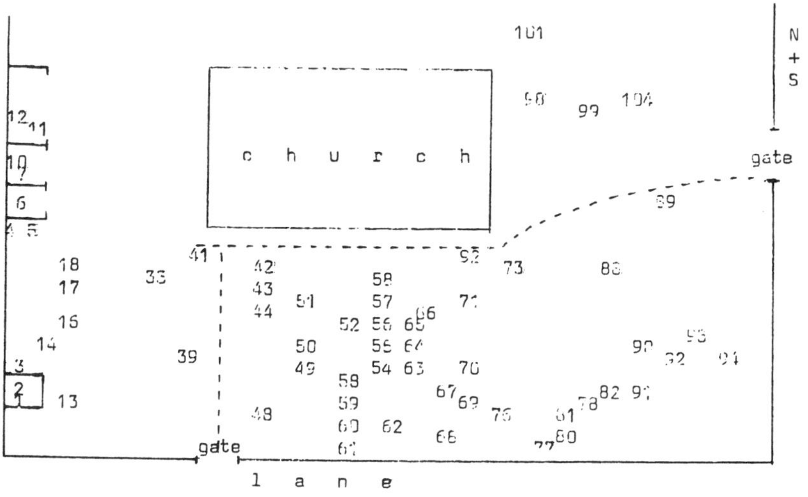

1 vault. John Moon manuf & tent Newbigging 17.1.1822 61, w Margt Robertson 4.8.1842 76, s Jas in Dundee 17.12.1839 43, s Geo here 23.12.1857 53, s rev John min 20.11.1862 71, da Susan 23.5.1863 69, s Adam surgeon 23. 2.1864 54, da Margt 31.10.1871 69 (h Jas Robertson), s Wm mert Dundee 1.10.1876 70, s Alex 12.11.1883 84, da Elspeth 24.3.1896 96 (h Jas Duncan) (see Fasti v 273: rev John Moon md Penelope (1da of Geo Moon))

2 next 1. John Moon tent & manuf Newbigging 17.1.1822 61, w Margt Robertson 4.8.1842 76, s Jas 17.12.1839 43; Geo Moon 27.8.1910 57; Margt Thomson 2.10.1913 63; Wm Moon 22.7.1929 82

3 FS tipped up. heir lyis ane famous and godlie man callit Geo Doig in Balmay (9).1618 65; G D, escutsheon for Doig; M R, escutcheon for Robertson (see F Davidson "Inventory" p 80 for details)

31 N E W T Y L E

4 FS tipped up. (marginal) Robt Mason late tent Pitnepie 20.4.1748 84, 1w Jean Jackson 20.4.1708 40 by whom he had 5 chn, 2w Isobel Spankie who survives him by whom he had two chn, by ss Geo & Alex; (central) R M, I I, I S; H M, G M, W M, A M, R M, A M, D M; oxenyoke; poem (quoted by Jervise, "Epitaphs" i 373)

5 FS tipped up. (marginal) Ihon Mitchell indweller Craighead 10.5.1678 78, w Grissell Grein 2.3.1675 82; I M, G G; poem (quoted by Jervise "Epitaphs"; see F Davidson "Inventory" p 8o no.5; see St Andrews Testaments)

6 vault. David Waddel fr Kinpurney 14.4.1838 64, w Jean Elder 23.2.1841 66; David Waddel 1804 20.4.1856 52, w Helen Morton 10.9.1856 49; Robt Waddel 16.8.1837 11.10.1915; David Waddel 24.4.1869 14.6.1938

7 vault. Hugh Watson for 55y tent Keillor b Bannatyne 4.10.1787 d the Den Perth 10.11.1865, w Margt Rose 7.3.1805 1.11.1866; Hugh Watson was one of the founders of the famous Aberdeen Angus breed of cattle

8 next 7, in Latin. mr Wm Blair of the family of Balgillo d 16.11.1656 58, by w Euphan Pattullo who has a da now aged 8y; arms of Blair & Patullo (see F Davidson, "Inventory")

9 next 8. Richd Jackson Jones, w Margt 18.5.1854 29 (da of Hugh Watson)

10 next 9. Wm Watson d Auchtertyre 3.12.1830 71, w Janet Wilkie 2.5.1835 81

11 vault. FS tipped up. (marginal) Here lyes interred below this stone the dust and ashes of Andrew Whitton and of his age Ninety even.... (central) Poor his living was in Auechteryre ane honest wright husband man, but now hes lying in the ground here. Also interred belou this ston a child of nonage whos name was John. His children seven remaining be and of his oyes (ed. grandchildren) thirty three; shield with A W, K G, 1730, plough

12 next 11. And Whitton of Couston 14.5.1861 68, mo Christian Robertson 12.3.1835 74, fa Robt 26.10.1840 82, w Agnes Arnot 4.12.1882 90 at Newtyle, s And 17.6.1917 79 (w Eliz Martin Webster at Couston 26.7.1924 82); Patk Webster Whitton d Henderston 7.11.1934 61 (see Jervise, "Epitaphs" i 374: firstnamed Andrew was succeeded in Couston & Scotston by s now local factor for lord Wharncliffe)

13 by Margt Skea in Mirside of Fullarton imo h Jas Edward 1761 44 ......(under turf)...; (west side) 1762. I E A E M K

14 1881. Jas Gray mason Newbigging 11.4.1879 76, w Elspeth Stevenson 3.1.1853 47, da Martin 11.3.1845 18, s Adam 28.8.1856 21, s Allam 28.6.1858 12

15 Wm Gray late tent Newbigging 4.3.1821 61, w Eliz Hunter 15.1.1822 59, chn Margt, Janet, Mary & Agnes, gchn Agnes Gray 4.9.1832 17 & Jas Gray 2.9.1834 8

16 Thos Alexander smith Newbigging 12.1785 60, w Elspeth Souttar 12.1797 71, by ss Wm smith in Newbigging & John smith in Lundie; (west side) crown, anvil, hammer, pincers, horseshoe; 1805; by Wm Alexander smith Newtyle & w Henrietta Doig, chn Jean & David d inf

17 David Martin of Denhead 5.1825 71, w Eliz Hill 31.5.1851 87

18 ob 1840. Geo Browster schoolmaster here for 52y d 17.2.1838 82, by pupils

19 1858. John Ferguson 26.11.1831 54, s Jas 22.1.1827 2, da Penelope 2.8.1828 inf, da Eliz 10.4.1833 19, da Janet 6.1.1851 31, by da Betty

20 1838. Walter Auld

21 1872. John Stevenson d Newbigging 25.2.1848 44, s John inf, w Elspeth Johnston 14.11.1902 90, da Jane 25.4.1925 84 (s John Stewart d Canada 1945 73)

22 John Ogilvie 12.8.1831 84, w Helen Hutchison 2.1824 77

23 1855. And Crichton fr Hatton b there 6.11.1794 d Newtyle 8.6.1853, by wid Helen Thoms

24 Geo Crichton tent Hatton 24.4.1824 85, w Eliz Miller 7.6.1844 87

25 1842. Jas Guild

26 1842. John Guild

27 1840. P L

28 And Stevenson schollmaster Eassie & Nevay for 33y d 30.5.1877 66, w Euphemia Ireland 7.4.1888 78, s Robt 1828 1w, da Cath 1834 4, s John 1838 2, s Jas 1838 4, s Robt 1840 8, s David 1840 6m, s Geo 1840 2, Rea in Ireland 1891 48, Alex 1897 50, s And 1902 67

29 Wm Butters blacksmith Ingleston, w Agnes Steele 27.4.1877, da Jean 26.11.1826 12, his mo Janet Mitchell 27.8.1819 57

30 1859. Wm Butters fr Millhole 29.6.1851 61, by w Agnes Steele & surviving family, da Marjory Rodger 26.6.1830 1y, s Jas Steele 29.11.1858 43, s Thos 9.8.1862 38; Thos Butters, w Jane Keay 17.3.1846

31 1839. W L

32 1839. Bob Chambers

33 by David Tullo fr Auchtertyre, w Margt Hair 29.3.1762 37, das Eliz 22.5.1763 7, Helen 1760 1y, Kath 1766 1y; D T,1766, M S; yoke, plough, harrow; Eliz T, Je T, He T, M T; Jam T, Ka T, M A

34 David Strathearn innkeeper here 5.11.1842 59, w Elspat Thomson 16.3.1866 73, da Cath 21.6.1842 17; David Strathearn 12.12.1874 43; Ann Strathearn 7.5.1880 51

35 And Whitton 30.3.1839 78, w Ann Crichton 1.4.1820 54, his bro David Whitton 4.8.1840 63, da Ann 8.2.1841 38, by s Wm in Denend; Wm Whitton 8.10.1884 84

36 Jas Wilkie & Helen Gruar, da Ann 27.1.1756

37 1820. by Jas Dundas & wife, da Margt 9.1.1852 8, s And 27.2.1869 inf

38 1844. A G

39 1832. by Jas Martin & his sisters, fa John d Boghead 31.1.1815 52, mo Agnes Henderson d Burnside 13.9.1819 61, bro Geo 18.2.1832 31; James' ss David & Peter d in childhood

40 Allan Robertson 3.9.1875 68, w Jane Ogilvie 2.1.1894 77, da Jane 3.10.1848 2, s Thos 23.2.1856 3m

41 And Millar d Ballantyne 22.10.1836 52, uncle Jas Millar d there 26.8.1836 79 (ed. Ballantyne is otherwise called Bannatyne)

42 pillar. Jas Burman late tent Mill of Newtyle & Balmaw b Mill of Newtyle 2.5.1777 d there 22.12.1839, w Cecelia Clark 30.8.1796 11.12.1870, chn Marjory, Cecelia & John d young, Ann 1816 1851, Peter writer 1814 d Australia 1841, Jas engineer 1818 1885 int Harrington, Cecelia 1826 1919 (wid of rev Jas Dalrymple of Cumberland, da Cecelia Clark 1863 1946), David Clark master mariner 7.2.1830 8.7.1906, Cath 1822 1877 int Dundee (wid of Richd Baird), Jessie 1824 d Carmyllie Touranga Upotiki New Zealand 17.11.1906 (wid of rev John Gow of Carmyllie)(see Ewing i 173: John Gow b NewKilpatrick 1815, md 1850, ord 1849 at Carmyllie, translated 1865 to N Zealand)

43 TS (marginal) David Jobsone sometime fr Hall Town of Newtyle, w Isobel

Burns there, yt s John 27.10.1720 21; death bed scene

(central) Jas Jobson tent Haltown of Newtyle 12.8.1764 70, w Jean Matthew 26.11.1741 43, she had ten chn viz. Jas, David, Jas, John, Chas, Thos, Isobel, Margt, Jean & Ann; David Jobson, wid Marjory Johnson 3.12.1843; Robt Jobson, w Jane Small 29.5.1830; above Robt Jobson d 9.3.1864; Wm Jobson, only da Janet 20.7.1862; Wm Jobson 26.1.1890; (at head) D J; (at foot) D B; (at left) G J, J J; (at right) - -, W J (see F Davidson, "Inventory", also Rogers ii 264 & Jervise "Epitaphs" i 140: the oldest of four stones erected to the memory of members of the same family - Jas Jobson & W Barbry Scot "frugall & vertuous" 24.3. 1684 67, indweler in the Haltown of Newtyl, s Jas 7.1660 9 - the family became very rich merchants in Dundee & Jane Jobson md the 1s of sir Walter Scott; see also Dundee Howff inscription 111 & St Andrews Testaments)

44 TS David Jobson fr West Mains of Auchterhouse 12.1804 41, da Magdalen d Dundee 12.12.1839 33; Jas Jobson indweller Haltowne of New Tyle 9.2. 1674 63; David Jobson of age 56y (ed. circa 1670?) (see F Davidson, "Inventory")

45 Adam Syme Free Church teacher here, w Jane Stewart 20.5.1816 22.2.1867

46 1863. Jas Millam 4.1854 77, w Mary Doig 24.5.1847 63, by s Peter

47 1841. by Jas Thomson 20.2.1860 75, w Eliz Douglas d Chapel of Keilor 11.12.1840 48, da Jane d Ward of Turin 18.12.1899 80

48 by Jane Ramsay 30.4.1879 73 & Mary Ramsay imo their uncle & aunts And Ramsay 27.12.1834 73, Margt Ramsay 28.12.1839, Jane Ramsay 11.12.1845 67 all tents Burnside

49 Wm Baxter weaver Lone-end of Balm- 7.3.1735 73, by w Elspet Wallace; G B, E B; loom & shuttle

50 Geo McIntosh 2.10.1854 65, w Elspeth Donaldson 26.7.1879 82, s Wm 2.1840 6, s David 7.1842 6, da Matilda 12.1843 1½, by da Janet

51 Anne Dalrymple schoolmistress Newbigging House 21.2.1839 63, by a few of her pupils

52 1827. by John Small tent Burnmouth, w Jean Johnston 17.10.1822 47, s David 11y, da Margt 19y, s Wm 14y, da Marjory 21y; John Small 9.4.1855 52

53 Robt Lindsay fr Henderston d Belmont Street 3.2.1839 73

54 1771. "Here lyes the dust of Robt Small/Who when in life was thick not tall;/But what's of greater consequence/ He was endowed with good sense. O how joyful the day in which /Death's pris'ner shall be free /And in triumph o'er all his foes /His God in mercy see". Revised 1838. (west

side) R S, H A; oxen yoke & plough; Jo S, El S, M S, R S, Jas S; erected at the instance of Robt Small fr Boghead imo fa Robt who was gathered with his fathers 11.3.1771 72 (see St Andrews Testaments: Robt Small in Boghead, 4.8.1775)

55 Janet Small 14.1.1838 59, by da Jean Miller (& h John Gill)

56 Jean Millar 4.7.1845 45

57 David Gill 8.8.1920 84, w Helen Hay Dutch 19.1.1911, s John d South Africa 5.1898 27, 1da Jeannie Miller 18.10.1946

58 Wm Gibson, w Jane Gill 2.4.1928 93, s Wm John d Brooklyn USA 20.2.1921 63

59 next 53. by Wm Thomson builder Dundee, w Janet Lindsay 30.9.1836 37 (da of Robt Lindsay fr Henderston), da Jessie Lindsay d West Ferry 15.7.1900 65

60 Robt Lindsay onetime tent Henderston then of Ardler d Sidlaw House Newtyle 7.7.1877 81

61 Peter Roy fr Locklones par Liff 10.5.1891 95 int Madura cem Clay County Kansas, w Mary Lindsay d Locklones

62 1715. cherub; P M , K S , M M ; of age 44

63 Jas Mitchell surgeon Newtyle 6.4.1842 43, w Agnes Pourie 25.1.1890, da Agnes 6.5.1840 10, s David d Port Elizabeth S Africa 29.1.1873 30

64 Alex Millar 2.3.1874 49, w Jane Ann Mitchell 8.12.1884 58, s John d Belize British Honduras 17.9.1886 20, s David d Melbourne Australia 10.12.1925 66, by s Alex 6.2.1932 71

65 coped FS tipped up. Iohn Mitchel vittaler in Balmav & h to Issobel Dog he d 17.11.1603 72y6m. "I fer God." 
(see F Davidson, "Inventory" p 19 no 2, sketch; Jervise, "Epitaphs" i 373)

66 FS Jas Anderson & w Agnes Small, by surviving chn Agnes, Susan, Isobel, Jean & Eliz; revised in 1828 by order of Isobel Anderson as a tribute of filial respect. shield with J A, J W, 1739

67 Wm Massie contractor Newtyle d East Mains of Oathlaw 26.6.1844 60, by s Wm fr East Mains of Oathlaw

68 1826. by Thos Easson, Newtyle & w Kath Kinmont, da Jean 21.2.1826 19, s Geo 19.5.1836 28

69 1840. Eliz Monro 7.11.1839 54, by s Robt Angus, Burnside (his uncle Geo Monro 14.11.1839 44, his aunt Mary Monro 2.1.1840 59)

70 1844. David Crockatt 1.10.1843 44, by w Ann Donaldson, s Christopher 1836 6m, s David 1840 8m, da Jane Ann 1844 2

71 Alex Ramsay 6.2.1830 71, w Isabella Young d Hill of Keillor 5.12.1829 73, da Margt 1.4.1858 65, by da Hellen(& h Chas Robertson) in 1861

72 Alex Johnstone 25.12.1825 47, w Jane Small 12.11.1864 79 (her sis Helen Small 20.7.1875 88), da Elspeth Stevenson 14.11.1902 90, by da Ann 8.2.1899 84

73 Jas Jeffrey here 1811 59, w Jean Sturton 1821 57, s John d Hill of Keillor 7.6.1863 73; (west side) T E, E C, 1781; loom

74 1840. John Miller. Geo Miller

76 Margt Ogilvie 15.4.1832 53, by h Jas Pirie tent Nether Mill Newtyle

77 FS (marginal) here lyes ane honest man cald David Wobster husband to

Catrin Blair indwellers in Balmav who departed the 18 July 1664 44; (central) D W ♡ C B; emblems

78 by John Sidey in Burnside, s Alex 18.8.1838 28, da Margt 5.10.1839 23

79 1852. D Coupar

80 by Alex Turner in Balkirrie & w Janet Moncur, s Jas 11.8.1821 11

81 1763. Jas Irland indweller Newbigging 15.12.1759 76, w Elspet Anderson 10.12.1761 65, by ss Jas & Geo; (west side) loom & shuttle; I I, I I, G I, I I, E I, K I (see St Andrews Testaments: Jas Ireland mason in Keilor, 23.4.1800)

82 Jas Clarke in Sauchieburn Kincardineshire, wid mrs Ann Nicoll 29.10. 1842 42; Wm Nicoll fr Nether Kinalty par Airlie, wid Margt Howe 12.7. 1849 87; late Robt Nicoll in Shannon House Sligo Ireland, da Isabella 17.8.1839 27 (see Airlie inscription no.20)

83 Wm Lindsay d Newbigging 2.4.1829 74. Wm Lindsay d High Keillor 14.1. 1835 45

84 1878. by Jas Heron, Betty Heron 7.3.1845 35, Alex Heron 4.3.1850 19, Eliz Heron 9.1.1827 4

85 by Ann Strathern, da Christian Kay 1.1840 5

86 Wm Wallace. 1845

87 1840. J L

88 1845. by Jas Saunders wood mert here, s Wm 22.4.1845 20y10m2w

89 1876. Alex Morrison 12.5.1814 39, w Hannah Nicol 18.2.1862 86, by s Alex

90 by rev John Muir min here (see Small i 340: United Secession Church in Newtyle, only min John Muir in 1838), nephew Wm Muir 13.4.1848 11½, wid Jessie Thomson 21.4.18(<u>95</u>) 8(<u>4</u>), niece Sarah Smith 2.3.1929 84

91 Wm Patterson here 18.6.1843 79, w Janet Howie 21.5.1844 86

92 by John Stephen fr Davidston & w Agnes Soutar d Coupar Angus 4.7.1873 79, s Jas 21.3.1848 30

93 Peter Anderson 2.9.1849 35, w Betsy Hendry 11.1.1901 85, by s Geo in Newbigging (w Ann Hendry 30.8.1905)

94 by Jas Ogilvie & Cath Blair, da Mary 10.1848 7, da Betsy 10.1848 4, s d 5.1860 inf

95 Eunice Edward native of Kingoldrum d here 2.1852 27

96 by John McNicoll 31.12.1871 84, w Ann Watson d Burnmouth 6.2.1852 61, da Mary d Lochee 9.8.1859 39, s Wm 30.3.1869 59

97 1838. J S

98 1871. John Stewart fr Newbigging (<u>1</u> or <u>7</u>).9.1861 87, s Peter 5.4.1853 29, da Margt 18.3.1839 8, da Fanny 6.9.1842 3, s Wm 2.4.1891 48, w Jane McLaren 1891 90

99 Peter Downie 1876 73, w Cath Kennedy, da Janet 29.3.1847 14, s John 21. 6.1851 21, by ss Peter & W.

100 1842. Thos Mole

101 Helen Smith 20.1.1872 77, s Jas 6.7.1842 16

102 1841. Jas Butchart

103 by Alex Fleming & Janet Kinnaird, s Jas 22.11.1819 2y

31 N E W T Y L E

104 David McIntosh 7.1830 38, by da Margt 21.10.1881 60 (h capt Wm Dixon)

The following nos. 105-116 are recorded by Jervise, "Epitaphs & Inscriptions" i 139-41 & 373-4, and some also by Rogers ii 263, but were not seen in 1977:

105 mural on south wall of church, in latin. Jas Alison sometime inhabitant of this par, indulgent fa, affectionate husband etc d 4.2.1737 (progenitor of late sir Alex bart & he was succeeded by s Patk who became proprietor of Stonee & Newhall near Coupar Angus etc etc)

106 near 8. 1813. Geo Watson esq Bannatyne House, w Jean Rose sole heiress of ancient families of Moray & Kinnaird of Culbin; "all who knew her loved her"

107 FS G M, K B, M B, 1675; Gilbert Mille d 100y, twentysix chn by two wives; poem in acrostic form (quoted)

108 Geo Mitchel indvaler in Balmav 1625 52, w C B; Andro Mitchel, w L R; A S, w Isobel Mitchel; poem

109 Jhon Moug 2.8.1632 66, w Margrat Halen; I M, M H; shield, arms impaled chevron with rose in base

110 Jas Ramsay in Aughtertyr 50y, w Janet Whitton 15.10.1673 52, s Jas 11. 11.1677 20; Wm Ramsay & Agnas Lounie in said toune, chn Jas, David, Geo & Janet int here; Wm Ramsay in Auchtertyre 36y; 1682; poem

111 near middle of churchyard. John Don indweller Hill of Keillor 6.1698 60 & Barbra Thom there 6.1698 65

112 near south wall. Alex Badan 18.7.1702 59 with four wives & four chn all d in Burnmouth; Jas Badan d Denhead 1715 36, w Agnes Horn (see St. Andrews Testaments: Alex Badine in Burnemouth, 18.11.1702)

113 David Baxter, w Ann Wilkie 1753 59; poem (poem quoted "Epitaphs" 141)

114 John Sliddrs 18.4.1702 75 & w Isobell Marten 5.1678 56 indwellers in Balmav; John Sliddrs & Janet Small, da Isoball d 9y; poem

115 Wm Jackson mert 16.3.1703 61 & w Anna Meal indwellers Newbigging with seven ss & das; poem

116 fragments. I O, - C; arms of Oliphant & ?Crichton?

117 fragment. - - - - - Olyphan and h- - - - - age ye - - - - - 1603

118 the only surviving stone of several used as paving in Church Street, this is a FS in the workshop at 30 Church St which would repay further study: (central) H G, I T; ?inkhorn, heart & dunce's cap?; latin text - - - - ; (marginal) - - - - - - - - - - - -

119 inscription at Glamis no.104: Andrew Deuchars 1840 51 int Newtyle

N o t e s

F Davidson, "Inventory of 17th Century Tombstones in Angus" details inscriptions 3,5,8,44,65,77

A Jervise, "Epitaphs & Inscriptions" i 139-41 & 373-4 notes inscriptions 4-5, 7-8,11-2,18, 51,54,65,105-116

Fasti v 271 ministers from 1566

Small i 340 Newtyle United Secession 1838

31 NEWTYLE

OPR with the Registrar General: 314 Newtyle
Births 1628-1722, 1728-1854
Marriages 1717-44, 1747-52, 1756-71, 1773-1854
Deaths 1773-86 (see also SRO CH2/284)

Church Records in SRO CH2/284 Newtyle (ie Newtyle West):
minutes 1648-57, 1663-1807, 1825-1950
Deaths 1758-71
collections 1808-37
discipline 1819-28
communion roll 1874-1910

CH3/247 Newtyle United Associate Congregation, UP :
KS minutes 1836-1872

CH3/248 Newtyle FC (later UF & East C of S)
KS minutes 1848-78, 1903-32
congregational committee minutes 1843-63
DC minutes 1864-1938, ms history

HR 627 post1863

Testaments: the following is a small random selection from the Register of the St Andrews Commissariot -
Thos Baxter servitor to sir Jas Haliburton of Pitcur, 1618
Agnes Bethune in Auchtertyre, 1685
mr Thos Black min at Newtyle, 1691
Thos Haldane portioner of Easter Kelour, 1613
David Small sometime in Burnmouth thereafter of Kirktoun of Newtyle, 1783
Robt Small in Newtyle, 1694
And Whittit in Auchtertyre, 14.10.1673
- and the following were noticed in the Register of the Edinburgh Commissariot
Christine Anderson somtyme spouse to John Anderson in Balcraig, 1590-1
John Anderson in Haltoun of Newtyle, 1589-90 & w Jonet Blair, 1577
Henry Anderson in Auchtertyre, 1608
John Christie in Kinpurney, 1591

Index

A.	54
Alexander	16
Alison	105
Anderson	66.81.93.Notes
Angus	69
Arnot	12
Auld	20
B.	107-8
Baden, Badine	112
Baird	42
Baxter	49.113.Notes
Blair	8.77.94.Notes
Bethune	Notes
Black	Notes
Browster	18
Burman	42
Burns	43
Butchart	102
Butters	29.30
C.	73
Chambers	32
Christie	Notes
Clark(e)	42.82
Crichton	23-4.35.116
Crockatt	70
Dalrymple	42.51
Deuchars	119
Dixon	104
Dog,Doig	3.16.46.65
Don	111
Donaldson	50.70
Douglas	47
Downie	99
Duncan	1
Dundas	37
Dutch	57
E.	73

31 N E W T Y L E

Easson 68
Edward 13.95
Elder 6

Ferguson 19
Fleming 103

G. 11.38.118
Gibson 58
Gill 55.57-8
Gow 42
Gray 14-5
Green 5
Gruar 36
Guild 25-6

Hair 33
Haldane,Halden 109.Notes
Haliburton Notes
Henderson 39
Hendry 93
Heron 84
Hill 17
Horn 112
Howe 82
Howie 91
Hunter 15
Hutchison 22

Ir(e)land 28.81

Jackson 4.115
Jeffrey 73
Jobson 43-4
Johnson 43
Johnston(e) 21.52.72
Jones 9

K. 13
Kay,Keay 30.85
Kennedy 99
Kinmont 68
Kinnaird 103

L. 27.31.87
Lindsay 53.59-61.83
Lounie 110

M. 62
McIntosh 50.104
McLaren 98
McNicoll 96
Marten/in 12.17.39.114
Mason 4
Massie 67
Matthew 43
Meal 115
Millam 46
Millar 41.56.64
Mille,Miller 24.55.57.74.107
Mitchel(l) 5.29.63-5.108
Mole 100
Moncur 80
Monro 69
Moon 1-2
Morrison 89
Morton 6
Moug 109
Muir 90

Nicol(l) 82.89

Ogilvie 22.40.76.94
Oliphant 116-7

Patterson 91
Pattullo 8
Pirie 76
Pourie 63

R. 3.108
Ramsay 48.70.110
Robertson 1-3.12.40.70
Rodger 30
Rose 7.106
Roy 61

S. 33.62.97.108
Saunders 88
Scott 43
Sidey 78
Skea 13
Sliddrs 114
Small 43.52.54-5.66.72.114.Notes
Smith 90.101
Sout(t)ar 16.92
Spankie 4
Steele 29-30
Stephen 92
Stevenson 14.21.28.72
Stewart 21.45.97
Strathe(a)rn 34.85
Sturton 73
Syme 45

T. 118
Thom 111
Thoms 23
Thomson 2.34.47.59.90
Tullo 33
Turner 80

W. 66
Waddel 6
Wallace 49.86
Watson 7.9-10.96.106
Webster 12 see Wobster
Whittit Notes
Whitton 11-2.35
Wilkie 10.36
Wobster 77

Young 70

32 OATHLAW

The original parish church was dedicated in 1380 to the Nine Maidens on a site now a field at the junction of the Esk & the Lemno, called Aitkenhauld at Finhaven (Finaven). In 1618 the chapel of St Mary at Oathlaw became the parish church & the parish was renamed Oathlaw. This church, in the burial ground, was replaced by a new building in 1815. It is well kept.
National Grid reference: 476 562

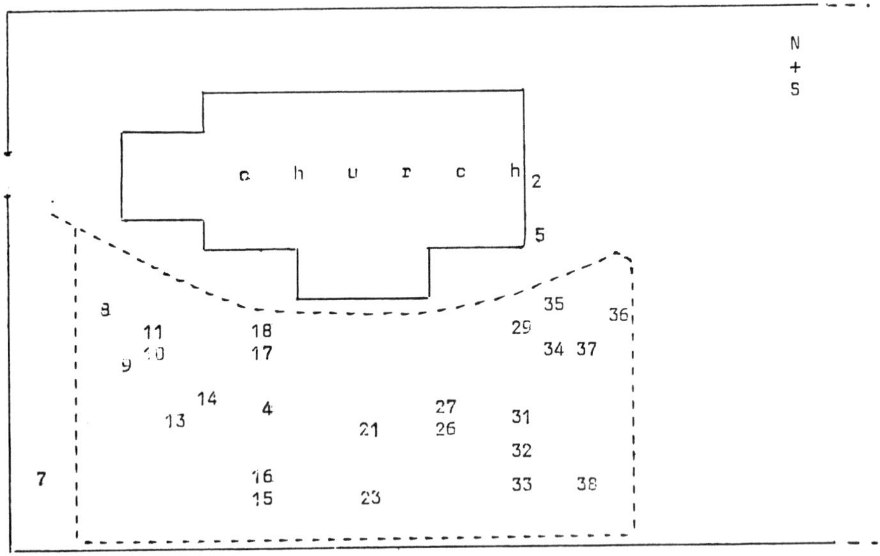

1 mural in church. capt Jas Webster (see Jervise "Epitaphs" i 334: his fa was provost of Forfar), w Mary Eliz Hillocks 2.1.1834, only chn David 10.1.1834 2y19d, & Mary 3.8.1834 3y7m19d. This tablet is (by permission of the heritors) erected by a sorrowing husband & father.

2 1831. David Hillocks at Mill of Finhaven 6.6.1839 86, w Isabella Brown 11.2.1831 79 (see Jervise "Epitaphs" i 335: parents of Mary Eliz above, he was long local factor in Finhaven, Careston & Hallyburton & she was da of a factor at Aboyne; his bro was fr East Newton then grain mert in Montrose d ca 1859 97, their fa was fr of Peebles near Arbroath - Jervise has Isabella Brown's age at death as 97y in error)

3 per Jervise i 336, not seen in 1971. Wm Cuthbert wright Carsburn 1768 72, s John d inf; poem

4 FS Thos Hood hammerman sometime indweller Wilds Hillok 18.1.1699 57 (probably in error, Jervise has 86y), w Janet Sutar & his chn; poem; crown & hammer

5 FS tipped up (brought from the old burial ground at Finhaven) (marginal in latin) dominus Rechard de Breic(h- -) vicar; incised effigy of priest (see PSAS 1908-9 p 311, F C Eeles "A slab at Oathlaw"; also Jervise, "Epitaphs" i 338 for sketch)

6 John Fairweather in this town, w Agnes Clerk 15.3.1734

7 Jas Webster fr Parkford 27.4.1884 78, w Martha Smith 18.3.1874 80, s Wm & da Mary d inf, da Jane 23.10.1907 75, da Isabella 30.5.1910 82 (wid of

John Dawson), s John fr Parkford for 44y succeeding his fa d 24.6.1913 83

8 David Cuthbert sometime tent & wright Carsburn 3.12.1768 72, by w Agnes Butchard & ss John, David & Wm, s Jas 14.1.1744 in none age; (west side) wrights tools; mantling; D C, A B; Is, Io, A, D, M, Ia, E, W Cuthberts; 1770

9 1852. by David & Grace Hendry, fa And 26.1.1852 61, sis Betsy 28.11. 1823 8

10 rev Alex Cromar min here for 4½y d 10.11.1835 39, w Jane Phillip d Collieston Mains 7.9.1874 64, (west side) s Geo Philip wine mert Arbroath 12.12.1862 31, da Jane 1.4.1863 32 int Petropolis Brazil (h David Ritchie in Rio de Janeiro), Barbara d Bargeddie Manse Lanarkshire 30.3.1881 (h rev A T Scott (see Fasti iii 226)), 1da Margt Milne d Hopeville Dowanhill Glasgow 27.2.1901 72 int Necropolis there (see Jervise "Epitaphs" i 337 & Fasti v 301: he was s of Patk Cromar fr Lumphanan, Jane was da of Geo Philip, Arbroath)

11 mr Thos Raiker b 11.6.1711, min here from 24.12.1740 d 30.1.1803,md 4.2.1742 to w May Prophet 5.3.1715 20.7.1798; poem (see Fasti v 301 & Jervise "Epitaphs" i 336: he was 7s of Robt excise officer Anstruther Wester, & she was da of Jas Profit mert Kirriemuir; see also Jervise "Land of the Lindsays" 167; microfilm "Scottish Excise Dept" in SRO; Brechin Testaments)

12 FS broken. David Dalgity sometime indweller here 20.4.1710, w Eliz Hutcham 20.1.1707 49; monogram DDE; (E)D, I D, D D, I D, M D, I D, A D

13 1810. Jas Wallace sometime tent Birkenbush 21.3.1796 63, by w Jean Ireland, chn David, Janet & Ann

14 FS John Marno sometime indweller Ovthlaw 11.1675 76; I M, M N; R M, I D

15 Alex Milne 18.2.1841 31, w Helen Kydd 6.3.1868 (or 1869) 58,(by sis Eliz Kydd) chn Belen & Jas d inf (see inscription no.16)

16 1833. Chas Milne 26.12.1851 84, w Ann Davidson 2.2.1834 63, chn Robt 4.7.1804 4, John & Isobel d nonage; Jean Milne 10.4.1883 84; Chas Milne 3.2.1889 82; (west side) Alex Milne 18.2.1841 31, chn Helen & Jas d inf, w Helen Kydd 6.3.1869 58

17 by Robt Doig fr Cossens, w Anne Tailor, fa Wm Doig 55y, mo Agnes Kid 65y, sis Isobel 30y, s Frederick 6y, gdas Eliz, Cath, Anne & Jessie Doig or Duff int here; (east side) emblems; renovated 1900 by mrs Chambers P L G Sutherland, ggda of Robt Doig

18 FS in latin. (Wm)Fode d Oct - - - - -, s Alex Fode 25.5.1618 (Jervise "Epitaphs" i 336 suggests Fode is a corruption of Fothie, Fithie or Fadie; Brechin Testaments, Alex Fod in Ordy par of Fynnevine, 1628); V F, I D

19 Chas Carnegy fr Battledykes 12.1844 67, w Douglas Stewart 8.1884 84, s David 7.1863 34, s Alex 3.1884 44, s Chas 12.1891 47, four chn inf

20 1820. by Jas Morris & w Margt Black, s Jas 20.10.1808 noneage, da Helen 21.7.1818 14

21 Here lys Wm Duncan & w Janet Davidson & s Chas 4.3.1733 23 who caued this stome to be erected imo his deceased parents & himself; (east side) W D, I D, C D; I B, I M

22 ob Robt Yeaman d Forfar 13.7.1869 49 int there, w Susan Scott d Forfar 1858 30 int here (fa Peter Scott fr Bourtreebush 5.1831, mo Jane Morris d Dundee 20.10.1875 76), by s Jas sometime in California USA,nat-

ive here b 15.9.1845 d Dundee 1.12.1906 61 (w Christina Keir b Dundee 9.3.1859 d there 19.5.1947 88)

23 by Patk Nish sometime in Mill of Finhaven, w Kathren Watson 28.11.1750 44, s John sometime tent Parkford 20.5.1800 73 (w Agnes Gibson 58y, s John of Newfordpark near Forfar sometime tent Parkford 18.12.1819 66); (west side) cherub, mantling; 1751; P N, K W; Io N, P N, T N, Ia N, An N, C N, A N, G N, E N, W N, A N

24 1851. Wm Ford fr Ballandarge 7.3.1848 67, s Geo 11.2.1823 4; (west side) Ann Lindsay 29.1.1823; Geo Stewart 12.11.1825

25 David Craik in Oathlaw 1840, w Margt Lawrance 1839, chn Chas Jas, Walter, Thos Raiker, Margt, Jean Eliz, gs John Morris 3.11.1891

26 Wm Hird sometime smith at Feneven 22.3.1774 60y5d, da Jean 3.1754 9m3w, da Barbarie 11.1758 4, by w Kathraine Gall; W H, K G; A, I, K, I, B, I, W, E, D; (west side) cherub; W H, K G: anvil; A, I, K, I, B, I, W, E, D Hirds; poem

27 Alex Low sometime smith Fenaven 18.3.1737 41; anvil, crown, hammer, tongs; A L, I S; I L, A L, D L, M L; Alex Low & Isobel Smith, two chn Alex & David d in their young & tender age

28 David Kydd sometime fr Bogindollo 21.3.1862 70, w Jane McDonald 13.9.1882 71, da Helen 3.1.1850 15w, s John 8.7.1859 24, da Elis 27.3.1860 17; Jane 28.7.1863 17

29 by Jas Fraser road contractor & surveyor & late fr Blairyfeddon, w Eliz Langlands 22.1.1826 64, s Jas fr Cairn & shoremaster Montrose 30.11.1829 35

30 1882. David Ritchie sometime fr Ordie 5.1.1875 81, s David 1843 4, John d Chicago 1876 37, s Robt M 4.8.1884 41, w Eliz Millar 19.11.1891 81

31 ob David Ritchie fr Ordie, only da Jane 9.4.1909 75; Wm Ritchie for 37y in succession to his fa fr Ordie d Forfar 13.5.1914 78; David Ritchie & Eliz, yt s Alex of Tigh Alasdair in Forfar late Wester Oathlaw & Barnyards 2.1.1937 84, w Eliz Keay 20.4.1951 94

32 fallen. (east side) monogram AM H D; W M, I I, W M, I M, M M, A M; (west side) by Wm Millar imo fa Andrew 1.8.1721 69

33 1882. by David Millar fr Wester Oathlaw, bros John, Wm & Jas, fa d 26.8.1844 70, mo d 26.11.1871 91, w Martha Waterston 9.11.1880 72; David Millar 20.2.1894 77

34 FS Robt Moor sometime indweller Bogardo 1.8.1694 76, w Euphan Ese, chn Robt, John, Kathren & Janet lye here (Jervise "Epitaphs" i 336 omits s Robt)

35 Alex Adams 27.9.1883 82, w Isabella Stuart 15.7.1863 58, s Wm 5.9.1836 15.1.1837, John 8.5.1842 24.9.1842, gda Margt Jane 22.6.1864 22m

36 FS 1799. John Brydon sometime tent Mill of Finhaven 20.1.1799 86, by w Isabel Low

37 Alex Jack crofter d here 24.12.1831 62, w Margt Black d Brechin 19.10.1845 73, erected in 1862 by ss Jas postman, Alex flesher, David fr Middle Drums all in Brechin & gs Alex of Inland Revenue (mo Mary Scott d Gillaburn 29.11.1841 22)

38 D M ♡ A A; by David MacKey sometime tent Ground of Feneven, w Agnes Allon 20.6.1760 58; John MacKey, da Battie 25.6.1766 1y, s David 29.4.1762 13m; (east side) I M, I H, 1763, anvil; I M, I M, W M; B M, D M, I M D C son to said A A & his spous K B

39 by wall of old manse. John Ferrier shipmaster d Riga 43y int there, w mrs Ferrier d Easter Oathlaw 25.9.1881 92

40 per Jervise i 374, not seen in 1971. 1732. here lyes Eliz Volum da to Iohn Volum & Iannet Cato in Main Shott of Finevan & Helen Volum their da d 10.6.1731 19y (see notes in "Epitaphs" i 374 & "Land of the Lindsays")

41 (inscription no. 104 at Glamis) Peter Deuchars 9.1785 18 & bro John 8. 1786 both int Oathlaw

N o t e s

F Davidson, "Inventory of 17th Century Tombstones in Angus" details nos. 4, 12,14,18,34 at pp 81-2

A Jervise, "Epitaphs & Inscriptions" notes inscriptions 1-4, 10-1, 14, 18 & 34, & 40

Testaments: the following were noticed in the Edinburgh Commissariot Register
Robt Finlayson in Akenhat, 1594
Jas Jack ferryman at Fynneven, 1602
- and the following in the Brechin Commissariot Register
David Dalgety in Chevishache of Finnevine, 1624
Isabel Doig relict of Thos Hood in Phinhaven, 1679

OPR with the Registrar General: 315 Oathlaw

Births	1717-42, 1745-66, 1768-9, 1771-1854
Marriages	1717-42, 1745-66, 1768-9, 1771-1854
Deaths	1720-42, 1783-90

Church Records in the SRO: CH2/287 minutes 1741-51
minutes & a/c 1772-1840
book of discipline 1808-60
communion roll 1849-59
HR 580 Oathlaw post 1880
CH3/497 Memus FC minutes 1843-65
communion roll 1857-70

Fasti v 300 Oathlaw of old Finaven, ministers from 1560

Ewing ii 157 Memus, ministers from 1844 (the congregation from Cortachy, Kirriemuir, Oathlaw & Fern met in a cartshed of West Memus farm.

Angus District Cemeteries Office, Forfar: ms references to pre-1855 burials.

I n d e x

Adams	35
Allon	38
B.	21.38
Black	20.37
Brown	2
Brydon	36
Butchard	8
C.	38
Carnegy	19
Cato	40
Chambers	17
Clerk	6
Craik	25
Cromar	10
Cuthbert	3.8
D.	14.18.32
Dalgity	12.Notes
Davidson	16.21
Dawson	7
Deuchars	41
Doig	17. Notes
Duff	17
Duncan	21
Ese	34
Fadie	18
Fairweather	6
Ferrier	39
Fithie	18
Fod(e)	18
Ford	24
Fraser	29
Gall	26
Gibson	23

32 O A T H L A W

H.	38
Hendry	9
Hillocks	1-2
Hird	26
Hood	4.Notes
Hutchan	12
I.	32
Ireland	13
Jack	37.Notes
Keay	31
Keir	22
Kid, Kydd	15.17.28
Langlands	29
Lawrance	25
Lindsey	24
Low	27.36
M.	21
McDonald	28
McKey	38
Marno	14
Millar	30.32-3
Milne	15-6
Moor	34
Morris	20.22.25
N.	14
Nish	23
Phil(l)ip	10
Prophet,Profit	11
Raiker	11
Ritchie	10.30.31
Scott	10.22.37
Smith	7.27
Stewart	19.24
Stuart	35
Sutar	4
Tailor	17
Volum	40
Wallace	13
Watson	23
Waterston	33
Webster	1.7
Yeaman	22

33a R E S C O B I E

The present parish church was built in 1820 on a knoll near the loch on the ancient site of the church dedicated to St Triduana the Virgin. It is well kept. Interments now take place in the new cemetery a few yards away.

National Grid reference: NO 509 521

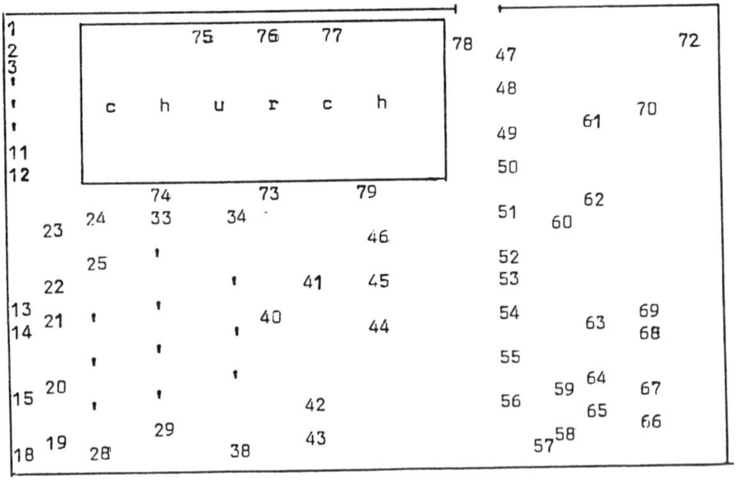

33a R E S C O B I E

Nos. 1-12 are a row of stones stacked upright against the west dyke:

1 by Wm Smith tent Finastown, w Jannet White; Alex Smith tent Finestown 6.12.1772 67, w Jean Dalgety 20.12.1772 75; "He studied the poor for to relieve..." (poem quoted by Jervise, "Epitaphs" i 159)

2 heir lyis a faithfvll brother Iames Pyot who depairtit in Turing 15.1. 1643 72, w Ianot Fitchit bvir to him thirteen bairns, Alex, Jas, John, Patk, Wm, Jaine Pyots - - - - (Daigite); shield with anvil, tongs & hammer (see Davidson "Inventory" p 82 & Jervise "Epitaphs" i 158)

3 FS heir lyes Alex Simpson 3.5.1616 (36 or 58)y - - - w Agnes Rynd (see Jervise "Epitaphs" i 157 for notes on the Rhynds of Carse & Clocksbriggs)

4 1755. by Alex Drimmie sometime tent Westertoun of Balgavies, w Eliz Smith 22.8.1754 63

5 A S, E M; I S, I S, - S; shield with 4 & scales for merchant, & share & coulter for farmer; 17--

6 cherub; I S ♡ M D; 1725; Io S, A S, Io S, Io S, D S, R S, M S, W S; emblems; (other side) Jas Sutar, w Marjory Dalgaty sometime in Kirktoun of Rescobie - - - - - da Margret Soutar 21.3.1724 2y

6a FS Heir lyis a faithfull sister Ianet Dal spous to David Dog of Resvale, vho lived with hir h 15y & d 8.4.1658 36 (Jervise "Epitaphs" i 158 notes Doigs owned Reswallie for a considerable period. It was nought in 1816 by Wm Powrie a Dundee mert...)

7 E F ; 1764

8 FS Jas Buack in Turin d 24.6.1--- 80, w Agnes Robert; emblems; I B, A R; I B, I B

9 cherub; by Thos Wallace in Rescobie Mill, w Margt Stroak 30.5.1759 51; Alex Wallace 12.9.1760 16; Thos Wallace 1.4.1761 23, chn Jas & Isobel d 12 & 19.7.1761; Thos Wallace 19.7.1762 55; acrostic poem (quoted by Jervise "Epitaphs" i 159)

10 1859. by Jas Robb fr Springfield Arbroath, mo Marjory Kerr 1813 47, fa David Robb sometime tent Hillside of Fenhaven 1849 84 both int here

11 1758. cherubs; A N, M S; T N, I W; shield with A N, H W, share & coulter; I, I, Al, An, J Nicols; A N, M N, I N, G N, M N, I N; H N, A N, I N, D N, T N; (other side) 1758. Alex Nicoll sometime tent Balmoshaner 15.2.1751 78, w Hellen Williamson 1.11.1750 66, by ss Alex & Thos

12 - - - - -

13 David Law quarrier Turin 23.9.1839 61

14 cherub; - - - - - Gro- - - 6.1706 of age (5)6, w Margret (Craike) 26. 12.1722 61; emblems

15 (on top) 17 A P, M S (31); - - - Isbil Webster w of Iams Peter sometime mil(ler) Miwrton Mill; Walter Donet miller in Burnsyd, w - - - Piter, chn John, Jean, Isbil Donet

16 1811. by Ann Smith, h Francies Anderson sometime tent Broadfold 13.(12). 1802 65, s Wm 9.1773 9d, da Ann 3.1787 21, Francis junior (da Ann 14.12. 1806 14), surviving chn And^n, Kathrine, Francis, Peter & Jannet; poem (quoted by Jervise, "Epitaphs" i 158)

17 1825. by Francis Anderson & Jannet Fawns in the Ground of Balgavies, chn Ann 14.12.1806 14, Walter 11.10.1823 27, John 3.12.1823 14

18 by Jas Martin 14.5.1902 89, w Jane Anderson 20.6.1887 73, chn Ann 14.1.1870 33, Chas Robt 28.12.1878 22, Robt, David & Jane d inf, s Jas 26.2.1921 80, da Helen 21.1.1938 84

19 17 I M, A S 63; loom & shuttle; I, D, A, I, W Malcom; (west side) Jas Malcom weaver Ground of Turrin 10.4.1764 8(5), w Agnes Smart 9.4.1762 73, chn David & Alex d nonage

20 1879. Jas Key late fr Rescobie 25.9.1840 60, w Ann Key 18.7.1862 73, chn And & Chas d inf, Jas 19.2.1868 40, Mary 23.12.1878 48

21 1848. by Jas Henderson mason Forfar, w Mary Milne 9.11.1847 45

22 1832. John Dewar wright Blackgate of Pitscandly one of the four elders in the parish who left the established church in 1843 d 8.10.1883 85, w Jannet Dewar 24.2.1831 38, da Agnes 16.4.1884 57

23 1839. by Chas Hill fr Burnside, w Kathrine Morison 26.6.1839 61; Chas Hill 3.4.1855 85

24 1834. by Thos Watson fr Clochtow & w Helen Renton, s Alex 4.7.1833 24

25 Geo Thom tent Auchteforfar 18.10.1857 90, w Jane Doig 1.11.1837 74

26 Wm Douglas fr Finneston 25.6.1857 72, w Isabella McLaren 12.6.1859 64, s Archd 24.10.1850 15, da Charlotte 11.6.1893 52

27 John Carr fr Hagmuir 22.6.1868 82, w Jean Ross 27.1.1871 68, da Annie 1842 11, s Jas 1851 10

28 Alex Christie quarrymaster Lunanhead 7.9.1877 66, "he was a good husband & a kind father", da Agnes 7.2.1848 3y9m, by family

29 1813. And Henderson tent Nethermuir of Turin 1.10.1838 83, w Jane Skair 26.1.1847 87, s Jas 14.2.1812 27, s Thos 2.6.1819 28, da Ann 2.5.1820 21, da Margt 4.8.1881

30 CT Wm Rogers min here 10.9.1842 59, w Agnes 30.7.1816 29 (fa rev Jas Lyon min Glammis) chn Wm, Jas & John all d, w Ann 19.6.1841 55 (fa John Oldham in Millthorpe); Margt Hannah Rogers d Edinburgh (16). 9.1843 22 (see no.74 infra, Glamis inscription 177, Fasti v 303 & 290)

31 And Osler fr Tulloes 17.1.1862 66, w Susan Couper 7.10.1859 47, chn And 29.9.1841 6m, da Agnes 8.1.1845 2, Helen 20.8.1848 3, Jannet 4.12.1851 10m, Isabella 7.9.1854 5; And Smith 31.3.1865 2; Margt Osler 30.12.1892 57; Susan C Osler 7.6.1895 48; David Osler 23.8.1887 56; Marjory Osler 21.2.1939 87

32 David Smith in West Mains Dunnichen 10.5.1882 61, w Jane Osler 8.7.1920 87

33 John Farquhar esq of Pitscandly 30.6.1808 67, w Susannah Floyd Lake 12.6.1857 89; Eliz Farquhar of Pitscandly 1764; Thos Farquhar of Pitscandly 15.3.1789; rev Wm Farquhar 4.3.1874, w Mary Ann Farquhar of Pitscandly 14.8.1825 1.12.1911; (east side) John Farquhar of Pitscandly, s John of Pitscandly 14.6.1844 49 (w Mary Ann Shillito 10.3.1855 63, da Emily Lake 21.1.1839 7, da Sarah Susannah of Pitscandly 1849 26), da Susannah Floyd 10.2.1822 23

34 David Grant fr Clochtow d Turin Home Farm 9.12.1894 89, w Isabella Rea d Turin Mains Forfar 6.9.1905 91, da Eliz 22.7.1854 12y7m, da Eliza 2.7.1859 2y1m, s Alex d Turin Home Farm 4.12.1899 45, da Mary Ann d Upper Tulloes 9.12.1924 72

35 John Taylor in North Mains of Turin in 1853 d Carsegounie 16.10.1905 89, w Ann Taylor 6.10.1853 43, s Colin 19.5.1872 10m, s John 21.6.1872 9, w Mary Mather 17.8.1895 63, da Joan 18.6.1909 48, gda Mary Ann Taylor 21.

2.1880 3y3½m; Peter Taylor d Carsegownie Muir 9.5.1926 68, w Isabella Spark 25.2.1931 70

36 rev Jas Esdaile DD Perth 8.1.1854 79, w Margt Blair d Manse of Rescobie on visit to her son 24.5.1843 67, eulogy; (west side) David Esdaile DD min here for 37y d Rothesay 10.6.1880 69, wid Mary Esdaile 6.9.1900 74, da Alice 29.12.1872 21, da Margt 26.8.1874 20, s Jas Blair d Seville Spain 19.11.1899 42, da Mary Mowbray 4.3.1925 75 (wid of rev Alex Walker min here) (see Fasti v 303 for rev David E founder with his bro Jas of the Ministers' daughters' college in Edinburgh, w Mary Chatterton da of John Lowson Arbroath)

37 1827. Jas Donald farmerly tent Craighall of Tannadyce 31.12.1845 63, w Jean Rattray 13.12.1826 49, s Jas mason Forfar repaired this stone in 1854 (s David 30.12.1844 14)

38 by David Mill in My- -e head imo wives & chn; D M, M M, I S, I M, A M; I M, W M, A M, I C, I M; I M 1704

39 ob David Dickson of Clocksbriggs officer of the order of the Legion of honor d Dunkirk France 11.1869 58, w Eliz Lindsay d Tours France 10.6.1855 40, 1da Marguerite Burness d Brussels 19.8.1897 (da Marguerite Isabella Gill 21.4.1926 50)

40 TS David Dickson of Clocksbriggs 12.9.1803 60, w Mary Cuthbert 8.7.1816 72, inf s David 1777 19w, s Jas officer on "The Generous Friebds" an East India ship lost in China Seas 1802 supposed d age 21y, da Isabella 11.4.1821 37, s maj David of Clocksbriggs 1778 1859 81, da Mary 1788 1866 76, s Alex sometime of Wemyss 1780 1864 84 (w Isabella Duffus Cargill 1786 1870 84) (see Jervise, "Epitaphs" i 157-8 for notes on the family)

41 TS broken. - - - - -(indwe)llar in Fannowha depairted in - - - - - - - ; A, W, A, M, D - - -; skull

42 FS Under this stone - - - - - of Cath Burns - - - - - hn Burns of Clocksbridges & w Margt Reind who departed this life 28.9.1718; shield; I B, M R, K B, 1717

43 by David Gray 10.9.1864 79, w Ann Gibson 6.12.1847 56, da Eliz 1.1.1850 18, Margt 15.7.1851 24

44 by Alex Mann master of quarries, w Jean Catanach 29.5.1839 51, s John 14.11.1821 5, da Helen 14.3.1837 14

45 by Jessie Jamieson 27.6.1891 81, mo Eliz Cruickshank 29.4.1858 84, bro Dond Hill 2.9.1849 42, h David Jamieson 30.1.1899 79

46 Dond Stewart fr West Mains in Turin 9.3.1880 80, w Jean Stewart 29.11.1840 37, s Alex d same day inf; Jas 25.3.1844 10; Wm 5.1.1848 10; Chas 10.2.1860 36

47 by - - - Elspeth spo- - - William A- - - skine som- - - in Turin; H T, E T, M T, I T; shield; I T, I T, I C; (west side) text; hourglass

48 hear lyes dust of a young man Thos Findly 9.10.1750 20, s of Thos Findly & Helan Millar sometime fr Mains of Carsbank; also by Alex, John, And, Patk & David Rochs; emblems; (west side) T F, I F; oxenyoke; 1750 share & coulter; T F ♡ H M; by Helen Millar, h Thos Findlay sometime fr Carsbank 16.10.1743 55, also by s Thos

49 1856. by John Whyte, w Margt Grant 30.7.1833 36, chn Alex 9.1833 5m, David 3.1838 10w, Wm 11.1859 31, gch David 7.1861 4

50 Jas Robb 12.2.1871 84, 2w Margt Nicol d Dykehead Burnside 8.4.1914 88, 1w Ann Millar at Boal this par, da Eliz 13.2.1837 10y6w (west side) s

Jas Nicol Robb d Dykehead 31.12.1(937) (s John Gordon d Dundee 10.10.1944 (w Margt Telfer) w Jessie Gordon 25.3.1956 90)

51 1843. John Gove 23.3.1853 55, w Agnes Oram 9.6.1858 58, s John 27.10.1841 10

52 by Margt Grant 13.8.1888 73, h Jas Wishart fr Haresburn 16.10.1882 72, da Ann Grant 19.11.1854 1y

53 by Wm Kinnear & Janet Stirling at West Mains of Turin, chn Elis 27.9.1807 1y9m, Jas 27.5.1815 5y9m, Janet 5.6.1815 4; 1816

54 1840. John Howe fr for 47y in Hearsburn d 10.1823 73, w Margt 10.1820 63, 1s John 4.1824 43, da Ann 15.2.1840 41 (h Jas Davidson)

55 1818. by John Howe & Margt Simpson in Haresburn, chn Elis 3.1.1783 1y9m, Wm 9.6.1792 6m, Alex 6.1.1817 23

56 1816. by Chas Pullar & Elis Kinnear in West Mains of Turin, chn Agnes 5.3.1794 2y8m, Mafgt 9.7.1815 12; Chas Pullar late tent West Mains of Turin erector of this stone d 6.8.1822 67, bro David there 5.8.1822 64 both int same grave; Jas Pullar late tent there 6.1.1838 49 (s of late Chas)

57 FS by Robt Hay, fa Alex & mo Eliz Nicol sometime at Milldens,his age 45y, her age 52y, also Margt Edison age 56y, his da Eliz age 17; A H, E N; R H, M E; I H, R H, M H, I H; A H, L H, E H; (marginal) - - - -- ed sumtyme in Mildens husband to Elis- - - - -

58 1797. by Wm Scott of Reswallie 19.4.1812 61, w Jean Sturrock 23.6.1813 62, chn Elis 24.9.1796 9m17d, Helen 17.12.1813 26, Wm 29.4.1814 26, Geo d Glasgow 21.1.1815 22 int Cathedral churchyard there; (west side) two sheaves of corn; W S, I S; Robt Scott d Seaforth near Arbroath 5.2.1822 36, w Ann Colvill d Knaphill near London 26.7.1873 83 int Kensal Green cem, da Ann 24.8.1814 9m11d (gch of Wm Scott & Jean Sturrock of Reswallie

59 Alex Craig late millwright at Kirkward of Ouchterlony 4.12.1855 63, w Ann Brown 29.11.1880 88, da Margt 13.10.1840 9y8m, da Isabella 4.11.1843 16y 8m, by surviving members of family

60 by David Robertson, fa Jas 22.8.1840 59, mo Betsy Tullo 22.10.1857 74, sis Barbara 1834 27, Margt Robertson 1837 8, chn Jas & Jean d inf

61 1841. David Millne 6.6.1840 75, w Eliz Weighton 5.5.1812 43, four chn David 2.8.1814 9, John 28.5.1818 27, Chas 11.11.1830 20, Jane 30.1.1838 43, Betsy 1.1.1873 69

62 1817. by Chas Brown & w Ann Adam, gch Betty Hood 29.3.1817 18; Chas Brown 12.1.1826 76

63 John Arthur schoolmaster here d Forfar 11.1859, w Betsy Gillespie d here 8.1841, chn Agnes 12.1874, Betsy 9.1845 (h Wm Proctor in Forfar), Helen 2.1844, Ann 4.1849, Margt 5.1889, Mary 10.1868 (h Jas Scott, Brechin), Isabella 6.1836, gda Helen Arthur Proctor d Forfar 6.1890

64 cherub; A P ♡ M S, 1735; share & coulter, pickaxe; E P, A P, I P, M P, M P, M P, I P, I P, W P; by Archd Peter in Milltoun of Rescobie imo chn viz. Archd, John, Margt,& Marie Petters; John Peter 2.6.1803 72, w Isobel Dickson 2.4.1801 66, revised by 5da Mary in Montrose; 1838; (west side) poem (quoted by Jervise, "Epitaphs" i 158)

65 by Jas Mathew, fa Wm sometime subtent Turrin 28.6.1755 63, mo Marget Gipson 21.12.1755 60; (west side) shield with W M, M G; I M, W M, A M, D M, I M, E M, A M; emblems

66 by John Macnab, fa Jas sometime in Ground of Carsbank 7.1.1728 77 (w Ja

et Samson 12.6.1727 73); (west side) I M, I S; I M, H M; Ketran, Margt, Euphan, Christian, Jean, Helan, Jas, John; emblems

67 by Jas Hutton 31.10.1883 77, w Eliz Roberts 3.1844, chn Wm 3y, David 8, John 10y, Eliz, Jeanie, And, Wm & Helen inf, also fa Wm & mo Isabella all int here

68 Alex Wood late smith Ward of Turin 9.7.1834 26, by w Isabel Robert

69 Alex Gibson 31.10.1853 27 of injuries received by an accident from the train of which he was the fireman; by enginemen & firemen Scottish Central Railway

70 urn. 1829. by John Annat 18.7.1892 86, fa Jas late wright at Hearsburn 19.4.1828 48, two siss Margt 29.4.1826 18 & Eliz 11.4.1827 15, w Betsy Salmond 24.9.1868 58, da Betsy 31.1.1878 44, sis Ann 1.3.1886 72, s Jas late joiner Ward of Turin 5.3.1912 66 (w Aimee Bennet d Forfar 8.7.1935 89)

71 (marginal) heir lyes Anges Dall spouse to F D d 12.1684 her age 58

72 I D 1758; by John Dalgity, fa David 6.1736 36, chn Isabell & Eliz; emblems; (west side) shield with trowel, hammer, saw, axe, dividers, pincers, square, share & coulter

73 mural. arms of Lindsay; H L, A S; M D L, M L; (in latin) mr Henry Lindsay late of Blairifeden 72y, w Alison Scrimseur 1651 (of family of Glaswal), by s mr David min here d 1677 72 (1w Marjory (da of Lindsay of Kinnettles), 2w Beatrix 1716 89 (da of Ogilvy of Carsbank) some chn - - - - - - - - - - - , by s rev David min Maryton); restored by KS here 1867 (see Jervise i 157 "restored in 1752"; Fasti v 302 & 406; Jervise,"Land of the Lindsays" 423)

74 mural. rev Wm Rogers min here 10.9.1842 59 in 34th y of ministry, 1w Agnes 30.7.1816 29 (1da of rev Jas Lyon min Glammis), 2w Ann 19.6.1841 55 (yt da of John Oldham in Millthorpe Notts) (see Fasti v 303 & 290;& also inscription no. 30 ante)

75 mu Chas Gray esq of Carse 28.4.1768 86, friend Jas Farquhar esq of Balmoor 31.12.1759 66, by w Eliz Farquhar to h & bro, & grandnephew & heir Walter Gray in 1769 (see Jervise "Epitaphs" i 156 notes this stone was removed from the old church and lay under the loft of the new church: Chas Gray was a Gray of Balbunno Perthshire, bought Carse ca 1741 & was succeeded by gnephew Walter Lowson (later Gray) s of a fr in Auchterhouse etc etc)

76 mural. Jas Gordon sometime teacher Rescobie par d in the pulpit of Forfar 15.6.1808 while delivering part of his probationary trials ... only s of Peter late teacher here, by widowed mo as expression of her irreparable loss

77 mural. John Farquhar esq of Pitscandly 30.6.1808 67, s Roby Jas 16.2.1819 21 (see inscription 33 ante; Jervise, "Epitaphs" i 155: col Farquhar of Mounie descended from Robt F of Mounie & Tonley once provost of Aberdeen, had three nieces as his co-heiresses; Eliz bought Pitscandly ca 1731 & md Jas 1s of Stormonth of Kinclune Angus who assumed the name of Farquhar, was out in the '45 & reprieved from execution)

78 FS tipped up & broken, in latin. (marginal) Thos Dall sometime in Balgaies 12.2.1675 63, w Agnes Bellie 2.3.1682 70, by s John in Milldens (& w Margt Finlo); (central) I D, M F

79 Thos Mills sometime - - - er in the (parochin) Rescobie 20.(10.1691) - -y; T M, I G; (other side) T M, skull, H S; angelic hands holding a curtain inscribed with text Eccles. 12 7

33a RESCOBIE

The following nos.80-82 were not seen in 1977 but are taken from Jervise,"Epitaphs" i 158:

80 John Coulie; 1731; poem (quoted)

81 John Walace in Finnestoun 5.1688 87, w Cath Piter 5.1687 60; text from Ovid,Metamorph. b.x.l.33-4

82 John Espline; 1717; poem (quoted)

Notes

F Davidson, "Inventory of 17th Century Tombstones in Angus" details inscriptions 2,3,6a,8,41 & 78 at pp 82-84

A Jervise, "Epitaphs & Inscriptions" i 155-61 & 384 has notes on inscriptions 1-3,6a,9,16,30,39-40,42,73-82

A Jervise, Society of Antiquaries, Scotland Library ms 350: 4.5.169-, Margt Rinde? - - Clocksbriggs; 27.3.1751, Alex Dicken, Clocksbriggs heir of Margt Rinde da of Thos Rinde of Clocksbriggs who was bro of the ggmo of said Alex Dicken lawful s of Alex D of West Dodd (1s of Alex D tent in Restennet afterwards of Dodd); David Dicken made settlement of Muirton Clocksbriggs & Rescobie on 27.9.1815

Testaments: the following were noticed in the Register of the Edinburgh Commissariot - Thos Broun in Carse, 1595
Marion Calbert spouse to And Whitburne in Pitscandlie, 1598
Alex Fairwedder in Mylnehill of Baldardy, & Bessie Symson,"
and the following is a random selection from the St Andrews Commissariot:
Isobel Barrie spouse to John Myle at Rescobie, 1686
Euphan Fairweather spouse to David Watterstone in Wodset of Lour, 1606
Patk Finlay in Hatton of Carse, 1761
Jas Lowson in Bagarton, 1744
Patk s of mr Patk Lyon of Carse, 1733
John Meek of Drimmie, 1741
Cath Peter spouse to John Wallace in Phinnestoun, 1687
John Wilson in Milldens, 1737

OPR with the Registrar General - 317 Rescobie Births 1688-1854
Marriages 1783-1854
Deaths 1784-91

Church Records in SRO: CH2/536 minutes & accounts 1677-1809
minutes 1809-1911
poors fund accounts 1809-61
accounts 1845-1917
HR 426 Rescobie minutes including statute road minutes 1828-1927 etc

Fasti v 302 ministers from 1567

Index

Adam	62	Bellie	78	C.	38.47
Anderson	16-8	Bennet	70	Calbert	Notes
Annat	70	Blair	36	Cargill	40
Arthur	63	Brown	59.62.Notes	Carr	27
		Buack	8	Catanach	44
B.	5	Burness	39	Christie	28
Barrie	Notes	Burns	42	Colvill	58

33a RESCOBIE

Coulie 80
Couper 31
Craig 59
Craike 14
Cruickshank 45

Dalgety 1-2.6.72
Dal(l) 6a.71.78
Davidson 54
Dewar 22
Dicken Notes
Dickson 39-40.64
Do(i)g 6a.25.
Donald 37
Donet 15
Douglas 26
Drimmie 4

E. 57
Edison 57
Esdaile 36
Espline 82

F. 7.78
Fairweather Notes
Farquhar 33.75.77
Fawns 17
Fin(d)lay/o 48.78.Notes
Fitchit 2

G. 79
Gibson 43.69
Gill 39
Gillespie 63
Gipson 65
Gordon 76
Gove 51
Grant 34.49.52
Gray 43.75

Hay 57
Henderson 21.29
Hill 23.45
Hood 62
Howe 54-5
Hutton 67

Jamieson 45

Kerr 10
Key 20
Kinnear 53.56

Lake 33
Law 13
Lindsay 39.73
Lowson 36.75.Notes
Lyon 30.74.Notes

M. 5.66
McLaren 26
Macnab 66

Malcom 19
Mann 44
Martin 18
Mather 35
Mathew 65
Meek Notes
Mill 38
Millar 48.50
Mills 79
Mil(l)ne 21.61
Morison 23
Myle Notes

Nicol(l) 11.50.57

Ogilvy 73
Oldham 30.74
Oram 51
Osler 31-2

Pet(t)er, Piter 15.64.81.Notes
Proctor 63
Pullar 56
Pyot 2

Rattray 37
Rea 34
Reind 42
Renton 24
Rhynd, Rinde 3.42.Notes
Robb 10.50
Robert 8.68
Roberts 67
Robertson 60
Roch 48
Rogers 30.74
Ross 27
Rynd, see Rhynd 3

S. 5.11.15.38.64.79
Salmond 70
Scott 58.63
Scrimseur 73
Semson 66
Shillito 33
Simpson, Symson 3.55.Notes
Skair 29
Smart 19
Smith 1.4.16.31.32
Soutar 6
Spark 35
Stewart 46
Stirling 53
Stormonth 77
Stroak 9
Sturrock 58
Sutar 6

T. 47
Taylor 35
Telfer 50

33a RESCOBIE

Thom	25	Watson	24	White	1
Tullo	60	Watterstone	Notes	Whyte	49
W.	11	Webster	15	Williamson	11
Walker	36	Weighton	61	Wilson	Notes
Wal(l)ace	9.81.Notes	Whitburn	Notes	Wishart	52
				Wood	68

33b BALMADIES

The Chapelyard is now cut off from public access being a locked walled ground in the middle of a field, neglected but the inscriptions are remarkably well preserved. All inscriptions are listed below.
National Grid refernce: NO 542 507

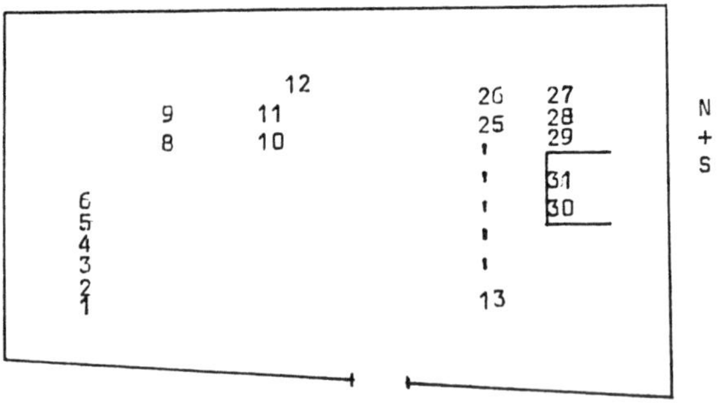

1 Geo Sharp mason Edinburgh d while superintending building of Balmadies mansion house 14.2.1821 42 much respected, by wid & family

2 1857. Robt Scott late tent Milldens of Auchterlony 14.10.1836 92, w Eliz Scott 14.11.1837 80, s Robt d Milldens 13.1.1875 82 (w Helen Elder d Forfar 29.9.1891 74)

3, 4 & 5 (touching) 1805. by Robt & Eliz Scott in East Milldens of Balmadies s David 13.5.1805 20, da Margt 1.8.1810 22, s Wm 11.8.1814 24

6 Wm Watson fr Mains of Ouchterlony 1.2.1879 75, w Margt Grant 24.11.1857 47

7 small. John Pierson Taylor

8 small. Jas Ogilvie; John Ogilvie (ed. early 18th century?)

9 small. Wm Grime

10 & 11 mr Archd Piersone of Westhal, w Eliz Gairden

12 sarcophagus. John Mudie of Pitmuies 26.5.1812 22.1.1876

13 1763. Jas Piersone of Balmadies, s mr John 16.2.1763 64 "a devout worshipper of his creator & sincere lover of all mankind"

14 mr Alex piersone of Balmadies, s John

15 mr Alex Piersone of Balmadies, s Archd

16 Susanna Smal

17 Alexander Piersone

18 William Piersone

19 the laird of Balmadies, s James Piersone d of smallpox 6.8.1714 about the 18 or 19 y of his age here int 9 ditto "a promising young gentleman"

20 cherub; 1746; (in latin) Jas Piersone of Balmadies 3.11.1666 30. 3.1745; eulogy (quoted by Jervise, "Epitaphs" i 160)

21 Margt d 11 or 12.5.1714 about 55y, here int 18.5.1714 (da to sir Alex Lindsay of Evlick) first md to the laird of Findoury, then to Jas Piersone of Balmadies to whom she bore seven sons "a virtuous & religious lady"

22 cherub; mrs Eliz Arbuthnot d of a deceiy about the 18 y of her age, here int some y before her mo's death, sister german to the present laird of Findourie "a beautiful virtuous & religious young lady" (see Jervise Epitaphs i 383 for funeral in 1704)

23 & 24. emblems; mr Alex Piersone of Balmadies 3.2.1626 13.3.1701 here int 26.3.1701, w dam Margt Murray 9.6.1625 12.9.1694 vas heir int 26.9.1694

25 Jas Piersone of Balmadies 7.12.1673

26 Jas Pierson, w Eliz Pierson 1669

27 cherub; Anne b 9.5.1723 old style d 9.7.1761 "greatly esteemed ..." (da of John Fraser of Kirkton) md mr Robt Pierson advocate in 10.1740, five chn Jas, John, Mary, Margt & David all alive in 1761

28 cherub; Robt Pierson of Balmadies advocate 4.4.1763 62y1m7d "an affectionate husband, a loving parent, an easy landlord, the poor man's friend, never intended to harm or injure any person..."

29 late Robt Pierson of Balmadies esq, yt da Margt 26.8.1746 10.11. 1771; tribute by her sister (see Jervise "Epitaphs"i 160: inscription composed by her betrothed the rev John Aitkin of St Vigeans, see Fasti v 450)

30 Jas Pierson & Margt Auchterlony, s Jas Alex 21st laird of The Guynd d at the Guynd 9.8.1873, succeeded his mo in 1849, by w w Eliz Townsend d at The Guynd 5.10.1887 (2da of Jas Murray Grant 12th laird of Glenmoriston)

31 John Ouchterlony esq of the Guynd, 2da Margt d at the Guynd 21.3. 1849 77 (wid of Jas Pierson esq); tribute

Notes

A Jervise, "Epitaphs & Inscriptions" i 159-61 & 383-5 notes most of the above inscriptions with notes on the Piersons, Arbuthnotts & Ochterlonies; see also "Land of the Lindsays" pp 335-7 for the Arbuthnotts of Findourie

dr John Pierson, "Familien Chronik der Pierson von Balmadies" (Berlin 1901) copy in Lord Lyon's library, Edinburgh

Rogers, "Monumental Inscriptions" has quoted nos. 29 & 31 in vol ii 267

33b BALMADIES

Testaments: the following was noted in the Edinburgh Commissariot Register -
Wm Daw in Balmady, 1581-2, relict Kath Symson last spouse to Geo Fischeild there, 1581-2
the following is a random selection from the Brechin Commissariot Register -
Alex Arbuthnot of Findowrie, 1745
Robt Arbuthnot of Findowrie, 1745
and the St Andrews Commissariot has -
Margt yt da of deceased mr Robt Pierson of Pitmuie advocate Forfar, 1772

Index

Aitkin	29	Gairden	11	Pierson(e)	10-1.13-5.17-21 23-31.Notes
Arbuthnot	21-2.Notes	Grant	6.30	Scott	2-5
Auchterlony see Ouchterlony		Grime	9	Sharp	1
Daw	Notes	Lindsay	21	Smal	16
Elder	2	Mudie	12	Symson	Notes
Fischeild	Notes	Murray	24	Townsend	30
Fraser	27	Ogilvie	3	Watson	6
		Ouchterlony	30-1		

34 RUTHVEN

The medieval parish church was dedicated to St Malnac. The present spired church on the same site was built in 1859. It is well kept.
National Grid reference:NO286 488

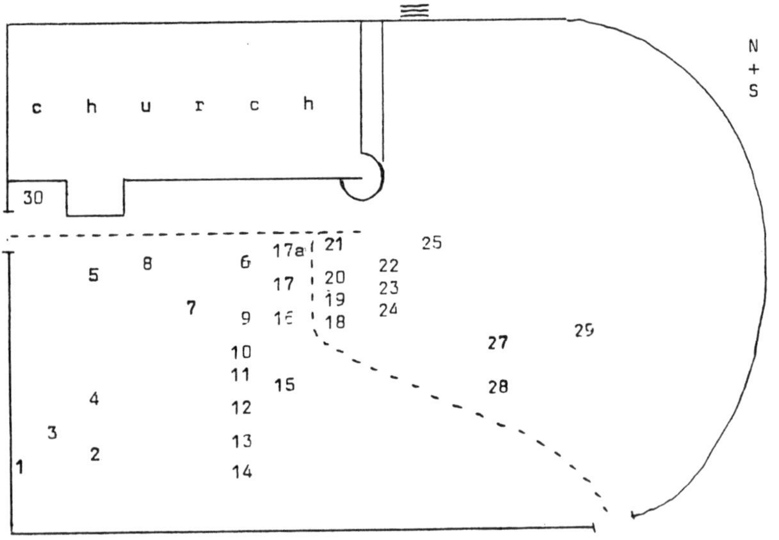

1 1808. by Wm Carr, fa David, mo Elis Robertson; David Carr shoemaker in the Bakie 17(9)8; Elus Robertson 1807 63

2 fallen - - - -

3 TS (marginal) by Geo Matheson tent Ballindoch, w Jean Mauer; (central) two cherubs; G M, I (M), I (M), M (M), E M, I M, R M; crown, cordiners' knife, ?stag's head, oxenyoke, share & coulter; (on east end) two angel trumpeters & rising skeleton; (on west end) latin text; poem

4 TS cherub; D B, M K; square & compasses, share & coulter; emblems; by David Brown in B(rid)gend of Ruthven imo parents, w & chn, Thos Brown 12.11. 1777 79, Helen Marshal 5.2.1777 78, Kathren Marshal 31.1.1773 42, Ann & Jane Brown d nonage

5 FS hear lys ane honest man Andr- - - - - - - Jhon - - - - - - - ckside - - - husband - - - zab- - the - - august 17(3 or 7)-; A W

6 FS raised oval containing H

7 1819. Gilbert Hay 13.7.1818 7y6m & Wm Salter 18.7.1818 9y5m, by fa Wm Salter & mo Kathrine Hutchison at Bellendoch

8 FS broken. David (Mustard or Satar) in Balbirnie 20.(3).1694 58, w Isobel Smith; ?miller's rhind; "My glas is run

9 FS (Jas or Thos) Mell- - - - - - to w Margrat - - -on. He lived in (Dri)loch & d 3.17(53) 42

10 by John Lesslie mason Balbirnie & w Jean Adam, da Margt 16.2.1823 1y3m, s Jas 30.3.1835 19; (west side) pillars, moon with face, sun with face; shield with square & compasses & three castles (for mason)

11 Peter Barty Lesslie fr Bridgend of Ruthven, w Jane Isobel Macdonald, s Peter Barty gunner 366 battery RGA 1914-19 d 22.11.1919 38

12 FS heir lys - - - - - - - - (ed. this could be as in Jervise, "Epitaphs" ii 186: heir lys ane honest man called David Bowacks & his lafvl spouse - - - Whyte)

13 gardener's tools; (west side) by B(e- - -) Farquhar gardener here, w Shuson Ratterey 25.11.1787 26

14 FS (marginal) Jas Wright sometime in Tillefargus, w Christian Irland d in the Maines of Ruthuens the last day of Agust 1695 77, bulded by her lauful son John Wright in the Mains of Ruthuens (ed. the preceding is exceedingly well executed); Heir lyes an honest man called Iohn Wright h to Janet Anderson, he lived in Brydiestone & d 18.12.171(4) -3y; Thos Wright, w (Janet or Anna) Gibb 4.1735 39; I W, C I; I W, J A

15 FS under turf (marginal) Thos Hunter; shuttle

16 FS (marginal) Jas Lounie 20.11.1679 7(7)y; I L, I H; shuttle

17 David Simson in Miltoun of Ruthven 7.1673 (3)5, w Margt Whitson - - - ; Thos Simson fewer in Derrie 15.3.1834 75, w Elis Mitchell 5.14.1844 86

17a - - - an honest man callit Jas Hay lived in Barbres Val(ls) d 7.17--, w (Margt Simpson)

18 FS to John Stewart residenter Dundee d in this par 7.9.18(3)4

19 FS broken. - - - - - - - - Breuer - - - /of Ruthven - - - /airted this 1(9). 5.(1692 or 1702) - - - -/her age was - -y - - -; - S ♡ I B; emblems

20 FS Eliz Rv- - - - - - d - - - 1691

21 FS Villam Fee d (8).1708 & w Margt Smith; W F ♡ M S; emblems

22 1856. by Geo Ballingall fr Cookston, w Jane Simpson 9.10.1855 28, s David S d Milnathort 20.11.1919 71

23 1874. David Simpson of Parkfield Scone 3.6.1870 74, w Helen Fell Simpson 14.9.1872 69, by gchn Geo, David & Peter Ballingall

24 1856. Thos Simpson late fr Milton of Ruthven 17.4.1833 64, w Janet Moncur 3.4.1829 61, chn John 17.12.1833 29, Agnes 1824 16, Jessie 1812 2½, by Alex & David Simpson frs Brigton & Keithock imo parents, bro & siss

25 Wm Kandow schoolmaster this par for 36y d 14.12.1798 73; the other half of this stone stands in the churchyard of Guthrie; his w Jean Brown 14.9.1801 70, by only surviving ch Jas schoolmaster Guthrie; 180- (see Guthrie inscription no. 54; Jervise, "Epitaphs" ii 186: Wm Kandow was s of a waulkmiller in Lintrathen - describes his school & teaching)

26 FS tipped up. hear lyes ane honest man called Thos Whyt he lived sumtym h to Isabel Coupar in the Bakside of Ruthven d 2.6.1731 78; T W, I C; emblems

27 1797. by John Reid, fa Jas fr Haughend 12.1.1797 57, sis Helen 10.1790 9, bro Wm - - - - 1790 11y; (east side) two cherubs; shield with share & coulter; emblems

28 1814. Bridgend of Ruthven; by Silvester Kermack, w Cathrine Douglas 4.11.1796 47, chn Isobel & John d inf; (west side) S K, C D

29 1842. by Peter & And Bruce, fa And late tent Hole of Ruthven 24.2.1842 77, mo Margt Roger 18.4.1853 75; And Bruce many y fr Hole of Ruthven d 25.4.1887 86; Margt Bruce 31.1.1889 84

30 rev mr Patk Crichtovn min here 36y & w Isobel Ratray ---- - - she d Oct (16-2) of aige 57; M P C & I R flanking hsield with arms (?of Crichton & Rattray?) (see Fasti v 274: he was s of Alex Crichton of Naughton, was still min here in 1644, da Margt md Alex Ramsay of Dalrulzian; see dr Campbell, "Balmerino & its Abbey")

31 The Wedderburn-Ogilvy enclosure at the east end of the church contains the remains of mrs Anna Wedderburn-Ogilvy 1853 75 last represntative of the Ogilvys in Coull, h Peter Wedderburn officer HEICS 1873 91 (yr s of Jas Wedderburn sometime physician in Jamaica & Margt Blackburn Colville heiress of Ochiltree & Crombie & gs of sir John Wedderburn of Blackness hanged at Kennington 28.11.1746)

N o t e s

A Jervise, "Epitaphs & Inscriptions" ii 183-7 notes inscriptions 3,8,12,14, 17,25,30

F Davidson, "Inventory of 17th Century Tombstones in Angus" details inscriptions 8,14,16-7,19 on pp 84-5

rev John G M'Pherson, "Summer Sundays in a Strathmore Parish" (Perth, 1885)

Wm Wilson,"Airlie, a Parish History" (1917) pp 180-9 has details of the Wedderburn-Ogilvy family

OPR with the Registrar General: 318 - Ruthven. Births 1744-81, 1788-1854
Marriages 1744-81, 1788-1854
Deaths 1744-98

Church Records in SRO : nil except HR 285 1726-

Fasti v 274 ministers from 1574

34 RUTHVEN

Index

Adam 10
Anderson 14

Ballingall 22-3
Bowacks 12
Breuer 19
Brown 4.25
Bruce 29

Carr 1
Colville 31
Coupar 26
Crichtoun 30

Douglas 28

Farquhar 13
Fee 21
Fell 23

Gibb 14

H. 6.16
Hay 17a
Hunter 15
Hutchison 7

Irland 14

Kandow 25
Kermack 28

Lesslie 10-1
Lounie 16

Macdonald 11
Marshal 4
Matheson 3
Mauer 3
Mell- 9
Mitchell 17
Moncur 24
Mustard 8

Ramsay 30
Ratray 30
Ratterey 13
Reid 27
Robertson 1
Roger 29
Ru- - - 20

S. 19
Satar 8
Salter 7
Sim(p)son 17.17a.22-4
Smith 8.21
Stewart 18

W. 5
Wedderburn 31
Wedderburn-Ogilvy 31
Whitson 17
Whyt(e) 5.12.26
Wright 14

35 STRACATHRO

The medieval parish church was dedicated to St Rule. The present plain building was erected in 1799 and is well kept in a trim burial ground. National Grid reference: NO 618 658

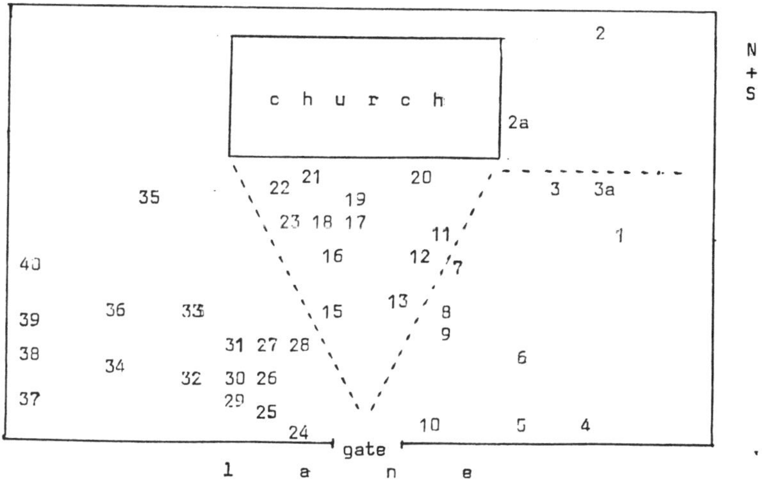

35 STRACATHRO

1 Wm Stiven d Damside of Dun 29.8.1867 72, da Mary Ann 14.10.1862 27, s Peter d Detroit Michigan US 1858 27, s Thos d Mhow East Indies 1861 28, mo in law mrs Scott d Hillside 1847 84, w Agnes Scott b 19.8.1799 d Drumforbes Lawrencekirk 31.7.1880 81

2 mural. John Hull Fell esq of Belmont near Uxbridge Middlesex d Cairnbank 31.1.1854 38, w Eliz 31.2.1854 41 (fa Thos Bowes esq of Darlington) only s Richd 25.1.1854 8, they leaving three das passed from life to death by the same disease (a malignant fever) taken one from the other after an illness of 3d each parent, the son d of same fever after illness of one day

2a 1856. by Geo Smith, sis Eliz 9.8.1854 53, his bro's chn Jas 2.2.1853 4m, & Isobell 19.9.1854 3m

3 1838. Jas Buchan in Inchbare 2.3.1843 68, w Ann Walker 6.1.1837 59

3a John Grant 26.6.1869 66, w Mary Young d Inchbare 15.5.1889 85, chn Alex d Asuncion Paraguay 5.9.1865 39, Annie 20.9.1872 36, Robt d Frankton NZ 23.12.1877 39, Nathan d Singapore 19.11.1878 38

4 Wm Lyon 5.6.1826 52, w Barbara Wattie 9.3.1844 81, chn Wm d inf, Cath 31.12.1819 22, Helen 18.12.1836 33, by chn David & Eliz; (west side) David d Varna Canada West 12.8.1876 75; Eliz Lyon d Dundee 22.10.1882 83; serjt Wm Lyon, Edzell, Crimean & Indian Mutiny veteran d Edzell 14.4.1899 68, w Jane Lowson b Barry 5.9.1836 d 28.2.1898 61

5 Adam Charters d at the Burn 22.4.1886 79, w Barbara Bowman 18.12.1885 88, ch Jas d by accident of a gun near Kintore 21.6.1844 9, Isobel Ann d 1886 (sic) inf; also of Agnes & Christian Bowman

6 John Hall sometime miller at Mill of Side 8.12.1743 45, w Jean Allan & three das Helen, Mary & Rachel; (west side) helmet, mantling, shield with square, axe, handplane & Miller's picks; I H, I A (illustrated A Reid, PSAS xliv 302 whose photograph shows a headstone, to north, with angel trumpeting over a skeleton, and to south, a headstone with M A C, plough, cherub)

7 Wm Buchan mert Inchbare 24.12.1827 51, w Jean Walker 20.10.1855 75, chn John 1815 3, Jas 2.7.1835 17, Robt 12.4.1855 32

8 1832. Patk Murray fr West Side of Edzell 25.12.1832 58, by w Ann Durrie 2.3.1862 76

9 1803. by David, Jas, Alex, John & Thos imo fa David Durie tent Newton 5.12.1789 69 (four das Kath, Ann, Jean, Margt 14.4.1800 21); Thos 22.3.1804 23; Jean 3.12.1804 37; John 25.2.1807 34; Alex 20.12.1811 48

10 by Alex Black capt 14th light dragoons, fa David 20.8.1806 55, mo Janet White 26.12.1825 74 (chn Eliz 28.11.1791 2, John 29.2.1796 15, Geo 11.12.1805 30)

11 TS next 12. sir Geo Mulgrave Ogilvy bart of Barras d Newtonmill 9.3.1837 57 (see Jervise, "Epitaphs" ii 240: he was nephew of dr Ogilvy of Newtonmill & last baronet of Barras etc)

12 TS next 11. Wm Ogilvy of Newtonmill 20.3.1817 71 (s of sir Wm bart & Ann (da of Isaac Foulerton esq of Charlton)), sis Isabella, sis Eliz; Cath 25.12.1812 28 (yt da of late sir David Ogilvy of Barras) (see Jervise, "Epitaphs" ii 240: Ogilvys of Barras were a branch of the Ogilvys of Inverquharity & the baronetcy was conferred in recognition of the share the laird of Barras & his lady had in hiding the Scottish Regalia in 1652)

13 broken & rivetted. helmet, shield with waulking shears; potted plants; Margt Will(sometime spouse to P(eter) S(ymmer) in Wakmill of Newtoun) who d 16.10.173(0) 59, chn Margt 1727 30 (spouse to And W(ylie), Ann Sym - - -; P S, M W, M S; (west side)"Adam & Eve, by eating the forbidden tree, Brought all mankind to sin & misery. The marriage of the soul & Christ/ No death disoliue it can,/But carnall marriages it maye /Of wife & of the man." Here lyes Mary Symmer 7.4.1782 30, h Jas Tindal mason Newton

14 FS rev Alex Guthrie min here d Stracathro 1661, he was s of laird of Pitforthie & bro of rev Wm of Fenwick, cousin of Jas Guthrie the martyr; by Jas Guthrie of Pitforthie in 1915 (see Fasti v 48 & iii 93; Brechin Testaments, mr Alex Guthrie min Stracathro & w Magdalen Carnegy, 1663)

15 FS rev Patk Turnbull ordained 15.7.1747 d 1.4.1782, w Margt Fergusson d Brechin 14.3.1818 97 (see Fasti v 418

16 1835. Geo Bruce late fr Side 30.11.1832 32, w Mary Paterson 20.1.1878 73, chn Alex & Geo d inf

17 TS Alex Don on Ballownie 1.8.1808 62, mo Janet Prophet 2.1799 81, w Jean Hood 6.2.1837 81, chn Jas 1796 inf, Hannah 9.7.1800 7, Janet 4.12.1804 26, John 24.2.1808 27, Thos 1.3.1822 52, Wm d Montreal 1.1850 58, Alex d Ballownie 11.1850 68 (s Robt 17.3.1838 7, w Jean Fullerton d Fettercairn 19.2.1871 78, s Alex in Fettercairn 13.5.1907 90 (w (Anne Don) d 15.2.1912 70), s Robt d Brechin 4.1853 65, Mary d Brechin 6.10.1861 7(3 or 5); Henry Don d Colombo Ceylon 18.-.18--; Anne Don 19.12.1889 wid of - - - - (see Jervise "Epitaphs" ii 243: Alex Don & Jean Hood also had s Jas surgeon general Bengal army who d Bearehill Brechin in 1864 leaving £1,800 to establish an infirmary there; also Alex Don, 1w Margt (fa David Skair of Balconnell & Burnside), 2w Janet (fa And Leighton fr Burnside), 3w Janet Prophet, s Alex d 1.8.1808)

18 This stone commemmorates the three generations of Don who farmed Ballownie for 109y

19 cross. Jeanie, John, Christian, Alice; Fettercairn; 1886

20 Dond Cruikshank of Gorton & w Cath Grant both int Strathspey (see Speyside Inscriptions, Inverallan no.80 & Cromdale 90), 1s Jas of Langley Park 1748 1830 (w Margt Helen Gerard 1770 1823), 2s Patk of Stracathro 1749 1797 (wives Eliz Davidson, Jane Lewis, Marjory Gerard). gs Jas of Langley Park 1798 1842, all int here, by ggs Augustus Walter Cruikshank of Langley Park in 1913(see Jervise "Epitaphs"ii)

21 rev Wm Gerard min here 23y b Old Aberdeen 9.1791 d manse here 7.1851, by Wm Gerard Don MD surgeon-major Army & of Bearehill Brechin in 1873 d 1920 84 deputy surgeon-general Army, ashes int in crypt of St Columba's church Pont Street London (see Fasti v 418: rev Wm d unm)

22 CT Colin Mackenzie esq of Strickathro 1.1767 (47) & bro dr John 12.1775 (see Jervise, "Epitaphs" ii 239: one was laird of Drumtochty; Colin "of Jamaica" bought Stracathro in 1764 from Peter Turnbull & after sold it to bro dr John, who sold to Patk Cruickshank who acquired a fortune in the West Indies & had five das md to Gordon of Cairnfield, two bros of sir Alex Ramsay of Balmain, maj Robertson of Kindace & to lieut col Mackay of Bigghouse etc etc)

23 Thos Fawns cattle dealer Ward of Keithock 23.4.1868 66, w Jean Graham d at Ward of Keithock 15.7.1843 32, two ss called George d inf, da Jean 27.8.1845 7, da Eliz 31.8.1845 15

24 by Ann imo fa John Hood 2.1800 77 & mo Mary William- - d 6.1782 49, also three of their chn David, Mary & one stillborn; (east side) Ann Hood 4.3.1821 62; Jean Hood 11.3.1827 57; crown & hammer

25 Wm Broun sometym in Mill of Siyd 1711, w Jean Esplean 1703; (west side) cherub; W B, I E, R B; I B, I C, E B (see Brechin Testaments: Wm Broun in the Mill of Syde, 29.8. & 2.5.1711)

26 John Towns sometime in Newtown 25.11.1758 76; K C; angel; potted plants; (west side) Kath Carnegie 6.1.1737 40 sometime w of John Towns tent Smiddhill; armorial plough, potted plants, angel & heart (see Alan Reid PSAS xlix 302 quotes poem, & has his death as 15.11.1738 in error)

27 rev Robt Hannah 7.4.1828 74 in 44th y of ministry (see Fasti v 418: Hanna (sic) d unm)

28 FS master John Glasfurd min Strickathroy, w Margt Ogilvy 11.6.1714 57, s John 20.5.1713 8; M I G, bible, M O (see Fasti v 418: their das Euphemia, Margt, Agnes; Brechin Testaments; Jervise ii 239)

29 FS Allex Mader in Boders, w Isobell Sime 17.12.169- (22); David Sime, w Elspet (Steuart) 9.12.99 60; A M ♡ I S; D S ♡ E S; broom & firetongs, two baker's peels; (see Brechin Testaments: Sara Peddie spouse to Arthour Mader yr in Bothers par Brechin, 1609; Margt Speid spouse to John Madder in Bothers, 1625; Christian Malder spouse to John Malder in Bothers, 1625; Jervise "Epitaphs" ii 241 says Mader is a form of Mathers & Boders or Bodwarts is now known as Cairnbank)

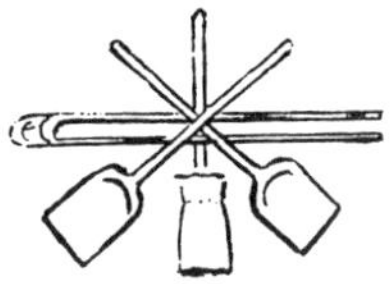

30 FS - - - - (divided down the centre vertically) - - - - -

31 TS (marginal) here lyes in the Lord master Alex Coutes min Strickathrow 14.4.1695 40, w Eliz - - - - - - - -; (central) M A C, E B; bible over two mullets (see Fasti v 418: Rev Alex Coutts b 1656, w Eliz Burnett, chn Alex & Ann; Brechin Testaments, mr Alex Coutts & spouse Eliz Burnet,1695 & 1696; Alan Reid, PSAS xlix; Jervise, "Epitaphs" ii 238 says he was the last episcopal clergyman of the parish)

32 Alex Duncan schoolmaster here 22.11.1763 63, w Ann Buchan 20.6.1777 63, by s Alex 4.4.1824 65 (ed;corrected to 75 by the mason) (w Mary Tindal 14.2.1815 67, da Ann 29.3.1819 41 (h Alex Bell, s Jas 15.1.1813 21m)) (see Jervise "Epitaphs" ii 242: a succeeding schoolmaster Alex Laing perished not far from his own house during a smowstorm 1.1854, cousin to Alex Laing the poet of Brechin also born in 1786)

33 FS Heir lyes Davi Burne sumtym at the Mill of Neuton & s David who succeeded to his fa as tent at the sed mill d 1681 6(3) (s Thos 1675); DB ◊ MS; D B,(K)D; poem (quoted by Jervise, "Epitaphs" ii 242); skull,crossbones, hourglass (see Alan Reid, PSAS xlix 302)

34 And Roberts wright d Trinity Muir 4.7.1861 59, w Jane Duncan d there 6.8.1863 61, s Alex d Cairnton 23.5.1841 14, s David d Cairnton 7.3.1842 14m; (west side) Jane Duncan, fa Chas Duncan 20.2.1853 81, mo Margt Stewart 13.11.1852 81

35 by Mary Grant, h Alex Brown d Newton 5.9.1803 48

36 by Alex Williamson, w Christian Grant 30.12.1793 27

37 1844. Geo Brown 6.2.1873 85, w Helen Mennie 9.9.1843 63,(sis Janet Mennie 18.3.1842 73)

35 S T R A C A T H R O

38 David Williamson, w Jessie Smith d Woodside Little Brechin 11.3.1928

39 next 38. Wm Smith 27.4.1863 80, w Anna Gordon 12.4.1839 60, s Wm 11.9.1841 17, da Margt 2.4.1851 30, s Jas 2.4.1903 84 (w Jane Duncan 9.8.1920 91) gch Jane Ann Findlay 4.1906 17

40 Jas Stewart d Backhill of Peat 22.4.1803 31, sis Elspet 2.7.1795 27, fa Chas 15.11.1796 54, sis Jean 5.4.1803 28, by w Margt Fraser

41 Archd Gibson of Auchinreoch 19.1.1858, sis Jane 18.2.1852, by bro Alex conservator of forests Western India d at Auchinreoch 18.1.1867 67 (see Jervise, "Epitaphs" ii 241 notes their fa was fr Morphie St. Cyrus, twice md with families by both wives: Alex at first in medical service India, Wm dr Montrose, Archd & Alex d unm & Auchinreoch left to Wm's gs (whose fa Patk was mert Peru))

The following nos. 42-5 were not seen in 1978 and are from Jervise, "Epitaphs" ii 238-45:

42 TS two shields charged with bearings of Fraser & Liddell; M P F, B L; 1609 (for rev Paul Fraser 22.8.1609, w Barbara Liddell, chn Isabel & da who both md - to Thos Erskine of Whitefield Dun & to Jas Schewan a relative (Barbara Liddell's 1h was David Schewan mert Brechin, s John burgess & baillie Dundee); see Brechin Testaments: rev Paul Fraser; Edinburgh Testaments: David Schewane citizen of Brechin,1573)

43 FS A T hammer; G T, K F, I T, G T

44 FS - - - - - -d 1667 & w Sibilia Hil d 1671 & Da- - - - - - year 1658, & David Wil his son d 1676 - - -

45 - - - - - & w - - - - - - - with Jas, And, Jean, Kath & Eliz Carnegys their chn who d in the yrs 1685 & 1686; A C, K D; I C, A C, I C, K C, E C

N o t e s

Priestoun at Dunlappie is reputed to be the site of an early Christian settlement and is the site of the medieval parish church on the west bank of the Westwater. The Edzell beaker in the Museum of Antiquities, Edinburgh was found here, and the site is fenced off by the Dept of the Environment. No ruins or inscriptions are visible. The parishes of Stracathro and Dunlappie were united in 1618. National Grid Reference: NO 592 679

Alan Reid,"Proceedings of Soc.Antiquaries, Scotland" xliv 302 also notes an old burying ground at Chapelton of Arnhall - no trace left except for stone inscribed"Anno 1668; eagle; ES + I S 1704",since about 1840 a lintel to a cottage door nearby. National Grid reference: NO 617 685

Jervise, "Epitaphs & Inscriptions" ii 236-45 notes stones nos. 2,11-4,17, 22-3,27-9,31-2, & 41-5

F Davidson, "Inventory of 17th Century Tombstones in Angus" details stones no. 29,31 & 33

F Cruickshank, "Historic Footmarks in Stracathro" (Brechin, 1891)

E G G Cruickshank & W Gordon, "Cruickshank Family in Strathspey & Stracathro" (Elgin, 1847)

Fasti v 417 - Stracathro & Dunlappie,ministers from 1581
v 419 - Dunlappie, ministers from 1574-1621

35 STRACATHRO

Episcopal Church, rev David Rose's register of baptisms from 7.1727 in Lochlee, Lebbnot, Navar, Edzell & Stracathro, ms copy in Brechin Diocesan Library deposited at Dundee University Library.

Testaments: The following was noticed among the St Andrews Commissariot Indices,
Thos Grymme in Wodsyd of Dunloppie, 1624
The following were noticed in the Register of the Edinburgh Commissariot,
Christian Davidson sometime spouse to David Proffeit in Eister-toun of Dunloppie, 1607
Marjorie Hill spouse to Chas Smyth in Easter Dunlappie, 1577 & his spouse Marionn Stratoun, 1577
Eufame Jameson relict of John Smyth in Eister-Dilloppie,
Isobel Whytelaw sometime spouse to Jas Murray fiar of Smiddiehill now in Westertoun of Dunlappie, 1606
Christian Stratoun spouse to Arthur Malder portioner of Ardo, 1609
The following is a small random seledtion from the Register of the Commissariot of Brechin:
Jean Arbuthnot spouse to Wm Burnett in Heuk of Pitrodie, 1610
Alex Bell in Adecat & spouse Isobel Peter, 1614
Alex Don in Ardo, spouse Euphemia Malder, 1630
And Drummond at Foord of Fochray & spouse Isobel Guthrie, 1670
Helen Fyfe relict of Hugh Petrie in Wester Keith, 1662
Violet Halkertoune spouse to Geo Barclay of Syde, 1581
Francis Low sometime tent Woodside of Dunlappie, wid Janet Fairweather, 1747
Jean Will spouse to John Dirow in Adocat, 1661

OPR with the Registrar General -	320 Stracathro		
	Births	1709-13, 1716-1854	
	Marriages	1709-15, 1764-1854	
	Deaths	nil	

Church Records in SRO:	CH2/339	minutes	1709-23, 1747-1936
		accounts	1808-1943
	HR 295	minutes	1842-1928

Index

Allan	6	D.	33.45
Arbuthnot	Notes	Davidson	20.Notes
		Dirow	Notes
Barclay	Notes	Don	17-8.21.Notes
Bell	32	Douglass	22
Black	10	Drummond	Notes
Bowes	2	Duncan	32.34.39
Bowman	5	Dur(r)ie	8-9
Brown	25.35.37		
Bruce	16	Esplean	25
Buchan	3.7.32	Erskine	42
Burne	33		
Burnett	31.Notes	F.	43
		Fairweather	Notes
C.	6.25	Fawns	23
Carnegie/y	14.26.45	Fell	2
Charters	5	Fergusson	15
Coutts	31	Findlay	39
Cruikshank	20.22.Notes	Foulerton see Fullerton	

35 S T R A C A T H R O

Fraser	40.42
Fullerton	12.17.
Fyfe	Notes
Gerard	20-1
Gibson	41
Glasfurd	28
Gordon	22.39
Graham	23
Grant	3a.20.35-6
Grymme	Notes
Guthrie	14.Notes
Halkertoune	Notes
Hall	6
Hanna(h)	27
Hil(l)	44.Notes
Hood	17.24
Jameson	Notes
Laing	32
Leighton	17
Lewis	20
Liddell	42
Low	Notes
Lowson	4
Lyon	4
Mackay	22
Mackenzie	22
Mader	29
Malder	29.Notes
Mathers	29
Mennie	37
Murray	8.Notes
Ogilvy	11-2.28
Paterson	16
Peddie	29
Petrie	Notes
Prophet,Proffeit	17.Notes
Ramsay	22
Roberts	34
Robertson	22
S.	33
Schewan	42
Scott	1
Sime	29
Skair	17
Smith	2a.38-9.Notes
Speid	29
Stewart	34.40
Stratoun	Notes
Stuart	29
Symmer	13
T.	43
Tindal	13.32
Towns	26
Turnbull	15.22
Walker	3.7
Wattie	4
White	10
Whytelaw	Notes
Wil(l)	13.44.Notes
William- -	24
Williamson	36.38
Wilson	13
Wylie	13
Young	3a

36 T A N N A D I C E

The pre-reformation church was dedicated to St Adamnan (St Ernan) in 1242. The present spacious building was erected in 1846 on the same site. The burial ground beside the river is well kept and the extension is still in use. National Grid reference: NO 475 580

1 on dyke. John Todd 1841, w Ann Archibald 5.4.1885 78, da Isabell 18.6.1888 48, s Jas 2.8.1889 49, da Mary 5.6.1907 70, da Margt 11.9.1922 81

2 John Cummin late in Tannadice d Forfar 29.12.1849 72; Alex Cummin 4.5. 1856 22; Eliz Stupart d Arbroath 5.9.1865 70, wid of John Cummin

3 CT (marginal) Robt Bruce in Meikle Coull 6.3.16(8)5 76, w Jean Eaton; (central) R B, R, I B, B, W B; (granite tablet attached) Geo Bruce, w Euphemia Bruce, ss David & Adam int here, da Mary 3.11.1832 40 (h Wm Robertson, Farnell), s Jas d Dundee, s Wm d West Hartlepool, gs John Robertson d Glasgow 1885; by gs Jas Robertson in 1896 (see par register: Robt Bruce in Ground of Murthill 1695/1707 had s Robt b 7.1700; Geo B int 12.1.1766 mortcloth fee £2.2/-)

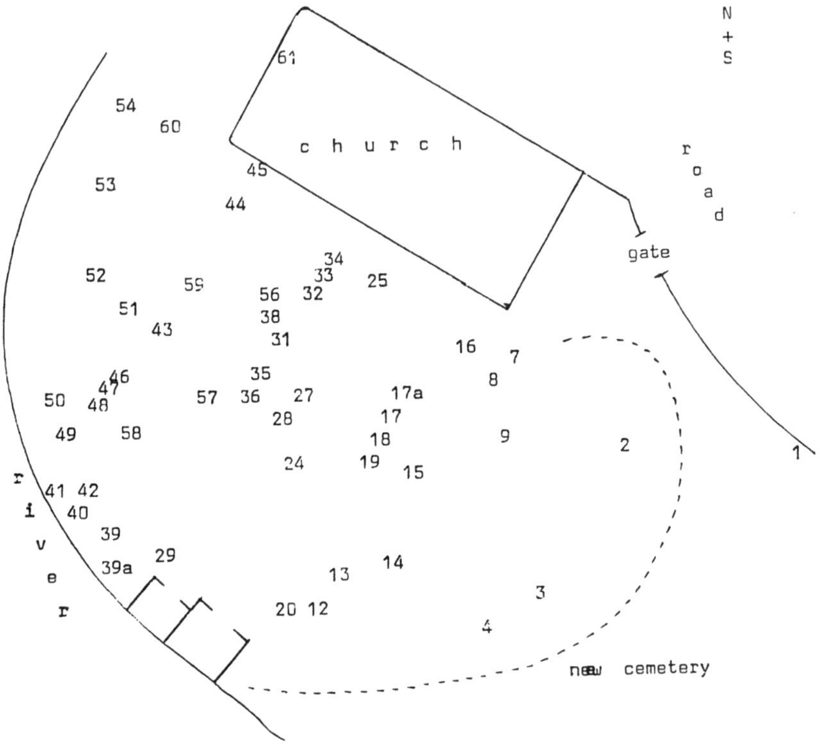

4 by Jas Tosh, w Isabella Simpson 12.12.1869 40 (sis Betsy Simpson 8.1.1847 16, fa Walter Simpson 11.6.1857 57, whose w Isabella Scrimger 8.5.1889 88); Mary Tosh Edwards 4.1.1956 89

5 by John Bain fr Newmill of Inshewan d Newmill Kinnordy 30.5.1892 64, fa Jas 9.11.1866 74, mo Jane McWilliam 5.12.1872 64 (ss Jas 29.12.1857 27 & Alex 3.6.1857 22) chn John 7y, Jane 5y & Mary 1y, w Ann Bearn 29.12.1913 87

6 by Alex McIntosh, w Margt Hendry 11.11.1872 59, da Betsy 11.1.1854 1y, s Chas 21.11.1870 15, da Jean 17.8.1871 26, gch Charlotte McIntosh Easton d inf; A McIntosh d Woodside farm Finavon 15.9.1896 85

7 Robt Watt sometime Drydrum of Barnyards 30.12.1745, yt s Lauchlan d non-age, by chn Jas, John, Robt, Wm, David, Alex & Isobel; (west side) 1761; R W, I I; I W, I W, R W, W W, D W, A W

8 1798. by Wm Allan smith Finhaven & w Jean Hood, fa David Allan sometim e weaver Braeheads Haugh of Finhaven 1768 55, mo Margt Low 1779 65, chn seven ss & two das, their forefathers above 200y int here; (west side) by Wm Allan late smith Finhaven now residenter Forfar, w Jean Hood 17.3.1816 65; crown, horseshoes, hand holding hammer

9 small. by Jas Watt

10 1861. Geo Miller lately fr Glen Ogle 30.6.1860 76, s John d inf, w Isobel

Guthrie 3.12.1867 78, da Margt Guthrie d Montrose 15.8.1897 80

11 1880. Jas Gray of Forfar d here 22.11.1847, w Margt Stevenson 28.9. 1879, s Alex 9.5.1912 69

12 Alex Whyte shoemaker Blackburn d Dundee 4.5.1881 87, w Ann Milne 15.1. 1859 71, fa 14.6.1832, mo 18.1.1843, bros Wm & John & siss Mary & Ann all int here, Jas 6.1.1872 71

13 1862. Jas Millar in Foreside of Cairn 21.2.1861 80, w Janet Lindsay 17.1.1837 50, da Jane 3.7.1893 76, s Robt 3.3.1806 79

14 1846. Jas Hendry late innkeeper Arbroath 20.12.1845 30, by w Jean Ferrier, "regretted as a father & a friend"

15 David Hebenton native of Tannadice d Forfar 2.5.1874 79, w Margt Edward d Forfar 4.3.1877 73, s And teacher General Assembly School Bishopmill Elgin d Bishopmill 10.2.1862 29; Thos d inf; Betsy 31.3.1878 39; Jas 22.5.1887 58; Edward 12.10.1887 45; David 11.3.1890 60

16 by Jas Gall sometime tent in Drumnecho 3.1755 70, chn Janet & Jas d 1736, Wm 1740, Robt 1741; (west side) I G ♡ K H; K G, I G, A G, - - - -; I G ♡ K B

17a Jas Guthrie fr Barnyards, w Eliz Webster 8.12.1910 78, chn Ann 3.8.1859 19m, Isabella 23.5.1864 4m, Jas 15.1.1868 7m, Jas 28.3.1869 10w, Margt 19.9.1870 8m, Janet 10.6.187(4) 6, Thos 10.7.1910 50

17 by Thos Guthrie fr East Mains of Finhaven, w Eliz Scrimger 5.4.1848 58

18 1786. by David Lighton fr Kairn & w Agnes San(g), s And 7.1776 nonage, da 12.1776 nonage, s Jas 7.1785 6

19 Thos Guthrie fr East Mains of Finhaven 13.2.1858 68, w Eliz Scrymgour 5.4.1848 58, da Isabella 6.3.1849 32 (h John Peter), s David Hillocks 21.1.1858 26; Ann 8.8.1862 44

20 by Alex Anderson smith Fearn, ch Margt 2.11.1825 3; (west side) Geo Anderson & Ann Duncan gfa & gmo of the erector of this stone who are int here

21 Andrew Hendry tailor here 16.11.1858 48, s David d here 27.7.1853 20, s Edward d here 18.7.1860 18, da Margt d Forfar 29.3.1874 37, s Jas d Brechin 5.12.1881 38, da Agnes Hendry or Bremner d London 16.12.1907 51 (da Edith Hendry Bremner d London 19.10.1950 58)

22 And Hendry, 2s John of Paris d London 8.5.1884 49, da Ann d London 8. 7.1917 89, w Agnes Gray d Brechin 1.2.1887 74

23 next 21 & 22. Wee Aggie 30.12.1887 7.8.1889

24 David Thomson in East Howmuir 8.2.1883 76, w Martha Sime 28.9.1897 90, da Hannah 22.1.1840 1y, s David d Gillingham Kent 25.9.1894 62, da Barbara d Auldbar 9.1.1808 68 (h Robt Lawson); Wm d Vancouver Island B C 12.8.1909 77

25 1678; I W, I W; Jas Wilson sometime in Baldoukie 25.4.1678 60, w Jean Wobster 27.3.1718 78, s Jas sometime in Baldoukie - - - - - - - his spouse Margt Wilson 16.12.1728 (18)y

26 1835. Jas Milne 13.12.1819 63, w Jennet Barclay 17.4.1822 61, chn Jane, Mary, Jas & Barbara, by ss John, David & Alex

27 by John Sime tent Burnside, w Jannet Cossens 27.11.1826 32, his fa David Sime 18.7.1815 59

28 David Sim 28.11.1848 64, w Mary Winter Sim 6.2.1864 61, s David 31.3. 1848 13, da Agnes 6.5.1848 16, da Mary Ann 23.10.1923 84

29 1838. John Grant 21.2.1836 88, w Sarah Robertson 13.2.1828 68, by ss John, Wm (three ss John 5.1824 4, David 5.1833 7w & Jas 4.1837 12) & Jas (da Sarah 3.1832 20m)

30 Robt Cooper fr Coul, w Jane McCowan 27.12.1836 52, da Christian Foote 30.3.1831 6, s Stewart 4.7.1833 14, da Jane Lindsay 2.3.1840 25

31 by Chas Sandeman blacksmith Boghaugh, fa Jas 20.5.1819 83, mo Eliz Kennedy 13.3.1821 71, bro Geo 11.1821 28; Chas Sandeman 1824; poems (quoted by Jervise, "Epitaphs" i 47)

32 by Wm Elmslie writer Edinburgh, mo Ann Wilkie 9.2.1821 47, fa Wm late schoolmaster Tannadyce 15.6.1821 61, bro Jas 13.12.1823 22

33 by David Dakers schoolmaster here, w Margret Binny 28.3.1728 68; penknives, inkstands, books; (east side) D D, M B; D D, E D; 1729 (see Jervise "Epitaphs" i 46: maternal ancestors of David Dakers Black esq of Kergord, author of the History of Brechin)

34 1787. by John Whammond fr Townhead of Tannadice & mo Jean Hunter, fa John Hunter 1.1786 47 (da Mary 12.1775 18m, s David 12.1775 3); imo John Wall & w Eliz Smith who had a laying stone here upon four pillars imo David Whamond in Townhead & w Agnes Wall & imo Jean Whamond 11.1781 2y8m & May 6.1786 10y11m (das of David Whamond in Oathlaw who was elder bro to John deceased)

35 David Cuthbert & Margt Mitchell, s Thos (w Ann Leuchars, s John 1837 (w Margt Adam 1869, s Thos 1881 (w Helen Bearn 1876, s John 1893), 1w Margt Smart 1848); John Cuthbert 13.11.1893 69, w Anne Perks 31.5.1881 46, chn Thos 6.11.1884 20, Walter Joseph 8.3.1885 20, Alice Maud 27.12.1887 18, Florence Annie 8.3.1888 28

36 next 35. by David Cuthbert tent Mains of Murthill, w Margt Mitchell 14.5.1767 68y6m, she bare him seven chn viz. Thos, David, Margt, Eliz, Helen, Jean & John, of whom Helen d 3y & John d 6w; (west side) cheese-press, plough; poem (quoted by Jervise, "Epitaphs" i 46)

37 by Wm Rue builder Montrose, w Ann Wilkie 12.12.1804 22 (ed. Montrose par marriage register spells his name as Rew)

38 1822. by Jas Williamson late tent East Baldardie, gfa Alex Williamson d there 1759 71, gmo Betty Hay 1774 77, bro Alex 14.5.1781 21, fa Alex d Baldardie 14.7.1800 74, mo Jean Arnot 4.2.1813 74

39a small. 1729

39 1852. by Thos Fenton engineer Glasgow, mo Mary Edward d the Whyteburn 3.9.1851 72, fa Jas d Whyteburn 30.12.1857 79, sis Betty 1803 10m, bro Joseph 1811 4, bro Chas 1820 inf

40 1880. by Wm Gordon shoemaker here, w Cath Fleming 4.5.1871 48 (sis Agnes Fleming 1.8.1860 26); Agnes, Wm, Chas & Wm d inf; Wm Gordon d Chicago USA 2.10.1896 82, s John F 17.7.1912 53 (s Wm d inf, w Helen Sturrock 1.1.1941 79)

41 Jas Knowles late innkeeper Brechin 24.11.1865 51, w Marjory Christie d Brechin 27.5.1887 73, s Geo 6.2.1871 32, da Marjory & s Jas d inf, da Margt 20.2.1874 25, yt s Chas D d Crown Hotel Brechin 13.11.1906 51, s Keith d there 21.3.1909 55

42 Joseph Hood 1857 49, w Janet Fyfe 1857 46, s Chas 1848 7m, da Isabella 1859 18, s John 1868 22

43 double headstone. John Hill in New Mill, son d 2.171(7) 10m; I H, E W, I H, - - - -. John Mitchell in Tannadice 6.1.1699, w Margt Guthrie in Tannadice; I M, M G, I M, - - - -

44 FS tipped up. D H ♡ E G; W H, R H, M H, K H; David, Eliz & Christian Hendry d 4.171(7) - - - - - (under turf) - - -

45 TS broken, tipped up. (marginal) John Wilkie som time in East Wood of Phinawin - - - - 60y; (central) John Wilkie here; Wm Wilkie in West Balgillo; Jas Wilkie in Craighall; Geo Wilkie in East Ogle; Walter Wilkie in West Hall; Elis Wilkie in Nether Balgillo & Duncan Wilkie here renewed this monument imo their - - - - - Wm Wilkie late tent (B)oghall who d July - - - yrs of his - - - - - Wilkie who - - - - aged 61y

46 1806. by David Fyffe tent Milltown of Murthle, w Agnes Mitchell 1778 33, chn David, Wm, Elis & Agnes; Wm d 5.1805 38 - - - - (under turf)

47 Wm Fyffe late tent New Mill of Craigessie 14.10.1836, chn Agnes, Wm & Eliz d young, da Isabella b Bombay 21.11.1873 (h John Stewart), w Mary Webster d Trusta Brechin 17.9.1894 86 (da of John Webster tent Dubton Brechin)

48 Robt Fyfe native Forfar late fr Nether Balgillo 12.12.1825 38, left a widow & two infant das

49 ob John Fyfe manuf Forfar 18.11.1845, w Eliz Mylne 2.6.1842, s Jas 7.5. 1810, s Robt 6.3.1812, das Eliz 9.3.1816, Mary 5.4.1818, s Jas 1.3. 1827; Chas Fyfe fr Nether Balgillo 25.12.1869; Isabella Barry Fyfe d Mylne Hall Forfar 18.3.1907; John Fyfe junior manuf Forfar 24.11. 1846, only s David Whyte in Mylne Hall Forfar 28.12.1911; Geo Fyfe d Forfar 28.8.1878, da Marianne d Hownam Manse Kelso 28.4.1906 (h rev W D Morris BD (but see Fasti ii 124 has her death 26.4.1904)); Janet 24.2.1857

50 upper part missing. - - - - -Andrew Copland late taxman Myer Stone Quarries 18.8.1801 43 & his mo Elis Shepherd 9.1801 40, three siss Mary d nonage, Elis 9.1801 11, Mary 10.7.1818 19

51 David Cant sometime wright Bournhead Coul 3.5.1733 71, w Magdelon Lou 3.4.1711 37; D C 1747 H W; axe, setsquares, dividers, saw; (west side) angel; arms

52 TS, large, tipped up. David Greige at the - - - -, w Jean Young 27.12. 1686 19; (central) monogram; poem (quoted by Jervise, "Epitaphs" i 46); A Y, E T, I Y, D Y, I Y; I Y, G Y, I Y, I Y, A Y

53 1846. by Alex & Wm Smith, mo Jean Smith 5.2.1833 66, fa Alex Smith late blacksmith here 2.5.1840 82; crown, anvil, horseshoes

54 by Walter O Ross, mo Grace Hird 1869, bro & sis John & Annie 1847, bro Chas d New Zealand 1874, gfa John Ross 1856, fa John 1883

55 four tablets. rev John Buist d here 9.12.1845 91 in 50th y of ministry native of Abdie Fife, yt da Margt b here 12.6.1812 d Edinburgh 1.8. 1846, w Margt Jafferson d Hamilton 4.3.1866 85, 1s Geo LLD FRS d Calcutta 1.10.1860 55 editor Bombay Times (w Jessie Hadow Hunter d Bombay Presidency 5.5.1845 27), 2s Jas mert Dundee b here 10.7.1810 d Dundee 28.3.1844, 3s John d here 7.6.1824 8, 4s & yts Chas d Dundee 3.12.1836 14, 1da Jean b here 3.3.1803 d Netherlea Hamilton 20. 5.1874, 2da Isabella b here 4.8.1806 d Netherlea Hamilton 5.3.1895 (see DNB for dr Geo; Fasti v 305: other chn were Eliz b 1808 md rev Joseph Loudon min Dalziel, Alex Jafferson b 10.2.1818; see also Norrie's "Dundee Celebrities" 190; Warden's "Angus" v 181)

56 TS tipped up. (marginal) - - - - - - departed this life the - - - - - of age 3y - - - - - - - chn to Andrew (Li)ghtoun and - - - - - (central) - L, A -; G L, I L, A L, M L, - - - (under turf)

57 TS tipped up. W S, M D, 1729; M S, W S, I S, - - - - (under turf); Wm S(uttie) sometime in Akenbatt d 1728 50, by w Margt Deuchars

58 Alex Whamond shoemaker Tannadice 22.12.1809 23.11.1880, w Jean Brown 1.12.1801 20.10.1883, chn Wm 13.8.1842 9.7.1851, John 13.12.1838 10.10.1859, Eliz 21.1.1836 12.4.1913

59 T L, I L; I L, E S; 1739; T L, I D, I L, D L, I L, G L, A L

60 TS - - - - - - - - - - - - - - - - ; (C)-, (C)-, M -, (A)-, - -, (I)-, D -

61 mural inside church. very rev John Machar DD second principal Queen's University Kingston Ontario & for 36y min St Andrews Church Kingston b Tannadice 12.1786 d Kingston 7.2.1863

Notes

A Jervise, "Epitaphs & Inscriptions" i 45-8 notes inscriptions 2,25,31,33,36, 52 & 55, also notes about Wm Herald admitted schoolmaster in 1.1824 d 1863 58.

Downie Park private burial ground, National Grid reference NO 420 580, is a small walled enclosure in a field of Turfachie farm. All inscriptions had been removed by 1978, but Jervise "Epitaphs" i 48 describes a tablet to lieut col Wm Rattray of Downie Park, late HEIC Bengal Artillery 30.10.1752 20.12.1819 67 who md a da of mr Rankin of Dudhope & whose remains were removed to the Rankin burial place in the Howff Dundee.

Testaments: the following were noticed in the Index to the Register of the Commissariot of Edinburgh -
John Adam in Over-Balgillie, 1592
Isobel Balbirny spouse to Jas Lundy in Densyd, 1577
Alex Cheild in Inschewin, spouse Kath Ferrier, 1588
Wm Currour in Kinnatie, relict Jonet Kinnear, 1606
Walter Esse of Muretoun, 1591-2; Walter Essie of Muretoun, 1603
and the following is a random selection from the St Andrews Commissariot -
Helen Carnegie spouse to Dond M'Claren in Cottoun of Kincardin, 1617
Janet Laing spouse to Andrew Bellie in Meikle Coule, 1639
Margt Mitchell spouse to John Wyllie in Cottertown of Muirhillok, 1619
Janet Morie spouse to And Whyte in Howmoor of Mooryhillock, 1712
Alex Skair in Muirhillok, 1618; Patk Simpson in Auchnagray, 1621

OPR with the Registrar General: 321 Tannadice - Births 1694-1854
Marriages 1717-43, 1756-68
Deaths 1722-73

Church Records in the SRO: CH2/1019 seat-roll accounts 1721-41
minutes & accounts 1720-46, 1750-74
minutes 1786-1877
communion roll, 1864 (or earlier)
GD 16/46 & 47 (Airlie muniments)
church, manse & school 1783-1872

Fasti v 304 - ministers from 1567

Ewing ii - see Memus, ministers from 1844 for FC adherents from the parishes of Cortachy, Kirriemuir, Oathlaw, Tannadice & Fern

Index

Adam	35.Notes
Allan	8
Anderson	20
Archibald	1
Arnot	38
B.	16
Bain	5
Balbirny	Notes
Barclay	26
Barry	49
Bearn	5.35
Bellie	Notes
Binny	33
Black	33
Bremner	22
Brown	58
Bruce	3
Buist	55
Cant	51
Carnegie	Notes
Cheild	Notes
Christie	41
Cooper	30
Copland	50
Cossens	27
Cummin	2
Currour	Notes
Cuthbert	35-6
D.	59
Dakers	33
Deuchars	57
Duncan	20
Easton	6
Eaton	3
Edward	15.39
Edwards	4
Elmslie	32
Essie	Notes
Fenton	39
Ferrier	14.Notes
Fleming	40
Fyf(f)e	42.46-9
G.	44
Gall	16
Gordon	40
Grant	29
Grey	11.22
Greige	52
Guthrie	10.17a.17.19.43
H.	16
Hay	38
Hebenton	15
Herald	Notes
Hend- -	44
Hendry	6.14.21-3.44
Hill	43
Hollocks	19
Hird	54
Hood	8.42
Hunter	34.55
I.	7
Jafferson	55
Kennedy	31
Kinnear	Notes
Knowles	41
L.	59
Lawson	24
Laing	Notes
Leuchars	35
Lighton	18.56
Lindsay	13.30
Lou, Low	8.51
Lundy	Notes
M'Claren	Notes
McCowan	30
McIntosh	6
McLaren	see M'Claren
McWilliam	5
Machar	61
Millar	10.13
Milne, Mylne	12.26.49
Mitchell	35-6.43.46.Notes
Morie	Notes
Morris	49
Mylne	see Milne
Perks	35
Peter	19
Rankin	Notes
Rattray	Notes
Rew, Rue	37
Robertson	3.29
Ross	54
Rue, Rew	37
S.	59.60
Sandeman	31
Sang	18
Scrimger	4.17.19
Scrymgour	19
Shepherd	50
Sim	28
Sime	24.27
Simpson	4.Notes
Skair	Notes
Smart	35
Smith	34.53

Stevenson	11
Stewart	47
Stupart	2
Sturrock	40
Suttie	57
Thomson	24
Todd	1
Tosh	4
W.	43
Wall	34
Watt	7.9
Webster	17a.47.25
Wham(m)ond	34.58
Whyte	12.Notes
Wilkie	32.37.45
Williamson	38
Wilson	25
Winter	28
Wyllie	Notes
Wobster	25. see Webster
Young	52

Kirkton of Menmuir
tablet
about 1730

CUMULATIVE INDEX
of SURNAMES

Numbers denote the burial grounds as listed at beginning and end of book.

Abbot 14
Abercrombie 30
Aberdein 3b
Acton 3a
Adam 2.3ab.8.10ab.11a.13abc 14.15.16a.17a.18.19.22 23a.25.30.33a.34.36
Adams 18.32
Adamson 1a.3a.13ab.14.18.23ac
Addison 3a.11a.13b.20a.23a.25
Adeson 19
Adie 17a.see Eadie
Aikenhead 11a
Aikman 2.30
Ailsa 7
Air 8.16a
Aird 3b
Airth 17a
Aitchison 11a
Aitken 3a.7.13b.20a.23a.33b
Aldie 13b
Alexander 1a.3a.10a.11a.13a.14.15 16a.17a,18.20a.22.23ac 24.25.27b.29.31
Alison 31.see Allison
Allan 1a.2.3a.6a.7.8.9.10a. 11b.13ab.14.16a.17a.18 28.35.36.see Allon
Allardice 1a.3a.7.13b.14.27c
Allerdice 1a.13b
Allison 11a.see Alison
Allon 16a.32.see Allan
Ammer 17a
Anderson 1a.3ab.6a.7.8.9.10.11a 12.13abc.14.15.16ab.17a 18.19.20ab.21.22.23ac 27c.28.30.31.33a.34.36
Andrew 8.13b
Angus 18.31
Annan 22
Annand 25
Annandall 27c
Annat 33a
Annordaill 30
Anthony 1a
Arbuthnot(t) 3a.4.18.21.22.28.30 33b.35
Archer 2.10a
Archibald 3a.10a.12.24.28.36
Arnet 22
Arnot(t) 2.3a.7.13ab.21.28.31.36
Arsbald 24. see Archibald
Arthur 18.33a
Auchinleck 30
Auchterlony see Ochterlony
Auld 31
Austin 22
Aymer 23a
Ayre 2a

Baden 31
Badenach/och 9.11a.14
Baillie 3a.7.14.18.20a
Bain 1a.11a.13a.36
Baird 3a.28.31
Baisler 8
Balardie 18
Balbirnie/y 1a.14.36
Balfour 3a.8.10a.13c.16a.27c
Balfour-Ogilvy 13c.27c
Balharry 9
Ballantyne 15
Ballie 3a.17a
Ballingall 13a.34
Ballo 8
Balneaves 18
Barclay 3a.13a.21.23a.30.35.36
Barnet(t) 2.3a.9.15.27c
Barrie 1a.13abc.14.17a.18.19.22 23ac.30.33a
Barron 5.30
Barry 1a.13abc.14.30.36
Barty 23c
Batchelor 8.13b.17a
Baxter 2.3a.12.14.18.22.23ac.31
Baylie 3a. see Baillie
Beal(e) 3a.23b
Bean 3a.4.28
Beanie 13a
Bearn 23c.36
Beaton 1a.13a
Beattie 7.13b.23a
Beddy 12
Beg(g) 15.20a
Begbie 17a
Belford 3ab
Bell 1a.3a.8.12.13ab.14.16ab.18 20a.21.23a.27c.28.35
Bellie 1a.3a.9.10a.13a.17a.28.33a 36
Bennet 8.10a.14.17a.23a.33a
Benny 3a.13a
Benzie 30
Bertie/y 1a.7.10a.16a.22
Bethune 31
Binnie/y 3a.8.12.13abc.36
Birnie 27c.28
Birse 3a.26b
Bishop 10a.18

CUMULATIVE INDEX

Numbers denote the burial grounds as listed at beginning and end of the book.

Bisset(t) 3a.13b
Black 1a.3ab.4.7.8.10a.12.13ab 16ab.18.19.23a.24.28.30 31.32.35.36
Blackadder 3a.14
Blackie 14
Blacklaw 16a
Blackwell 19
Blackwood 13a
Blaer,Blair 3a.9.11ab.13abc.14.17a. 18.19.25.28.30.31.33a
Blear 14
Blewhoise,Blewass 7
Blues 3a
Blyth 20a
Boack 28 .see Bowack,Buack
Boath 8.13ab
Bonar 2
Booth 17a
Both 22
Bouden 20a
Boutchart 13a.21.see Butchart
Bo(w)ack 3a.8.20a.28.34
Bowan 27b
Bower 13a.14.17ab.19
Bowes 35
Bowes-Lyon 14
Bowie 3a.21
Bowman 3a.6a.8.13a.23ac.24.26b 35
Boyack see Bowack
Boyd 2
Boyle 8.13b.16a
Brake 10a
Brand 8.10a.13ab.23c
Brandon 13a
Brane 27c
Brechin 7.27c
BreMar 17a
Bremner 3a.11a.13b.36
Brewer 8.13a.34
Bridges 23c
Brodie 3a.14.15.16b
Bromley 27c
Brough 3a.15.18
Brouster 22.31.see Browster
Brown 1a.2.3a.5.6b.8.9.11a.13ab 14.16a.17a.18.19.20a.21.22 23ac.25.26a.30.32.33a.34 35.36
Brownhill 13d
Bruce 6a.8.10ab.11a.13a.14.16 17a.18.19.20a.22.25.27c 34.35.36
Brydon 3b.32
Buchan 4.13b.14.16a.23a.29.35
Buchanan 3a.20a.27c
Buack, Buick 8.33a see Bowack
Budworth 14
Bue 23a
Buist 36
Burgess 3b.7
Bumet 3a
Bunch 19
Burman 31
Burn(e) 3a.6a.7.10a.14.35
Burnes(s) 10a.11a.27c.33a
Burnet(t) 1a.2.3a.4.8.11a.13b. 26b.27c.35
Burns 1a.3a.8.13ac.15.18.23c 31.33a
Burslem 3a
Burt 13a
Burton 2.13a
Butchard 32
Butchart 9.13ab.17b.21.30.31
Butter 14.17a.23a
Butters 31
Byars, Byers 1a.3a.13ab
Cabel,Cable 1a.13ab.14
Cadenhead 27c
Caird 8.13b.16a.23c.27bc.see Keard
Cairncroft 19
Cairncross 3a.20a.25
Cairns 2.3a.13ab
Caithness 3a.10a.26b.27c
Calbert 33a. see Culbert
Calder 3a.13ab
Caldonhead 3a
Caldwell 3a
Callendar 3a
Cameron 3a.6b.13a.15.16a.22.23c
Campbell 4.10b.11a.13bd.14.15.18 20a.23c.26a.28
Candow see Kandow
Cant 8.13a.22.36
Capel 28
Car see Carr
Cardean 2.
Care 23a
Cargill 13ab.15.18.25.27c.33a
Carle 13a
Carnegie/y 3a.4.7.10ab.11ab.12.13ac 16a.21.24.27bc.28.32.35 36
Carnegy-Arbuthnot 28
Carr 3a.10a.11b.13b.17a.22 33a.34
Carrie 3a.22.23ac
Carruthers 22
Carter 27b
Catenoch 1a.3a.7.8.26a.33a
Cathro 12.13b.14.21

CUMULATIVE INDEX

Cato	32
Cattenach	8.see Catenoch
Caution	3a
Caw	10b
Cay	3a.14.see Kay,Keay
Chalmers	1ab.3a.14.23ac
Chambers	2.31.32
Channer	23d
Chapl(a)in	2.4.9.13b.25
Chapman	3a
Charles	15
Charters	35
Cheild	36
Chisholm	9.11a.14.26a
Christie	3ab.8.9.10a.11a.13ab 14.16a.18.27c.30.31 33a.36
Christison	3a.7.10a.24.26ab.28.29
Chrystal	14
Clark(e)	3ab.4.7.9.13b.14.15. 16a.18.20a.21.22.23ac 25.26b.27bc.30.31
Clayton	23a
Cleator	3a
Cleland	8
Clerk	32.see Clark
Cloudsley	7.27c
Clyne	28
Coathill	11a
Cobb	4.7.11b.13a.27b.28.29
Cobban	11a.20a
Cobbie	13a
Cobe	17a
Cochrane	18
Cock	13a.16a
Cockpen	27b
Col(l)ace	20a.18
Collie	3a
Collier	26b
Collins	3b
Colvill(e)	1a.7.11a.20a.22.23c. 33a.34
Colvin	3b
Conacher	18
Constable	2.8.17a.18
Cook	7.10a.13b.18
Cooper	1a.10a.16a.27b.30.36
Copland	13b.36
Cormack	7
Cossens	36
Coullie	7.11a.22.33a
Counsell	17a
Coupar	3a.8.9.13ab.14.17a.18 19.27c.33a.34
Cout(t)ie	3a.8.14.17a
Coutts	3ab.11a.13b.23ac.26ab 35
Cove	4.8
Coventry	2.14
Cowan	3a
Cowel	8
Cowie	1a.3ab.22.23a.27c
Cownie	13b.23c
Cowpar	see Coupar
Crab(b)	1a.3a.13ab.14.23ac.27c
Craig	3a.9.11a.12.13ab.14.17a 18.19.33a
Craigie	18
Craik	1a.3a.10a.13ab.25.32.33a
Cram(m)ond	1a.3a.13c
Crane	3b.18
Craw	1a.3a
Crawforn	23a
Cree	27c
Creech	25
Crichton	3a.5.9.11a.13b.15.18.20a 30.31.34
Crighton	3a.17a
Cristy	see Christie
Croall	11a.see Croll
Crockat/et(t)	3a.13b.27c.31
Crofts	3c
Croll	14.27b.see Croall
Cromar	7.32
Cromb	23a
Crooks	7
Crowe	12
Croydon	3a
Crui(c)kshank(s)	7.12.14.23ac.27c.33a.35
Culbert	19. see Calbert
Cummin	36
Cummings	14
Cunningham	3a.14
Currie	3a
Currier	14
Curro(u)r	9.36
Cuthbert	1a.13ab.14.16b.20a.23c.28 32.36 see Cudbert 23a
Cut(t)hill	1a.3a.13a.16a.30
Daa	14.see Daw
Daer	11a
Dais	11a.17b.see Deas
Dakers	3a.36.see Deuchars
Dalbreck	23c
Dalgairns	9
Dalgetie/y	1a.8.11a.12.13a.14.23a.32 33a
Dall	1a.8.13a.20a.22.33a
Dalrymple	31
Dand	13a.23c
Dargie	20a
Darling	16a.23a
Davidson	1a.3a.6b.8.9.10a.13ab.14. 17a.21.23c.24.25.27bc.28-9. /32.33a.35
Davie	2.14.25
Davi(e)s	11a.24.26b

Daw, Daa	14.20a.33b
Dawson	2.13b.17a.32
Dear	1a.3a.11ab.23c
Deas	3a.7.17b
Dempster	1a.7.8.10a.13d.14.17a.20b 28
Dens	25
Deuchar/s	2.3a.4.8.11a.12.13a.14.18 22.23c.25.27c.31.32.36
Dewar	33a
Dewars	13b
Dick	2.8.13ab.14.17a.18.19.21
Dicken	33a
Dickson	3a.10a.13abc.16a.23a.25.33a
Dieack	26a
Dingwall	17a
Dir(r)ow	3a.16a.35
Dixon	9.31
Doig, Dog	3a.8.9.11a.13ab.14.16a.21 23a.25.30.31.32.33a
Dollan	13b
Don	3a.10a.13a.23ac.27c.28.31 35
Donald	1a.6ab.10a.13ab.14.23c.26b 33a
Donaldson	3a.7.8.9.10a.14.16a.20ab. 23ac.17b.30.31
Donet	33a
Doors, Dores	7
Doroe	10a
Dorward/t	1a.3a.8.11ab.16a.20a.22.27c 29
D(o)ugal	23a.25
Dougatt	18.see Ducat,Dugat,Duguid
Douglas	1b.3a.8.13bc.21.23a.25.27c 31.33a.34.35
Dounie	15.see Downie
Dow	10b.12.13b
Dowie	13a
Dowker	3a.see Deuchar
Down, Doun	8
Downie	3a.13a.15.19.31
Drimmie	33a
Dron	17ab
Drummond	14.17a.35
Dryburns	14
Dryden	17a
Ducat	11a.see Dougatt,Dugat,Duguid
Ductor	18
Duchars	see Beuchars
Duff	14.17a.21.23c.25.26a.32
Duffus	13b
Dufs	26a
Ducat	30.see Dougatt, Dugat,Duguid
Duguid	14.see Ducat
Duke	3a.10a.12.13a.21.23ac.26b
Dumbraik	8
Dunbar	3a.13ab.14.23c.24.26a
Duncan	3ab.4.5.6ab.7.8.9.10ab 12,13ab,14,16a.17a.18 19.20a.22.23ac.24.25. 26b.27b.28.29.31.32. 35.36
Dundas	3a.10a.11a.20b.23a.31
Dunn	8.18.25
Duquhare	11a.see Deuchar,Dyker
Dures	27c
Durie	3ab.7.10ab.27c.35
Durward	27c.see Dorward
Dutch	31
Duthie	3ab.8.10b.13ab.22.23a 27c
Dyce	13b
Dyker	11a.see Deuchar
Dysert/art	13a.18
Eadie	1a.7.13b
Easson	9.13b.14.21.31
Easton	10a.13a.36.see Eston
Eaton	3a.7.36
Edgar	3a.12
Edison	7.33a
Edward/s	2.3ab.6ab.7.9.10a.13bc 14.15.19.20b.23c.25. 26ab.31.36
Ego	5
Eilon	8
Elder	13ab.14.17a.31.33b
Elliott	14.15
Ellis	13b
Ellson	14
Elmslie	36
Elphinston	1a
Enderdeal	24.see Inverdale
Enererity	11a.see Innerarity
Erskine	3ac.7.13b.28.35
Esdaile	33a
Ese,Essie	32.36
Eslo	20a
Esplin(e)	1a.4.5.8.13b.16ab.20a 25.33a.35
Eston	11a.13a.see Easton
Ewan	23c
Ewart	5
Fadie	32
Fairlie/y	3a.8
Fairweather	1a.2.3a.4.8.9.13ab.14 16a.17a.20ab.21.22.23c. 27bc.28.30.32.33a.35
Falconer	7.10a.14.20ab.25.26a. 27c
Fanes	3a
Fanum	1a
Farguson	19.see Ferguson,Farquhar-son
Farmer	13b

Farar 9
Farquhar 1a.3a.8.22.27c.28.33a.34
Farquharson 3a.8.9.14.15.18.19 23c.24.25.26a.30
Farries 24
Fauld 8
Fawns 33a.35
Fearn 27c
Fee 34
Fell 34.35
Fenton 2.3a.6a.9.12.13ab.14 15.16a.19.23ac.25.27c 36
Fergus(s)on 3ab.6b.8.11a.13ad.14 18.19.27c.31.35
Ferney 21
Ferrier 3ab.8.10a.11a.13ab. 20ab.22.32.36
Fethie 14
Fettes 3a.8.27c.28
Fiddes 3a
Fiddler 3a
Fife,Fyffe 3ac.4.7.8.11a.13ab.14 18.20ab.22.23a.25.27c 29.35.36
Findlater 2
Fin(d)lay 1a.3a.4.6ab.8.12.13ab 16a.19.21.22.23c.26b. 27bc.33a.35
Findlayson 4.9.12.28
Findlow 7.8.27c.see Findlay
Fischeild 33b
Fish 13b
Fisher 3a
Fitchett 1a.3a.10a.33a
Fithie 14.32
Fitzclarence 7
Fitzhard 13b
Flaxman 1a
Fleming 3a.6b.8.11a.14.15.17a 21.31.36
Fletcher 3a
Flowris 30
Fod(e),Food 13b.32
Foord 13a.21.see Ford,Furde
Foote 3a
Forbes 3a.7.8.9.11a.13ab.16a 18.20a.23c.27bc
Ford 1a.8.32.see Foord,Fod
Fordell 19
Ford(ou)n 12
Foreman 27c
Forrest 3a.21.23ac
Forrester 9.23a.30.see Froster
Forsyth 4.7.13ab
Fotheringham 1a.3a.23d
Foulerton see Fullerton
Foulis,Fowlis 8
Fowler,Fouller 11b.13b.21
Fraser 3ab.4.13ab.17a.20a.32. 33b.35
Frisley 13a
Froster 6a.see Forrester
Fullerton 3ab.7.9.10a.14.27bc.35
Furde 21.see Ford
Fyffe see Fife
Gairden 33b.see Gardyne
Gairdner 3a.see Gardner
Galdie 3a.27b
Gall 3a.6ab.8.9.12.13ab.26b 32.36
Galletlly 18.see Gellatley
Galloway 18.25
Gamley 13b
Garden 3a.8.23d.26a.see Gardyne
Gard(i)ner 3a.4.13b.18
Gardyne 3a.8.20a.22.23d.26a.27b 33b
Garland 8.21
Garvack 25
Garvie 3a.20b.27c
Gaul 3a.see Gall
Gavin 20a
Gearrie 7
Geddes 8.14
Geekie 3a.6b.18
Gelaty 11b.see Jelatie
Gellatley 14.25
Gemlo 16a
Gerard 35
George 27c
Gib(b) 1a.3a.9.10b.18.22.24.26a 34
Gibbon 2.25
Gibson 1a.6b.7.8.11a.13b.14.15 17a.21.23a.27c.28.31.32 33a.35
Giekie 18.see Geekie
Gilchrist 13b
Gill 31.33a
Gillam 3a
Gillespie 27c.33a
Gillie 27c
Gillies 3a.4.14.27b
Gilrey 18
Gipson 33a
Girvan 13b
Glasfurd 35
Glass 13a
Gleig,Gleag 7.10a.17a.27c
Glen 3a.6a.8.27c
Glend(a)y 2.14.23ac
Glendel 3a
Glenny 25
Gold 10ab.11a.29

Goodfellow 11b.29
Goodle 17a
Goodlet,Gudlet 18.23a.22
Goodwin 3a
Gordon 1a.2.3a.6ab.10a.11a.13ab 14.15.16a.18.20b.27c.29 33a.35.36
Gorme 27c
Gossens 6a
Gothill 20a
Goudie 7
Gourlay 6a.28
Gove 33a
Gow 9.18.31
Gowans 1a.3a.20a.23c
Gownie 8
Gowrie 13a.25
Grace 18
Gracie 14.23c
Graham 1b.2.3a.10a.16a½27bc.30.35
Grant 3a.6a.9.10a.11a.12.13ab.15 17a.23ac.24.25.26b.27b.28 33ab.35.36
Grave 2
Graw 16a
Gray,Grey 2.3a.7.8.9.10a.11a.13abc 14.18.19.20a.23c.26b.27c 30.31.33a.36
Great 2
Green 31
Greenhill 9.12.14
Gregory 13b.18.28
Greig 3a.13b.22.27bc.36
Grewar,Gruar 6a.15.23a.31
Grey see Gray
Grierson 13b
Grieve 2.3a.14.27c
Grig 13a.20a
Grim(e),Grymme 3a.33b.35
Grimmond 2
Gruar see Grewar
Grub(b) 3a.13a.20a.27b
Grymme see Grim
Gudlet see Goodlet
Guild 9.14.21.31
Gurley 1a
Guthrie 3ab.4.5.8.11a.13abc.14 16ab.21.23c.28.35.36

Haaket 18.see Halket
Hackney 17a.18.see Halkney
Hag(g)art 14.18.23c
Hain 16a
Hair 13a.31.see Air
Haldane 19.31
Haliburton 9.30.31.see Hallyburton
Halkerton 27c.35
Halket 9.14.see Haaket
Halkney 13b.17a.18.see Hackney
Hall 1a.11a.13b.14.18.20a.25.35
Hallyburton 7.18.30.see Haliburton
Hamilton 5.11b.13ad.14
Hammack 14
Hampton 3a
Hanna(h) 35
Hanton 6b
Hardy 3a.9
Hariel,Heriel 13a
Harris 6a.12.14.20a
Hart 26b
Harvey 3a.21
Hastings 3a.13ab
Hawkins 8.13d
Hawtyn 30
Hay 3a.8.9.10a.14.16a.17b 18.22.23c.25.33a.34. 36
Headrick 8.9
Heathcote 23b
Hebenton 3a.12.13b.16a.36
Heemin 17a
Heggie 23c
Henderson 1a.2.3ab.9.10a.13ab 14.15.17a.21.23c.31 33a
Hendry 2.3a.6ab.9.13ab.14. 16a.17a.31.32.36
Henry 3a.20a
Hepburn 19
Herald 13b.18.19.22.23c.36
Hereis 13a
Heriel,Hariel 13a
Heron 18.31
Herue 27c
Hewitt 4
Hick 23c
Hickson 2
High 10a.14.29
Hill 2.3a.7.9.13abc.14.17a 18.20ab.25.27c.18.30 31.33a.35.36
Hillocks 13ab.32.36
Hindmarsh 18
Hindy 23a
Hird 8.13a.32.36
Hitherwick 3a
Hobart 13b.see Holbert
Hobb 3a.13a
Hodge 3a.11a.22
Hodgson 2
Hodgston 27c
Hogg 3a.11a.14.24.27c
Hoggen 27c.see Huggans
Holbert 6b.see Hobart
Home 13ab
Honey/ie 1a.14
Hood 1a.2.3a.4.8.10a.11a. 12.14.18.19.20a.22. 23ac.25.27c.32.33a. 35.36

Horn 13b.14.21.31
Hosea 3b
Hostler see Osler
Houseby 4
How(e) 1a.5.6ab.12.13a.14.16a.23ac.31.33a
Howie 3a.31
Huggans 27c.see Hoggen
Hume 17a.23c
Hunter 1a.3a.6a.8.9.11a.12 13abcd.14.17a.18.25 28.31.34.36
Huntly 1a.18
Hurry 13ab
Husband 14
Hutche(o)n 1a.3a.13ab.14.20a.23a 24.32
Hutchison 8.9.14.30.31.34
Hutton 8.10a.13b.18.33a

Imlach 16a
Inchik 9
Inglis 16.10a.26b
Ingram 26b
Innerarity 1a.3a.11a.23b.see Enerarity
Innes 26a
Inverdale 13b.see Enderdeal
Inverwick 13b
Ireland 13b.14.16a.18.20a.31 32.34
Irnes 2
Irons 8.13a.14.23c
Irvin(e) 1a.2.3a.16a.28
Ivory 23c

Jack 3a.6a.7.9.11b.13b.15 18.19.30.32
Jackson 10a.16b.31
Jacob 23c
Jafferson 23a.36
Jaffray 1a.see Jeffrey
Jamie 3a.10ab.27c
Jam(i)eson 3a.9.11a.13b.20a.23c 26b.33a.35
Jamson 7
Jap(e),Japp 3a.7.8.13b.27bc
Jarron/en 1a.3a.8.13a.16a.17a
Jarvis 3a.7.see Jervis
Jeali 9
Jeffrey 14.31.see Jaffray
Jelatie 11b.see Gelaty
Jenkins 3a
Jervis 3a.7.see Jarvis
Jobson 18.31
Joe 3a
Johnson 28.31
Johnston 3a.9.11a.13ab.14.20a 21.23a.25.31
Joiner 21
Jollie/y 1a.3ab.10a.13b.17a.24.26a 27bc.28.29
Jones 23a.31
Joy 27b
Junor 3a

Kaithness 3a
Kandow,Kendow 6b.16a.25.34
Kanzow 15
Kar 11b.see Car,Carr
Kay,Kea(y),Key 8.9.13abc.17a.18.31.32.33a
Keard 16a.see Caird
Kebel 13a.see Cabel
Ked 17b
Keeler 3a
Keir,Keer 3a.17a.32
Keith 13ab.28
Kellie 16a
Kendow 6b.see Kandow
Kenear 13a.see Kinnear,Kenner
Kennedy 1a.5.6a.7.8.11a.12.13b.23c 25.31.36
Kennedy-Erskine 7
Kenner 17a.see Kinnear,Kenear
Kent 8
Kermack 23c.34
Kermath 14
Kerr 1a.3a.9.11a.13ab.14.16a 17ab.21.33a.see Care
Kerrie 22.see Carrie
Key 13a.33a.see Kay
Kid(d),Kyd 1a.3a.6a.9.13ab.14.17a.18 21.23c.30.32
Kiell 23a
Kilgour 14
King 1a
Kinloch 23ad
Kinmonth/d 14.31
Kinnaird 17a.31.see Kynnard
Kinnear 2.3ab.9.10a.12.13b.14.17a 21.25.26b.33a.36
Kinoch 2
Kirkland 3c.7.23c.27c
Knight 7.23c
Knowles 27c.36
Knox 3a.13a.22.28
Kyd see Kid
Kyninmonth see Kinmond
Kynnard 17a.see Kinnaird

La(c)kie 8.14.19.23c.27b
Laing 3ab.4.8.9.15.17a.20a.24 26b.27c.35.36
Laing-Meason 14
Laird 13ab.14.17a.21
Lake 33a
Lakie 14.see Lackie
Lamb 3ab.7.8.11a.15.16a.23a.27c

CUMULATIVE INDEX

Numbers denote the burial grounds as listed at beginning and end of the book.

Lam(m)ie 9.10a
L'Amy 9.10a.14
Lamond 2.15.23a.25
Landale 11a.13b
Landreth 27c
Landsay 27c.see Lindsay
Langlands 1a.8.13ab.14.16a.23c
Langson 7
Langwill 3a
Larons 13a.see Lawrence
Lauder,Lawdor 18.22
Law 3ac.7.10a.11a.13ab.24.33a
Lawie 10b
Lawson 3a.9.13ab.16a.21.23ac.25.36
Lawrence 3a.8.13a.16a.27c.32
Lawrie 3a.10a
Layell see Lyall,Lyell.11a
Layon 2
Leang 23a.see Laing
Learmonth 14
Leask,Leisk 13a.20b
Leckie 13b.16a
Lee 14.see Ley
Lees 23c.see Leys
Leighton see Lighton
Leishman 3a
Leith 11a
Leitch 16a.24
Lennox 3a
Les(s)lie/y 3a.8.11a.22.28.34
Leuchars 6a.36
Lewis 35
Ley 10a.27c.see Lee
Leys 13b.18.see Lees
Liddell 35
Lighton,Leighton 3ab.12.13b.24.25.28.29 35.36
Lindsay 3ab.4.5.6ab.7.8.9.10a.11a 12.13ab.14.17a.19.21.23ac. 24.25.27c.31.32.33ab.36
Linn 17a
Linton 3a
Littleboy 10b
Littlejohn 3a.13b
Liveston 13b.see Livingston
Livie 3a.13b
Livingston 13a.see Liveston
Lockhart 13b.30
Logan 22
London 25
Long 2
Longair 17a
Longland(s) 8.22
Lonmuir 3a
Lord 26b
Lorimer 19
Lothian 23c
Loudon 2.3a.9.13a.17a.23a
Louk see Luke
Lounie 31.34
Lourance see Lawrence, Larons
Low(e) 2.3ab.4.6ab.7.9.10ab 11a.13ab.14.17a.18.19 20a.23ac.24.25.26ab 27bc.28.30.32.35.36
Lowson 13b.17a.20a.22.23c.25 33a.35
L(o)unan 2.13c.21.27c
Lucas 5.6a
Luke 9.14.30
Lumgair 22
Lunan see Lounan
Lundie 13a.14.36
Lyall,Lyel(l) 3abc.4.6a.7.10a.11a 12.13b.16a.23abc.24. 27c
Lyon 1b.2.3a.9.12.13ab.14 15.20a.21.23ac.33a.35

McAdam 10a
McAllie 1a
McAndrew 2.15
McArthur 6b.18.26a
McBain 3a.23a
McBeth 8
M'Claren 36
McCowan 36
McCombie 11a.15
McCraw 2
McCulloch 3a
McDonald 3a.5.6a.10b.13b.14.15 18.23c.25.27c.32.34
McDonel 26a
McDougal(l) 13b.15.18.25
McDougan 1a
McEwan 3a
McFadyen 3a.10b
McFarlane 14.15.17a
McGill 3a
McGilvray 17a
McGonachie 4.27c
McGregor 1a.7.17a.25
McGrigor 23a
Machan 23c
Machar 3a.10a.36.see Machir
McHardie 23c.25
Machir 7.25.27c.see Machar
McInnes/is 15.25
McIlwraith 26b
McInroy 8.10b
McIntosh 3a.6a.12.13ab.14.15. 18.30.31.36
McIntyre 3a.14
McKay 3a.13b.14.20ab.21.22 23a.25.27c.30.32.35

CUMULATIVE INDEX

McKenzie 1a.3a.6b.7.13b.15.16 18.23c.27bc.35
McKey 32
McKiddie/y 14
McKillop 23a
Mackie 10a.12.13a.20a
McKinley 3a
McKinnon 13b
McKintosh 12.14.see McIntosh
McLachlan 18
McLagan 13b
McLaren 1a.2.6b.13b.17a.23c 31.33a.36
McLean 13bc.14
McLeish 4.13b.18
McLeod 3a.14
McNab 25.33a
McNeill 7
McNicol(l) 6b.7.15.19.23ac.25.21
McPherson 6b.14.23c.27b
McPherson-Grant 27b
McQuattie 17a.see McWattie
McQuiver 7
McReay 13a
McRitchie 13b
McWattie 8.see McQuattie
McWilliam 36
Maden,Maiden 7.23c
Mader 3a.7.35.see Mather
Maich 3a
Maiden see Maden
Main 3b
Mair 24.28
Maitland 11b
Malco(l)m 2.7.8.12.13abc.14.17a 19.22.26b.33a
Malder see Mather.35
Malloch 13b.23c
Mands 13a
Mann 1a.3a.11a.13ab.14.16a 20ab.22.23c.33a
Manuel 17a
Marechan 20a
Marishal 14.see Marshall
Marnie 12
Marno 32
Marnoch 11a
Marr 3a.13b
Marshall 2.6b.13b.14.17a.18 20a.34
Martin 3ab.13b.14.18.21.30 31.33a
Mason 13b.20b.31
Massie 31
Masson 8
Masterton 13a
Mather 12.13a.20b.33a.35
Mathers 3a.7.11a.13a.23c.28 35
Matheson 34
Mat(t)hew 1a.2.7.9.11a.16a.22.23c 31.33a
Mathie 3a.11ab.13a
Maule 3a.12
Mawer 30.34
Maxwell 3b.8.11a.17a.22.30
May 28
Meal 31
Mealmaker 6a
Mearns 28
Mechie 5.see Michie
Medden 7
Mee 9
Meek 14.27c.33a
Meffan 13b
Melba 17b
Meldrum 3b.13b.14
Mell 34
Melville 8.9
Melvin 21
Memes 3a
Menelaws 16a
Mennie 35
Menzies 1a
Metcalfe 8.13d
Methven 20a
Michie,Mechie 3a.5.9.10a
Middleton 3a.6b.10a.16a.22.26b.27c
Mill(s) 1a.3a.6a.7.8.9.11a.12. 13ab.16a.17a.18.19.20ab 21.22.23c.26a.27c.30.33a
Millam 31
Millar/er 1a.2.3a.7.8.9.11b.13ab 14.16a.17a.18.19.23ac.25 27c.30.31.32.33a.36
Milligan 22
Millikin 3a
Miln(e) 1a.2.3a.6ab.7.8.10a.11a 13ab.14.15.16a.17ab.19. 20a.21.22.23ac.24.25.26a 27b.28.32.33a.36
Mitchel(l) 1a.2.3ac.6a.7.8.9.10a. 11ab.12.13abc.14.15.17ab 19.22.23ac.24.25.26b.27c 28.30.31.34.36
Mitchelson 14.17ab
Mitcheton 23a
Moffat/et 8.13b
Moir 3a.7.22.23c.26a.28
Mole 31
Moleson 1a.28
Mol(l)ison 3a.12.13a.14.16b.20a.22 24.28.29
Molleson 10a.12
Moncrieff 23c
Moncur 2.13b.14.31.34
Monro(y) 3ab.31

CUMULATIVE INDEX

Numbers denote the burial grounds as listed at beginning and end of the book.

Montgomerie	17a
Mood	18
Moodie	14.see Mudie
Moon	31
Moonlight	12
Moor	32
Mordoch,Murdo	8
Mores	27c
Morgan	13ab.15.16a.22
Morie	36
Morley	23d
Morren	3a
Morris,Morrice	7.8.13ab.18.27c.30.32.36
Mor(r)ison	3a.6b.7.13ab.16a.17a.18. 23a.31.33a
Morton	1a.17a.21.22.30.31
Moug	3a.31
Mowatt	28
Mudie	3a.8.11a.13a.16ab.22.23a. 33b.see Moodie
Muir,Mure	14.23ac.31
Muirton	3a
Mundell	2
Mungo	17a
Munro	see Monro
Murdo(ch)	8
Murison	.12.13a.28
Murray	3a.4.7.13bc.14.15.16a.18 19.26a.27bc.30.33b.35
Mustard	2.3a.11a.18.23c.34
Myle(s)	2.17a.18.23ac.33a
Mylne	see Milne
Nairn	3a.16b
Napier	3ab.7
Nash	13c
Neave	13b.14.30
Nedry	10a.see Niddrie
Nail(l)	2.14.19
Neilson	27c
Neish, Nish	3a.13a.16a.17a.28.32
Nesbitt	18
Ness	13b
Nevay	13ab.14.17b.30
Newall	14
Newton	2.25
Nicol(l)	1a.2.3a.6a.7.8.9.10b.11a 13abc.14.16a.17a.18.19. 20ab.21.22.23ac.15.26a. 27bc.28.31.33a.see Nokel
Nicolson	11a
Niddrie	24.27b.see Nedry
Nisbet	14
Niven	23c.30
Noel	11b
Nokel	27c.see Nicol,Nuckle
Norie,Norrie	3a.7.8.17a.27b
Nucator	18
Nuckle	27b.see Nicol
Oakenhead	3a.11a
Oastler	see Osler
Och	18.see Ogg
O(u)chterlony	1a.3a.8.12.20a.33b
Ogg	10a.see Och
Ogilvie/y	1a.2.3a.5.6ab.8.11a.13abc 14.15.16ab.17a.18.19.20a. 23acd.25.27c.30.31.33ab.3
Oldham	33a
Oliphant	31
O'Neil	3a
Ortchartson	14
Orchar	13b
Ord	8
Ordie	28
Orem	14.17a.33a
Orkney	7
Ormand,Ormond	8.13a.21.22
Orrock	17a
Os(t)ler	9.14.23ac.33a
Oswald	3a
Otman	14
Ouchterlony	see Ochterlony
Palmer,Palmor	2.3a.22.23a
Panmure	3a
Pat(t)erson	1a.2.3ab.7.11a.13ab.14.1 20a.21.22.23c.24.27c.30. 35
Paton	15.16a.20a
Pat(t)ullo	2.8.13a.18.31
Peacock	13b
Pearson	28
Peddie	13a.35
Pedrane	18
Pellow	14
Pennycook	3a
Perks	36
Perron	3a
Pert	13b
Peter,Piter	1a.3a.4.8.11a.12.13ab.1 23c.25.33a.36
Peterkin	3a
Peters	13b.16a
Petr(i)e	1a.7.9.13ab.14.16ab.18. 22.27c.35
Phillip(s)	15.23c.32
Philp	1a.6ab.13a.14.18.22.23a
Pickard	14
Pickeman	7.12
Piddy	9
Pierson	33b
Pierss	3a
Pig(g)ott	2.13ab
Pirie	7.26a.31
Pitcarns	27c
Pitkaithly	18
Playfair	2.14
Poraz	6a

Porter 8.9.13b.17b
Potter 13b.16a
Pourie 31
Poustie 27c
Powers 13b
Preshaw 3a
Prestack 27c
Pringle 3a
Pritchard 22
Proctor 3a.12.13b.14.21.33a
Prophet 23a.32.35
Prott 27c
Pulkace 7
Pullar 8.18.30.33a
Pyett,Pyot 11a.16a.19.33a
Pyper 3a
Purvise 27c

Rae 9.13b.17a.21.see Rea
Rait(t) 3a.11b.20a.28
Raiker 32
Ralston 14
Ramsay 2.3a.6a.8.9.11a.13ab 14.16a.17a.18.19.21 22.23ac.24.25.29.31 34.35
Rankin 2.36
Ranny 13a
Raphael 14
Rattray 2.3a.6b.13a.14.15.18 23ac.33a.34.36
Rea 13b.14.33a.see Rae
Read,Reed 13b.3a.see Reid
Reddell 27c
Reich 14
Reid 1a.2.3a.6a.7.11a.12 13ab.14.15.16a.17a 18.19.21.22.23ac.25 26b.28.34
Reidie 30
Rennie/y 3a.11a.13ab.16a.20a 22.27c
Renwick 27c
Rew 20b.36
Rhind/Rhynd,Rind 14.17a.30.33a
Richard 4
Richardson 17b
Riche 21.see Ritchie
Richter 3a
Rickard,Riccard 3a.10a.12.13a.23a. 24.28
Riddoch 3a
Ritchie,Riche 3a.4.8.13abc.16a.18 20ab.21.22.23a.32
Riven 30
Rob(b) 3ac.6a.7.13ab.22.23ac 27c.33a
Rob(b)ie 3b.5.6a.13b.14.21. 23ac.24

Robert 6a.7.12.13a.21.33a
Roberts 3b.11a.13ab.14.19.22 33a.35
Robertson 1a.2.3a.6a.7.8.9.10a.11a 12.13abc.14.15.17a.18.21 22.23c.25.27c.30.31.33a 34.35.36
Robie 10a.see Robbie
Robson 21
Roch,Rock 13a.14.18.33a
Roderick 13b
Roddick 23a
Ro(d)ger 2.3a.9.13ab.14.18.19.20a 31.34
Rogers 33a
Rollo 18
Rollock 2.3a
Ronald 3a
Rood 19
Rorer 18
Rose 3a.10a.24.31
Ross 1a.3a.7.10ab.11a.13ab.14 20a.23a.26a.27c.30.33a.36
Rough 14.16a.20a
Row(e) 20a.24
Roy 9.22.31
Rue 36.see Rew
Ruehie 20a
Runcie 20b
Russell 11a.27c
Rutherford 18
Ruxton 3a.11a
Rynd 30.33a.see Rhynd

Sadler 17a
StClair 17b.see Sinclair
Salmon(d) 13a.16a.17a.22.33a
Salter 2.34
Sam(p)son 3a.7.8.11b.13ab.14.23a.25 see Semson
Sand 17a
Sanders 30
Sand(i)eman 2.3a.36
Sandison 23a
Sands 13a
Sang 36
Satar 34
Saunders 1a.18.31
Sayers 25
Scheres,Seres 3a
Schewan 35
Scott 1a.3ab.7.8.10a.11a.12.13abc 14.16a.17a.18.20a.22.23c. 27c.28.30.31.32.33ab.35
Scrymgeour 14.16a.19.20a.23acd.33a.36
Seato(u)n 4.13c
Sedgwick 1a
Selby 7
Semon 18

CUMULATIVE INDEX

Numbers denote the burial grounds as listed at beginning and end of the book.

Semson 33a
Seres 3a
Seymour 24
Shand 3a.11a
Shank 3a
Sharp 3a.9.33b
Shaw 5.6ab.13bc.14.15.18
Shearer 11a
Shedden 13a
Shepherd 3a.7.8.13b.14.18.27b.36
Sherratt 27c
Sherriff(s) 8.13b
Shiell 28
Shilgreene 11a
Shillito 33a
Shingar 9
Shiphart 9
Shirburn 3a
Shires(s),Seres 3a.16a
Shirrell 5
Shoreswood 3a
Sidey 18.31.see Sydie
Sievwright 3a.11a.13a
Silver 10b
Sim 2.13b.18.22.27c.36
Sime, Syme 3a.6a.13a.21.27b.28.31.35 36
Sim(p)son 3a.7.11b.13ab.14.16a.20a 23c.27c.30.33ab.34.36
Sinclair 1a.9.13b.14.see StClair
Singer(s) 3a
Skair,Skeir 3c.20a.28.33a.35.36
Skea 3a.31
Skene 3b.4.13c.26b
Skinner 3a.13ac.23c
Skirling 8.20a.21
Slidder 18.31
Smale 2
Small 2.13ac.14.16a.18.19.25.31 33b
Smart 3a.6b.10ab.11a.12.13b.14 18.19.23c.24.25.28.29.33a 36
Smith 1a.2.3ab.6ab.7.8.9.10ab. 11a.13ab.14.161b.17a.18.19 20a.21.22.23abc.24.25.26b 27a.28.30.31.32.33a.34.35. 36
Smyttan 3a
Snowie 13a
Somer 1a
Somerville 28
Soppet 3a
Soot 18
Sorbel 13a
Soutar,Soutter 3ab.6a.7.8.9.11b.13ab.14 15.18.21.23a.31.32.33a
Spaddie 3a
Spalding 3a.17a.18.23c.25
Spaldon 14.30
Spankie 7.27c.31
Spark 16b.27c.33a
Speed,Speid 3ab.8.13a.29.35
Spens/ce 1a.3a.9.11a.13ab.15 16a.20a.22.23ac.29
Spottiswood 9
Stark 13a
Steele,Steill 2.3a.6a.7.8.9.11a 13abc.15.18.25.30.31
Stephen,Steven 1a.3a.7.8.10b.11a 13a.14.16a.17ab.18. 20ab.26b.31
Stevens 23a .see Stivens
Stevenson 2.3a.7.8.14.18.22.23a 27c.31.36
Steurd 10a
Stewart 1a.2.3ab.6a.7.8.9.10a 11b.13b.14.15.18.21 23ac.24.26b.27c.28.29 30.31.32.33a.34.35.36
Stil 2.25
Stirling 1a.8.13b.17a.21.33a
Stiven see Stephen
Stivens 14.see Stephens
Stocks 14
Stockwell 3a
Stool 7.see Stuill
Storach 30
Stormont(h) 2.5.10a.12.14.19.23 26b.33a
Storrock 1a.8.see Sturrock
Storrier 15.30
Stott 3a.7
Strachan 3a.6a.7.9.10a.11a.13a 16a.17a.18.20ab.21.22 23a.27bc
Strang 13ab
Strathearn 31
Strat(t)on 3a.7.12.30.35
Stroak 33a
Stuart 3a.13a.32.35
Stubbles 9.18
Stupart 36
Stuill 22.see Stool
Sturrock 3a.8.13abc.14.17a.28 33a.26.see Storrock
Sturton 31
Sutar see Soutar
Sutherland 13ab
Sutter 11a
Suttie 13ab.14.36
Sydie 9.see Sidey
Syme see Sime
Symers 11a.18.24

CUMULATIVE INDEX

Symington 3a
Symmer 12.35
Symon,Semon 13b.18
Symson 1a.33ab.see Simpson
Tailor see Taylor
Talbert 21.24
Tamson 23a
Tannoch 14
Tarbat/et 8.13ab
Tasker 13b.18.26b
Taviotdale 27b
Taws 8.16a
Taylor 1a.3ab.10a.11a.12.13b 14.16ab.17a.22.27bc 29.30.32.33a.see Tyler
Telfer 33a
Tendil 12.see Tindal
Tevendale 7
Thain 9.13b.17a.18.27c
Thom(s) 6b.8.13ab.16a.17a.18 19.21.25.31.33a
Thomas 2.23a
Thompson 11a
Thomson 1a.2.3ab.4.6a.7.8.9 10a.11a.13ab.14.15 16a.18.20a.22.23ac 25.26b.27b.28.31.36
Thornton 1a.8.13abc.14.16a
Tindal(l),Tendil 1a.3a.10a.12.14 17a.18.35
Toad 18
Tod(d) 3a.22.23a.36
Tohow 26a
Torbat 13b.see Tarbat
Torn 13a
Torry 13b
Tosh 3a.6a.12.13ab.14.18 20a.24.28.36
Touch 13b
Towns 27c.28.35
Townsend 33b
Trail(l) 3a.12.13b
Trest 17b
Trimble 3a.see Turnbull
Trotter 14.18
Troup 3a
Tullo(a) 24.31.33a
Tulloch 3a.16a.18
Turnbull 13b.14.35.see Trimble
Turner 3a.31
Tyler,Tylior 11a.28 .see Taylor
Tytler 12
Tyre 4
Tyrie 16a.23a.30
Ure 13ac
Urquhart 1a.14.20a
Val(l)entine 3a.7.10ab.14.25.27b.30
Vallance 20a
Veilant 30
Volom,Volum 6a.14.32
Wach 16a.see Waugh
Waddell 14.18.31
Waighe 17b.see Waugh
Waith,Weath 3a
Waker 18
Walker 3a.5.6a.7.8.10a.11a.13ab 16a.17ab.19.20a.21.22.23ac 28.30.33a.35
Wall(s) 3a.9.36
Wallace 1a.2.3a.8.10a.13ab.14.16a 20b.23c.25.27c.31.32.33a
Walles/as 17a.24
Wan 8
Wan(d)less 15.18
Ward 11a.13b
Warden 8.13b.25
Wardroper 30
Watchman 16a
Wat(t)erston 13ab.32.33a
Watson 1a.2.3ab.4.9.12.14.16a. 17a.18.19.22.23ac.27c.28 30.31.32.33ab
Wat(t) 1a.3a.6a.7.8.11b.13ab.14 16a.17a.18.21.22.26b.30 36
Wattie 35
Waugh,Wach,Waighe 16a.17b.28
Weath,Waith 3a
Weaver 17a
Webster 1a.3a.5.7.12.13ab.14.16a 19.20a.22.23ac.24.28.29 31.32.33a.36
Wedderburn 28.34
Wedderburn-Ogilvy 34
Weighton 33a
Weir 8.10b.16b.18.27c
Wells 13b
Welsh 3a.13ab.22.26a
Wemyss 12
Whamond 3a.9.11a.36
Wheatley 6a
Whitaker 18
Whitburn(s) 13a.14.23a.33a
White 2.3a.6a.7.8.9.13a.14.20a 27c.33a.35.see Whyte
Whitson 3a.15.16a.34
Whit(t)et 18.31
Whitton 2.3b.13b.14.30.31
Whyte 2.3a.5.8.9.13abc.14.17a 20a.23c.26b.33a.34.36
Whytlaw 13a.35
Wiggen 21

C U M U L A T I V E   I N D E X

Numbers denote the burial grounds as listed at beginning and end of the book.

Wightman	9.14
Wighton	2.9.11b.13b.17a.21.25
Wilkie	2.8.12.13b.14.16a.17a.18 23ac.25.30.31.36
Will	3a.10ab.11a.16a.23c.24 26b.27b.29.35
Williamson	3a.11a.13ab.25.33a.35.36
Willie	see Wyllie
Willis	13a
Willocks/x	3a.10a.27c
Wilson	3ab.5.6ab.8.9.11a.13ab 17a.19.20a.22.23ac.25 27c.33a.35.36
Windrim	3a.16a.22
Winter	6a.13ab.30.36
Wise,Wyse	16a.30
Wiseman	8
Wishart	1a.3a.7.8.13a.22.27c.28 29.33a
Wobster	3a.23a.31.36
Wolom,Volom	6a.14.32
Wood	1a.3a.4.13ac.14.23a 33a
Wright,Wrycht	2.3a.6b.9.14.19.20a 25.27c.34
Wyl(l)ie	1a.3ab.4.7.10a.11a. 12.13ac.14.20a.23a 25.27c.28.29.35.36
Wynram,Windrim	3a.16a.22
Wyse	see Wise
Yates	13b.see Yeats
Yeaman	13b.22.32
Yeats	23a.see Yates
Yeulo,Yoolow	18
Young	1ab.2.3a.6a.7.8.9. 11a.13a.14.17a.19 20ab.21.22.23a.24 28.30.31.35.36
Yule	25

1979.

This volume could not have been completed without the meticulous work, over many years, of Sydney Cramer and John Fowler Mitchell. Thankyou!

S T R A T H M O R E
A N G U S

1a Aberlemno
1b Aldbar
2 Airlie
3a Brechin cathedral
3b Brechin cemetery
3c Magdalen chapel
4 Careston (Fuirdstone)
5 Clova
6a Cortachy
6b Glen Prosen
7 Dun
8 Dunnichen
9 Eassie
10a Edzell
10b Newdosk
11a Farnell
11b Kinnaird (Cuikston)
12 Fern
13a Forfar parish church
13b Forfar St John's
13c Forfar cemetery
14 Glamis
15 Glenisla
16a Guthrie
16b Kirkbuddo
17a Inverarity
17b Meathie-Lour
18 Kettins
19 Kingoldrum
20a Kinnell old church
20b Friockheim cemetery
21 Kinnettles
22 Kirkden (Idvie)
23a Kirriemuir parish church
23b Kirriemuir St Mary's
23c Kirriemuir cemetery
23d Kinloch mausoleum
24 Lethnot
25 Lintrathen
26a Lochlee old church
26b Lochlee parish church
27a Logie-Pert parish church
27b Logie-Montrose
27c Pert
28 Menmuir
29 Navar
30 Nevay (St. Ringane's)
31 Newtyle
32 Oathlaw (Finhaven)
33a Rescobie
33b Balmadies
34 Ruthven
35 Stracathro
36 Tannadice

The Scottish Genealogy Society has published similar collections for:

Berwickshire
Clackmannanshire
Dunbartonshire
Fife
Lanarkshire, Upper Ward
Lothian, West
Peeblesshire
Perthshire
Renfrewshire
Stirlingshire
Speyside

Over a period of years the Scottish Genealogy Society has published several volumes of pre-1855 gravestone inscriptions.

The Society currently has over 200 titles on genealogy and related subjects for sale. All enquiries about the availability and price of these volumes should be addressed to:

The Scottish Genealogy Society
15 Victoria Terrace
Edinburgh
EH1 2JL

Telephone/Fax: 0131 220 3677

Internet at: ***http://www.scotland.net/scotgensoc/***

E-mail at: **scotgensoc@sol.co.uk**